The Complete Guide to
National Symbols and Emblems

The Complete Guide to National Symbols and Emblems

Volume 1

James Minahan

GREENWOOD PRESS
An Imprint of ABC-CLIO, LLC

A B C ☰ C L I O

Santa Barbara, California • Denver, Colorado • Oxford, England

Library of Congress Cataloging-in-Publication Data

Minahan, James.
    The complete guide to national symbols and emblems / James Minahan.
        p. cm.
    Includes bibliographical references and index.
    ISBN 978-0-313-34496-1 (set : alk. paper) — ISBN 978-0-313-34497-8 (set ebook) —
ISBN 978-0-313-34498-5 (vol. 1 : alk. paper) — ISBN 978-0-313-34499-2 (vol. 1 ebook) —
ISBN 978-0-313-34500-5 (vol. 2 : alk. paper) — ISBN 978-0-313-34501-2 (vol. 2 ebook)
    1. Emblems, National—Encyclopedias.   2. National characteristics—Encyclopedias.   I. Title.
    CR191.M56   2010
    929.903—dc22   2009036963

14 13 12 11 10   1 2 3 4 5

This book is also available on the World Wide Web as an eBook.
Visit www.abc-clio.com for details.

Greenwood Press
An Imprint of ABC-CLIO, LLC

ABC-CLIO, LLC
130 Cremona Drive, P.O. Box 1911
Santa Barbara, California 93116–1911

This book is printed on acid-free paper ∞

Manufactured in the United States of America

For Emili Roig Navarra
¡Gracies!

Contents

Alphabetical List of Entries

Guide to Related Topics

Asia and Oceania

Aceh
Afghanistan
American Samoa
Australia
Bangladesh
Bhutan
Bougainville
Brunei
Cambodia
China
China, Republic of.
　　See Taiwan
Cook Islands
East Timor
East Turkestan
Fiji
French Polynesia
Guam
Hong Kong
India
Indonesia
Japan
Kashmir
Kazakhstan
Kiribati
Korea, North
Korea, South
Kyrgyzstan
Laos
Macau
Malaysia
Maldives
Marshall Islands
Micronesia
Mongolia

Myanmar
Nagaland
Nauru
Nepal
New Caledonia
New Zealand
Niue
Norfolk Island
North Korea. *See* Korea, North
Northern Mariana Islands
Pakistan
Palau
Papua New Guinea
Philippines
Pitcairn
Samoa
Singapore
Solomon Islands
South Korea. *See* Korea, South
Sri Lanka
Tahiti. *See* French Polynesia
Taiwan
Tajikistan
Tamil Eelam
Thailand
Tibet
Tokelau
Tonga
Turkmenistan
Tuva
Tuvalu
Uzbekistan
Vanuatu
Vietnam
Wallis and Futuna
West Papua

Central and South America

Argentina
Belize
Bolivia
Brazil
Chile
Colombia
Costa Rica
Ecuador
El Salvador
Falkland Islands
French Guiana
Guatemala
Guyana
Honduras
Nicaragua
Panama
Paraguay
Peru
Santa Cruz
Suriname
Uruguay
Venezuela
Zulia

Europe

Abkhazia
Åland Islands
Albania
Andorra
Armenia
Austria
Azerbaijan
Azores
Bashkortostan
Bavaria
Belarus
Belgium
Bosnia and Herzegovina
Brittany
Bulgaria
Canary Islands
Catalonia
Chechnya
Cornwall
Corsica
Croatia
Cyprus

Czech Republic
Denmark
Estonia
Euskal Herria
Faroe Islands
Finland
Flanders
France
Galicia
Georgia
Germany
Gibraltar
Greece
Guernsey
Hungary
Iceland
Ireland
Isle of Man
Italy
Jersey
Kosovo
Latvia
Liechtenstein
Lithuania
Luxembourg
Macedonia
Madeira
Malta
Moldova
Monaco
Montenegro
Netherlands
Northern Cyprus
Northern Ireland
Norway
Poland
Portugal
Romania
Russia
San Marino
Sapmi
Sardinia
Scania
Scotland
Serbia
Slovakia
Slovenia
South Ossetia

Spain
Sweden
Switzerland
Tatarstan
Transnistria
Turkey
Ukraine
United Kingdom
Vatican City
Wales
Wallonia

Middle East and North Africa

Algeria
Bahrain
Egypt
Iran
Iraq
Israel
Jordan
Kurdistan
Kuwait
Lebanon
Libya
Mauritania
Morocco
Oman
Palestine
Qatar
Sahrawi
Saudi Arabia
Sudan
Syria
Tunisia
United Arab Emirates
Western Sahara. *See* Sahrawi
Yemen

North America and the Caribbean

Anguilla
Antigua and Barbuda
Aruba
Bahamas
Barbados
Bermuda
British Virgin Islands
Canada
Cayman Islands

Cuba
Curaçao
Dominica
Dominican Republic
Greenland
Grenada
Guadeloupe
Haiti
Jamaica
Martinique
Mexico
Montserrat
Netherlands Antilles
Nevis
Puerto Rico
Quebec
Saint Barthelemy
Saint Kitts and Nevis
Saint Lucia
Saint Maarten
Saint Martin
Saint Pierre and Miquelon
Saint Vincent and the Grenadines
Trinidad and Tobago
Turks and Caicos Islands
United States
Virgin Islands

Sub-Saharan Africa

Ambazania
Angola
Benin
Botswana
Burkina Faso
Burundi
Cabinda
Cameroon
Cape Verde
Casamance
Central African Republic
Chad
Comoros
Congo, Democratic Republic
Congo, Republic
Côte d'Ivoire
Djibouti
Equatorial Guinea
Eritrea

Preface

This volume was compiled to give a detailed guide to the symbols we see every day, the waving flags that adorn the entrances to hotels and auditoriums, the colorful uniforms at international sports events, the exotic national dishes increasingly available to everyone, the anthems that accompany official visits or event winners at the Olympic Games, national airlines seen at world airports, and the many other national symbols we encounter on a daily basis on the Internet. This guide is presented as a unique reference source to the symbols that are daily becoming more visible around the world.

The world's nations and territories represent a perplexing diversity of symbols chosen to represent them and their cultures. Containing over 200 entries, this guide highlights the many national symbols that represent each of the world's independent nations and many of the dependent nations and territories that increasingly function as autonomous political entities. The worth of this volume in part derives from its up-to-date information on national symbols and other aspects of each country and territory.

Each national entry is divided into several parts or headings: the name and alternative name or names of the country or territory, including the English-language version; the latest population estimate; the name and nickname of the inhabitants; the national or official language and other spoken languages; the religions represented; the national flag; the national coat of arms or seal; the national motto; the capital city; the type of government; the national emblems or symbols; the national colors; the national anthem, generally in English translation; the patron saint or saints (where applicable); the national currency; the national Internet identifier; the vehicle identification plate or sticker code; the national passport; the national airlines (the flag carrier or carriers, if any, and other important airlines); national flora and fauna and national resources; national foods and dishes; national sports teams; national heroes or personifications; the national holiday or independence day; important festivals and fairs; and significant events in the formation of each national identity.

The national population figures are the author's estimates for the year 2009. These figures are designated by "(2009e)" alongside the appropriate statistics. The population figures represent information gleaned from a large number of sources representing the latest census results, official estimates, and figures published by international bodies, such as the United Nations. Information on spoken languages and religious affiliation are mostly derived from official government publications or other recognized reference material.

Information on the national flags, coats of arms, seals, and national mottos are mostly taken from official publications or specialized reference volumes and Web sites. Although flag enthusiasts are very interested in official measurements and sizes, the information included here is more concerned with the colors and symbolism of flags and the other official symbols of each nation.

Few of the world's countries developed in isolation; rather, they were and are shaped by their relations with neighboring governments and peoples. In our ever-increasingly globalized world, influences often come from countries and cultures geographically distant. To facilitate the reader's identification of countries mentioned in the text, the name of each country appears with an asterisk (*) on first reference within a section. An extensive subject index at the end of the volume provides a convenient way to access desired information.

This volume was compiled to provide a precise guide to the national symbols that represent all nations, but that to most of us present a colorful but incomprehensible chaos. In order to make the book as comprehensive as possible not only independent nations are included but also dependent states and territories and many other territories that actively seek greater autonomy, including recognition of their own national symbols.

A special thank-you to all the national governments, tourist offices, information offices, embassies, and consulates that so kindly forwarded information. And my forgiveness to those governments or other national representatives that ignored my requests and pleas.

Introduction

The world's population quadrupled during the 20th century, and the number of independent states grew from about 35 in 1900 to around 200 in 2000. Each of these countries, along with many still-dependent territories, has adopted symbols to represent its people and culture. National symbols are outward displays of each country or territory's national characteristics. These symbols developed as part of each national group's culture, reflecting the historical, ethnic, religious, and territorial influences that became part of it.

National symbols are not exclusive to the world's independent states. Many national groups and dependent territories also employ national symbols that characterize their particular histories and aspirations. Included are a representative sample of the many nonindependent territories that are seeking greater visibility as separate political entities, most importantly through their use of national symbols that represent their aspirations and distinct histories. The nonindependent territories included in this study are those that are attempting, with the support of a sizable portion of their respective populations, to attain more independence and greater recognition as distinct national entities. National symbols are an important political statement, embodying the history, geography, and aspirations of each culture. These symbols are so important that one of the first acts of a conqueror or dictator is to suppress the legitimate or traditional national symbols as a means of subjugation.

The most widely recognized symbols are national flags, but as the number of countries proliferated, so did the number of different, often unique, symbols that were adopted to represent them. With the dawn of the information age, these national symbols and many others took on even more importance. Government departments, diplomatic missions, tourist boards or departments, trade delegations, and tens of thousands of Web sites now use national symbols to represent the focus country or territory.

In these volumes, the world's countries and territories are presented with useful background material and detailed information on their national symbols. Included in each national survey are the official name; the national population; the inhabitants' name or names, including nicknames; languages and religions; the national flag; the national coat of arms or seal; the capital city; the type of government; and the significant events that shaped each national identity. Other national information, where applicable, includes the national motto; the national emblem or symbol; the national colors; the national anthem; the patron saint or saints; the national currency; the Internet identifier; the vehicle identification initials; the national passport; the national airline; the national flower, tree, plant, animal, bird, and fish;

national resources; national foods and dishes; national sports teams; national heroes or personifications; the national holiday or holidays; and annual festivals and fairs.

Each national survey begins with the short name of the country and the official name in all official languages, with translation into English when necessary. The country or territory's population is given with author's estimates for 2009 (2009e) based on official census figures or calculations. The demonym, the name used to describe the inhabitants, is given, along with alternatives and any nicknames. The languages and religions of the inhabitants are listed, with any official status indicated. The capital cities and types of government of the various countries and territories are also included.

Each country or territory's national symbols begin with the national flag, the most visible and widely known of all international symbols. The coat of arms or seal at times reflects the design of the national flag but is usually an amalgam of symbols representing economic activities, geographic features, flora and fauna, and other additions, such as a national motto.

The national emblems or symbols are included, but, as with many national symbols, the category is not applicable to every country or territory. Examples of well-known national emblems or symbols are such landmarks as the Eiffel Tower in France, the Hagia Sofia in Turkey, and the Statue of Liberty in the United States; the trident symbol that represents Ukraine; and the zebra that represents Botswana. National colors are also very popular symbols, used in correspondence, on airplanes and ships, and in the uniforms or kits worn by national sports teams.

The national anthem is another very important national symbol. English translations are included for nearly all of the anthems, mostly gathered from specialized publications or Web sites. The translations have been edited to clarify meaning or to conform to American grammar and spelling. A few of the anthems are presented in the original language when an English translation was not available.

Lesser-known symbols, such as patron saints, national currencies, and national Internet identifiers, all of which are considered important national representations, are included as well. Initials from vehicle identification plates or stickers, usually one to three letters that identify a vehicle's origin, are becoming more important as national barriers to cross-border travel disappear.

The national symbols most identified with modern international travel are passports and airlines. Information on the front cover of national passports is included with each national entry. The colors of the national passports have been omitted, because they change much more often than the actual cover presentation. National airlines, sometimes referred to as a country's roving ambassadors, are often called flag carriers—the national airline designated as the official airline by the addition of the national flag as part of the paint job or airline livery. Following a spate of bankruptcies, many national airlines have disappeared, but others have emerged as replacement national carriers. Many countries now have more than one national airline carrying the national colors and the national flag as part of the airline's livery.

Symbols of a country's flora and fauna are also very important representations. The national flower, tree, plant, animal, bird, fish or sea creature, fruit, insect, and stone are presented when applicable. Many of these symbols are popularly accepted but have not been officially adopted, which is indicated by a notation of *unofficial* in parentheses. Many countries have no national symbols that represent their national flora and fauna.

A country's national resources also represent the country or territory, as its economic well-being, or lack thereof, is often all too visible, whether in the evident poverty of some resource-poor countries or the showy opulence of countries rich in natural resources. National resources may be the visible signs of a country's history, geography, and culture as seen by tourists and visitors. National dishes and national foods are also symbolic of a country's culture and history.

One of the most obvious representations of national pride are each country's national sports teams. International sports venues, such as regional games, international sports meetings, and the Olympic Games, are characterized by the colorful and distinctive national flags of the participating nations, which are usually reflected in the kits or uniforms worn by the participants. National sports federations are represented by logos decorated with national symbols and colors, while national uniforms or kits carry national color combinations and usually other representations of the country or territory they represent. The international sports teams of each country or territory are listed in each entry.

A country's national personification and national heroes are icons that loom large in most cultures. Our own Uncle Sam is used or alluded to in magazines, newspapers, cartoons, film, and television. Many other countries have equivalent characterizations that represent their cultures. Most countries have a national holiday, often the date of independence or a date that recalls other events in the national history; some even have more than one, which are noted in each national entry. Festivals and fairs are also representative of the nation's culture, history, or present circumstances. Most of the festivals and fairs are annual or semiannual, although some are celebrated at greater intervals.

The last part of each national survey is made up of the significant events that formed each national culture or identity. The dates and events are presented in chronological order to give a timeline of each national history, from its inception to the present day.

Asia and Oceania

The national symbols of the region of Asia and Oceania often reflect the long and turbulent histories of the countries in the region or the colors and designs brought by European colonial powers. The color red is predominant in the flags and coats of arms of most of Asia, harking back to the colors of indigenous religions or the symbolic use of red as the color of revolution. Both red, as a traditional color, and blue also predominate in Oceania, the latter either as a tribute to a former colonial power, the United Kingdom, or to represent the Pacific Ocean, the home of many small island nations. Other symbols, such as national foods, flora and fauna, and music and dance, vary greatly, even among the culturally related nations of the various regions of Asia and the Pacific. The former Soviet republics of Central Asia adopted symbols related to their ancient traditions and use the colors of Islam, Turkey, and the pale blue that represents the various Turkic peoples.

A number of the territories included in this section are not independent nations but are dependent or overseas territories with their own identities and symbols. Many are the remnants of the former European empires. The other nonindependent nations that are included are Aceh; Bougainville; East Turkestan; Kashmir; Nagaland; Tamil Eelam; Tibet; and West Papua. These territories are not officially dependent states or territories, a large portion of each of their populations support the aim of actively seeking greater self-government and recognition of their distinct cultures, including their own national symbols. Tuva, although geographically in Asia, is included in the European section as it forms a member state of the Russian Federation, which is generally considered part of Europe although a large part is actually in northern Asia.

ACEH

OFFICIAL NAME

Nanggröe Aceh Darussalam (Bahasa Indonesia); Special Territory of Aceh (English)

NICKNAME

The Verandah of Mecca

POPULATION

4,250,000 (2009e)

INHABITANTS' NAME/NICKNAME

Acehnese

LANGUAGE/LANGUAGES

Acehnese, Indonesian (official); Alas, Kluet, Jamee, others

RELIGION/RELIGIONS

Shia Muslim, 65 percent; Sunni Muslim, 17 percent; Christian, 2 percent; Hindu, Buddhist, animist, other or no religion

NATIONAL FLAG

The flag of GAM (Gerakan Aceh Merdeka/Free Aceh Movement) the historical flag of

Aceh, has a red field bearing a centered white crescent moon and five-pointed star between two horizontal black stripes outlined in white. The flag, in use for more than five centuries, is considered the national flag of Aceh. The crescent and star symbolize Islam and submission to Allah; the red stands for bravery, loyalty, and truth; and the white fimbriations symbolize purity.

COAT OF ARMS/SEAL

The ancient symbol of Aceh, adopted by the GAM separatists, consists of a shield below a crescent moon and five-pointed star. The shield is supported by a lion and a mythical winged horse with a human head, both holding *rincongs* (Acehnese daggers) crossed over the shield. Below the shield is a banner with the name of the state in Acehnese and Arabic.

MOTTO

The Verandah of Mecca; *Panacacita* (Five Goals) is on the shield of the Indonesian special region

CAPITAL CITY

Bandar Aceh

TYPE OF GOVERNMENT

Special territory with an autonomous government within the Republic of Indonesia since the end of the separatist war in 2005

NATIONAL EMBLEM

Mesjid Baiturrahman, the Grand Mosque of Aceh; the *rincong*, the traditional Acehnese dagger

NATIONAL COLORS

Red, white, and black

CURRENCY

Indonesian rupiah

VEHICLE IDENTIFICATION PLATES/STICKERS

RI Indonesia (official); ACH Aceh (unofficial)

PASSPORT

Acehnese are Indonesian citizens and travel on Indonesian passports.

NATIONAL FLOWER

Rafflesia (unofficial; the world's largest flower)

NATIONAL ANIMAL

Lion (unofficial; the lion is not native to southeast Asia. The mythical image was brought to the region from the Middle East and is also used as a national symbol by Singapore*). Sumatran Tiger (unofficial).

NATIONAL BIRD

Aceh pheasant (unofficial)

NATIONAL RESOURCES

Aceh has substantial natural resources, including coal, gold, tin, platinum, oil, and natural gas. Aceh's main income-earners are petroleum and natural gas, fertilizer, estate produce, and agriculture. The natural gas reserves are believed to be among the largest in the world.

FOODS

Ayam tangkap, chicken with bay leaves and spices, is the traditional Acehnese dish. Other specialties include *gulai ikan kembung khas aceh,* Acehnese mackerel curry; *roti jala,* a dish of beef, potatoes, coconut milk, and spices served with *roti,* a type of crepe or flatbread; *sop konro,* a stew of beef and vegetables; *rending,* a dish of beef cooked in coconut milk; *ayam aceh,* Aceh-style chicken cooked in coconut milk and spices; *bakso ayam wortel,* fried balls of minced chicken and carrot; *chermoula,* grilled lamb chops with spices; *molokhryis nil dsmsk,* a soup of ground *molokhia* (Egyptian spinach) and anchovies; and *kuah titchrah,* white fish curry with chilies.

SPORTS/SPORTS TEAMS

Association football is the most popular sport, although Aceh is not permitted to play at an international level.

TEAM SPORTS

Persiraja Banda Aceh Football Team is considered the national team, nickname Lantak Laju.

NATIONAL HEROES
OR PERSONIFICATIONS

Iskander Muda, the Acehnese sultan who extended Acehnese possessions to much of Sumatra and the Malay Peninsula in the 17th century; Tengku Tjhik di Tiro, a late 19th-century ruler who inaugurated the modern Acehnese resistance movement against foreign aggression

NATIONAL HOLIDAY/INDEPENDENCE DAY

Independence Day, December 4 (unofficial; commemorates the declaration of independence issued on December 4, 1976); Iskander Muda Day, December 27; Tengku Tjhik di Tiro Day, January 25

FESTIVALS/FAIRS

Aceh Cultural Festival, August; Tari dan Seuruné Kalée (Festival of Dance and Culture), March

SIGNIFICANT EVENTS IN FORMATION
OF NATIONAL IDENTITY

400–600 C.E. A powerful Buddhist state flourishes in Aceh.

Seventh century The state declines and its power is curtailed by the emergence of Hindu empires in Java and Sumatra.

12th century Large numbers of Arab migrants settle the coastal regions. The religion of Islam, brought to the region by the Arabs, spreads throughout northwestern Sumatra.

14th century The Muslim sultanate of Aceh is established and retains strong ties to the Muslim states to the west.

16th–17th centuries Led by Iskander Muda, the Acehnese sultanate expands to control much of Sumatra and parts of the Malay Peninsula, including territory in modern Thailand*. Dutch and Portuguese colonization of the region is fiercely resisted from the 16th century.

1824 The Sultanate of Aceh is recognized as an independent nation by the United Kingdom* and the Netherlands*.

1873 The Dutch, after conquering neighboring islands and territories, declare war on the Kingdom of Aceh on May 26, 1873. The Acehnese War would drag on for more than 80 years.

1941–1945 The Acehnese, never fully conquered by the Dutch, rebel again as World War II breaks out. The invading Japanese drive the Dutch from Aceh in 1942, but the conservative Acehnese reject Japanese overtures and continue to fight the invaders. When Japanese forces capitulate to the allied powers in August 1945, the Dutch make no attempt to return to Aceh, although they do return to Java and to all other parts of their former colonial empire.

1949–1953 Aceh remains free of outside rule until the Dutch sign over their colonial claim to newly independent Indonesia on December 27, 1949, leading to open rebellion in Aceh in early 1950. The Acehnese refuse to recognize Indonesian authority and proclaim their independence of Indonesia on September 21, 1953.

1956 In an effort to undermine Acehnese nationalism, the Indonesian government grants the region some limited autonomy, but the Acehnese continue to resist, particularly against government plans to settle tens of thousands of non-Acehnese from other parts of Indonesia.

1960s The Acehnese separatist war resumes in the 1960s, led by Hassan di Tiro, heir to the sultans of Aceh. The separatist organization GAM, the Free Aceh Movement, receives support and arms from Muslim countries in Africa and the Middle East.

1976 Indonesia's centralization and a lack of autonomy pushes the Acehnese leadership to again declare independence on December 4, 1976. The declaration is not recognized by the international community.

1980s In 1989, in an effort to defeat the separatists, the Indonesian government sends special military units to the region. The campaign, marked by massive human rights abuses, rape, and pillage, garners even greater support for Acehnese separatism.

2004 The Acehnese war continues until the region, the closest to the epicenter, is overwhelmed by a tsunami caused by an undersea quake. The tsunami destroys much of the region, killing more than 230,000 and leaving another 500,000 homeless. The nationalist leaders call an immediate ceasefire to allow aid to reach their desperate people.

2005 On July 16, 2005, negotiators announce a comprehensive peace deal to end the 30-year separatist war. The leaders of GAM renounce their goal of full independence and dissolve the armed wing of the organization. They accept an autonomous state in association with Indonesia. The Indonesian government agrees to a full military pullout and to free elections for the autonomous government, which are won by the former separatists. One important part of the agreement allows Aceh to retain 70 percent of the benefits from its natural resources. Some smaller separatist groups reject the agreement and continue to demand full independence.

2005–2007 The reconstruction of Aceh delays the implementation of many of the autonomy agreement's statutes, bringing protests and threats from several separatist groups that did not participate in the negotiations.

2008–2009 Acehnese cultural leaders call for the revival of traditional and religious culture in Aceh. Many of the region's local customs had been very strong prior to their erosion by the region's long history of conflict.

2009 Tensions between the Indonesian military and former Acehnese rebels reaches levels not seen since the peace agreement of 2005 as local Acehnese political parties, for the first time, are able to participate in parliamentary elections.

See also Indonesia

AFGHANISTAN

OFFICIAL NAME
Jamhūrī-ye Islāmī-ye Afġānistān (transliteration from Farsi); De Afġānistān Islāmī Jomhoriyat (transliteration from Pashto); Islamic Republic of Afghanistan (English)

POPULATION
23,725,000 (2009e)

INHABITANTS' NAME/NICKNAME
Afghan(s), Afghani(s)

LANGUAGE/LANGUAGES
Pashto, Dari (Afghan Persian) (both official); Uzbek, Turkmen, Balochi, Pashai, Nuristani, Brahui, others

RELIGION/RELIGIONS
Sunni Muslim, 80 percent; Shia Muslim, 19 percent; other or no religion

NATIONAL FLAG
The national flag is a vertical tricolor of black, red, and green bearing the national coat of arms in white on the red stripe. The three colors represent the three different stages of Afghanistan's modern history. The black symbolizes the colonial era, when the country was ruled by foreigners; the red represents the fight for independence; and the green symbolizes Afghan independence.

COAT OF ARMS/SEAL
A new coat of arms, adopted in 2009, has a central circle divided horizontally with a green lower half, representing Islam and the

natural wealth of Afghanistan, with a yellow and white representation of a mosque, representing the country's adherence to Islam. Above the green is a white sun with 27 golden rays. Around the central emblems are wreaths of wheat, representing Afghanistan's agriculture and productivity. Below the central circle is a blue cog wheel, symbolizing Afghanistan's industries, and banners in the national colors.

CAPITAL CITY

Kabul

TYPE OF GOVERNMENT

Islamic republic

NATIONAL EMBLEM

Two very large and ancient Buddhist statues, destroyed by the Taliban as offensive to Islam in 2001. Many countries and organizations have pledged support for the rebuilding of the monumental statues.

NATIONAL COLORS

Red, black, and green

NATIONAL ANTHEM

The anthem was adopted in 2004, following the fall of the Taliban government.

Soroud-e-Melli (National Anthem)

This land is Afghanistan
It is the pride of every Afghan
The land of peace, the land of the sword
Its sons are all brave
This is the country of all tribes
The land of the Baluch and Uzbeks,
Pashtuns and Hazaras,
Turkmen and Tajiks with them,
Arabs and Gojars, Pamirian,
Nuristan, Barahawi, and Qizilbash,
Also Aimak and Pashaye
This land will shine forever
Like the sun in the blue sky
In the chest of Asia

It will remain as the heart forever
We will follow the one God
We all say, Allah is great; we all say, Allah is great

CURRENCY

Afghan afghani

INTERNET IDENTIFIER

.af

VEHICLE IDENTIFICATION PLATES/STICKERS

AFG

PASSPORT

The passport cover has the name of the country in Farsi (Persian) and Pashto, the coat of arms, the name of the country in English, and the word *passport* in English.

AIRLINES

Ariana Afghan Airlines; Safi Airways

NATIONAL FLOWER

Red poppy (unofficial)

NATIONAL TREE

Mulberry (unofficial)

NATIONAL ANIMAL

Gazelle (unofficial; seriously endangered)

NATIONAL RESOURCES

Natural resources include gold, copper, zinc, coal, iron ore, precious and semiprecious stones, talc, barites, sulfur, lead, and salt. There are potentially significant petroleum and natural gas reserves. Opium, the poppy derivative that is the basis for heroin and other drugs, is illegal but is the country's most important export and its most profitable product.

FOODS

Qaubilli pilau, a rice dish with beef or lamb, is considered the national dish.

Lamb kebab served with rice is also a very popular dish and is considered by some as a national dish, along with *sabse borani,* spinach with onions and yogurt; *mourgh* (Afghan chicken), chicken breast prepared with garlic, yogurt, and lemon juice; *aush,* a dish of noodles, lentils, meat, and yogurt; *samoosi yirakot,* stuffed vegetable turnovers; *kofta nakhod,* meatballs of beef and onion cooked with chickpeas; and *baklava,* a dessert of thin dough layered with crushed nuts.

SPORTS/SPORTS TEAMS

The national sport is *buzkashi,* a sport similar to polo and played by horsemen in two teams, each attempting to retain control of a goat carcass. Afghan national teams also participate in many sports at an international level.

TEAM SPORTS

Badminton

Afghanistan Men's Badminton Team; Afghanistan Women's Badminton Team

Basketball

Afghanistan Basketball Team; Afghanistan Women's Basketball Team

Cricket

Afghanistan Cricket Team

Field Hockey

Afghanistan Field Hockey Team

Football

Afghanistan Football Team, nickname Team Melli (the Team or the National Team); Afghanistan Women's Football Team, nickname Team Melli (the Team or the National Team); Afghanistan Under-19 Football Team, nickname Team Melli (the Team or the National Team); Afghanistan Futsal Team

Volleyball

Afghanistan Volleyball Team; Afghanistan Women's Volleyball Team

INDIVIDUAL SPORTS

Afghanistan Athletics Team; Afghanistan Boxing Team; Afghanistan Canoeing Team; Afghanistan Cycling Team; Afghanistan Fencing Team; Afghanistan Gymnastics Team; Afghanistan Judo Team; Afghanistan Rowing Team; Afghanistan Table Tennis Team; Afghanistan Tae Kwon Do Team; Afghanistan Weight Lifting Team; Afghanistan Wrestling Team

NATIONAL HEROES OR PERSONIFICATIONS

Mahmud of Ghazni, creator of an early medieval empire; Ahmad Shah Adbali, the founder of the Durrani dynasty; Ahmad Shah Durrani, the creator of the modern state of Afghanistan in 1747; Amanullah Khan, who attempted to modernize the country but was ousted in 1929

NATIONAL HOLIDAY/INDEPENDENCE DAY

Independence Day, August 19

FESTIVALS/FAIRS

Nau Roz (Afghan New Year Festival), January–March (variable; based on the Islamic calendar); Labor Day, May 1

SIGNIFICANT EVENTS IN FORMATION OF NATIONAL IDENTITY

2000–1200 B.C.E. Aryan peoples enter northern Afghanistan.

Sixth century B.C.E. Most of Afghanistan is brought under Persian rule.

330 B.C.E. The Greeks, under Alexander the Great, conquer the region.

300–185 B.C.E. Buddhism is introduced.

First century C.E. The vast Kushan Empire, centered in modern Afghanistan, flourishes as a Buddhist culture.

600 C.E.–800 C.E. Islam emerges.

1219 Afghanistan is overrun and devastated by the invading Mongols of Genghis Khan.

1747 Most of Afghanistan is united under the Durrani dynasty of Ahmad Shah Durrani.

1881 The British establish a loose colonial control of Afghanistan.

1919 The Kingdom of Afghanistan achieves independence from British rule.

1933–1978 A period of stability under King Zahir Shah, probably the longest in Afghanistan's history, ends in 1973 in a bloodless coup and results in the establishment of a republic. The royal family is murdered in 1978 when communists, with the support of the Soviet Union, take control of the country.

1970s Growing opposition to a series of unstable communist governments and conflicts between government factions bring Afghanistan into the Cold War. The United States* supports and arms numerous anticommunist groups, mostly Muslim groups opposed to the communist government's official atheism.

1979–1989 In 1979, Soviet troops invade Afghanistan to prop up the weak communist regime. The Soviet occupation results in up to five million refugees, mostly resettled in camps in neighboring Pakistan*. In 1989, faced with mounting losses and international pressure, the Soviet military withdraws.

1990s After the Soviet withdrawal, the United States and its allies lose interest and do little to rebuild the war-ravaged country. Fighting continues among the various factions, splitting the country into ethnic and regional fiefdoms controlled by local warlords. More refugees, including many of the country's educated elite, flee the country's instability and violence. Continued chaos and corruption allow the rapid growth of the Taliban, a collection of Muslim, mostly Pashto, groups that finally win control of the fragmented country in 1996. The Taliban institutes an extremely harsh regime based on strict interpretation of Sharia (Islamic law). Women are banned from seeking jobs or education, modern clothing is forbidden, music is outlawed, and any infringement of the Taliban version of Sharia is punished instantly. Opium production, seen as anti-Islamic, is nearly eradicated. The Taliban is accused of training and arming various Islamic terrorist groups active in the 1990s, including the Al-Qaeda group.

2001–2008 Following the September 11 attacks on the United States, the United States military launches Operation Enduring Freedom, a widely supported campaign to destroy the Al-Qaeda terrorist network in Afghanistan and to overthrow the radical Taliban government. The success of the military operation allows the formation of a pro-Western Afghan government, but the country continues to grapple with a Taliban insurgency in the south and widespread instability, corruption, and tribalism. An estimated four million refugees return to the country.

2009 Opium production once again flourish and account for a third to two-thirds of the country's national economy, making Afghanistan the world's largest producer. Flawed elections give the Western-supported government an electoral victory but much of the country remains outside government control or is under military control by the armed forces sent by many countries as part of the fight against local warlords, Islamic fundamentalists, and remnants of the Taliban.

AMERICAN SAMOA

OFFICIAL NAME
Amerika Samoa/Samoa Amelika (Samoan); American Samoa (English)

POPULATION
69,800 (2009e)

INHABITANTS' NAME/NICKNAME
American Samoan(s); Samoan(s)

LANGUAGE/LANGUAGES
English, Samoan (both official); Tongan, others

Religion/Religions

Christian Congregationalist, 50 percent; Roman Catholic, 20 percent; other or no religion

Territorial/National Flag

The flag is blue with a white triangle, edged in red, based on the fly. The triangle extends to the hoist and bears the American eagle in proper colors and facing towards the hoist. The eagle grasps the symbol of power of the Samoan high chiefs, the *uatogi* (a war club), and the symbol of wisdom of the councils, the *fue* (ritual stick). The colors of the flag are both traditionally Samoan and American, and the American eagle, holding traditional Samoan emblems, represents the protection and friendship of the United States.

Coat of Arms/Seal

The Seal of American Samoa is based in traditional local design. The *fue,* the ritual stick or fly switch, represents wisdom, while the *to'oto'o,* or staff, represents authority. Samoan chiefs use both symbols to indicate their rank. The *tanoa* (kava bowl) represents service to the chief.

Motto

Samoa ia muamua le Atua (Samoan); Samoa, let God be first (English)

Capital City

Pago Pago is the capital; Fagatogo is the seat of government.

Type of Government

Representative democracy as a self-governing territory of the United States*

National Emblem

Fue and *to'oto'o* (the ritual stick or fly switch and the staff of authority)

National Colors

Blue, red, and white

National Anthem

The official anthem of the United States, "The Star-Spangled Banner," was translated into Samoan in 2006. The official territorial anthem is "Amerika Samoa," written in the Samoan language with an English translation.

> **Amerika Samoa (Samoan)/American Samoa Anthem (English)**
> American Samoa
> You are my beloved country
> Your name I shan't search for
> You are my hope
> You are the jewel of the Pacific
> That is the lure of the five islands
> Your name forever holds
> Your legends of yore
> Tutuila and Manu'a Ala mai
> Stand up and be counted
> Serve and bow down to your country
> Let it be blessed and grow
> American Samoa
> The land of the free

Patron Saint

The Holy Family

Currency

U.S. dollar

Internet Identifier

.as

Vehicle Identification Plates/Stickers

USA United States (official); AS American Samoa (unofficial)

Passport

American Samoans are U.S. citizens and travel on passports of the United States.

NATIONAL FLOWER

Paogo, or *ula-fala*

NATIONAL TREE

Coconut Palm (shown on license plates)

NATIONAL ANIMAL

Flying fox (unofficial)

NATIONAL BIRD

American eagle (shown on National Flag)

NATIONAL RESOURCES

Natural resources include fish, pumice, pumicite, sandy beaches, a pleasant climate, and interesting scenery. The relatively undiscovered islands have become popular with sophisticated tourists seeking new destinations in the Pacific.

FOODS

The Samoan *umu,* an above-ground stone oven, is the traditional method of preparing Samoan food, consisting of chicken, pork, taro, coconut, breadfruit, fish and shellfish, and various vegetables wrapped in banana leaves. Other specialties include *palusami,* taro leaves baked in coconut cream; *oka,* raw fish marinated in coconut cream; octopus cooked in coconut cream and served in a half coconut shell; *talo ta'amu,* a baked root vegetable with coconut cream; and *masi samoa,* a type of bread made of flour, eggs, and coconut milk.

SPORTS/SPORTS TEAMS

The most popular sports are American football, wrestling, and *killikiti,* Samoan cricket. American football is considered the de facto national sport. American Samoa national teams participate in many sports at an international level.

TEAM SPORTS

Baseball

American Samoa Baseball Team; American Samoa Softball Team

Basketball

American Samoa Basketball Team; American Samoa Women's Basketball Team

Football

American Samoa Football Team; American Samoa Women's Football Team; American Samoa Rugby Union Team; American Samoa Touch Football Team; American Samoa Women's Touch Football Team; American Samoa Rugby League Team; American Samoa American Football Team.

Hockey

American Samoa Field Hockey Team

Table Tennis

American Samoa Table Tennis Team

Tennis

Pacific Oceania Davis Cup Team; Pacific Oceania Fed Cup Team (Pacific Oceania teams represent a number of Pacific island nations)

Volleyball

American Samoa Men's Volleyball Team; American Samoa Women's Volleyball Team; American Samoa Men's Beach Volleyball Team; American Samoa Women's Beach Volleyball Team

INDIVIDUAL SPORTS

American Samoa Amateur Boxing Team; American Samoa Archery Team; American Samoa Athletics Team; American Samoa Canoeing Team; American Samoa Judo Team; American Samoa Sailing Team; American

Samoa Swim Team; American Samoa Tae Kwon Do Team; American Samoa Weight Lifting Team; American Samoa Wrestling Team

NATIONAL HEROES OR PERSONIFICATIONS

Samuel Sailele Ripley, leader of the Mau Movement after World War I; Mariota Tiumalu Tulasosopo, the chief who led the autonomy movement in the 1950s and 1960s and wrote the official anthem; Paramount Chief Letluli Olo Misilagi, known as Freddie Letuli, who perfected the traditional fire-knife dance; Eni Fa'una'a Hunkin Faleomavaega, the longest-serving representative in the United States House of Representatives and an author on Samoan perspectives.

NATIONAL HOLIDAY/INDEPENDENCE DAY

Flag Day, April 17

FESTIVALS/FAIRS

The Flag Day Festival on April 17 is an annual event and the largest festival in the territory, with traditional dancing and singing, colorful parades, arts and crafts exhibitions, and *fautasi,* traditional longboat races.

SIGNIFICANT EVENTS IN FORMATION OF NATIONAL IDENTITY

200 B.C.E. By 200 B.C.E. Samoa is the center of a flourishing Polynesian culture based on agriculture, fishing, and extensive trade with Tonga*, Fiji*, and other Pacific islands.

1300 C.E. About 1300 C.E., to alleviate overcrowding in Samoa, settlers from the islands colonize Tokelau*, which explains the cultural and linguistic ties between the two island groups.

1722 European explorers first reach Samoa when, in 1722, a Dutch ship under Captain Jacob Roggeveen sights the islands.

19th century In the early 19th century, Christian Rarotongan missionaries from the Cook Islands* are followed by a group of Western missionaries led by John Williams of the Congregationalist London Missionary Society in the 1830s, officially bringing Christianity to Samoa and bringing an end to the Samoans' traditional religion.

1871–1872 The government of New Zealand* recommends immediate British annexation of the Samoa Islands to prevent colonization by other powers. Commander Richard Meade of the *USS Narragansett* signs a treaty that grants the United States rights to a coaling station in Pago Pago.

1889–1899 The Samoa Islands become a tripartite protectorate of Germany*, the United Kingdom*, and the United States. The 1899 Treaty of Berlin finally settles international rivalries, and the United States and Germany divide the Samoan archipelago.

1900–1904 The United States formally occupies its portion—a smaller group of eastern islands with the deep-water harbor of Pago Pago.

1911 The U.S. Naval Station Tutuila is renamed American Samoa. The name is applied to the entire eastern group of the Samoa Islands.

1929–1930 The U.S. Congress formally accepts the cession of Manu'a and Tutuila by their chiefs, retroactive to 1904. In 1930, the Congress sends a committee to investigate the status of American Samoa and the Samoans, led by Americans who had a part in the overthrow of the Hawaiian Kingdom.

1941–1945 During World War II, U.S. Marines in American Samoa outnumber the local population, exerting a huge cultural influence on the society.

1946–1951 An attempt to incorporate American Samoa is defeated in Congress, primarily through the efforts of American Samoan chiefs, led by Tulasosopo Mariota. These chiefs' efforts lead to the creation of a local legislature, the American Samoa *fono,* which meets in the village of Fagatogo, the de facto and de jure capital of the territory.

1951 American Samoa remains under the rule of the U.S. Department of the Navy until its transfer to the jurisdiction of Department of the Interior in 1951.

1960–1967 In time, a locally elected official replaces the Navy-appointed governor. Although technically considered unorganized, in that the U.S. Congress has not passed an Organic Act for the territory, American Samoa is self-governing under a constitution that becomes effective July 1, 1967.

2000–2009 The islanders' employment falls into three relatively equal categories of approximately 5,000 workers each: the public sector, two tuna canneries, and the private sector.

See also Samoa

AUSTRALIA

OFFICIAL NAME
Commonwealth of Australia

POPULATION
21,370,000 (2009e)

INHABITANTS' NAME/NICKNAME
Australian(s); Aussie(s)

LANGUAGE/LANGUAGES
English (de facto official); Aboriginal languages, Chinese, Italian, Greek, others

RELIGION/RELIGIONS
Roman Catholic, 27 percent; Anglican, 21 percent; other Protestant, 21 percent; Buddhist, 1.5 percent; Muslim, 1.5 percent; other or no religion

NATIONAL FLAG
The flag is a Blue Ensign with a large, white, seven-pointed star on the lower hoist and the Union Jack as a canton on the upper hoist; on the fly is a representation of the Southern Cross constellation. The Union Jack symbolizes Australia's history as six British colonies and the principles on which the federation is based. The points of the Commonwealth Star represent the original six colonies, plus another for any future territories. The Southern Cross is the most visible constellation and represents justice, prudence, temperance, and fortitude.

COAT OF ARMS/SEAL
A shield bears the symbols of Australia's six states, surrounded by a border representing federation. An emu and a kangaroo support the shield. Above the shield is the seven-pointed Commonwealth Star, also called the Star of Federation, above a blue and gold wreath.

CAPITAL CITY
Canberra

TYPE OF GOVERNMENT
Federal parliamentary democracy

NATIONAL EMBLEM
Commonwealth Star (Star of Federation)

NATIONAL COLORS
Gold and green

NATIONAL ANTHEM
"Advance Australia Fair" was adopted as the official anthem in 1984. Up to that time, the anthem of the Commonwealth of Nations, "God Save the Queen," was the official anthem of the federation.

Advance Australia Fair

Australians all, let us rejoice,
For we are young and free;
We've golden soil and wealth for toil,
Our home is girt by sea;
Our land abounds in Nature's gifts
Of beauty rich and rare;
In history's page, let every stage
Advance Australia fair!
In joyful strains then let us sing,
"Advance Australia fair!"

Beneath our radiant Southern Cross,
We'll toil with hearts and hands;

To make this Commonwealth of ours
Renowned of all the lands;
For those who've come across the seas
We've boundless plains to share;
With courage let us all combine
To advance Australia fair.
In joyful strains then let us sing
"Advance Australia fair!"

PATRON SAINT
Mary, Help of Christians

CURRENCY
Australian dollar

INTERNET IDENTIFIER
.au

VEHICLE IDENTIFICATION PLATES/STICKERS
AUS

PASSPORT
The passport cover has the coat of arms, the name of the country in English, and the word *passport*.

AIRLINES
Qantas; JetStar

NATIONAL FLOWER
Golden wattle

NATIONAL TREE
Gum tree

NATIONAL ANIMAL
Kangaroo (on the coat of arms); Koala (unofficial)

NATIONAL BIRD
Emu (on the coat of arms)

NATIONAL FISH
Short-finned eel (unofficial)

NATIONAL RESOURCES
Natural resources include bauxite, coal, iron ore, copper, tin, gold, silver, uranium, nickel, tungsten, mineral sands, lead, zinc, diamonds, natural gas, and petroleum. Australia's varied scenery, vibrant culture, sandy beaches, and pleasant climate support an important tourist industry.

FOODS
Meat pie with sauce, fish and chips, and Pavlova (a cream cake dessert) are considered national dishes. Other specialties include apricot chicken; barbecued shrimp; chicken pie; grilled lobster with lime butter; kangaroo fillet with red currant sauce; macadamia tart; and roasted lamb.

SPORTS/SPORTS TEAMS
Australians have a range of sporting interests; therefore, there is no official national sport. However, cricket, because of its historic associations, is often considered the national sport. Various forms of football are also very popular, particularly Australian-rules football, which also is often considered the de facto national sport. Australia national teams participate in many sports at an international level.

TEAM SPORTS
Badminton
Australia Badminton Team

Baseball
Australia Baseball Team; Australia Softball Team

Basketball
Australia Basketball Team, nickname the Boomers; Australia Women's Basketball Team, nickname the Opals; Australia Under-21 Basketball Team, nickname the Crocs or Crocodiles; Australia Women's Under-21

Basketball Team, nickname the Sapphires; Australia Under-19 Basketball Team, nickname the Emus; Australia Women's Under-19 Basketball Team, nickname the Gems; Australia Men's (Intellectual Disability) Basketball Team, nickname the Boomerangs; Australia Women's (Intellectual Disability) Basketball Team, nickname the Pearls; Australia Wheelchair Basketball Team, nickname the Rollers; Australia Women's Wheelchair Basketball Team, nickname the Gliders

Bowls

Australia Bowls Team, nickname the Jackaroos; Australia Women's Bowls Team, nickname the Sapphires

Cricket

Australia Cricket Team, nickname the Baggy Greens or the Aussies; Australia Women's Cricket Team, nickname the Baggy Greens or the Aussies; Australia A Cricket Team

Curling

Australia Curling Team; Australia Women's Curling Team

Football

Australia Football Team, nickname the Socceroos; Australia Women's Football Team, nickname the Matildas; Australia Under-23 Football Team, nickname the Olyroos; Australia Under-20 Football Team, nickname the Young Socceroos; Australia Women's Under-20 Football Team, nickname the Young Matildas; Australia Under-17 Football Team, nickname the Joeys; Australia Futsal Team; Australia Australian-Rules Football Team, nickname All-Australia Team; Australia Women's Australian-Rules Football Team, nickname All-Australia Team; Australia Rugby Union Team, nickname the Wallabies; Australia Women's Rugby Union Team, nickname the Wallaroos; Australia A Rugby Union Team; Australia Rugby League Team, nickname the Kangaroos; Australia Women's Rugby League Team, nickname the Jillaroos; Australia Rugby Union Team (Sevens), nickname Australia Sevens; Australia Women's Rugby Union Team (Sevens); Australia Under-21 Rugby Union Team, nickname the Junior Wallabies; Australia Schoolboy Rugby Union Team; Australia InterRules Football Team; Australia Women's InterRules Football Team; Australia Wheelchair Rugby Team, nickname the Steelers; Australia American-Rules Football Team, nickname the Australia Outback; Australia Men's Touch Football Team; Australia Women's Touch Football Team.

Golf

Australia Men's Pitch and Putt Team; Australia Women's Pitch and Putt Team

Handball

Australia Handball Team; Australia Women's Handball Team

Hockey

Australia Field Hockey Team, nickname the Kookaburras; Australia Women's Field Hockey Team, nickname the Hockeyroos; Australia Under-21 Field Hockey Team, nickname the Burras; Australia Ice Hockey Team, nickname the Mighty Roos; Australia Junior Ice Hockey Team; Australia Women's Ice Hockey Team; Australia Roller Hockey Team; Australia Women's Roller Hockey Team

Korfball

Australia Korfball Team

Lacrosse

Australia Lacrosse Team, nickname the Sharks; Australia Women's Lacrosse Team, nickname the Stars; Australia Under-19 Lacrosse Team, nickname the Crocodiles; Australia Women's Under-19 Lacrosse Team, nickname the Stars; Australia Women's Under-17 Lacrosse Team, nickname Team Koala; Australia Box Lacrosse Team, nickname the Boxaroos

Netball
Australia Netball Team

Polo
Australia Polo Team

Racing
A1 Team Australia; Australia Speedway Team

Table Tennis
Australia Table Tennis Team

Tennis
Australia Davis Cup Team; Australia Fed Cup Team

Volleyball
Australia Volleyball Team; Australia Women's Volleyball Team; Australia Beach Volleyball Team; Australia Women's Beach Volleyball Team

Water Polo
Australia Men's Water Polo Team, nickname the Sharks; Australia Women's Water Polo Team, nickname the Sharks

INDIVIDUAL SPORTS
Australia Aikido Team; Australia Amateur Boxing Team; Australia Archery Team; Australia Athletics Team; Australia Canoeing Team; Australia Chess Team; Australia Cycling Team; Australia Equestrian Team; Australia Fencing Team; Australia Gymnastics Team; Australia Judo Team; Australia Modern Pentathlon Team; Australia Rowing Team; Australia Sailing Team; Australia Shooting Team; Australia Swim Team, nickname the Dolphins; Australia Tae Kwon Do Team;

Australia Triathlon Team; Australia Weight Lifting Team; Australia Wrestling Team

WINTER SPORTS
Australia Alpine Ski Team; Australia Bandy Team; Australia Biathlon Team; Australia Curling Team; Australia Women's Curling Team; Australia Ice Hockey Team, nickname the Mighty Roos; Australia Junior Ice Hockey Team; Australia Women's Ice Hockey Team; Australia Luge Team; Australia Skating Team

NATIONAL HEROES OR PERSONIFICATIONS
Bronzed, healthy Aussie; Digger (Aussie soldier); Little Boy from Manly; Ned Kelly, an outlaw and folk hero; gold miners of the Eureka Rebellion; Henry Lawson, one of the most famous and most popular of all Australian writers; "Banjo" Paterson, a bush poet and nationalist patriot; Jack Lang, one of the pioneers of Australian independence

NATIONAL HOLIDAY/INDEPENDENCE DAY
Australia Day, January 26

FESTIVALS/FAIRS
Melbourne Cup Carnival, annual horse race and festival, first Tuesday in November; National Multicultural Festival, February; Sydney Gay and Lesbian Mardi Gras, February; National Folk Festival, April; Dreaming Festival, June

SIGNIFICANT EVENTS IN FORMATION OF NATIONAL IDENTITY
40,000 B.C.E. The Australian mainland has been inhabited for more than 42,000 years by the indigenous Australians, the Aborigines. Their tribal cultures differed greatly across the continent, but all cultures included reverence for the land and its bounty.

1600–1770 After occasional visits or sightings by fishermen from the islands to the north, Australia begins to be visited by European explorers and merchants in the 17th century. In 1770, the British claim the eastern coast of the continent. The first settlers are criminals, debtors, and often their families, sentenced to be transported to the penal colonies established in Australia.

1770–1848 As the settlements grow and new areas are explored, another five largely self-governing colonies are established alongside the first, called New South Wales. The transportation of convicts to the colonies ceases in 1848 after a determined campaign by the settlers.

1850 The indigenous population, estimated at 350,000 at the time of European settlement, declines rapidly over the subsequent 150 years, mainly due to infectious diseases, forced resettlement, loss of traditional lands, and cultural disintegration.

1869–1976 The indigenous Australians suffer discrimination and other forms of racism from the beginning of European settlement. The removal of children, as practiced by the federal government, state government, and church missions, continues from approximately 1869 to 1969, with some children being taken from their homes into the 1970s. The policy, to place the children in adoptive homes where they would learn to live like the majority of the Australian population, leads to massive abuses and furthers the deterioration of the Aborigines' traditional cultures. In 1962, indigenous Australians are finally allowed to vote in commonwealth elections, and in state elections shortly after. The Aborigines continue to suffer high unemployment, discrimination, substance abuse, educational problems, and high rates of violent crimes. On February 13, 2008, Prime Minister Kevin Rudd formally apologizes to the indigenous peoples of Australia for former government policies and their stolen generations.

1901 The six Australian colonies join in a federation, the Commonwealth of Australia. A new Australian Capital Territory is formed from a part of New South Wales in 1911, and the capital of the federation is moved there to the planned city of Canberra. From the time of federation, Australia maintains a stable liberal democracy closely allied to the United Kingdom*.

1914–1945 Australia supports the United Kingdom in World War I, suffering a heroic defeat, along with New Zealand, at Gallipoli in Turkey*. Many Australians regard this defeat as the true birth of the Australian nation—its first major military campaign. A second nation-building campaign, the Kokoda Track Campaign, takes place during World War II.

1946–1980 Following World War II, the government begins a massive program of European immigration. After narrowly preventing a Japanese invasion and suffering direct attacks on Australian territory for the first time, the government and the people see that the country must "populate or perish." Government policy favors immigration from Europe, specifically the United Kingdom and Ireland*. A policy known as the White Australian policy is instituted, which restricts the number of immigrants from some regions, particularly the Asian countries to the north, but also disenfranchises the already marginalized Aborigines. In 1973, the White Australia policy is abolished. Henceforth, numerous government policies promote racial harmony based on multiculturalism.

The dismantling of the White Australia immigration policy in the decades after World War II begins an era of large-scale immigration by non-European peoples.

1986–1999 The final constitutional ties between Australia and the United Kingdom are severed with the passing of the Australia Act in 1986. In 1999, Australian voters reject by a majority of 54 percent a motion to become a republic with a president appointed by two-thirds vote of both houses of parliament.

2008 Many Australians now see their nation as an Asian-Pacific nation, with only weakening links to Europe. Proposals for the severing of ties to the Commonwealth of Nations and for the creation of a distinct Australian republic continue to be discussed at all levels of Australian society.

2009 Immigration remains a politically sensitive issue, with many Australians favoring a quota system or other means to manage the large number of immigrants, most from nearby Asia.

BANGLADESH

OFFICIAL NAME
Gônoprojatontri Bangladesh (Bengali); People's Republic of Bangladesh (English)

POPULATION
148,388,200 (2009e)

INHABITANTS' NAME/NICKNAME
Bangladeshi(s)

LANGUAGE/LANGUAGES
Bengali (Bangla) (official); English, indigenous languages, others

RELIGION/RELIGIONS
Sunni Muslim, 73 percent; Hindu, 15 percent; Shia Muslim, 5 percent; Christian, animist, other or no religion

NATIONAL FLAG
The flag has a green field bearing a centered red disk representing the sun slightly offset to the hoist. The red disk represents the sun rising over Bengal and also the blood of those who died for the independence of Bangladesh. The green field stands for the lushness of the land of Bangladesh.

COAT OF ARMS/SEAL
The coat of arms of 1972 is round, colored in gold and white. Within a circle is a stylized depiction of a water lily, the national plant. Above the blossom of the lily are four five-pointed stars, as well as leaves of the jute tree and one rice ear on either side. The four stars represent the political principles of the state: nationalism, democracy, Islamic socialism, and confession to Islam. The water lily represents the many rivers that run through Bangladesh and the agriculture that is possible because of the rivers.

CAPITAL CITY
Dhaka

TYPE OF GOVERNMENT
Parliamentary republic

NATIONAL EMBLEM
Red sun

NATIONAL COLORS
Green and red

NATIONAL ANTHEM
The anthem dates from 1906, during the attempted British partition of Bengal, a time of great unrest in the region. It was adopted as the official anthem at independence in 1971.

> **Amar Shonar Bangla (Bengali); My Beloved Bangladesh (English)**
>
> My Bengal of gold, I love you.
> Forever your skies, your air set my heart in tune
> As if it were a flute.
> In spring, O mother mine, the fragrance from your mango groves
> Makes me wild with joy,
> Ah, what a thrill!
>
> In autumn, O mother mine,
> In the full-blossomed paddy fields
> I have seen spread all over sweet smiles.
> Ah, what a beauty, what shades, what an affection,
> and what a tenderness!
> What a quilt have you spread at the feet of banyan trees
> And along the banks of rivers!
>
> O mother mine, words from your lips
> Are like nectar to my ears.
>
> Ah, what a thrill!
> If sadness, O mother mine, casts a gloom on your face,
> My eyes are filled with tears!

CURRENCY
Bangladeshi taka

INTERNET IDENTIFIER
.bd

VEHICLE IDENTIFICATION
PLATES/STICKERS
BD

PASSPORT
The passport cover has the name of the country in Bengali and English, the coat of arms, and the word *passport* in English and Bengali.

AIRLINES
Biman Bangladesh Airlines; GMG Airlines

NATIONAL FLOWER
Shapla (white water lily)

NATIONAL TREE
Jute; banyan (unofficial)

NATIONAL ANIMAL
Bengal tiger

NATIONAL BIRD
Doyel (oriental magpie robin)

NATIONAL FISH
Hilsa shad

NATIONAL RESOURCES
Natural resources include natural gas, arable land, timber, coal, and fisheries. Production of jute, once the major export, has declined since World War II. Agricultural products and garments are now the major exports. Recent investment in the natural gas fields promises a better economic future. Remittances sent by expatriate Bangladeshis living in other countries are also a major source of foreign currency and an important asset of the country.

FOODS
The culinary tradition of Bangladesh has close relations to Indian and Middle Eastern cuisines, as well as many unique traits. Rice and fish are traditional favorites, leading to a common saying that "fish and rice make a Bengali" (*machhe bhate bangali*). National specialties include *biryani,* a dish of rice with meat and vegetables; *kalia,* a dish of meat, onions, garlic, chilies, and spices; *maker taukari,* fish curry; *reshmi kabab,* chicken with onions, garlic, and spices; *tikya kabab,* beef with lentils, onions, and garlic; vindaloo, a spicy meat dish; and *misto doi,* sweet yogurt.

SPORTS/SPORTS TEAMS
Cricket is the most popular sport, but others, such as kabaddi, football, and field hockey, are also very popular. Kabaddi was defined as the national sport by law in 1972. Bangladesh national teams participate in many sports at the international level.

TEAM SPORTS
Badminton
Bangladesh Badminton Team

Cricket
Bangladesh Cricket Team, nickname the Tigers; Bangladesh Women's Cricket Team, nickname the Tigers

Football
Bangladesh Football Team

Hockey
Bangladesh Field Hockey Team

Kabaddi
Bangladesh Kabaddi Team

Table Tennis
Bangladesh Table Tennis Team

Tennis
Bangladesh Davis Cup Team

Volleyball
Bangladesh Volleyball Team

INDIVIDUAL SPORTS

Bangladesh Amateur Boxing Team; Bangladesh Archery Team; Bangladesh Athletics Team; Bangladesh Chess Team; Bangladesh Cycling Team; Bangladesh Fencing Team; Bangladesh Gymnastics Team; Bangladesh Judo Team; Bangladesh Modern Pentathlon Team; Bangladesh Rowing Team; Bangladesh Shooting Team; Bangladesh Swim Team; Bangladesh Tae Kwon Do Team; Bangladesh Weight Lifting Team; Bangladesh Wrestling Team

NATIONAL HEROES
OR PERSONIFICATIONS

Kazi Nazrul Islam was a poet, musician, revolutionary, and philosopher best known for pioneering poetic works espousing intense spiritual rebellion against orthodoxy and oppression. Popularly known as the *Bidrohi Kobi* (Rebel Poet), Nazrul is officially recognized as the national poet of Bangladesh and is also commemorated in India. Sheikh Mujibur Rahman, the autonomy and independence leader in the 1960s and 1970s, is revered as the founder of Bangladesh; Rabindranath Tagore, poet and novelist of the early 20th century; Jasim Uddin, known as the people's poet.

NATIONAL HOLIDAY/
INDEPENDENCE DAY

Independence Day, March 26

FESTIVALS/FAIRS

The two Eids, Eid al-Fitr and Eid al-Adha, are the two largest festivals in the Islamic calendar. The day before Eid al-Fitr is called Chäd Rat, "the night of the moon," and is celebrated with fireworks. Other Muslim festivals are also observed, as are major Hindu festivals, such as Durga Puja and Saraswati Puja.

SIGNIFICANT EVENTS IN FORMATION
OF NATIONAL IDENTITY

2000 B.C.E.–1000 B.C.E. Traces of civilizations in the region date back four thousand years to when the area was settled by Dravidian, Tibeto-Burman, and Austro-Asiatic peoples.

Seventh century B.C.E.–sixth century C.E. Indo-Aryan invaders establish the kingdom of Gangaridai, possibly in the seventh century B.C.E., Bengal forms part of the Gupta Empire.

12th century–16th century Sufi missionaries first introduce Islam to the region, and subsequent conquests by Muslim armies help to spread the new religion across the area. In the 16th century, the Muslim Mughal Empire takes control, and Dhaka becomes an important Mughal center of religion and administration.

15th century–1757 Armed incursions by Europeans result in turmoil and the conquest of Bengal by the troops of the British East India Company in 1757.

1857–1943 Many Bengali soldiers under British command participate in the bloody rebellion of 1857, following rumors that new bullets had been covered in pork fat forbidden to Muslims. The Great Bengal Famine, the worst in Bengali history, claims some three million lives in 1943 during the Second World War.

1947 Bengal is divided along religious lines, the western, mainly Hindu portion going to India* and the eastern, majority Muslim region forming part of the new Muslim state of Pakistan*, which has territory on both the east and west of newly independent India.

1948–1951 East Bengal, as the Muslim portion is known, forms a province of Pakistan with its capital at Dhaka. Land reforms in 1950 eliminate many of the feudal traditions in the region, but in spite of a larger population and greater economic potential, East Bengal, also called East Pakistan, remains dominated by the upper classes of the ethnically distinct western part of the country.

1952–1962 The Bengali-dominated Awami League emerges as the political voice of the disadvantaged Bengalis of Pakistan.

1960s The Awami League leads agitation for autonomy for East Pakistan. Leaders of the movement, including the president, Sheikh Mujibur Rahman, are jailed for subversion and other crimes against the state.

1970 A massive cyclone devastates much of East Pakistan in 1970, its effects made worse by a very poor response by the central government. The growing anger among the Bengali-speaking population flares into violence when Sheikh Mujibur Rahman, whose Awami League wins a majority in parliament in the 1970 elections, is blocked from taking office.

1971 The government launches Operation Searchlight, a sustained military invasion of East Pakistan. Some ten million Bengali refugees flee into India to escape the terror and violence. Estimates of the numbers who die in systematic massacres range from about three hundred thousand to more than three million. The Indian Army and the Bengali fighters achieve a decisive victory over the Pakistani troops.

1973–1975 A series of bloody coups and countercoups follow until a military government reinstates multiparty politics. Political instability, coupled with frequent cyclones and poor harvests, leaves Bangladesh as one of the world's poorest countries.

1982–1991 In 1982, an anticommunist military dictatorship takes control of the country and rules until 1990. Multiparty democracy is again embraced, with the widow and daughter of two of the country's murdered rulers leading the two largest political parties.

2007–2009 In 2007, widespread violence results in a caretaker government being appointed to oversee the next general election. Much of the violence stems from extensive corruption, disorder, and political violence and manipulations.

BHUTAN

Official Name

'Brug Rgyal-khabDru Gäkhap (Dzongkha); Kingdom of Bhutan (English)

Nickname

Land of the Thunder Dragon

Population

672,300 (2009e)

Inhabitants' Name/Nickname

Bhutanese

Language/Languages

Dzongkha (official); Tibetan, Nepalese, English, others

Religion/Religions

Drukpa Kagyu—the Nyingmapa school of Tibetan Buddhism, 75 percent; Hindu, 23 percent; other or no religion

National Flag

A white dragon symbolizes purity. The two colors of the flag, red and yellow, divided diagonally, represent spiritual and temporal power within Bhutan. The orange part of the flag represents the Drukpas monasteries and Buddhist religious practice, while the saffron yellow field denotes the secular authority of the dynasty. The flag's central dragon represents Druk, the Tibetan name for the kingdom of Bhutan. The jewels clamped in the dragon's claws symbolize wealth. The snarling mouth represents the strength of the male and female deities protecting the country.

Coat of Arms/Seal

The national emblem, contained in a circle, is composed of a double diamond thunderbolt, or *dorji,* placed above a lotus, surmounted by a jewel and framed by two dragons. The thunderbolt represents the harmony between secular and religious power. The lotus symbolizes purity; the jewel expresses sovereign power; and the two dragons, male and female, stand for the name of the country, which they proclaim with their great voice, "the thunder."

CAPITAL CITY

Thimphu

TYPE OF GOVERNMENT

Constitutional monarchy

NATIONAL EMBLEM

Druk, the Thunder Dragon

NATIONAL COLORS

Yellow and red

NATIONAL ANTHEM

The original melody of the anthem is based on a folk song, which is also the music for a traditional dance, making the Bhutanese anthem possibly the only national anthem that is based on the music of a traditional dance.

> **Druk Tsendhen (Dzongkha); The Glorious Dragon Kingdom (English)**
>
> In the Thunder Dragon Kingdom, where cypresses grow,
> Refuge of the glorious monastic and civil traditions,
> The King of Druk, precious sovereign,
> His being is eternal, his reign prosperous
> The enlightenment teachings thrive and flourish
> May the people shine like the sun of peace and happiness!

PATRON SAINT/PROTECTOR

The Thunder Dragon

CURRENCY

Bhutanese ngultrum

INTERNET IDENTIFIER

.bt

VEHICLE IDENTIFICATION PLATES/STICKERS

BHT

PASSPORT

The passport cover has the name of the country in Dzongkha and English, the coat of arms, and the word *passport* in Dzongkha and English.

AIRLINE

Drukair (Royal Bhutan Airlines)

NATIONAL FLOWER

Blue poppy

NATIONAL TREE

Bhutan cypress

NATIONAL ANIMAL

Takin

NATIONAL BIRD

Common raven

NATIONAL RESOURCES

Natural resources include timber, hydropower, gypsum, and calcium carbonate. An ancient culture, unique cities and monuments, and mountain scenery support a small but growing tourist industry. Although Bhutan's economy is one of the world's smallest, it has grown very rapidly in recent years, with Bhutan's standard of living now one of the highest in South Asia.

FOODS

Ema datshi, a dish of cheese and chilies, is considered the national dish. Other national specialties include *phaksha pa,* a dish of cured, dried pork; *kewa datshi,* potatoes and cheese; *tshoem,* beef with mushrooms and curry; *kewa phagsha,* spicy pork with potatoes; *hasha maroo,* minced chicken with chilies; and *hapai hantue,* buckwheat dumplings with a lettuce and poppy seed filling.

Sports/Sports Teams

Bhutan's national sport is archery, and competitions are held regularly in most parts of the country. Another traditional sport is *digor*, which is best described as shot put combined with horseshoe throwing. Football is also very popular. Bhutan national teams participate in many sports at an international level.

Team Sports

Badminton
Bhutan Badminton Team

Cricket
Bhutan Cricket Team

Football
Bhutan Football Team, nickname Thimphu XI; Bhutan Futsal Team

Kabaddi
Bhutan Kabaddi Team

Table Tennis
Bhutan Table Tennis Team

Volleyball
Bhutan Volleyball Team

Individual Sports

Bhutan Amateur Boxing Team; Bhutan Archery Team; Bhutan Athletics Team; Bhutan Canoeing Team; Bhutan Shooting Team; Bhutan Tae Kwon Do Team; Bhutan Weight Lifting Team

National Heroes or Personifications

Shabdrung Ngawang Namgyal, the first king of united Bhutan in the 17th century; King Jigme Singye Wangchuck, who brought Bhutan into the modern world

National Holiday/ Independence Day

National Day, December 17

Festivals/Fairs

Paro Festival, March–April; Thimpu Drupchen, September–October

Significant Events in Formation of National Identity

600 B.C.E.–500 B.C.E. A state created by the Monpa, the indigenous people of the region, is established.

747 C.E.–10th century The earliest event widely chronicled in Bhutan is the passage of the Buddhist saint Padma Sambhava in the year 747. By the 10th century, the country's political development is heavily intertwined with its religious history.

13th century–16th century In the 13th century, the Mongols overrun the region, leaving behind a feudal hierarchy of local overlords.

17th century Bhutan exists as a patchwork of minor, often warring fiefdoms until the early 17th century. A Buddhist lama and military leader, Shabdrung Ngawang Namgyal, begins to unify Bhutan and to defend the country against frequent Tibetan invasions.

1710–1774 Taking advantage of continuing chaos and petty wars, the Tibetans invade Bhutan in 1710 and again in 1730.

1864–1865 Ongoing skirmishes and tensions finally erupt in the Duar War over control of the territory known as the Bengal Duars. Bhutan is defeated, and the peace treaty cedes the Duars to the United Kingdom* and ends all hostilities between Bhutan and British India.

1870s–1880s In the 1870s, a civil war begins in Bhutan between two rival regions. Ugyen Wangchuck reunites the country under one rule.

1907–1910 Ugyen Wangchuck is chosen as the hereditary king of Bhutan by an assembly of leading monks, government officials, and heads of important noble families.

1947–1949 A treaty similar to that signed with the British in 1910 is negotiated with newly independent India* in 1949.

1950s The Chinese invasion of Tibet* in 1951 ends Bhutan's long relationship with its northern neighbor. Bhutan begins a program of modernization that is largely sponsored and financed by India. King Jigme Dorji Wangchuck establishes the country's national legislature in 1953, ending the tradition of absolute monarchy.

1971–1972 Bhutan becomes a member of the United Nations. In July 1972, Jigme Singye Wangchuck ascends to the throne at the death of his father, Dorji Wangchuck.

1980s A Citizenship Act in 1985 requires residents to prove that their parents had lived in Bhutan in 1958. These measures are aimed at the large Nepali immigrant population in the south of the country.

1998–1999 The king introduces significant political and economic reforms. In 1999, the king lifts a ban on television and the Internet, ending centuries of self-imposed isolation.

2003 In late 2003, the Bhutanese Army successfully launches a large-scale operation to flush out anti-Indian insurgents who are operating training camps in southern Bhutan. Indian pressure on Bhutan to refuse passage or aid to the numerous national insurgencies in northeastern India has became part of Bhutan's modern political life.

2007 The revised 2007 treaty with India includes language "reaffirming their respect for each other's independence, sovereignty, and territorial integrity," an element that was absent from the earlier 1949 version. The Indo-Bhutan Friendship Treaty of 2007 thus puts to rest any questions that might have existed in regard to the complete independence and sovereignty of Bhutan.

2008–2009 The country's first democratic elections are held in March 2008. A new king is crowned, ensuring the continuity of the Himalayan kingdom.

BOUGAINVILLE

OFFICIAL NAME
Autonomous Region of Bougainville, Province of the North Solomons

POPULATION
136,700 (2009e)

INHABITANTS' NAME/NICKNAME
Bougainvillean(s)

LANGUAGE/LANGUAGES
Rotokas (Bougainvillean), Papuan, others

RELIGION/RELIGIONS
Christian, 94 percent; indigenous beliefs, Buddhist, other or no religion

NATIONAL FLAG
The national flag, and the official flag of the autonomous region, was first raised on May 17, 1990, as part of Bougainville's unilateral declaration of independence. A blue background surrounds a white outer ring, an inner ring with green triangles, a black circle, and a red and white *upei,* a traditional male initiation hat. The blue stands for the sea that surrounds the island, the white for seashells, the green for islands, the black for the people, and the *upei* for the nation's culture and traditions.

COAT OF ARMS/SEAL
The coat of arms is a depiction of the central disk shown on the national flag.

MOTTO
Persevere

CAPITAL CITY
Buka; there are plans to move the capital back to Arawa, which is claimed as the capital by Bougainvillian nationalists although the city was badly damaged by fighting in the 1990s.

TYPE OF GOVERNMENT

Parliamentary democracy, as an autonomous province of Papua New Guinea*

NATIONAL EMBLEM

Upei (ceremonial headdress worn during marriage, initiation, and other traditional events)

NATIONAL COLORS

Green and yellow

NATIONAL ANTHEM

The Bougainville Anthem is the unofficial anthem of the autonomous region and is based on the anthem adopted in 1990.

Bougainville Anthem

The crisis came about
so that we could identify
ourselves with God.
Material goods had led us astray
from God our Father.
The Crisis resulted for us to know God:
God's painful path.
Through the painful experiences
we have life everlasting in Jesus Christ.

CURRENCY

Papua New Guinea kina

VEHICLE IDENTIFICATION PLATES/STICKERS

PNG Papua New Guinea (official); BOU Bougainville (unofficial)

PASSPORT

Bougainvillans are citizens of Papua New Guinea and travel on that country's passports.

NATIONAL FLOWER

Bougainvillea (unofficial)

NATIONAL ANIMAL

Flying fox (fruit bat) (unofficial)

NATIONAL BIRD

Reef heron (unofficial)

NATIONAL RESOURCES

Natural resources include gold, silver, timber, fish, cacao, and copra. The economy suffered greatly from the blockade imposed by the government of Papua New Guinea in 1980s and 1990s, and the environment still suffers severe damage from indiscriminate mining operations from 2000 to 2009. Sandy beaches, friendly people, a pleasant climate, and unspoiled nature could support an important tourist industry.

FOODS

The yam or sweet potato is considered the national food and is cooked and served in many ways. Fish prepared in coconut milk is also considered a national dish. A stew of flying fox (fruit bat) with vegetables is another typical dish.

SPORTS/SPORTS TEAMS

Association football (soccer) is the most popular sport. Canoeing and other traditional sports are also very popular. The Bougainville national team participates in football at an international level.

TEAM SPORTS

Football

Bougainville Football Team

NATIONAL HEROES OR PERSONIFICATIONS

Francis Ona, the leader of the independence movement, died in 2005 after a short illness. He had refused to formally join the peace process; Joseph Kabui, secessionist leader and first president of the autonomous state of Bougainville.

NATIONAL HOLIDAY/INDEPENDENCE DAY

Independence Day, May 17

FESTIVALS/FAIRS

Bougainville Festival, an annual festival of culture, food, and tradition, February

SIGNIFICANT EVENTS IN FORMATION OF NATIONAL IDENTITY

31000 B.C.E.–1000 B.C.E. The islands are inhabited by peoples from the south. A second wave of migrants, belonging to the Lapita culture, arrives from the west around 1000 B.C.E.

1568 C.E. On February 17, 1568, the archipelago is encountered by Spanish explorer Alvaro de Mendaña y Neyra, who names it the Islas de Salomon (Solomon Islands*).

1768–1884 French explorer Louis-Antoine de Bougainville, whose name is given to the largest island of the group, visits the islands. Germany puts forth its claim to northeastern New Guinea, the Bismarck Archipelago, and the Solomon Islands in 1884.

1885 The Germans proclaim a protectorate over the Solomon Islands, the islands of Buka, Bougainville, Choiseul, Santa Isabel, and Ontong Java. In 1899, the Germans transfer all the Solomon Islands except Bougainville and Buka to British control in exchange for Western Samoa (Samoa*).

1914–1919 Australian forces defeat the German colonial forces and take control of the former German possession. By the terms of the Treaty of Versailles in 1919, the islands remain under Australian authority as a League of Nations mandate. Petitions by Bougainvilleans for separation from the ethnically and linguistically distinct Papua New Guinea are rejected.

1942–1945 Japanese forces invade the Australian mandate in 1942. At the end of the war, the Australians again take control of the islands, which are again grouped with Papua New Guinea despite Bougainvillean protests.

1964–1969 The first attempts are made to explore the islands' resources. When they are found to be rich in copper, and possibly gold, Bougainville Copper Ltd., a subsidiary of Australia's Rio Tinto, opens a copper mine at Panguna in 1969.

1969–1975 The first independence movement begins in the late 1960s, with grievances focusing on the Panguna mine and the power given to the mining company over the lives of many Bougainvilleans. Negotiations with the government of Papua New Guinea over autonomy for the island and a share of the copper profits collapse in early 1975.

1975 In May 1975, an interim government of Bougainville announces plans for secession. Negotiations again fail, and on September 1, 1975, the leaders issue a unilateral declaration of independence of the Republic of the North Solomons, just two weeks before Papua New Guinea's formal independence from Australia*.

1975–1976 The leaders of the new republic unsuccessfully seek recognition through the United Nations. They attempt to unite with the other Solomon Islands, which remain under British rule, but are rebuffed. Reluctantly, they agree to major autonomy as part of Papua New Guinea.

1976–1988 Relations between the islands and the government of Papua New Guinea remain tense but peaceful until 1981, when disputes over the copper mine again raise tensions. In 1987, a landowners association demands a monetary settlement from the mine owners in compensation and for clean up of the massive pollution caused by mining operations. The group's demands amount to half the profits from the mine since 1969.

1988–1989 Francis Ona forms the Bougainville Revolutionary Army, which commits numerous acts of arson and sabotage. The group cuts power to the mine by blowing up the local power station. The mine, the largest open-cut mine in the world, is forced to shut down operations in 1989.

1989–1991 Human rights abuses by members of the Papua New Guinea police and military forces on the island lead to open warfare. Papua New Guinean forces leave the islands to the Bougainville Revolutionary Army. On May 17, rebel leaders declare the independence of the Republic of Bougainville. The Papua New Guinean government imposes a blockade on the islands that would remain for nine years. The island falls into anarchy and civil war.

1991–1996 Skirmishes with Papua New Guinean forces and fighting among Bougainvillean factions devastate the islands. In 1994, government forces take control of the capital, Arawa. A new government in Papua New Guinea announces its intention to find a peaceful solution. After failed negotiations and little progress, however, the government orders the invasion of Bougainville in March 1996.

1997–2000 A cease-fire is negotiated with mediation by New Zealand*. Some factions enter into talks with the government, which lead to agreements to withdraw government military forces and provisions for the deployment of an international force led by Australia and New Zealand. In 2000, provincial government is organized and a reconciliation process is begun at the tribal level.

2002–2005 The island province is granted widespread autonomy. A Bougainville Autonomous Region is established in 2005, with the approval of most of the former rebel leaders. The autonomy agreement ends the bloodiest war in the Pacific since World War II. More than 20,000 people died, including many Bougainvillean civilians.

2008–2009 A small group of nationalist fighters continues to fight in the center of the island, obstructing plans to reopen the giant copper mine. A referendum on independence, part of the present peace settlement, is planned for sometime in the 2010s.

See also Papua New Guinea

BRUNEI

OFFICIAL NAME
Negara Brunei Darussalam (Malay); Sultanate of Brunei Darussalam (English)

NICKNAME
Darussalam (Malay); Abode of Peace (English)

POPULATION
382,600 (2009e)

INHABITANTS' NAME/NICKNAME
Bruneian(s)

LANGUAGE/LANGUAGES
Malay (Bahasa Melayu) (official); English, Chinese, others

RELIGION/RELIGIONS
Muslim, 67 percent (official); Buddhist, 15 percent; Christian, 10 percent; other or no religion

NATIONAL FLAG
The flag has a yellow field crossed by diagonal white and black stripes behind the country's coat of arms. Yellow, in Southeast Asia, represents royalty, in this case the Sultan of Brunei. The white and black stripes represent Brunei's chief ministers.

COAT OF ARMS/SEAL
The coat of arms, known as the National Crest, consists of a crescent, symbolizing Islam, joined with a parasol, symbolizing the monarchy, and two gloves on upturned hands, representing the benevolence of the government. Below the crescent is a ribbon with an Arabic inscription that translates as "State of Brunei, Abode of Peace" and the country's motto.

MOTTO
Always in service with God's guidance (English translation)

CAPITAL CITY
Bandar Seri Begawan

TYPE OF GOVERNMENT
Absolute monarchy

NATIONAL EMBLEM
The National Crest

NATIONAL COLORS
Yellow, black, and white

NATIONAL ANTHEM

The anthem was written and composed in 1947, almost 40 years before independence. It was officially adopted in 1951.

Allah Peliharakan Sultan (Malay); God Bless the Sultan (English)

God bless His Majesty
With a long life
(May he) rule the realm justly and in majesty
And lead our people (into) eternal happiness
(May) the kingdom and sultan live in peace
Lord, save Brunei, the Abode of Peace

CURRENCY

Brunei ringgit

INTERNET IDENTIFIER

.bn

VEHICLE IDENTIFICATION PLATES/STICKERS

BRU

PASSPORT

The passport cover has the word *passport* and the name of the country in Malay, the coat of arms, and the word *passport* and the name of the country in English.

AIRLINE

Royal Brunei Airlines

NATIONAL FLOWER

Simpor

NATIONAL TREE

Mangrove (unofficial)

NATIONAL ANIMAL

Orangutan (unofficial)

NATIONAL BIRD

Kingfisher (unofficial)

NATIONAL FISH

Koran angelfish (unofficial)

NATIONAL RESOURCES

Natural resources include petroleum, natural gas, timber, and fisheries. Protected natural rainforests cover about 75 percent of the land, a protected biodiversity almost unique in Southeast Asia.

FOODS

Rice is the staple food, often eaten with shell-fish, and curries. A coconut cream–based meat curry, called *santan,* is considered the national dish. Other national dishes include *bak kut the,* a spicy soup of beef or mutton ribs; *murtabak,* a type of crepe filled with minced mutton, onions, and spices; *beriani,* a chicken curry dish; *kurma,* chicken cooked in coconut cream; *gulai daun singkong tumbuk,* grilled red snapper with coconut milk and greens; and *urap,* vegetables with coconut.

SPORTS/SPORTS TEAMS

Association football (soccer) is very popular, as are basketball and rugby union. Brunei national teams participate in many sports at an international level.

TEAM SPORTS

Badminton
Brunei Darussalam Badminton Team

Baseball
Brunei Darussalam Baseball Team; Brunei Darussalam Softball Team

Basketball
Brunei Darussalam Basketball Team; Brunei Darussalam Women's Basketball Team

Cricket
Brunei Darussalam Cricket Team

Football
Brunei Darussalam Football Team, nickname the Wasps or Harimau Bintang (the Leop-

ards); Brunei Darussalam Women's Football Team; Brunei Darussalam Rugby Union Team; Brunei Darussalam Futsal Team

Hockey

Brunei Darussalam Field Hockey Team

Kabaddi

Brunei Darussalam Kabaddi Team

Table Tennis

Brunei Darussalam Table Tennis Team

Tennis

Brunei Darussalam Davis Cup Team; Brunei Darussalam Fed Cup Team

Volleyball

Brunei Darussalam Volleyball Team

INDIVIDUAL SPORTS

Brunei Darussalam Amateur Boxing Team; Brunei Darussalam Canoeing Team; Brunei Darussalam Cycling Team; Brunei Darussalam Equestrian Team; Brunei Darussalam Fencing Team; Brunei Darussalam Swim Team; Brunei Darussalam Tae Kwon Do Team; Brunei Darussalam Weight Lifting Team

NATIONAL HEROES OR PERSONIFICATIONS

Awang Alak Betatar, who adopted Islam and became the first Muslim sultan of Brunei as Sultan Muhammad; his brother, the second sultan, Sultan Ahmad; Sultan Sharif Ali, the third sultan, a descendant of the Prophet Muhammad who came from Arabia and married the daughter of Sultan Ahmad

NATIONAL HOLIDAY/
INDEPENDENCE DAY

National Day, February 23

FESTIVALS/FAIRS

National Day Festival, February; Birthday of the Sultan, July 15; Anniversary of the Al-

Qu'ran, variable dates based on the lunar calendar; Chinese New Year, variable dates based on the lunar calendar

SIGNIFICANT EVENTS IN FORMATION
OF NATIONAL IDENTITY

Seventh century–eighth century   A trading state, called Po-ni, exists at the mouth of the Brunei River and maintains trading and diplomatic relations with China and other Asian nations.

14th century   Po-ni comes under the influence of the powerful Majapahit Empire, based in Java. The book of Nagarakertagama, written in 1365, mentions the state of Berune as a vassal state of Majapahit.

1405–1521   Brunei establishes close relations with the Muslim kingdom of Malacca. The present dynasty is established. The rulers of Brunei adopt Islam, which becomes the state religion, although many ethnic groups inhabit the kingdom. The reign of the fifth sultan, Bolkiah, from 1485 to 1521, is considered Brunei's golden age. The kingdom includes much of present Borneo; the Sulu Archipelago, now part of the Philippines*; and the islands off the northwest tip of Borneo. Brunei establishes colonies as far away as Manila Bay.

1521   The first Europeans visit the kingdom as part of Ferdinand Magellan's expedition that sailed around the world. The European visitors are amazed at the advanced and wealthy society of Brunei.

1565–1580   Spanish colonizers and the forces of Brunei first clash in 1565. The Spanish succeed against Bruneian resistance and capture Manila Bay in the Philippines in 1571. Spanish forces capture the Sulu Islands in 1578. Later the same year, they attack and take control of Brunei's capital city. The Spanish demand that Christian missionaries be allowed to visit the kingdom. The Spanish are driven out, and soon after, Sulu is retaken. Spanish attacks on the kingdom from Manila in 1578 and 1580 are unsuccessful.

1580–1700   Brunei enters a period of decline due to internal conflicts and the rising influence of European colonial powers in the region. European encroachment disrupts the traditional trade routes and relations between regional states.

1661–1673 Civil war breaks out following confusion over the succession to the throne. The war rages for 12 years.

1839–1841 An English adventurer, James Brooke, arrives in Borneo and aids the sultan in putting down a rebellion. As a reward, he is made governor of Sarawak in northwest Borneo. Brooke gradually expands the territory under his control and even threatens to take control of Brunei. Brunei's present geography, divided into two regions separated by Malaysian territory, is due to Brooke's territorial expansion and the cession of Sarawak to Brooke in 1841.

1847 Brunei signs a trade relations agreement with the British.

1888 Brunei is proclaimed a British protectorate.

1931 Exploration for oil begins in Brunei and adjacent areas.

1941–1945 Brunei is occupied by Japanese forces. The British do not attempt to defend Brunei, in spite of an agreement to do so. In 1945, several influential Bruneians call for an end to the British protectorate.

1959 A new constitution is adopted, making Brunei an internally self-governing member of the British Commonwealth.

1962 An attempt to introduce a partially elected legislative body with limited powers is abandoned after opposition and a brief rebellion.

1984 The small state gains full independence on January 1, 1984. The sultanate, fearful of Malaysian or Indonesian interference, joins several international organizations, including the United Nations.

1990 A new state ideology is launched to promote the unity of the diverse groups that make up Bruneian society.

2004 A royal wedding, celebrated throughout Brunei, ensures the stability and continuance of the Brunei dynasty. The sultan convenes the appointed parliament, which has not met since independence in 1984, although it lacks any authority other than to advise the sultan.

2008–2009 Brunei is considered a "not free" country by journalists and some international organizations, although local press criticism of the government or the monarchy is rare. Brunei is one of the wealthiest countries in Southeast Asia.

CAMBODIA

OFFICIAL NAME
Preăh Réachéanachâkr Kâmpŭchea (Khmer); Royaume du Cambodge (French); Kingdom of Cambodia (English)

POPULATION
14,308,300 (2009e)

INHABITANTS' NAME/NICKNAME
Khmer(s), Cambodian(s)

LANGUAGE/LANGUAGES
Khmer (Cambodian) (official); French, Vietnamese, others

RELIGION/RELIGIONS
Theravada Buddhist, 94 percent; Muslim, 3 percent; Christian, 2 percent; other or no religion

NATIONAL FLAG
The national flag has three horizontal stripes of blue, red, and blue, the red twice the width of the blue stripes. In the center is a white depiction of Angkor Wat. The blue symbolizes the monarchy, the red represents the nation, and the white stands for religion—initially Brahmanism, and now the Buddhist majority.

COAT OF ARMS/SEAL
The nation's coat of arms is the royal coat of arms and the symbol of the Cambodian monarchy. Depicted, all in gold, on the coat of arms are two mythical animals: a *gajasimha*a lion with an elephant trunk, on the left, and a *singha,* a lion, which is not native to the region but features in Cambodian mythology,

on the right. Supported by the animals are two five-tiered parasols. Between the parasols is a royal crown with a ray of light at its top. Beneath the crown are two pedestaled platters bearing a sacred sword surmounted by a Khmer symbol for *Aum*. The Khmer language phrase at the base of the royal coat of arms is made up of the words *preah'jao* (royal or auspicious ruler), *krung* (kingdom), and *Kampuchea* (Cambodia).

MOTTO

Nation, Religion, King (English translation)

CAPITAL CITY

Phnom Penh

TYPE OF GOVERNMENT

Constitutional monarchy

NATIONAL EMBLEM

Ankor Wat (depicted on the national flag)

NATIONAL COLORS

Red and blue

NATIONAL ANTHEM

The anthem, the royalist anthem of Cambodia, was originally adopted in 1941. In 1970, the monarchy was abolished and a different anthem was adopted. After the communist victory in 1975, the royal symbols, including the anthem, were reinstated for a short while until they were replaced with socialist symbols. Following the overthrow of the communist government in 1993, the royal anthem was again made the official anthem. The name of the anthem is derived from the name of an ancient Khmer kingdom.

> Nokoreach
>
> Heaven protect our king
> And give him happiness and glory
> To reign over our souls and our destinies,
> The one being, heir of the sovereign builders
> Guiding the proud old kingdom.

> Temples are asleep in the forest,
> Remembering the splendor of Moha Nokor.
> Like a rock, the Khmer race is eternal,
> Let us trust in the fate of Kampuchea,
> The empire that challenges the ages.

> Songs rise up from the pagodas
> To the glory of the holy Buddhist faith.
> Let us be faithful to our ancestors' belief.
> Thus heaven will lavish its bounty
> Towards the ancient Khmer country, the
>   Moha Nokor.

PATRON SAINT

Saint John the Apostle is the patron saint of the Catholic Church in Cambodia.

CURRENCY

Cambodian riel

INTERNET IDENTIFIER

.kh

VEHICLE IDENTIFICATION PLATES/STICKERS

K

PASSPORT

The passport cover bears the name of the country in Khmer and English, the coat of arms, and the word *passport* in Khmer and English.

AIRLINE

President Airlines

NATIONAL FLOWER

Rumdul

NATIONAL TREE

Palmyra palm

NATIONAL ANIMAL

Kouprey (Cambodian ox)

NATIONAL BIRD

Giant ibis

NATIONAL FISH
Giant barb

NATIONAL RESOURCES
Natural resources include oil and gas, timber, gemstones, some iron ore, manganese, phosphates, hydropower potential, and arable land. The country's wealth of ancient ruins, fascinating cities, and unique culture are helping the growth of tourism. Remittances from the Cambodian diaspora are an important source of hard currency.

FOODS
Samlor kako, a soup of meat and vegetables, is considered the national dish. A curry dish called *gahree,* which can be served in many ways and with variable ingredients, is considered a national dish and shows Indian influence. Another popular dish, *kuyteay* or beef noodle soup, shows Chinese influence on the cuisine. Other specialties include *amok trei,* fish and coconut curry; *true kno manor,* pork with pineapple; *saik chrouk ch'ranouitk,* pork skewers with shredded coconut; *pakon char poat koun,* shrimp with baby corn; *num ta leng sap,* a vegetable pancake; *salor ko-ko sap,* vegetable stew with coconut and spices; and *kuay nanuan,* a dessert of bananas cooked in coconut milk.

SPORTS/SPORTS TEAMS
Association football (soccer) is very popular. Traditional martial arts sports—*bokator, pradal serey* (Khmer kickboxing), and Khmer wrestling—are practiced throughout the country. Traditional boat racing is considered a national sport. Cambodia national teams participate in many sports at an international level.

TEAM SPORTS
Badminton
Cambodia Badminton Team

Baseball
Cambodia Baseball Team

Basketball
Cambodia Basketball Team

Football
Cambodia Football Team; Cambodia Rugby Union Team; Cambodia Futsal Team

Hockey
Cambodia Field Hockey Team

Table Tennis
Cambodia Table Tennis Team

Volleyball
Cambodia Volleyball Team; Cambodia Women's Volleyball Team; Cambodia Men's Volleyball Team (Disabled); Cambodia Women's Volleyball Team (Disabled)

INDIVIDUAL SPORTS
Cambodia Amateur Boxing Team; Cambodia Archery Team; Cambodia Athletics Team; Cambodia Canoeing Team; Cambodia Equestrian Team; Cambodia Fencing Team; Cambodia Gymnastics Team; Cambodia Judo Team; Cambodia Swim Team; Cambodia Tae Kwon Do Team; Cambodia Weight Lifting Team; Cambodia Wrestling Team

NATIONAL HEROES OR PERSONIFICATIONS
Preah Thaong (Kaundinya) and Neang Neak (Soma) are symbolic personas in Khmer culture. They are considered to have founded the ancient Khmer state of Funan. Many Khmer wedding customs can be traced to the legendary marriage of Preah Thaong and Neang Neak.

Jayavarman VII, the king who ruled during Cambodia's golden age in the 12th and 13th centuries, is considered a national hero;

Norodom Sihanouk, the former king and head of state who abdicated in 2004.

NATIONAL HOLIDAY/ INDEPENDENCE DAY

Independence Day, November 9

FESTIVALS/FAIRS

Bonn Om Teuk (Boat Racing Festival) is the most popular festival. It is held each year at the end of the rainy season.

SIGNIFICANT EVENTS IN FORMATION OF NATIONAL IDENTITY

First century C.E.–sixth century C.E. Funan and Chenla control large parts of present Cambodia, Vietnam*, Thailand*, and Laos*.

9th century–13th century The Cambodian kingdom of Kambuja, which would give its name to modern Cambodia, experiences a golden age.

14th century–15th century The Khmer Empire declines but remains powerful. The center of power is Angkor, where a series of capitals is constructed during the empire's zenith. Angkor Wat, the most famous and best-preserved religious complex, stands as a relic of the empire's past. The monarchy survives until 1431, when Thai forces capture and sack the Khmer capital.

1594–1863 The Cambodians attempt to regain their past glory, but wars with the Thais and Vietnamese result in lost territory and finally in defeat in 1594. Spanish and Portuguese expeditions visit the kingdom in the 16th century, but French influence becomes paramount in the region.

1863–1906 King Norodom, installed by the Thais, seeks the protection of the French.

1953–1965 After World War II, Cambodia continues as a French protectorate, part of French Indochina, until independence in 1953 as a constitutional monarchy under King Norodom Sihanouk. The kingdom adopts a policy of neutrality, but by the mid-1960s, the eastern provinces are used as bases by the Viet Cong and North Vietnamese during the Vietnam War.

1969–1970 The United States* begins bombing along the Cambodian-Vietnamese border, which Sihanouk opposes, as it could draw Cambodia into the Southeast Asian war. Sihanouk is ousted by a military coup. He realigns himself with the communist Khmer Rouge rebels, who have been slowly gaining ground in the mountains. He urges his followers to help overthrow the pro-United States government, hastening the onset of civil war in the country.

1971–1973 Strikes by U.S. forces continue on both sides of the border, and the United States briefly invades Cambodia to disrupt the Viet Cong. The civil war widens, leaving thousands dead and more than 2 million as refugees.

1975 The Khmer Rouge captures Phnom Penh and takes power under leader Pol Pot. Immediately, the Khmer Rouge orders the evacuation of all cities and towns, sending the entire population into the countryside to work as farmers. Thousands starve, die of disease, or are killed during the evacuation and its aftermath. Prince Sihanouk resigns as head of state.

1976–1978 The communists seek to completely restructure Cambodian society. Old traditions are abolished, and religion is suppressed. Agriculture is collectivized and industries abandoned. Life is strict and brutal. Executions are common for speaking a foreign language, wearing glasses, mourning a loved one, or scavenging for food. Former military personnel, businessmen, and politicians are hunted down and killed, along with their families. Estimates of the number of dead range from 1 million to 3 million.

1978–1979 The North Vietnamese launch a full-scale invasion of Cambodia, capturing Phnom Penh on January 7, 1979, and driving the Khmer Rouge before them. A new, pro-Vietnamese communist government is installed.

1991–1993 A conference is convened in Paris to sign a comprehensive settlement and to prepare the country for free elections. Prince Sihanouk and other exiled leaders return. Elections lead to a coalition government and a new constitution that establishes a multiparty liberal democracy within the framework of a constitutional monarchy under King Norodom Sihanouk.

2004 The National Assembly approves an agreement with the United Nations for the establishment of a tribunal to try senior Khmer Rouge officials responsible for the killing fields of Cambodia in the 1970s and 1980s. King Norodom Sihanouk resigns and is replaced as king.

2008 The first trials of senior Khmer Rouge leaders by the tribunal begin. Cambodia is widely criticized for its very high level of corruption. International aid is often illegally transferred into private accounts, adding to the wide disparity of income between the affluent minority and the very poor majority.

2009 Cambodia's flourishing sex industry draws tourists to the region. The government begins to close down brothels, with a new emphasis on karaoke bars and clubs, where former prostitutes work as hosts and hostesses.

CHINA

OFFICIAL NAME

Zhōnghuá Rénmín Gònghéguó (transliteration from Mandarin Chinese); People's Republic of China (English)

POPULATION

1,321,552,900 (2009e)

INHABITANTS' NAME/NICKNAME

Chinese

LANGUAGE/LANGUAGES

Chinese (Potonghua, also known as Mandarin), Yue (Cantonese), Wu (Shanghainese), Minbei (Fuzhou), Minnan (Hokkien-Taiwanese), Xiang, Gan, and Hakka dialects, others

RELIGION/RELIGIONS

Nonreligious or adherents of traditional belief systems, Confucianist, or Taoist, 60 per-cent; Buddhist, 33 percent; Christian, 3 to 4 percent; Muslim, 1 to 2 percent; others

NATIONAL FLAG

Called the Five-Starred Red Flag, the flag is a red field bearing a large, yellow, five-pointed yellow star and four smaller yellow stars on the upper hoist. The red background symbolizes the blood of the heroes who died during the revolution. The yellow stands for the glorious culture and history of China and the brightness of the communist future. The large yellow star symbolizes the leadership of the Communist Party of China, and the four smaller stars stand for the four classes that originally existed in the People's Republic: workers, peasants, petty bourgeoisie, and national bourgeoisie.

COAT OF ARMS/SEAL

The National Emblem of the People's Republic of China contains a representation of Tiananmen Gate, the entrance gate to the Forbidden City from Tiananmen Square in Beijing, in a red circle. Above this representation are the five stars found on the national flag, representing the union of Chinese peoples. Many have interpreted this as the union of the five major nationalities in China, while others interpret the stars as signifying five social classes. The border of the circle contains sheaves of wheat, reflecting the Maoist philosophy of an agricultural revolution. At the center of the bottom portion of the border is a cogwheel that represents industrial workers.

CAPITAL CITY

Beijing

TYPE OF GOVERNMENT

Socialist republic

NATIONAL EMBLEM

Great Wall of China; Forbidden City

NATIONAL COLORS

White and red

NATIONAL ANTHEM

The anthem was written in 1935, during the Chinese Civil War, and was adopted following the communist victory in 1949.

> **Yiyonggjun Jinxingpu (transliteration from Chinese); March of the Volunteers (English)**
>
> Arise, ye who refuse to be slaves!
> With our flesh and blood, let us build our new Great Wall!
> The Chinese nation faces its greatest danger.
> From each one the urgent call for action comes forth.
> Arise! Arise! Arise!
> Millions with but one heart,
> Braving the enemy's fire.
> March on!
> Braving the enemy's fire.
> March on! March on! March on!

CURRENCY

Chinese yuan

INTERNET IDENTIFIER

.cn

VEHICLE IDENTIFICATION PLATES/STICKERS

No official international designation; CN (unofficial)

PASSPORT

The passport cover features the coat of arms, the name of the country, and the word *passport* in Chinese; and, in smaller print, the name of the country and the word *passport* in English.

AIRLINES

Air China; China Southern Airlines; China Eastern Airlines; Hainan Airlines; Shanghai Airlines; Xiamen Airlines

NATIONAL FLOWER

Rock's peony

NATIONAL TREE

Chinese pine

NATIONAL ANIMAL

Giant panda

NATIONAL BIRD

Crane

NATIONAL RESOURCES

Natural resources include coal, iron ore, petroleum, natural gas, mercury, tin, tungsten, antimony, manganese, molybdenum, vanadium, magnetite, aluminum, lead, zinc, uranium, and hydropower potential (the world's greatest). China also has the world's largest population, with an increasingly well-educated workforce. Historic cities, a fascinating culture, monuments, and modern commercial cities support a large tourist industry.

FOODS

The size of the country accounts for the large number of regional cuisines. Rice is a critical part of much of Chinese cuisine, particularly in the southern part of the country. However, in many parts of China, particularly the north, wheat-based products predominate, including noodles and steamed buns. Soup is usually served at the start of a meal and at the end of a meal in southern China.

In most dishes in Chinese cuisines, food is prepared in bite-sized pieces, ready for direct picking up and eating, including vegetables, meats, and tofu. By contrast, fish are traditionally cooked and served whole, with diners directly pulling pieces from the fish with chopsticks, unlike in some other cuisines, in which fish are first filleted. This is because it is desirable for fish to be served as fresh as possible.

SPORTS/SPORTS TEAMS

Table tennis is a national passion and is considered the national sport. Other popular sports are association football (soccer), basketball, and volleyball. China national teams participate in many sports at an international level.

TEAM SPORTS

Badminton

China Badminton Team

Baseball

China Baseball Team; China Softball Team

Basketball

China Basketball Team; China Women's Basketball Team; China Wheelchair Basketball Team; China Women's Wheelchair Basketball Team

Cricket

China Cricket Team

Curling

China Curling Team

Football

China Football Team, nickname the Dragons, Team China, Guozu (Foot), or Guojia Dui (Team); China Women's Football Team nickname Steel Roses or Forceful Roses; China Under-20 Football Team; China Under-23 Football Team; China Women's Under-19 Football Team; China Rugby Union Team; China Women's Rugby Union Team; China Wheelchair Rugby Team; China Beach Soccer Team; China Futsal Team; China Australian-Rules Football Team, nickname the Blues; China Rugby Union Team (Sevens), nickname China Sevens or China 7s; China Women's Rugby Union Team (Sevens) nickname China Sevens or China 7s

Handball

China Men's Handball Team; China Women's Handball Team; China Beach Handball Team; China Women's Beach Handball Team

Hockey

China Ice Hockey Team; China Women's Ice Hockey Team; China Junior Ice Hockey Team; China Field Hockey Team

Kabaddi

China Kabaddi Team

Korfball

China Korfball Team

Racing

A1 Team China; China Speedway Team

Table Tennis

China Table Tennis Team

Tennis

China Davis Cup Team; China Fed Cup Team

Volleyball

China Men's Volleyball Team; China Women's Volleyball Team; China Men's Beach Volleyball Team; China Women's Beach Volleyball Team

INDIVIDUAL SPORTS

China Aikido Team; China Amateur Boxing Team; China Archery Team; China Athletics Team; China Cycling Team; China Equestrian Team; China Fencing Team; China Gymnastics Team; China Judo Team; China Modern Pentathlon Team; China Rowing Team; China Sailing Team; China Shooting Team; China Swim Team; China Tae Kwon Do Team; China Triathlon Team; China Weight Lifting Team; China Wrestling Team

WINTER SPORTS

China Alpine Ski Team; China Bandy Team; China Biathlon Team; China Ice Hockey Team; China Women's Ice Hockey Team; China Junior Ice Hockey Team; China Luge Team; China Skating Team

NATIONAL HEROES OR PERSONIFICATIONS

Bao Gong, a famous politician and legendary hero of the late 10th and 11th centuries; Ta Yu, a legendary hero who saved the Middle Kingdom from a flood by creating a multiplicity of channels to divert the torrent; Lin Zexu, who stood up to the British before the Opium War in the mid-19th century; Mao Zedong, sometimes called Mao Tse-tung, the founder of the People's Republic of China

NATIONAL HOLIDAY/INDEPENDENCE DAY

National Day, October 1 (anniversary of the founding of the People's Republic)

FESTIVALS/FAIRS

Lantern Festival, variable dates based on the lunar calendar; Dragon Boat Festival, variable dates; Double Seventh Festival, variable dates; Mid-Autumn Festival, variable dates; Double Ninth Festival, variable dates; Winter Solstice Festival, variable dates; Spring Festival, variable dates

SIGNIFICANT EVENTS IN FORMATION OF NATIONAL IDENTITY

Neolithic Era Chinese civilization originates in small city-states along the Yellow River.

1600 B.C.E.–1100 B.C.E. China's written history begins with the Shang Dynasty.

1122 B.C.E.–256 B.C.E. Culture, characterized by literature, philosophy, architecture, and the decorative arts, develops during the Zhou Dynasty that follows the Shang. It is the longest-lasting dynasty and spans a period of cultural consolidation and the evolution of Chinese script.

221 B.C.E.–205 B.C.E. The feudal Zhou breaks up into distinct city-states. The various warring kingdoms are united in the first Chinese empire. Successive dynasties develop elaborate bureaucratic systems that permit the Chinese emperor to directly control the vast territories of the empire. The Great Wall of China is begun.

206 B.C.E.–220 C.E. The Han Dynasty emerges and is the first to embrace the philosophy of Confucianism. The dynasty is characterized by great advances in the arts and sciences and expansion of the empire's borders.

220 C.E.–1279 C.E. Various dynasties hold power, extending China's borders near to their present size. Many Asian nations become vassals of the powerful empire before the Mongols conquer China. Before the Mongol invasion, censuses show approximately 120 million inhabitants; after the conquest is complete in 1279, the area's inhabitants number roughly 60 million. Kublai Khan establishes the Yuan Dynasty and rules China from a centralized capital at Beijing.

1368–1644 The Mongols are defeated and pushed back to the steppes north of the empire's territory. A new dynasty, the Ming, takes power. The Chinese population urbanizes rapidly. Foreign contacts and trade increase rapidly. The last construction of the Great Wall is undertaken.

1644–1911 The Manchus, a tall, rugged people from the steppe lands, conquer China and establish the Qing Dynasty. The new rulers adopt the Confucian form of traditional Chinese government and eventually rule in the manner of the traditional Han Chinese dynasties. The Manchus, only a small minority of the population, govern the vast empire and extend Chinese authority to Xinjiang, Tibet*, and Mongolia*. Europeans force the declining dynasty to sign unequal treaties and to open Chinese ports to European traders. Corruption, cynicism, and quarrels within the imperial family further weaken the empire, which is defeated in wars with the French and Japanese in the 1880s and 1890s. At the beginning of the 20th century, the Boxer Rebellion erupts across northern China in an effort to return China to the old ways. A coalition of European troops invades to defeat the Boxers and demand further concessions from the Chinese government.

1911–1945 A revolution overthrows the Manchu dynasty, and a republic is proclaimed. Slavery is abolished, although the practice continues in many areas. China breaks apart into provinces and regions controlled by local warlords. In the 1920s, communists and nationalists gain support for a united China. Under Mao Zedong, the communists fight a civil war with the nationalists that continues through the Japanese invasion and occupation in the 1930s and 1940s.

1945–1949 The civil war resumes following Japan's defeat in World War II. The communist victory drives the last nationalist forces to Taiwan*, and the People's Republic of China is proclaimed. Radical land reform and persecution of the former upper classes marks the first years of the regime.

1950s–1960s An estimated 70 million people die during the chaotic movements initiated by the communist government, the Cultural Revolution, the Anti-Rightist Campaign of the 1950s, and the Great Leap Forward. Minorities, particularly religious groups, suffer persecution, as do intellectuals and others considered antigovernment. Strict controls are established over everyday life.

1976–1989 Mao Zedong's death, in 1976, begins a process of liberalization, particularly of the economy. China's eastern maritime provinces lead a booming economy. Consumer goods become widely available, and poverty is eradicated in many areas. The communist party allows capitalist economic systems to flourish, but only at the cost of a quiescent population.

1989 Protests against communist party excesses and against the leadership result in massive protests in Tiananmen Square in Beijing. After days of protests and calls for democracy and an end to communism in China, the government orders a brutal oppression of the protests.

1989–2002 After the Tiananmen Square massacre, a new generation of communist leaders concentrates on improving China's economy. Two foreign colonies, Hong Kong* and Macau*,

are returned to Chinese sovereignty. A burgeoning economy makes China a world economic power.

2008 China stages the Olympics in Beijing, the most expensive and elaborate Olympics in history. The show is carefully stage-managed to showcase the new China: modern, sleek, capable, and ready to rejoin the world as a major power. Criticism of the communist government remains rare, although minorities such as the Tibetans and the Uighurs of Xinjiang grow more openly hostile to Chinese rule.

2009 There is renewed criticism of the Chinese government for blocking access to many popular Internet Web sites. Antigovernment protests in Tibetan-inhabited regions and international concern over China's methods for controlling the Tibetans continue to mar the country's efforts to present itself as a peaceful, modern world power.

See also East Turkestan; Hong Kong; Macau; Taiwan; Tibet

China, Republic of. *See* Taiwan

COOK ISLANDS

OFFICIAL NAME

Kūki 'Āirani (Cook Islands Maori); Cook Islands (English)

POPULATION

19,500 (2009e for Cook Islands). Nearly 60,000 self-identified Cook Islanders live in New Zealand*.

INHABITANTS' NAME/NICKNAME

Cook Islander(s); Cook Islands Maori(s); Rarotongan(s)

LANGUAGE/LANGUAGES

English, Cook Islands Maori (both official); others

RELIGION/RELIGIONS

Cook Islands Christian, 56 percent; Roman Catholic, 16 percent; Seventh-day Adventist,

8 percent; Mormon, 3.5 percent; other or no religion

NATIONAL FLAG

The flag is a blue field with 15 white, five-pointed stars in a circle on the fly and the Union Jack as a canton on the upper hoist. The stars represent the 15 islands in the Cook Islands group. The Union Jack represents past ties to the United Kingdom* and the present as an independent state in association with New Zealand.

COAT OF ARMS/SEAL

The coat of arms of the Cook Islands has a blue shield at its center. The shield contains the 15 stars found on the national flag. A *maroro* (flying fish) and a *kakaia* (white tern) are on each side of the shield, one supporting a cross as a symbol for Christianity, the other holding a *momore taringavaru* (Rarotongan club) as a symbol of the richness of Cook Islands' tradition. Orators used to hold the club during traditional discourses. Above the shield is a *pare kura* (*ariki* headdress) of red feathers, symbolizing the importance of the traditional rank system. The name of the nation appears on a banner below the shield.

CAPITAL CITY

Avarua

TYPE OF GOVERNMENT

Parliamentary republic as an associated state with New Zealand

NATIONAL EMBLEM

A circle of stars representing the 15 islands

NATIONAL COLORS

Green and white

NATIONAL ANTHEM

Officially, as a territory associated with New Zealand, the Cook Islands' national anthem is that of New Zealand. The territorial anthem was adopted in 1982.

> **Te Atua Mou'e (Cook Islands Maori); God is Truth (English)**
> To God Almighty
> Ruler of the isles of the sea
> Hearken our call
> Protect us
> Crown us with liberty
> May peace and love reign supreme
> Throughout the land.

PATRON SAINT

Saint Joseph is the patron saint of the dioceses of Rarotonga.

CURRENCY

Cook Islands dollar; New Zealand dollar

INTERNET IDENTIFIER

.ck

VEHICLE IDENTIFICATION PLATES/STICKERS

NZ New Zealand (official); CK Cook Islands (unofficial)

PASSPORT

Cook Islanders are New Zealand citizens and travel on New Zealand passports.

AIRLINE

Air Rarotonga

NATIONAL FLOWER

Tiare Maori (Cook Islands gardenia)

NATIONAL TREE

Flame tree (unofficial)

NATIONAL ANIMAL

Dolphin (unofficial)

NATIONAL BIRD

Kakaia (white tern)

NATIONAL FISH

Maroro (flying fish); whitecheek surgeonfish (unofficial)

NATIONAL RESOURCES

Natural resources are negligible, other than copra. Fresh and canned fruits and fruit juices, clothing, pearl shells, handicrafts, and jewelry are the principal exports. Tourism and food processing are the major industries. Beginning in 1980s, the islands also became a popular tax haven and offshore banking center, but in 2003, the government moved to increase regulation of offshore banks as a result of international pressure. Government spending is important to the economy, and some 60 percent of the labor force works in the public sector. Most imports, largely foodstuffs, textiles, and fuels, come from New Zealand. Cook Islanders living in New Zealand outnumber those living in the islands and are an important source of income through remittances.

FOODS

Mitiore, shellfish fermented in a coconut shell, is considered the national dish. *Tiopu kuru,* known as breadfruit stew, is a mixture of breadfruit, onions, garlic, saltwater, cooked pork or chicken, chicken stock, and coconut cream. It is popular throughout the islands. *Poke,* a cake of bananas and coconut, is a popular dessert.

SPORTS/SPORTS TEAMS

Rugby union is the country's most popular sport. Association football (soccer) and rugby league are also very popular. Cook Islands national teams participate in many sports at an international level.

TEAM SPORTS

Badminton

Cook Islands Badminton Team

Baseball

Cook Islands Softball Team

Basketball

Cook Islands Basketball Team; Cook Islands Women's Basketball Team

Cricket

Cook Islands Cricket Team

Football

Cook Islands Football Team; Cook Islands Women's Football Team; Cook Islands Rugby Union Team; Cook Islands Rugby Team (Sevens), nickname Cook Islands Sevens or Cook Islands 7s; Cook Islands Beach Soccer Team; Cook Islands Futsal Team; Cook Islands Touch Football Team; Cook Islands Women's Touch Football Team; Cook Islands Rugby League Team; Cook Islands Women's Rugby League Team

Handball

Cook Islands Handball Team; Cook Islands Women's Handball Team

Netball

Cook Islands Netball Team

Table Tennis

Cook Islands Table Tennis Team

Tennis

Pacific Oceania Davis Cup and Fed Cup Teams (Pacific Oceania teams represent a number of English-speaking Pacific countries)

Volleyball

Cook Islands Men's Volleyball Team; Cook Islands Women's Volleyball Team

INDIVIDUAL SPORTS

Cook Islands Amateur Boxing Team; Cook Islands Athletics Team; Cook Islands Canoeing Team; Cook Islands Judo Team; Cook Islands Sailing Team; Cook Islands Swim Team; Cook Islands Triathlon Team; Cook Islands Weight Lifting Team

NATIONAL HEROES OR PERSONIFICATIONS

Sir Albert Henry, pro-independence politician and first premier of the islands in 1965; Laka/Aka, the hero who undertakes a long and dangerous journey to the Cook Islands to obtain the highly prized feathers of a red parrot as gifts for his son and daughter (Marquesan version of the Polynesian legend); Sir Thomas Davis, known as Papa Tom, former Cook Islands prime minister and patron of Cook Island arts, literature, and traditional canoe voyages. He oversaw the economic reforms that resulted in unprecedented economic prosperity in the 1980s.

NATIONAL HOLIDAY/INDEPENDENCE DAY

Constitution Day, first Monday in August

FESTIVALS/FAIRS

Annual Te Maeva Nui celebrations the week before Constitution Day; Vaka Eiva (Canoeing Festival), mid- to late November; Tiare (Floral Festival), first week of December

SIGNIFICANT EVENTS IN FORMATION OF NATIONAL IDENTITY

1000 B.C.E. The northern islands of the archipelago are settled by people from Tonga* and Samoa*.

Sixth century C.E. Polynesian people, who migrated from nearby Tahiti, to the southeast, first settle in the Cook Islands. According to legend, the first voyage is to collect the extremely valuable red feathers of the local parrots.

Sixth century–16th century About 1,000 high-ranking adventurers from Raiatea, in present-day French Polynesia*, establish their rule over the islands as a local aristocracy. The islanders later send groups to colonize the large islands they called Aotearoa, later known as New Zealand.

1595–1606 A Spanish explorer sights Pukapuka, in the northern group of the archipelago. Another Spaniard is the first European to set foot on Rarotonga, the main island of the group, in 1606. He calls the island Gente Hermosa, meaning "beautiful people."

1773–1779 British navigator Captain James Cook visits the islands in 1773 and 1779 and names them the Hervey Islands. The archipelago is later called the Cook Islands.

1821–1858 British missionaries arrive in the islands. Christianity quickly takes hold in the island culture. The London Missionary Society sets up a virtual "missionary kingdom" in the islands, dictating the local administration, what clothing is to be worn, and many other aspects of island life.

1858–1888 The Kingdom of Rarotonga is established. The kingdom seeks British protection against French encroachments from Tahiti.

1901 The islands are transferred to newly independent New Zealand's authority.

1945–1947 After the Second World War, New Zealand grants the islands increased authority and autonomy.

1962 The government of New Zealand offers the islands four alternatives—full independence; full integration with New Zealand; internal self-government with New Zealand responsible for security and foreign affairs; or membership in a (still nonexistent) Polynesian Federation. By a nearly unanimous vote, the Cook Islands Assembly chooses internal autonomy in association with New Zealand.

1965 The protectorate status ends and the Cook Islands become a self-governing state, with New Zealand responsible for security and external relations. The new status ends 65 years of missionary lawmakers followed by 77 years of paternalistic British, then New Zealander, authority.

1974 The state's first premier, Sir Albert Henry, becomes increasingly nationalistic as neighboring island groups opt for independence. He calls a referendum on independence but is blocked by the legislature.

1978 In parliamentary elections, Henry uses public funds to fly Cook Islanders in from New Zealand in support of his reelection and his bid for full independence. The government annuls the vote, and Sir Albert is convicted of conspiracy, stripped of his knighthood, and heavily fined.

1979 The Cook Islands government adopts a new flag more closely resembling that of New Zealand to replace the nationalist flag of the Henry government. The nationalist movement adopts the former flag, a circle of fifteen gold stars on a green field.

1991–2005 Full diplomatic relations are established with China* in 1997 and with France* in 2000. As of 2005, the country has established full diplomatic relations with 18 other countries. Although no longer responsible for foreign relations, New Zealand retains responsibility for the security of the country.

2008 A small majority of the members of the House of Ariki, the local parliament, attempt to dissolve the government and take control. The situation soon normalizes, with the members returning to their regular duties.

2009 The important tourist industry slows due to global economic problems.

See also New Zealand

EAST TIMOR

OFFICIAL NAME

Repúblika Demokrátika Timór Lorosa'e (Tetum); República Democrática de Timor-Leste (Portuguese); Democratic Republic of Timor-Leste/East Timor (English)

POPULATION

1,102,300 (2009e)

INHABITANTS' NAME/NICKNAME

Timorese; East Timorese; Maubere(s)

LANGUAGE/LANGUAGES

Tetum, Portuguese (both official); Indonesian, English, indigenous languages, others

RELIGION/RELIGIONS

Roman Catholic, 90 percent; Muslim, 5 percent; Protestant, 1 percent; other or no religion

NATIONAL FLAG

The flag has a red field with two isosceles triangles at the hoist, their bases overlapping. One triangle is black with a centered white, five-pointed star. The other triangle is yellow and forms a border between the red field and the black triangle. The yellow represents the traces of colonialism in the country's history, the black represents the obscurantism that needs to be overcome, and the red represents the struggle for national liberation. The white star, called "the light that guides," stands for peace.

COAT OF ARMS/SEAL

The coat of arms is an inverted shield bearing a white star over a book flanked by agricultural products; below are a traditional bow and arrow and a modern weapon. Beneath the shield is the national motto. The shield, outlined in gold and red, is surrounded by a white circle with the name of the country in red.

MOTTO

Unidade, acção, progresso (Portuguese); Unity, Action, Progress (English)

CAPITAL CITY

Dili

TYPE OF GOVERNMENT

Republic

NATIONAL COLORS

Red, yellow, and black

NATIONAL ANTHEM

The anthem was adopted when independence was declared as the Portuguese left the colony in 1975. When the country regained its independence in 2002, after nearly three decades of Indonesian rule, the anthem was again used.

Patria, Patria (Portuguese); Fatherland, Fatherland (English)

Fatherland, fatherland, East Timor our nation
Glory to the people and to the heroes of our liberation
Fatherland, fatherland, East Timor our nation
Glory to the people and to the heroes of our liberation
We vanquish colonialism, we cry "Down with imperialism!"
Free land, free people, no, no, no to exploitation.
Let us go forward, united, firm and determined
In the struggle against imperialism, the enemy of people,
until final victory, onward to revolution.

PATRON SAINT

Saint Mary

CURRENCY

U.S. dollar; Timorese centavo coins

INTERNET IDENTIFIER

.tl

VEHICLE IDENTIFICATION PLATES/STICKERS

TL

PASSPORT

The passport cover has the name of the country in Portuguese and English, the coat of arms, and the word *passport* in Portuguese and English.

AIRLINE

Air Timor

NATIONAL ANIMAL

Crocodile

NATIONAL RESOURCES

Natural resources include gold, petroleum, natural gas, manganese, and marble. The exploitation by East Timor and Australia* of petroleum and natural gas in the Timor Gap region promises to become a major resource. A large and potentially lucrative coffee industry sells high-quality coffee to fair-trade retailers and on the open market.

FOODS

Rice is the staple food in the country and is served with most meals. *Dukkah*, lamb, beef, or pork marinated and served with pomegranate juice and molasses, is considered the national dish.

SPORTS/SPORTS TEAMS

Association football (soccer) is the most popular sport. Traditional sports, weight lifting, and martial arts, such as karate and judo, are also popular. East Timor national teams participate in many sports at an international level.

TEAM SPORTS

Badminton

East Timor Badminton Team

Basketball

East Timor Basketball Team; East Timor Women's Basketball Team

Football

East Timor Football Team, nickname Os Sol Leventar (the Rising Sun); East Timor Futsal Team

Table Tennis

East Timor Table Tennis Team

Volleyball

East Timor Men's Volleyball Team; East Timor Women's Volleyball Team; East Timor Men's Beach Volleyball Team

INDIVIDUAL SPORTS

East Timor Amateur Boxing Team; East Timor Athletics Team; East Timor Canoeing Team; East Timor Cycling Team; East Timor Tae Kwon Do Team; East Timor Weight Lifting Team

NATIONAL HEROES OR PERSONIFICATIONS

José Ramos-Horta, a leader of the independence movement; Xanana Gusmão, independence leader and first president of East Timor; Bishop Filipe Ximenes Belo, head of the Roman Catholic Church in East Timor from 1983 and the winner, along with Ramos-Horta, of the Nobel Peace Prize, for their work toward a just and peaceful solution to the East Timor conflict

NATIONAL HOLIDAY/ INDEPENDENCE DAY

Independence Day, November 28

FESTIVALS/FAIRS

Independence Festival, November; Feast of Saint Mary, August.

SIGNIFICANT EVENTS IN FORMATION OF NATIONAL IDENTITY

3000 B.C.E.–1000 C.E. Austronesians migrate to the island, displacing the earlier Melanesian peoples. Malay peoples settle the coastal regions.

14th century Timor is incorporated into Chinese and Indian trading networks as an exporter of sandalwood, honey, wax, and slaves.

1556–1702 European explorers encounter a number of small principalities and chiefdoms. Portuguese Catholic missionaries establish the first European settlement. The Dutch gain control of the many islands making up the Indonesian Archipelago, except for half of Timor, which remains under Portuguese control. The territory officially becomes a Portuguese territory.

1767 Dili becomes the capital and center of Portuguese administration. Outside of Dili and a few other lowland areas, Portuguese authority is largely restricted. The Portuguese introduce the Portuguese language, Roman Catholicism, the Roman alphabet, a printing press, and formal schooling. Maize is introduced as a food crop, and coffee becomes the major export crop.

1859–1913 The border between Portuguese Timor and Dutch Timor is settled. The colony, seen as little more than a trading post, is neglected and underdeveloped. A Timorese rebellion is quashed by colonial troops hastily brought from Macau* and Mozambique*, leaving more than three thousand East Timorese dead. The Treaty of Lisbon formally divides the island between the two colonial powers.

1941–1942 Although Portugal* remains neutral in the Second World War, Australian and Dutch troops occupy the colony to prevent a Japanese invasion, which comes in February 1942.

1942–1945 Four hundred Dutch and Australian commandos are trapped on the island and wage a guerilla war against the Japanese. When the commandos are finally evacuated, the East Timorese are accused of aiding the guerillas, and punishments are severe. By the time the Japanese surrender, between 40,000 and 60,000 East Timorese have died, the economy is in ruins, and famine is decimating the surviving population.

1946–1950 The Portuguese return to claim their Timorese colony. Dutch West Timor becomes part of independent Indonesia*.

1974 The leftist revolution in Portugal begins the process of the decolonization of Portugal's overseas territories. Political parties are legalized, with three major groups advocating independence, incorporation into Indonesia, or continued association with Portugal.

1975 Leaders of the independence movement unilaterally declare the independence of East Timor on November 28. Indonesian troops invade just days later.

1975–1998 East Timorese groups fight the imposition of Indonesian rule. Indonesian rule is harsh, and between 100,000 and 200,000 die during the 24 years of occupation, mostly from hunger and disease, but also in massacres and atrocities carried out by the Indonesian military against suspected rebels.

1998–1999 A less authoritative government in Indonesia offers East Timor limited autonomy within Indonesia. A referendum on the province's future, organized under strong international pressure, shows a clear majority favoring independence. Pro-Indonesian militias and Indonesian troops carry out a campaign of terror. Hundreds are killed, and thousands flee or are forced into West Timor. Most of the province's schools, power plants, banks, water supply systems, and churches are destroyed. An Australian-led mission lands to reestablish order and to place East Timor under United Nations control.

2001–2003 Elections are held and a constitution drafted. East Timor becomes formally independent on May 20, 2002. Many pro-Indonesian East Timorese flee reprisals and take refuge in West Timor.

2005 East Timor and Australia, after years of boundary disputes, agree to defer the disputed portion of the boundary for 50 years and to split petroleum revenues evenly outside the joint areas covered by a 2002 treaty.

2006 Unrest starts over the dismissal of a group of soldiers and quickly turns into rioting. Fierce fighting between government troops and disaffected soldiers spreads. International peacekeepers from several countries arrive in the country.

2007 The peaceful handover of power from one political party to another after elections is a significant milestone.

2008 The development of East Timor's offshore oil fields promises a brighter future for the country. Some 30,000 people remain in refugee camps around Dili, with another 70,000 in other parts of the country. Followers of a former military police commander attack President Ramos-Horta, who sustains gunshot injuries. An attack on Prime Minister Gusmão is thwarted.

2009 Poverty and violence continue to affect the majority of the population 10 years after the 1999 independence referendum.

EAST TURKESTAN

OFFICIAL NAME

Xinjiang Uygur Zizhiqu (transliteration from Chinese); Sincañ Uyghur Aptonom Rayon (Uighur); Sinjiang Uighur Autonomous Region (English); Sherqiy Türkistan/Doğu Türkistan (Uighur); Eastern Turkestan/East Turkestan (English); Mulkul Uyghuriye (Uighur); Uighuristan (English)

POPULATION

20,635,500 (2009e)

INHABITANTS' NAME/NICKNAME

Uighur(s); East Turkestani(s)

LANGUAGE/LANGUAGES

Mandarin Chinese, Uighur (both official); Kazakh, Kyrghyz, Mongol, Tatar, others

RELIGION/RELIGIONS

Muslim (mostly Sunni), 45 percent; Buddhist, 6 percent; other or no religion

NATIONAL FLAG

The East Turkestan flag of the Uighurs, called the Kokbayraq flag, is a pale blue field bearing a white crescent moon and a single five-pointed star. Except for the background color, it is identical to the flag of the Turkish Republic. The blue represents the sky of East Turkestan, while the crescent moon and star represent Islam. It is used by the East Turkestan government-in-exile.

COAT OF ARMS/SEAL

The seal of the Republic of East Turkestan government-in-exile is a blue oval bearing nine points on each side of a gold crescent moon, points up, enclosing Arabic script reading "*Bismillahir rahmanir rahim*," or "in the name of Allah, the compassionate source of all mercy" below three golden stars. The 18 dots or points represent the 18 clans living in East Turkestan, while the three stars represent the three fallen republics proclaimed in East Turkestan. A new coat of arms proposed for the independent East Turkestan consists of a pale blue crest or shield bearing a white crescent moon and star above a white mountain between two gray wolves. Below is a banner with the national motto and nine stars representing the nine major Uighur tribes. The moon and stars represent Islam, the mountain stands for the Tian Shan Mountains and also the determination of the East Turkestan peoples to survive and endure, and the two wolves represent the country's ties to the other Turkic peoples.

CAPITAL CITY

Urumqi (Ürümqi)

TYPE OF GOVERNMENT

Nominally autonomous region of the People's Republic of China*; proposed democratic republic with a government-in-exile

NATIONAL EMBLEM

White crescent moon and star on a pale blue background

NATIONAL COLORS

Pale blue and white

NATIONAL ANTHEM

The anthem is the anthem of the East Turkestan government-in-exile and, like the flag and coat of arms, is forbidden in China.

Uyghur On Ikki Muqami (Uighur); Uighur March (English)

Our blood has flown on the way of salvation
For you, O my homeland, we devote our lives
We have saved you by crossing rivers of blood
We had the faith to liberate you

For you, we have united and fought
In the past, our great ancestors ruled the
  world

My homeland, we cleansed your eyes and
  saved you with our blood
Now, we shall not allow our enemies destroy
  you, because our name is Türk

Attila, Ghengis, Timor shook the world
Our names shall become famous, too, because
  we are their descendents
Our spirits left our bodies and our blood
  flowed, we avenged our enemies
Our country shall live and never perish, our
  future shall flourish

CURRENCY

Chinese yuan

VEHICLE IDENTIFICATION PLATES/STICKERS

China (no official initials); DT (unofficial Doğu Türkistan/East Turkestan)

PASSPORT

Uighurs are Chinese citizens; when allowed to travel, they use Chinese passports.

NATIONAL FLOWER

Aigul (unofficial)

NATIONAL TREE

Cotton tree (unofficial)

NATIONAL ANIMAL

Wild camel (unofficial)

NATIONAL BIRD

Common buzzard (unofficial)

NATIONAL RESOURCES

Natural resources include uranium, beryllium, oil, natural gas, gold, diamonds, precious stones, iron, lead, copper, silver, sulfur, tin, mica, arable land, and grazing land, The region's oil reserves have only begun to be exploited but could be the basis of a viable economy in the region. The famed Silk Road that runs through the region's historic cities could support a thriving tourist industry.

FOODS

Lagman, noodles made from wheat flour and served topped with stir-fried meat and vegetables in meat sauce, is considered the national dish. *Sumsa,* lamb pastries cooked in a special oven, are also popular across the region. *Narin,* boiled meat served with dumplings, is a regional specialty. Other specialties include *shurpa,* a lamb soup; *youtazi,* a steamed, multilayered bread; *guxnan,* pan-grilled lamb pies; *pamirdin,* baked pastries filled with minced lamb, carrots, and onion; *gül tavaq,* a dish of cold chopped vegetables; and *manty,* small pastries stuffed with minced meat.

SPORTS/SPORTS TEAMS

Association football (soccer) is the most popular sport. Traditional sports, such as games played on horseback and wrestling, are also very popular.

TEAM SPORTS

Football

East Turkestan National Football Team, created in 1959; outlawed by authorities of the People's Republic of China in 1989

NATIONAL HEROES OR PERSONIFICATIONS

Kutluk Bilge Kul, who established the first Uighur national state in 744; Rabiya Kadir, a jailed millionaire accused of separatism in 2007; Isa Alptekin, leader of the First East Turkestan Republic in the 1930s; Muhammad Emin Bughra, nationalist leader exiled in 1949; Mehmet Emin Batur, a leader of the East Turkestan autonomy movement; Hgojaniyaz Haji, the president of the East Turkestan Islamic Republic in 1933–1934. His tomb and monument in Urumchi was destroyed during the Cultural Revolution in

the 1960s, but like most mosques and monuments destroyed during that time, the Chinese government refuses permission to repair or restore the tomb.

NATIONAL HOLIDAY/INDEPENDENCE DAY

National Day, November 12

FESTIVALS/FAIRS

Grape Festival, August; Corban Festival, dates vary according to the Islamic lunar calendar.

SIGNIFICANT EVENTS IN FORMATION OF NATIONAL IDENTITY

4000 B.C.E. Well-preserved mummies with Caucasoid features, often with reddish or blond hair, are evidence of a non-Chinese population in the area thousands of years ago. They are probably part of a large Indo-European migration into Central Asia.

645 B.C.E. The first reference is made in Chinese writings of the nomadic peoples northwest of the Chinese border.

220 B.C.E.–100 B.C.E. A number of powerful states emerge along the trade route between East and West known as the Silk Road.

60 B.C.E. China establishes the Protectorate of the Western Regions as a dependent state west of the Pamir Mountains.

13 C.E. A rebellion throws off Chinese authority, beginning centuries of Chinese encroachments and war.

400–609 A vast Turkic empire ruled by the Gokturks includes the region until, defeated by the Chinese in 606, the empire disappears.

744–840 A Uighur national state is established in 744 under Kutluk Bilge Kul, now a revered national hero. His son subdues neighboring Turkic peoples and extends the borders of the state to Lake Baikal in the north and to Tibet* in the south. At the height of its power and prestige in the late eighth century, the state falls to Kyrgyz invaders.

934 Islam, introduced by Arab traders, spreads along the Silk Road and is embraced by the Uighurs.

14th century Numerous small states are created and gain fame as centers of Muslim learning and tolerance. Disparate ethnic and religious groups populate Uighur cities. As centers of trade, they boast extensive libraries, elaborate mosques, and opulent public buildings and palaces.

1756–1862 China's Manchu rulers dispatch a huge army to conquer the region. Between 1759 and 1862, the Uighurs rebel 42 times.

1863–1878 A widespread rebellion, encouraged by Russian and British agents, loosens China's grip on the region. A Uighur kingdom is created and establishes relations with the Ottoman Empire, Russia*, and the United Kingdom*. The Chinese reconquer the territory, a campaign marked by savage reprisals. Thousands flee to nearby Russian territory.

1884–1911 Xinkiang, meaning "new domain" or "new territory," is annexed to Manchu China. The Uighurs, considered a rebellious people, are subjected to a campaign to destroy their pride and self-respect. Forced labor, hunger, and mistreatment force thousands more to cross into Russian territory.

1911 The overthrow of the Manchu dynasty begins new period of instability.

1934 A rebellion drives all Chinese officials from the region. The first national republic is proclaimed as the Islamic Republic of East Turkestan, which is soon ended by the return of Chinese troops.

1937–1945 Renewed rebellion arises while China is engaged in war with Japan* in the east. The second republic, called the Republic of East Turkestan, is declared. The Soviets, fearing unrest in their own Central Asian territories, persuade the leaders to negotiate with the Nationalist Chinese of Chiang Kai-shek. After months of negotiations, they agree to autonomy and begin to disarm. The Nationalists betray the accord and begin a brutal retribution.

1945–1949 The Nationalist betrayal costs Chiang Kai-shek a major defeat in the ongoing Chinese Civil War; the entire region, still recovering from the devastation, goes over to the communists without a fight. Some nationalist leaders establish a government in exile in Turkey*.

1949–1955 Ignoring promises of autonomy, the Chinese government begins to settle non-Muslims in the region to dilute the local population. In 1955, the region is organized as a nominally autonomous region.

1966–1976 The brutalities of the Cultural Revolution come to Xinjiang. Radical cadres destroy thousands of mosques and other Muslim monuments.

1976–1993 Isolated from the outside world, Xinjiang becomes a dumping ground, with thousands of labor camps to hold dissidents and rebels. Goods produced in the labor camps are often exported as China experiences a great economic awakening.

1993–1999 East Turkestani nationalists plead their case at the United Nations but receive little support. An uprising is again put down, with reports of many executions and more than 10,000 people, both activists and sympathizers, arrested.

1999 Representatives of the government-in-exile and most nationalist groups attend a conference of the Uighur National Congress in an effort to end factionalism and to present a united front.

2001 In the wake of the September 11 attacks on New York by Islamic radicals, the Chinese government characterizes East Turkestani nationalists as Islamic terrorists, although the nationalists describe their movement as anticolonial, not Islamic. The United States*, seeking better relations with the People's Republic of China, lists the nationalist groups as terrorist organizations.

2003–2008 Chinese authorities destroy the contents of several noted Muslim libraries in reprisal for continued anti-Chinese violence. Thousands of historic houses are torn down to make way for redevelopment, which is decried as an attack on Uighur heritage.

2008 In the run-up to the Summer Olympics in Beijing, while world attention is on pro-Tibetan protests, Uighur groups stage protests in several countries. Four days before the opening of the Olympics, a bomb explodes in the region, killing 16 policemen.

The region has the highest longevity rate in China, due to the region's weather and environment and the living and working habits of the population. By Chinese statistics, more than 90 percent of the area's Muslims live below the poverty line.

2009 A Swedish court accepts that Abel Hakimjan, an ethnic Uighur, is not a terrorist, despite spending more than five years in the U.S. military prison at Guantanamo Bay. He is granted permission to remain permanently in Sweden*. Another 17 Uighurs still refuse repatriation to China because they fear persecution there. In mid-2009 ethnic violence between Uighurs and Han Chinese leaves over 200 dead. The two ethnic groups are increasingly segregated as fear of violence and antigovernment demonstrations continue to destabilize the region.

See also China

FIJI

OFFICIAL NAME

Matanitu TūVaka-koya ko Viti (Fijian); Republic of the Fiji Islands (English)

POPULATION

832,700 (2009e)

INHABITANTS' NAME/NICKNAME

Fijian(s)

LANGUAGE/LANGUAGES

English, Bau Fijian (both official); Hindustani (Hindi/Urdu), others

RELIGION/RELIGIONS

Christian, 52 percent; Hindu, 33 percent; Muslim, 7 percent; Sikh, other or no religion

NATIONAL FLAG

A sky blue field bears the Union Jack as a canton on the upper hoist and the Fijian shield centered on the fly. The blue symbolizes the Pacific Ocean, which plays an important role in the lives of the Fijians. The Union Jack represents the country's historic ties to the United Kingdom*. The white shield, quartered in red, has images of Fiji's agricultural products below a heraldic British lion, gold on red.

COAT OF ARMS/SEAL

The coat of arms is made up of a shield, as on the national flag, supported by two Fijian warriors, one holding a spear and the other a pineapple mace. A heraldic lion holds a cacao pod across the top of the shield, while sugarcane, a coconut palm, and bunch of bananas are represented in three of the shield's sections. The fourth contains a reproduction of the dove of peace. Below the shield is a banner with the national motto.

MOTTO

Rerevaka na kalou ka doka na tui (Fijian); Fear God and honor the queen (English)

CAPITAL CITY

Suva

TYPE OF GOVERNMENT

Republic (under military rule)

NATIONAL EMBLEM

Tabua (a whale's tooth)

NATIONAL COLORS

White and black

NATIONAL ANTHEM

The anthem is based on a hymn titled "Dwelling in Beulah Land," and the words were adopted just before independence in 1970. There are two official versions, in Fijian and in English.

Meda Dau Doks (Fijian); God Bless Fiji (English)

Blessing grant, O God of nations, on the isles
of Fiji
As we stand united under noble banner blue
And we honor and defend the cause of free-
dom ever
Onward march together
God bless Fiji

Chorus

For Fiji, ever Fiji, let our voices ring with
pride
For Fiji, ever Fiji, her name hail far and wide,
A land of freedom, hope, and glory, to endure
whatever befall
May God bless Fiji
Forever more!

Blessing grant, O God of nations, on the isles
of Fiji
Shores of golden sand and sunshine, happi-
ness and song
Stand united, we of Fiji, fame and glory ever
Onward march together
God bless Fiji.

PATRON SAINT

Saint Peter Channel is the patron saint of the
South Pacific.

CURRENCY

Fijian dollar

INTERNET IDENTIFIER

.fj

VEHICLE IDENTIFICATION PLATES/STICKERS

FJI

PASSPORT

The passport cover has the name of the country in Fijian and English, the coat of arms,
and the word *passport* in Fijian and English.

AIRLINE

Air Pacific

NATIONAL FLOWER

Tagimoucia (official); hibiscus (unofficial)

NATIONAL TREE

Coconut palm (unofficial)

NATIONAL ANIMAL

Crested iguana (unofficial)

NATIONAL BIRD

Collared lory

NATIONAL FISH

Clown triggerfish (unofficial)

NATIONAL RESOURCES

Natural resources include timber, fish, gold,
copper, offshore oil potential, and hydropower.
The sugar industry, long the mainstay of the
Fijian economy, is subsidized by the European
Union (EU) and is considered a major asset.

FOODS

Fijian cuisine is quite diverse, with a fusion
of traditional dishes and Indian cuisine and
spices. *Palusami*—parcels of taro leaves satu-
rated with coconut milk, stuffed with onions
and fish meat, and cooked on hot rocks in
an earth oven—is the national dish. *Lovo,*
meat, vegetables, or seafood cooked in an
underground earth oven, is another typical
meal. Chicken curry; and goat curry are also
very popular. *Kava,* often called *yakona,* is
the national drink. Other specialties include
vakalolo, a dessert of freshly grated cassava
and coconut mixed with ginger and cloves
and cooked in banana leaves.

SPORTS/SPORTS TEAMS

Rugby union is the country's most popular sport, particularly rugby union sevens.
Association football (soccer) has grown in
popularity over the past decade. Fiji national
teams participate in many sports at an international level.

TEAM SPORTS

Badminton

Fiji Badminton Team

Baseball

Fiji Baseball Team

Basketball

Fiji Basketball Team; Fiji Women's Basketball Team

Cricket

Fiji Cricket Team

Football

Fiji Football Team; Fiji Women's Football Team; Fiji Rugby Union Team, nickname the Bati; Fiji Women's Rugby Union Team; Fiji Rugby Union Team (Sevens), nickname Fiji Sevens or Fiji Barbarians; Fiji Women's Rugby Union Team (Sevens), nickname Fiji Sevens or Fiji 7s; Fiji Rugby League Team; Fiji Futsal Team; Fiji Touch Football Team; Fiji Women's Touch Football Team; Fiji Women's Under-19 Football Team

Hockey

Fiji Field Hockey Team

Netball

Fiji Netball Team

Table Tennis

Fiji Table Tennis Team

Tennis

Fiji Davis Cup Team; Fiji Fed Cup Team; Pacific Oceania Fed Cup and Davis Cup teams (Pacific Oceania teams represent a number of Pacific island nations)

Volleyball

Fiji Men's Volleyball Team; Fiji Women's Volleyball Team

INDIVIDUAL SPORTS

Fiji Amateur Boxing Team; Fiji Archery Team; Fiji Athletics Team; Fiji Cycling Team; Fiji Judo Team; Fiji Karate Team; Fiji Sailing Team; Fiji Shooting Team; Fiji Swim Team; Fiji Tae Kwon Do Team; Fiji Triathlon Team; Fiji Weight Lifting Team

NATIONAL HEROES OR PERSONIFICATIONS

Ratu Sir Lala Sukuna, Fiji's first modern statesman; Sitiveni Ligamamada Rabuka, the leader of two coups to reassert ethnic Fijian supremacy; Shamina Ali, a Fiji Indian political and women's rights activist

NATIONAL HOLIDAY/INDEPENDENCE DAY

Fiji Day/Independence Day, second Monday of October

FESTIVALS/FAIRS

Holi, the Hindu Festival of Colors, February–March; Ratu Sir Lala Sukuna Festival, May; Muhammad's Birthday, July–August; Fiji Day Festival, October

SIGNIFICANT EVENTS IN FORMATION OF NATIONAL IDENTITY

3500 B.C.E.–1000 B.C.E. Melanesian and Polynesian settlers colonize the islands around 1000 B.C.E. The large number of islands is divided into chiefdoms or kingdoms, many with distinct ethnic or cultural backgrounds.

1643 C.E. Dutch explorer Abel Tasman visits Fiji.

1774 British explorer Captain James Cook visits the Lau Archipelago.

1800–1874 European whalers, traders, and missionaries arrive in the islands. In the 1850s, a local chief, or *ratu*, Cakobau, gains control of the western islands during a period of unrest and lavish overspending. Cakobau and other chiefs cede Fiji to the British Crown in exchange for financial aid.

1875–1876 A measles epidemic leaves a third of the Fijian population dead. The Great Council of

Chiefs is established as an advisory body to the local British administration.

1879 Indentured laborers arrive from India*, the first of more than 61,000 that are eventually brought to the islands.

1881 The first sugar mill is built, as sugar production becomes the main economic activity.

1916 A ban is placed on the importation of Indian laborers to the islands. The first Indian joins the European planters and Fijian chiefs on the legislative council.

1929 Wealthy Indo-Fijians are enfranchised for the first time.

1963 The indigenous Fijians and women are enfranchised, with indigenous representation in the Legislative Council in more than just an advisory or ceremonial role.

1965–1970 Differences between indigenous Fijians and Indo-Fijians block the adoption of a constitution until 1970, when Fiji is granted independence.

1987–1990 A general election is won by a coalition of Indo-Fijian political parties. Lieutenant Colonel Sitiveni Rabuka overthrows the government and stages a second coup some months later to consolidate ethnic Fijian control of the government. A new constitution institutionalizes ethnic Fijian supremacy.

1997 Fijians and Indo-Fijians agree to a new constitution.

2000 A civilian coup topples the new elected government. Troops mutiny in the capital. The constitution is reinstated and new elections held.

2006 A coup overthrows the government and a military government is formed. The coup is widely criticized internationally.

2007 The interim government suspends the Grand Council of Chiefs. The civilian presidency is restored.

2008 The interim government pledges to hold elections in 2009. A series of court cases challenging the constitutionality of the 2006 coup and its aftermath continue to cause controversy.

2009 In early 2009, the military ruler of Fiji rejects a demand from the Commonwealth of Nations to prepare for the promised elections.

FRENCH POLYNESIA

Official Name

Polynésie Française (French); Pōrīnetia Farāni (Tahitian); French Polynesia (English); Tahiti et ses Îles (French); Tahiti Nui (Tahitian); Great Tahiti or Tahiti and Her Islands (English)

Population

262,300 (2009e)

Inhabitants' Name/Nickname

French Polynesian(s); Tahitian(s)

Language/Languages

French (official); Tahitian, other Polynesian languages, others

Religion/Religions

Evangelical Christian, 46 percent; Roman Catholic, 38 percent; Mormon, 6 percent; other or no religion

National Flag

The flag of the islands, a French overseas collectivity, has stripes of red, white, and red, the white twice the width of the red stripes, bearing the coat of arms centered. The red and white are taken from historic Tahitian flags and represent the traditions and history of the people. The coat of arms represents the people of the five island groups that make up the territory.

Coat of Arms/Seal

The coat of arms is a white circle bearing a Polynesian canoe with red sails on a blue and white sea below a rising sun of 10 rays. The canoe and the sails are outlined in brown, with two figures atop each prow and five small stars representing the five island groups in French Polynesia. The canoe represents the Polynesian seafaring tradition.

MOTTO

Tahiti nui mare'are'a (Tahitian); Great Tahiti of the Golden Haze (English)

CAPITAL CITY

Papeete

TYPE OF GOVERNMENT

An overseas collectivity (overseas country) of the French Republic

NATIONAL EMBLEM

Tiki (carved figure)

NATIONAL COLORS

Red and white

NATIONAL ANTHEM

The official anthem is the French anthem, "La Marseillaise." The anthem of French Polynesia was adopted in 1993 and represents the territory at international venues.

> **La Ora 'O Tahiti Nui (Tahitian); Long Live Tahiti Nui (English)**
>
> God created my country
> Garland of multiple islands
> With such delicate fragrances
> Linked up as an everlasting braid
> Today let me praise you
> Listen to your children's voice
> Crying out "Lavish your love"
> So that Tahiti Nui can live.

CURRENCY

Comptoirs Français du Pacifique franc (French) French-Pacific Banking Agreement franc most commonly known as CFP franc or simply, franc

INTERNET IDENTIFIER

.pf

VEHICLE IDENTIFICATION PLATES/STICKERS

F (official France); TAH (unofficial Tahiti/French Polynesia)

PASSPORT

Tahitians are French citizens and travel on French passports.

AIRLINE

Air Tahiti Nui

NATIONAL FLOWER

Tiare Tahiti (Tahitian gardenia); Hibiscus (unofficial)

NATIONAL TREE

Breadfruit (unofficial)

NATIONAL RESOURCES

Natural resources include timber, fish, cobalt, black pearls, and hydropower. The islands are dependent on imported goods. Tourism, and the financial assistance of mainland France* represent the major assets of the regional economy. Sandy beaches, island scenery, and a unique culture support a well-developed tourist industry.

FOODS

Traditional Tahitian food is cooked in an underground oven called an *ahimaa*. Pork, fish, breadfruit, taro, and other foods are wrapped in banana leaves and cooked on the preheated volcanic rocks. Other specialties include *poisson cru*, raw fish marinated in lime juice and coconut; *poulet tahitienne*, chicken cooked with lime juice, pineapple, and oranges; *poulet fafa*, chicken with taro leaves; *pua toro*, a type of corned beef; *fafaru*, fish fermented in seawater; *fe'I*, baked plantains; *poi*, baked and mashed taro root; and *po'e*, a fruit pudding dessert.

SPORTS/SPORTS TEAMS

Association football (soccer) is the most popular sport. Traditional sports, such as canoeing, surfing, and athletics, remain very popular. French Polynesia national teams, under the name Tahiti, participate in many sports at an international level.

TEAM SPORTS

Basketball

Tahiti Basketball Team; Tahiti Women's Basketball Team

Football

Tahiti Football Team; Tahiti Women's Football Team; Tahiti Rugby Union Team; Tahiti Beach Soccer Team; Tahiti Under-19 Football Team; Tahiti Women's Under-19 Football Team; Tahiti Futsal Team

Table Tennis

Tahiti Table Tennis Team

Volleyball

Tahiti Men's Volleyball Team; Tahiti Women's Volleyball Team

INDIVIDUAL SPORTS

Tahiti Amateur Boxing Team; Tahiti Archery Team; Tahiti Athletics Team; Tahiti Judo Team; Tahiti Sailing Team; Tahiti Swim Team; Tahiti Tae Kwon Do Team; Tahiti Triathlon Team; French Polynesia Tahiti Weight Lifting Team

NATIONAL HEROES OR PERSONIFICATIONS

King Pomare II, the king of Tahiti when Europeans first visited the islands; Pouvanaa o Oopa, a decorated First World War hero and leader of the nationalist movement; Oscar Manutahi Temaru, three-time president of French Polynesia between 2004 and 2009

NATIONAL HOLIDAY/ INDEPENDENCE DAY

Internal Autonomy Day, June 29; Bastille Day, July 14

FESTIVALS/FAIRS

Heiva Festival, July; Raiatea Carnival, September; Tiare Festival (Flower Festival), December; Marquesas Festival, December

SIGNIFICANT EVENTS IN FORMATION OF NATIONAL IDENTITY

200 C.E.–1400 C.E. Settlers arrive by canoe from the west to settle the Marquesas. Settlers from these islands reach Tahiti and the Society Islands around 800 C.E. Over the centuries, the Polynesians spread through the islands, which are organized as small chiefdoms.

1400–1600 Large chiefdoms are established on Tahiti, Bora Bora, and Raiatea, often warring among themselves.

1521–1797 European contact begins with the Portuguese sailing into the Tuamoto Archipelago. British explorer Samuel Wallis visits Tahiti in 1767. Mutineers from the *HMS Bounty* reach the islands in 1788. Protestant missionaries settle in the islands in 1797, beginning the islanders' conversion to Christianity.

1812–1834 King Pomare II and his people convert to Protestantism. French Catholic missionaries arrive in the islands.

1841–1843 Queen Pomare IV seeks French assistance against British encroachments. A French protectorate is declared, which allows Catholic missionaries to work undisturbed.

1843–1885 French claims are extended to the other island groups.

1940 During the Second World War, the islands remain under the control of the Free French authorities. Many Polynesians serve as soldiers in the French forces.

1946 Polynesians are granted French citizenship, and the islands' status is changed from colony to overseas territory.

1962–1976 French nuclear testing begins over protests from the Polynesians. The influx of Europeans to the islands and the callous use of the islands for nuclear testing initiate a protest movement that becomes a nationalist movement demanding autonomy for the islands.

1977–1984 French Polynesia is granted partial autonomy in 1977. In 1982, a majority in the territorial assembly announces support for independence. The autonomy statute is expanded in response to rising nationalist demands, which are tempered by an increase in the generous French subsidies that sustain one of the highest standards of living in the South Pacific.

1991 The imposition of new taxes sets off riots that quickly become a mass pro-independence movement, forcing the resignation of the local administration.

1992–1996 A moratorium on nuclear testing is announced, but tests resume in 1995. The next year, France finally signs the Treaty of Rarotonga that creates a nuclear-free zone in the South Pacific.

2004–2008 French Polynesia becomes a full overseas collectivity of France. Polynesian support for independence is widespread, but French economic subsidies may be too much for the islanders to forfeit.

2009 Oscar Temaru is again elected regional president, the seventh change of presidents since the first general elections in 2004. Frequent changes of alliance among the small, powerful political elite result in regular changes of government.

GUAM

Official Name
Guåhan (Chamorro); Territory of Guam (English)

Population
175,900 (2009e)

Inhabitants' Name/Nickname
Guamanian(s)

Language/Languages
English, Chamorro (both official); Filipino (various Filipino languages), other Pacific Island languages, other Asian languages, others

Religion/Religions
Roman Catholic, 85 percent; other or no religion

National Flag
A blue field bordered in red bears the territorial seal, centered and also bordered in red. The almond shape of the centered emblem represents the slingshot stones used in Chamorro history. The scene is of a Chamorro canoe, a *proa*, sailing in Agana Bay, with the name Guam in red letters. The red border represents the blood shed by Guam's people in defense of liberty. The sailing canoe symbolizes the courage of the first settlers, who traveled by canoe across great distances. A coconut palm growing in barren sand represents the determination of the earliest settlers to overcome whatever natural obstacles they encountered.

Coat of Arms/Seal
The seal of Guam appears at the center of the Guamanian flag. The coconut palm, known in Guam as the tree of life, is a symbol of Guam's determination.

Motto
Where America's day begins

Capital City
Hagåtña

Type of Government
Representative democracy as an incorporated territory of the United States*

National Emblem
Coconut palm (shown on the Guam flag); *Latte* stone

NATIONAL COLORS

Blue, white, and black

NATIONAL ANTHEM

The anthem was originally written and composed in 1919. The Chamorro version was written later. As a dependency of the United States, the official anthem is "The Star-Spangled Banner."

Fanohge Chamoru (Chamorro); Stand Ye Guamanians (English)

Stand ye Guamanians for your country
And sing her praise from shore to shore
For her honor, for her glory
Exalt our island forever more.
For her honor, for her glory
Exalt our island forever more.

May everlasting peace reign o'er us
May heaven's blessing to us come
Against all perils, do not forsake us
God protect our isle of Guam.
Against all perils, do not forsake us
God protect our isle of Guam.

PATRON SAINT

Saint Marian Kamalen

CURRENCY

U.S. dollar

INTERNET IDENTIFIER

.gu

VEHICLE IDENTIFICATION PLATES/STICKERS

USA United States (official); GU Guam (unofficial)

PASSPORT

Guamanians are American citizens and travel on American passports.

AIRLINE

Continental Micronesia is based in Guam but is part of Continental Airlines and uses aircraft painted in Continental livery

NATIONAL FLOWER

Puti tai nobiu (great Bougainvillea)

NATIONAL TREE

Ifil (*Ifit*); coconut palm (unofficial)

NATIONAL ANIMAL

Carabao (water buffalo) (unofficial)

NATIONAL BIRD

Ko'ko' (Guam rail) (unofficial)

NATIONAL RESOURCES

Natural resources are negligible. The one natural resource, fish, is largely undeveloped. Guam's economy depends primarily on tourism, the U.S. military base presence, and other federal spending.

FOODS

Typical American food is available throughout Guam. Local dishes considered island specialties include *hineksa agata,* red rice; shrimp patties; *kelaguin manok,* a dish of chopped chicken, grated coconut, lemon juice, and hot peppers; *kelaguin uhang,* shrimp and sweet green peppers with coconut; *kelaguin guihan,* fish with lemon and onions; *su tang hu,* a soup of chicken and rice; *chalakilis,* chicken cooked with corn, garlic, onions, and coconut milk; and *golai'agon suni,* spicy spinach with coconut milk.

SPORTS/SPORTS TEAMS

Baseball is the most popular sport in Guam. American football, association football (soccer), and basketball are also popular. Guam national teams participate in many sports at an international level.

TEAM SPORTS

Baseball

Guam Baseball Team; Guam Men's Softball Team; Guam Women's Softball Team

Basketball

Guam Basketball Team; Guam Women's Basketball Team

Football

Guam Football Team; Guam Women's Football Team; Guam Rugby Union Team; Guam Futsal Team; Guam Women's Under-19 Football Team; Guam American Football Team

Racing

Guam Speedway Team

Table Tennis

Guam Table Tennis Team

Tennis

Pacific Oceania Davis Cup and Pacific Oceania Fed Cup teams (Pacific Oceania teams represent a number of Pacific countries)

Volleyball

Guam Men's Volleyball Team; Guam Women's Volleyball Team

Water Polo

Guam Men's Water Polo Team; Guam Women's Water Polo Team

INDIVIDUAL SPORTS

Guam Amateur Boxing Team; Guam Archery Team; Guam Athletics Team; Guam Canoeing Team; Guam Cycling Team; Guam Judo Team; Guam Modern Pentathlon Team; Guam Sailing Team; Guam Swim Team; Guam Tae Kwon Do Team; Guam Triathlon Team; Guam Weight Lifting Team; Guam Wrestling Team

WINTER SPORTS

Guam Biathlon Team

NATIONAL HEROES OR PERSONIFICATIONS

Chief Gadao, a legendary chief from southern Guam featured in stories and legends, is the personification of Guam. Other national heroes are Mata'pang, a chief accused of murder who escaped the Spanish manhunt for many years; Hurao, a chief who led the fight against Spanish colonization; and Chief Kiphua, the first important chief to adopt Christianity

NATIONAL HOLIDAY/INDEPENDENCE DAY

Discovery Day, first Monday in March

FESTIVALS/FAIRS

Malojloj Festival, May; Liberation Day, July

SIGNIFICANT EVENTS IN FORMATION OF NATIONAL IDENTITY

3000 B.C.E.–1500 B.C.E. Ancient seafaring peoples, probably from present Indonesia*, settle the Mariana Islands. Later waves of settlers come from Polynesia and Melanesia.

1500 B.C.E.–800 C.E. The islanders develop a complex culture.

1521–1565 Ferdinand Magellan, sailing for Spain*, sights the Mariana Islands and makes landfall on Guam, which he claims for Spain. The Spanish government annexes the island, although no Europeans are resident there.

1670–1698 An uprising against Spanish rule initiates 25 years of intermittent war, known as the Chamorro Wars. European diseases devastate the population. The Chamorros resist conversion to Catholicism and are driven into segregated villages. The entire populations of Saipan and Rota, in the Northern Marianas*, are forcibly removed to Guam.

1700–1850 The population of the Mariana Islands, estimated at 100,000, is reduced to 4,000 by 1700 and to 1,500 by 1850. Spain develops Guam as a waystation for treasure galleons traveling between the Philippines* and Mexico*. The islanders develop a culture incorporating both Chamorro and Spanish characteristics.

1898–1920 Guam is ceded to the United States following the Spanish-American War, while the other islands in the group are sold to Germany*, effectively dividing the archipelago. The new American administration outlaws slavery in Guam. Japan* takes control of the Northern Marianas during the First World War. The Chamorro population begins to recover from the devastation of Spanish rule.

1941 Until the beginning of the Second World, villages remain the basic social and economic units of the Chamorro population. At the outbreak of war, Japanese troops from nearby islands overrun Guam. Chamorros from the Japanese Marianas are brought to Guam to assist the Japanese administration, creating a lasting rift between Guamanians and other Mariana Islanders.

1944–1950 The Americans return to retake Guam in some of the heaviest fighting of the war. Guamanians become citizens of the United States, but without the right to vote in national elections.

1960s A referendum on the reunification of the Mariana Islands wins approval in the Northern Marianas, but Guamanians, still resentful of the northerners' wartime conduct as Japanese administrators, vote against the measure.

1972–1979 Limited self-government is introduced. Guam gains representation in the U.S. House of Representatives. Land, sacred in Chamorro tradition, becomes a sensitive issue, as demands are raised for lands confiscated by the U.S. military and later abandoned, but never returned to the Chamorro people. In 1979, the Guamanians vote five to one against a new constitution that fails to address the land issue.

1980s Feeling neglected and misunderstood by the U.S. government and other world nations, the Chamorro Guamanians begin a concerted effort to revive their flagging culture and to win greater self-government.

1992 Typhoon Omar devastates Guam, leaving 90 percent of the island's buildings damaged. The reconstruction effort revives the land question. Land confiscated from local people for military use but no longer needed by the military becomes a nationalist issue. Between the federal and local government, more than two-thirds of the island is in government hands.

1997–2000 Nationalist leaders request that Guam be added to the United Nations' list of non-self-governing territories, which would produce official U.N. support for decolonization. Guamanians demand commonwealth status as a state associated with the United States, similar to the statutes enjoyed by Puerto Rico* and the Northern Marianas.

2000–2008 Proposals to transfer 8,000 U.S. Marines from Okinawa to Guam alarm the Guamanians. Guam's multicultural society poses particular challenges to the Chamorros struggling to preserve their identity and culture. Increasing numbers of young Guamanians relocate to the U.S. mainland.

2009 Tourism and the military presence on the island remain the mainstays of the economy, despite government efforts to diversify.

HONG KONG

OFFICIAL NAME

Xianggang Tebie Xingzhengqu (transliteration from Chinese); Hong Kong Special Administrative Region (English)

POPULATION

6,988,600 (2009e)

INHABITANTS' NAME/NICKNAME

Hong Kong Chinese; Hongkonger(s)

LANGUAGE/LANGUAGES

Chinese (Cantonese), English (both official); other Chinese dialects, others

RELIGION/RELIGIONS

Buddhist (includes Taoist, Buddhist, and other influences), 90 percent; Christian, 7 percent; other or no religion

REGIONAL FLAG

The flag is a red field with the flower of the Hong Kong orchid tree (*Bauhinia blakeana*) in white. Red is the color of festivals and nationalism, and the flag uses exactly the same hue as that of the People's Republic of China*, representing the new ties between Hong Kong and China. The juxtaposition of the white and red represents the "one country, two systems" principle applied to the region.

Coat of Arms/Seal

The Hong Kong coat of arms or emblem features the same design elements as the regional flag of Hong Kong, but in a circular setting. The outer white ring is contains the official name of the territory in traditional Chinese characters and the English short form, Hong Kong.

Capital City

Victoria (unofficial, as Hong Kong has no designated capital)

Type of Government

Autonomous government as a special territory of the People's Republic of China. The Central People's Government is responsible for the territory's defense and foreign affairs, while Hong Kong maintains its own legal system, police force, customs policy, monetary system, immigration policy, and delegates to international organizations and events.

National Emblem

Dragon; The Star Ferry, the picturesque ferries that connect mainland Kowloon with the Victoria on Hong Kong Island

National Colors

Red and white

National Anthem

The anthem of the People's Republic of China is the official anthem.

Currency

Hong Kong dollar

Internet Identifier

.hk

Vehicle Identification Plates/Stickers

HK

Passport

The passport cover has the names of the special region and the People's Republic of China in Chinese, followed by the name *Hong Kong* and, in smaller letters, *Special Administrative Region, People's Republic of China* in English, the coat of arms of the People's Republic of China, the word *passport* in Chinese and English, and the standard biometric symbol.

Airlines

Cathay Pacific Airways; Dragonair

National Flower

Bauhinia orchid

National Tree

Hong Kong bauhinia orchid tree

National Resources

Natural resources include an outstanding deepwater harbor and deposits of feldspar. Hong Kong's major asset is a well-educated and sophisticated population that sustains a world trading and banking center. Tourism is also very important.

Food

Dim sum, various appetizers or small dishes of stuffed dumplings, meats, shellfish, and buns with various fillings, is considered the most famous Hong Kong tradition. Other specialties include *liang*

gua neu rou, stir-fried beef with bitter gourd; *long jing xia ren,* shrimp cooked in tea; *lu zi wne ji,* chicken with chestnuts; *ba bao zhou,* sweet rice with beans; *bai cai xiang gu bao,* a stew of Chinese cabbage; *dong gua tang,* white gourd soup; *ning meng jian zhu bu,* fried pork with lemon; *nan yu ja pai gu,* deep-fried pork ribs with red bean curd; and *tian suan he tao,* walnuts in sweet and sour sauce.

SPORTS/SPORTS TEAMS

Association football (soccer) is the most popular sport in Hong Kong. Many other sports are also practiced. Hong Kong national teams participate in many sports at an international level. Some of Hong Kong's sports teams use the name Hong Kong China as a geographic designation even though they represent only Hong Kong at international events.

TEAM SPORTS

Badminton

Hong Kong Badminton Team

Baseball

Hong Kong China Baseball Team; Hong Kong Softball Team

Basketball

Hong Kong Basketball Team; Hong Kong Women's Basketball Team; Hong Kong Wheelchair Basketball Team (known as Hong Kong China Wheelchair Basketball Team)

Bowls

Hong Kong Bowls Team

Cricket

Hong Kong Cricket Team

Football

Hong Kong Football Team; Hong Kong Women's Football Team; Hong Kong Under-23 Football Team; Hong Kong Rugby Union Team; Hong Kong Women's Rugby Union Team; Hong Kong Futsal Team; Hong Kong Touch Football Team; Hong Kong Women's Touch Football Team; Hong Kong Rugby Union Team (Sevens), nickname Hong Kong Sevens; Hong Kong Women's Rugby Union Team (Sevens), nickname Hong Kong Sevens or 7s; Hong Kong Women's Under-19 Football Team

Handball

Hong Kong Handball Team; Hong Kong Women's Handball Team; Hong Kong Beach Handball Team; Hong Kong Women's Beach Handball Team

Hockey

Hong Kong Ice Hockey Team; Hong Kong Field Hockey Team

Korfball

Hong Kong Korfball Team (also known as Hong Kong China Korfball Team)

Lacrosse

Hong Kong Lacrosse Team; Hong Kong Women's Lacrosse Team

Netball

Hong Kong Netball Team

Table Tennis

Hong Kong Table Tennis Team

Tennis

Hong Kong Davis Cup Team; Hong Kong Fed Cup Team

Volleyball

Hong Kong Men's Volleyball Team; Hong Kong Women's Volleyball Team; Hong Kong Men's Beach Volleyball Team; Hong Kong Women's Beach Volleyball Team

INDIVIDUAL SPORTS

Hong Kong Amateur Boxing Team; Hong Kong Archery Team; Hong Kong Athletics Team; Hong Kong China Canoeing Team; Hong Kong Cycling Team; Hong Kong Equestrian Team; Hong Kong Fencing Team; Hong Kong Judo Team; Hong Kong Karate Team; Hong Kong Modern Pentathlon Team; Hong Kong Rowing Team; Hong Kong Sailing Team; Hong Kong Shooting Team; Hong Kong Swim Team; Hong Kong Tae Kwon Do Team; Hong Kong Triathlon Team; Hong Kong Weight Lifting Team

WINTER SPORTS

Hong Kong Ice Hockey Team; Hong Kong Skating Team

NATIONAL HEROES OR PERSONIFICATIONS

Martin Lee, founder of the Democratic Party, the leading prodemocracy political party in the territory; Anson Chan, a prodemocracy leader and the first woman to head Hong Kong's civil service; Bruce Lee, internationally known actor and athlete who died in 1973

NATIONAL HOLIDAY/
INDEPENDENCE DAY

Hong Kong Day, July 1

FESTIVALS/FAIRS

Dwan Wu (Dragon Boat Festival), variable dates based on the lunar calendar; Spring Lantern Festival, variable dates; Tam Kung Festival, variable dates; Seven Sisters Festival, variable dates; Mid-Autumn Festival, variable dates; Dong Zhi (Winter Solstice Festival), variable dates

SIGNIFICANT EVENTS IN FORMATION
OF NATIONAL IDENTITY

Seventh century C.E.–13th century Han Chinese migrating south from the Chinese heartland settle the region. Major settlements are established during the Sung Dynasty.

1513 Portuguese sailor Jorge Alvares is the first European to visit the territory.

1699 An East India Company expedition reaches the China coast. British merchants found a trading post in Canton, up the Pearl River.

1839–1841 The refusal of the Qing Dynasty authorities to import opium results in the First Opium War. Hong Kong Island is occupied by a British force and is formally ceded at the end of the war.

1860 Following China's defeat in the Second Opium War, Kowloon and some mainland territory are ceded to the United Kingdom*.

1898 China leases the adjacent northern districts and Lantau Island to the United Kingdom for 99 years. The areas become known as the New Territories. Hong Kong is a major trading center of the British Empire.

1910–1940 The Kowloon-Canton Railway opens, increasing trade through the busy port. A British educational system is introduced. The Chinese population has very little contact with the wealthy Europeans living in the colony.

1941–1945 Japanese troops invade and take control of the colony. Hong Kong's population declines from 1.6 million in 1940 to just 600,000 in 1945. The United Kingdom resumes control at the end of the war.

1945–1965 Hong Kong quickly recovers. Waves of immigrants arrive, seeking refuge from the ongoing Chinese Civil War. With the communist victory in 1949, millions crowd into Hong Kong to escape persecution. Large corporations from formerly international Shanghai shift their operations to Hong Kong. The colony becomes the sole point of contact between isolationist Red China and the West.

1965–1967 Hong Kong is heavily industrialized, and living standards rise steadily. The continued arrival of refugees swells the population. Procommunist groups stage a violent uprising.

1980s With the lease on the New Territories due to expire within two decades, talks on Hong Kong sovereignty begin. An agreement is signed for the transfer of Hong Kong to Chinese sovereignty in 1997.

1997 Hong Kong becomes a special autonomous region of the People's Republic of China with a high degree of self-government for at least 50 years after the transfer, per the transfer agreement. Some people leave the territory for Europe or North America.

2003 More than half a million people march in Hong Kong to protest infringements of their rights and freedoms. The majority of Hong Kong Chinese were born between 1949 and 1997 and feel loyalty to their small state, rather than to the huge Chinese republic of which they are now a part.

2008 The education minister of Hong Kong lifts restrictions that forced four-fifths of the territory's secondary schools to teach in Cantonese Chinese, as English makes a comeback in multicultural Hong Kong.

2009 Hong Kong's booming economy begins to slow due to a global economic recession. Many educated workers leave for Canada*, the United States*, and the United Kingdom.

INDIA

OFFICIAL NAME
Bhārat Gaṇarājya (transliteration from Hindi); Republic of India (English)

POPULATION
1,133,105,800 (2009e)

INHABITANTS' NAME/NICKNAME
Indian(s)

LANGUAGE/LANGUAGES
Hindi (in the Devanagari script), English (both official); numerous regional languages are official within the various states; Hindustani, others

RELIGION/RELIGIONS
Hindu, 80 percent; Muslim, 13 percent; Christian, 2.5 percent; Sikh, 2 percent; Buddhist, Jain, others

NATIONAL FLAG
The national flag is a horizontal tricolor of equal stripes of deep saffron, white and green. In the center of the white stripe is the *chakra,* a navy blue wheel with 24 spokes symbolizing life in movement and death in stagnation. The saffron color stands for courage and sacrifice, the white for purity and truth, and the green for growth and auspiciousness.

COAT OF ARMS/SEAL
The national emblem is derived from the time of the Emperor Ashoka and is a replica of the Lion of Sarnath in Uttar Pradesh. The lion was erected on the spot where Buddha first proclaimed his gospel of peace and emancipation. The symbol is contemporary India's reaffirmation of its ancient commitment to world peace and goodwill. The national motto is inscribed below the emblem in Devanagari script.

MOTTO
Satyameva javate (transliteration from Hindi); Truth Alone Triumphs (English)

CAPITAL CITY
New Delhi

TYPE OF GOVERNMENT
Federal republic

NATIONAL EMBLEM
Chakra; Taj Mahal

NATIONAL COLORS
White and blue

NATIONAL ANTHEM

The anthem was written to include many of India's ethnic and cultural groups. It was adopted as the national anthem in 1950

Jana-Gana-Mana (Hindi); Thou Art the Ruler of the Minds of All People (English)

Thou art the ruler of the minds of all people,
Dispenser of India's destiny.
Thy name rouses the hearts of Punjab, Sind,
 Gujarat and Maratha,
Of the Dravida and Orissa and Bengal;
It echoes in the hills of the Vindhyas and
 Himalayas,
Mingles in the music of Yamuna and Ganga
 and is chanted by
The waves of the Indian Sea.
They pray for thy blessings and sing thy
 praise.
The saving of all people waits in thy hand,
Thou dispenser of India's destiny,
Victory, victory, victory to thee.

NATIONAL SONG

The national song has equal status to the national anthem within India.

Vande Maratam (Hindi); Mother, I Salute Thee! (English)

My obeisance to Mother India!
With flowing beneficial waters
Filled with choicest fruits
With sandal-scented winds
Green with the harvest
O Mother! My obeisance to you!
Ecstatic moonlit nights
The plants blooming with flowers
Sweet speaker of sweet languages
Fount of blessings,
Mother, I salute you!

PATRON SAINT

Our Lady of Bandel; Our Lady of Banda; Our Lady of the Assumption; Saint Rose of Lima; Saint Thomas the Apostle

CURRENCY

Indian rupee

INTERNET IDENTIFIER

.in

VEHICLE IDENTIFICATION PLATES/STICKERS

IND

PASSPORT

The passport cover has the word *passport* in Hindi and English, the coat of arms with the national motto in Hindi, and the name of the country in Hindi and English.

AIRLINES

Air India; Jet Airways; Kingfisher Airlines

NATIONAL FLOWER

Lotus

NATIONAL TREE

Banyan

NATIONAL ANIMAL

Royal Bengal tiger; Indian elephant (unofficial)

NATIONAL BIRD

Indian peacock

NATIONAL RESOURCES

Natural resources include coal, iron ore, manganese, mica, bauxite, titanium ore, chromite, natural gas, diamonds, petroleum, limestone, and arable land. India's fascinating cultures, ancient monuments, wonderful scenery, historic cities, and beaches support a thriving tourist industry. Remittances from Indians living outside the country are an important resource and a source of foreign currency and investment.

FOODS

Indian cuisine is characterized by a very wide variety of regional cuisines and its sophisticated use of spices and herbs. The staple food in the south and east is rice, and wheat is the most popular in the north. Specialties include dal, crushed lentil stew with various vegetables; tandoori, spiced chicken baked in a special oven called a tandoor; *sambar,* a southern Indian stew made with lentils, vegetables, and spices; and vindaloo, from the Portuguese *vinha d'alhos,* a dish originally from Goa of marinated pork cooked with vinegar, chilies, garlic, and spices.

SPORTS/SPORTS TEAMS

Field hockey is India's national sport, although cricket is the most popular sport in the country. Association football (soccer) is gaining popularity. India national teams participate in many sports at an international level.

TEAM SPORTS

Badminton
India Badminton Team

Baseball
India Baseball Team; India Softball Team

Basketball
India Basketball Team, nickname the Young Cagers; India Women's Basketball Team; India Wheelchair Basketball Team

Bowls
India Bowls Team

Cricket
India Cricket Team, nickname the Men in Blue; India Under-19 Cricket Team; India Women's Cricket Team

Football
India Football Team, nickname the Wonder Boys, the Bhangra Boys, or Yoddha-E-Hind (the warriors of Hind); India Women's Football Team, nickname the Wonder Girls; India Under-19 Football Team; India Women's Under-19 Football Team; India Rugby Union Team; India Wheelchair Rugby Team; India Beach Soccer Team

Hockey
India Ice Hockey Team; India Field Hockey Team; India Women's Field Hockey Team

Kabaddi
India Kabaddi Team

Korfball
India Korfball Team

Netball
India Netball Team

Polo
India Polo Team

Racing
A1 Team India; India Speedway Team

Table Tennis
India Men's Table Tennis Team; India Women's Table Tennis Team

Tennis
India Davis Cup Team; India Fed Cup Team

Volleyball
India Fistball Team; India Men's Volleyball Team; India Women's Volleyball Team; India Men's Beach Volleyball Team; India Women's Beach Volleyball Team

INDIVIDUAL SPORTS

India Amateur Boxing Team; India Archery Team; India Athletics Team; India Canoeing Team; India Cycling Team; India Equestrian Team; India Fencing Team; Indian Gymnastics Team; India Judo Team; India Karate Team; India Modern Pentathlon Team; India Rowing Team; India Sailing Team; India Shooting Team; India Swim

Team; India Tae Kwon Do Team; India Triathlon Team; India Weight Lifting Team; India Wrestling Team

WINTER SPORTS

India Bandy Team; India Biathlon Team; India Ice Hockey Team; India Luge Team; India Skating Team

NATIONAL HEROES
OR PERSONIFICATIONS

Bharat Mata (Mother India) is the personification of India as the mother goddess.

National heroes include Mohandas Gandhi, called Mahatma, the leader of the Indian independence movement in the 1930s and 1940s, known as the father of the nation; Jawaharlal Nehru, a leader of the independence movement and India's first prime minister; Indira Gandhi, the Indian prime minister assassinated in 1984; and Rajiv Gandhi, the former Indian prime minister assassinated in 1991.

NATIONAL HOLIDAY/
INDEPENDENCE DAY

Republic Day, January 26

FESTIVALS/FAIRS

Holi, the Festival of Colors or Spring Festival, March; Diwali Festival, on a new moon in October–November; Baisakhi Festival, the major Sikh festival, April; Durga Puja Festival, in the Bengal region, October. There are also many regional festivals in India's many states and territories.

SIGNIFICANT EVENTS IN FORMATION
OF NATIONAL IDENTITY

3300 B.C.E.   The Indus Valley civilization flourishes in western India.

1000 B.C.E.–600 B.C.E.   The Vedas, the oldest texts of Hinduism, are composed. The Vedic period lays the foundation for later Hindu civilizations.

320 B.C.E.–232 B.C.E.   Most of South India is united in the Maurya Empire that flourishes under Asoka the Great.

180 B.C.E.–50 B.C.E.   A series of invasions from Central Asia leaves many new ethnic and religious groups across northern India.

Third century C.E.–sixth century C.E.   The period of the Gupta Empire in the north, known as the Golden Age of India, sees great advances in the fields of mathematics, science, religion, astronomy, and philosophy.

10th century–11th century   Southern India, under the Chola Empire, experiences its golden age, with achievements in architecture, sculpture, bronze working, and Tamil literature.

10th century–12th century   Invasions from Central Asia bring a new series of rulers to northern India, much of which falls under the rule of the Delhi Sultanate and later the Muslim Mughal Empire. The Mughals extend their boundaries to include much of the subcontinent.

16th century–18th century   European explorers and traders visit Indian ports and, taking advantage of the fractious relations between the region's many kingdoms, establish colonies. Over the next century, most colonies are captured by the British, except a handful of small coastal enclaves.

1850–1857   The British East India Company controls most of the subcontinent, using divide-and-rule tactics to control the many territories, kingdoms, and principalities. The first great uprising, called the Indian Rebellion or the Sepoy Mutiny, breaks out in northern India. In the aftermath, all power is transferred from the British East India Company to the British crown.

1920   Indian nationalists initiate mass movements and civil disobedience to campaign against British rule.

1947–1949   At the end of the Second World War, India becomes independent, but as two separate countries, secular India and Muslim Pakistan*. The immediate aftermath of partition is serious rioting among Hindus, Muslims, and Sikhs and population transfers between the two new countries involving more than 12 million people. Partition violence and the first Indo-Pakistan War leaves some half a million people dead.

1950s–1960s India is instrumental in forming the Non-Aligned Movement of countries seeking to remain neutral during the Cold War. India fights a second war with Pakistan in 1965. Anti-Indian nationalist movements emerge in several Indian states and territories.

1971–1974 The third Indo-Pakistan war breaks out, which leads to the independence of East Pakistan as Bangladesh*. The Green Revolution greatly expands agriculture to feed a rapidly expanding population. India tests its first nuclear bomb.

1980–1984 Violent separatist organizations become active in several regions. Indira Gandhi, India's prime minister, orders the army to attack the Sikhs' Golden Temple, where separatists are thought to be storing arms. The death of many civilians and the damage to the Sikhs' most holy site enflame tensions. Gandhi is assassinated by her Sikh bodyguards, setting off anti-Sikh rioting that leaves thousands dead after weeks of pillage, rape, and arson. Tensions in Kashmir* between Hindus and Muslims turn to violence.

1984–1991 Indira's Gandhi's oldest son, Rajiv, becomes the next prime minister. During his time in office, he opposes Tamil separatist activity in India and Sri Lanka*. He, too, is assassinated, by a Tamil suicide bomber in 1991 after he leaves office.

1999 Attempts to conclude a lasting peace with Pakistan are derailed by the outbreak of the fourth Indo-Pakistan War in the Kashmir region.

2003–2008 New economic policies begin a period of accelerated economic growth and the lessening of India's endemic poverty. A new round of talks begins between India and Pakistan over Kashmir and other questions.

Muslim militants attack large hotels and other tourist facilities in Mumbai, killing and injuring many Indians and foreign tourists. The attacks, the most violent in many decades, shock an Indian public accustomed to cheerful political and economic news.

2009 The government announces the launch of a program to give each citizen, including the estimated 100 million internal migrants until now invisible to the authorities, a biometric identity card that would allow them to vote and receive services even away from their home region or state.

INDONESIA

Official Name
Republik Indonesia (Indonesian); Republic of Indonesia (English)

Population
237,012,900 (2009e)

Inhabitants' Name/Nickname
Indonesian(s)

Language/Languages
Indonesian (Bahasa Indonesia) (official); many regional languages (including Javanese, the most widely spoken), Dutch, English, others

Religion/Religions
Muslim, 86 percent; Protestant, 5.5 percent; Roman Catholic, 3 percent; Hindu, 2 percent; Buddhist, 1 percent; other or no religion

National Flag
The flag, known as *Sang Merah Putih* (the Red and White), is a horizontal bicolor of red over white. Red symbolizes bravery, and white symbolizes the spiritual element in life.

Coat of Arms/Seal
The coat of arms is called *garuda pancasila*. It consists of a central shield containing five emblems representing the *pancasila*, the five principles of the national philosophy. Behind the shield is the *garuda,* the vehicle of the god Vishnu and Indonesia's national symbol. A banner held in its claws bears the country's national motto.

MOTTO

Bhinneka tunggal ika (Indonesian); Unity in Diversity (English)

CAPITAL CITY

Jakarta

TYPE OF GOVERNMENT

Presidential republic

NATIONAL EMBLEM

The *garuda*

NATIONAL COLORS

Red and white

NATIONAL ANTHEM

The anthem began as the song of a political group of the independence movement in 1928. It was adopted at independence in 1945.

Indonesia Raya (Indonesian); Great Indonesia (English)

Indonesia, my native land, the land where I
  shed my blood.
There I stand, being a soldier of my mother.
Indonesia, my nationality, my nation and my
  country.
Let us exclaim, "United Indonesia!"
Live my land, live my state,
My nation, my people, all.
Build its spirit, build its bodies
For great Indonesia!

Chorus

Great Indonesia, independent and free,
My land, my country, which I love.
Great Indonesia, independent and free,
Live great Indonesia!

Indonesia, an eminent country, our wealthy
  country.
There we shall be forever.
Indonesia, the country of our ancestors, a
  relic of all of us.
Let us pray for Indonesia's prosperity.

May her soil be fertile and spirited her soul,
The nation and all the people.
Conscious be her heart and her mind
For Indonesia the Great!

Chorus

Indonesia, a sacred country, our victorious
  country.
There we stand, guarding our true mother.
Indonesia, a beaming country, a country we
  love with all our heart.
Let's make a vow, "Indonesia be there
  forever!"
Blessed be her people and her sons,
All her islands, and her seas.
Fast be the country's progress and the prog-
  ress of her youth
For Indonesia the Great!

CURRENCY

Indonesian rupiah

INTERNET IDENTIFIER

.id

VEHICLE IDENTIFICATION PLATES/STICKERS

RI

PASSPORT

The passport cover has the Indonesian word for passport at the top, the coat of arms, and the name of the country in Indonesian.

AIRLINES

Garuda Indonesia; Lion Air

NATIONAL FLOWER

Moon orchid

NATIONAL BIRD

Garuda (mythical)

NATIONAL ANIMAL

Komodo dragon

NATIONAL RESOURCES

Natural resources include petroleum, tin, natural gas, nickel, timber, bauxite, copper, fertile soils, coal, gold, and silver. Historical monuments and cities, sandy beaches, a pleasant climate, and unique cultures are the attractions that support Indonesia's important tourist industry.

FOODS

Rice is the main staple and is served with side dishes of meat, fish, and vegetables. Spices, chilies, coconut milk, fish, and chicken are the fundamental ingredients of Indonesian cuisine. Indonesian specialties include *rijsttafel,* a Dutch tradition adopted by Indonesians, a smorgasbord of 12 meat, fish, vegetable, and curry dishes; *sate,* chunks of beef, fish, pork, chicken, or lamb cooked on hot coals and served with peanut sauce; *gado-gado,* a salad of raw and cooked vegetables with a mild peanut and coconut sauce; *babi guling,* a Balinese dish of roast suckling pig; and *soto ayam,* chicken noodle soup.

SPORTS/SPORTS TEAMS

Association football (soccer) and badminton are the two most popular sports in Indonesia. Traditional sports, such as *sepak takraw,* a game resembling volleyball, and *pencak silat,* a martial art, remain very popular. Indonesia national teams participate in many sports at an international level.

TEAM SPORTS

Badminton

Indonesia Badminton Team

Baseball

Indonesia Baseball Team; Indonesia Softball Team

Cricket

Indonesia Cricket Team

Football

Indonesia Football Team, nickname Merah Puthi (Red and White) or Garuda; Indonesia Under-23 Football Team; Indonesia Under-21 Football Team; Indonesia Under-19 Football Team; Indonesia Rugby Union Team, nickname the Rhinos; Indonesia Futsal Team; Indonesia Australian-Rules Football Team, nickname the Bintangs (the Stars)

Hockey

Indonesia Field Hockey Team

Kabaddi

Indonesia Kabaddi Team

Korfball

Indonesia Korfball Team

Polo

Indonesia Polo Team

Racing

A1 Team Indonesia; Indonesia Speedway Team

Table Tennis

Indonesia Table Tennis Team

Tennis

Indonesia Davis Cup Team; Indonesia Fed Cup Team

Volleyball

Indonesia Men's Volleyball Team; Indonesia Women's Volleyball Team; Indonesia Men's Beach Volleyball Team; Indonesia Women's Beach Volleyball Team

INDIVIDUAL SPORTS

Indonesia Aikido Team; Indonesia Amateur Boxing Team; Indonesia Archery Team; Indonesia Athletics Team; Indonesia Canoeing Team; Indonesia Cycling Team; Indonesia Equestrian Team; Indonesia Fencing Team; Indonesia Gymnastics Team; Indonesia Judo

Team; Indonesia Karate Team; Indonesia Modern Pentathlon Team; Indonesia Rowing Team; Indonesia Sailing Team; Indonesia Shooting Team; Indonesia Swim Team; Indonesia Tae Kwon Do Team; Indonesia Triathlon Team; Indonesia Weight Lifting Team; Indonesia Wrestling Team

NATIONAL HEROES OR PERSONIFICATIONS

Ibu Pertiwi, roughly translated as Motherland, is the personification of Indonesia. The *garuda,* the mythical bird that serves as the god Vishnu's mount, is another personification.

National heroes include Gajah Mada, the 14th-century leader who guided the Majaphaphit Empire to its age of glory; Sukarno, a leader of the independence movement and first president of Indonesia; and Mohammad Hatta, a leader of the independence movement.

NATIONAL HOLIDAY/INDEPENDENCE DAY

Independence Day, August 17

FESTIVALS/FAIRS

Festival Indonesia, August; Fishing Festival, June; Nyale Festival, February; Tabut Festival, August

SIGNIFICANT EVENTS IN FORMATION OF NATIONAL IDENTITY

4000 B.C.E. Austronesian peoples migrate to the islands from Southeast Asia.

200 B.C.E. Dvipantara, a Hindu kingdom, is established in Java and Sumatra.

700 C.E. Wet-field rice cultivation is introduced. Small towns and kingdoms flourish.

700–1100 Several Indian-influenced Hindu kingdoms rise and fall in Java and Sumatra.

1200s Islam is introduced by Muslim traders and within two centuries becomes the predominant religion in the islands.

1509–1532 A Portuguese expedition visits the region. The Portuguese send a second expedition

to find the Spice Islands. The first European trading posts are established. Christianity is introduced to the Molucca (Maluku) Islands.

1595–1596 British and Dutch expeditions sail through the islands.

1602–1750 The Dutch East India Company is created as a vehicle for trade with the islands. A number of trading posts are established. The Dutch East India Company takes control of the islands, often through wars with local states.

1800–1900 The Dutch government takes control of the colony of the Dutch East Indies. Dutch conquest of the Indonesian states continues into the 20th century.

1908–1912 The first nationalist movement is formed to combat Dutch rule. The Islamic League becomes the first mass nationalist organization.

1942–1945 Japanese troops occupy the East Indies. At the end of the Second World War, the Netherlands* resumes control. A draft constitution for an Indonesian republic is drafted. Indonesia is declared independent of Dutch rule.

1945–1946 The Dutch favor a United States of Indonesia, with broad autonomy for the member states.

1948–1949 A communist attempt to take over the government is defeated. The Dutch transfer power to a new federation.

1550 The federation is dissolved and a unitary state declared, the Republic of Indonesia. Separatist revolts break out in several regions.

1961 Indonesia annexes the former Dutch territory of New Guinea, over the objections of the inhabitants.

1965–1966 A violent anticommunist campaign leads to the deaths of more than half a million people.

1975 Indonesian troops invade East Timor* to overthrow a nationalist government in the former Portuguese territory. East Timor is incorporated as a province.

1997–1999 Indonesia's economy slumps during the Asian financial crisis, creating hardship for many. Clashes between Muslims and Christians in the Maluku Islands leave thousands dead and hundreds of thousands displaced. East Timor votes to secede, setting off violence between nationalists and the Indonesian military.

2004 An earthquake-triggered tsunami hits western Indonesian, leaving 160,000 dead and massive destruction. Nationalists in the hardest-hit province, Aceh*, agree to a peace accord and to special status within Indonesia.

2004–2007 Indonesia stabilizes relations and borders with neighboring states, including East Timor. A growing separatist movement in West Papua*, the former Dutch territory in the east, has the potential for future problems, as does Aceh*, where some groups continue to demand independence.

2009 In spite of predictions, Indonesia weathers the world economic crisis and continues to see economic growth and greater stability.

See also Aceh; West Papua

JAPAN

OFFICIAL NAME
Nippon-koku/Nihon-koku (transliteration from Japanese); Japan (English)

POPULATION
127,512,300 (2009e)

INHABITANTS' NAME/NICKNAME
Japanese

LANGUAGE/LANGUAGES
Japanese (de facto official); Korean, English, others

RELIGION/RELIGIONS
Shinto and Buddhist, 84 percent; Christian, other or no religion

NATIONAL FLAG
The flag, known as Nisshōki (sun flag) or Hinomaru (sun disk) in Japanese, is a white field with a large red disk centered. The red disk represents the rising sun. The flag was the de facto national flag until its official adoption in 1999.

COAT OF ARMS/SEAL
The coat of arms, called the Imperial Seal of Japan, is a deep yellow chrysanthemum with black or red outlines and background. The central disk is surrounded by one set of 16 petals in front of another set.

CAPITAL CITY
Tokyo

TYPE OF GOVERNMENT
Constitutional monarchy and parliamentary democracy

NATIONAL EMBLEM
Imperial Chrysanthemum (the national coat of arms); Mount Fuji

NATIONAL COLORS
Red and white

NATIONAL ANTHEM
The anthem has been used since the early 1880s as the de facto national anthem. It was officially adopted as the national anthem in 1990. There is some opposition to the anthem, both within Japan and in other countries, for its association with militarism and for the lyrics.

> **Kimi ga Yo (Japanese); May your reign last forever (English)**
> May your peaceful reign
> Continue for a thousand,
> eight thousand generations,
> Until the pebbles
> Grow into boulders
> Lush with moss.

PATRON SAINT
Saint Francis Xavier; Our Lady of Japan; Saint Peter Baptist

CURRENCY
Japanese yen

INTERNET IDENTIFIER
.jp

VEHICLE IDENTIFICATION PLATES/STICKERS
J

PASSPORT
The passport cover has the name of the country and the word *passport* in Japanese, the chrysanthemum symbol, and the name of the country and the word *passport* in English.

AIRLINES
Japan Airlines; ANA All Nippon Airways

NATIONAL FLOWER
Cherry blossom; chrysanthemum (both unofficial)

NATIONAL TREE
Cherry (unofficial)

NATIONAL ANIMAL
Pheasant (unofficial)

NATIONAL RESOURCES
The natural resources of Japan are negligible, other than some mineral resources and fisheries. Japan's major asset is a dynamic and well-educated population. Ancient monuments, historic cities, varied scenery, and a unique culture support a flourishing tourist industry.

FOODS
National specialties include teriyaki, marinated beef, chicken or fish seared on a hot grill; sukiyaki, thin slices of beef, tofu, and vegetables cooked in soy sauce and then dipped in egg; tempura, battered and deep-fried seafood and vegetables; sushi, vinegary rice balls served with raw seafood and vegetables; and sashimi, thin slices of raw seafood dipped in soy sauce.

SPORTS/SPORTS TEAMS
Traditionally, sumo is considered Japan's national sport, and it remains one of the most popular spectator sports. Martial arts, such as judo, karate, and aikido, are also very popular. Association football is gaining popularity. Japan national teams participate in many sports at an international level.

TEAM SPORTS
Badminton
Japan Badminton Team

Baseball
Japan Baseball Team; Japan Softball Team; Japan Women's Softball Team

Basketball
Japan Basketball Team; Japan Women's Basketball Team; Japan Under-21 Basketball Team; Japan Wheelchair Basketball Team; Japan Women's Wheelchair Basketball Team

Bowls
Japan Bowls Team

Cricket
Japan Cricket Team; Japan Women's Cricket Team

Curling
Japan Curling Team

Football
Japan Football Team, nickname Nippon Daihyo (Blue Samurai), Okada Japan, or the Blues; Japan Women's Football Team, nickname the Blues; Japan Under-20 Football Team; Japan Women's Under-19 Football Team; Japan Rugby Union Team, nickname

the Cherry Blossoms or Brave Blossoms; Japan Women's Rugby Union Team, nickname the Cherry Blossoms; Japan Australian-Rules Football Team, nickname Samurai or Tozai Tsunami; Japan Rugby League Team, nickname the Samurais; Japan Futsal Team; Japan Rugby Union Team (Sevens), nickname Japan Sevens, Japan 7s, or Samurai; Japan American Football Team; Japan Wheelchair Rugby Team; Japan Beach Soccer Team; Japan Touch Football Team; Japan Women's Touch Football Team

Handball

Japan Handball Team; Japan Women's Handball Team; Japan Beach Handball Team; Japan Women's Beach Handball Team

Hockey

Japan Field Hockey Team; Japan Women's Field Hockey Team; Japan Ice Hockey Team; Japan Women's Ice Hockey Team; Japan Junior Ice Hockey Team

Kabaddi

Japan Kabaddi Team

Korfball

Japan Korfball Team

Lacrosse

Japan Lacrosse Team; Japan Women's Lacrosse Team; Japan Under-19 Lacrosse Team; Japan Women's Under-19 Lacrosse Team

Racing

A1 Team Japan; Japan Speedway Team

Table Tennis

Japan Table Tennis Team

Tennis

Japan Davis Cup Team; Japan Fed Cup Team

Volleyball

Japan Men's Volleyball Team; Japan Women's Volleyball Team; Japan Men's Beach Volleyball Team; Japan Women's Beach Volleyball Team; Japan Fistball Team

INDIVIDUAL SPORTS

Japan Aikido Team; Japan Amateur Boxing Team; Japan Archery Team; Japan Athletics Team; Japan Canoeing Team; Japan Equestrian Team; Japan Fencing Team; Japan Gymnastics Team; Japan Judo Team; Japan Karate Team; Japan Modern Pentathlon Team; Japan Rowing Team; Japan Sailing Team; Japan Shooting Team; Japan Swim Team; Japan Tae Kwon Do Team; Japan Triathlon Team; Japan Weight Lifting Team; Japan Wrestling Team

WINTER SPORTS

Japan Alpine Ski Team; Japan Biathlon Team; Japan Curling Team; Japan Luge Team; Japan Skating Team

NATIONAL HEROES OR PERSONIFICATIONS

Two groups of historic figures are considered the personifications of Japan and the Japanese. The first are the geisha, the famed entertainers of Japanese history; the second are the samurai, the nation's historical warriors.

National heroes include Hideyoshi Toyotomi, the unifier of Japan in the 16th century; Oda Nobunaga, a military leader of the 16th century; Sakamoto Ryoma, a leader in the struggle for the creation of a modern government in the mid-19th century; and Sadayakki Kawakami, a famous geisha and actress in the late 19th and early 20th centuries.

NATIONAL HOLIDAY/INDEPENDENCE DAY

The Emperor's Birthday, December 23

FESTIVALS/FAIRS

Sapporo Snow Festival, April; Sanja Matsuri, June; Kyoto Gion Matsuri, July; Tanabata (Star Festival), July; Nebuta Matsuri, August; Awadori Festival, October; Hadaka Matsuri, winter

SIGNIFICANT EVENTS IN FORMATION OF NATIONAL IDENTITY

10,000 B.C.E.–300 B.C.E. Hunters and gathers inhabit Japan. The mythological Jimmu, the descendent of the sun goddess, Amaterasu, lays the foundations of the Japanese Empire.

300 B.C.E.–300 C.E. Wet-rice farming is introduced. Migrants from China* and Korea* settle in the islands. A primarily agricultural culture spreads across the islands.

300–645 The emergence of powerful clans unifies the country and establishes the imperial dynasty that continues to the present.

710–794 The emperor's power is strengthened. The adoption of Buddhism as the state religion gives monasteries political power.

800–1192 A great flowering of classical Japanese culture includes the invention of a syllabary for writing the Japanese language. The emperor's power declines with the rise of the warrior class and provincial warlords, who take control of the government.

1274–1281 Kublai Khan's Mongol invasions are repelled with the help of *kamikaze* (divine winds or storms) that wreck the Mongol fleets.

1333–1467 A new military government is established. Japanese leaders patronize Zen Buddhism and promote ink painting, garden design, and the tea ceremony.

1467–1600 Civil war leads to disintegration. Shipwrecked Portuguese sailors introduce firearms in 1543. Francis Xavier introduces Christianity in 1549. The process of unification begins after a century of civil war.

1600–1868 Japan initiates an age of peace and national isolation, which limits foreign trad-

ers to a single port at Nagasaki. Christianity is suppressed, and a rigid social hierarchy ensures peace and security. U.S. Commodore Matthew Perry and his steam frigates arrive in Japan in 1853. The Japanese agree to open the country's doors for the first time in two centuries. The Meiji Restoration begins, the emperor is restored, and Japan becomes a modern nation-state.

1895–1910 Japan becomes a military power through wartime victories over China and Russia* and the conquest of Korea.

1931–1945 Japan's liberal leadership is replaced by a military intent on creating a new Japanese Empire. Japan attacks China and takes Manchuria in 1931 and joins the Axis in 1940. The Japanese attack on Pearl Harbor in 1941 brings the United States* into the Second World War. The United States uses atom bombs dropped on Hiroshima and Nagasaki to bring the war to a rapid end in 1945.

1945–1952 The Americans occupy Japan and restore a democratic government. Women gain equality and the right to vote.

1950s–1970s The Japanese economy booms, and Japanese export brands become household names around the world.

1990s Controversy over Japan's role in the world becomes a major issue, with isolationists demanding that the government concern itself with Japan's peace and economic security without participating in world events.

2000–2008 Japan's developed democratic system continues to oversee a very prosperous and highly developed nation. Its industrialized, free-market economy is the second largest in the world, although agriculture is highly protected.

Japan technically remains at war with Russia, as no peace treaty has been signed since the Second World War, due to the conflict over a group of small islands in northern Japan taken by the Soviet Union in the last days of the war.

2009 Japan's exports, the backbone of its economy, plunge dramatically as the world economy slows. New levels of unemployment and violence frighten the normally complacent Japanese public.

KASHMIR

OFFICIAL NAME

State of Jammu and Kashmir (part of India); State of Jammu and Kashmir (Azad Jammu and Kashmir or Free Kashmir (part of Pakistan)

POPULATION

13,865,500 (2009e)

INHABITANTS' NAME/NICKNAME

Kashmiri(s)

LANGUAGE/LANGUAGES

Indian Kashmir: Kashmiri written in the Sharada script (official); Hindi, English, Dogri Pahari, Balti, Ladakhi, Punjabi Gojri, Dadri, others; Pakistani Kashmir: Northern Hindko, Pashto, others

RELIGION/RELIGIONS

Sunni Muslim, Hindu, Buddhist, Christian, others

NATIONAL FLAG

The flag of the Kashmiri nationalists is a horizontal bicolor of red over green bearing a white triangle at the hoist. The unofficial flag of the Indian state is red field bearing a white stylized native plow and three vertical white stripes. The plow represents Kashmir's determination and prosperity and the three stripes represent the three regions of Jammu, Kashmir, and Ladakh. The flag of Pakistani Kashmir is a green field bearing eight narrow white and green stripes at the bottom, an orange canton on the upper hoist, and a white crescent moon and five-pointed star on the upper fly. The green field represents the majority Muslim population, the orange canton stands for the large Hindu minority, the white and green stripes represent the snow-topped mountains and the central Vale of Kashmir, and the crest and star represent Islam.

COAT OF ARMS

The unofficial seal of the Indian state of Jammu and Kashmir is an oval representing a vase made of two Kashmir plows, holding a lotus flower above the name of the state all within a red wreath. The vase represents the Vale of Kashmir, the plows the traditions of the region and their determination to prosper, and the flower symbolizes the region and is the unofficial national flower.

CAPITAL CITY

Indian Kashmir: Jammu (winter) and Srinagar (summer)
 Pakistani Kashmir: Muzaffarabad

TYPE OF GOVERNMENT

Kashmir is a formerly autonomous state disputed by pro-independence Kashmiris, India*, and Pakistan*. Divided by a United Nations cease-fire line in 1948, each region has special status within the states of India and Pakistan. China* controls a small mountainous territory in the north called Aksai Chin.

NATIONAL EMBLEM

The Vale of Kashmir

NATIONAL COLORS

Red, green, and white

CURRENCY

Indian Kashmir: Indian rupee
 Pakistani Kashmir: Pakistani rupee

VEHICLE IDENTIFICATION PLATES/STICKERS

IND (India) (official): JK Jammu and Kashmir (Indian Kashmir) (unofficial)
 PAK (Pakistan) (official); AJK Pakistani Kashmir (unofficial)

PASSPORT

Kashmiris travel on Indian or Pakistani passports.

NATIONAL FLOWER

Lotus (Indian Kashmir, unofficial); Rhododendron (Pakistani Kashmir, official)

NATIONAL TREE

Almond (Pakistani Kashmir, official)

NATIONAL ANIMAL

Kashmir stag (Pakistani Kashmir, official)

NATIONAL BIRD

Black-necked crane (Pakistani Kashmir, official)

NATIONAL RESOURCES

Natural resources include lignite, limestone, copper, iron ore, gypsum, ochre, zinc, slate, graphite, sulfur, and marble. In spite of abundant mineral wealth, Kashmir's economy is centered on agriculture. Remittances from the large number of Kashmiris living outside the area are a major asset.

FOODS

The style of cooking Kashmiri food is different for Hindus and Muslims. Traditional specialties include *dum aloo,* boiled potatoes with spices; *traman,* a type of fresh cheese; *rogan josh,* lamb cooked in spices; *zaam dod,* a type of curds or cottage cheese; *yakhayn,* lamb cooked with curds and mild spices; and *rista-gustava,* balls of minced meat in tomato and curd curry.

SPORTS/SPORTS TEAMS

Cricket and association football (soccer) are the most popular games in the region. Polo is the official sport of Pakistani Kashmir. Jammu and Kashmir national teams participate in cricket and football at an international level.

TEAM SPORTS

Cricket
Jammu and Kashmir Cricket Team

Football
Jammu and Kashmir Football Team

NATIONAL HEROES OR PERSONIFICATIONS

Sultan Zain-ul-Abadin, the ruler of independent Kashmir during its golden age in the 15th century; Muhammad Abdullah, known as the Lion of Kashmir; Rajinder Singh, a Kashmiri soldier killed in the fighting; Arundhati Roy, a noted author who demands that India and Pakistan rethink their policies in the disputed territory

NATIONAL HOLIDAY/INDEPENDENCE DAY

Independence Day, October 24 (marks the declaration of independence when the British withdrew in 1947; unofficial/illegal in Indian and Pakistani Kashmir)

FESTIVALS/FAIRS

Makar Sankranti (Lohri), January; Baisakhi (Harvest Festival), April; Parsi Navroz Festival, one week after the New Year; Muharram, January

SIGNIFICANT EVENTS IN FORMATION OF NATIONAL IDENTITY

Third century B.C.E. Ashoka, the ruler of the Maurya Empire is thought to have founded Srinagar, which becomes the center of a Buddhist kingdom.

Eighth century C.E. The Buddhists rule until the eighth century C.E. They leave behind their culture and monasteries, especially in Ladakh.

14th century Aryan Muslim tribes from Central Asia conquer the region. Islam becomes the dominant belief system in Kashmir.

15th century A Muslim sultanate is created in the great valley, the Vale of Kashmir, which begins a great cultural golden age.

1586–1756 Invading Moghuls from the Indian lowlands overrun Kashmir, ending the independence and culture of the region. An independent Kashmir is reestablished but falls to invading Pushtuns.

1819 Sikhs from the Punjab region conquer Kashmir. The Sikhs place a Hindu as ruler of Jammu but rule the rest of Kashmir directly.

1846–1885 The First Sikh War breaks out. The victorious British overthrow Sikh rule and sell Kashmir to Gulab Singh of Jammu, who remained carefully neutral during the conflict. Independent Kashmir is a buffer state between Russian influence to the north and British possessions to the south. The British install an adviser in Srinagar to regulate relations with British India.

1900 The rule of the Hindu rulers becomes increasingly despotic and disagreeable to the state's Muslim majority.

1939–1940 Muhammad Abdullah, called the Lion of Kashmir, creates the first Kashmiri national political organization, the Kashmir National Conference, which is considered the inception of the modern Kashmiri national movement. Inspired by Mohandas "Mahatma" Gandhi's movement in India, the Kashmiris begin a peaceful movement for change.

1945–1947 At the end of the Second World War, the British prepare to leave India, which is partitioned into Muslim Pakistan and secular India. Despite pro-Pakistani sentiment among Kashmiri Muslims, the Hindu raja, Hari Singh, refuses to accede to either Pakistan or India.

1947 Muslim tribals from Pakistan invade Kashmir amid a pro-independence uprising by Kashmiri Muslims. A provisional government deposes Hari Singh, who flees to Delhi. The independence of Kashmir is declared on October 24, 1947. Hari Singh signs a cession treaty with India in Delhi. The first Kashmiri War breaks out between invading Indian and Pakistani troops and Kashmiri irregulars.

1948–1949 The United Nations establishes a cease-fire line as a temporary measure and passes a resolution calling on India and Pakistan to organize a plebiscite on Kashmir's future.

1950 India rejects the United Nations' plan and organizes Indian-held Kashmir as a state of the Indian Union, the only state with a Muslim majority. Pakistan creates Azad Kashmir in Pakistani-occupied territory. Muhammad Abdullah, continuing to demand a referendum on independence, spends years in Indian jails.

1971–1984 India and Pakistan again go to war during the secession of Bangladesh from Pakistan. India removes the state government and begins direct rule in Kashmir in order to suppress a spreading uprising.

1988 The Kashmir revolt sweeps across Indian Kashmir. The uprising becomes a chaotic mixture of Indian army brutality against the civilian population, Pakistani support for Muslim terrorism, and Kashmiri factions often fighting each other and unable to agree on a plan for the region's future.

1999–2001 Pakistani and Indian troops clash along the cease-fire line, fighting spreads to become the first Indian-Pakistani conflict since 1947. Kashmiri nationalists reiterate that Kashmir is an indivisible entity, not a territorial dispute between India and Pakistan. They again call on all parties to respect the 1949 United Nations plan for a plebiscite on Kashmir's future.

2001 Several Kashmiri nationalist groups are listed as terrorist groups by the U.S. government following the September 11 attacks on New York.

2005–2008 A devastating earthquake hits Kashmir, leaving more than 70,000 dead and widespread destruction. The Kashmir war continues to disrupt the territory on both sides of the cease-fire line.

2009 Many Kashmiri activists embrace nonviolent protest as a means of winning the independence they have sought for more than two decades. In spite a lessening of separatist violence, many protesters are killed by indiscriminate firing on crowds by Indian security forces.

See also India; Pakistan

KAZAKHSTAN

OFFICIAL NAME

Qazaqstan Respublïkasi (transliteration from Kazakh); Respublika Kazakhstan (transliteration from Russian); Republic of Kazakhstan (English)

POPULATION

15,645,100 (2009e)

INHABITANTS' NAME/NICKNAME

Kazakhstani(s); Kazakh(s)

LANGUAGE/LANGUAGES

Kazakh (state language); Russian (official); Ukrainian, Uzbek, German, Tatar, Uighur, others

RELIGION/RELIGIONS

Muslim, 47 percent; Russian Orthodox, 44 percent; Protestant, 2 percent; other or no religion

NATIONAL FLAG

The flag consists of a sky-blue background charged with a steppe eagle beneath a 32-rayed golden sun in the center and a traditional Kazakh pattern running down the hoist side. The pattern represents the arts and cultural traditions of the old Kazakh khanate and the Kazakh people. The sky blue represents the Turkic peoples and also the culture and ethnic unity of the country. The sun represents the source of energy and is a symbol of wealth and abundance. The sun's rays are like grain, which is the basis of abundance and prosperity. The eagle represents the power of the state and is a symbol of independence, freedom, and the flight to the future.

COAT OF ARMS/SEAL

The coat of arms has a circular form with the same blue and yellow colors as the national flag. Blue represents the blue sky and yellow is a symbol of agriculture. To the left and right of the coat of arms, two winged unicorns look away from each other. In the upper part of the coat of arms, a star and rays surround a *shangrak*, the crown of a Kazakh yurt, which symbolizes both the wealth of heritage and a hopeful future. The name of the country in Kazakh is in the lower part.

CAPITAL CITY

Astana

TYPE OF GOVERNMENT

Presidential republic

NATIONAL EMBLEM

Kazakh yurt

NATIONAL COLORS

Blue and yellow

NATIONAL ANTHEM

The anthem adopted at independence was replaced with the present anthem in 2006. It is based on a patriotic song written in 1958.

Mening Qazaqstanym (Kazakh); My Kazakhstan (English)

Sky of golden sun,
Steppe of golden seed,
Legend of courage—
Take a look at my country.
From antiquity
Our heroic glory emerged,
They did not give up their pride
My Kazakh people are strong!

Chorus

My country, my country,
As your flower I will be planted,
As your song I will stream, my country!
My native land—My Kazakhstan!

The way was opened to posterity
I have a vast land.
Its unity is proper,

I have an independent country.
It welcomed the time
Like an eternal friend,
Our country is happy,
Such is our country.

Chorus

My country, my country,
As your flower I will be planted,
As your song I will stream, my country!
My native land—My Kazakhstan!

PATRON SAINT

Blessed Mary

CURRENCY

Kazakhstani tenge

INTERNET IDENTIFIER

.kz

VEHICLE IDENTIFICATION PLATES/STICKERS

KZ

PASSPORT

The passport cover has the name of the country in Kazakh and English, the coat of arms, and the word *passport* in Kazakh and English.

AIRLINE

Air Astana

NATIONAL FLOWER

Asian lily (unofficial)

NATIONAL ANIMAL

Unicorn (on the coat of arms) (unofficial)

NATIONAL BIRD

Steppe eagle (golden eagle)

NATIONAL RESOURCES

Natural resources include major deposits of petroleum, natural gas, coal, iron ore, manganese, chrome ore, nickel, cobalt, copper, molybdenum, lead, zinc, bauxite, gold, and uranium. The high prices for crude oil have allowed the country to diversity and develop other industries, such as textiles.

FOODS

Kazi and *chuzhuk,* horsemeat sausages; *kaurdak,* mutton stew; *besbarmak,* a dish of horse meat or mutton with dumplings; and *shashlyk,* skewered mutton cooked over charcoal, are considered the national dishes. *Plov,* a rice dish with mutton, shredded turnip, and onion, is a staple dish in all the Central Asian republics. *Lepeshka,* a round, unleavened bread, is the national bread.

SPORTS/SPORTS TEAMS

Association football (soccer) is the most popular sport, and boxing is also popular. Traditional sports, such as *kyz kuu,* are still played on horseback. Kazakh national teams participate in many sports at an international level.

TEAM SPORTS

Badminton

Kazakhstan Badminton Team

Baseball

Kazakhstan Baseball Team; Kazakhstan Softball Team

Basketball

Kazakhstan Basketball Team; Kazakhstan Women's Basketball Team

Curling

Kazakhstan Curling Team

Football

Kazakhstan Football Team; Kazakhstan Women's Football Team; Kazakhstan Under-21

Football Team; Kazakhstan Rugby Union Team; Kazakhstan Women's Rugby Union Team; Kazakhstan Futsal Team; Kazakhstan Rugby Union Team (Sevens), nickname Kazakhstan Sevens or Kazakhstan 7s; Kazakhstan Women's Rugby Union Team (Sevens), nickname Kazakhstan Sevens or Kazakhstan 7s; Kazakhstan Rugby League Team

Handball

Kazakhstan Handball Team; Kazakhstan Women's Handball Team

Hockey

Kazakhstan Ice Hockey Team; Kazakhstan Junior Ice Hockey Team; Kazakhstan Women's Ice Hockey Team; Kazakhstan Field Hockey Team

Kabaddi

Kazakhstan Kabaddi Team

Racing

Kazakhstan Speedway Team

Table Tennis

Kazakhstan Table Tennis Team

Tennis

Kazakhstan Davis Cup Team; Kazakhstan Fed Cup Team

Volleyball

Kazakhstan Men's Beach Volleyball Team; Kazakhstan Women's Beach Volleyball Team; Kazakhstan Men's Volleyball Team; Kazakhstan Women's Volleyball Team

INDIVIDUAL SPORTS

Kazakhstan Amateur Boxing Team; Kazakhstan Archery Team; Kazakhstan Athletics Team; Kazakhstan Canoeing Team; Kazakhstan Cycling Team; Kazakhstan Equestrian Team; Kazakhstan Fencing Team; Kazakhstan Gymnastics Team; Kazakhstan Judo Team; Kazakhstan Karate Team; Kazakhstan Modern Pentathlon Team; Kazakhstan Rowing Team; Kazakhstan Sailing Team; Kazakhstan Shooting Team; Kazakhstan Swim Team; Kazakhstan Tae Kwon Do Team; Kazakhstan Triathlon Team; Kazakhstan Weight Lifting Team; Kazakhstan Wrestling Team

WINTER SPORTS

Kazakhstan Alpine Ski Team; Kazakhstan Bandy Team; Kazakhstan Biathlon Team; Kazakhstan Curling Team; Kazakhstan Ice Hockey Team; Kazakhstan Junior Ice Hockey Team; Kazakhstan Women's Ice Hockey Team; Kazakhstan Luge Team; Kazakhstan Skating Team

NATIONAL HEROES OR PERSONIFICATIONS

Janybek Khan, a founder of the medieval Kazakh Khanate; Kerei Khan, a founder of the medieval Kazakh Khanate; Abul Khair Khan, a leader of the western Kazakh horde in the early 18th century; Ablai Khan, a ruler of the Kazakh Khanate in the 18th century; Kenesary Khan, the leader of the Kazakh resistance to Russian rule in the 19th century; Akhmet Baytursinuli, leader of the autonomous Kazakh state from 1917 to 1920, who also adapted Arabic script for the Kazakh alphabet; Alikhan Bokeikhanov, the first president of the Alash state in 1917; Mirjaqip Dulatuli, leader of the Alash state and author of the first novel in the Kazakh language; Alia Moldagulova and Manshuk Mametova, heroine soldiers of World War II

NATIONAL HOLIDAY/INDEPENDENCE DAY

Independence Day, December 16

FESTIVALS/FAIRS

Nauryz, March; Kurban (the end of Uraza or Ramadan), variable dates; Khan Tengri Mountain Festival, August; World Food

Kazakhstan Fair, November; Golden Eagle Festival, October

SIGNIFICANT EVENTS IN FORMATION OF NATIONAL IDENTITY

500 B.C.E. The Sakas, a nomadic people, populate the vast steppe region.

200 B.C.E. The eastern tribes come under the control of Hsiung-Nu, a union of nomadic peoples in the Chinese border areas.

550 C.E.–750 C.E. The Turkic peoples displace or absorb the earlier inhabitants. Cities and towns are established along the famed trade route known as the Silk Road.

10th century The Turkic tribes unite in a powerful state called Karakan, known for its wealth and culture.

1218–1219 The Mongols invade the Karakan state. Its sophisticated cities and advanced irrigation system are destroyed, and the survivors are scattered across the vast Kazakh steppe.

1456–1500 A division of the Mongol hordes settles the steppe and slowly absorbs the remaining Turkic peoples, as well as adopting the Turkic language and culture. Traders bring Islam to the area from the south.

16th century Russian explorers and traders visit the region, beginning a gradual Russian encroachment. The Kazakh language, culture, and way of life are consolidated.

17th century The Kazakhs divide into three hordes, or tribal federations.

1715–1742 The first official Russian expedition establishes contact with the khans of the Kazakh hordes. The three hordes, pressured militarily, accept Russian protection between 1731 and 1742.

1822–1855 The Russians consolidate their authority by abolishing the hordes, setting off a series of Kazakh uprisings. As a reaction to Russian attempts to promote Christianity, the majority of the Kazakhs adopt Islam.

1896–1911 The completion of the railways brings more than a million Slavic settlers to the region.

1916 During the First World War, the Russians attempt to conscript the Kazakhs for labor duty. A Kazakh rebellion spreads to other areas of Central Asia. Kazakh attacks on Slavic settlers are revenged by the slaughter of thousands of Kazakhs.

1917–1920 The Russian Revolution allows Kazakh leaders to create a separate Kazakh republic, called Alash after the probably mythical ancestor of the Kazakhs. The Bolsheviks take control of the region in 1920.

1930s Between 1916 and 1939, more than 1.5 million Kazakhs die and another 1 million flee to Chinese territory. Kazakhstan is established as a separate republic of the Soviet Union.

1986–1988 Riots break out over plans to replace the republic's Kazakh chairman with an ethnic Russian. The riots initiate a resurgence of Kazakh nationalism that grows quickly with the liberalization of Soviet life in 1987–1988.

1991 The collapse of the Soviet system allows the union republics to become independent states. Kazakhstan is the last to declare independence under the former communist leader Nursultan Nazarbayev.

2000–2008 The high price of oil helps Kazakhstan convert to a market economy. Kazakhstan's parliament passes a law granting Nazarbayev lifetime power and privileges, amid international criticism of Kazakhstan's failure to create a democratic system. Elections are judged unfair, although less fraudulent than previous polls.

2009 A spate of arrests of prominent Kazakhs forces many others to flee the country as human rights abuses and corruption increase.

KIRIBATI

OFFICIAL NAME

Kiribati (Gilbertese); Republic of Kiribati (English)

POPULATION

102,300 (2009e)

INHABITANTS' NAME/NICKNAME

I-Kiribati

LANGUAGE/LANGUAGES

English (official), Gilbertese/I-Kiribati (de facto official); others

RELIGION/RELIGIONS

Roman Catholic, 52 percent; Congregational, 40 percent; Seventh-day Adventist, Mormon, Church of God, Muslim, Baha'i, others

NATIONAL FLAG

The flag is divided horizontally. The upper half is red with a gold frigate bird flying over a gold rising sun with 17 gold rays. The lower half is blue with three wavy white stripes. The frigate bird symbolizes command of the sea. The blue and white waves represent the Pacific Ocean and the three island groups that make up the country, the Tungaru, Phoenix, and Line islands. The 17 rays represent the 16 Tungaru Islands and Banaba.

COAT OF ARMS/SEAL

The coat of arms is a copy of the flag as a shield: a yellow frigate bird over a rising sun on a red background with white and blue wavy lines. A yellow banner under the shield is inscribed with the country's national motto.

MOTTO

Te mauri te raoi ao te tabomoa (Gilbertese); Health, peace, and prosperity (English)

CAPITAL CITY

Tarawa

TYPE OF GOVERNMENT

Republic

NATIONAL COLORS

Blue, red, and yellow

NATIONAL ANTHEM

The anthem was adopted at independence in 1979.

Teirake Kaini Kiribati (Gilbertese); Stand up, Kiribati! (English)

Stand up, Kiribati! Sing with jubilation!
Prepare to accept responsibility
And to help each other!
Be steadfastly righteous!
Love all our people!
Be steadfastly righteous!
Love all our people!

The attainment of contentment
And peace by our people
Will be achieved when all our hearts beat as
  one.
Love one another!
Promote happiness and unity!
Love one another!
Promote happiness and unity!

We beseech you, O God, to
protect and lead us in the days to come.
Help us with your loving hand.
Bless our government and all our people!
Bless our government and all our people!

CURRENCY

Kiribati dollar; Australian dollar

INTERNET IDENTIFIER

.ki

VEHICLE IDENTIFICATION PLATES/STICKERS

KIR

PASSPORT

The passport cover has the name of the country, Kiribati, the coat of arms, and the word *passport* in English.

AIRLINE

Air Kiribati

NATIONAL TREE

Breadfruit tree (unofficial)

NATIONAL BIRD

Frigate bird

NATIONAL FISH

Yellowfin tuna (unofficial)

NATIONAL RESOURCES

Kiribati has few natural resources, other than phosphates. Commercially viable phosphate deposits were exhausted at the time of independence. Copra and fish now represent the bulk of production and exports. Tourism, especially ecotourism, is becoming a major source of income. Tourists are drawn to the sandy beaches, out-of-the way lifestyle, island culture, and year-round pleasant climate. Foreign financial aid, largely from the United Kingdom* and Japan*, is a valuable and valued resource.

FOODS

National dishes are *pandanus*, a fruit boiled, thinly sliced, and spread with coconut cream; and *pahl sami*, coconut cream with sliced onions and curry powder, wrapped in taro leaves, and cooked in seaweed. *Pahl sami* can be eaten by itself or served with roast pork or chicken.

SPORTS/SPORTS TEAMS

Association football (soccer), cricket, and volleyball are the favorite sports in the islands.

TEAM SPORTS

Basketball

Kiribati Basketball Team; Kiribati Women's Basketball Team

Cricket

Kiribati Cricket Team

Football

Kiribati Football Team

Table Tennis

Kiribati Table Tennis Team

Tennis

Pacific Oceania Davis Cup; Pacific Oceania Fed Cup Teams (Pacific Oceania teams represent a number of island nations in the Pacific)

Volleyball

Kiribati Men's Volleyball Team; Kiribati Women's Volleyball Team

INDIVIDUAL SPORTS

Kiribati Archery Team; Kiribati Athletics Team; Kiribati Tae Kwon Do Team; Kiribati Weight Lifting Team; Kiribati Wrestling Team

NATIONAL HEROES OR PERSONIFICATIONS

Ieremia Tabai, Kiribati's first president from 1979 to 1991; Teburoro Tito, the president of Kiribati from 1994

NATIONAL HOLIDAY/INDEPENDENCE DAY

Independence Day, July 12

FESTIVALS/FAIRS

Independence Day celebration, July; Youth Festival, August

SIGNIFICANT EVENTS IN FORMATION OF NATIONAL IDENTITY

1000 C.E.–1300 C.E.   Micronesian seafaring people settle the islands. Invaders from Tonga* and later from Fiji* bring Polynesians and Melanesians to the islands. Intermarriage blurs cultural differences and results in a homogenous culture and language throughout the islands.

16th century–18th century   European whalers, slave traders, and merchants begin to visit the islands. Often-fatal European diseases devastate the population. The European visitors often foment local conflicts. The islands are named the

Gilbert Islands after Thomas Gilbert, who sails through the archipelago in 1788.

1837–1892 The first British settlers and missionaries arrive in the islands. The majority of the population converts to Christianity. To restore order among the islanders and the many European whalers and traders, the chiefs of the islands and those of the nearby Ellice Islands consent to become British protectorates.

1900 Banaba (Ocean Island) is annexed after the discovery of phosphate-rich guano deposits.

1916–1937 The Gilbert and Ellice Islands become a British Crown colony. Kiritimati (Christmas Island) and the Phoenix Islands are added to the colony in 1919 and 1937.

1941–1945 Japanese forces capture the major islands during the Second World War. American forces attack the Japanese fortifications on Tarawa in some of the bloodiest fighting in the Pacific. The islands' capital, Betio, is destroyed in the fighting.

1960s The United Kingdom and the United States* use some of the more remote islands in the archipelago for nuclear and hydrogen bomb tests.

1971–1979 The Gilbert and Ellice Islands become self-governing. Ethnic and cultural differences lead to the separation of the two island groups in 1975, with each becoming internally self-governing. The Gilbert Islands, renamed Kiribati, become independent.

1983 The United States relinquishes all claims to the Phoenix and Line groups.

1988 Overcrowding becomes a problem in the central islands. The government begins to resettle excess population to the outer islands.

1994 The Kiribati government announces its intent to unilaterally move the international date line far to the east, so that all the islands will be in the same time zone and can keep the same business week.

1999 Kiribati becomes a member of the United Nations.

2002 A controversial new law allows the government to shut down nongovernmental newspapers.

2008–2009 Kiribati government officials request Australia* and New Zealand* to accept Kiribati citizens as permanent refugees in case of a national disaster. Kiribati is expected to be the first country to lose land territory due to rising sea levels caused by global warming.

KOREA, NORTH

OFFICIAL NAME

Chosŏn Minjujuŭi Inmin Konghwaguk (transliteration from Korean); Democratic People's Republic of Korea (English)

POPULATION

23,546,800 (2009e)

INHABITANTS' NAME/NICKNAME

Korean(s); North Korean(s)

LANGUAGE/LANGUAGES

Korean (official); Chinese, Japanese, others

RELIGION/RELIGIONS

Buddhism, Confucianism, shamanist, Chongdogyo, Christian, others. Religious activities have been forbidden since 1945 and replaced by cult worship of rulers Kim Il Sung and Kim Jong Il.

NATIONAL FLAG

The flag consists of a red field with narrow blue stripes at the top and bottom, separated from the red by thin white lines. A white disk on the red field bears a single red, five-pointed star. The blue stripes symbolize the people's desire for peace, the red symbolizes the revolutionary spirit of the struggle for socialism, and the white, a traditional Korean color, stands for the purity of the ideals of the People's Republic and national sovereignty. The red star of communism symbolizes the happy future of the people, building socialism under the leadership of the Korean People's Party.

COAT OF ARMS/SEAL

The coat of arms, called the National Emblem of the Democratic People's Republic of Korea, depicts a hydroelectric power plant under Mount Paektu below the beaming light of a five-pointed red star. Ears of rice form a round frame surrounding the whole, bound with a red banner inscribed with the name of the country in Hangul characters.

CAPITAL CITY

Pyongyang

TYPE OF GOVERNMENT

Single-party dictatorship

NATIONAL EMBLEM

Kim Il Sung badge worn by all citizens on the left shoulder.

NATIONAL COLORS

Red and white

NATIONAL ANTHEM

Songs that praise former leader Kim Il Sung and his son and successor Kim Jong Il have mostly replaced the official anthem.

Aegukka (Korean); The Song of Patriotism (English)

Let morning shine on the silver and gold of
   this land,
Three thousand leagues packed with natural
   wealth.
My beautiful fatherland.
The glory of a wise people
Brought up in a culture brilliant
With a history five millennia long.
Let us devote our bodies and minds
To supporting this Korea forever.

Embracing the atmosphere of Mount Baekdu,
Nest for the spirit of labor,

The firm will, bonded with truth,
Will go forth to the entire world.
The country established by the will of the
   people,
Breasting the raging waves with soaring
   strength.
Let us glorify forever this Korea,
Limitlessly rich and strong.

PATRON SAINT

Saint Joseph; Mary, the Blessed Virgin

CURRENCY

North Korean won

INTERNET IDENTIFIER

.kp (unofficial)

VEHICLE IDENTIFICATION PLATES/STICKERS

KP

PASSPORT

The passport cover has the name of the country in Korean, the coat of arms, and the word *passport* in Korean.

AIRLINE

Air Koryo

NATIONAL FLOWER

Magnolia (official): *Kimjongilia*; *Kimilsungia* (both unofficial, named for the country's former and present leaders)

NATIONAL ANIMAL

Siberian tiger

NATIONAL RESOURCES

Natural resources include coal, lead, tungsten, zinc, graphite, magnesite, iron ore, copper, gold, pyrites, salt, fluorspar, and hydropower. The country's economy has been geared toward military manufacturing since 1995.

FOODS

National dishes include kimchi, a highly spiced relish of pickled cabbage or white radish with turnips, onions, and other ingredients; *bibimbap*, boiled rice with vegetables; *bulgogi*, marinated, charcoal-broiled beef; *galbi*, marinated, charcoal-broiled beef ribs; and *haemultang*, seafood stew.

SPORTS/SPORTS TEAMS

Athletics and traditional sports are encouraged, but association football (soccer) is the country's most popular sport. Democratic People's Republic of Korea national teams participate in many sports at an international level.

TEAM SPORTS

Badminton

Democratic People's Republic of Korea Badminton Team

Baseball

Democratic People's Republic of Korea Baseball Team; Democratic People's Republic of Korea Softball Team

Basketball

Democratic People's Republic of Korea Basketball Team; Democratic People's Republic of Korea Women's Basketball Team

Football

Democratic People's Republic of Korea Football Team, nickname Chollima; Democratic People's Republic of Korea Women's Football Team; Democratic People's Republic of Korea Women's Under-19 Football Team

Handball

Democratic People's Republic of Korea Handball Team; Democratic People's Republic of Korea Women's Handball Team

Hockey

Democratic People's Republic of Korea Ice Hockey Team; Democratic People's Republic of Korea Junior Ice Hockey Team; Democratic People's Republic of Korea Women's Ice Hockey Team; Democratic People's Republic of Korea Field Hockey Team

Table Tennis

Democratic People's Republic of Korea Table Tennis Team

Volleyball

Democratic People's Republic of Korea Men's Volleyball Team; Democratic People's Republic of Korea Women's Volleyball Team

INDIVIDUAL SPORTS

Democratic People's Republic of Korea Amateur Boxing Team; Democratic People's Republic of Korea Archery Team; Democratic People's Republic of Korea Athletics Team; Democratic People's Republic of Korea Canoeing Team; Democratic People's Republic of Korea Cycling Team; Democratic People's Republic of Korea Fencing Team; Democratic People's Republic of Korea Gymnastics Team; Democratic People's Republic of Korea Judo Team; Democratic People's Republic of Korea Karate Team; Democratic People's Republic of Korea Modern Pentathlon Team; Democratic People's Republic of Korea Rowing Team; Democratic People's Republic of Korea Shooting Team; Democratic People's Republic of Korea Swim Team; Democratic People's Republic of Korea Weight Lifting Team; Democratic People's Republic of Korea Wrestling Team

WINTER SPORTS

Democratic People's Republic of Korea Ice Hockey Team; Democratic People's Republic of Korea Junior Ice Hockey Team; Democratic

People's Republic of Korea Women's Ice Hockey Team; Democratic People's Republic of Korea Skating Team

NATIONAL HEROES OR PERSONIFICATIONS

Kim Il Sung, leader of the country from 1949 to 1994; Kim Jong Il, his son and the leader of the country since 1994

NATIONAL HOLIDAY/INDEPENDENCE DAY

Founding of the Democratic People's Republic of Korea, September 9

FESTIVALS/FAIRS

Arirang Festival, held around Kim Il Sung's birthdate in April

SIGNIFICANT EVENTS IN FORMATION OF NATIONAL IDENTITY

10,000 B.C.E.–1200 B.C.E. Altaic-speaking tribes from south-central Siberia populate the peninsula in successive waves.

Second century B.C.E. The adoption of the Chinese writing system has profound effects on the Korean population.

50 C.E.–1392 C.E. The Korean Peninsula is divided into three kingdoms: Silla, Koguryo, and Paekche. Buddhism is introduced to Korea in the fourth century. The peninsula is unified under the rule of the Silla kingdom in 668. The Silla is succeeded by the Koryo dynasty in 935. The Chosan dynasty takes power in 1392, following a century of rule by the Mongols.

16th century Portuguese ships visit the kingdom. Portuguese missionaries corrupt the name Koryo to Korea. Pyongyang becomes a center of missionary activity, with many converts to Christianity.

1592–1597 Japanese invasions disrupt the kingdom.

1850–1890 European gunboat diplomacy and Japanese encroachments are met with the closure of Korea's ports to foreigners and a refusal to maintain relations with other countries, earning Korea the nickname "the Hermit Kingdom."

1905–1938 Japanese troops fighting Russia* in nearby Manchuria occupy the kingdom. Japan* annexes Korea in 1910, treating it as a colony. Tight control and a ruthless program to supplant the Korean culture and language with Japanese characterize the colonial administration. Korean resistance is brutally suppressed.

1939–1945 More than 5 million Koreans are conscripted as forced labor during the Second World War. Tens of thousands of young men are forced into the Japanese military. An estimated 200,000 women and girls are forced into sexual slavery for the military as the euphemistically named "comfort women."

1945–1948 At the end of the Second World War, Japan surrenders and the United States* occupies the southern part of the peninsula, while the Soviet Union takes control of Korea north of the 38th parallel. The division is intended to be temporary, until the Allies set up a trusteeship administration for the whole peninsula.

1948 Cold War politics prevents the unification of Korea. Two distinct nations are established, with opposing political, economic, and social systems. In the north, the People's Republic of Korea is established under Kim Il Sung, who is cultivated and supported by the Soviet Union.

1950–1953 Guerilla warfare, border clashes, and naval battles lead to full-scale war, the Korean War, between the two Koreas. The new United Nations sends troops to aid South Korea, led by the United States. Large numbers of Chinese "volunteers" cross into North Korea. The battle line stabilizes along the 38th parallel. An armistice is signed but is never followed by a peace treaty.

1953–1990 Kim Il Sung remains the leader of the country, which is the most closed society in the world. Religion is mostly replaced by worship of the communist dictator. Thousands of dissidents are sent to prison labor camps. Very few foreigners are allowed to visit the country.

1991–2005 The collapse of the Soviet Union, North Korea's major supplier, along with a series of natural disasters, causes widespread famine that leaves between 300,000 and 800,000 dead.

The regime reluctantly allows international food aid to arrive in the country.

2002–2009 The United States, Russia, Japan, China, and the Democratic People's Republic of Korea form a working group to find a solution to North Korea's blatant nuclear program. Chronic food shortages and malnutrition continue to plague the general population of the People's Republic. The government confirms the launch of several short-range missiles in defiance of world opinion and increasingly tight economic and diplomatic sanctions.

KOREA, SOUTH

OFFICIAL NAME
Daehan Minguk (transliteration from Korean); Republic of Korea (English)

NICKNAME
Land of the Morning Calm

POPULATION
49,689,100 (20089e)

INHABITANTS' NAME/NICKNAME
Korean(s); South Korean(s)

LANGUAGE/LANGUAGES
Korean (official); English, Japanese, others

RELIGION/RELIGIONS
Christian, 26 percent; Buddhist, 24 percent; other or no religion

NATIONAL FLAG
The flag, called *Taegukgi,* is a white field with a centered disk of red and blue and four black trigrams, one in each corner. The center disk, the *taeguk,* represents the origin of all things in the universe, the ying and the yang, which hold the opposing principles of negative and positive, good and evil, and so on in perfect balance and continuous movement within infinity. The white represents the cleanliness of the Korean people. The four trigrams represent various celestial bodies, seasons, directions, and virtues.

COAT OF ARMS/SEAL
The coat of arms has the same *taeguk* symbol as the national flag, surrounded by stylized petals and a banner bearing the name of the country in Hangul letters. The ying and yang represent peace and harmony. The petals symbolize Korea's national flower, the *Hibiscus syricus,* or rose of Sharon.

CAPITAL CITY
Seoul

TYPE OF GOVERNMENT
Presidential republic

NATIONAL EMBLEM
Taeguk (yin-yang symbol)

NATIONAL COLORS
White, blue, and red

NATIONAL ANTHEM
The anthem was written and composed in 1937 and became the official anthem of the Korean government-in-exile. It was adopted as the national anthem at independence in 1948.

> **Aegukga (Korean); The Patriotic Song (English)**
>
> Until the day when the East Sea's
> waters and Mount Baekdu are dry
> and worn away,
> God protect and preserve us.
> Long live our nation!
>
> The pine tree atop Namsan
> stands firmly unchanged under wind
> and frost as if wrapped in armor,
> as is our resilient spirit.
>
> Autumn sky is void and vast, high and
> cloudless,

the bright moon is our heart,
undivided and true.

With this spirit and this mind, give all loyalty,
in suffering or in joy, love the country.
Three thousand *Li* of splendid rivers
and mountains, filled with roses of Sharon,
Great Korean people, stay true to the
Great Korean way.

PATRON SAINT

Saint Joseph; Mary the Blessed Virgin

CURRENCY

South Korean won

INTERNET IDENTIFIER

.kr

VEHICLE IDENTIFICATION PLATES/STICKERS

ROK

PASSPORT

The passport cover has the name of the country and the word *passport* in Korean, the coat of arms, and the name of the country and the word *passport* in English.

AIRLINES

Korean Air Lines; Asiana Airlines

NATIONAL FLOWER

Rose of Sharon

NATIONAL TREE

Gingko (official); magnolia (unofficial)

NATIONAL ANIMAL

Korean tiger (unofficial)

NATIONAL BIRD

Black-billed magpie (unofficial)

NATIONAL RESOURCES

Natural resources include coal, tungsten, graphite, molybdenum, lead, and hydropower potential. The dynamic, well-educated population is a major resource, making South Korea a major economic power. Korean brand names are known throughout the world. Tourism is also very important and stems from the country's many ancient monuments, historic cities, unique culture, and proximity to major Asian population centers.

FOODS

Kimchi, a marinated and highly spiced relish of cabbage, cucumber, or white radish with onions, turnips, salt, chestnuts, red pepper, and often fish, is considered the national dish. Other specialties include *banchan,* a variety of small side dishes that accompany steam-cooked white rice; *bulgogi,* marinated beef cooked over charcoal; and *haemultang,* a seafood stew. *Yakju,* refined pure liquor fermented from rice, is considered the national drink.

SPORTS/SPORTS TEAMS

Association football (soccer) is the most popular sport in Korea. Tae kwon do, a martial art, was declared the national sport in 1971. Republic of Korea national teams participate in many sports at an international level.

TEAM SPORTS

Badminton

Republic of Korea Badminton Team

Baseball

Republic of Korea Baseball Team; Republic of Korea Softball Team

Basketball

Republic of Korea Basketball Team, nickname Asian Tigers, Taeguk Warriors, or Red Devils; Korea Wheelchair Basketball Team

Curling

Republic of Korea Curling Team

Football

Republic of Korea Football Team, nickname the Taeguk Warriors; Republic of Korea Women's Football Team, nickname the Taeguk Warriors; Republic of Korea Under-20 Football Team; Republic of Korea Women's Under-19 Football Team; Republic of Korea Rugby Union Team; Republic of Korea Wheelchair Rugby Team; Republic of Korea American Football Team; Republic of Korea Futsal Team

Handball

Republic of Korea Men's Handball Team; Republic of Korea Women's Handball Team

Hockey

Republic of Korea Ice Hockey Team; Republic of Korea Junior Ice Hockey Team; Korea Men's Field Hockey Team; Korea Women's Field Hockey Team

Kabaddi

Republic of Korea Kabaddi Team

Korfball

Republic of Korea Korfball Team

Lacrosse

Korea Lacrosse Team; Korea Under-19 Lacrosse Team

Netball

Republic of Korea Netball Team

Racing

A1 Team Korea; Republic of Korea Speedway Team

Table Tennis

Republic of Korea Table Tennis Team

Tennis

Republic of Korea Davis Cup Team; Republic of Korea Fed Cup Team

Volleyball

Republic of Korea Men's Volleyball Team; Republic of Korea Women's Volleyball Team; Republic of Korea Beach Volleyball Team; Republic of Korea Women's Beach Volleyball Team

INDIVIDUAL SPORTS

Republic of Korea Amateur Boxing Team; Republic of Korea Archery Team; Republic of Korea Athletics Team; Republic of Korea Canoeing Team; Republic of Korea Cycling Team; Republic of Korea Equestrian Team; Republic of Korea Fencing Team; Republic of Korea Gymnastics Team; Republic of Korea Judo Team; Republic of Korea Karate Team; Republic of Korea Modern Pentathlon Team; Republic of Korea Rowing Team; Republic of Korea Sailing Team; Republic of Korea Shooting Team; Republic of Korea Swim Team; Republic of Korea Tae Kwon Do Team; Republic of Korea Triathlon Team; Republic of Korea Weight Lifting Team; Republic of Korea Wrestling Team

WINTER SPORTS

Republic of Korea Biathlon Team; Republic of Korea Curling Team; Republic of Korea Ice Hockey Team; Republic of Korea Junior Ice Hockey Team; Republic of Korea Luge Team; Republic of Korea Skating Team

NATIONAL HEROES OR PERSONIFICATIONS

Kim Yushin, leader of the Silla unification of Korea in the seventh century; Taejo of Goryeo, the founder of the Goryeo Dynasty, which ruled Korea from the 10th to 14th centuries; Yi Seong-gye, first king of the Chosan Dynasty in the late 14th century; Yi Sun-sin, called Admiral Yi, the naval leader noted for victories over the invading Japanese fleets in the late 16th century

NATIONAL HOLIDAY/ INDEPENDENCE DAY

Liberation Day, August 15

FESTIVALS/FAIRS

Baekje Cultural Festival, October; Jagaichi Festival; October; Cheongdo Bullfighting Festival, April; Seoul International Cartoon and Animation Festival, May; Boryeong Mud Festival, July; Jagaichi Festival, October; Namdo Food Festival, October

SIGNIFICANT EVENTS IN FORMATION OF NATIONAL IDENTITY

10,000 B.C.E.–1200 B.C.E. Altaic-speaking tribes from south-central Siberia settle the Korean Peninsula in successive waves.

Second century B.C.E. The adoption of the Chinese writing system has profound effects on the Korean population.

50 C.E.–935 C.E. The Korean Peninsula is divided into three kingdoms: Silla, Koguryo, and Paekche. Buddhism is introduced to Korea in the fourth century, The peninsula is unified under the rule of the Silla kingdom in 668–676. An advanced Buddhist culture flourishes.

935–1392 The Silla dynasty is succeeded by the Koryo dynasty in 935. The Chosan dynasty takes power in 1392, following a century of rule by the Mongols. The capital moves to Seoul.

16th century Portuguese ships visit the kingdom. Portuguese missionaries corrupt the name Koryo to Korea. Pyongyang becomes a center of missionary activity with many converts to Christianity.

1592–1597 Japanese invasions disrupt the kingdom. The dominance of Korean sea power under Admiral Yi is decisive in Japan's retreat.

1850–1890 Foreign threats are met with the closure of Korea's ports to foreigners and a refusal to maintain relations with other countries, earning Korea the nickname "the Hermit Kingdom."

1905–1938 Japanese troops fighting Russia* in nearby Manchuria occupy the kingdom. Japan* annexes Korea in 1910, ending the centuries-long rule of the Chosan Dynasty. All Korean resistance is brutally suppressed. Official Japanese policy is to convert the Koreans to the Japanese language and culture, violently if necessary.

1939–1945 More than 5 million Koreans are conscripted as forced labor as the Second World War begins. Tens of thousands of young men are forced into the Japanese military. An estimated 200,000 women and girls are forced into sexual slavery for the military as the euphemistically named "comfort women."

1945–1948 At the end of the Second World War, Japan surrenders and the United States* and the Soviet Union occupy the peninsula. The division is intended to be temporary until the Allies can set up a trusteeship administration for the whole peninsula.

1948 Cold War politics prevents the unification of Korea. Two distinct nations are established, with a democratic government in the south and a socialist people's republic in the north. Syngman Rhee is installed as the first president of the Republic of Korea.

1950–1953 Guerilla warfare, border clashes, naval battles, and finally a full-scale invasion by North Korea begin the Korean War. Large numbers of Chinese "volunteers" cross into North Korea to aid the communist cause. The battle line stabilizes along the 38th parallel, and an armistice is signed but never followed by a peace treaty. The peninsula remains split at the 38th parallel, where a demilitarized zone is established.

1960 A student uprising leads to the resignation of autocratic and corrupt Syngman Rhee. Under President Park Chung-hee, the country experiences rapid economic growth, but at the cost of political suppression.

1980 A military coup triggers widespread demonstrations, particularly in the city of Gwangju, where special forces fire on demonstrators in an act known as the Gwangju Massacre.

1988   Seoul hosts the 1988 Summer Olympics, a cause for celebration and a symbolic break with the political turmoil of the 1980s.

2000   South Korean officials meet with representatives of North Korea. Concerns include the ongoing famine in the North and the communist government's efforts to produce nuclear weapons.

2004   The country's economy continues to grow, giving South Koreans a standard of living comparable to that in many parts of the European Union.

2008   The government prepares to launch a vehicle into space from the new Naro Space Center.

2009   A growing number of Koreans adhere to new religious movements that have developed as a reaction to the influence of Christianity and Western culture.

KYRGYZSTAN

OFFICIAL NAME

Kyrgyz Respublikasi (transliteration from Kyrgyz); Kyrgyzskaya Respublika (transliteration from Russian); Kyrgyz Republic (English)

POPULATION

5,312,500 (2009e)

INHABITANTS' NAME/NICKNAME

Kyrgyz, Kyrgyzstani(s)

LANGUAGE/LANGUAGES

Kyrgyz, Russian (both official); Uzbek, Dungun, others

RELIGION/RELIGIONS

Muslim, 75 percent; Russian Orthodox, 20 percent; other or no religion

NATIONAL FLAG

The national flag is a red field bearing a central yellow sun with 40 rays, representing the 40 tribes of the Kyrgyz nation. In the center of the sun is a red ring crossed by two sets of three lines, a stylized symbol of the crown, or *tunduk,* of a traditional Kyrgyz yurt, symbolizing Kyrgyz traditions and the people of Kyrgyzstan. The color red represents the peace and openness of the country.

COAT OF ARMS/SEAL

The coat of arms is a circle of mostly blue, the color of courage and generosity. The central part of the circle depicts the Tian Shan mountains and a rising sun above a white eagle with fluttering wings. Around the circle are wheat and cotton, the country's two major crops, and the name of the country in Kyrgyz in the Cyrillic alphabet.

CAPITAL CITY

Bishkek

TYPE OF GOVERNMENT

Parliamentary republic

NATIONAL EMBLEM

The *tanduk,* the stylized crown of a Kyrgyz yurt; Sun emblem as shown on the national flag

NATIONAL COLORS

Red and yellow

NATIONAL ANTHEM

Instead of adopting the Soviet-era anthem, as did neighboring states, Kyrgyzstan adopted a new anthem at independence in 1991.

Kyrgyz Respublikasynyn Mamlekettik Gimni (Kyryz); National Anthem of the Kyrgyz Republic (English)

High mountains, valleys and fields
Are our native, holy land.
Our fathers lived amidst the Ala-Too,
Always saving their motherland.

Chorus

Come on, Kyrgyz people,
Come on to freedom!
Stand up and flourish!
Create your fortune!

We are open for freedom for ages.
Friendship and unity are in our hearts.
The land of Kyrgyzstan, our native state,
Shining in the rays of consent.

Chorus

Come on, Kyrgyz people,
Come on to freedom!
Stand up and flourish!
Create your fortune!

Dreams of the people came true,
And the flag of liberty is over us.
The heritage of our fathers we will
Pass to our sons for the benefit of people.

Chorus

Come on, Kyrgyz people,
Come on to freedom!
Stand up and flourish!
Create your fortune!

CURRENCY

Kyrgyz som

INTERNET IDENTIFIER

.kg

VEHICLE IDENTIFICATION PLATES/STICKERS

KS

PASSPORT

The passport cover has the name of the country in Kyrgyz, Russian, and English; the coat of arms; and the word *passport* in the same three languages.

AIRLINE

Kyrgyzstan Airlines

NATIONAL FLOWER

Tulip (unofficial)

NATIONAL BIRD

White eagle (unofficial)

NATIONAL RESOURCES

Natural resources include abundant hydropower, significant deposits of gold and rare earth metals, and locally exploitable coal, oil, and natural gas, along with deposits of nepheline, mercury, bismuth, lead, and zinc. Although the export of minerals is growing, agriculture remains very important to the country. Abundant water is a very valuable resource in the generally dry region of Central Asia.

FOODS

Besh barmak, boiled horse meat with dumplings; *plov,* a rice dish with shredded meat; *laghman,* a noodle soup with mutton and vegetables; *shopur,* a meat soup with potatoes and vegetables; *manty,* steamed noodle dough stuffed with meat or vegetables; and *chiburekki,* a doughnut-like fried pastry, are all considered national dishes.

SPORTS/SPORTS TEAMS

Association football (soccer) is very popular, as are traditional games played on horseback, such as *ulak tatrysh,* a team game resembling polo or rugby. Kyrgyzstan national teams participate in many sports at an international level.

TEAM SPORTS

Badminton

Kyrgyzstan Badminton Team

Basketball

Kyrgyzstan Basketball Team; Kyrgyzstan Women's Basketball Team

Football

Kyrgyzstan Football Team; Kyrgyzstan Women's Football Team; Kyrgyzstan Rugby Union Team; Kyrgyzstan Women's Rugby Union Team; Kyrgyzstan Futsal Team

Handball

Kyrgyzstan Handball Team

Hockey

Kyrgyzstan Field Hockey Team

Table Tennis

Kyrgyzstan Table Tennis Team

Tennis

Kyrgyzstan Davis Cup Team; Kyrgyzstan Fed Cup Team

Volleyball

Kyrgyzstan Men's Volleyball Team; Kyrgyzstan Women's Volleyball Team

INDIVIDUAL SPORTS

Kyrgyzstan Amateur Boxing Team; Kyrgyzstan Archery Team; Kyrgyzstan Athletics Team; Kyrgyzstan Canoeing Team; Kyrgyzstan Cycling Team; Kyrgyzstan Equestrian Team; Kyrgyzstan Fencing Team; Kyrgyzstan Gymnastics Team; Kyrgyzstan Judo Team; Kyrgyzstan Karate Team; Kyrgyzstan Modern Pentathlon Team; Kyrgyzstan Rowing Team; Kyrgyzstan Sailing Team; Kyrgyzstan Shooting Team; Kyrgyzstan Swim Team; Kyrgyzstan Tae Kwon Do Team; Kyrgyzstan Wrestling Team

WINTER SPORTS

Kyrgyzstan Bandy Team; Kyrgyzstan Alpine Ski Team; Kyrgyzstan Luge Team

NATIONAL HEROES OR PERSONIFICATIONS

Manas, the mythical hero of the Kyrgyz national poem, is considered the father of the Kyrgyz nation. The *Epic of Manas* has more than half a million lines, 20 times longer than Homer's *Odyssey* and *Iliad* combined. Other national heroes include Kurman-jan Datka, known as Queen of the South, a leader of the resistance to Russian domination; Kasym Tynystanov, creator of the Kyrgyz alphabet and a leading intellectual, who was arrested and executed by the Soviet authorities in 1937; and Sayakbay Karalaev, a renowned *manaschi,* or reciter of the *Epic of Manas.*

NATIONAL HOLIDAY/ INDEPENDENCE DAY

Independence Day, August 31

FESTIVALS/FAIRS

Nooruz (Kyrgyz New Year), March; Orozo Alt, variable dates; Kurman Alt, variable dates; Independence Day celebrations, August

SIGNIFICANT EVENTS IN FORMATION OF NATIONAL IDENTITY

201 B.C.E. The Kyrgyz, a tribal people of Turkic and Iranian background, occupy the upper Yenisey River valley in central Siberia.

7th century C.E.–13th century C.E. The Kyrgyz tribal federation reaches its greatest expansion after defeating the Uighur Khanate in 840. By the 12th century, the tribes have adopted Islam. The rise of the Mongols threatens the tribal peoples, and a great migration begins to the south.

13th century The region becomes an important part of the trade route known as the Silk Road.

15th century–16th century The Kyrgyz tribes settle the highland region of the Tian Shan Mountains.

16th century–19th century In the early 19th century, the southern tribes come under the Uzbek Khanate of Kokand, while Russians move into the northern region in 1855.

1876–1891 The Kyrgyz tribes fall under Russian rule, setting off a series of revolts against czarist troops. Many Kyrgyz migrate to escape the Russians. The completion of a rail link to Europe brings thousands of Slavic settlers.

1916 During World War I, Russian attempts to draft the Central Asians initiate a serious revolt across the vast region. Thousands of Slavic settlers are slaughtered. The rebellion rekindles a sense of unity among the Kyrgyz tribes.

1917 The Russian Revolution leads to the collapse of czarist authority. Central Asian leaders form a provisional government of Turkestan.

1919–1924 The Bolshevik Red Army conquers Central Asia. Kyrgyz guerrilla groups continue to harass the new Soviet authorities for several years. Islam is suppressed.

1936–1953 The Kyrgyz territory becomes a full union republic of the soviet Union. The Kyrgyz national epic *Manas* is banned in 1952. Soviet leader Joseph Stalin's death in 1953 ends an era of arbitrary rule and terror.

1960s The beginnings of a Kyrgyz cultural revival are smothered by intense pressure to assimilate into Soviet life. Settlers from other areas of the Soviet Union make the Kyrgyz a minority in their own homeland.

1985–1990 Events in faraway Moscow begin to be felt in the region. A hesitant national movement emerges, and democratization begins.

1991 The collapse of the Soviet Union allows the various union republics to declare independence. Poorly prepared Kyrgyzstan is declared independent in August 1991.

1995 The Kyrgyz celebrate 1,000 years of their national epic, *Manas*. The United Nations honors the celebration by declaring 1995 the Year of the Manas Millennium.

1996 The new constitution is amended to make Russian the second official language.

2000–2006 Although Kyrgyzstan lacks the petroleum and other resources of its neighbors, its abundant water becomes a valuable asset in water-starved Central Asia. Large demonstrations protest flawed elections and the increasingly authoritarian methods of the government.

2008–2009 Serious disputes delay boundary agreements with neighboring states. Present concerns include the privatization of state-owned enterprises, the expansion of the democratic process, and interethnic relations. The country's supply of freshwater, the largest in the region, gives it the potential for greater prosperity in the future.

LAOS

OFFICIAL NAME
Sathalanalat Paxathipatai Paxaxon Lao (transliteration from Lao); Republique Democratique Populaire Lao (French); Lao People's Democratic Republic (English)

POPULATION
6,704,500 (2009e)

INHABITANTS' NAME/ NICKNAME
Laotian(s); Lao(s)

LANGUAGE/LANGUAGES
Lao (official); French, English, various regional languages

RELIGION/RELIGIONS
Buddhist, 65 percent; indigenous beliefs, 32 percent; Christian, 1.5 percent; other or no religion

NATIONAL FLAG
The flag consists of three horizontal stripes of red, blue, and red, the blue twice the width of the red stripes. In the center is a white disk. The color red represents the blood shed in the struggle for independence, and the blue symbolizes the wealth of the country. The white disk represents the moon over the river Mekong, as well as the unity of Laos under the communist government.

COAT OF ARMS/SEAL

The coat of arms is a circular disk depicting the national shrine Pha That Luang, the dam at the Nam Ngun reservoir, a forest, a stylized rice field, and a cogwheel. The center is surrounded by stalks of fully ripened rice and red banners bearing the national motto on one side and the slogan "Unity and Prosperity" on the other. In the middle is the name of the country in Lao script.

MOTTO

Peace, independence, democracy, unity, and prosperity

CAPITAL CITY

Vientiane

TYPE OF GOVERNMENT

Socialist republic

NATIONAL EMBLEM

The gilded stupa of Pha That Luang

NATIONAL COLORS

Red, blue, and white

NATIONAL ANTHEM

The anthem was written and composed in 1941 and was adopted when the Kingdom of Laos was created in 1947. New words were written following the 1975 communist revolution.

Pheng Xat Lao (Lao); Hymn of the Lao People (English)

For all time the Lao people have glorified
  their fatherland,
United in heart, spirit, and vigor as one.
Resolutely moving forward,
Respecting and increasing the dignity of the
  Lao people
And proclaiming the right to be their own
  masters.
The Lao people of all origins are equal
And will no longer allow imperialists and trai-
  tors to harm them.
The entire people will safeguard the
  independence
And the freedom of the Lao nation.
They are resolved to struggle for victory
In order to lead the nation to prosperity.

CURRENCY

Laotian kip

INTERNET IDENTIFIER

.la

VEHICLE IDENTIFICATION PLATES/STICKERS

LAO

PASSPORT

The passport cover has the name of the country in Lao and French, the coat of arms, and the word *passport* in Lao and French.

AIRLINE

Lao Airlines

NATIONAL FLOWER

Champa (plumeria)

NATIONAL TREE

Dok champa

NATIONAL PLANT

Rice

NATIONAL ANIMAL

Asian elephant (unofficial)

NATIONAL RESOURCES

Natural resources include timber, hydropower, gypsum, tin, gold, and gemstones. The communist government began liberalizing controls and encouraging private enterprise in 1986, which has dramatically stimulated the Lao economy. The Lao economy is heavily dependent on investment and trade with its larger and richer neighbors. Tourism, particularly ecotourism, is becoming a valuable resource.

FOODS

The Lao national dish is *laap,* a spicy mixture of marinated meat or fish with a variable combination of greens, herbs, and spices. Other national specialties include *tam mak houng,* a spicy salad of greens and papayas; *pho,* a soup of rice and noodles, often with beef or pork and vegetables; and *khai phaan,* a water green from the Mekong River.

SPORTS/SPORTS TEAMS

Association football (soccer) is the most popular sport. Athletics is also widely practiced. Laos national teams participate in many sports at an international level.

TEAM SPORTS

Badminton

Laos Badminton Team; Laos Women's Badminton Team

Basketball

Laos Basketball Team; Laos Women's Basketball Team

Football

Laos Football Team; Laos Women's Football Team; Laos Rugby Union Team; Laos Futsal Team

Table Tennis

Laos Table Tennis Team

Volleyball

Laos Men's Volleyball Team; Laos Women's Volleyball Team

INDIVIDUAL SPORTS

Laos Amateur Boxing Team; Laos Archery Team; Laos Athletics Team; Laos Canoeing Team; Laos Cycling Team; Laos Judo Team; Laos Karate Team; Laos Shooting Team; Laos Swim Team; Laos Tae Kwon Do Team; Laos Wrestling Team

NATIONAL HEROES OR PERSONIFICATIONS

Fa Ngum, founder of the first important Lao kingdom; Photisarath, a Lao ruler who suppressed spirit worship and promoted Buddhism; Setthatirath, a Lao leader who successfully resisted Burmese invaders, only to be murdered by conspirators; Sisavangvong, the king of Luang Prabang from 1904–1946 and king of Laos from 1946–1959; Prince Souvanna Phouma, the neutralist prime minister off and on from 1951 until the communist revolution in 1975

NATIONAL HOLIDAY/INDEPENDENCE DAY

Republic Day, December 2

FESTIVALS/FAIRS

Lao Handicraft Festival, November; Lao Industry and Handicrafts Products Trade Fair, June; Boun Khoun Khao (Rice Harvest Festival), January–February; Boun Khao Chi, February; Boun Phrawetsandone, March; Boun Phimai Lao (Lao New Year), April; Khao Padabdin Festival, August–September.

SIGNIFICANT EVENTS IN FORMATION OF NATIONAL IDENTITY

Ninth century C.E. The Lao people migrate to the Mekong River basin from northwestern Vietnam*. Buddhism spreads to the region.

1353 The kingdom of Lan Xang is established by Fa Ngum, the forerunner of the modern Lao state.

16th century King Photisarath helps establish Theravada Buddhism as the predominant religion by suppressing traditional spirit worship.

17th century—18th century Lan Xang begins a period of decline. Siam, now called Thailand*, establishes control over most of the Lao homeland.

The region is divided into three smaller kingdoms under Thai authority: Luang Prabang in the north, Vientiane in the center, and Champassak in the south.

1828 The Vientiane Lao rebel against Thai rule and are defeated. Vientiane is incorporated directly into the Thai kingdom of Siam.

1893–1904 France*, having taken control of neighboring Vietnam, absorbs Laos into its French Indochina via treaties with Thailand.

1940–1946 Japanese forces occupy Indochina during World War II. Following the Japanese defeat, Lao nationalists declare independence, but French military forces return and reestablish French authority.

1946–1954 During the First Indochina War, communists organize the Pathet Lao resistance organization dedicated to Lao independence. French defeat leads to the independence of the Lao people in a united kingdom in 1954.

1962–1975 Laos attempts to remain neutral as the Second Indochina War, also called the Vietnam War, spreads across the region. Pathet Lao guerrillas fight government forces in a local civil war as Laos is drawn into the war by U.S. and Vietnamese incursions into the neutral country. The communists of Pathet Lao take control of Laos.

1975 The new government imprisons many members of the previous government and imposes communist ideals, but remains mostly a puppet regime run from communist Vietnam. About 10 percent of the population flees the country.

1986–1991 As Soviet subsidies end, the government introduces some economic reform. Following the Soviet collapse, the Lao government gives up centralized economic management but maintains its monopoly on political activity.

2001–2008 The government's more moderate policies allow many refugees to return to Laos. Efforts to modernize the country and the economy include greater emphasis on foreign languages. The government plans to introduce English at the primary-school level by 2010.

2009 International organizations report that about 69 percent of Laotian children lack basic health care. Persecution of the Hmong minority continues to drive Hmong refugees to the United States* and other countries.

MACAU

OFFICIAL NAME

Aomen Tebie Xingzhengqu (transliteration from Chinese); Regiao Administrativa Especial de Macau (Portuguese); Macau Special Administrative Region (English)

POPULATION

532,400 (2009e)

INHABITANTS' NAME/NICKNAME

Macanese; Macau Chinese

LANGUAGE/LANGUAGES

Chinese (Cantonese), Portuguese (both official); Mandarin, English, Hokkien, others

RELIGION/RELIGIONS

Most Macanese believe in Chinese folk religions, which include the faiths of Confucianism, Taoism, Buddhism, and worship of folk gods and goddesses (especially Kuan Yin and Matsu), as in other Chinese communities. There is also a small Christian—mostly Roman Catholic—community, as well as practitioners of other religions or none.

REGIONAL FLAG

The flag is a green field with a white lotus flower above a stylized depiction of Governor Nobre de Carvalho Bridge and green and white stripes representing water. Above the lotus is an arc of five-pointed gold stars, one larger centered star and two smaller stars on each side. The color green represents Macau's ties to Portugal*. The lotus is Macau's official flower. The bridge is one of Macau's most recognizable structures and links the Macau Peninsula and the island of Taipa. The water represents Macau's position as a port. The five stars repeat the stars on the flag of the People's Republic of China*, symbolizing the relationship between Macau and China.

COAT OF ARMS/SEAL

The coat of arms has the same lotus, bridge, water, and stars as the flag, within a disk with a wide white border inscribed with the complete name of the territory (Macau Special Administrative Region of the People's Republic of China) in traditional Chinese characters above and the Portuguese short name, Macau, beneath.

CAPITAL CITY

Macau (de facto, as Macau has no designated capital)

TYPE OF GOVERNMENT

As a special administrative region of the People's Republic of China, Macau is autonomous except for defense and foreign relations. Macau maintains its own legal system, police force, monetary system, customs, and immigration policies and participates in international organizations and events as a separate nation.

NATIONAL EMBLEM

Governor Nobre de Carvalho Bridge; Ruins of St. Paul cathedral; Lotus

NATIONAL COLORS

Green and white

NATIONAL ANTHEM

The official anthem of the territory is the anthem of the People's Republic of China, "March of the Volunteers."

PATRON SAINT

John the Baptist

CURRENCY

Macanese pataca

INTERNET IDENTIFIER

.mo

VEHICLE IDENTIFICATION PLATES/STICKERS

MO

PASSPORT

The passport cover has the full name of the territory, Macao Special Administrative Region of People's Republic of China, in Chinese, Portuguese, and English; the coat of arms of the People's Republic of China; and the word *passport* in Chinese, Portuguese, and English.

AIRLINE

Air Macau

NATIONAL FLOWER

White lotus

NATIONAL RESOURCES

Macau has a small population and limited natural resources. The economy is based on tourism, much of it geared toward gambling. The well-educated population also supports a thriving banking and financial services industry. Textile manufacturing is the leading industrial activity. Macau is one of the world's wealthiest territories.

FOODS

Macanese cuisine is a mixture of Chinese, Portuguese, Indian, and Malay influences. Specialties include *caldo verde,* a rich vegetable soup; *bacalhau,* salt cod prepared in various ways; *galinha à Portuguesa,* Portuguese-style chicken; *galinha à Africana,* chicken cooked in an African style; and *porc tamarindo,* pork cooked in a broth with hot red peppers.

SPORTS/SPORTS TEAMS

Association football (soccer) and basketball are the two most popular sports. Macau national teams participate in many sports at an international level. Some sports teams carry the designation Macau China although they represent only the territory of Macau at international sporting events.

TEAM SPORTS

Badminton

Macau Badminton Team

Basketball

Macau Basketball Team; Macau Women's Basketball Team

Football

Macau Football Team, nickname Macau Team; Macau Women's Football Team; Macau Rugby Union Team; Macau Under-18 Football Team; Macau Futsal Team

Hockey

Macau Ice Hockey Team; Macau Field Hockey Team

Korfball

Macau China Korfball Team

Racing

Macau Speedway Team

Table Tennis

Macau Table Tennis Team

Volleyball

Men's Volleyball Team; Macau Women's Volleyball Team

INDIVIDUAL SPORTS

Macau Aikido Team; Macau Amateur Boxing Team; Macau Archery Team; Macau Athletics Team; Macau China Canoeing Team; Macau Cycling Team; Macau Fencing Team; Macau Judo Team; Macau Karate Team; Macau Shooting Team; Macau Swim Team; Macau Tae Kwon Do Team; Macau Triathlon Team; Macau Weight Lifting Team

WINTER SPORTS

Macau Ice Hockey Team

NATIONAL HEROES OR PERSONIFICATIONS

Leonel de Sousa, a 16th-century Portuguese governor of the new colony; Anders Ljungstedt, a Swedish-born merchant and historian, the first to refute the Portuguese claim that Ming China ever formally ceded Macau to Portugal

NATIONAL HOLIDAY/INDEPENDENCE DAY

Macau Day, December 20; National Day (China), October 1

FESTIVALS/FAIRS

Chinese New Year, variable dates; Macau Arts Festival, March–April; Dragon Boat Festival, May–June; Mid-Autumn Festival, September–October; Macau International Music Festival, October; Macau Grand Prix, November

SIGNIFICANT EVENTS IN FORMATION OF NATIONAL IDENTITY

220 B.C.E.–500 C.E. The territory appears in archives among the rural counties under various Chinese dynasties. Beginning in the fifth century C.E., ships begin to stop in the anchorage for fresh water and food or to shelter from storms.

1277–1500 Members of the Song Dynasty and some 50,000 followers seek refuge in the area from invading Mongols. The port prospers as fishermen and boat people migrate there.

1513 A Portuguese ship from Portuguese-controlled Malacca arrives in the delta of the Pearl

River, and the crew claims Lintin Island for the king of Portugal.

1557 The Portuguese establish a trade settlement at Macau with Chinese permission and a small annual payment. Macau becomes an important part of Portugal's Asian trade routes.

1685 Macau's golden age ends when the Chinese emperor decides to allow other countries to trade in Chinese ports, ending Macau's near-monopoly in trade with China.

1842–1844 China cedes nearby Hong Kong*, with its splendid harbor, to the British, further damaging Macau's position as a trade port. Macau is joined with East Timor* as an overseas province of Portugal.

1851–1864 Portugal gains control of Taipa and Coloane, two islands just south of mainland Macau. The Chinese government recognizes Portuguese authority over the colony of Macau.

1940–1945 Macau briefly enjoys an economic resurgence during World War II, when the Japanese occupy the Chinese mainland and British Hong Kong but respect Portugal's neutrality.

1949 The victory of the communists in the Chinese Civil War leaves the status of Macau uncertain as the new government denounces unequal treaties forced on China by foreigners. Tens of thousands of refugees flood into the territory.

1966–1967 Rioting breaks out that forces Portugal to sign documents to prohibit activities by agents or representatives of the Republic of China in Taiwan*. A Portuguese proposal to return Macau to Chinese sovereignty is declined.

1979–1985 Portugal and the People's Republic of China establish diplomatic relations. China acknowledges Macau as a Chinese territory under Portuguese administration. Macau's famous casinos become the cornerstone of a tourist boom, mostly from Hong Kong.

1986–1999 China and Portugal hold talks over the status of Macau. The territory is returned to Chinese sovereignty as a special autonomous region in 1999. China promises not to impose its economic or political system on the territory, which will remain autonomous except for foreign and defense affairs until 2049.

1999–2008 Macau undergoes a building boom and uses reclaimed land for new casinos, hotels, and other tourist amenities as the Monte Carlo of Asia.

2009 A new state security law takes effect in Macau, with harsh punishments for treason, advocating secession, and subversion against the Chinese government. The law, heavily criticized internationally for its ambiguous, catchall language, also punishes "preparatory acts" having to do with these crimes.

See also China; Hong Kong

MALAYSIA

OFFICIAL NAME
Malaysia (official name)

POPULATION
27,455,600 (2009e)

INHABITANTS' NAME/NICKNAME
Malaysian(s)

LANGUAGE/LANGUAGES
Bahasa Malaysia/Malay (official); English, Cantonese, Mandarin, Hokkien, Hakka, Hainan, Foochow, Tamil, Telugu, Malayalam, Punjabi, Thai, others

RELIGION/RELIGIONS
Muslim, 61 percent (official); Buddhist, 20 percent; Christian, 9 percent; Hindu, 6.5 percent; other or no religion

NATIONAL FLAG
The flag, known as the Jalur Gemilang (Stripes of Glory), has 14 stripes of red and white with a blue canton on the upper hoist, bearing a gold crescent moon and a 14-pointed gold star. The 14 stripes represent the equal status of the 13 states and

the federal government. The crescent moon represents Islam, and the star with 14 points represents the unity of the states and the government.

COAT OF ARMS/SEAL

The coat of arms has a central shield or crest with representations of the various states of Malaysia. Two Malayan tigers support the shield. Above the shield are a gold crescent moon and a 14-pointed star representing, respectively, Islam and the 13 states and federal government. Below the shield and tigers is a banner inscribed with the national motto in Romanized Malay and in the Jawi script.

MOTTO

Bersekutu bertambah mutu (Malay); Unity is Strength (English)

CAPITAL CITY

Kuala Lumpur; some ministries and government offices have relocated to Putrajaya, the planned new capital south of Kuala Lumpur

TYPE OF GOVERNMENT

Parliamentary democracy as a federal constitutional elective monarchy

NATIONAL EMBLEM

Pak Belang (Harimau Malaya); Malayan tiger

NATIONAL COLORS

Yellow and black

NATIONAL ANTHEM

The melody derives from the anthem of one of the states, Perak, and became a popular love song before being selected as the national anthem, with new words, in 1957. The love song, called *"Terang Bulan,"* is now forbidden in Malaysia.

Negara Ku (Malay); My Country (English translation)

My country, my native land
The people living united and progressive
May God bestow blessings and happiness
May our ruler have a successful reign
May God bestow blessings and happiness
May our ruler have a successful reign

CURRENCY

Malaysian ringgit

INTERNET IDENTIFIER

.my

VEHICLE IDENTIFICATION PLATES/STICKERS

MAL

PASSPORT

The passport cover has the Romanized version of the Malay word for passport, *passport,* and the name of the country, Malaysia, and the coat of arms.

AIRLINES

AirAsia; Malaysian Airlines

NATIONAL FLOWER

Bunga raya (rose hibiscus)

NATIONAL TREE

Bunga raya (rose hibiscus)

NATIONAL ANIMAL

Malayan tiger

NATIONAL BIRD

Rhinoceros hornbill

NATIONAL FISH

Golden arowana (unofficial)

NATIONAL RESOURCES

Natural resources include tin, petroleum, timber, copper, iron ore, natural gas, bauxite, and arable land. The well-educated and industrious population changed the traditionally agricultural country, which became an industrialized nation between the 1960s and the 1990s. Tourism, based on the country's unique culture, historic cities and monuments, and sandy beaches and pleasant climate, is a very important resource.

FOODS

Satay, skewered meat or chicken cooked over charcoal and served with a spicy peanut sauce, and *nasi lemak,* rice soaked in coconut cream and then steamed, are considered the national dishes. Other specialties are *roti canai,* Malaysian flatbread; *char kway teow,* a noodle dish with soy sauce, chilies, prawns, cockles, eggs, bean sprouts, and Chinese chives; and *laksa,* a spicy noodle soup with meat, chicken, fish, or shrimp.

SPORTS/SPORTS TEAMS

Association football (soccer) is the most popular sport in Malaysia. Traditional sports, such as archery and athletics, are also popular. Malaysia national teams participate in many sports at an international level.

TEAM SPORTS

Badminton
Malaysia Badminton Team

Baseball
Malaysia Baseball Team; Malaysia Softball Team

Basketball
Malaysia Basketball Team; Malaysia Women's Basketball Team; Malaysia Wheelchair Basketball Team

Bowls
Malaysia Bowls Team

Cricket
Malaysia Cricket Team; Malaysia Women's Cricket Team

Football
Malaysia Football Team, nickname Harimau Malaya or the Tigers; Malaysia Women's Football Team, nickname Harimau Malaya; Malaysia Under-23 Football Team, nickname Harimau Muda; Malaysia Under-20 Football Team, nickname Harimau Muda; Malaysia Women's Under-19 Football Team; Malaysia Rugby Union Team; Malaysia Beach Soccer Team; Malaysia Futsal Team; Malaysia Touch Football Team; Malaysia Australian-Rules Football Team, nickname the Warriors

Hockey
Malaysia Field Hockey Team; Malaysia Ice Hockey Team

Kabaddi
Malaysia Kabaddi Team

Netball
Malaysia Netball Team

Polo
Malaysia Polo Team

Racing
A1 Team Malaysia; Malaysia Speedway Team

Table Tennis
Malaysia Table Tennis Team

Tennis
Malaysia Davis Cup Team; Malaysia Fed Cup Team

Volleyball
Malaysia Men's Volleyball Team; Malaysia Women's Volleyball Team; Malaysia Men's

Beach Volleyball Team; Malaysia Women's Beach Volleyball Team

INDIVIDUAL SPORTS

Malaysia Aikido Team; Malaysia Amateur Boxing Team; Malaysia Archery Team; Malaysia Athletics Team; Malaysia Canoeing Team; Malaysia Cycling Team; Malaysia Equestrian Team; Malaysia Fencing Team; Malaysia Gymnastics Team; Malaysia Judo Team; Malaysia Karate Team; Malaysia Modern Pentathlon Team; Malaysia Rowing Team; Malaysia Sailing Team; Malaysia Shooting Team; Malaysia Swim Team; Malaysia Tae Kwon Do Team; Malaysia Triathlon Team; Malaysia Weightlifting Team; Malaysia Wrestling Team

WINTER SPORTS

Malaysia Ice Hockey Team

NATIONAL HEROES OR PERSONIFICATIONS

Pak belang (the Malayan tiger) is the national personification, representing bravery and strength.

National heroes include Tuanku Abdul Rahman Putra, first ruler of the Federation of Malaya; Abdul Razak, prime minister in the 1970s, responsible for Malaysia's successful economic policies; Hussein Onn, called *Bapa Perpaduan* (Father of Unity); and Mahathir bin Mohamad, prime minister from 1981 to 2003.

NATIONAL HOLIDAY/ INDEPENDENCE DAY

Malaysia Day, August 31

FESTIVALS/FAIRS

Hari Raya Aidilfitri, variable dates; Chinese New Year, variable dates; Deepavali (Hindu Festival of Light), variable dates; Thaiponggol (Harvest Festival), January; Penang International Dragon Boat Festival, August

SIGNIFICANT EVENTS IN FORMATION OF NATIONAL IDENTITY

Second century B.C.E.–third century C.E. Numerous Malay kingdoms divide the Malay Peninsula.

3rd century–11th century The Malays adopt Hinduism and Buddhism and the Indian Sanskrit language and script. Islam first comes to the peninsula with Indian traders from south India*.

14th century Islam is introduced to many of the Malay peoples by traders from Arabia.

15th century–17th century The Sultanate of Malacca is established in the early 15th century and expands to control parts of present Malaysia, Thailand*, and Indonesia* at its height. The Portuguese conquer Malacca in 1511. Portugal*, Johor, and Aceh*, in present Indonesia, struggle for control of the peninsula until the Dutch take Malacca in 1641.

1786–1874 The British establish a colony on the island of Penang. In 1824, the British take control of Malacca in a treaty with the Dutch that divides the Malay Archipelago between the United Kingdom* and the Netherlands*. The British establish the Straits Settlements as a crown colony.

1874–1914 The Malay states not under direct British rule accept British advisers and guidance. Only Johor remains independent at the turn of the new century but finally accepts a British adviser in 1914. The British gain control of North Borneo and Sarawak.

1945–1960 The Japanese invasion during the Second World War initiates popular support for independence. A post-war plan to unite Malaya in a single colony flounders due to Malay objections to traditional rulers' loss of power and the plan to grant citizenship to a large Chinese minority. Malay communists launch a guerrilla war to force the British to leave Malaya. The Federation of Malaya becomes independent in 1957.

1963–1969 The federation is joined with the British colonies of North Borneo (Sabah) and Sarawak and Singapore* to form Malaysia. Conflicts with Indonesia over the territories in Borneo disrupt the new nation. Serious race riots occur involving Malays and Chinese in Kuala Lumpur and other cities.

1970s–1980s The country experiences significant economic growth and changes from an agricultural to an industrial country.

2000–2007 Demonstrations break out, demanding electoral reforms and opposing official corruption. Chinese and Hindus protest government policies that favor ethnic Malays. Unrest in the Borneo states is exacerbated by demands for greater rights and equality.

2009 The government relaxes many of the laws that favor ethnic Malays over other sectors of the population.

MALDIVES

OFFICIAL NAME
Dhivehi Raajje ge Jumhuriyyaa (Dhivehi); Republic of Maldives (English)

POPULATION
366,500 (2009e)

INHABITANTS' NAME/NICKNAME
Maldivian(s)

LANGUAGE/LANGUAGES
Dhivehi (official); English, others

RELIGION/RELIGIONS
Sunni Muslim (official); the open practice of other religions is forbidden

NATIONAL FLAG
The flag has a red field with a large green rectangle in the center bearing a vertical white crescent. The red represents the courage of the nation's heroes and their willingness to sacrifice their blood in defense of the country. The green represents the many coconut palms in the islands. The crescent moon is a Muslim symbol representing the state of the unified Muslim faith in the islands.

COAT OF ARMS/SEAL
The coat of arms consists of a tall coconut palm, a gold crescent moon and five-pointed star, two national flags crossed at the base of the palm tree, and a banner with the historical name of the country in Arabic script. The coconut palm represents the livelihood of the people. The crescent moon and star symbolize the people's Muslim faith and its authority.

CAPITAL CITY
Malé

TYPE OF GOVERNMENT
Republic

NATIONAL EMBLEM
White crescent moon

NATIONAL COLORS
Red, green, and white

NATIONAL ANTHEM
The original anthem was replaced in 1972 on the occasion of Queen Elizabeth II's official visit to the islands.

> **Gaumii Salaam (Dhivehi); National Salute (English)**
>
> We salute you in this national unity.
> We salute you, with many good wishes in the national tongue,
> Bowing the head in respect to the national symbol.
> We salute the flag that has such might;
> It falls into the sphere of victory, fortune, and success
> With its green and red and white together, and therefore we salute it,
>
> To those heroes who sought out honor and pride for the nation
> We give salute today in auspicious verses of remembrance.
> May the nation of the Maldivian Islanders advance under guard and protection

And the name of the Maldivian Islanders become great.

Thus we pledge as we salute.

We wish for their freedom and progress in
this world

And for their freedom from sorrows, and thus
we salute.

With full respect and heartfelt blessing towards religion and our leaders,

We salute you in uprightness and truth.

May the state ever have auspicious honor and
respect.

With good wishes for your continuing might,
we salute you.

CURRENCY
Maldivian rufiyaa

INTERNET IDENTIFIER
.mv

VEHICLE IDENTIFICATION PLATES/STICKERS
MV (unofficial)

PASSPORT
The passport cover has the name of the country in Dhivehi (Thaana script) and English,
the coat of arms, and the word *passport* in
Dhivehi and English.

AIRLINE
Maldivian Airways

NATIONAL TREE
Coconut palm

NATIONAL FISH
Whale shark (unofficial)

NATIONAL RESOURCES
Other than fish, the country's national resources are negligible. The country relies on
a mixture of tourism, fishing, and shipping.
Tourism is the largest industry, followed by
fishing. The limited land area makes agriculture and manufacturing less important.

FOODS
Traditional Maldivian cuisine is based on
three ingredients: coconut, fish, and rice. Pro-
cessed and dried tuna, called Maldive fish,
is considered the national food. *Kavaabu,*
a deep-fried mixture of rice, tuna, coconut,
lentils, and spices, and *curry,* beef, chicken or
fish cooked in a sauce with curry leaves and
served with rice, are also local specialties.
The national dish is *garudhiya,* boiled tuna
served with lemon, onion, chilies, and rice.

SPORTS/SPORTS TEAMS
Cricket and association football (soccer) are
the most popular sports. Maldives national
teams participate in many sports at an international level.

TEAM SPORTS
Badminton
Maldives National Badminton Team

Basketball
Maldives Basketball Team; Maldives Wom-
en's Basketball Team

Football
Maldives Football Team; Maldives Women's
Football Team; Maldives Futsal Team

Cricket
Maldives Cricket Team

Kabaddi
Maldives Kabaddi Team

Netball
Maldives Netball Team

Table Tennis
Maldives Table Tennis Team

Volleyball
Maldives Men's Volleyball Team

INDIVIDUAL SPORTS
Maldives Athletics Team; Maldives Shooting Team; Madives Swim Team; Maldives Weight Lifting Team

NATIONAL HEROES OR PERSONIFICATIONS
Koimala, first king of all the Maldive Islands in the 12th century; Muhammad Thakurufaanu al-Auzam, ruler of the Maldives after expelling the Portuguese in 1573; Sultan Muhammad Shamsuddeen Iskander III, who gave the country its first constitution in 1932

NATIONAL HOLIDAY/INDEPENDENCE DAY
Independence Day, July 26

FESTIVALS/FAIRS
Eid-Ul al'H'aa (the local name of the Islamic holiday Eid al-Adha), variable dates based on the Islamic lunar calendar; Prophet's Birthday, variable dates; Independence Day celebrations, July; Republic Day celebrations, variable dates.

SIGNIFICANT EVENTS IN FORMATION OF NATIONAL IDENTITY
Prehistory The islands are known in India* and Sri Lanka* through cultural and economic ties. Local kings rule the islands, which were originally populated from southern India. Buddhism comes to the islands around 250 B.C.E.

12th century According to Maldives legend, an Indian prince named Koimala comes to the islands as their ruler. Malé is named for him and becomes the capital of the islands. Arab invaders introduce Islam.

1558–1573 Portuguese invaders kill the sultan and take control of the islands. After 15 years, they are defeated and expelled by Muhammad

Thakurufaanu al-Auzam, who reunites the islands under his rule.

1887 Maldives becomes a British protectorate, with the rule of the sultans continuing under British advice.

1953–1959 Rebels attempt to overthrow the sultan and declare a republic, but the movement is defeated. In 1959, the inhabitants of the three southernmost atolls rebel and declare a separate republic, which is later brought back under the rule of the sultan.

1965–1968 The islands become independent as the Sultanate of the Maldives. A republic replaces the monarchy.

1970–1980 Tourism begins to be developed as an economic activity in the islands. Queen Elizabeth II of the United Kingdom visits the country in 1972.

1988 Tamil mercenaries from Sri Lanka briefly take over the government before being driven out by forces sent from India.

2004 Maldives is devastated by the tsunami that followed the Indian Ocean earthquake.

2005–2008 Political parties are recognized and legalized as part of a broad political reform. The country's first multiparty presidential elections are held in October.

2009 There is growing concern that global warming could lead to higher water levels that would cover many of the country's atolls and islands.

MARSHALL ISLANDS

OFFICIAL NAME
Aolepān Aorōkin Majeḷ (Marshallese); Republic of the Marshall Islands (English)

POPULATION
63,400 (2009e)

INHABITANTS' NAME/NICKNAME
Marshallese

LANGUAGE/LANGUAGES

English, Marshallese (both official); other Pacific Island languages, Asian languages, others

RELIGION/RELIGIONS

Protestant, 81 percent; Roman Catholic, 8.5 percent; other or no religion

NATIONAL FLAG

The flag is a blue field with a rising diagonal band of orange over white from the lower hoist to the upper fly and a white star on the upper hoist. The blue represents the Pacific Ocean, and the star represents the Marshall Islands' place in the ocean; its 24 rays represent the electoral districts, while the four elongated rays represent the principal population centers. The orange and white bands represent the equator, just to the south of the islands, and also the two island chains that make up the island nation, the Ratak and Ralik chains. The two colors also represent peace and courage.

COAT OF ARMS/SEAL

The coat of arms consists of a blue circle showing an angel with outstretched wings, symbolizing peace. Behind the angel are two islands with an outrigger canoe and a palm tree. Above the angel are the stripes and star of the national flag. The circle is bordered in white with a stylized edge resembling a nautical chart. Inscribed on the upper part of the border is "Government of the Marshall Islands," and on the bottom is the national motto in Marshallese.

MOTTO

Jepilpilin ke ejukaan (Marshallese); Accomplishment through joint effort (English)

CAPITAL CITY

Majuro

TYPE OF GOVERNMENT

Presidential republic

NATIONAL COLORS

Blue, orange, and white

NATIONAL ANTHEM

The anthem was adopted at independence in 1986. Former president Ambala Kabua wrote the lyrics.

Forever Marshall Islands

My island (heart) lies o'er the ocean,
Like a wreath of flowers upon the sea,
With the light of the Maker from far above,
Shining with the brilliance of rays of life,
Our Father's wondrous creation,
Bequeathed to us, our motherland;
I'll never leave my dear home sweet home,
God of our forefathers protect and bless
  forever Marshall Islands.

CURRENCY

U.S. dollar

INTERNET IDENTIFIER

.mh

VEHICLE IDENTIFICATION PLATES/STICKERS

MH

PASSPORT

The passport cover has the name of the country in Marshallese and English, the coat of arms, and the word *passport* in English and Marshallese.

AIRLINE

Air Marshall Islands

NATIONAL FLOWER

Flame of the forest (unofficial)

NATIONAL TREE

Palm tree

NATIONAL RESOURCES

Natural resources include coconut products, marine products, and deep-seabed minerals. U.S. government financial assistance is the mainstay of the economy, and many Marshallese work at the Ronald Reagan Ballistic Defense Test Site on Kwajalein. Remittances from Marshallese living in the United States* are a source of foreign currency and investment.

FOODS

National dishes include Micronesian chicken; barramundi cod baked in banana leaves; fruit bat pie; banana cake; banana pancakes; rice pudding; macadamia nut pie; Jakarta roasted chicken; and hot and spicy prawns.

SPORTS/SPORTS TEAMS

Baseball and basketball are popular games introduced by U.S. personnel stationed on the islands. Association football (soccer) is also very popular. Marshall Islands national teams participate in many sports at an international level.

TEAM SPORTS

Baseball

Marshall Islands Baseball Team; Marshall Islands Softball Team

Basketball

Marshall Islands Basketball Team; Marshall Islands Women's Basketball Team

Football

Marshall Islands Football Team

Table Tennis

Marshall Islands Table Tennis Team

Tennis

Pacific Oceania Davis Cup Team; Pacific Oceania Fed Cup Team (Pacific Oceania teams represent a number of Pacific island countries)

Volleyball

Marshall Islands Men's Volleyball Team; Marshall Islands Women's Volleyball Team

INDIVIDUAL SPORTS

Marshall Islands Athletics Team; Marshall Islands Swim Team; Marshall Islands Tae Kwon Do Team; Marshall Islands Weight Lifting Team; Marshall Islands Wrestling Team

NATIONAL HEROES OR PERSONIFICATIONS

Ambata Kabua, a president of the republic who wrote the lyrics to the national anthem; Kessai Note, president of the republic from 2000 to 2008 and the first commoner (rather than traditional chief) to be elected to the presidency

NATIONAL HOLIDAY/INDEPENDENCE DAY

Independence Day, October 21

FESTIVALS/FAIRS

Coconut Cup Sailing Regatta, April; Outrigger Marshall Islands Cup (traditional canoe races), April; Constitution Day Festival, May; Lutok Koppan Alele, September; Chamber of Commerce Christmas Festival, December.

SIGNIFICANT EVENTS IN FORMATION OF NATIONAL IDENTITY

200 B.C.E. Micronesian seafarers settle the islands, calling the atolls Aelon Kein Ad, meaning "our islands." The atolls are ruled as local chiefdoms by an aristocratic class of nobles.

1521–1529 C.E. Portuguese and Spanish navigators visit the islands. European diseases devastate the island population.

1592 Spain* lays formal claim to the islands, which are mostly ignored.

1788 The islands are called the Marshall Islands for British Captain John Marshall who sails through the atolls with convicts bound for Australia*.

1864–1885 A German trading company establishes a base in the islands, trading for copra and other island products. Other German trading companies soon follow. Germany* annexes the islands for a payment of $4.5 million in compensation to Spain. Administration of the islands is left to the powerful trading companies. Forced labor and other mistreatment ravage the population.

1886–1887 Germany declares a protectorate over the Marshall Islands. The Jaluit Company, a German company, is given the right to administer the islands.

1914–1920 Japanese forces take control of the islands during World War I. The League of Nations gives Japan* a mandate to administer the islands. Several large military installations are built.

1940–1944 The Japanese fortify the islands when the Second World War begins. U.S. troops take the islands in heavy fighting in 1944.

1946–1947 The United States begins a program of nuclear testing on Bikini Atoll. The inhabitants are evacuated but promised they can return when the tests are finished. The Marshall Islands become part of the Trust Territory of the Pacific Islands, created by the United Nations under U.S. administration.

1948–1954 The inhabitants of Eniwetok Atoll are forced to evacuate as the United States expands its nuclear tests. The most powerful hydrogen bomb ever tested by the United States is detonated over Bikini Atoll.

1965–1969 The Congress of Micronesia is created in preparation for self-government of the trust territory. The U.S. government begins the long-term decontamination of Bikini.

1970s The islanders are told they can return to Bikini but are later found to have dangerous levels of radiation in their bodies and are again evacuated. Many develop severe health problems. The Marshall Islands withdraws from the Congress of Micronesia in order to gain greater independence. A new government is formed under Amata Kabua.

1980–1986 The inhabitants of Eniwetok Atoll are allowed to return. The islands are officially re-named the Republic of the Marshall Islands. The islanders vote to approve a compact of free association with the United States, which gives the islands independence but retains financial aid and other forms of support by the U.S. government, which promises to decontaminate the islands and pay compensation for damage.

1990 The United Nations terminates the trusteeship. Studies show the Marshall Islands will be underwater by 2030 because of global warming.

2000–2007 A new compact of free association is signed with the United States in 2003. The islands become a tax haven but are forced by international criticism to tighten laws. Chaotic elections in 2007 are challenged in court.

2008–2009 A new president takes office in 2008, promising to press the United States over unpaid claims by islanders stemming from the nuclear tests in the 1940s and 1950s. The threat of global warming and rising sea levels is a major concern.

MICRONESIA

OFFICIAL NAME
Federated States of Micronesia

POPULATION
110,700 (2009e)

INHABITANTS' NAME/NICKNAME
Micronesian(s)

LANGUAGE/LANGUAGES
English (official); Ulithian, Woleaian, Yapese, Pohnpeian, Kosraean, Chuukese (official at state or local levels); Japanese, others

RELIGION/RELIGIONS
Roman Catholic, 50 percent; Protestant, 47 percent; other or no religion

NATIONAL FLAG
The flag has a pale blue field with four five-pointed white stars arranged in a diamond

pattern in the center. The blue represents the Pacific Ocean that surrounds the Micronesian islands, and the four stars represent the four island groups in the federation: Chuuk, Pohnpei, Kosrae, and Yap.

COAT OF ARMS/SEAL

The coat of arms is a circle with a centered floating coconut with a green sprout on a blue sea. Above the coconut on a light blue sky are the four stars of the national flag. Below the coconut is a banner inscribed with the national motto and the year 1979. Surrounding the circle is a yellow border resembling ship's rope, around which is written "Government of the Federated States of Micronesia," with a blue border resembling the border of a nautical chart.

MOTTO

Peace, Unity, Liberty

CAPITAL CITY

Palikir

TYPE OF GOVERNMENT

Constitutional federation of four states

NATIONAL COLORS

Pale blue and white

NATIONAL ANTHEM

The anthem was adapted from the melody of a German patriotic song of the early 19th century. It was adopted as the national anthem in 1991.

Patriots of Micronesia

'Tis here we are pledging,
with heart and with hand,
Full measure of devotion
to thee, our native land,
Full measure of devotion
to thee, our native land.

Now all join the chorus,
let union abide.

Across all Micronesia
join hands on every side,
Across all Micronesia
join hands on every side.

We all work together,
with hearts, voice, and hand,
Till we have made these islands
another promised land,
Till we have made these islands
another promised land.

PATRON SAINT

Mary, Queen of Peace; Saint Peter Channel (patron saints of Oceania)

CURRENCY

U.S. dollar

INTERNET IDENTIFIER

.fm

VEHICLE IDENTIFICATION PLATES/STICKERS

FSM

PASSPORT

The passport cover has the name of the country in English, the coat of arms, and the word *passport*.

NATIONAL FLOWER

Plumeria (unofficial)

NATIONAL TREE

Coconut palm

NATIONAL RESOURCES

Natural resources include forests, marine products, deep-seabed minerals, and phosphates. Tourism is growing, supported by island scenery, sandy beaches, a pleasant climate, and the ruined city of Nan Madol; however, travel distance and a lack of air connections hamper the industry. Remittances from Micronesians living in the United States* are a major source of income.

FOODS

Local specialties include bonnie pepper chicken, chicken cooked with carrots, cabbage, and bonnie peppers; shrimp in coconut sauce; island fish stuffed with onions and wrapped in banana leaves for cooking; Micronesian chicken, chicken breasts cooked with lemon, onions, beer, soy sauce, and cloves; and fruit bat soup.

SPORTS/SPORTS TEAMS

Baseball and association football (soccer) are the most popular sports. Micronesia national teams participate in many sports at an international level.

TEAM SPORTS

Baseball

Federated States of Micronesia Baseball Team; Federated States of Micronesia Men's Softball Team; Federated States of Micronesia Women's Softball Team

Basketball

Federated States of Micronesia Basketball Team; Federated States of Micronesia Women's Basketball Team

Football

Federated States of Micronesia Football Team, nickname the Four Stars

Table Tennis

Federated States of Micronesia Table Tennis Team

Tennis

Pacific Oceania Davis Cup Team; Pacific Oceania Fed Cup Team; (Pacific Oceania teams represent a number of Pacific island countries)

Volleyball

Federated States of Micronesia Men's Volleyball Team; Federated States of Micronesia Women's Volleyball Team

INDIVIDUAL SPORTS

Federated States of Micronesia Athletics Team; Federated States of Micronesia Sailing Team; Federated States of Micronesia Swim Team; Federated States of Micronesia Weight Lifting Team; Federated States of Micronesia Wrestling Team

NATIONAL HEROES OR PERSONIFICATIONS

Olifat, or Wolphat, a Micronesian trickster figuring in many tales and legends, is the national personification; Emanuel "Manny" Mori, elected five times to congress and in 2007 elected as president of the federation

NATIONAL HOLIDAY/ INDEPENDENCE DAY

Constitution Day, May 10

FESTIVALS/FAIRS

Yap Day Festival, March; Independence Day celebrations, November; Micronesia Festival, May

SIGNIFICANT EVENTS IN FORMATION OF NATIONAL IDENTITY

2000 B.C.E.–500 C.E. The seafaring ancestors of the Micronesians settle the islands from the Philippines* and Indonesia*. The first settlements are on Yap; later arrivals from Melanesia settle Kosrae, Pohnpei, and Chuuk. Small chiefdoms are established on each major island.

500–1500 A centralized kingdom with its capital at Nan Madol is established on Pohnpei. Nan Madol, built on a series of islands connected by canals, would later be called the Venice of the Pacific. The state collapses and disappears.

1521 Ferdinand Magellan sails through the region. Portuguese and Spanish ships visit the islands, which are claimed by Spain*.

1600–1800 The islands, with little treasure in the European sense, are mostly ignored. European diseases ravage the islands, and slavers, called blackbirders, raid the islands for captives to sell.

1899–1920 The Spanish government sells the islands to Germany*. German trading companies become the islands' administrators, often known for harsh and arbitrary rule. The Japanese take the islands at the outbreak of the First World War. The islands become part of a Japanese League of Nations mandate and are heavily fortified. Japanese immigrants settle on many of the larger islands.

1941–1947 Used as stationary aircraft carriers, the islands are devastated in heavy fighting in the Second World War. The islands become a United Nations trust territory under the administration of the United States.

1979 Four of the trusteeship's districts ratify a new constitution to become the Federated States of Micronesia. Palau*, the Marshall Islands*, and the Northern Mariana Islands* choose not to become part of the new federation.

1986–2004 A compact is signed with the United States that ends the trusteeship and paves the way for the independence of the federation. The United States undertakes to ensure the security of the islands and to provide other services and aid. The pact is renewed in 2004.

2004–2008 The U.S. government provides about $100 million in annual assistance and remains the federation's major trading partner. A movement in Chuuk to separate from the federation remains a threat to the geographically extensive nation.

2009 Global warming and rising sea levels threaten to swamp many of the low-lying islands.

MONGOLIA

OFFICIAL NAME
Mongol uls (transliteration from Mongolian); Mongolia (English)

POPULATION
3,014,700 (2009e)

INHABITANTS' NAME/NICKNAME
Mongolian(s); Mongol(s)

LANGUAGE/LANGUAGES
Khalkha Mongolian (official); other Mongol languages, Turkic languages, English, Russian, others

RELIGION/RELIGIONS
Tibetan Buddhist, 50 percent; shamanist (indigenous beliefs), Christian, Muslim, other or no religion

NATIONAL FLAG
The flag has three vertical stripes of red, pale blue and red. Centered on the red stripe at the hoist is the national emblem, the *soyombo*, a yellow columnar design of abstract and geometric representations of the elements—fire, the sun, the moon, earth, water—and the *taijitu*, the yin-yang symbol.

COAT OF ARMS/SEAL
The coat of arms consist of a circle with a blue background representing the sky. At the center of the circle is a combination of the *soyombo* and the wind horse that symbolizes Mongolia's independence, sovereignty, and spirit. Below the horse is a green mountain range, with the wheel of destiny in the center. Below the wheel is a *khadag,* a ceremonial scarf. The outer rim of the circle features a *fumen nusan,* representing eternity, and above it, a *chandmani,* representing Buddhism's Three Jewels, which in Mongolian tradition grants wishes and represents the past, present, and future.

CAPITAL CITY
Ulan Bator

TYPE OF GOVERNMENT
Parliamentary republic

NATIONAL EMBLEM
The *soyombo*

NATIONAL COLORS
Red and white

NATIONAL ANTHEM
The anthem was officially adopted in 1950, although the lyrics have undergone several changes. In 2006, the lyrics were revised to commemorate Genghis Khan.

National Anthem of Mongolia
Our sacred revolutionary country
Is the ancestral home of all Mongols
We will never yield at the foot of an enemy
And we will prosper for eternity

With all the honest nations of the world
Forming into unified ranks
With an iron will and all our strength
Let us develop our beloved Mongolia

The fortunate people of brave Mongolia
Have freed themselves from suffering to enjoy
  happiness
The pillar of happiness, the key to
  development
Let our majestic nation live forever!

With all the honest countries of the world
Forming into unified ranks
With an iron will and all our strength
Let us develop our beloved Mongolia

CURRENCY
Mongolian tögrög or tugrug

INTERNET IDENTIFIER
.mn

VEHICLE IDENTIFICATION PLATES/STICKERS
MGL (official); MNG (unofficial). The older designation, MNG, is still widely used, however the official designation is now MGL.

PASSPORT
The passport cover has the national emblem and the name of the country in the Mongolian script, the word *passport* in English, and the name of the country, Mongolia, at the bottom.

AIRLINE
Mongolian Airlines MIAT

NATIONAL FLOWER
Lotus (unofficial)

NATIONAL ANIMAL
Gobi bull; Mongol horse (unofficial)

NATIONAL RESOURCES
Natural resources include oil, coal, copper, molybdenum, tungsten, phosphates, tin, nickel, zinc, fluorspar, gold, silver, and iron. The Mongolian economy is centered on agriculture and mining. The majority of the population outside the urban areas engages in herding.

FOODS
Boodog, a whole goat roasted from the inside with hot coals, is considered the national dish. *Suutei tsai,* a salty tea with milk, is the national drink. Other national specialties include *buuz,* a type of dumpling stuffed with meat; *khuushuur,* a meat pastry; *khorkhog,* a stew of meat and vegetables; and *boortsog,* a sweet biscuit.

SPORTS/SPORTS TEAMS
Traditional sports—wrestling, archery, and horseracing—are the most popular in the country. Association football (soccer) and basketball are mostly confined to large urban areas. Mongolia national teams participate in many sports at an international level.

TEAM SPORTS
Badminton
Mongolia Badminton Team

Baseball
Mongolia Baseball Team; Mongolia Softball Team

Basketball

Mongolia Basketball Team; Mongolia Women's Basketball Team

Football

Mongolia Football Team; Mongolia Women's Football Team; Mongolia Rugby Union Team

Hockey

Mongolia Ice Hockey Team; Mongolia Field Hockey Team

Netball

Mongolia Netball Team

Racing

Mongolia Speedway Team

Table Tennis

Mongolia Table Tennis Team

Tennis

Mongolia Davis Cup Team

Volleyball

Mongolia Men's Volleyball Team; Mongolia Women's Volleyball Team

INDIVIDUAL SPORTS

Mongolia Amateur Boxing Team; Mongolia Archery Team; Mongolia Athletics Team; Mongolia Canoeing Team; Mongolia Cycling Team; Mongolia Equestrian Team; Mongolia Gymnastics Team; Mongolia Judo Team; Mongolia Karate Team; Mongolia Shooting Team; Mongolia Swim Team; Mongolia Tae Kwon Do Team; Mongolia Weight Lifting Team; Mongolia Wrestling Team

WINTER SPORTS

Mongolia Bandy Team; Mongolia Biathlon Team; Mongolia Ice Hockey Team; Mongolia Skating Team

NATIONAL HEROES OR PERSONIFICATIONS

Modu Chanyu, the unifier of the Mongol peoples and founder of the Xiongnu (Hun) Empire; Genghis Khan, the leader who united the Mongols and created the Mongol Empire in the 12th and 13th centuries; Kublai Khan, the founder of the Mongol Yuan Dynasty that ruled Mongolia and China* in the 13th century; Altan Khan, Mongol military leader in the 16th century; Damdin Sükhbaatar, leader of the 1921 war of liberation

NATIONAL HOLIDAY/INDEPENDENCE DAY

Independence Day/Revolution Day, July 11

FESTIVALS/FAIRS

Goyol Fashion Festival, December; Naadam Festival of the Three Games of Men, July; Tsagaan Sar (White Month), February; Thousand Camel Festival, February; Nomads Festival, September

SIGNIFICANT EVENTS IN FORMATION OF NATIONAL IDENTITY

208 B.C.E.–10th century C.E.   The nomadic peoples of the vast steppe lands form tribal groups. The threat to China leads to the construction of the Great Wall of China.

20 B.C.E.–174 B.C.E.   The Mongol tribes form a loose confederation under Modu Chanyu.

10th century–12th century   The Mongols are divided into numerous tribes, often in transient alliances but more often involved in intertribal wars.

12th century–13th century   A local chief named Temüjin finally succeeds in uniting the warring Mongol tribes. In 1206, he takes the name Genghis Khan and begins a series of military campaigns that sweep through much of Asia to form the Mongol Empire. Under his successors, the empire stretches from present Poland* in the west to Korea* in the east and Vietnam* in the south, with a population of more than 100 million people.

1259–1368 Following Genghis Khan's death in 1259, the empire is divided. One of the divisions includes the Mongol homeland and China, which the Mongols ruled as the Yuan Dynasty, created by Kublai Khan. The Yuan Dynasty ends in 1368 with the emergence of the Chinese Ming Dynasty. Ming armies pursue the Mongols back into Mongolia, which is laid waste, pushing the Mongols back into anarchy and their former tribal existence.

16th century Intermittent war with the Chinese Empire continues to disrupt the Mongol tribes. Tibetan Buddhism becomes the majority religion.

17th century The powerful Manchu people conquer Inner Mongolia by 1636 and move south to conquer China in 1644. The Chinese force the Khalka Mongols to submit to Chinese rule in 1691.

1800–1911 The Manchu rulers divide the region into small feudal and ecclesiastical provinces. Harsh taxes and corruption result in widespread poverty. The fall of the Manchu Qing Dynasty in China is followed by the declaration of Mongolia's independence in the territory known as Outer Mongolia. Chinese military leaders prevent the Mongols of Inner Mongolia from uniting with the new state.

1919–1921 Russian protection of the Mongol state ends with the Russian Revolution, opening the way for Chinese occupation and incorporation into the Republic of China. In 1921, aided by the Soviet Union, the Mongols rebel and drive the Chinese from the country.

1924–1937 Mongolia is proclaimed the Mongolian People's Republic, with close ties to the Soviet Union. Stalinist purges, the destruction of Buddhist monasteries, and persecution of noncommunists cost the lives of more than 30,000 people.

1949–1960 Following the communist victory in China's civil war, the Chinese finally recognize Mongolia's independence. The country maintains its alliance with the Soviet Union following the Soviet-Chinese split in the late 1950s.

1990s The introduction of a more liberal regime in the Soviet Union in the late 1980s influences Mongolian politics and begins the process that leads to the peaceful Democratic Revolution and the introduction of multiparty politics.

1996 Elections result in the peaceful transition of power from the former communists to a coalition of opposition parties.

2000–2008 The former communists return to power following an election but retain Mongolia's democratic system. Two days after parliamentary elections in 2008, civilian demonstrations accusing the government of fraud turn to violent rioting, leaving several dead and many wounded.

2009 Some Mongols voice support for the reunification of Mongolia, including the large territory known as Inner Mongolia in China.

MYANMAR

OFFICIAL NAME
Pyi-daung-zu Myan-ma Naing-ngan-daw (Myanmarese); Union of Myanmar (English)

POPULATION
56,783,800 (2009e)

INHABITANTS' NAME/NICKNAME
Myanmarese or Burmese

LANGUAGE/LANGUAGES
Burmese or Myanmarese (official); Jingpo, Shan, Karen, Mon (recognized regional languages); English, others

RELIGION/RELIGIONS
Buddhist, about 89 percent; Christian, 4 percent; Muslim, 4 percent; traditional beliefs, Hindu, other or no religion

NATIONAL FLAG
The flag is a red field with a blue canton on the upper hoist charged with a white cogwheel and rice plant surrounded by 14 small, white, five-pointed stars. The red stands for the courage of the people, blue is for peace,

and white is for purity. The cogwheel represents industry, the rice plant represents agriculture, and the 14 stars symbolize the union of 14 states.

COAT OF ARMS/SEAL

The coat of arms has a central white cogwheel around a map of the country. On each side of the cogwheel is a blue *chinthe* (mythical creature half lion and half dragon) facing outward. The cogwheel and lions are surrounded by traditional flower designs. Above the cogwheel is a white, five-pointed star and below is a red banner bearing the a form of the name of the country in the Pali script, the Union of Socialist Myanmar.

CAPITAL CITY

Naypyidaw; many ministries and departments remain in Yangon, formerly called Rangoon

TYPE OF GOVERNMENT

Military dictatorship under a military junta

NATIONAL EMBLEM

Chinthe (mythical creature half lion and half dragon)

NATIONAL COLORS

Red, blue, and white

NATIONAL ANTHEM

The anthem was used as a national symbol during the Japanese occupation in World War II. It was officially adopted in 1947, just prior to independence, with several changes of lyrics since then.

> **Kaba Ma Kyei (Till the End of the World, Myanmar)**
>
> Till the end of the world, Myanmar!
> We love our land because this is our real inheritance.
> We will sacrifice our lives to protect our country.

> This is our nation, a land of our own
> For our nation's good, we will shoulder the task
> Standing as one in duty to our precious land.

CURRENCY

Myanmarese kyat

INTERNET IDENTIFIER

.mm

VEHICLE IDENTIFICATION PLATES/STICKERS

MYA

PASSPORT

The passport cover has the name of the country in Myanmarese, the coat of arms, the name of the country in English, and the word *passport* in Myanmarese and English.

AIRLINE

Myanma Airways

NATIONAL FLOWER

Paduak flower

NATIONAL TREE

Paduak (rosewood)

NATIONAL ANIMAL

Burmese tiger

NATIONAL BIRD

Peacock

NATIONAL RESOURCES

Natural resources include petroleum, timber, tin, antimony, zinc, copper, tungsten, lead, coal, some marble, limestone, precious stones, natural gas, and hydropower. The country is one of the poorest nations in Southeast Asia, suffering from decades of stagnation, mismanagement, and isolation. The lack of an educated workforce skilled in modern technology contributes to the growing economic problems. Under British rule until 1948, the country was the wealthiest and most advanced in Southeast Asia. Illegal drugs are now one of the most lucrative industries. Remittances from Myanmarese living outside the country are a major source of foreign currency.

Foods

Mohinga, a soup of fish, vegetables, and rice vermicelli, is considered the national dish. *Lahpet,* pickled tea leaves, is also considered a national dish. Other specialties include *lethok son,* a spicy salad of rice and vegetables; *oh-no khauk swe,* a dish of curry, rice noodles, chicken, and coconut milk; *kya zan hinga,* a soup of dried shrimp, glass noodles, wood-ear mushrooms, egg, dried flowers, and onions; *Shan khauk swe,* Shan-style rice noodles with chicken or pork, onions, garlic, tomatoes, chilies, and peanuts; and *ng-abaung doke,* a Mon dish of vegetables and shrimp cooked in banana leaves.

Sports/Sports Teams

The national sport is *chinglone,* a team sport played with a cane ball. Traditional boxing is also very popular. Myanmar national teams participate in many sports at a national level.

Team Sports

Badminton
Myanmar Badminton Team

Baseball
Myanmar Baseball Team

Basketball
Myanmar Basketball Team; Myanmar Women's Basketball Team

Cricket
Myanmar Cricket Team

Football
Myanmar Football Team; Myanmar Women's Football Team; Myanmar Futsal Team; Myanmar Under-19 Football Team; Myanmar Women's Under-19 Football Team

Hockey
Myanmar Field Hockey Team

Table Tennis
Myanmar Table Tennis Team

Volleyball
Myanmar Men's Volleyball Team; Myanmar Women's Volleyball Team

Individual Sports

Myanmar Amateur Boxing Team; Myanmar Archery Team; Myanmar Athletics Team; Myanmar Canoeing Team; Myanmar Cycling Team; Myanmar Equestrian Team; Myanmar Fencing Team; Myanmar Gymnastics Team; Myanmar Judo Team; Myanmar Karate Team; Myanmar Rowing Team; Myanmar Sailing Team; Myanmar Shooting Team; Myanmar Swim Team; Myanmar Tae Kwon Do Team; Myanmar Weight Lifting Team

National Heroes or Personifications

Bogyoke Aung San, a nationalist leader instrumental in securing independence in 1948; Zarganar, leader of the 1988 democracy movement; Tabinshwehti, the king responsible for unifying the country in 1539; Mahabandoola, a resourceful military leader during the First Anglo-Burmese War in the 1820s; Aung San Suu Kyi, leader of the democracy movement; U Wisara, who died in prison after a 166-day hunger strike to protest a rule that forbade him to wear his Buddhist robes while imprisoned by the British

National Holiday/Independence Day

Union Day, February 12; Independence Day, January 4

Festivals/Fairs

Thingyan (Water Festival), April; Kasone Festival, May; Thadingyut (Full-Moon Day or Festival of Lights), usually October

Significant Events in Formation of National Identity

900 B.C.E. The Mons, related to the Khmers of Cambodia*, are thought to be the earliest settlers of the region. The Mon kingdom embraces Theravada Buddhism.

First century B.C.E. The Phu settle the central Irrawaddy River basin, but the Mon kingdom continues to expand.

9th century C.E.–11th century C.E. The Bamar people, later known as the Burmans, migrate to the region from eastern Tibet*. In 1044, the Burmans overwhelm the Mon kingdom while adopting much of the more advanced Mon culture.

13th century The Burmans' power and expansion is ended by the Mongol invasion. In the subsequent centuries, a number of small kingdoms are created, many by the Burman peoples of the region. The period is characterized by near constant warfare.

1486–1752 The Burman Konbaung Dynasty unifies lower Burma and creates a powerful state that focuses on warfare with the Mons, the Shans to the north, and the Thais to the east.

1782–1885 Constant war with the Thai kingdom, Siam, is inconclusive, but conquests in Manipur and Assam bring the Burmans into conflict with the British in India*. The British defeat the Burmans in the First Anglo-Burmese War in the 1820s, taking much territory. The Second Anglo-Burmese War, in 1852, ends with the British occupying the Burman heartland in the Irrawaddy Valley. The Third Anglo-Burmese War ends in 1885 with the remaining Burmese territories falling under British rule. The British pacify the Shans, Kachins, and Chins in the regions around Burma.

1886–1946 The British import Indian and Chinese workers, who soon outnumber the Burmese in urban areas. In 1937, British Burma and its associated territories are separated from British India. Burmese nationalists, promised independence, initially support Japan* during World War II.

1947–1948 Aung San, the influential leader of the independence movement, creates a provisional government. Political rivals assassinate him and his ministers. Burma, called the Union of Burma, becomes independent. Rebellions break out among the Karens and other non-Burman peoples who had been under separate British administrations and had rejected inclusion in Burma.

1948–1962 Instability, rebellions in the non-Burman regions, and political rivalries disrupt the country. A military coup takes control of the government and creates a socialist state under a military dictatorship that continues to the present.

1962–1988 Continuing ethnic rebellions, sporadic student demonstrations, and protests led by Buddhist monks are all brutally suppressed in the 1960s and 1970s and the early 1980s. Forced labor, particularly widespread in non-Burman regions, is used to build roads and other projects.

1988 Widespread protests over economic mismanagement and political oppression initiate pro-democracy demonstrations across the country. Hundreds are killed as the military attacks peaceful protests. The name of the country is changed to Myanmar.

1990 Bowing to international pressure, the military government allows free elections. The National League for Democracy, led by Aung San Suu Kyi, the daughter of the independence-war hero, wins a majority in the legislature. The government annuls the results, arrests Aung San Suu Kyi, and suppresses the democracy movement.

1992 Several of the rebellious ethnic groups, exhausted from decades of fighting the government, sign cease-fire agreements.

1997 The countries of the Association of Southeast Asian Nations organization (ASEAN) allow Myanmar to become a member state, believing erroneously that membership would moderate the military government's behavior.

2005 The International Labor Organization denounces the military government for the continuous forced labor of its citizens.

2007 Small demonstrations by dissidents denouncing corruption and oppression lead to widespread protests. The military ends the demonstrations, and many well-known dissidents disappear into government prisons. Buddhist monks take the lead in new demonstrations that are also attacked by security forces.

2008 The government announces that a referendum will be held on a new draft constitution, possibly followed by elections, in 2010. A massive cyclone strikes the country. The government's slow and hesitant response to the disaster, which leaves thousands dead and many more injured and homeless, brings widespread criticism and protests. Hundreds of political activists are given sentences of up to 65 years in a series of secret trials.

2009 Neighboring Thailand* expels hundreds of Muslim Rohingya refugees who had fled from Myanmar. The government continues to deny the existence of the large Rohingya minority.

NAGALAND

OFFICIAL NAME

State of Nagaland; Nagalim

Nagalim is the Nagas' name for their homeland, including territory in India* and Myanmar*. Technically, both names are the same; *lim* is simply a Naga word for land. However, in 1963, India created a state called Nagaland covering a small portion of the traditional Nagaland. To avoid confusion, *Nagalim* is now used to refer to the entire Naga homeland currently divided between India and Myanmar.

POPULATION

2,104,200 (2009e)

INHABITANTS' NAME/NICKNAME

Naga(s)

LANGUAGE/LANGUAGES

English, Nagamese (both official); Ao, Sema, Konyak, Hindi, others

RELIGION/RELIGIONS

Christian, 90 percent (mostly Baptist); Hindu, 7 percent; Muslim, 2 percent; other or no religion

NATIONAL FLAG

The flag adopted when the Nagas declared independence in 1947 is a pale blue field bearing a rainbow of red, yellow, and green from lower hoist to upper fly below a white, six-pointed star on the upper hoist. The blue represents the sky over Nagalim, the rainbow signifies the promise of the future, and the star stands for the major divisions of the Naga nation and for liberty and independence. Indian states do not have official flags but do have seals or coats of arms.

COAT OF ARMS/SEAL

The seal of the Indian state of Nagaland is a circle with a black and white bull standing on green ground against a white background and surrounded by wide red circle, bearing the words *Unity* at the top and *Government of Nagaland* at the bottom.

CAPITAL CITY

Kohima

TYPE OF GOVERNMENT

State government within India

NATIONAL EMBLEM

Black and white horned bull's head

NATIONAL COLORS

Blue and white

NATIONAL ANTHEM

The national anthem, "God Bless Our Nagaland," was adopted in 1947 but has since been banned by Indian authorities. Lyrics are unavailable.

CURRENCY
Indian rupee

VEHICLE IDENTIFICATION PLATES/STICKERS
IND India (official); FRN Federal Republic of Nagalim (unofficial)

PASSPORT
Nagas are Indian citizens and travel on Indian passports.

NATIONAL FLOWER
Kew hi (unofficial)

NATIONAL ANIMAL
Naga bull

NATIONAL BIRD
Hornbill

NATIONAL RESOURCES
Natural resources include timber, petroleum, coal, gold, iron ore, semiprecious stones, and copper. Petroleum is the most important natural resource, but exploitation has been stopped due to Naga opposition. Agriculture is the most important economic activity in Nagaland, with more than 90 percent of the population employed in farming. Forestry is also an important source of income. Cottage industries, such as weaving, woodwork, and pottery, are also an important source of revenue. Tourism is important but largely limited due to insurgency during the past five decades.

FOODS
Pork with bamboo shoots is considered the national dish. Assam curry is also very popular, along with chicken Naga, a very hot chicken dish with Jolokia peppers, and Naga pork, a dish of diced pork, tomatoes, red chilies, and garlic.

SPORTS/SPORTS TEAMS
Cricket and association football (soccer) are the most popular sports. Many traditional sports are still practiced. Nagaland national teams participate in cricket and football at an international level.

TEAM SPORTS
Cricket
Nagaland Cricket Team

Football
Nagaland Football Team

NATIONAL HEROES OR PERSONIFICATIONS
Angami Zapu Phizo, leader of the independence movement, called Father of the Nagas; Isaac Chishi Swu, leader of the Nationalist Socialist Council of Nagaland and proponent of independence for Greater Nagalim

NATIONAL HOLIDAY/ INDEPENDENCE DAY
Independence Day, August 14

FESTIVALS/FAIRS
Hornbill Festival, first week of December; Sekrenyi (Harvest Festival), November; Aoleang Monyu Festival, April; Moatsu Mong Festival, May; Tsukhenyie Festival, March

SIGNIFICANT EVENTS IN FORMATION OF NATIONAL IDENTITY
10th century B.C.E.–13th century C.E. The Naga tribes migrate to the region from their original homes in present Mongolia*.

13th century Invaders from present Myanmar record the fierce resistance of the Naga tribes.

1832 The British move into the mountains, giving the Nagas their first contact with Europeans. After a violent clash, the British withdraw.

1851–1881 Construction of a British road from Manipur to Burma necessitates the subjugation of the Naga tribes. A British force burns Kohima and kills more than a hundred Nagas. Slaughter-and-withdraw becomes the British policy for dealing with the hostile Nagas.

1881–1925 British and American missionaries convert the majority to Christianity and introduce modern education through mission schools. A written form of the lingua franca begins the process of molding a distinct Naga identity.

1929 Christian Naga leaders demand the unification of Naga territories in India and Burma.

1942–1945 The Japanese, during the Second World War, promise independence, persuading some Naga leaders to fight against the British. The fighting causes a serious split in the Naga leadership. At the end of the war, the Nagas open negotiations on separate independence.

1947 The Naga leaders, pressed by the British, refuse to join India. Mohandas Gandhi, the Indian leader, promises independence should they not wish to join India. On August 14, 1947, one day before India is to receive independence, the Naga leadership declares the independence of Nagaland. Nagaland is not specifically included in the India Independence Act. Gandhi is assassinated, and the Indian government refuses to fulfill his promise.

1950–1955 Atrocities committed by the Indian army, an economic blockade, and official harassment end when the Naga leaders finally submit. In 1951, the dissatisfied Nagas organize a plebiscite that overwhelmingly reaffirms the 1947 declaration of independence. The Naga rebellion resumes.

1956–1975 The Federal Republic of Nagaland is organized. Indian troops are given broad powers to fight the rebels with mass killings, rape, and displacement of populations. By 1975, tens of thousands of people have died in the war.

1960–1963 The Indian government, unable to subdue the Nagas, grants autonomy as a district within the state of Assam and then full statehood in 1963. The Nagas offer to end the rebellion in exchange for a democratic referendum on independence but are rebuffed, and the rebellion continues.

1995–1999 Nagaland is declared a disturbed area, allowing security forces to take drastic measures to bring the state under control. A cease-fire is signed in 1998. An underground referendum shows overwhelming support for independence.

2000–2001 The Indian government rejects Naga demands for negotiations before new elections are held in the state of Nagaland and demands that the cease-fire be extended to Naga-populated areas in neighboring states. A Baptist-sponsored conference reaches an agreement to end intertribal conflicts as a step toward the unification of the Naga homeland.

2007–2009 A new state government is elected. Factional disputes and renewed violence are met by the imposition of direct rule by the Indian government.

See also India

NAURU

OFFICIAL NAME
Ripublik Naoero (Nauruan); Republic of Nauru (English)

POPULATION
9,300 (2009e)

INHABITANTS' NAME/NICKNAME
Nauruan(s)

LANGUAGE/LANGUAGES
English, Nauruan (both official); others

RELIGION/RELIGIONS
Christian 73 percent (one-third Protestant, two-thirds Roman Catholic); Baha'i, 10 percent; other or no religion

NATIONAL FLAG

The flag is a blue field with a narrow horizontal yellow stripe in the center and a white, 12-pointed star on the lower hoist. The blue represents the Pacific Ocean, the yellow stripe represents the equator, and the white star represents Nauru's location in the seas just south of the equator. The 12 rays represent the island's original 12 tribes. The color white symbolizes the phosphates that brought the nation prosperity.

COAT OF ARMS/SEAL

The coat of arms consists of a shield divided and separated in the middle. The upper section depicts the chemical symbol for phosphorus against a golden woven background. The lower left section has a black frigate bird on a perch above blue and white ocean waves. The lower right section has a branch of calophyllum flowers on a blue background. The shield is surrounded by images of tribal chief gear, which was worn to ceremonies—ropes from palm leaves, feathers of the frigate bird, and shark teeth. The star centered above the shield is taken from the flag. The ribbon above it bears the name of the island in the Nauruan language. The ribbon under the shield bears the national motto.

MOTTO

God's Will First

CAPITAL CITY

No official capital; the largest town is Yaren

TYPE OF GOVERNMENT

Republic

NATIONAL EMBLEM

Frigate bird

NATIONAL COLORS

Blue and yellow

NATIONAL ANTHEM

The anthem, composed by an Australian, was adopted upon independence from Australia* in 1968.

Nauru Bwiema (Nauruan); Song of Nauru (English)

Nauru our homeland, the land we dearly love,
We all pray for you and we also praise your name.
Since long ago you have been the home of our great forefathers
And will be for generations yet to come.
We all join in together to honor your flag,
And we shall rejoice together and say;
Nauru for evermore!

CURRENCY

Australian dollar

INTERNET IDENTIFIER

.nr

VEHICLE IDENTIFICATION PLATES/STICKERS

NAU

PASSPORT

The passport cover has the name of the country in Nauruan and English, the coat of arms, and the word *passport* in Nauruan and English.

AIRLINE

Our Airline

NATIONAL FLOWER

Calophyllum

NATIONAL TREE

Calophyllum

NATIONAL BIRD

Black frigate bird

NATIONAL FISH

Ibija (milkfish) (unofficial)

NATIONAL RESOURCES

Natural resources are limited to phosphates and fish. Nauru's economy depends almost entirely on declining phosphate deposits; there are few other resources, and most necessities are imported. The government places a percentage of phosphate earnings in the Nauru Phosphate Royalties Trust. The trust manages long-term investments, intended to support the citizens once the phosphate reserves have been exhausted. However, a history of bad investments, financial mismanagement, overspending, and corruption has reduced the trust's fixed and current assets. Remittances from Nauruans living outside the country are a source of foreign currency. Financial aid from Australia is also very important.

FOODS

Sweet potatoes, coconut, fish, and pork are the main ingredients of Nauruan cuisine. Fresh fish served with rice is considered the national dish. Other specialties include chicken *fafa*, a chicken and taro leaf dish; *pahua taloro*, clams in coconut sauce; shrimp in coconut milk; *ufi*, baked yams with coconut cream; *uru*, roasted breadfruit; and *po'e*, a dessert pudding with fruit.

SPORTS/SPORTS TEAMS

Australian-rules football is the most popular sport. Softball and cricket are also very popular. Nauru national teams participate in many sports at an international level.

TEAM SPORTS

Badminton

Nauru National Badminton Team

Baseball

Nauru National Softball Team

Basketball

Nauru National Basketball Team; Nauru Women's National Basketball Team

Football

Nauru National Football Team, nickname the Chiefs; Nauru National Australian-Rules Football Team, nickname the Chiefs

Table Tennis

Nauru National Table Tennis Team

Tennis

Pacific Oceania Davis Cup Team; Pacific Oceania Fed Cup Team (Pacific Oceania teams represent a number of Pacific island countries)

Volleyball

Nauru Men's National Volleyball Team; Nauru Women's National Volleyball Team

INDIVIDUAL SPORTS

Nauru National Amateur Boxing Team; Nauru National Athletics Team; Nauru National Judo Team; Nauru National Weight Lifting Team; Nauru National Wrestling Team

NATIONAL HEROES OR PERSONIFICATIONS

Aweida, the island king in the late 19th century; Hammer DeRoburt, who led Nauru to independence and became first president of the republic; Bernard Dowiyogo, second president of the republic and a sharp critic of French nuclear testing in the Pacific

NATIONAL HOLIDAY/INDEPENDENCE DAY

Independence Day, January 31

FESTIVALS/FAIRS

Independence Day delectations, January; Amram Festival, October (celebrates the important birth of the 1,500th Nauruan in

1933, which signaled the revival of the small nation)

SIGNIFICANT EVENTS IN FORMATION OF NATIONAL IDENTITY

2000 B.C.E.–1700 C.E. Micronesian and Polynesian seafaring peoples settle the island. Traditionally, 12 clans represent the people, with descent and clan membership through the female line.

1798 A British whaler sights the island, which is called Pleasant Island. From the 1830s, whalers and trading ships visit to restock and trade, with the islanders often trading food for firearms and alcohol.

1878–1888 A civil war breaks out using imported firearms. The cost of the war is widespread destruction and a reduction of the island population from 1,400 to just 900 inhabitants. The war ends with annexation of the island by Germany*.

1900–1920 Phosphates are discovered by a British prospector. The first shipment of phosphates leaves the island in 1907. Australian troops take the island during the First World War. Nauru becomes a League of Nations mandate under Australian administration.

1933 The birth of a baby to the Amram family, marking the growth of the decimated population back up to 1,500.

1942–1947 Japanese forces occupy the island and deport 1,200 Nauruans for forced labor in Micronesia*, where nearly 40 percent of the deportees die. The island becomes a United Nations trust territory under Australian administration. Phosphate mining leaves many parts of the island a wasteland. The reduction in population, to less than 1,500, raises fears that the Nauruans could disappear as a distinct nationality.

1967–1980 The people of Nauru purchase the assets of the phosphate mining company. Nauru gains independence. The phosphate mines give the Nauruans one of the highest standards of living in the Pacific and, per capita, in the world.

1989–2009 Nauru takes legal action against Australia for its failure to remedy mining-related damage to the island during its tenure as the trustee power. Diminishing phosphate reserves bring about an economic decline and increased political instability.

NEPAL

OFFICIAL NAME

Sanghiya Loktāntrik Ganatantra Nepāl (Nepali); Federal Democratic Republic of Nepal (English)

POPULATION

29,564,500 (2009e)

INHABITANTS' NAME/NICKNAME

Nepali(s)

LANGUAGE/LANGUAGES

Nepali (official); Maithali, Bhojuri, Tharu, Tamang, Newar, Magar, Awadhi, English, others. Many local languages are recognized as regional languages.

RELIGION/RELIGIONS

Hindu, 80 percent; Buddhist, 11 percent; Muslim, 4 percent; Kirant, 3.5 percent; other or no religion

NATIONAL FLAG

The flag is the only national flag that is not rectangular, its shape, two triangles one above the other, based upon two triangular pennants that belonged to rival branches of the Rana dynasty, which formerly ruled the country. The flag is crimson, with a white moon in the upper part that traditionally represents the royal house and a sun in the lower part that traditionally symbolizes another branch of the Rana family, members of which acted as prime ministers until 1961. The charges are now said to represent the hope that Nepal itself will last as long as the sun and the moon.

COAT OF ARMS/SEAL

The seal is a circle with a depiction of Mount Everest, green hills representing the Nepali highlands, and a yellow color representing the fertile *terai* region, with a white map of Nepal in silhouette. Above is a small national flag; around the edge is a garland of rhododendrons; and below are male and female hands clasped to symbolize gender equality. Under the circle is a crimson banner inscribed with the national motto in Sanskrit.

MOTTO

Janani janmabhūmiśca svargādapi garīyasī (transliteration from Devangari script Nepali); The mother and the motherland are greater than the heavens (English)

CAPITAL CITY

Katmandu

TYPE OF GOVERNMENT

Republic

NATIONAL EMBLEM

Mount Everest

NATIONAL COLORS

Crimson and blue

NATIONAL ANTHEM

The anthem was adopted in 2007 to replace the former royal anthem when Nepal became a republic.

Sayaun Thunga Phool Ka (Nepali); Hundreds of Flowers (English)

We are hundreds of flowers, the one garland—Nepali
Sovereign, spread out from Mechi to Mahakali.
Amassing nature's millions of resources
By the blood of heroes, independent and immovable.
Land of knowledge, land of peace, *terai*, hills, mountains
Indivisible this beloved, our motherland Nepal.
The diverse races, languages, faiths, and cultures are so extensive
Our progressive nation, long live Nepal.

CURRENCY

Nepali rupee

INTERNET IDENTIFIER

.np

VEHICLE IDENTIFICATION PLATES/STICKERS

NEP (unofficial)

PASSPORT

The passport cover has the name of the country in Nepali and English, the coat of arms, and the word *passport* in Nepali and English.

AIRLINE

Nepal Airlines

NATIONAL FLOWER

Gali guran (rhododendron)

NATIONAL ANIMAL

Dzo (Nepalese cow)

NATIONAL BIRD

Impeyen pheasant

NATIONAL RESOURCES

Natural resources include quartz, water, timber, hydropower, scenic beauty, and small deposits of lignite, copper, cobalt, and iron ore. Nepal is among the poorest and least developed countries in the world, with almost one-third of its population living below the poverty line. Agriculture is the mainstay of the economy, providing a livelihood for three-fourths of the population. Security concerns relating to the Maoist conflict have led to a decrease in tourism, a key source of foreign exchange. Nepalis living outside the country are a major source of foreign currency.

FOODS

Dahl baht, a dish of rice and lentils, is considered the national dish. Other national specialties include *tarkan,* a spiced vegetable dish; *gurr,* a Sherpa dish of pounded potato mixed with spices and then grilled; rotis, flatbreads made of wheat or rice flour; and *chiya,* tea brewed with milk, sugar, and spices, considered the national drink. Other common dishes are *alu tarkari,* potato curry; *payajra dhulo masu,* a curry of onion and minced meat; *alu achar,* marinated potatoes; *momos,* dumplings filled with minced meat; *alu tama,* potatoes with marinated bamboo shoots; *thukpa,* a vegetable and noodle stew; and *kheer,* a dessert made of very fine pasta.

SPORTS/SPORTS TEAMS

Field hockey is the most popular sport. Association football (soccer) and cricket are also popular. Nepal national teams participate in many sports at an international level.

TEAM SPORTS

Badminton

Nepal Badminton Team

Basketball

Nepal Basketball Team; Nepal Women's Basketball Team

Cricket

Nepal Cricket Team; Nepal Women's Cricket Team

Football

Nepal Football Team; Nepal Women's Football Team; Nepal Under-19 Football Team; Nepal Women's Under-19 Football Team

Hockey

Nepal Field Hockey Team

Kabaddi

Nepal Kabaddi Team

Table Tennis

Nepal Table Tennis Team

Volleyball

Nepal Fistball Team; Nepal Men's Volleyball Team; Nepal Women's Volleyball Team

INDIVIDUAL SPORTS

Nepal Amateur Boxing Team; Nepal Archery Team; Nepal Athletics Team; Nepal Canoeing Team; Nepal Cycling Team; Nepal Gymnastics Team; Nepal Judo Team; Nepal Karate Team; Nepal Modern Pentathlon Team; Nepal Swim Team; Nepal Shooting Team; Nepal Tae Kwon Do Team; Nepal Triathlon Team; Nepal Weight Lifting Team; Nepal Wrestling Team

NATIONAL HEROES OR PERSONIFICATIONS

Prithvi Narayan Shah, the first ruler to unify Nepal in the late 18th century; Bhimsen Thapa, prime minister of Nepal under six kings and an anti-British leader in the late 18th and early 19th centuries; Amar Singh Thapa, military leader in the Anglo-Nepalese War in the 19th century; King Tribhuvan, the monarch who ended rule by the hereditary prime ministers in the 1950s; Tenzing Norgay, who scaled Mount Everest with Edmund Hillary in 1953; Pasang Lhamu Sherpa, the first Nepali woman to climb Mount Everest in 1993

NATIONAL HOLIDAY/INDEPENDENCE DAY

National Day, December 28

FESTIVALS/FAIRS

Dasain, September–October; Ghanta Karna Chaturdasi Festival, July–August; Gai Jatra (the Procession of Cows), August; Tihar (the Festival of Lights), October; Gunla, March

SIGNIFICANT EVENTS IN FORMATION OF NATIONAL IDENTITY

1000 B.C.E.–450 B.C.E.   Small kingdoms and clan confederations emerge in the region. One of the confederations, known as Shakya, is known for a prince named Siddharta Gautama who renounces his privileges to lead the life of an ascetic, later known as the Buddha.

100 C.E.–1100 C.E.   Nepal is ruled by local dynasties but often comes under the authority of rulers of the early Indian empires. In the 11th century, Nepal abandons Buddhism for the Indian Hindu religion.

1482   Nepal is divided into three kingdoms.

1765–1768   The Gorkha king, Prithvi Narayan Shah, unifies the Nepali kingdoms, which is commemorated as the birth of modern Nepal.

1815–1816   British encroachments lead to the Anglo-Nepalese War and the loss of territory to British India.

1846   A period of instability and violence leads to the creation of the Rana lineage. The king becomes only a figurehead, while the hereditary prime minister holds power.

1923   A treaty with the United Kingdom* formally recognizes Nepal's independence. Slavery is abolished in the kingdom.

1951–1959   King Tribhuvan ends the Rana hegemony and establishes closer ties to India*. A democratic system leads to years of wrangling between the king and the government and is replaced by a system without political parties.

1989–1991   The People's Movement forces the king to accept constitutional reforms and establish a multiparty parliament.

1996   Communists attempt to replace the monarchy with a people's socialist republic, initiating the Nepal Civil War, which leads to more than 12,000 deaths.

2001   A massacre in the royal palace leaves the king, queen, and heir apparent among the dead. The king's brother takes the throne, dismisses the government, and attempts to defeat the long-running Maoist rebellion.

2006–2008   A democracy movement gains support, and the king agrees to relinquish power back to the people. The new House of Representatives abolishes the monarchy and declares Nepal a federal republic.

2009   Despite massive human rights abuses during the 10-year conflict that ended in 2006, not a single person has yet been prosecuted for the political disappearances, killings, and torture commonly employed by both the government and the rebels.

NEW CALEDONIA

OFFICIAL NAME

Territoire des Nouvelle-Calédonie et Dependances (French); Territory of New Caledonia and Dependencies (English)
   Kanaky (Melanesian/independence name)

POPULATION

244,800 (2009e)

INHABITANTS' NAME/NICKNAME

New Caledonian(s); Kanak(s)

LANGUAGE/LANGUAGES

French (official); Melanesian languages, Polynesian languages, Vietnamese, others

RELIGION/RELIGIONS

Roman Catholic, 60 percent; Protestant, 30 percent; Muslim, 3 percent; other or no religion

NATIONAL FLAG

The official flag of the territory is the French tricolor. The flag of the independence movement, the de facto flag of the territory since 1998, is a horizontal tricolor of blue, red, and green, with a large yellow disk on the hoist bearing a traditional roof ornament in black. Blue symbolizes the sky, the surrounding ocean, and the sovereignty in the Pacific Ocean of the Kanak people. Red symbolizes the blood shed in the struggle for independence, socialism, and the unity of the Kanak people. Green symbolizes the land of the ancestors, the soil, and the country. The yellow disk represents the sun, on which is inscribed a *flèche faitière*, a kind of arrow that adorns the roofs of Kanak houses, thrust through *tutut* marine shells.

COAT OF ARMS/SEAL

The emblem, in black and white, consists of a large nautilus shell in front of a *koumac* or *flèche faitière,* taken from the independence flag, and the depiction of an araucaria tree.

CAPITAL CITY

Nouméa

TYPE OF GOVERNMENT

Overseas collectivity of France*

NATIONAL EMBLEM

The *koumac* (Kanak Melanesian) or *flèche faitière* (French), a kind of arrow that adorns the roofs of Kanak houses

NATIONAL COLORS

Gray and red

NATIONAL ANTHEM

The French national anthem, "La Marseillaise," is the official anthem. The anthem of New Caledonia was officially presented in June 2008.

> **Soyons Unis, Devenons Freres (French); Let Us Be United, Let Us Become Brothers (English)**
>
> Ô Terre sacrée de nos ancêtres,
> Lumière éclairant nos vies,

Tu les invite à nous transmettre
Leurs rêves, leurs espoirs, leurs envies.
A l'abri des pins colonnaires,
A l'ombre des flamboyants,
Dans les vallées de tes rivières,
Leur coeur toujours est présent.

Refrain 1

Hnoresaluso ke'j omome
Ha deko ikuja ne enetho
Hue netitonelo kébo kaagu
Ri nodedrane

Refrain 2

Soyons unis, devenons frères,
Plus de violence ni de guerre.
Marchons confiants et solidaires,
Pour notre Pays.
Terre de Parole et de Partage
Tu proposes à l'étranger,
Dans la tribu ou le village,
Un endroit pour se reposer.
Tu veux loger la tolérance,
L'équité et le respect,
Au creux de tes bras immenses,
Ô Terre de liberté
Refrain 1
Refrain 2
Ô Terre aux multiples visages
Nord, Sud, Iles Loyauté,
Tes trois Provinces sont l'image
De ta grande diversité
Nous tes enfants, tu nous rassembles,
Tempérant nos souvenirs.
D'une seule voix, chantons ensemble:
Terre, tu es notre avenir.
Refrain 1
Refrain 2

PATRON SAINT

Mary, on the feast of her Assumption

CURRENCY

CFP Franc

INTERNET IDENTIFIER

.nc

VEHICLE IDENTIFICATION PLATES/STICKERS

F France (official); KA Kanaky (unofficial)

PASSPORT

New Caledonians are French citizens and travel on French passports.

AIRLINE

Air Caledonie International (Aircalin)

NATIONAL FLOWER

Frangipani (unofficial)

NATIONAL TREE

Pin colonnaire (araucaria)

NATIONAL BIRD

Kagu (unofficial)

NATIONAL RESOURCES

Natural resources include nickel, chrome, iron, cobalt, manganese, silver, gold, lead, and copper. New Caledonian soils contain a considerable wealth of industrially critical elements and minerals, including about one-quarter of the world's nickel resources. Mining is therefore a significant industry that greatly benefits the territory's economy. Tourism, particularly from France, Australia*, and New Zealand*, is based on the island's unique culture, sandy beaches, and pleasant climate.

FOODS

Civet de roussette, a stew of flying fox (fruit bat) with vegetables and herbs, and *bougna,* a Melanesian dish of chicken, lobster, or fish with yams, sweet potatoes, and bananas cooked in banana leaves, are considered the national dishes. Other national specialties include *bouchons,* small steamed meatballs; *bonbons piments,* mashed peas; *sarcives,* pork cooked with honey and soy sauce; *chou-gratin,* pumpkin with coconut cream; *riz zambrocal,* a rice dish with beans and salt meat or sausage; *riz mais,* a rice dish with ground corn; *cari,* a type of curry made with tomatoes, chopped onion, garlic, and spices and served with meat, fish, or vegetables; and *paste goyavier,* a dessert made of guava.

SPORTS/SPORTS TEAMS

Association football and rugby are the favorite sports. New Caledonia national teams participate in many sports at an international level.

TEAM SPORTS

Baseball
New Caledonia Baseball Team

Basketball
New Caledonia Basketball Team; New Caledonia Women's Basketball Team

Cricket
New Caledonia Cricket Team

Football
New Caledonia Football Team, nickname Les Cagous (the Kagus); New Caledonia Women's Football Team, nickname Las Cagous (the Kagus); New Caledonia Under-19 Football Team; New Caledonia Women's Under-19 Football Team; New Caledonia Rugby Union Team; New Caledonia Rugby League Team; New Caledonia Wheelchair Rugby Team; New Caledonia Futsal Team

Handball
New Caledonia Men's Handball Team; New Caledonia Women's Handball Team

Table Tennis
New Caledonia Table Tennis Team; New Caledonia Judo Team

Tennis

New Caledonia is an associate member of the Pacific Oceania Davis Cup and Fed Cup teams.

Volleyball

New Caledonia Men's Volleyball Team; New Caledonia Women's Volleyball Team

National Heroes or Personifications

Jean-Marie Tjibaou, leader of the independence movement; Edmond Nekiriai, founder of the Kanak Socialist National Liberation Front (FLNKS); Nidoïsh Naisseline, independence leader

National Holiday/Independence Day

Bastille Day, July 14; New Caledonia Day, September 24

Festivals/Fairs

Festival of the Yam, March; Giant Omelette Festival, March–April; Avocado Festival, June

Significant Events in Formation of National Identity

1500 b.c.e.–1500 c.e. A Melanesian people known as the Lapita settle the islands. Later, Polynesian seafarers settle in the islands and mix with the Melanesians.

1774–1793 British mariner James Cook sights the largest of the islands, naming it New Caledonia after the Scottish Highlands. The Loyalty Islands are encountered.

1800–1850 British and American whalers and sandalwood traders often visit the islands, introducing diseases that ravage the population. Firearms and alcohol are traded for food, further damaging the local population. Slave traders called blackbirders raid the islands, taking slaves for plantations in Fiji* and Queensland.

1850–1860 The French government claims the islands, which are annexed and become part of the French Settlements in Oceania, governed from Tahiti in French Polynesia*, until they become a separate colony in 1860. A serious Kanak rebellion threatens French control and is met by the destruction of entire villages and unconditional surrender.

1864–1922 The French consider the islands uninhabited and therefore suitable for use as a penal colony. More than 20,000 prisoners are transported to New Caledonia. European colonists and Asian contract workers settle the territory, pushing the indigenous peoples into the less fertile regions. Kanak uprisings are frequent. By 1922, the last prisoners are released, and most choose to remain.

1936 The population of indigenous Kanaks drops to fewer than 30,000, raising the question of Kanak survival.

1950s Kanak nationalism begins as European settlement increases while other Melanesian peoples move toward independence. French citizenship is extended to all inhabitants in 1953. A referendum on the territory's future shows majority support for continued ties to France.

1970s The Kanaks become a minority in their homeland as the non-Kanak population continues to grow. Serious pro-independence riots sweep the islands in 1978. Many local Europeans support the demand for independence, and pro-independence groups garner 35 percent of the vote for the local legislature, which is dismissed. Troops are dispatched to maintain order.

1980s The restored assembly votes to declare independence on September 24, 1983, exactly 130 years after the French occupation began. Serious violence between Kanaks and anti-independence settlers spreads, and the government postpones plans for independence. Increased autonomy is granted in 1988.

1998–2008 A referendum on autonomy and future independence is approved. The accord provides for separate citizenship and official symbols and begins an irreversible devolution leading to a referendum on independence sometime after 2014.

2009 A strong earthquake rocked the islands, but no serious damage or tsunami occurs.

See also France

NEW ZEALAND

OFFICIAL NAME

New Zealand (English); Aotearoa (Māori)

NICKNAME

Land of the Long White Cloud

POPULATION

4,274,400 (2009e)

INHABITANTS' NAME/NICKNAME

New Zealander(s); Kiwi(s)

LANGUAGE/LANGUAGES

English, Māori (both official); Hungarian, Italian, others

RELIGION/RELIGIONS

Anglican, 15 percent; Roman Catholic, 12 percent; Presbyterian, 11 percent; Methodist, 3 percent; Pentecostal, 2 percent; Baptist, 1.5 percent; other or no religion

NATIONAL FLAG

The flag is based on the British Blue Ensign, a blue field with the Union Jack on the upper hoist and the Southern Cross, represented by four red stars outlined in white, on the fly. The Union Jack represents New Zealand's historic ties to the United Kingdom*, and the Southern Cross symbolizes New Zealand's location in the southern hemisphere.

COAT OF ARMS/SEAL

The coat of arms consists of a central shield containing, in the first quadrant, four stars on blue representing the Southern Cross constellation; in the second quadrant, a golden fleece on red representing the farming industry; in the third quadrant, a sheaf of wheat representing agriculture; and in the fourth quadrant, two hammers representing industry and mining. In the center of the shield is a broad, vertical white stripe with three ships, representing the importance of sea trade and the immigration of the majority from outside the country. The shield is crowned, alluding to the queen of the United Kingdom as the monarch of New Zealand, and two figures support the shield, a woman representing the European-descended population and a man representing the indigenous Maoris. Below is a white banner inscribed with the name of the country.

CAPITAL CITY

Wellington

TYPE OF GOVERNMENT

Parliamentary democracy

NATIONAL EMBLEM

Silver fern

NATIONAL COLORS

Black and white

NATIONAL ANTHEM

The anthem was written and composed in the 1870s and became the national anthem in 1940. The Commonwealth anthem, "God Save the Queen," has equal status but is used only on special occasions.

> **God Defend New Zealand**
>
> Men of ev'ry creed and race
> Gather here before thy face
> Asking thee to bless this place
> God defend our free land
> From dissension, envy, hate
> And corruption guard our state
> Make our country good and great
> God defend New Zealand.
>
> Peace, not war, shall be our boast
> But should our foes assail our coast

Make us then a mighty host
God defend our free land
Lord of battles, in thy might
Put our enemies to flight
Let our cause be just and right
God defend New Zealand

Let our love for thee increase
May thy blessings never cease
Give us plenty, give us peace
God defend our free land
From dishonor and from shame
Guard our country's spotless name
Crown her with immortal fame
God defend New Zealand.

May our mountains ever be
Freedom's ramparts on the sea
Make us faithful unto thee
God defend our free land
Guide her in the nations' van
Preaching love and truth to man
Working out thy glorious plan
God defend New Zealand
God defend New Zealand.

PATRON SAINT

Our Lady Help of Christians

CURRENCY

New Zealand dollar

INTERNET IDENTIFIER

.nz

VEHICLE IDENTIFICATION PLATES/STICKERS

NZ

PASSPORT

The passport cover has the name of the country in English, the coat of arms, the word *passport* in English, and the standard biometric symbol.

AIRLINE

Air New Zealand

NATIONAL FLOWER

Kowhai

NATIONAL TREE

Kauri

NATIONAL PLANT

Silver fern

NATIONAL ANIMAL

Sheep

NATIONAL BIRD

Kiwi

NATIONAL FISH

John Dory (unofficial)

NATIONAL RESOURCES

Natural resources include natural gas, iron ore, sand, coal, timber, hydropower, gold, limestone, and arable land. A well-educated population gives New Zealand a prosperous society that consistently ranks high in quality-of-living polls. The service sector is the largest portion of the economy, followed by industry and farming. The important tourist industry is based on varied scenery and activities.

FOODS

Hangi, Maori food cooked in earth ovens, is a national cooking method. A Maori boil-up, a dish of pork, potatoes, *kumara* (sweet potato), and dumplings, is considered the national dish. Traditional New Zealand dishes include pork and *puha* (sonchus), fish and chips, meat pies, custard squares, and Pavlova, a dessert of meringue and cream with kiwi fruit. Colonial goose, a stuffed leg of lamb often served at holidays, was a New Zealand invention and a substitute for turkey before the birds were commercially farmed in the country.

SPORTS/SPORTS TEAMS

Rugby union is the unofficial national sport. Other popular sports are cricket, bowls, and association football (soccer). New Zealand national teams participate in many sports at an international level.

TEAM SPORTS

Badminton

New Zealand Badminton Team

Baseball

New Zealand Baseball Team, nickname Black Socks; New Zealand Softball Team, nickname Black Socks; New Zealand Women's Softball Team, nickname White Socks

Basketball

New Zealand Basketball Team, nickname the Tall Blacks; New Zealand Women's Basketball Team, nickname the Tall Ferns; New Zealand Wheelchair Basketball Team

Bowls

New Zealand Bowls Team

Cricket

New Zealand Cricket Team, nickname the Black Caps or the Kiwis; Women's Cricket Team, nickname the White Ferns; New Zealand A Cricket Team

Curling

New Zealand Curling Team

Football

New Zealand Football Team, nickname All Whites; New Zealand Women's Football Team, nickname Football Ferns; New Zealand Under-20 Football Team; New Zealand Rugby Union Team, nickname the All Blacks; Women's Rugby Union Team, nickname the Black Ferns; New Zealand Rugby Union Team Sevens, nickname New Zealand Sevens or 7s; New Zealand Women's Rugby Union Team Sevens, nickname New Zealand Sevens or 7s; New Zealand Rugby League Team, nickname the Kiwis or the All Golds; New Zealand Women's Rugby League Team; New Zealand Maori Rugby League Team; New Zealand Maori Women's Rugby League Team; New Zealand Australian-Rules Football Team, nickname the Falcons; New Zealand Under-23 Football Team, nickname the Oly-Whites; New Zealand Under-17 Football Team, nickname the Young All Whites; New Zealand Under-21 Rugby Union Team; New Zealand Under-19 Rugby Union Team; New Zealand Schoolboy Rugby Union Team; New Zealand Junior All-Blacks Rugby Team; New Zealand Wheelchair Rugby Team, nickname the Wheel Blacks; New Zealand American Football Team; New Zealand Beach Soccer Team; New Zealand Futsal Team; New Zealand Touch Football Team; New Zealand Women's Touch Football Team; Aotearoa Maori Women's Rugby Union Team Sevens, nickname Maori Sevens or 7s

Handball

New Zealand Handball Team; New Zealand Women's Handball Team; New Zealand Beach Handball Team; New Zealand Women's Handball Team

Hockey

New Zealand Men's Ice Hockey Team, nickname the Ice Blacks; New Zealand Woman's Ice Hockey Team, nickname the Ice Ferns; New Zealand Junior Ice Hockey Team, nickname the Junior Ice Blacks; New Zealand Men's Field Hockey Team, nickname the Black Sticks; New Zealand Women's Field Hockey Team, nickname the Black Sticks

Korfball

New Zealand Korfball Team

Lacrosse

New Zealand Lacrosse Team; New Zealand Women's Lacrosse Team; New Zealand Under-19 Lacrosse Team; New Zealand Women's Under-19 Lacrosse Team

Netball

New Zealand Netball Team, nickname the Silver Ferns

Racing

A1 Team New Zealand; New Zealand Speedway Team

Table Tennis

New Zealand Table Tennis Team

Tennis

New Zealand Davis Cup Team; New Zealand Fed Cup Team

Volleyball

New Zealand Volleyball Team; New Zealand Women's Volleyball Team; New Zealand Men's Beach Volleyball Team; New Zealand Women's Beach Volleyball Team

Water Polo

New Zealand Men's Water Polo Team; New Zealand Women's Water Polo Team

INDIVIDUAL SPORTS

New Zealand Aikido Team; New Zealand Amateur Boxing Team; New Zealand Archery Team; New Zealand Athletics Team; New Zealand Canoeing Team; New Zealand Cycling Team; New Zealand Equestrian Team; New Zealand Fencing Team; New Zealand Gymnastics Team; New Zealand Judo Team; New Zealand Karate Team; New Zealand Modern Pentathlon Team; New Zealand Rowing Team; New Zealand Sailing Team; New Zealand Shooting Team; New Zealand Swim Team; New Zealand Tae Kwon Do Team; New Zealand Triathlon Team; New Zealand Weight Lifting Team; New Zealand Wrestling Team

WINTER SPORTS

New Zealand Alpine Ski Team; New Zealand Biathlon Team; New Zealand Bobsleigh and Tobogganing Team; New Zealand Curling Team; New Zealand Men's Ice Hockey Team, nickname the Ice Blacks; New Zealand Woman's Ice Hockey Team, nickname the Ice Ferns; New Zealand Junior Ice Hockey Team, nickname the Junior Ice Blacks; New Zealand Luge Team; New Zealand Skating Team

NATIONAL HEROES OR PERSONIFICATIONS

The traditional national personification is Zealandia, portrayed as the daughter of Brittania, personification of Great Britain or the United Kingdom.

National heroes include Sir Edmund Hillary, the first man to climb Mount Everest in the 1950s; Maurice Wilkins, scientist and discoverer of the DNA molecule structure and Nobel prize winner; Kate Sheppard, leader of the suffragist movement; Ernest Rutherford, nuclear scientist and Nobel prize winner; and Mable Howard, first woman cabinet member in the 1940s.

NATIONAL HOLIDAY/ INDEPENDENCE DAY

Waitangi Day, February 6; ANZAC Day, April 25

FESTIVALS/FAIRS

Pasifika Festival, March; World of Wearable Art, September; Blossom Festival, September; Kaikoura Seafest, October; Otago Festival of the Arts, October; Coromandel Pohutukawa Festival, November; New Zealand International Arts Festival, August–September

SIGNIFICANT EVENTS IN FORMATION OF NATIONAL IDENTITY

800 C.E.–1300 C.E. The first seafaring Polynesians discover and begin to settle the two large islands. Continuous settlement begins, with large numbers arriving in seagoing sailing canoes.

1300–1600 The Polynesian settlers develop the distinct Maori culture. The population is divided into clans that often war or cooperate.

1642–1647 Dutch mariner Abel Tasman sites the land mass and names it Staten Landt. Part of the coastline appears in subsequent maps and charts as Zeelandia Nova.

1769–1790 British explorer James Cook claims the territory for the British Crown. Settlers begin arriving from Europe to take up whaling, sealing, and the timber trade. The Maori suffer the first of many introduced epidemics.

1806–1822 The first European women arrive in New Zealand, followed by Christian missionaries. Maori resistance to European encroachments leads to the first Maori raids on settlements.

1839–1846 The Treaty of Waitangi is signed in 1840, with some Maori chiefs accepting British sovereignty with rights established for the Maoris. Attacks by Maoris continue to disrupt settlement.

1848 Settlers from Scotland* arrive on the South Island.

1850s–1870s Amid continuing Maori wars, the colonial government confiscates much land for settlement. The first Maori king is installed in 1858. Maori armed resistance ends in 1872.

1884 King Tawhiao travels to England with a petition for Queen Victoria but is refused access.

1893 New Zealand women become the first in the world to receive the vote.

1901 The territory of the Cook Islands* is annexed, along with other Pacific islands. New Zealand enters both world wars, sending troops to aid the United Kingdom. New Zealand becomes an independent dominion of the British Commonwealth.

1949–1962 New Zealand votes to retain ties to the Commonwealth as an independent state. The New Zealand Maori Council is established.

1980s New Zealand's nuclear-free declaration bars warships from the United States* and opens a rift between the two longtime allies. Maori-rights activists become more aggressive in demanding communal rights.

2004–2009 The first specifically Maori political party forms. Maori television begins broadcasting. The Maori sovereignty movement seeks more recognition of Maori culture. New Zealanders, in international polls, are characterized by satisfaction with their country and their lifestyle.

NIUE

OFFICIAL NAME
Niuē Fekai (Niuean); Niue (English)

POPULATION
1,700 (2009e). The Niuean population living in New Zealand* is estimated to number more than 13,000.

INHABITANTS' NAME/NICKNAME
Niuean(s)

LANGUAGE/LANGUAGES
Niuean, English (official)

RELIGION/RELIGIONS
Ekalesia Niue (closely related to the London Missionary Society), 61 percent; Mormon, 9 percent; Roman Catholic, 7 percent; other or no religion

NATIONAL FLAG
The flag is a yellow field with a Union Jack on the upper hoist, bearing a large, five-pointed yellow star in the center and four smaller stars on each quadrant of the Saint George cross of the British flag. The yellow symbolizes the warmth and friendship between Niue and New Zealand. The Union

Jack symbolizes Niue's historic ties to the United Kingdom*.

COAT OF ARMS/SEAL

Niue uses the coat of arms of New Zealand within a white disk, with "Public Seal of Niue" above the coat of arms and the name of the country written beneath.

NATIONAL EMBLEM

Spinner dolphin

CAPITAL CITY

Alofi

TYPE OF GOVERNMENT

Constitutional monarchy in free association with New Zealand

NATIONAL COLORS

Yellow and green

NATIONAL ANTHEM

The anthem is based on a popular Christian hymn. The official anthems are the anthem of New Zealand and "God Save the Queen," which is co-official in New Zealand territories.

> **Ko e Iki he Lagi (Niuean); The Lord in Heaven (English)**
>
> The Lord in Heaven
> Who loves
> Niue
> Who rules kindly
> The Almighty
> Who rules completely over Niue
> Over Niue, Over Niue
> Over Niue, Over Niue
> Over Niue, Over Niue
> Over Niue
> Who rules completely over Niue
> Who rules over Niue

CURRENCY

New Zealand dollar

INTERNET IDENTIFIER

.nu

VEHICLE IDENTIFICATION PLATES/ STICKERS

NZ New Zealand (official); NU Niue (unofficial)

PASSPORT

Niueans are New Zealand citizens and travel on New Zealand passports.

NATIONAL FLOWER

Hibiscus

NATIONAL TREE

Coconut palm (unofficial)

NATIONAL ANIMAL

Spinner dolphin

NATIONAL RESOURCES

Natural resources are negligible, other than fish and arable land. The economy suffers from the typical Pacific island problems of geographic isolation, few resources, and a small population. Generous subsidies from New Zealand and remittances from Niueans living in New Zealand are very important to the economy. Tourism, mostly based on diving and snorkeling, is becoming a very important industry.

FOODS

Mitiore, shellfish fermented in a coconut shell, is considered the national dish. *Umukai,* which involves baking food in an underground oven, is reserved for holidays and is usually accompanied by dancing and entertainment.

SPORTS/SPORTS TEAMS

Rugby and association football (soccer) are the most popular sports. Niue national teams participate in many sports at an international level.

TEAM SPORTS

Basketball

Niue Basketball Team; Niue Women's Basketball Team

Cricket

Niue Cricket Team

Football

Niue Football Team; Niue Rugby Union Team; Niue Rugby League Team; Niue Women's Rugby League Team; Niue Rugby Union Sevens Team, nickname Niue Sevens or Niue 7s; Niue Women's Rugby Union Sevens Team, nickname Niue Sevens or Niue 7s; Niue Touch Football Team; Niue Women's Touch Football Team

Netball

Niue Netball Team

Table Tennis

Niue Table Tennis Team

Volleyball

Niue Men's Volleyball Team; Niue Women's Volleyball Team

INDIVIDUAL SPORTS

Niue Judo Team; Niue Weight Lifting Team

NATIONAL HEROES OR PERSONIFICATIONS

Puni-mata, the first king of Niue in the 18th century; Tui-toga, the first Christian king in the late 19th century; Fata-a-Iki, the king from 1896, who forbade the sale of land to foreigners and the sale of liquor to Niueans and is responsible for Niue's British protectorate status, which precluded annexation by another European power

NATIONAL HOLIDAY/INDEPENDENCE DAY

Waitangi Day, February 6 (New Zealand national holiday); Constitution Day, October 19

FESTIVALS/FAIRS

Niue Show Days, variable dates.

SIGNIFICANT EVENTS IN FORMATION OF NATIONAL IDENTITY

900 C.E.–1600 C.E. Seafaring Polynesians from Samoa* settle the island. A new wave of settlers invades or occupies the island from Tonga*.

18th century The island is divided into small family units or chiefdoms, although two divisions emerge on each side of the island, often leading to conflicts. British Captain James Cook lands on the island but retreats in the face of armed warriors yelling taunts. He calls the island Savage Island.

19th century British missionaries introduce Christianity in 1846. The idea of kingship comes to the inland through contact with Samoa and Tonga. Puni-mata, who reigns from 1875 to 1887, is known for adopting Christianity.

1900–1901 Niue becomes a British protectorate and in 1901 is annexed by New Zealand.

1903 Cultural and linguistic differences lead to Niue's separation from the Cook Islands*.

1974 Self-government is granted with a new constitution in 1974. Citizenship rights lead many to leave the small island for life in New Zealand.

2004 Niue is hit by Cyclone Heta, which causes extensive damage and derails economic progress.

2008–2009 The island's population, 5,200 in 1966, continues to drop as Niueans leave for New Zealand. International aid, mainly from New Zealand, makes the island the highest per-capita recipient of aid in the world.

See also New Zealand

NORFOLK ISLAND

OFFICIAL NAME

Territory of Norfolk Island

POPULATION

2,100 (2009e); estimates of the number of Norfolk Islanders living in Australia vary from about 5,000 to 15,000

INHABITANTS' NAME/NICKNAME

Norfolk Islander(s)

LANGUAGE/LANGUAGES

English, Norfolk (both official); Norfolk is a mixture of 18th century English and Tahitian.

RELIGION/RELIGIONS

Anglican, 35 percent; Roman Catholic, 11 percent; Uniting Church, 11 percent; Seventh-day Adventist, 3 percent; other or no religion

NATIONAL FLAG

The flag has three equal vertical stripes of green, white, and green bearing a green Norfolk pine centered on the white stripe. The green represents the abundant vegetation and fertility of the island. The Norfolk pine is the official tree of the island.

COAT OF ARMS/SEAL

The coat of arms has a central crest bearing a rocky mount with a book and a Norfolk pine on a white triangle below a purple background bearing two white five-pointed stars. A lion and a kangaroo, each holding an anchor, support the shield. Above the shield are a heraldic helmet and a smaller lion holding a covered golden cup. Below is a banner inscribed with the Norfolk motto. The lion and the kangaroo represent the island's historic ties to the United Kingdom* and Australia*.

MOTTO

Inasmuch

CAPITAL CITY

Kingston

TYPE OF GOVERNMENT

Self-governing parliamentary democracy in association with Australia

NATIONAL EMBLEM

Norfolk pine

NATIONAL COLORS

Green and white

NATIONAL ANTHEM

The official anthem is that of Australia. The local anthem is a hymn with lyrics taken from the Bible.

Come Ye Blessed, or Pitcairn Anthem

(Spoken)
Then shall the King
Say unto them
On his right hand:

(Verse)
Come ye blessed of my Father
Inherit the kingdom prepared for you
From the foundation of the world
I was hungered and ye gave me meat,
I was thirsty and ye gave me drink
I was a stranger and ye took me in,
Naked and ye clothed me,
I was sick and ye visited me,
I was in prison and ye came unto me
In as much ye have done it unto one of the
 least of
These my brethren
Ye have done it unto me,
Ye have done it unto me.

CURRENCY

Australian dollar

INTERNET IDENTIFIER

.nf

VEHICLE IDENTIFICATION PLATES/STICKERS

AUS Australia (official); NF Norfolk Island (unofficial)

PASSPORT

Norfolk Islanders are Australian citizens and travel on Australian passports.

AIRLINE

Norfolkair

NATIONAL FLOWER

Norfolk flax (unofficial)

NATIONAL TREE

Norfolk pine

NATIONAL FISH

Hammerhead shark (unofficial)

NATIONAL RESOURCES

Natural resources, other than fish, are negligible. Tourism is the primary economic activity and has steadily increased over the years. Norfolk Island prohibits the importation of fresh fruit and vegetables, so most produce is grown locally. Beef is both produced locally and imported. There are no major arable lands or permanent farmlands, though about 25 percent of the island is a permanent pasture. Remittances from Norfolk Islanders living mostly in Australia are a source of foreign currency and investment.

FOODS

Fish, beef, and *kumera* (sweet potato) are the basis of the island's cuisine, with specialties such as stuffed paw-paw, papaya stuffed with minced meat; *kumera* with yam and coconut, mashed sweet potato, yam, and coconut wrapped in a banana leaf and baked; *kumera* with bananas, mashed fruit mixed with flour and baked; and banana and coconut soup with herbs and spiced prawns.

SPORTS/SPORTS TEAMS

Rugby is the most popular sport, but association football (soccer) is also becoming popular. Norfolk Island national teams participate in many sports at an international level.

TEAM SPORTS

Badminton

Norfolk Island Badminton Team

Basketball

Norfolk Island Basketball Team; Norfolk Island Women's Basketball Team

Bowls

Norfolk Island Bowls Team

Football

Norfolk Island Football Team; Norfolk Island Rugby Union Team; Norfolk Island Rugby League Team

Netball

Norfolk Island Netball Team

Tennis

Pacific Oceania Davis Cup Team; Pacific Oceania Fed Cup Team (Pacific Oceania teams represent a number of Pacific island nations)

INDIVIDUAL SPORTS

Norfolk Island Archery Team; Norfolk Island Athletics Team; Norfolk Island Judo Team; Norfolk Island Triathlon Team; Norfolk Island Weight Lifting Team

NATIONAL HEROES OR PERSONIFICATIONS

Philip Gidley King, founder of the first European colony on Norfolk Island; William Hutchinson, a British convict transported to Norfolk Island who later became superintendent of works

NATIONAL HOLIDAY/ INDEPENDENCE DAY

Bounty Day, June 8

FESTIVALS/FAIRS

Jazz Festival in the Pines, December; Country Music Festival, February; Theater Festival, October; Bounty Day celebrations, June

SIGNIFICANT EVENTS IN FORMATION OF NATIONAL IDENTITY

14th century C.E.–15th century C.E. Maori settlers arrive from New Zealand* or the Kermadec Islands. Their colony survives for several generations before mysteriously disappearing.

1774–1814 British Captain James Cook, on his second expedition to the Pacific, sights the island, which he names for the Duchess of Norfolk. The first settlement is established on the uninhabited island as a penal colony but is later abandoned.

1825 A second attempt is made to establish a penal colony.

1855–1856 The island is again abandoned as a penal colony. Islanders from overcrowded Pitcairn* are settled on the island, which is made a separate territory under the governor of New South Wales.

1897–1914 The island's self-government is revoked. Norfolk Island becomes a territory of Australia.

1979 The island is granted autonomy under a parliamentary government. Norfolk Islanders are not represented in the Australian parliament.

2006–2009 A review of the island's status is undertaken, but it is decided that no changes would be made at the present time. About half the island's population traces its ancestry to the settlers from Pitcairn.

See also Australia

North Korea. *See* Korea, North

NORTHERN MARIANA ISLANDS

OFFICIAL NAME

Sankattan Siha Na Islas Mariånas (Chamorro); Commonwealth of the Northern Mariana Islands (English); Northern Marianas (informal usage)

POPULATION

85,300 (2009e)

INHABITANTS' NAME/NICKNAME

Mariana Islander(s)

LANGUAGE/LANGUAGES

English, Chamorro, Carolinian (all official); Japanese, others

RELIGION/RELIGIONS

Roman Catholic, 26 percent; Protestant, 19 percent; other or no religion

NATIONAL FLAG

The flag has a blue field with a centered, white, five-pointed star, a stone and a decorative wreath. The blue field represents the Pacific Ocean, and the white star represents the islands surrounded by the ocean. The *latte* stone, a traditional foundation stone, represents the islands' links to the past. The wreath, called a *mwarmwar,* represents the link between the islands and their sacred history.

COAT OF ARMS/SEAL

The coat of arms is a circle with the star, *latte* stone, and *mwarmwar* of the national flag. Below the images is inscribed "United States, 1976" and "Official Seal" in white on the blue background. Around the edge of the circle is the name of the territory, also in white letters.

CAPITAL CITY

Saipan

TYPE OF GOVERNMENT

Commonwealth in free association with the United States*

NATIONAL EMBLEM

Latte stone

NATIONAL COLORS

Blue and white

NATIONAL ANTHEM

"The Star-Spangled Banner" is the official anthem. The commonwealth's official song was adopted in 1996.

Gi Talo Gi Halom Tasi (Chamorro); Satil Matawal Pacifiko (Carolinian); In the Middle of the Sea (English)

In the middle of the sea
Is where my home is
That is where I will spend my days
It is my desire
If I ever leave this place
One day I will return
For I can never leave you
O land of mine

Chorus

A thousand times and more
I will honor and salute you
Beautiful islands of the Mariånas
Glory be to you

PATRON SAINT

Saint Joseph

CURRENCY

U.S. dollar

INTERNET IDENTIFIER

.mp

VEHICLE IDENTIFICATION PLATES/STICKERS

USA United States (official); NMI Northern Mariana Islands (unofficial)

PASSPORT

Mariana Islanders are American citizens and travel on American passports.

NATIONAL FLOWER

Plumeria

NATIONAL TREE

Flame tree

NATIONAL BIRD

Paluman tottut (Mariana fruit-dove)

NATIONAL RESOURCES

Natural resources are negligible, other than fish and limited arable land. Tourism, particularly from Japan, is an important industry and is based on the island scenery, pleasant climate, and mixed island and American culture. Remittances from Mariana Islanders living outside the country are an important source of investment. Subsidies paid to the islands' government by the U.S. federal government are very important to the economy.

FOODS

Kelaguin manok, a dish of chicken and shredded coconut served with a spiced sauce, is considered the national dish. Other specialties include shrimp patties; *kelaguin uhang,* a dish of shrimp, sweet pepper, coconut, and lemon; *kelaguin benadu,* a dish of venison and sweet peppers; *kadun niguk,* a soup of vegetables, curry, and coconut; *pado'lalo',* a dish of eggplant, green onions, and coconut milk; *hineksa agaga,* a rice dish with *achiote* juice and onion; and *cari,* a chicken dish with mango and coconut.

SPORTS/SPORTS TEAMS

Baseball, basketball, and association football (soccer) are the most popular sports. Northern Mariana Islands national teams participate in many sports at an international level.

TEAM SPORTS

Baseball

Northern Mariana Islands Baseball Team; Marianas Softball Team; Saipan Softball Team

Basketball

Northern Mariana Islands Basketball Team; Northern Mariana Islands Women's Basketball Team

Football

Northern Mariana Islands Football Team, nickname Blue Ayuyus

Table Tennis

Northern Mariana Islands Table Tennis Team

Tennis

Pacific Oceania Davis Team; Pacific Oceania Fed Team (Pacific Oceania teams represent a number of Pacific island countries)

Volleyball

Northern Mariana Islands Men's Volleyball Team; Northern Mariana Islands Women's Volleyball Team

INDIVIDUAL SPORTS

Northern Mariana Islands Athletics Team; Northern Mariana Islands Judo Team; Northern Mariana Islands Swim Team; Northern Mariana Islands Weight Lifting Team; Northern Mariana Islands Wrestling Team

NATIONAL HEROES OR PERSONIFICATIONS

Mata'pang, a local chief who led the resistance to Spanish rule in the 17th century

NATIONAL HOLIDAY/
INDEPENDENCE DAY

Commonwealth Day, January 8

FESTIVALS/FAIRS

Flame Tree Arts Festival. April; Liberation Day Festival, July; Taste of the Marianas, May; Saipan Marathon, January; San Jose Fiesta, May

SIGNIFICANT EVENTS IN FORMATION OF NATIONAL IDENTITY

3000 B.C.E.–1500 B.C.E. Ancient seafaring peoples, probably from present Indonesia* or the Philippines*, settle the Mariana Islands. Later waves of settlers come from Polynesia* and Melanesia*.

1500 B.C.E.–800 C.E. The islanders develop a complex and sophisticated culture.

1521–1565 Ferdinand Magellan, sailing for Spain*, sights the Mariana Islands and makes landfall on Guam*, which he claims for Spain. The Spanish government annexes the entire Mariana archipelago.

1670–1698 An uprising against Spanish rule initiates 25 years of intermittent war known as the Chamorro Wars, characterized by brutality and massacres. European diseases devastate the population.

1700–1850 The population of the Mariana Islands, estimated at 100,000, is reduced to just 4,000 by 1700 and to just 1,500 by 1850.

1898–1920 Guam is ceded to the United States following the Spanish-American War, while the other islands in the group are sold to Germany*, effectively dividing the archipelago. Japan* takes control of the Northern Marianas during the First World War. The Chamorro population begins to recover from the devastation of Spanish rule.

1941 Japanese troops from the nearby islands overrun Guam at the outbreak of the War. Chamorros from the Japanese Marianas are taken to Guam to assist the Japanese administration, creating a lasting rift between Guamanians and Mariana Islanders.

1944–1950 The Americans return to retake the islands in some of the heaviest fighting of the war. The Northern Marianas become a United Nations trust territory administered by the United States.

1960s A referendum on the reunification of the Mariana Islands wins approval in the Northern Marianas, but Guamanians, still resentful of the northerners' wartime conduct as Japanese administrators, vote against the measure.

1970s–1980s The Mariana Islanders decide against seeking independence and forge closer ties to the United States.

1992 Typhoon Omar devastates the islands. The reconstruction effort revives the land question. Land confiscated from local people for military use but no longer needed by the military becomes a political issue.

2000–2009 The islands' multicultural society poses particular challenges to the Chamorros struggling to preserve their identity and culture. Increasing numbers of young Mariana Islanders move to the U.S. mainland.

PAKISTAN

OFFICIAL NAME
Islāmī Jumhūrīyah Pākistān (transliteration from Urdu); Islamic Republic of Pakistan (English)

POPULATION
172,845,200 (2009e)

INHABITANTS' NAME/NICKNAME
Pakistani(s)

LANGUAGE/LANGUAGES
Urdu (national), English (official); Balochi, Pashto, Punjabi, Siraiki, Sindhi (recognized regional languages); Brahui, Burushaski, others

RELIGION/RELIGIONS
Sunni Muslim, 77 percent; Shia Muslim, 20 percent; Christian, Hindu, other or no religion

NATIONAL FLAG
The flag, known as *Parcham-e-Sitāra-o-Hilāl*, the Flag of the Crescent and Star, consists of a dark green field charged with a large white crescent and a white, five-pointed star and a vertical white stripe at the hoist. The green represents the country's Muslim majority; the white represents the non-Muslim religious minorities. The white crescent moon symbolizes progress, and the star symbolizes light and knowledge. The flag is a symbol of Pakistan's commitment to Islam, the Muslim world, and the rights of religious minorities.

COAT OF ARMS/SEAL
The coat of arms, called the state emblem, is green and white and has a central crest or shield with four quarters, with each quadrant containing a major crop at the time of Pakistan's independence: cotton, jute, tea, and wheat. The floral wreath around the shield represents Pakistan's Mughal cultural heritage. Above the shield is a crescent moon and star, the symbols of Islam. Below is a banner inscribed with the national motto in Urdu.

MOTTO
Ittehad, tanzim, yaqeen-e-muhkam (Urdu); Unity, discipline, and faith (English)

CAPITAL CITY
Islamabad

TYPE OF GOVERNMENT
Islamic republic

NATIONAL EMBLEM
Minar-e-Pakistan (The Tower of Pakistan)

NATIONAL COLORS
Green and white

NATIONAL ANTHEM
The anthem was selected by a committee after independence and was officially adopted in 1953.

Pak sarzamin shad bad (Urdu); Blessed Be the Sacred Land (English)

Blessed be the sacred land
Happy be the bounteous realm
Symbol of high resolve
Land of Pakistan
Blessed be thou citadel of faith

The order of this sacred land
Is the might of the brotherhood of the people
May the nation, the country, and the state

Shine in glory everlasting
Blessed be the goal of our ambition

This Flag of the Crescent and Star
Leads the way to progress and perfection
Interpreter of our past, glory of our present
Inspiration of our future
Symbol of the Almighty's protection

PATRON SAINT

Saint Thomas the Apostle

CURRENCY

Pakistani rupee

INTERNET IDENTIFIER

.pk

VEHICLE IDENTIFICATION PLATES/STICKERS

PK

PASSPORT

The passport cover has the name of the country in Urdu and English, the state emblem, the word *passport* in Urdu and English, and the standard biometric symbol.

AIRLINES

PIA Pakistan International Airlines, Shaheen Air International, AirBlue

NATIONAL FLOWER

Jasmine

NATIONAL TREE

Deodar cedar

NATIONAL ANIMAL

Markhor (goat-antelope)

NATIONAL BIRD

Chukar (Red-legged partridge)

NATIONAL FISH

Bat ray (unofficial)

NATIONAL RESOURCES

Natural resources include arable land, extensive natural gas reserves, limited petroleum, poor-quality coal, iron ore, copper, salt, and limestone. Ancient monuments, historic cities, unique cultures, and varied scenery support the tourist industry, which has declined due to unrest and religious conflicts in the country. Remittances from Pakistanis living outside the country are a source of foreign currency and investment.

FOODS

Nihari, a stew of beef or lamb with spices that is usually eaten in the morning, is considered the national dish. Other specialties include pilaf, a dish of rice or cracked wheat cooked in broth, usually with meat or vegetables; *biryani,* a rice dish with meat and vegetables; *haleem,* a dish of cracked wheat, lentils, and meat, with many variations; *keema,* minced meat curry with peas or potatoes; *sag gosht,* a spinach and lamb curry; and *shami kebab,* patties of fried minced meat.

SPORTS/SPORTS TEAMS

Field hockey is the national game, but cricket is the most popular. Association football (soccer) is becoming popular, particularly among the young. Pakistan national teams participate in many sports at an international level.

TEAM SPORTS

Badminton

Pakistan Badminton Team

Baseball

Pakistan Baseball Team; Pakistan Softball Team

Basketball

Pakistan Basketball Team; Pakistan Women's Basketball Team

Cricket

Pakistan Cricket Team; Pakistan Women's Cricket Team

Football

Pakistan Football Team, nickname the Greenshirts; Pakistan Women's Football Team, nickname the Greenshirts; Pakistan Australian-Rules Football Team, nickname the Dragoons; Pakistan Rugby Union Team

Handball

Pakistan Handball Team

Hockey

Pakistan Field Hockey Team

Kabaddi

Pakistan Kabaddi Team

Lacrosse

Pakistan Lacrosse Team

Netball

Pakistan Netball Team

Polo

Pakistan Polo Team

Racing

A1 Team Pakistan

Table Tennis

Pakistan Table Tennis Team

Tennis

Pakistan Davis Cup Team; Pakistan Fed Cup Team

Volleyball

Pakistan Volleyball team; Pakistan Fistball Team

Water Polo

Pakistan Water Polo Team

INDIVIDUAL SPORTS

Pakistan Amateur Boxing Team; Pakistan Archery Team; Pakistan Athletics Team; Pakistan Canoeing Team; Pakistan Cycling Team; Pakistan Equestrian Team; Pakistan Gymnastics Team; Pakistan Judo Team; Pakistan Karate Team; Pakistan Modern Pentathlon Team; Pakistan Rowing Team; Pakistan Sailing Team; Pakistan Shooting Team; Pakistan Swim Team; Pakistan Tae Kwon Do Team; Pakistan Triathlon Team; Pakistan Weight Lifting Team; Pakistan Wrestling Team

NATIONAL HEROES
OR PERSONIFICATIONS

Muhammad Ali Jinnah, known as Quaid-I-Azam or Father of the Nation, the Muslim independence leader in the 1930s and 1940s; Dr. Abdul Qadeer Khan, the man responsible for making Pakistan a nuclear power; Abdul Sattar Edhi, a philanthropist responsible for a network devoted to the people; Muhammad ibn Qasim, the Arab leader who introduced Islam to the area in the eighth century

NATIONAL HOLIDAY/
INDEPENDENCE DAY

Republic Day, March 23

FESTIVALS/FAIRS

Festival of Norouz, March; Independence Day celebrations, August; Pakistan Day celebrations, March; Mela Chiraghan (Festival of Lamps), March; Lok Mela (Folk Festival), October; Basant (Kite Festival), spring

SIGNIFICANT EVENTS IN FORMATION
OF NATIONAL IDENTITY

2600 B.C.E.   The Indus Valley civilization flourishes in the fertile regions along the Indus River.

1700 B.C.E.   Aryan invaders from Central Asia overwhelm the sophisticated cities of the Indus

River region. Their strict caste system and belief in many gods lay the basis of the Hindu religion.

Sixth century B.C.E. Dissatisfied with the rigid caste system of Hinduism, many adopt the Buddha's teaching of equality. Most of present Pakistan becomes part of the Persian Empire.

711 C.E. Arab invaders, led by Muhammad ibn Qasim, bring the new Muslim religion to the subcontinent.

1526 The Muslims of the Mughal Empire unite much of the Indian subcontinent.

1858 The British overthrow Mughal rule and take control of India*.

1906–1940 The Muslim League is founded as a forum for India's large Muslim population. The platform soon espouses Muslim separatism. The league endorses the idea of a separate nation for India's Muslims.

1947–1949 India is partitioned at independence into secular India and Muslim Pakistan, the latter led by Muhammad Ali Jinnah. Pakistan is made up of two large territories separated by India. The partition, involving huge population transfers, massacres, and extreme violence that leaves hundreds of thousands dead, embitters feelings on both sides. Muhammad Ali Jinnah, the first leader of independent Pakistan, dies in 1948. Pakistan and India fight a brief war over the disputed state of Kashmir*.

1951–1956 The civilian government is overthrown and replaced by military rule. A new constitution proclaims Pakistan an Islamic republic. The military will retain a prominent place in Pakistani politics.

1965 Pakistan again goes to war with India over Kashmir, which is claimed by both nations. Kashmiri separatists reject both claims and fight for independence.

1971–1972 East Pakistan, ethnically and historically distinct from West Pakistan, proclaims its independence as Bangladesh* following a brutal independence war that eventually involves war between India and Pakistan.

1991 Islamic Sharia law is formally incorporated into the legal code.

1998 In response to India's nuclear tests, Pakistan also develops and tests nuclear weapons, adding a serious global concern to the long enmity between the two countries. Another war is fought with India in northern Kashmir.

1999 A military coup brings General Pervez Musharraf to power.

2001–2002 Pakistan becomes a close ally of the United States* following the terrorist attacks in New York. Pakistani troops fight to remove Taliban and Al-Qaeda fundamentalists who are infiltrating the country. The military government takes steps to curb religious extremism.

2007 Former Prime Minister Benazir Bhutto returns to Pakistan from exile and dies in a bomb attack at an election campaign rally.

2008 Amid continuing political upheavals, President Musharraf resigns following an agreement by the two major political parties to begin impeachment proceedings. Tensions over the Kashmir conflict continue to be paramount concerns in the country. India accuses Pakistan of involvement in the terrorist attacks in Mumbai, which the government denies.

2009 Militants attack a bus carrying the Sri Lanka* national cricket team, leaving five policemen dead and seven players injured. Increasing violence and Islamic militancy threaten the stability of the republic.

PALAU

OFFICIAL NAME

Beluu er a Belau (Palauan); Republic of Palau (English)

POPULATION

20,900 (2009e)

INHABITANTS' NAME/NICKNAME

Palauan(s)

LANGUAGE/LANGUAGES

English, Palauan (both official); several recognized regional languages

RELIGION/RELIGIONS

Roman Catholic, 49 percent; Protestant, 22 percent; Modekngei (mixed Christian and traditional beliefs), 9 percent; other or no religion

NATIONAL FLAG

The flag is a sky blue field charged with a large yellow disk offset to the hoist. The blue represents the Pacific Ocean that surrounds Palau, as well as Palau's transition from foreign rule to self-determination. The yellow disk represents the full moon, a sign of national unity. The full moon is considered by Palauans to be the optimum time for human activity.

COAT OF ARMS/SEAL

The coat of arms is a circle with a centered depiction of a Palauan communal meetinghouse, or *bai,* with the sea, the sky, and a flag, all in black and white. Around the flag is the name of the country in Palauan and English.

CAPITAL CITY

Melekeok

TYPE OF GOVERNMENT

Presidential republic

NATIONAL EMBLEM

Decorated gable of a *bai,* a communal meeting house

NATIONAL COLORS

Blue and yellow

NATIONAL ANTHEM

The anthem was adopted in 1980, when independence was first requested, and became the national anthem upon independence in 1994.

Belau rekid (Palauan); Our Palau (English)

Palau is coming forth with strength and
  power,
By her old ways abides still every hour.
One country, safe, secure, one government
Under the glowing, floating soft light stands.
Let's build our economy's protecting fence
With courage, faithfulness and diligence
Our life is anchored in Palau, our land
We with our might through life and death
  defend
In spirit let's join hands, united, one
Care for our homeland . . . from forefathers on
Look after its concord, its glory keep
Through peace and love and heart's devotion
  deep
God bless our country, our island home
  always
Our sweet inheritance from ancient days
Give us strength and power and all the rights
To govern with to all eternity

CURRENCY

U.S. dollar

INTERNET IDENTIFIER

.pw

VEHICLE IDENTIFICATION PLATES/STICKERS

PAL

PASSPORT

The passport cover has the name of the country in Palauan and English, the coat of arms, and the word *passport* in Palauan and English.

NATIONAL FLOWER

Plumeria

NATIONAL TREE

Temple tree

NATIONAL BIRD

Biib (Palau fruit dove)

NATIONAL RESOURCES

Natural resources include forests, minerals (especially gold), marine products, and deep-seabed minerals. The economy consists primarily of tourism, subsistence agriculture, and fishing. Tourism is supported by one of the world's greatest concentrations of coral reefs, exotic fish, and other marine life. The government is the major employer of the work force, relying heavily on financial assistance from the United States*. Remittances from Palauans living outside the country are an important source of foreign currency.

FOODS

Local specialties include shrimp in coconut sauce; island fish stuffed with onions and wrapped in banana leaves for cooking; island chicken, chicken breasts cooked with lemon, onions, beer, soy sauce, and cloves; fruit bat soup; coconut fritters; and chicken stew.

SPORTS/SPORTS TEAMS

Baseball and association football (soccer) are the most popular sports. Palau national teams participate in many sports at an international level.

TEAM SPORTS

Baseball

Palau Baseball Team; Palau Softball Team

Basketball

Palau Basketball Team; Palau Women's Basketball Team

Football

Palau Football Team

Tennis

Pacific Oceania Davis Cup Team; Pacific Oceania Fed Cup Team (Pacific Island teams represent several Pacific island nations)

Volleyball

Palau Men's Volleyball Team; Palau Women's Volleyball Team

INDIVIDUAL SPORTS

Palau Archery Team; Palau Athletics Team; Palau Swim Team; Palau Table Tennis Team; Palau Triathlon Team; Palau Wrestling Team

NATIONAL HEROES OR PERSONIFICATIONS

Elicita Morei, leader of the women's liberation movement and anti–nuclear weapons activist; Ngiratkel Etpison, considered the father of tourism in the islands and the president from 1989 to 1992; Kuniwo Nakamura, the president who oversaw Palau's transition to full independence in 1994

NATIONAL HOLIDAY/INDEPENDENCE DAY

Constitution Day, July 9

FESTIVALS/FAIRS

Festival of Pacific Arts, July; Underwater Palau International Photo Festival, March; Constitution Day celebrations, July

SIGNIFICANT EVENTS IN FORMATION OF NATIONAL IDENTITY

2500 B.C.E.–1500 C.E. Seafaring settlers, probably from present Indonesia*, settled the islands. The colonists develop a complex society based on fishing and farming. Palauan culture is matrilineal, with land and wealth passed from mother to daughter.

1543–1783 European mariners probably sight the islands in the mid-1500s. An English sea captain shipwrecked on the islands in 1783 names the group the Pelew Islands. Various European countries make vague claims to the region.

1885–1920 The Spanish government asserts its claim, and Palau becomes part of the Spanish East Indies governed from the Philippines*. Germany* also claims the islands. After the Spanish-American War in 1898, Spain* sells the islands to Germany. After World War I, the islands pass to Japan* as a League of Nations mandate.

1922–1945 The Japanese promote economic development and support immigration by Japanese, Okinawans, and Koreans. Fishing and copra are established as the main industries in Palau. The islands are the scene of intense fighting in the Second World War.

1947 Palau becomes part of the United Nations Trust Territory of the Pacific Islands under U.S. administration. The islands, subsidized by government aid, develop a separate local economy.

1970 Palauans indicate to the U.S. government their wish for separation from Micronesia*.

1979–1981 As the trust territory moves toward independence, Palau and the Marshall Islands* opt for separate status. The Republic of Palau is created.

1983–1990 Successive referendums on a proposed compact with the United States fail to win a majority of the votes. The compact would have given Palau management of its own affairs, while the United States would retain responsibility for defense.

1993–1994 Voters approve a compact agreement and become an independent state. Under the compact, the country receives financial and other aid from the United States, which retains responsibility for defense and the right to operate military bases. Palau becomes a member state of the United Nations.

2003 Palau signs the Comprehensive Test Ban Treaty and becomes a nuclear-free zone.

2006–2009 Government ministries begin moving to a new capital at Melekeok.

PAPUA NEW GUINEA

OFFICIAL NAME

Papua Niugini (Pidgin); Independent State of Papua New Guinea (English)

POPULATION

6,450,800 (2009e)

INHABITANTS' NAME/NICKNAME

Papua New Guinean(s)

LANGUAGE/LANGUAGES

English, Tok Pisin, Hiri Motu (all official); Melanesian Pidgin serves as the lingua franca. An estimated 820 indigenous languages are spoken.

RELIGION/RELIGIONS

Roman Catholic, 22 percent; Lutheran, 16 percent; Anglican, 5 percent; other Protestant, 23 percent; indigenous beliefs, other or no religion

NATIONAL FLAG

The flag has two triangles of red over black, divided from upper hoist to lower fly. The *kumul,* or bird of paradise, flies across the red half, symbolizing the country's emergence into nationhood. On the black is depicted the five stars of the South Cross constellation, representing ties to Australia* and other South Pacific nations. Red, black, and yellow are traditional colors in Papua New Guinea.

COAT OF ARMS/SEAL

The coat of arms consists of a bird of paradise over a traditional spear and a *kundu* drum. The images symbolize the country's ties to nature and history and its willingness to defend its freedom.

MOTTO

Unity in Diversity

CAPITAL CITY

Port Moresby

TYPE OF GOVERNMENT

Parliamentary democracy

NATIONAL EMBLEM
Bird of paradise

NATIONAL COLORS
Red, black, and yellow

NATIONAL ANTHEM
The anthem, composed by an Australian soldier before independence, was adopted when Papua New Guinea gained independence in 1975.

O Arise, All You Sons
O arise all you sons of this land,
Let us sing of our joy to be free,
Praising God and rejoicing to be
Papua New Guinea.

Shout our name from the mountains to seas
Papua New Guinea;
Let us raise our voices and proclaim
Papua New Guinea.

Now give thanks to the good Lord above
For his kindness, his wisdom and love
For this land of our fathers so free,
Papua New Guinea.

Shout again for the whole world to hear
Papua New Guinea;
We're independent and we're free,
Papua New Guinea.

PATRON SAINT
Michael the Archangel

CURRENCY
Papua New Guinea kina

INTERNET IDENTIFIER
.pg

VEHICLE IDENTIFICATION PLATES/ STICKERS
PNG (unofficial)

PASSPORT
The passport cover has the Pidgin name of the country, Papua Niugini, and the full English name, Independent State of Papua New Guinea, with the coat of arms and the word *passport* in English.

AIRLINE
Air Niugini

NATIONAL FLOWER
Passion flower (unofficial)

NATIONAL TREE
Strangler fig (unofficial)

NATIONAL ANIMAL
Pig (unofficial)

NATIONAL BIRD
Kumul (bird of paradise)

NATIONAL FISH
Papuan black bass (unofficial)

NATIONAL RESOURCES
Natural resources include gold, copper, silver, natural gas, timber, oil, and fisheries. Papua New Guinea is richly endowed with natural resources, but exploitation has been hampered by rugged terrain and the high cost of developing infrastructure. Agriculture provides a subsistence livelihood for most of the population. Tourism is becoming an important industry, based on the country's remarkable variety of cultures and varied scenery and ecology. Annual financial aid, particularly from Australia, is an important resource.

FOODS
Mumu, a dish of pork, sweet potatoes, rice, and greens, is considered the national dish. Other local specialties include curried fish, a dish of fresh fish, pineapple, onion, garlic, and curry; fried sweet potatoes and bananas; chicken and greens in coconut milk; vegetables in coconut milk; sago grubs with peanut sauce; chicken on a stick; flying fox

(fruit bat) with prunes and cream sauce; and *paua sup*, made of python, pork, onions, and chilies.

Sports/Sports Teams

The unofficial national sport is rugby league. Other popular sports are association football (soccer), cricket, and Australian-rules football. Papua New Guinea national teams participate in many sports at an international level.

Team Sports

Baseball

Papua New Guinea Baseball Team; Papua New Guinea Softball Team

Basketball

Papua New Guinea Basketball Team; Papua New Guinea Women's Basketball Team

Bowls

Papua New Guinea Bowls Team

Cricket

Papua New Guinea Cricket Team; Papua New Guinea Women's Cricket Team

Football

Papua New Guinea Football Team, nickname the Golden Birds of Paradise; Papua New Guinea Women's Football Team; Papua New Guinea Rugby League Team, nickname the Kumuls; Papua New Guinea Rugby Union Team; Papua New Guinea Australian-Rules Football Team, nickname the Mosquitoes; Papua New Guinea Women's Australian-Rules Football Team, nickname the Mosquitoes; Papua New Guinea Futsal Team; Papua New Guinea Touch Football Team; Papua New Guinea Women's Touch Football Team

Hockey

Papua New Guinea Field Hockey Team

Korfball

Papua New Guinea Korfball Team

Netball

Papua New Guinea Netball Team

Tennis

Papua New Guinea Davis Cup Team; Pacific Oceania Davis Cup Team; Pacific Oceania Fed Cup Team (Pacific Oceania teams represent a number of Pacific island countries)

Volleyball

Papua New Guinea Men's Beach Volleyball Team; Papua New Guinea Women's Beach Volleyball Team; Papua New Guinea Men's Volleyball Team; Papua New Guinea Women's Volleyball Team

Individual Sports

Papua New Guinea Amateur Boxing Team; Papua New Guinea Archery Team; Papua New Guinea Athletics Team; Papua New Guinea Canoeing Team; Papua New Guinea Judo Team; Papua New Guinea Sailing Team; Papua New Guinea Shooting Team; Papua New Guinea Swim Team; Papua New Guinea Tae Kwon Do Team; Papua New Guinea Weight Lifting Team

National Heroes or Personifications

Michael Somare, leader of the independence movement and four-time prime minister; Tore Lokoloko, popular politician and leader of the 1975 transition to independence; John Guise, a leader of the independence movement in the 1970s

National Holiday/Independence Day

Independence Day, September 16

Festivals/Fairs

Enga Cultural Festival, August; Mount Hagen Festival, August; Tumbuan Mask Festival, August; Goroka Festival, September; Hiri Moale Festival, September; Papua

New Guinea Arts and Cultural Festival, November

SIGNIFICANT EVENTS IN FORMATION OF NATIONAL IDENTITY

500 B.C.E. Austronesian migrants settle the coastal regions, displacing the original inhabitants, who still dominate the highlands. The island is called Papua, a Malay word describing the Melanesians' frizzy hair. Traders from Southeast Asia visit the island to trade for the rare bird of paradise plumes prized in Asian courts.

16th century Portuguese and Spanish explorers visit the islands. Spanish mariner Inigo Ortiz de Retes names the main island Nueva Guinea, due to the resemblance of the islanders to the people of Guinea* in Africa.

1768 French explorer Louis-Antoine de Bougainville sails through the islands, giving his name to the most northerly of the Solomon Islands*.

19th century British mariners claim the region for the United Kingdom*. The British establish a protectorate over southeast New Guinea, while Germany* annexes the northern part of the island.

1906 Administration of the British protectorate is transferred to newly independent Australia as the Territory of Papua.

1914 Australian forces occupy German New Guinea when the First World War begins. At the end of the war, Australia is given a League of Nations mandate to administer the territory, which remains separate from Australian Papua.

1933 Gold prospectors lead expeditions into the highlands, where they encounter cultures unchanged since the Stone Age.

1942 During the Second World War, Japanese forces occupy the island.

1949–1961 The two territories unite in a United Nations trust territory called the Territory of Papua and New Guinea. A local legislative council is established in 1954, the first step towards self-government. The first election involving the indigenous population is held.

1971–1975 The territory is renamed Papua New Guinea and is granted self-government under Michael Somare. Full independence is granted in 1975.

1989–1997 Separatist rebels on Bougainville* begin a prolonged war for independence from Papua New Guinea. A truce is signed leading to an autonomous Bougainville state in association with Papua New Guinea.

2001 The Bougainville Peace Agreement guarantees a referendum on independence in 10 to 15 years.

2004–2009 An Australian study warns that the country is on course for social and economic collapse. The continuing population drift to the urban centers accelerates, with problems of squatter settlements, ethnic disputes, unemployment, and social problems, particularly violent crime.

PHILIPPINES

OFFICIAL NAME

Republika ng Pilipinas (Filipino); Republic of the Philippines (English)

POPULATION

90,618,100 (2009e)

INHABITANTS' NAME/NICKNAME

Filipino(s); Pinoy(s)

LANGUAGE/LANGUAGES

Filipino (standardized Tagalog), English (both official); recognized regional languages include Tagalog, Bikol, Cebuano, Ilocano, Hiligaynon, Kapampangan, Waray-Waray, Pangasinan, and others.

RELIGION/RELIGIONS

Roman Catholic, 81 percent; Protestant, 8 percent; Muslim, 5 percent; other or no religion

NATIONAL FLAG

The flag is a horizontal bicolor of blue over red, with a white equilateral triangle at the hoist. In the center of the triangle is a gold sun with eight primary rays, each containing three individual rays; and at each corner of the triangle is a five-pointed gold star. The blue stands for peace, truth, and justice; the red stands for patriotism and valor; and the white triangle symbolizes equality and fraternity. The sun's eight primary rays represent the original eight provinces, while the three stars represent the three major geographical divisions of the country.

COAT OF ARMS/SEAL

The coat of arms is a shield or crest bearing the three five-pointed gold stars on the upper portion, the eight-rayed sun in a central oval, and a lower portion divided vertically blue and red. On the blue is the eagle of the United States* and on the red is the lion of Spain*, representing the historical rulers of the country.

MOTTO

Maka-Diyos, makatao, makakalikasan, at makabansa (Filipino); For God, people, nature, and country (English)

CAPITAL CITY

Manila

TYPE OF GOVERNMENT

Unitary presidential republic

NATIONAL EMBLEM

Eight-rayed golden sun

NATIONAL COLORS

Blue, red, and white

NATIONAL ANTHEM

The anthem, written during the uprising against Spanish rule in 1898, originally had Spanish lyrics; after the Philippines came under the rule of the United States, an English version was written; and finally, a version in Tagalog appeared in the 1940s. The Tagalog (Filipino) version is now the only official version.

Lupang Hinirang (Filipino); Beloved Land (English)

Beloved land,
Pearl of the Orient,
The heart's fervor
In your bosom is ever alive.
Chosen land,
You are the cradle of the brave,
To the conquerors
You shall never surrender.

Through the seas and mountains,
Through the air and your blue sky,
There is splendor in the poem
and song of beloved freedom.

The sparkle of your flag
Is shining victor,
Its stars and sun
will never dim.

Land of glory, the sun of our affections,
Life is heaven in your arms;
When someone oppresses you, it is our
   pleasure
To die for you.

PATRON SAINT

Our Lady of Safe Travel; Saint Rose of Lima; Our Lady of the Turumba; Immaculate Heart of Mary.

CURRENCY

Filipino peso

INTERNET IDENTIFIER

.ph

VEHICLE IDENTIFICATION PLATES/STICKERS

RP

PASSPORT

The passport cover has the short name of the country in Filipino, Pilipinas, the coat of arms, and the word for passport in Filipino, adopted from Spanish, *pasaporte.*

AIRLINES
Philippine Airlines; Cebu Pacific

NATIONAL FLOWER
Sampaguita (Arabian jasmine)

NATIONAL TREE
Rosewood

NATIONAL ANIMAL
Carabao (Philippines water buffalo)

NATIONAL BIRD
Philippines eagle (monkey-eating eagle)

NATIONAL FISH
Milkfish (unofficial)

NATIONAL FRUIT
Mango (unofficial)

NATIONAL LEAF
Anáhaw (Footstool palm) (unofficial)

NATIONAL RESOURCES
Natural resources include timber, petroleum, nickel, cobalt, silver, gold, salt, and copper. Remittances from Filipinos living outside the country, the largest diaspora in the world, are an important source of foreign currency and investment. Tourism, built around the country's historic cities, monuments, island life, sandy beaches, and pleasant climate, is one of the most important industries.

FOODS
Lechon, roasted whole pig, is considered the national dish. Other national dishes include adobo, a marinade method of preparing meat or chicken; *sinigana,* meat or fish prepared in a tamarind broth; *kare-kare,* a stew of oxtail with peanuts served with *bagoong* (fermented shrimp paste); *machado,* pork cooked in tomato sauce; *pochero,* beef or pork cooked in tomato sauce with bananas and vegetables; *bangus,* a dish of fresh milkfish; and *pancit,* a noodle dish of Chinese origin with many different varieties.

SPORTS/SPORTS TEAMS
Basketball is the most commonly played sport. *Sipa,* a team sport played both indoors or outdoors, is the traditional sport. Association football (soccer) and baseball are also popular. Philippines national teams participate in many sports at an international level.

TEAM SPORTS

Badminton
Philippines Badminton Team

Baseball
Philippines Baseball Team; Philippines Softball Team

Basketball
Philippines Basketball Team, nickname Team Pilipinas; Philippines Women's Basketball Team, nickname Team Pilipinas; Philippines Wheelchair Basketball Team

Cricket
Philippines Cricket Team

Football
Philippines Football Team, nickname Azkals (the Street Dogs); Philippines Women's Football Team, nickname Azkals (the Street Dogs); Philippines Under-19 Football Team; Philippines Women's Under-19 Football Team; Philippines Rugby Union Team, nickname the Volcanoes; Philippines Rugby League Team; Philippines Futsal Team; Philippines Beach Soccer Team

Handball
Philippines Handball Team

Hockey
Philippines Field Hockey Team

Kabaddi
Philippines Kabaddi Team

Polo
Philippines Polo Team

Racing
Philippines Speedway Team

Table Tennis
Philippines Table Tennis Team

Tennis
Philippines Davis Cup Team; Philippines Fed Cup Team

Volleyball
Philippines Men's Volleyball Team; Philippines Women's Volleyball Team; Philippines Men's Beach Volleyball Team; Philippines Women's Beach Volleyball Team

Water Polo
Philippines Water Polo Team

INDIVIDUAL SPORTS
Philippines Aikido Team; Philippines Amateur Boxing Team; Philippines Archery Team; Philippines Athletics Team; Philippines Cycling Team; Philippines Equestrian Team; Philippines Fencing Team; Philippines Gymnastics Team; Philippines Judo Team; Philippines Karate Team; Philippines Modern Pentathlon Team; Philippines Rowing Team; Philippines Sailing Team; Philippines Shooting Team; Philippines Swim Team; Philippines Tae Kwon Do Team; Philippines Triathlon Team; Philippines Weight Lifting Team; Philippines Wrestling Team

WINTER SPORTS
Philippines Skating Team

NATIONAL HEROES OR PERSONIFICATIONS
Juan de la Cruz is the personification of the Philippines and the collective Filipino psyche; Gabriela represents the women of the Philippines.

National heroes include José Rizal, the leader of the national movement in the late 19th century; Gabriela Silang, the first Filipina to lead a revolt against the Spanish in the mid-18th century; Andrés Bonifacio, a leader of the anti-Spanish revolution in the 1890s; and Melchora Aquino, known as Tandang Sora, the Grand Woman of the Revolution or the Mother of Balintawak.

NATIONAL HOLIDAY/INDEPENDENCE DAY
Independence Day, June 12

FESTIVALS/FAIRS
Christmas Festival, December–January; Holy Week, February–March; Hari-Raya Puasa (Thanksgiving Festival), variable dates; Penafrancia Fluvial Festival, April; Carabao Festival, May

SIGNIFICANT EVENTS IN FORMATION OF NATIONAL IDENTITY
5000 B.C.E.–1000 B.C.E. Seafaring Malays from the present Indonesia* colonize the islands, displacing the earlier Negrito peoples.

200 B.C.E. A large wave of immigrants arrives from the west. They become the ancestors of most of the present population.

9th century–12th century The Malay peoples of the islands establish trade relations with China* and Japan* and maintain cultural ties to India* and the Malay Archipelago region. Migrants from Borneo settle in the southern islands.

14th century–15th century Islam is introduced in Sulu and the southern islands. The Muslim sultanates of Jolo and Maguindanao are founded in the Sulu Archipelago and Mindanao.

1521–1580 Ferdinand Magellan, leading a Spanish flotilla, encounters the islands. Ruy Lopez de

Villalobos arrives in the islands in 1543. He calls them the Philippines in honor of Philip, the son of the Spanish king. The Spaniards institute forced labor of all indigenous males ages 16 to 60.

17th century The galleon trade between Manila and Mexico* begins, mostly carrying goods from China and silver from Mexico. Due to the profits earned from the trade, Spain lacks interest in developing the Philippines, Spanish control is restricted to the northern islands because of fierce Muslim resistance in the south.

1774 Filipinos are allowed to enter the Catholic priesthood.

1884 The annual tribute extracted from all Filipino males is ended and the required forced labor of 40 days a year is reduced to 15.

1896–1898 A nationalist uprising breaks out. Spanish authorities execute nationalist leader José Rizal. The Philippines are declared independent of Spain. The Spanish surrender, and a U.S. military government is established. Spain sells the colony to the United States for $20 million.

1899–1905 Denied their promised independence, hostilities break out between the Filipinos and the U.S. military. American troops moving into the south fight the Moro War against the Muslim sultanates.

1935 The Philippines Commonwealth is created as an autonomous state associated with the United States.

1941 Japanese bombers attack the Philippines following the attack on Pearl Harbor. The Japanese conquest begins a brutal occupation.

1946 The United States declares the Philippines independent. The Filipinos acknowledge the act as the nation's second independence.

1965–1969 Ferdinand Marcos is elected president. Fighting breaks out between Muslim separatists and the Filipino military. A communist insurgency begins. Marcos' rule becomes increasingly dictatorial as he is reelected every four years in fraudulent elections. He is supported by the United States for his anticommunist rhetoric.

1972–1976 Muslims launch an all-out war of independence. Marcos places the entire country under martial law and stifles dissent. A Muslim autonomous region is created in the south, but the war continues.

1981 Martial law is lifted in preparation for a visit by the Pope. Marcos is finally ousted after looting the public treasury.

1986–1987 Peace talks between the government and Muslim rebel groups fail to resolve the separatist war in the south. Communist rebels become more active.

2000–2009 Instability and political upheavals continue to hamper efforts to combat poverty and raise living standards to match those of neighboring countries. Fighting by Muslim rebels continues in the south following many failed negotiations. The U.S. government urges the Philippine government to again initiate negotiations with Muslim groups in the south in an effort to curb the rise of Islamic fundamentalist organizations in the region.

PITCAIRN

OFFICIAL NAME
Pitkern Ailan (Pitkern); Pitcairn Islands (English)

POPULATION
48 (2009e)

INHABITANTS' NAME/NICKNAME
Pitkerner(s)

LANGUAGE/LANGUAGES
English, Pitkern (both official). Pitkern is a mixture of 18th century English dialect mixed with a Tahitian dialect.

RELIGION/RELIGIONS
Seventh-day Adventist, 100 percent

NATIONAL FLAG
The flag is a blue field charged with the Union Jack on the upper hoist and the coat of arms on the fly.

COAT OF ARMS/SEAL

The coat of arms features a shield depicting the anchor and bible from the *HMS Bounty*. This represents the ancestral history of the islanders, as most are descended from the sailors who mutinied on the *Bounty* in 1789. The design of the shield is green and blue, representing the island rising from the ocean. The helmet and crest are above the shield, with a flowering slip of *miro* and a Pitcairn Island wheelbarrow.

CAPITAL CITY

Adamstown

TYPE OF GOVERNMENT

British overseas territory

NATIONAL ANTHEM

The official anthem is "God Save the Queen," although the local anthem is used most often for official purposes.

Come Ye Blessed (shared with Norfolk Island*)

Then shall the King
Say unto them
On his right hand:
Come ye blessed of my Father
Inherit the kingdom prepared for you
From the foundation of the world
I was hunger'd and ye gave me meat,
I was thirsty and ye gave me drink
I was a stranger and ye took me in,
Naked and ye clothed me,
I was sick and ye visited me,
I was in prison and ye came unto me
In as much ye have done it unto one of the
  least of
These my brethren
Ye have done it unto me,
Ye have done it unto me.

CURRENCY

New Zealand dollar

INTERNET IDENTIFIER

.pn

VEHICLE IDENTIFICATION PLATES/STICKERS

GB Great Britain (official); PN Pitcairn (unofficial). Pitcairn has no official license plates. The PN code is normally used by Pitkerners living in New Zealand and Australia.

PASSPORT

Pitkerners are British citizens and travel on British passports.

NATIONAL FLOWER

Miro flower

NATIONAL TREE

Miro (portia tree)

NATIONAL RESOURCES

Natural resources include *miro* trees (used for handicrafts) and fish. Manganese, iron, copper, gold, silver, and zinc have been discovered offshore. Pitcairn postage stamps are a major source of revenue for the island.

NATIONAL HEROES OR PERSONIFICATIONS

Fletcher Christian, the leader of the *Bounty* mutiny and the subsequent settlement of Pitcairn Island by the mutineers, and their Tahitian companions.

NATIONAL HOLIDAY/INDEPENDENCE DAY

Birthday of Queen Elizabeth II, second Sunday of June; Bounty Day, January 23

FESTIVALS/FAIRS

Bounty Day celebrations, January 23

SIGNIFICANT EVENTS IN FORMATION OF NATIONAL IDENTITY

1767 Pitcairn Island is encountered by a British expedition and is given the family name of 15-year-old midshipman Robert Pitcairn, the first to sight the island.

1790 The famous mutiny on the *HMS Bounty* takes place. Mutineers and their Tahitian companions settle on the second largest of the uninhabited islands. The other three islands are sighted and charted.

1838 Pitcairn becomes the first Pacific island to become a British colony.

1855–1856 The island becomes overcrowded, and the entire population of 193 is moved to Norfolk Island. Later, a number of the settlers return to Pitcairn.

1890s The islanders convert to Seventh-day Adventism following a visit by missionaries.

1902–1938 The islands are annexed to the United Kingdom*. In 1938, the four become a single administrative unit named for the only inhabited island, Pitcairn.

2004 Allegations of a long history and tradition of sexual abuse of young girls culminates in charges against 13 men, six of whom are convicted and sentenced to a prison set up for that purpose on the island.

2008–2009 Emigration, primarily to New Zealand*, has thinned the population from a peak of 233 in 1937 to fewer than 50 in 2009.

See also United Kingdom

SAMOA

OFFICIAL NAME
Malo Sa'oloto Tuto'atasi o Samoa (Samoan); Independent State of Samoa (English)

POPULATION
221,500 (2009e)

INHABITANTS' NAME/NICKNAME
Samoan(s)

LANGUAGE/LANGUAGES
Samoan, English (both official); others

RELIGION/RELIGIONS
Congregational, 35 percent; Roman Catholic, 19 percent; Methodist, 15 percent; Mormon, 13 percent; Assembly of God, 6 percent; Seventh-day Adventist, 4 percent; other or no religion

NATIONAL FLAG
The flag consists of a red field with a blue rectangle in the canton charged with five white stars that form the Southern Cross constellation. Red and white are traditional colors used for centuries. The blue represents historic ties to the United Kingdom* and New Zealand*, and the stars represent the constellation and the Holy Cross.

COAT OF ARMS/SEAL
The coat of arms has a central silver shield with the lower two-thirds blue, charged with five silver stars representing the constellation of the Southern Cross. The upper third depicts a green sea with a green coconut palm. Above the shield is a gold cross, and behind are the concentric circles and olive branches representing the United Nations. Below the shield is a banner inscribed with the national motto.

MOTTO
Fa'avae i le atua Samoa (Samoan); Samoa is founded on God (English)

CAPITAL CITY
Apia

TYPE OF GOVERNMENT
Parliamentary republic

NATIONAL COLORS
Blue, white, and red

NATIONAL ANTHEM
The anthem honors the country's national flag. It was adopted at independence from New Zealand in 1962.

> **Samoa Tula'I (Samoan); The Banner of Freedom (English)**
>
> Samoa, arise and raise your flag, your crown!
> Samoa, arise and raise your flag, your crown!

Look at those stars that are waving on it:
This is the symbol of Jesus, who died on it for Samoa.
Oh, Samoa, hold fast your power forever.
Do not be afraid; God is our foundation, our freedom.
Samoa, arise: Your flag is waving, your crown!

CURRENCY

Samoan tala

INTERNET IDENTIFIER

.ws

VEHICLE IDENTIFICATION PLATES/STICKERS

WS

PASSPORT

The passport cover has the name of the country in Samoan and English, the coat of arms, and the word *passport* in Samoan and English.

AIRLINE

Polynesian Blue

NATIONAL FLOWER

Teuil a

NATIONAL TREE

Coconut palm

NATIONAL FISH

Zebra moray (unofficial)

NATIONAL RESOURCES

Natural resources include hardwood forests, hydropower, and fish. Tourism is a major source of income, with the number of visitors growing each year. Traditionally, Samoa has been dependent on foreign development aid, remittances from Samoans living outside the country, and agriculture.

FOODS

The traditional Samoan feast, *fia fia*, comprises suckling pig, chicken, fish, and vegetables, wrapped in taro leaves and cooked in an *umu*, a earth-pit oven. Specialties include *palusami*, taro leaves baked in coconut cream; *oka*, raw fish marinated in coconut cream; octopus cooked in coconut cream and served in a half coconut shell; *talo ta'amu*, a baked root vegetable with coconut cream; *sua arisa*, a rice soup; and *fa'alifu fa'I*, boiled green bananas with coconut milk and onions.

SPORTS/SPORTS TEAMS

The most popular sports are rugby union and *kilikiti*, or Samoan cricket. Samoa national teams participate in many sports at an international level.

TEAM SPORTS

Badminton

Samoa Badminton Team

Baseball

Samoa Baseball Team; Samoa Softball Team

Basketball

Samoa Basketball Team; Samoa Women's Basketball Team

Cricket

Samoa Cricket Team

Football

Samoa Football Team; Samoa Women's Football Team; Samoa Rugby Union Team, nickname Manu Samoa; Samoa Women's Rugby Union Team, nickname Manu Samoa; Samoa Rugby League Team; Samoa Women's Rugby League Team; Samoa Rugby Union Team Sevens, nickname Samoa Sevens; Samoa Futsal Team; Samoa Touch Football Team; Samoa Women's Touch Football Team; Samoa Australian-Rules Football Team, nickname the Bulldogs

Hockey

Samoa Field Hockey Team

Netball

Samoa Netball Team

Table Tennis

Samoa Table Tennis Team

Tennis

Pacific Oceania Davis Cup Team; Pacific Oceania Fed Cup Team (Pacific Oceania teams represent a number of Pacific island countries)

Volleyball

Samoa Men's Beach Volleyball Team; Samoa Women's Beach Volleyball Team; Samoa Men's Volleyball Team; Samoa Women's Volleyball Team

INDIVIDUAL SPORTS

Samoa Amateur Boxing Team; Samoa Archery Team; Samoa Athletics Team; Samoa Canoeing Team; Samoa Judo Team; Samoa Rowing Team; Samoa Sailing Team; Samoa Shooting Team; Samoa Swim Team; Samoa Tae Kwon Do Team; Samoa Weight Lifting Team; Samoa Wrestling Team

NATIONAL HEROES OR PERSONIFICATIONS

Mata'afa, the king who resisted German rule in the early 20th century; John Williams, a missionary responsible for the introduction of Christianity in the early 1800s; Robert Louis Stevenson, author of *Treasure Island*, who chose Samoa for his home in the 19th century; Olaf Nelson, half-Swedish leader of the Mau Movement in the 1920s; Tupua Tamesese, leader of the Mau Movement killed on Black Saturday

NATIONAL HOLIDAY/INDEPENDENCE DAY

Independence Day, June 1

FESTIVALS/FAIRS

Tuila Festival, September; Samoa Jazz Festival, September; Fautasi Outrigger Canoe Race, June; Independence Day celebrations, June

SIGNIFICANT EVENTS IN FORMATION OF NATIONAL IDENTITY

1000 B.C.E. The islands are settled by seafaring colonists from Southeast Asia.

200 B.C.E. Samoa is the center of a flourishing Polynesian community, with trade links to Fiji* and Tonga*.

1300 C.E. Overcrowding leads to the Samoan colonization of Tokelau*.

1722 A Dutch ship is the first European vessel to sight the islands.

1768 French explorer Louis-Antoine de Bougainville names the islands the Navigator Islands after encountering large seagoing canoes.

1857 The Germans establish a trading settlement that becomes the most popular trading post in the Pacific.

1889 The Treaty of Berlin guarantees Samoa independence under its own king, who would be advised by American, British, and German consuls. Robert Louis Stevenson dies at his home in Samoa.

1899 A new treaty divides the Samoa Islands into German Samoa and American Samoa*.

1914–1920 New Zealand troops take control of German Samoa at the outbreak of the First World War. Samoa becomes a League of Nations mandate administered by New Zealand.

1929 The nonviolent Mau Movement begins to demand self-determination. A Mau march in December 1929 is fired on by New Zealand soldiers, leading to many deaths, on what becomes known as Black Saturday.

1947 After the Second World War, Samoa becomes a United Nations trust under New Zealand administration. A legislative council with a Samoan majority is created.

1962 Samoa becomes independent as Western Samoa, the first Polynesian state to win independence. Samoa joins the Commonwealth in 1970.

1991 Universal suffrage is granted, ending the voting privileges of the chiefly class.

1997 The name of the country is officially changed from Western Samoa to Samoa.

2007 King Malietoa Tanumafili II dies after 45 years on the throne. He was appointed king for life at independence in 1962, becoming the third-longest reigning monarch, after King Khumibol Adulyadej of Thailand* and Queen Elizabeth of the United Kingdom*.

2000–2009 Samoa consciously guards its heritage. Economic problems lead to renewed emigration to New Zealand. Samoa is devastated by a large tidal wave in September.

See also American Samoa

SINGAPORE

OFFICIAL NAME
Republic of Singapore (English); Republik Singapura (Malay); Hsin-chia-p'o Hung-ho-kuo (Mandarin); Singapore Kudiyarasu (Tamil)

NICKNAME
The Lion City

POPULATION
4,972,300 (2009e)

INHABITANTS' NAME/NICKNAME
Singaporean(s)

LANGUAGE/LANGUAGES
English, Malay, Mandarin (Chinese), Tamil (all official); Hokkien, Cantonese, Teochew, others

RELIGION/RELIGIONS
Buddhist, 42 percent; Christian, 15 percent; Muslim, 14 percent; Taoist, 8 percent; Hindu, 4 percent; other or no religion

NATIONAL FLAG
The flag is a horizontal bicolor of red over white, charged with a white crescent moon and five white stars in a circle on the upper hoist. White symbolizes unity and purity, and red symbolizes universal brotherhood and equality. The crescent moon and stars symbolize a growing nation and the ideals of democracy, peace, progress, equality, and justice.

COAT OF ARMS/SEAL
The coat of arms has a central red crest or shield with the crescent moon and circle of stars from the national flag. A lion supports the shield on the left and a tiger on the right. Below is a black banner with the country's motto in Malay inscribed in gold letters.

MOTTO
Majulah Singapura (Malay); Onward, Singapore (English)

CAPITAL CITY
Singapore

TYPE OF GOVERNMENT
Parliamentary republic

NATIONAL EMBLEM
Lion

NATIONAL COLORS
Red and white

NATIONAL ANTHEM
The anthem was originally written in Malay when Singapore formed part of Malaysia*, and although independent Singapore has four official languages, the anthem is still sung only in Malay.

Majulah Singapura (Malay); Onward, Singapore (English)
Come, fellow Singaporeans
Let us progress toward happiness together

May our noble aspiration bring
Singapore success

Come, let us unite
In a new spirit
Let our voices soar as one
Onward, Singapore
Onward, Singapore

CURRENCY
Singapore dollar

INTERNET IDENTIFIER
.sg

VEHICLE IDENTIFICATION PLATES/STICKERS
SGP

PASSPORT
The passport cover has the name of the country in English, the coat of arms, the word *passport,* and the standard biometric symbol.

AIRLINE
Singapore Airlines

NATIONAL FLOWER
Vanda Miss Joaquim orchid

NATIONAL ANIMAL
Lion (the lion is not native to southeast Asia. The image was brought to the region by traders from the Middle East; merlion (a mythical creature half lion and half fish)

NATIONAL BIRD
Crimson sunbird

NATIONAL FISH
Guppy (unofficial)

NATIONAL RESOURCES
Natural resources include fish and a deep-water port. With few natural resources, Singapore is built on trade and manufacturing. A well-educated population is the country's major resource. Tourism is also very important to the economy.

FOODS
Rojak, a salad of fruit and vegetables with peanut sauce, is considered the national dish. Hainanese chicken rice, of Chinese origin, is also considered a national dish. Other specialties include *curry laksa,* a thick soup of meat and noodles cooked in coconut curry; *assam laksa,* noodles cooked in sour fish broth; chili crab, crab cooked in a thick, spicy tomato sauce; *rending,* beef cooked in coconut milk; *satay,* skewered marinated meat cooked over charcoal and served with peanut sauce, cucumber, rice, and onions; and the Singapore Sling, a national drink invented in the early 20th century at the famous Raffles Hotel.

SPORTS/SPORTS TEAMS
Association football (soccer), swimming, badminton, basketball, and table tennis are the most popular sports. Singapore national teams participate in many sports at an international level.

TEAM SPORTS
Badminton
Singapore Badminton Team

Baseball
Singapore Baseball Team; Singapore Softball Team

Basketball
Singapore Wheelchair Basketball Team; Singapore Basketball Team; Singapore Women's Basketball Team

Cricket
Singapore Cricket Team

Football

Singapore Football Team, nickname the Lions; Singapore Women's Football Team, nickname the Lionesses; Singapore Rugby Union Team; Singapore Women's Rugby Union Team; Singapore Touch Football Team; Singapore Women's Touch Football Team; Singapore Rugby League Team; Singapore Australian-Rules Football Team, nickname the Wombats; Singapore Rugby Union Team (Sevens), nickname Singapore Sevens; Singapore Women's Under-19 Football Team

Hockey

Singapore Field Hockey Team

Kabaddi

Singapore Kabaddi Team

Korfball

Singapore Korfball Team

Lacrosse

Singapore Lacrosse Team

Netball

Singapore Netball Team

Polo

Singapore Polo Team

Racing

A1 Team Singapore; Singapore Speedway Team

Table Tennis

Singapore Table Tennis Team

Tennis

Singapore Davis Cup Team; Singapore Fed Cup Team

Volleyball

Singapore Men's Volleyball Team; Singapore Women's Volleyball Team

INDIVIDUAL SPORTS

Singapore Aikido Team; Singapore Amateur Boxing Team; Singapore Archery Team; Singapore Athletics Team; Singapore Canoeing Team; Singapore Cycling Team; Singapore Equestrian Team; Singapore Fencing Team; Singapore Gymnastics Team; Singapore Judo Team; Singapore Karate Team; Singapore Rowing Team; Singapore Sailing Team; Singapore Shooting Team; Singapore Swim Team; Singapore Tae Kwon Do Team; Singapore Triathlon Team; Singapore Weight Lifting Team

NATIONAL HEROES OR PERSONIFICATIONS

Lee Kuan Yew, the country's first prime minister and the man responsible for Singapore's present prosperity; Sir Stamford Raffles, the British colonial founder of Singapore; Fandi Ahmad, a former soccer star and national idol; Lim Bo Seng, a resistance fighter against the Japanese during the Second World War

NATIONAL HOLIDAY/ INDEPENDENCE DAY

National Day, August 9

FESTIVALS/FAIRS

Singapore Food Festival, July; Singapore Biennale, September–November; Chinese New Year, January–February; Chingay, January–February; Singapore Fashion Festival, March–April; Singapore Arts Festival, June; Dumpling Festival, June; Deepavali, October

SIGNIFICANT EVENTS IN FORMATION OF NATIONAL IDENTITY

2nd century C.E.–14th century C.E. The island is mentioned as an outpost of the Srivijava state of Sumatra called Temasek, meaning "sea town." The town grew on trade, then declined in the 14th century.

16th century–19th century Singapore forms part of the Sultanate of Johor. The Portuguese take control of the island in 1613, followed by the Dutch, but the island is of little importance and is mostly inhabited by fishermen.

1819–1832 Thomas Stamford Raffles lands on the main island. He signs a treaty with the Sultan of Johor to develop the island as a trading post. Singapore, Malacca, and Penang become the British colony of the Straits Settlements. The busy new port attracts thousands of migrants from China*, India*, and other parts of Asia.

1869 The opening of the Suez Canal leads to a great expansion of trade.

1922 Singapore becomes the main British naval base in East Asia.

1941–1945 Invading Japanese besiege the island, which finally falls. At the end of the Second World War, the island comes under British military administration.

1959 Self-government is granted, with Lee Kuan Yew as prime minister.

1963 Singapore joins the Federation of Malaya, Sabah, and Sarawak to form the Federation of Malaysia.

1965 Singapore leaves the federation amid growing political and ethnic tensions to become an independent republic.

1990 Lee Kuan Yew stands down after 31 years of leading Singapore to become a modern, prosperous trading nation.

2001 Singapore and Malaysia agree to end long-standing disputes, ranging from the water supply to use of airspace, and agree to build a new bridge and tunnel to connect the island to the Malaysian mainland.

2008–2009 Singapore is the sixth wealthiest country in the world, with a lifestyle comparable to the other advanced countries of the world. Singapore's strict laws on public cleanliness, including prohibitions on chewing gum and smoking in public, make the city one of the world's cleanest. The government announces plans to open casinos as way to attract more tourists.

SOLOMON ISLANDS

OFFICIAL NAME
Solomon Islands

POPULATION
554,600 (2009e)

INHABITANTS' NAME/NICKNAME
Solomon Islander(s)

LANGUAGE/LANGUAGES
English, Pijin (Pidgin English), 120 indigenous languages

RELIGION/RELIGIONS
Church of Melanesia, 33 percent; Roman Catholic, 19 percent; South Seas Evangelican, 17 percent; Seventh-day Adventist, 11 percent; United Church, 10 percent; Christian Fellowship Church, 2.5 percent; other or no religion

NATIONAL FLAG
The flag is blue over green, divided diagonally by a thin yellow stripe. On the blue triangle, at the upper hoist, is a square of five white, five-pointed stars. The blue represents the surrounding ocean, the green represents the land, and the yellow represents sunshine. The five stars stand for the five major island groups that make up the country.

COAT OF ARMS/SEAL
The coat of arms has a central yellow shield with an eagle, turtles, and a war shield and arrows, symbols of the various provinces. Above the shield is a heraldic helmet with a traditional canoe and a hibiscus flower. An alligator and a shark support the shield above a brown stand and a yellow banner inscribed with the national motto.

MOTTO
To lead is to serve

CAPITAL CITY
Honiara

TYPE OF GOVERNMENT
Parliamentary democracy and constitutional monarchy as part of the Commonwealth

NATIONAL COLORS
Blue, yellow, and green

NATIONAL ANTHEM
The anthem was written and composed for adoption by the country at independence in 1978.

God Save Our Solomon Islands

God bless our Solomon Islands from shore to shore
Bless all our people and all our lands
With your protecting hands
Joy, peace, progress, and prosperity
That men shall brothers be, make nations see
our Solomon Islands, our Solomon Islands
Our nation Solomon Islands
Stands forever more

PATRON SAINT
Saint Michael the Archangel

CURRENCY
Solomon Islands dollar

INTERNET IDENTIFIER
.sb

VEHICLE IDENTIFICATION PLATES/STICKERS
SOL

PASSPORT
The passport cover has the name of the country in English, the coat of arms, and the word *passport*.

AIRLINE
Solomon Airlines

NATIONAL FLOWER
Hibiscus

NATIONAL ANIMAL
Crocodile

NATIONAL BIRD
Black frigate bird

NATIONAL FISH
Whitetip reef shark

NATIONAL RESOURCES
Natural resources include fish, forests, gold, bauxite, phosphates, lead, zinc, and nickel. The Solomon Islands is mostly undeveloped, with three-quarters of the population engaged in subsistence farming. Tourism is becoming an important resource, with various attractions including sandy beaches, a pleasant climate, and unique cultures. Remittances from Solomon Islanders living outside the country are an important source of foreign currency and investment.

FOODS
Taro and rice are the staples and are served at almost every meal. Tuna, coconut, crab, and other fish and shellfish are part of the cuisine. Tapioca, sweet potatoes, cassava, and other vegetables are also a daily part of island food. *Poi,* made of fermented taro root, is the most typical food. It can be eaten as porridge or served with meat and fish.

SPORTS/SPORTS TEAMS
Rugby and association football (soccer) are the most popular sports. Solomon Islands national teams participate in many sports at an international level.

TEAM SPORTS
Baseball
Solomon Islands Baseball Team; Solomon Islands Softball Team

Basketball

Solomon Islands Basketball Team; Solomon Islands Women's Basketball Team

Football

Solomon Islands Football Team; Solomon Islands Women's Football Team; Solomon Islands Under-19 Football Team; Solomon Islands Women's Under-19 Football Team; Solomon Islands Rugby Union Team; Solomon Islands Rugby Team (Sevens), nickname Solomon Islands Sevens or 7s; Solomon Islands Beach Soccer Team, nickname the Bilikiki Boys; Solomon Islands Futsal Team; Solomon Islands Touch Football Team; Solomon Islands Women's Touch Football Team; Solomon Islands Rugby League Team

Hockey

Solomon Islands Field Hockey Team

Table Tennis

Solomon Islands Table Tennis Team

Tennis

Pacific Oceania Davis Cup Team; Pacific Oceania Fed Cup Team (Pacific Oceania teams represent a number of Pacific island countries)

Volleyball

Solomon Islands Men's Volleyball Team; Solomon Islands Women's Volleyball Team

INDIVIDUAL SPORTS

Solomon Islands Amateur Boxing Team; Solomon Islands Archery Team; Solomon Islands Athletics Team; Solomon Islands Judo Team; Solomon Islands Sailing Team; Solomon Islands Tae Kwon Do Team; Solomon Islands Triathlon Team; Solomon Islands Wrestling Team

NATIONAL HEROES OR PERSONIFICATIONS

Jacob Vouza, a coast watcher during World War II who was captured and tortured by the Japanese without divulging information; Biuku Gasa and Eroni Kumana, the two islanders who found and aided then-Lieutenant John F. Kennedy, the future U.S. president, and his shipwrecked crew during World War II; Peter Kenilorea, the political leader who led the islands to independence in 1978

NATIONAL HOLIDAY/INDEPENDENCE DAY

Independence Day, July 7

FESTIVALS/FAIRS

Independence Day celebrations, July; Easter Week, March–April; Festival of the Sea, December; Music Festival, May

SIGNIFICANT EVENTS IN FORMATION OF NATIONAL IDENTITY

4000 B.C.E. Austronesian peoples settle the islands, displacing the earlier Papuan groups.

1200 B.C.E.–800 B.C.E. Polynesian seafaring peoples settle on the islands and mix with the earlier inhabitants.

1568 A Spanish expedition sailing from Peru sights the islands.

1800 Missionaries begin work in the islands. Blackbirding, the often brutal rounding up of villages for labor on sugar plantations in Fiji* and Queensland, continually disrupts island life.

1890s The evils of the labor trade prompt the United Kingdom* to declare a protectorate over the southern islands in 1893. Other islands, including the German Solomon Islands, are added to the protectorate.

1900–1940 Missionaries convert most of the population to Christianity. British and Australian firms establish large-scale coconut plantations.

1942–1945 Japanese forces overrun the islands. The returning Allies fight from island to island, with particularly hard fighting on Guadalcanal.

1946 British rule is restored. An independence movement, Marching Rule, is created.

1976–1978 The islands become fully self-governing, Two years later, the islands are granted full independence.

1988 The Solomon Islands joins Vanuatu* and Papua New Guinea* to form the Spearhead Group that aims to preserve Melanesian culture.

1997–1998 Violence between the islanders of Guadalcanal and Malaita leads to violence as 20,000 Malaitans are forcibly driven out of Guadalcanal. Fighting breaks out between militias formed on each island.

2000 Peacekeepers from Australia* and New Zealand* are deployed to end the fighting. Economic problems add to the disruption of island life.

2007–2009 The violence gradually diminishes, but poverty and conflicts over land and resources continue to threaten the unity of the island nation.

South Korea. *See* Korea, South

SRI LANKA

OFFICIAL NAME

Shri Lanka Prajatantrika Samajavadi Janarajaya (transliteration from Sinhala); Ilangai Jananayaka Socialisa Kudiarasu (transliteration from Tamil); Democratic Socialist Republic of Sri Lanka (English)

POPULATION

21,311,400 (2009e)

INHABITANTS' NAME/NICKNAME

Sri Lankan(s)

LANGUAGE/LANGUAGES

Sinhala, Tamil (both official); English, Malay, Portuguese, Dutch, others

RELIGION/RELIGIONS

Buddhist, 70 percent; Muslim, 7.5 percent; Hindu, 7 percent; Christian, 6 percent; other or no religion

NATIONAL FLAG

The flag has a yellow border around two vertical stripes of green and saffron at the hoist and a rectangular red panel bordered yellow on the fly containing a yellow lion holding a sword upright and four *bo* leaves, one in each corner. The lion represents the Sinhalese, the *bo* leaves stand for Buddhism, and the sword stands for sovereignty. The green stripe represents the Muslim faith and the Moorish minority; the saffron represents the mostly Hindu Tamils.

COAT OF ARMS/SEAL

The seal is a circular device resting on an ornate base featuring a central red circle with the gold lion of the national flag within concentric circles decorated in traditional motifs.

CAPITAL CITY

Colombo

TYPE OF GOVERNMENT

Democratic socialist republic

NATIONAL COLORS

White, red, and blue

NATIONAL ANTHEM

The anthem is the result of a contest at the time of independence and was first performed in 1952. There are official Sinhala and Tamil versions.

> **Sri Lanka Matha (Sinhala); Mother Lanka (English)**
>
> Mother Lanka, we salute thee!
> Plenteous in prosperity, thou,
> Beauteous in grace and love,
> Laden with corn and luscious fruit,
> And fragrant flowers of radiant hue,
> Giver of life and all good things,
> Our land of joy and victory,
> Receive our grateful praise sublime,
> Lanka! we worship thee.
> Thou givest us knowledge and truth,

Thou art our strength and inward faith,
Our light divine and sentient being,
Breath of life and liberation.
Grant us, bondage free, inspiration.
Inspire us for ever.
In wisdom and strength renewed,
Ill-will, hatred, strife all ended,
In love enfolded, a mighty nation
Marching onward, all as one,
Lead us, Mother, to fullest freedom.

PATRON SAINT

Mary Immaculate; Our Lady of Lanka

CURRENCY

Sri Lankan rupee

INTERNET IDENTIFIER

.ik

VEHICLE IDENTIFICATION PLATES/STICKERS

CL

PASSPORT

The passport cover has the name of the country in Sinhala, Tamil, and English; the coat of arms; and the word *passport* in the three languages.

AIRLINE

SriLankan Airlines

NATIONAL FLOWER

Nil Mahanel

NATIONAL TREE

Na (ironwood); *Bo* (sacred fig) (unofficial)

NATIONAL BIRD

Sri Lanka junglefowl

NATIONAL FISH

Two-spot barb (unofficial)

NATIONAL RESOURCES

Natural resources include limestone, graphite, mineral sands, gems, phosphates, clay, and hydropower. Tourism is an important resource, with attractions such as ancient cities and monuments, sandy beaches, unique cultures, and a pleasant climate. Remittances from Sri Lankans, particularly Tamils, living outside the country are an important source of foreign currency and investment.

FOODS

Rice and curry is the national dish with many varieties. Other specialties include *kiribath,* rice cooked in coconut milk; *dahl,* spiced lentils; *papadums,* thin crisp wafers made from chickpea or rice flour; Sri Lankan fish curry, a mixture of spices and herbs cooked with fresh fish; *hoppers,* a type of bread with a wafer-crisp edge served with an egg baked on top; *jaggery,* a fudge made of the sap of the *kitul* palm; springhoppers, steamed circlets made of rice flour and eaten like pasta; and *pittu,* a mixture of lightly toasted fresh rice meal and grated coconut steamed in a bamboo mold.

SPORTS/SPORTS TEAMS

Cricket is the country's most popular sport, along with association football. Volleyball, which is also very popular, was declared the national sport in 1991. Sri Lanka national teams participate in many sports at an international level.

TEAM SPORTS

Badminton
Sri Lanka Badminton Team

Baseball
Sri Lanka Baseball Team

Basketball
Sri Lanka Basketball Team; Sri Lanka Women's Basketball Team

Cricket

Sri Lanka Cricket Team, nickname the Lions; Sri Lanka Women's Cricket Team, nickname the Lions

Football

Sri Lanka Football Team, nickname the Lions or the Brave Reds; Sri Lanka Rugby Union Team, nickname the Elephants; Sri Lanka Rugby Union Team (Sevens), nickname Sri Lanka Sevens or Sri Lanka 7s; Sri Lanka Women's Rugby Union Team (Sevens), nickname Sri Lanka Sevens or Sri Lanka 7s

Hockey

Sri Lanka Field Hockey Team

Kabaddi

Sri Lanka Kabaddi Team

Netball

Sri Lanka Netball Team

Racing

Sri Lanka Speedway Team

Table Tennis

Sri Lanka Table Tennis Team

Tennis

Sri Lanka Davis Cup Team; Sri Lanka Fed Cup Team

Volleyball

Sri Lanka Men's Beach Volleyball Team; Sri Lanka Men's Volleyball Team; Sri Lanka Women's Volleyball Team

INDIVIDUAL SPORTS

Sri Lanka Amateur Boxing Team; Sri Lanka Archery Team; Sri Lanka Athletics Team; Sri Lanka Cycling Team; Sri Lanka Equestrian Team; Sri Lanka Gymnastics Team; Sri Lanka Judo Team; Sri Lanka Modern Pentathlon Team; Sri Lanka Rowing Team; Sri Lanka Sailing Team; Sri Lanka Shooting Team; Sri Lanka Swim Team; Sri Lanka Tae Kwon Do Team; Sri Lanka Weight Lifting Team; Sri Lanka Wrestling Team

NATIONAL HEROES OR PERSONIFICATIONS

Gongalegoda Banda, a leader of the 1848 rebellion and a pretender to the throne of Kandy; C.W.W. Kannangara, a leader of the independence movement in the early 20th century; Henry Pedris, a young militia officer unjustly executed by the British in 1915; Ponnambalam Arunachalam, a Tamil leader in the late 19th century; Puran Appu, a leader of the 1848 uprising

NATIONAL HOLIDAY/INDEPENDENCE DAY

Independence Day, February 4

FESTIVALS/FAIRS

New Year, April 13; Esala Perahera, July–August; Deepavali (Festival of Lights), October–November; Vesak, June

SIGNIFICANT EVENTS IN FORMATION OF NATIONAL IDENTITY

Sixth century B.C.E. The first Sinhalese settlers arrive from the northern Indian mainland to quickly drive the native peoples into the forested highlands.

Third century B.C.E. Buddhism is introduced, and a great Buddhist civilization develops with advanced culture, great cities, and a succession of rulers. Tamil migration begins from southern India*.

1200–1500 The Sri Lankan kingdom declines. A Tamil kingdom is established in the north of the island.

1505–1796 Portuguese explorers visit the island, marking the beginning of European interest in South Asia. The Portuguese control the coastal regions until the 1600s, when the Dutch take control of the island known as Ceylon.

1796–1815   The island is ceded to the British in 1796 and becomes a crown colony in 1802. The various kingdoms are united in 1815.

1833–1900   English is made the official language of the island. Large numbers of indentured workers are brought from nearby Tamil areas of India to work European plantations. A serious uprising against British rule extends across the island. The leaders are later captured and executed.

1931   The British grant voting rights and introduce power sharing between the Sinhalese and Tamils in local governments.

1948–1949   Ceylon becomes independent under a Sinhalese-dominated government that disenfranchises Indian Tamil plantation workers.

1956–1958   A wave of Sinhalese nationalism leads the government to make Sinhalese the sole official language and take other measures to bolster the Sinhalese Buddhist culture on the island. Tamil protests at the new laws lead to ethnic violence and rioting.

1972   The name of the country is changed to Sri Lanka, the ancient name of the island. Buddhism is made the official religion.

1976   A resistance group, the Liberation Tigers of Tamil Eelam*, forms as tensions increase in Tamil-majority districts in the north and east.

1983–1985   The growing civil war extends across the island, called the Eelam War after the proposed Tamil state in northern and eastern Sri Lanka.

1995–2002   War rages across the north and east, with atrocities committed by both sides. A cease-fire is signed under Norwegian auspices.

2004   More than 30,000 die when a tidal wave, generated by a powerful undersea earthquake, devastates the east coast of the island.

2006–2009   Violence resumes amid new demands for the creation of Tamil Eelam. Fighting continues in the north and east, disrupting normal life in those areas. The government officially withdraws from the 2002 cease-fire agreement and engages the Tamil rebels on several fronts. Growing international concern focuses on the thousands of civilians trapped in battle zones in the north and east of the country. The defeat of the Tamil Tiger rebels in mid-2009 gives the government a chance to extend its control to many areas of the north and east.

Tahiti. *See* French Polynesia

TAIWAN

OFFICIAL NAME
Jhonghuá Mínguó (transliteration from Chinese); Republic of China (English)

POPULATION
23,091,200 (2009e)

INHABITANTS' NAME/NICKNAME
Taiwanese; Taiwan Chinese; Chinese

LANGUAGE/LANGUAGES
Mandarin (official); Taiwanese (Taiyu/Min), Hakka dialects, English, others

RELIGION/RELIGIONS
Buddhist or Taoist, 93 percent; Christian, 4 percent; other or no religion

NATIONAL FLAG
The flag is a red field with a large blue rectangle as a canton on the upper hoist, charged with a white sun with 12 rays. The red represents the red earth, the blue represents the sky, the white sun and rays represent the spirit of progress, and the 12 rays represent the 12 hours of the Chinese day. The flag adopted by the Taiwanese nationalists who support the idea of an independent republic, called the "hearts-in-harmony" flag, has three vertical stripes of green, white, and green, the white twice the width of the green stripes and charged with a central device of four hearts in red. The green symbolizes the natural beauty of Taiwan and the need to protect the environment; the white stands for the purity of the Taiwanese people and their desire to pre-

serve the beauty and traditions of the island; and the red hearts, joined in the center, stand for the four population groups, the Hakka, Hoklo, aborigines, and mainlanders.

COAT OF ARMS/SEAL

The coat of arms is a blue circle charged with the white sun and 12 rays of the national flag. Called the "blue sky with a white sun," the design is taken from the historical flag of the Kuomintang, which ruled Taiwan until 2000.

CAPITAL CITY

Taipei

TYPE OF GOVERNMENT

Semipresidential republic

NATIONAL EMBLEM

White 12-rayed sun

NATIONAL COLORS

Red, blue, and white

NATIONAL ANTHEM

The country has two anthems; one is the official anthem of the Republic of China, and the other is *Gúoqî ge* (Flag-Raising Song), which is used at the Olympics and other international events to satisfy mainland China's rejection of anything representing the rival Republic of China.

> **Zhōnghuá Mínguó gúogē (Chinese); National Anthem of the Republic of China, or Three Principles of the People (English)**
>
> Three principles of the people,
> Our aim shall be:
> To found a free country,
> *World peace,* be our stand.
> Lead on, comrades,
> Vanguards ye are.
> Hold fast your aim,
> Without rest day or night.
> Be earnest and brave,
> Your country to save,

> One heart, one soul,
> One mind, one goal.

PATRON SAINT

Mary, Queen of China

CURRENCY

New Taiwan dollar

INTERNET IDENTIFIER

.tw

VEHICLE IDENTIFICATION PLATES/ STICKERS

RC Republic of China (official); TW Taiwan (unofficial)

PASSPORT

The passport cover has the name of the country, Republic of China, in Chinese and English; the coat of arms; the name Taiwan; and the word *passport* in Chinese and English.

AIRLINES

China Airlines; EVA Air

NATIONAL FLOWER

Ume (plum blossom)

NATIONAL TREE

Camphor tree (unofficial)

NATIONAL ANIMAL

Taiwanese rock macaque (unofficial)

NATIONAL BIRD

Mikado pheasant (official); Red-crowned crane (unofficial)

NATIONAL FISH

Seema (Taiwanese salmon)

NATIONAL RESOURCES

Natural resources include small deposits of coal, gold, marble, fisheries, natural gas, limestone, and asbestos. The island nation, boycotted for decades by mainland China*, developed an export economy based on its well-educated and skilled workforce. Taiwan now has one of the highest standards of living in Asia, equal to that of the countries of the European Union (EU), and has accumulated the world's fifth-largest reserve of foreign currency. Tourism is an important industry, with tourists drawn to the historic cities and monuments, unique culture, and varied scenery.

FOODS

Ba-wan, translucent dough filled with pork, bamboo shoots, and shiitake mushrooms, is considered the national dish. Other Taiwanese specialties include *taiyangbing,* known as suncake, a small, elaborately wrapped pastry intended for gifts; *chou doufu,* "stinky tofu," fried or cooked and served with vegetables and sauces; *niurou mian,* beef noodle soup; *ó-á-chian,* a type of omelet made with eggs, oysters, and Garland chrysanthemum leaves; *san bei,* a chicken dish made with rice wine, sesame oil, and soy sauce; and *koe-á bah,* a steamed pork patty with pickled cucumber.

SPORTS/SPORTS TEAMS

Baseball is the most popular sport and is considered the national sport. Association football (soccer) and basketball are also very popular. The island nation competes internationally under the euphemism Chinese Taipei, as the People's Republic of China objects to the names Republic of China and Taiwan.

TEAM SPORTS

Badminton
Chinese Taipei Badminton Team

Baseball
Chinese Taipei Baseball Team; Chinese Taipei Softball Team

Basketball
Chinese Taipei Basketball Team; Chinese Taipei Women's Basketball Team; Chinese Taipei Wheelchair Basketball Team

Curling
Chinese Taipei Curling Team

Football
Chinese Taipei Football Team; Chinese Taipei Women's Football Team; Chinese Taipei Under-23 Football Team; Chinese Taipei Under-20 Football Team; Chinese Taipei Women's Under-19 Football Team; Chinese Taipei Futsal Team; Chinese Taipei Rugby League Team; Chinese Taipei Rugby Union Team

Handball
Chinese Taipei Handball Team; Chinese Taipei Women's Handball Team

Hockey
Chinese Taipei Ice Hockey Team; Chinese Taipei Field Hockey Team

Korfball
Chinese Taipei Korfball Team

Netball
Chinese Taipei Netball Team

Racing
Chinese Taipei Speedway Team

Table Tennis
Chinese Taipei Table Tennis Team

Tennis
Chinese Taipei Davis Cup Team; Chinese Taipei Fed Cup Team

Volleyball
Chinese Taipei Women's Volleyball Team; Chinese Taipei Men's Volleyball Team; Chinese Taipei Fistball Team

INDIVIDUAL SPORTS

Chinese Taipei Aikido Team; Chinese Taipei Amateur Boxing Team; Taipei Archery Team; Chinese Taipei Athletics Team; Chinese Taipei Canoeing Team; Chinese Taipei Cycling Team; Chinese Taipei Equestrian Team; Chinese Taipei Fencing Team; Chinese Taipei Gymnastics Team; Chinese Taipei Judo Team; Chinese Taipei Karate Team; Chinese Taipei Modern Pentathlon Team; Chinese Taipei Rowing Team; Chinese Taipei Sailing Team; Chinese Taipei Shooting Team; Chinese Taipei Swim Team; Chinese Taipei Tae Kwon Do Team; Chinese Taipei Triathlon Team; Chinese Taipei Weight Lifting Team; Chinese Taipei Wrestling Team

WINTER SPORTS

Chinese Taipei Biathlon Team; Chinese Taipei Curling Team; Chinese Taipei Ice Hockey Team; Chinese Taipei Luge Team; Chinese Taipei Skating Team

NATIONAL HEROES OR PERSONIFICATIONS

The Chinese goddess Mazu, the Mother-Ancestor, is revered as the protector of Taiwan.

National heroes include Zheng Cheng-gong, a military leader who drove the Dutch from Taiwan in 1662 after 50 years of European rule; Dr. Sun Yat-sen, considered the Father of Modern China and founder of the Kuomintang; Chiang Kai-shek, the military and political leader who led the Republic of China through the Second World War but ultimately failed to defeat the communists and led the exodus to Taiwan in 1949; and Chiang Ching-kuo, premier and president of the republic in the 1970s and 1980s, when the government became much more tolerant and finally admitted native Taiwanese to positions of power.

NATIONAL HOLIDAY/INDEPENDENCE DAY

Republic Day (founding of the Republic of China), October 10

FESTIVALS/FAIRS

Dragon Boat Festival, June; Mid-Autumn Festival, September–October; Lantern Festival, February–March; Lunar New Year, variable dates; Ghost Festival, August; Double Ninth Day celebrations, variable dates

SIGNIFICANT EVENTS IN FORMATION OF NATIONAL IDENTITY

3000 B.C.E. The Changbin culture flourishes on the island, which is inhabited by Malay peoples.

Seventh century C.E. Small groups of migrants from the Chinese mainland begin to settle on the sparsely populated island. Over the following centuries, the migration continues until the Malay Kaoshan people are pushed into the eastern mountains.

1540s A separate kingdom is established on the island. Portuguese sailors name the island Ilha Formosa (Beautiful Island). The Japanese mount an unsuccessful invasion of the kingdom.

16th century Thousands of refugees fleeing mainland upheavals settle on the island, making the Chinese population the dominant majority.

17th century The Dutch take control of Taiwan and rule for 50 years before being driven out in 1662.

18th century Forces of the Manchu dynasty in China conquer the kingdom.

1874–1895 Japan* sends a military force to test Taiwan's defenses. Taiwan is organized as a province of the Chinese Empire in 1887. Following the Sino-Japanese war, Taiwan is ceded to Japan.

1915 A Taiwanese uprising is brutally put down by Japanese troops.

1921 The first cultural association is founded.

1947–1949 Following the Japanese defeat in the Second World War, Taiwan comes under the rule of the government of the Republic of China. The Kuomintang, or Chinese Nationalist Party, the main political group in the republic, is defeated by the communists and flees to Taiwan with over

2 million other refugees. The government of the Republic of China is reestablished at Taipei.

1949–1969 The period known as the white terror continues for years, with the killing or imprisonment of tens of thousands of opposition supporters, pro-independence activists, and other dissidents.

1971 The People's Republic of China assumes the Republic of China's seat at the United Nations Security Council. Taiwan is expelled from the world body.

1996 A "New Name, New Flag, New Anthem" campaign is launched to rename the Republic of China, replace the flag of the Republic of China, and the National Anthem of the Republic of China, all of which were brought to Taiwan when the Kuomintang government retreated to the island in 1949.

2000 The opposition Democratic Progressive Party defeats the Kuomintang in elections. The movement to replace the Republic of China with the Republic of Taiwan brings threats of invasion from the mainland.

2005 The People's Republic of China passes an antisecession law authorizing the use of force should Taiwan declare independence. Over 1.5 million people march through Taipei in protest.

2007–2008 The island applies for membership in the United Nations under the name Taiwan and is rejected by the General Assembly. Direct flights between Taiwan and the mainland begin after nearly six decades. The president apologizes for the killing and imprisonment of tens of thousands of political dissidents in the 1950s and 1960s.

2009 Visits by high-ranking Chinese officials seeking to improve relations are met with protests by pro-independence groups.

See also China

TAJIKISTAN

Official Name
Jumhurii Tojikiston (Tajik); Republic of Tajikistan (English)

Population
7,225,600 (2009e)

Inhabitants' Name/Nickname
Tajik(s); Tajikistani(s)

Language/Languages
Tajik (official); Uzbek, Russian, Kyrgyz, others

Religion/Religions
Sunni Muslim, 85 percent; Shia Muslim, 5 percent; other or no religion

National Flag
The flag is a horizontal tricolor of red, white, and green. The white stripe is 1.5 times the size of the red and green stripes and is charged with a centered golden crown and seven golden stars. The color red represents the unity of the country and brotherhood with other nations; the white represents the unity of the people, cotton, the major crop, and the snow and ice in the high mountains; and the green represents nature and green valleys. The crown and stars represent Tajikistan's sovereignty, friendship between all nationalities, and the union of workers, peasants, and the intellectual classes. The crown refers to the Farsi (Persian) word *taj,* meaning "crown," which is the basis of the country's name.

Coat of Arms/Seal
The coat of arms is a circle bearing a red rising sun with rays above the Pamir Mountains and the crown and stars of the national flag encircled by depictions of the country's two most important crops, cotton and wheat. Below is a book, representing learning and the future.

Capital City
Dushanbe

TYPE OF GOVERNMENT

Unitary presidential republic

NATIONAL COLORS

Red, white, and green

NATIONAL ANTHEM

The anthem was adopted at independence in 1991, when new lyrics were added to the melody of the Soviet-era anthem.

Surudi Milli (Tajik); Our Beloved Country (Engiish)

Our beloved country,
We are happy to see your pride.
Let your happiness and prosperity last forever.
We have reached this day since ancient times,
We stand under your flag.

Chorus

Long live my homeland, my free Tajikistan!
You are a symbol of our ancestors' hope
Our honor and dignity,
You are an eternal world for your sons,
Your spring will never end,
We remain loyal to you.

Chorus

Long live my homeland, my free Tajikistan!
You are a mother for all of us,
Your future is our future,
Your meaning is the meaning of our souls and
   bodies,
You give us happiness forever,
Because of you, we love the world!

Chorus

Long live my homeland, my free Tajikistan!

CURRENCY

Tajik somoni

INTERNET IDENTIFIER

.tj

VEHICLE IDENTIFICATION PLATES/STICKERS

TJ

PASSPORT

The passport cover has the name of the country in Tajik and English, the coat of arms, and the word *passport* in both languages.

AIRLINES

Tajik Air; Somon Air

NATIONAL ANIMAL

Snow leopard

NATIONAL RESOURCES

Natural resources include hydropower, some petroleum, uranium, mercury, brown coal, lead, zinc, antimony, tungsten, silver, gold, and arable land. The poorest country in Central Asia, Tajikistan depends on international assistance. The primary resources are foreign aid, cotton, aluminum, and remittances from Tajiks living outside the country.

FOODS

Ow palov, a dish of rice or cracked wheat with meat and shredded turnip or carrot, is considered the national dish. Other Tajik specialties include *shashlik,* skewered meat cooked over charcoal; *lipioshka,* a round, flat, unleavened bread; *manty,* a type of large dumpling filled with minced meat, onions, and spices; *samsa,* small meat-filled pastries; *chiburekki,* deep-fried dough cakes; and *halwa,* a sweet of sugar, rose water, and saffron threads.

SPORTS/SPORTS TEAMS

Association football (soccer) and wrestling are the most popular sports. Tajikistan national teams participate in many sports at an international level.

TEAM SPORTS

Basketball

Tajikistan Basketball Team; Tajikistan Women's Basketball Team; Tajikistan Futsal Team

Football

Tajikistan Football Team, nickname the Crown; Tajikistan Women's Football Team nickname the Crown

Hockey

Tajikistan Field Hockey Team

Table Tennis

Tajikistan Table Tennis Team

Tennis

Tajikistan Davis Cup Team; Tajikistan Fed Cup Team

Volleyball

Tajikistan Men's Volleyball Team; Tajikistan Women's Volleyball Team

INDIVIDUAL SPORTS

Tajikistan Amateur Boxing Team; Tajikistan Athletics Team; Tajikistan Canoeing Team; Tajikistan Fencing Team; Tajikistan Judo Team; Tajikistan Modern Pentathlon Team; Tajikistan Shooting Team; Tajikistan Swim Team; Tajikistan Tae Kwon Do Team; Tajikistan Weight Lifting Team

NATIONAL HEROES OR PERSONIFICATIONS

Rostam, a mythical hero from Shahnama famed for his leadership against invading Turks and Arabs; Ismail Somani, the founder of the Tajik nations; Somoni, the ninth-century Tajik king who built a Central Asian empire, considered the father of the nation; Sangak Safarov, the leader responsible for defeating the Islamic rebels in the 1990s civil war

NATIONAL HOLIDAY/INDEPENDENCE DAY

Independence Day (or National Day), September 9

FESTIVALS/FAIRS

Navruz, the Tajik New Year, March; Eid-e-Ramazon (Eid al-Fitr), variable dates; Eid-i-Kurbon (Festival of Sacrifice, or Eid al-Adha), variable dates; Independence Day celebrations, September

SIGNIFICANT EVENTS IN FORMATION OF NATIONAL IDENTITY

1000 B.C.E. The region forms part of the Persian Empire. Persian culture and language become part of the local culture.

Eighth century C.E. The Tajiks emerge as a separate ethnic group speaking a dialect of Persian. Invading Arabs conquer the region, bringing with them the new religion of Islam. Tajik cities become way stations on the Silk Road trading routes.

13th century–14th century Genghis Khan conquers the region with the destruction of cities and irrigation systems. Tamerlane, the heir to the Mongols, builds a great empire in Central Asia.

1860–1900 The territory is divided; the northern districts come under Russian rule, while the south forms part of the independent Emirate of Bukhara.

1914–1916 The beginning of the First World War is distant until Russian authorities attempt to conscript Central Asians in 1916, setting off a widespread rebellion.

1917–1920 The Russian Revolution ends czarist rule. The Central Asian rebellion continues until the invading Red Army crushes it.

1924–1929 Tajikistan becomes a separate autonomous republic within Soviet Uzbekistan and a separate union republic within the Soviet Union in 1929.

1930s The forced collectivization of Tajik farms and herds sets off armed resistance that continues for several years before it is finally crushed.

1960s The republic becomes the third-largest cotton-producing region in the Soviet Union. Aluminum production is introduced.

1970s Outside influences, particularly from ethnically and linguistically related Iran*, lead to the formation of Islamic groups and attacks on nationalities settled in the region under Soviet rule. In 1978, some 13,000 Tajiks take part in anti-

Russian rioting, the largest in Soviet Central Asia since the 1920s.

1988–1989 The liberalization of Soviet politics allows a renewed interest in Tajik culture and the formation of unofficial political groups. The Tajik government declares Tajik the official state language.

1990–1991 Prodemocracy protests, fueled by rumors that more non-Tajiks are to be settled in the region, disrupt the republic. Tajikistan becomes the last of the Central Asian republics to declare independence as the Soviet Union dissolves.

1992–1996 Anti-government demonstrations escalate until civil war erupts between pro-government forces and Islamic groups. The war kills over 20,000 people, forces hundreds of thousands to flee, and devastates the already fragile economy.

2004 The Russian military presence in the country is enlarged.

2008 The country appeals for aid following the harshest winter in half a century, which leads to famine and an energy crisis. Russia* and other countries begin sending aid to avert a possible famine.

2009 The country's lack of natural resources hampers the slow economic recovery after the civil war in the 1990s. The government signs an agreement with the United States* to allow the transport of nonmilitary supplies to Afghanistan* over Tajik territory.

TAMIL EELAM

OFFICIAL NAME
North-East Autonomous Zone of Sri Lanka; Tamil Eelam

POPULATION
3,091,600 (2009e)

INHABITANTS' NAME/NICKNAME
Tamil(s); Sri Lanka Tamil(s)

LANGUAGE/LANGUAGES
Tamil (de facto official); English, others

RELIGION/RELIGIONS
Hindu, 88 percent; Christian, 6 percent; Muslim, 5.5 percent; other or no religion

NATIONAL FLAG
The flag of the proposed state of Tamil Eelam is a red field with a large yellow sun at the bottom and nine yellow rays. Red represents the realization that freedom is not complete until the establishment of Tamil Eelam. Yellow symbolizes the Tamils' aspirations to freely govern themselves in their own homeland as a fundamental political and human right.

COAT OF ARMS/SEAL
The coat of arms is that of the Liberation Tigers of Tamil Eelam (LTTE): a red circle with the depiction of a leaping tiger surrounded by rounds of ammunition and knives, symbolizing the armed nature of the Tamil uprising.

CAPITAL CITY
Trincomalee (claimed); Kilinochchi (administrative)

TYPE OF GOVERNMENT
Unrecognized parliamentary republic

NATIONAL EMBLEM
Leaping tiger

NATIONAL COLORS
Red and yellow

NATIONAL ANTHEM
Vanati, a rebel leader killed in 1991, wrote the anthem of the Liberation Tigers of Tamil Eelam.

She, the Woman of Tamil Eelam

Her forehead shall be adorned
not with *kunkumczm* (but) with red blood.
All that is seen in her eyes

is not the sweetness of youth (but) the tombs
of the dead.
Her lips shall utter
not useless sentences (but) firm declarations of
those who have fallen.
She has embraced not men, (but) weapons!
Her legs are searching not for a relationship
with relatives
(but) looking towards the liberation of the
soil of Tamil Eelam
Her gun will fire shots.
No failure will cause the enemy to fall!
It will break the fetters of Tamil Eelam!
Then from our people's lips a national anthem
will sound!

CURRENCY
Sri Lankan rupee

INTERNET IDENTIFIER
.te (unofficial)

VEHICLE IDENTIFICATION
PLATES/STICKERS
CL Sri Lanka (official); TE Tamil Eelam
(unofficial)

PASSPORT
Tamils are Sri Lankan citizens and travel on
Sri Lankan passports.

NATIONAL FLOWER
Karthigai poo

NATIONAL TREE
Palmyra

NATIONAL ANIMAL
Tiger

NATIONAL RESOURCES
Natural resources include limestone, graphite, mineral sands, gems, phosphates, clay,
and hydropower. The disruptions of the war
have made financial assistance from Tamils
in India* and remittances from Sri Lankan
Tamils living outside Sri Lanka* important
sources of foreign currency.

FOODS
Idiyappam, also known as string hoppers, a
type of tiny rice noodle, is considered a national dish. Rice with curry of many different varieties is the other most popular dish.
Toddy, made from palm tree sap, is considered the national drink. Other specialties include *appam,* a thin bread made of rice flour;
ittapam, a thick, flat, round bread normally
served with *sambar,* a vegetable stew with
pigeon peas; *dahl,* spiced lentils with vegetables; and *paniyaram,* a steamed batter made
of black lentils and rice put through a mold.

SPORTS/SPORTS TEAMS
Association football (soccer) and wrestling
are the most popular sports. The Tamil Eelam national team participates in football at
a regional level.

TEAM SPORTS
Football
Tamil Eelam Football Team

NATIONAL HEROES OR PERSONIFICATIONS
Vanati, a military leader killed in the Battle
of Elephant Pass in 1991; Velupillai Pirapa-
haran, the leader of the LTTE; King Canili,
who led the resistance to the Portuguese invasion of the island in the 16th century; Ya-
lupillai Prabhakaran, the leader of the Tamil
rebellion until his death in May 2009; Kal-
inga Magha, the king who invaded northern
Sri Lanka from India to establish a powerful
Tamil kingdom on the island in the 13th century; Ponnambalam Arunachalam, a Tamil
political leader in the 19th century

NATIONAL HOLIDAY/
INDEPENDENCE DAY
Remembrance Day, July 24

FESTIVALS/FAIRS

Puththandu (Tamil New Year), April-May; Pongal (Harvest Festival), January; Saha Sivarathiri, February-March; Kataragama Festival, June

SIGNIFICANT EVENTS IN FORMATION OF NATIONAL IDENTITY

2000 B.C.E.–1700 B.C.E. Aryan invaders overrun much of northern India, pushing the indigenous Dravidian peoples to the south. Many cross the narrow strait to the large island off the coast later known as Sri Lanka.

Fifth century B.C.E. Buddhist Aryans, the Sinhalese, from northern India conquer the island, which becomes the center of an advanced Buddhist kingdom.

235 B.C.E.–101 B.C.E. Tamil invaders from southern India invade and conquer Sri Lanka. They rule as an aristocratic elite until the resurgent Sinhalese overthrow Tamil rule.

1017 C.E. Tamils of the Chola kingdom cross the isthmus to again conquer Sri Lanka. Tamil settlers colonize the north and spread down the eastern coast. A century of sporadic violence between Tamils and Sinhalese begins.

12th century–13th century A great flowering of Tamil culture ends with the Muslim invasion of southern India in 1279.

1509 The Portuguese encounter the island and establish trading posts. They eventually take control of the island's government.

1796 The British take control of the island, which they call Ceylon, adding the Tamil-populated region to the Madras government in the Tamil region of nearby India.

1815–1850 Plantation agriculture is introduced. Indentured Tamil laborers from British India become a large minority among the Tamil population. To differentiate between the groups, the newcomers become known as Indian Tamils.

1900–1945 Ethnic strife continues to disrupt island life. Only the British presence prevents even more violence.

1948–1949 Ceylon becomes an independent state under Sinhalese domination. The Indian Tamils are disenfranchised.

1956–1958 A wave of Sinhalese nationalism leads to the declaration of Sinhalese as the sole official language and restrictions on Tamil culture and education and the Hindu religion. Anti-Tamil riots leave over two hundred dead and thousands of refugees.

1972 The name of the country is changed from Ceylon to the Sinhalese name, Sri Lanka. Buddhism becomes the official religion.

1976–1977 Amid mounting ethnic tensions, Tamil nationalists form the Liberation Tigers of Tamil Eelam (LTTE). Anti-Tamil riots again sweep the island.

1983 Civil war erupts between Tamils and Sinhalese.

1991 The LTTE is implicated in the assassination of Indian premier Rajiv Gandhi in southern India.

1995–2001 Fighting races across the north and east. Tamils bomb the holiest Buddhist shrine of the Sinhalese.

2002–2004 A peace agreement is signed, although rebels continue to demand an independent Tamil Eelam. A massive tidal wave hits eastern Sri Lanka, killing over 30,000 people.

2006–2009 Peace talks resume. Government troops clear the eastern provinces as thousands flee. The war on the island continues, with neither side willing to negotiate a settlement. Government victories in the east and north in mid-2009 lead to widespread suffering among the civilian population trapped by the fighting.

See also Sri Lanka

THAILAND

OFFICIAL NAME

Ratcha Anachak Thai (transliteration from Thai); Kingdom of Thailand (English)

POPULATION

63,627, 200 (2009e)

INHABITANTS' NAME/NICKNAME

Thai(s)

LANGUAGE/LANGUAGES

Thai (official)

RELIGION/RELIGIONS

Buddhist, 94 percent; Muslim, 5 percent; other or no religion

NATIONAL FLAG

The flag, known as the *trairanga* or tricolor, has five horizontal stripes of red, white, blue, white and red, with the middle blue stripe twice the width of the others. Red and white are the traditional colors of Siam, or Thailand. Red represents the nation and the people, white represents the predominant Buddhist religion, and blue represents the king.

COAT OF ARMS/SEAL

The coat of arms, the national emblem, features the *garuḍa*, a figure from both Buddhist and Hindu mythology. In Thailand, this figure is used as a symbol of the royal family and authority. This version of the figure is referred to as *krut pha*, meaning "*garuḍa* acting as the vehicle (of Vishnu)." The *garuḍa* is a mythical figure with a human torso and arms, a demonic face, and a bird's legs, wings, and tail. It is dressed in gold, with a crown, bracelets, armbands, a necklace, and a loincloth.

CAPITAL CITY

Bangkok

TYPE OF GOVERNMENT

Parliamentary constitutional monarchy

NATIONAL EMBLEM

Phya khrut (royal *garuḍa*); white elephant

NATIONAL COLORS

Blue, red, and white

NATIONAL ANTHEM

The anthem was adopted in 1932, and the lyrics were changed at the time when the country changed its name from Siam to Thailand in 1939. A royal anthem is also used.

> **Phleng chat thai (Thai); Thailand National Anthem (English)**
>
> Thailand embraces in its bosom all people of Thai blood.
> Every inch of Thailand belongs to the Thais in every respect.
> It has long maintained its sovereignty,
> Because the Thais have always been united.
> The Thai people are peace-loving,
> But they are no cowards at war.
> They will allow no one to rob them of their independence,
> Nor will they suffer tyranny.
> All Thais are ready to give up every drop of blood
> For the nation's safety, freedom and progress.

CURRENCY

Thai baht

INTERNET IDENTIFIER

.th

VEHICLE IDENTIFICATION PLATES/STICKERS

T

PASSPORT

The passport cover has the name of the country and the word for passport in Thai, the national emblem, the short name of the country and the word *passport* in English, and the standard biometric symbol.

AIRLINES

Thai Airways International; Air Asia

NATIONAL FLOWER
Ratchaphruek (cassia flower)

NATIONAL TREE
Ratchaphruek tree

NATIONAL ANIMAL
Asian elephant

NATIONAL BIRD
Siamese fireback pheasant

NATIONAL RESOURCES
Natural resources include tin, rubber, natural gas, tungsten, tantalum, timber, lead, fish, gypsum, lignite, fluorite, and arable land. Rice and manufactured goods are the country's major exports. Tourism is very important, supported by historic cities and monuments, unique cultures, sandy beaches, a pleasant climate, and exotic and varied scenery.

FOODS
Pad thai, rice noodles pan-fried with fish sauce, lime, tamarind, chopped peanuts, and egg, often combined with chicken, seafood, or tofu, is considered the national dish. Other national specialties include *nuea sawan* (heavenly beef), thinly sliced beef with fish sauce, soy sauce, coriander, and palm sugar; *gai pud king,* stir-fried chicken with ginger; *kai look koei* (son-in-law eggs), hard-boiled eggs sautéed with shallots, tamarind, brown sugar, and fish sauce; *khao pad,* fried rice with meat, seafood, or coconut and vegetables; *pad prik,* stir-fried beef with chilies; and *gai pad grapao,* minced chicken with garlic, chilies, and basil.

SPORTS/SPORTS TEAMS
Association football (soccer), volleyball, and traditional sports, such as kickboxing, are popular sports. Thailand national teams participate in many sports at an international level.

TEAM SPORTS
Badminton
Thailand Badminton Team

Baseball
Thailand Baseball Team; Thailand Softball Team

Basketball
Thailand Basketball Team; Thailand Wheelchair Basketball Team; Thailand Women's Basketball Team

Cricket
Thailand Cricket Team; Thailand Women's Cricket Team

Football
Thailand Football Team, nickname Changsuk (the War Elephants); Thailand Women's Football Team, nickname Changsuk (the War Elephants); Thailand Under-23 Football Team, nickname Changsuk (the War Elephants); Thailand Women's Under-19 Football Team, nickname Changsuk (the War Elephants); Thailand Rugby Union Team; Thailand Women's Rugby Union Team; Thailand Futsal Team; Thailand American Football Team; Thailand Beach Soccer Team; Thailand Touch Football Team; Thailand Women's Touch Football Team; Thailand Rugby Union Team (Sevens), nickname Thailand Sevens or Thailand 7s; Thailand Women's Rugby Union Team (Sevens), nickname Thailand Sevens or Thailand 7s

Hockey
Thailand Ice Hockey Team; Thailand Field Hockey Team

Kabaddi
Thailand Kabaddi Team

Netball
Thailand Netball Team

Polo
Thailand Polo Team

Racing
Thailand Speedway Team

Table Tennis
Thailand Table Tennis Team

Tennis
Thailand Davis Cup Team; Thailand Fed Cup Team

Water Polo
Thailand Water Polo Team

Volleyball
Thailand Volleyball Team; Thailand Women's Volleyball Team; Thailand Men's Beach Volleyball Team; Thailand Women's Beach Volleyball Team

INDIVIDUAL SPORTS

Thailand Aikido Team; Thailand Amateur Boxing Team; Thailand Athletics Team; Thailand Canoeing Team; Thailand Cycling Team; Thailand Equestrian Team; Thailand Fencing Team; Thailand Gymnastics Team; Thailand Judo Team; Thailand Karate Team; Thailand Rowing Team; Thailand Sailing Team; Thailand Shooting Team; Thailand Tae Kwon Do Team; Thailand Triathlon Team; Thailand Weight Lifting Team

WINTER SPORTS

Thailand Ice Hockey Team; Thailand Luge Team; Thailand Skating Team

NATIONAL HEROES OR PERSONIFICATIONS

King Narai, responsible for the nation's first period of greatness in the seventh century; Pho Khun Si Indrathit, who established the powerful Sukhothai kingdom in 1238; King Ramathibodi I, who introduced Buddhism and a legal code based on Hindu principles; Taksin, the military leader who reunited the country following the Burmese invasion in 1767–69; King Chulalongkorn, the modernizer of the kingdom in the late 19th century

NATIONAL HOLIDAY/INDEPENDENCE DAY

Birthday of King Phumiphon (Bhumibol), December 5

FESTIVALS/FAIRS

Royal Plowing Ceremony, May; Chakkri Festival, April; Songkran, April; Summer Music and Sport Festival, March; Thai Fruit Festival, May; Green Adventure festival, June; Loy Krathong Festival, November

SIGNIFICANT EVENTS IN FORMATION OF NATIONAL IDENTITY

1000 B.C.E.–1100 C.E. Various cultures dominate the region in a succession of kingdoms.

1238 The first modern Thai state, Sukhothai, is founded in 1238. The Thai alphabet is created.

1365–1767 The successor state of Ayutthaya promotes Theravada Buddhism as the official religion. Burmese invasions in the 1750s and 1760s finally end with the fall of the kingdom in 1767.

1769–1782 King Taksin the Great reunites much of the fallen kingdom. In 1782, King Rama I the Great establishes the capital at Bangkok under the Chakri dynasty.

1868–1910 King Chulalongkorn employs Western advisers to modernize Siam.

1932–1939 A bloodless coup forces the king to introduce a constitutional monarchy and a parliamentary government. Siam changes its name to Thailand.

1941–1945   Japanese forces land and use Thailand to invade neighboring British territories. Thailand declares war on the Allies. At the end of the war, Thailand is forced to return territory taken from Cambodia*, Laos*, and Malaya.

1947–1991   A military coup sets the stage for numerous coups interspersed with civilian governments. The only constant is the Thai monarchy, which is revered and remains aloof from politics.

1997–1998   The Asian financial crisis hits Thailand hard. Tens of thousands of migrant workers are sent back to their countries.

2004   Thousands of people are killed, including hundreds of tourists, when massive waves caused by a powerful undersea quake devastate coastal communities. A wave of separatist violence in the southern Muslim provinces leads to the imposition of martial law in the whole country.

2006–2009   A coup initiates another period of military rule. Martial law is lifted in more than half the country. Elections in 2008 mark the first steps back to civilian rule. Political instability continues with frequent changes of government, although the monarchy remains a stabilizing force.

TIBET

OFFICIAL NAME

Bod-rang-skyong-ljongs (transliteration from Tibetan), Zizâng Zizhiqû (transliteration from Chinese), Tibet Autonomous Region (English)

Bõ (Tibetan; refers to traditional Tibet, including both the present province-level area in China* and the traditional provinces of Amdo, Kham, and Ü-Tsang, which were incorporated into Chinese provinces in the 18th century)

POPULATION

2,892,300 (2009e)

INHABITANTS' NAME/NICKNAME

Tibetan(s)

LANGUAGE/LANGUAGES

Mandarin Chinese, Tibetan (both official); Monya, Lhoba, Mongol, others

RELIGION/RELIGIONS

Buddhist, 93 percent; other or no religion

NATIONAL FLAG

The flag of the Tibetan government-in-exile has a central yellow sun with 12 red and blue rays at the top, hoist, and fly. A white triangle at the bottom, representing a snowy mountain, its point touching the center of the sun, is charged with two white snow lions with green manes and tails, holding the national symbols. The flag is bordered on all sides but the fly by narrow yellow stripes. The meeting point of the mountain and the sun represent Tibet's geographical position in the heart of the Asian continent. The golden rising sun symbolizes freedom, happiness, and prosperity. The 12 rays stand for the 12 descendants of the six aboriginal tribes of Tibet. The two colors of the rays symbolize two guardian deities known as *Mar Nag Nyi,* who are the special protectors of the flag. Red is for the male deity, Chhyo-kong, and blue for the female, Sung-ma. The yellow border indicates the spread of the golden ideals of Buddhism.

COAT OF ARMS/SEAL

The coat of arms of the Tibetan government-in-exile maintains several elements of the flag of Tibet and contains much Buddhist symbolism. The primary elements are the sun and moon above the Himalayas, which represent the nation of Tibet, often known as the Land Surrounded by Snow Mountains. On the slopes of the mountains stand a pair of white snow lions. Held between the two lions is the eight-spoked *dharmacakra,* which represents the Noble Eightfold Path of

Buddhism. Inside the wheel, a three-colored swirling jewel represents the practice of the 10 exalted virtues and the 16 humane modes of conduct.

CAPITAL CITY

Lhasa

TYPE OF GOVERNMENT

Autonomous region of the People's Republic of China; the Central Tibetan Administration government-in-exile is a parliamentary theocracy under the Dalai Lama and is based at Dharamsala in northwestern India, the closest part of India to the border with Tibetan region of China*

NATIONAL EMBLEM

Potala Palace, former residence of the Dalai Lama, in Lhasa

NATIONAL COLORS

Red, yellow, white, and blue

NATIONAL ANTHEM

The anthem is based on a historical piece of sacred music. It has been used by Tibetans in exile since the Chinese invasion of 1950.

Gyallu (English translation)

The source of temporal and spiritual wealth
  of joy and boundless benefits,
The wish-fulfilling jewel of the Buddha's
  teaching, blazes forth radiant light
The all-protecting Patron of the Doctrine and
  of all sentient beings by his actions stretches
  forth his influence like an ocean
By his eternal *vajra*-nature his compassion
  and loving care extend to beings everywhere

May the celestially appointed government of
  Gawa Gyaden achieve the heights of glory
And increase its fourfold influence and
  prosperity
May a golden age of joy and happiness spread
  once more through these regions of Tibet
And may its temporal and spiritual splendor
  shine once again

May the Buddha's teaching spread in all the
  10 directions and lead all beings in the
  universe to glorious peace
May the spiritual sun of the Tibetan faith and
  people emitting countless rays of auspicious
  light
Victoriously dispel the strife of darkness

CURRENCY

Chinese yuan

VEHICLE IDENTIFICATION PLATES/STICKERS

China has no official vehicle code; TBT Tibet (unofficial) is used by Tibetans living in other countries.

PASSPORT

Most Tibetans are Chinese citizens, and when they are allowed to travel, they use passports of the People's Republic of China.

NATIONAL FLOWER

Peony

NATIONAL TREE

Bodhi tree

NATIONAL ANIMAL

Snow lion (a mythical creature found in traditional Tibetan culture)

NATIONAL RESOURCES

Natural resources include hydropower, oil and natural gas potential, arable land, chromium, industrial crystal, corundum, copper, magnesite, boron, sulfur, mica, lithium, gold, iron, lead, uranium, and timber. Traditionally, the Tibetans depended on agriculture, but in recent years, other opportunities have become available. Tourism, based on the region's mountain scenery, unique culture, spiritual resources, and historic monuments, is increasingly important. Remittances from Tibetans living in other parts of the world are an important source of foreign currency and investment.

FOODS

Momos, steamed dumplings made of *tsampa,* barley flour, and filled with different combinations of meat, onions, shallots, garlic, and cilantro, are considered the national dish. Other specialties include *thenthuk,* a stew of noodles and vegetables; *thukpa,* Tibetan noodles with vegetables; *luksha shamdeh,* a Tibetan version of lamb curry; *mar jasha* (butter chicken), chicken cooked with spices, curry, and butter; *kongpo shaptak,* a dish of beef, red onions, garlic, ginger, tomatoes, *chucu* (blue cheese), and chilies; *shamday,* beef or lamb curry with potatoes; and *dri,* tea with salt and butter, which is considered the national drink.

SPORTS/SPORTS TEAMS

Association football (soccer) is the most popular sport. The Tibet national team participates in football at an international level.

TEAM SPORTS

Football

Tibet Football Team, nickname the Forbiddens

NATIONAL HEROES OR PERSONIFICATIONS

The Tibetan historical national hero is Gesar. The *Epic of King Gesar* is the central epic poem of Tibet.

National heroes include the Dalai Lama, the spiritual leader of the world's Tibetan Buddhists and temporal leader of the Tibetan government-in-exile; Milarepa, famed poet and yogi of the 11th and 12th centuries; and Songsten Gampo, the ruler that unified Tibet in the seventh century;

NATIONAL HOLIDAY/ INDEPENDENCE DAY

Independence Day, February 18; Tibetan Uprising Day, March 10; Birthday of His Holiness the Dalai Lama, June 6

FESTIVALS/FAIRS

Tibetan New Year, December; Monlam, the Great Prayer Festival, January; Butter Lantern Festival, January; Sagar Dawa Festival, April; Shoton Festival, August; Bathing Festival, July; Ongkor Festival (Bumper Harvest Festival), August; Horse Fair and Archery Festival, June–July

SIGNIFICANT EVENTS IN FORMATION OF NATIONAL IDENTITY

200 B.C.E. The Tibetans are chronicled as nomadic, pastoral people in the steppe lands northwest of China. Later migrations take them into the mountains and the high plateau of Tibet.

630 C.E.–10th century The introduction of Buddhism leads to the creation of a sophisticated theocratic kingdom. Diplomatic and trade ties are established with China. At the height of its power, in the eighth century, the kingdom controls the Silk Road trade routes and extracts tribute from vassal states.

10th century The kingdom disintegrates, and invading Mongols conquer much of Inner Tibet and eventually extend Mongol control to the high plateau, Outer Tibet.

16th century Religious reforms make Tibetan Buddhism more secluded and meditative as a way to enlightenment.

17th century China, under the Manchus, incorporates Inner Tibet into China. The fifth Dalai Lama, to eliminate the need for a standing army, negotiates a protectorate agreement with China in 1650. In 1720, nominal Chinese rule is extended to Outer Tibet.

1885 British explorers, with Chinese permission, try to enter Tibet but are turned back by the Tibetans.

1903–1906 When the Tibetans rebuff British demands for trade concessions, the British dispatch an expedition to occupy Lhasa. The British force the Tibetans to open several cities to trade. In 1906, without consulting the Tibetans, the British sign a treaty with China recognizing Chinese sovereignty over Tibet.

1912 Following the Chinese revolution, the Chinese are driven out of Tibet and independence is declared on February 18, 1912.

1918 The Tibetans defeat an attempted Chinese invasion. A Buddhist theocracy is created under the rule of the Dalai Lama, the leader of the Tibetan Buddhist religion.

1931–1933 A brief border war with China ends with a further loss of territory.

1945–1950 At the end of the Second World War, the Chinese Civil War, suspended during the war, is resumed. The communist victory in 1949 leads to a communist invasion of Tibet in 1950.

1954–1959 Mass Chinese immigration begins to colonize Inner Tibet under direct Chinese rule. The Tibetans of Inner Tibet revolt in 1956. The revolt spreads to Outer Tibet in 1959.

1959 The Chinese People's Army invades Tibet, sending the Dalai Lama and over 85,000 refugees fleeing over mountain passes into India*. A government-in-exile is organized at Dharmsala, in northern India. By 1965, the number of refugees rises to over 200,000.

1960–1980 Determined to crush Tibetan resistance, the Chinese destroy 6,000 ancient lamaseries and other historic monuments, and over 100,000 Tibetans die in mass executions, forced labor, and other abuses. Mass Chinese immigration to Tibet begins.

1989 The Dalai Lama is awarded the Noble Peace Prize for his nonviolent struggle to regain Tibetan independence.

2006 The Chinese inaugurate a railway connection between China and Tibet, facilitating the transfer of excess Chinese population to Tibet.

2008 Hundreds of monks in Lhasa begin a peaceful protest on the anniversary of the Tibetan uprising of 1959. Protests spread outside the autonomous region to Inner Tibet. News reports reach the outside world of up to 80 people dead when security forces end the protests, before China closes Tibet to foreigners and asks tourists to leave the region. Several pro-Tibetan protests are publicized in the run-up to the 2008 Summer Olympics in Beijing, in spite of very tight security.

2009 A number of protesters are reportedly killed as the government deals harshly with the continuing demonstrations.

See also China

TOKELAU

OFFICIAL NAME
Tokelau

POPULATION
1,500 (2009e); more than 8,000 Tokelauans live in New Zealand

INHABITANTS' NAME/NICKNAME
Tokelauan(s)

LANGUAGE/LANGUAGES
Tokelauan, English (both official)

RELIGION/RELIGIONS
Congregationalist, 70 percent; Roman Catholic, 28 percent; other or no religion

NATIONAL FLAG
The flag has a blue field with a stylized yellow Polynesian canoe in full sail and four yellow stars. The blue represents the Pacific Ocean that surrounds the country, yellow represents the riches of the land and the culture, and the stars represents the three main islands and also Swains Island, administered by the United States* but claimed by Tokelau.

COAT OF ARMS/SEAL
The national emblem is a traditional Tokelauan lidded clay pot in terra-cotta color with a cross of white links on the front. Below is a terra-cotta banner with the national motto. The pot symbolizes the people of the islands, and the cross represents their Christian faith.

MOTTO

Tokelau mo te atua (Tokelauan); Tokelau for the Almighty (English)

CAPITAL CITY

Fakaofo (unofficial); officially, none, as each of the three atolls has its own administrative center

TYPE OF GOVERNMENT

Representative democracy as a dependency of New Zealand*

NATIONAL COLORS

Blue and yellow

NATIONAL ANTHEM

The New Zealand anthems, "God Defend New Zealand" and "God Save the Queen," are the official anthems. Tokelau is moving toward free association status and is in the process of adopting an official anthem.

CURRENCY

New Zealand dollar

INTERNET IDENTIFIER

.tk

VEHICLE IDENTIFICATION PLATES/STICKERS

NZ New Zealand (official); TK Tokelau (unofficial), mostly used by Tokelauans living in New Zealand

PASSPORT

Tokelauans are New Zealand citizens and travel on New Zealand passports.

NATIONAL TREE

Coconut palm (unofficial)

NATIONAL RESOURCES

Tokelau's small size (three villages), isolation, and lack of resources greatly restrain economic development and confine agriculture to the subsistence level. Major resources are annual financial aid from New Zealand and remittances from the 8,000 Tokelauans living in New Zealand.

The principal sources of revenue are sales of copra, postage stamps, souvenir coins, and handicrafts. Selling the Tokelau Internet domain name .tk has become a major industry.

FOODS

Fish and coconuts are abundant, but other local foods are seasonal or scarce. Local stores stock imported food from New Zealand, mainly rice, flour, and sugar. *Poi*, made from taro roots, is the staple food, served as porridge or with meat, vegetables, or seafood. It is considered the national dish.

SPORTS/SPORTS TEAMS

Tokelau national teams participate in many sports at an international level.

TEAM SPORTS

Basketball

Tokelau Basketball Team; Tokelau Women's Basketball Team

Cricket

Tokelau Cricket Team

Football

Tokelau Football Team; Tokelau Rugby League Team; Tokelau Women's Rugby League Team; Tokelau Touch Football Team; Tokelau Women's Touch Football Team; Tokelau Rugby Union Team; Tokelau Rugby Union 7s Team, nickname the 7s

Volleyball

Tokelau Men's Volleyball Team; Tokelau Women's Volleyball Team

NATIONAL HEROES OR PERSONIFICATIONS

Mauimua, Mauiloto, and Mauimuli, the three legendary brothers who represent the three islands of Tokelau.

Faipule Kurea Nasau, the Ulu of Tokelau, the titular head of the nation, is a popular national hero.

NATIONAL HOLIDAY/
INDEPENDENCE DAY

Waitangi Day, February 6 (New Zealand national holiday); Aho o Fafine (Women's Day) and Aho o Aumaga (Men's Day), December-January

FESTIVALS/FAIRS

Tokelau Easter Festival, March–April

SIGNIFICANT EVENTS IN FORMATION
OF NATIONAL IDENTITY

1050 C.E.–1200 C.E. The three atolls are settled by seafaring Polynesians, probably from Samoa*, the Cook Islands*, and Tuvalu*. The settlers develop an island culture and a local mythology with the god Tui Tokelau. The three atolls function largely independently under chiefly clans.

1765–1835 A British expedition sights the islands, beginning European contact. European diseases devastate the population. A expedition from the United States* comes across the largest of the three atolls in 1835.

1845–1870 Missionaries arrive in the islands and use native teachers to convert the islanders.

1863 Peruvian slave traders raid the islands and take nearly all the able-bodied men. Most of the captives die of disease, and very few ever return to Tokelau.

1877–1926 The islands come under British protection. The Union Jack is officially raised in 1889. Eventually, the islands are transferred to New Zealand administration.

2000–2006 Tokelauans work to draft a constitution and develop institutions and patterns of self-government as Tokelau moves toward free association with New Zealand, as Niue* and the Cook Islands have done.

2006 A United Nations-sponsored referendum on self-determination fails when the pro-vote fails to reach the two-thirds mark. A second referendum fails by just 16 votes.

2007 The sale of Tokelau's Internet domain name, .tk, gives the island nation an added 10 percent to its annual income, plus computers and Internet access for its entire population.

2008–2009 United Nations decolonization officials push for full independence in 2010, although 95 percent of Tokelauans want to retain their ties to New Zealand.

See also New Zealand

TONGA

OFFICIAL NAME

Pule'anga 'o Tonga (Tongan); Kingdom of Tonga (English)

POPULATION

111,400 (2009e)

INHABITANTS' NAME/NICKNAME

Tongan(s)

LANGUAGE/LANGUAGES

Tongan, English (both official); others

RELIGION/RELIGIONS

Methodist, 41 percent; Roman Catholic, 16 percent; Mormon, 14 percent; other or no religion

NATIONAL FLAG

The flag is a red field with a white canton on the upper hoist containing a red equilateral cross. The original national flag was a white field with a centered red cross, which was judged too similar to that of the International Red Cross, so the present flag was adopted.

COAT OF ARMS/SEAL

The coat of arms has a central crest with the royal arms, which are divided into quarters: the upper left bears three white stars on yellow, representing the three island groups that make up the country; the upper right is red with a crown, symbolizing the monarchy; the lower left is a white dove and an olive branch on blue, signifying peace; and the lower right has three crossed swords on yellow, representing the three dynasties or kingly family lines. Behind the crest are two Tongan flags, and above are a laurel wreath and a royal crown. Below the crest is a white banner with the national motto in Tongan.

MOTTO

Ko e 'otua mo Tonga ko hoku tofi'a (Tongan); God and Tonga are my inheritance (English)

CAPITAL CITY

Nuku'alofa

TYPE OF GOVERNMENT

Monarchy

NATIONAL COLORS

Red and white

NATIONAL ANTHEM

The anthem was first performed in 1874. The literal meaning of the title is "song of the king of the Tonga Islands."

> *Ko e fasi 'o e tu'l 'o e 'Otu Tonga* (Tongan);
> **National Anthem of Tonga (English)**
> Oh, almighty God above!
> You are our Lord,
> It is you, the pillar
> And the love of Tonga.
> Look down on our prayer
> That is what we do now
> And may you answer our wish
> To protect Tupou.

CURRENCY

Tongan pa'anga

INTERNET IDENTIFIER

.to

VEHICLE IDENTIFICATION PLATES/STICKERS

TO

PASSPORT

The passport cover has the words *Tongan passport*, in both Tongan and English, above the coat of arms.

AIRLINE

Peau Vava'u

NATIONAL FLOWER

Heilala

NATIONAL BIRD

Pacific imperial pigeon

NATIONAL FISH

Tricolor parrotfish (unofficial)

NATIONAL RESOURCES

Natural resources include fish and arable land. Most Tongans live by subsistence farming, a large nonmonetary sector, and heavy dependence on remittances from the more than 100,000 Tongans living in Australia*, New Zealand*, and the United States*.

FOODS

Cassava balls, made with grated cassava, onion, herbs, and eggs and then fried, are considered the national dish. Other island specialties are *mango otai*, grated mango mixed with finely grated coconut; *lechoza*, a salad of papaya, or pawpaw; and *kokoda*, raw fish marinated in coconut milk, onion, and lemon juice.

SPORTS/SPORTS TEAMS

Rugby and association football (soccer) are the most popular sports. Tonga national teams participate in many sports at an international level.

TEAM SPORTS

Basketball

Tonga Basketball Team; Tonga Women's Basketball Team

Football

Tonga Football Team; Tonga Women's Football Team; Tonga Rugby League Team, nickname Mate Ma'a; Tonga Women's Rugby League Team; Tonga Rugby Union Team, nickname 'Ikale Tahi (the Sea Eagles); Tonga Women's Rugby Union Team, nickname 'Ikale Tahi (the Sea Eagles); Tonga Rugby Union Team (Sevens), nickname Tonga Sevens or Tonga 7s; Tonga Touch Football Team; Tonga Women's Touch Football Team

Hockey

Tonga Field Hockey Team

Lacrosse

Tonga Lacrosse Team

Table Tennis

Tonga Table Tennis Team

Tennis

Pacific Oceania Davis Cup Team; Pacific Oceania Fed Cup Team (Pacific Oceania teams represent a number of Pacific Island countries)

Volleyball

Tonga Men's Volleyball Team; Tonga Women's Volleyball Team

INDIVIDUAL SPORTS

Tonga Amateur Boxing Team; Tonga Athletics Team; Tonga Canoeing Team; Tonga Judo Team; Tonga Rowing Team; Tonga Tae Kwon Do Team; Tonga Weight Lifting Team; Tonga Wrestling Team

NATIONAL HEROES OR PERSONIFICATIONS

George Tupou I, the king who united the islands in 1845; and Queen Salote Tupou III, the monarch who negotiated Tongan independence from the United Kingdom* in 1970

NATIONAL HOLIDAY/INDEPENDENCE DAY

Emancipation Day, June 4

FESTIVALS/FAIRS

Heilala Festival, July–August

SIGNIFICANT EVENTS IN FORMATION OF NATIONAL IDENTITY

12th century   Tonga was the starting point for many seafaring settlers traveling to other Pacific islands and was known, along with the paramount chiefs, the Tu'i Tonga, in many parts of the Pacific.

1616–1643   Dutch explorers sight the islands are sighted.

1773–1777   Visits to the islands by British Captain James Cook establishes European contact.

1797–1826   The London Missionary Society and a Methodist expedition fail to establish Christianity in the islands until the Methodists finally established a mission in 1826.

1831–1875   George Tupou I converted to Christianity in 1831, declares Christianity the official religion on the main island in 1839, thus gaining missionary backing for his campaign to unite the island, which he does in 1845, ending decades of war and disorder. In 1875, he declares Tonga a constitutional monarchy.

1900   Tonga becomes a British protectorate but remains unique among Pacific nations, as it never completely loses its local monarchical government. Tonga remains the only monarchy in the Pacific.

1970 Under the terms of negotiations by Queen Salote Tupou III, Tonga ends its protectorate status and becomes an independent state.

1999 Tonga joins the United Nations.

2006–2009 The British close their diplomatic representation in the islands. The descendant of the first monarch, King George Tupou V, along with his family, some powerful noble families, and a growing nonroyal elite, lives a modern life, with the rest of the population living in relative poverty. The king announces he will relinquish the near-absolute power of the monarchy and fulfill a pledge to introduce democratic reforms.

TURKMENISTAN

OFFICIAL NAME

Türkmenistan (Turkmen); Turkmenistan (English)

POPULATION

5,321,800 (2009e)

INHABITANTS' NAME/NICKNAME

Turkmen(s); Turkmenistani(s)

LANGUAGE/LANGUAGES

Turkmen (official); Russian, Uzbek, Dari (recognized regional languages); Ukrainian, Farsi, others

RELIGION/RELIGIONS

Muslim, 89 percent; Eastern Orthodox, 9 percent; other or no religion

NATIONAL FLAG

The flag has a green field with a red vertical stripe near the hoist containing five carpet *guls* (traditional designs used in producing rugs) stacked above two crossed olive branches. Next to the stripe is a white crescent moon and five small, white, five-pointed stars. The green and red are colors historically associated with the Turkic peoples. The crescent moon symbolizes hope for a shining future, and the stars represent the country's five provinces. The five carpet designs represent the five major tribes or houses and form motifs in the country's state emblem and flag.

COAT OF ARMS/SEAL

The coat of arms is an eight-pointed green star with gold edges, the Star of Rub El Hizb, a symbol of Islam. A central red disk has the five *guls* of the national flag around a smaller blue disk with a depiction of an Akhal-Teke horse. Around the central disk are sheaves of wheat, representing the bread used to welcome guests. Above the red disk are the crescent moon and stars of the national flag.

CAPITAL CITY

Ashgabat

TYPE OF GOVERNMENT

Single-party parliamentary republic

NATIONAL EMBLEM

Akhal-Teke horse (Turkmen horse)

NATIONAL COLORS

Yellow and black

NATIONAL ANTHEM

The anthem was adopted in 1997 to replace the Soviet-era anthem. The president, known as "Türkmenbaşhi," is honored in the anthem.

Türkmenbaşyň guran beýik binasy (Turkmen); Independent, Neutral, Turkmenistan State Anthem (English)

Chorus

The great creation of Türkmenbaşhi
Native land, sovereign state
Turkmenistan, light and song of soul
Long live and prosper forever and ever!

I am ready to give my life for my native
  hearth

The spirit the ancestors' descendants are famous for
My land is sacred. My flag flies in the world
A symbol of the great neutral country flies.

Chorus
The great creation of Türkmenbaşhi
Native land, sovereign state
Turkmenistan, light and song of soul
Long live and prosper forever and ever!

My nation is united and is veins of tribes
Ancestors' blood, undying flows
Storms and misfortunes of times are not
  dreadful for us
Let us increase fame and honor!

Chorus
The great creation of Türkmenbaşhi
Native land, sovereign state
Turkmenistan, light and song of soul
Long live and prosper forever and ever!

Mountains, rivers and beauty of steppes
Love and destiny, revelation of mine
Let my eyes go blind for any cruel look at you
Motherland of ancestors and heirs of mine!

CURRENCY
Turkmen manat

INTERNET IDENTIFIER
.tm

VEHICLE IDENTIFICATION PLATES/ STICKERS
TM

PASSPORT
The passport cover has the name of the country in Turkmen and English, the coat of arms, and the word *passport* in Turkmen and English.

AIRLINE
Turkmenistan Airlines

NATIONAL FLOWER
Hyacinth (unofficial); *Rosa eglanteria*

NATIONAL ANIMAL
Akhal-Teke horse

NATIONAL BIRD
Seven-headed eagle (a important creature in Turkmen mythology)

NATIONAL RESOURCES
Natural resources include petroleum, natural gas, sulfur, and salt. About half the country's land is planted in cotton. Natural gas and petroleum are the other major exports.

FOODS
Plov, rice or cracked wheat browned in oil and cooked in a seasoned broth, usually served with shredded turnips and mutton, is considered the national dish. Other national specialties include *eksili çhorba,* called sour soup, a mixture of cracked wheat, chickpeas, red lentils, cubed eggplant, tomato purée, and spices; *ezo gelin çhorbasi,* a soup of red lentils and mint; *kuzu pirzola,* Turkmen-style lamb chops; *borcht,* cabbage soup; *shashlik,* skewered meat cooked over charcoal; and *manty,* large pasta dumplings filled with minced meat.

SPORTS/SPORTS TEAMS
Association football (soccer) is the most popular sport. Traditional sports, such as wrestling and games played on horseback, remain very popular. Turkmenistan national teams participate in many sports at an international level.

TEAM SPORTS
Badminton
Turkmenistan Badminton Team

Basketball
Turkmenistan Basketball Team; Turkmenistan Women's Basketball Team

Football

Turkmenistan Football Team, nickname the Dark Horses or the Green Men; Turkmenistan Women's Football Team, nickname the Dark Horses; Turkmenistan Futsal Team

Hockey

Turkmenistan Field Hockey Team

Table Tennis

Turkmenistan Table Tennis Team

Tennis

Turkmenistan Davis Cup Team; Turkmenistan Fed Cup Team

Volleyball

Turkmenistan Men's Volleyball Team; Turkmenistan Women's Volleyball Team

INDIVIDUAL SPORTS

Turkmenistan Amateur Boxing Team; Turkmenistan Athletics Team; Turkmenistan Canoeing Team; Turkmenistan Cycling Team; Turkmenistan Equestrian Team; Turkmenistan Fencing Team; Turkmenistan Judo Team; Turkmenistan Modern Pentathlon Team; Turkmenistan Rowing Team; Turkmenistan Shooting Team; Turkmenistan Swim Team; Turkmenistan Tae Kwon Do Team; Turkmenistan Weight Lifting Team

NATIONAL HEROES OR PERSONIFICATIONS

Magtymguly Pyragy, a poet and spiritual leader who struggled to win independence for his people in the 18th century; Mametveli Kemine, a satirical poet who criticized the clergy and landowners in the late 18th and early 19th centuries; and Saparmurat Atayevich Niyazov, the first president of independent Turkmenistan from 1991 until his death in 2006

NATIONAL HOLIDAY/INDEPENDENCE DAY

Independence Day, October 27; Holiday of the Turkmen Horse, April 27

FESTIVALS/FAIRS

Kurban Bairam, February; Navruz (Turkmen New Year), March; Revival and Unity Festival, May; Independence Day celebrations, October; Ramadan Bairam, November

SIGNIFICANT EVENTS IN FORMATION OF NATIONAL IDENTITY

Sixth century B.C.E. The region, according to Arab and Hindu legends, is the birthplace of the Aryan race. Persian rule is established.

Fourth century C.E. Alexander the Great of Macedonia* conquers Central Asia. The majority of the population makes up various nomadic tribes, with a Persianized urban population at the oasis cities.

Seventh century Invading Arabs conquer the region and introduce Islam. Merv (Mary), the seat of the Muslim administration, becomes one of the great centers of Muslim learning and Arab-Persian culture.

10th century–13th century Nomadic Turkic tribes, the ancestors of the present Turkmens, settle the region. Mongol peoples arrive in the region from the northeast. The Mongols of Genghis Khan conquer Central Asia.

15th century–17th century The Turkmen tribes are divided between Persia in the south and the Uzbek states in the north.

1881 The Turkmens are defeated at the Battle of Gok Tepe, and thousands are slaughtered. Russia* conquers Central Asia, which becomes part of the Russian Empire.

1916 Russian attempts to conscript Central Asians during World War I lead to a widespread uprising.

1918–1921 In the aftermath of the Russian Revolution, the Turkmens fight against the Red Army's attempts to conquer Central Asia. The defeated Turkmens fall under communist rule.

1925–1936 Turkmenistan is created as a full union republic within the Soviet Union, even though the tribes have a very shallow understanding of Turkmen nationality. Most Turkmen loyalty is to clans or tribal groups. Sporadic rebellions and violence accompany the Soviet collectivization of the Turkmens' prized herds of horses.

1948 Over 100,000 people are killed when an earthquake destroys Ashgabat.

1960–1967 Cotton production expands dramatically.

1985 Saparmurat Niyazov becomes leader of the Turkmen Communist Party.

1987–1989 The liberalizing of Soviet society allows Turkmen intellectuals to form a people's front organization, which is banned by the Turkmen Communist Party in 1990.

1991 Despite continued control by the local communist government of Saparmyat Niyazov, Turkmenistan declares independence as the Soviet Union collapses.

1992 A new constitution enshrines Niyazov as head of state and head of government with wide powers of authority.

1997–1998 Ownership of land is legalized. A pipeline for natural gas is opened to neighboring Iran*.

1999–2002 Niyazov becomes president for life. President Niyazov renames the months of the year after himself, his mother, and his spiritual guide. A Stalinist-style police state with a presidential cult leads to widespread oppression.

2006–2008 An agreement is signed for a pipeline to carry Turkmen gas to China*. President Niyazov dies. Presidential elections are held. The country reverts to the old calendar. The new president orders the removal of a huge rotating statue of Niyazov from the center of Ashgabat.

2009 A new constitution allows some liberalization of the culture and economy.

TUVA

OFFICIAL NAME

Tyva Respublika (transliteration from Russian/Tuvan); Tuva Republic (English)

POPULATION

310,400 (2009e)

INHABITANTS' NAME/NICKNAME

Tuvans(s); Tuvinian(s); Uriankhai(s)

LANGUAGE/LANGUAGES

Tuvan, Russian (both official); Kalkh Mongoian, others

RELIGION/RELIGIONS

Lamaism (Tibetan Buddhism), Eastern Orthodox, shamanism, Protestant, other or no religion

NATIONAL FLAG

The national flag is a pale blue field bearing a yellow triangle at the hoist outlined by narrow white stripes that extend in parallel stripes to the fly. The yellow symbolizes Tuva's mineral wealth and Buddhism; the blue, a traditional Turkic color, stands for tradition and the sky over Tuva, and the white symbolizes silver and virtue. The two stripes symbolize the Bolshoy Yenisei and Maly Yenisei rivers that meet at the Tuvan capital, Kyzyl, to form the Yenisei River.

COAT OF ARMS/SEAL

The coat of arms is a pale blue field with a yellow border in a traditional Tuvan style. In the center is a yellow and white horseman, symbolizing Tuva's sovereignty and spirit. On the upper right is a yellow sun and rays and below the horseman is a white banner with the name Tuva in Cyrillic letters. The yellow symbolizes mineral wealth, gold, and Buddhism. The blue symbolizes the Tuvan sky and the traditions and morals of the Tuvan nomads. The white symbolizes silver and virtue and also represents the silver streamers Tuvan women wear on their arms to greet visitors.

CAPITAL CITY
Kyzyl

TYPE OF GOVERNMENT
A parliamentary democracy as a member republic of the Russian Federation

NATIONAL COLORS
Pale blue and yellow

NATIONAL ANTHEM
The official anthem is the anthem of Russia*. The national anthem of Tuva, which was also the official anthem of independent Tuva before 1944, was adopted as part of the Tuva republican symbols.

**Tooruktug Dolgay Tandym (Tuvan);
The Forest is Full of Pine Nuts (English)**

When I walk in my forest
I will always be satisfied
Because my forest is rich with animals and
    everything I need.
There in the mountains, the cliffs, the taiga,
    I was born.
Because of that I am strong.
I will raise my livestock and be rich.
Nine different animals—If I herd them and
    feed them
And take care of them as my own—I'll be
    rich.

CURRENCY
Russian ruble

INTERNET IDENTIFIER
.ru Russia

VEHICLE IDENTIFICATION PLATES/
STICKERS
RUS Russia (official): TY Tuva (unofficial)

PASSPORT
Tuvans are Russian citizens and travel on Russian passports

NATIONAL TREE
Siberian pine (unofficial)

NATIONAL ANIMALS
Bactrian camel; reindeer (both unofficial)

NATIONAL BIRD
Saker falcon (unofficial)

NATIONAL RESOURCES
Natural resources include coal, iron ore, gold, cobalt, timber, and arable land. Wildlife is varied and provides opportunities for employment and tourism.

FOODS
Pooza, small steamed or fried pastries filled with minced lamb, is the national dish. Other regional specialties include *guriltai shol,* a soup of mutton, onion, and strips of dough; *khorkhog,* lamb cooked with onions in broth; *sulla,* leg of lamb prepared with rice, onions, butter, and spices; *kumiss,* made from ewe milk is somewhat like yogurt. The national drink is *suutug shai,* salted tea with milk.

SPORTS/SPORTS TEAMS
Traditional sports remain very popular, including horse racing, archery, and *khuresh,* a Tuvan form of wrestling.

NATIONAL HEROES OR PERSONIFICATIONS
Kaadyr-ool Bicheldei, the leader of the Tuvan linguistic and cultural revival in the 1990s; Sainho Namtchylak, an internationally known singer of traditional Tuvan songs; Sherig-ool Oorzhak, the president of Tuva from 1990 to 2007; Sholban Kara-ool, a former champion wrestler and, since 2007, the chairman of the Tuvan government.

NATIONAL HOLIDAY/INDEPENDENCE DAY
Tuva National Day, August 16

FESTIVALS/FAIRS

Naadym Festival, July; Ustu-Huer Festival (Summer Festival), July; Shagas, the new lunar moon festival, various dates.

SIGNIFICANT EVENTS IN FORMATION OF NATIONAL IDENTITY

Sixth century C.E. Tuvan tradition tells of the ancient Tuvan tribes being united under the rule of a Tuvan khanate.

9th century-10th century The Yenisei Kyrgyz people invade and take control of Tuva. The Tuvans are mentioned by early travelers as nomadic herders living in clan groups ruled by hereditary or elected chiefs.

1208–1368 The Mongols conquer the Tuva region, which becomes part of the vast Mongol empire that stretches from China* to Europe. The Eastern Mongols, a tribal confederation, conquers the Tuvans as the Mongol empire dissolves.

1368–1500s The Eastern Mongols rule the region as part of their khanate although the Tuvans retain their culture and language.

18th century The Tibetan form of Buddhism is introduced to the region. Many adopt the new religion while retaining their earlier shamanistic beliefs.

1757–1758 The Manchu Qing Dynasty of China sends a large army to take control of Mongolia and Tuva, which is incorporated into Chinese Mongolia as the Uriankhai region.

1860–1900 Russian explorers visit the region following a Russian-Chinese treaty that allows Russians to maintain trading posts in the region. Over the next few decades several thousand Russians settle in Tuva.

1911 The Chinese Revolution leaves Tuva effectively independent. With Russian support Tuvan nationalists organize a national government and declare Tuva an independent state.

1914–1920 The Tuvan government accepts Russian protectorate status when war breaks out in 1914. The Russian Revolution sweeps through the region in 1917 allowing the Tuvans to again assert their independence but by 1920 Tuva is under firm Bolshevik control.

1921–1944 Pressure from neighboring countries allow the Tuvans to organize an independent state despite Soviet objections. Tuvan independence is recognized by China and other regional states. In 1944, Soviet troops occupy the country, which is then annexed to the Soviet Union.

1961–1980 Tuva is granted the status of an autonomous republic within the Soviet Russian Federation. The Tuvans are forbidden contacts with neighboring peoples but the edict is difficult to endorse. The Tuvans urbanize during the 1970s and 1980s.

1987–1990 The liberalization of Soviet life allows the Tuvans to again establish ties to Mongolia* and the peoples of Soviet Asia. Tuvan nationalism is resurrected with radicals leading attacks on ethnic Russians living in the region, leaving many dead and wounded. Thousands of Russians flee as Russian troops arrive to restore order.

1992 Tuva, called the Republic of Tuva, joins the new Russian Federation as a member state. Nationalists agree to suspend their campaign for independence in exchange for a pledge that a self-determination clause is included in the new Russian constitution.

1992–2000 Efforts are begun to rebuild Tuva's Buddhist monasteries and shrines, mostly demolished under Soviet rule. In 1993, the Tuvan parliament amends the republic constitution to include a provision for secession from the Russian Federation, but under pressure from the Russian government the clause is removed two years later.

2000–2009 Although nationalist sentiment is widespread and a majority support reinstating Tuva's former status as an independent state—twice interrupted by annexation by Russians in 1914 and 1944—economic restraints and dependence on Russian government subsidies curtail support for immediate independence.

TUVALU

OFFICIAL NAME

Fakavae Aliki-Malo I Tuvalu (Tuvaluan); Constitutional Monarchy of Tuvalu (English)

POPULATION

11,900 (2009e)

INHABITANTS' NAME/NICKNAME

Tuvaluan(s)

LANGUAGE/LANGUAGES

Tuvaluan, English (both official); Samoan, Kiribati, others

RELIGION/RELIGIONS

Church of Tuvalu (Congregationalist), 97 percent; Seventh-day Adventist, 2 percent; other or no religion

NATIONAL FLAG

The flag has a sky blue field with the British Union Jack as a canton on the upper hoist and nine gold, five-pointed stars on the fly. The blue represents the Pacific Ocean around the islands. The stars represent the nine inhabited islands and are arranged in the geographical position of the islands. Originally, there were only eight inhabited islands; thus the name Tuvalu, meaning "eight islands."

COAT OF ARMS/SEAL

The coat of arms has a crest or shield with a gold border decorated with a pattern of eight mussels and eight banana leaves, representing the eight original islands. The center of the shield has wavy blue and gold lines representing the Pacific Ocean at the bottom, a meetinghouse on green earth, and a blue sky. Below the shield is a gold banner inscribed with the national motto.

MOTTO

Tuvalu mo te atua (Tuvaluan); Tuvalu for the Almighty (English)

CAPITAL CITY

Funafuti

TYPE OF GOVERNMENT

Parliamentary democracy and constitutional monarchy

NATIONAL COLORS

Blue, yellow, and white

NATIONAL ANTHEM

The anthem was adopted at independence in 1978. Its title is the national motto.

Tuvalu mo te Atua (Tuvaluan); Tuvalu for the Almighty (English)

"Tuvalu for the Almighty"
Are the words we hold most dear.
For as people or as leaders
Of Tuvalu we all share
In the knowledge that God
Ever rules in heav'n above,
And that we in this island land
Are united in his love.
We build on a sure foundation
When we trust in God's great law;
"Tuvalu for the Almighty"
Be our song for evermore!

Let us trust our lives henceforward
To the King to whom we pray,
With our eyes fixed firmly on him
He is showing us the way.
"May we reign with him in glory"
Be our song for evermore,
for his almighty power
Is our strength from shore to shore.
Shout aloud in jubilation
To the King whom we adore.
"Tuvalu free and united"
Be our song for evermore!

CURRENCY

Tuvaluan dollar; Australian dollar

INTERNET IDENTIFIER

.tv

VEHICLE IDENTIFICATION PLATES/STICKERS

TUV

PASSPORT

The passport cover has the name of the country in Tuvaluan and English, the coat of arms, and the word *passport* in the two languages.

NATIONAL TREE

Banana

NATIONAL FISH

Longnose butterflyfish (unofficial)

NATIONAL RESOURCES

The country has no known mineral resources and few exports. Subsistence farming and fishing are the primary economic activities. Fewer than 1,000 tourists on average visit Tuvalu annually, due to its relative inaccessibility. Job opportunities are scarce, and public sector workers make up the majority of those employed. Remittances from Tuvaluans outside the country are a major source of foreign currency and investment.

FOODS

Palusami, a dish of taro leaves, coconut cream, lemon juice, and chopped onions, is considered the national dish. Other specialties include taro cakes, made of cooked, mashed taro mixed with onions, flour, and milk and then fried in oil; taro chips, thinly sliced taro fried in oil; taro and coconut soup, made of taro leaves, onions, coconut cream, spices, and chilies; and *poke,* a dessert of bananas and coconut.

SPORTS/SPORTS TEAMS

Association football (soccer), volleyball, and rugby are the most popular sports. Tuvalu national teams participate in many sports at an international level.

TEAM SPORTS

Badminton

Tuvalu Badminton Team

Basketball

Tuvalu Basketball Team; Tuvalu Women's Basketball Team

Football

Tuvalu Football Team; Tuvalu Futsal Team; Tuvalu Rugby League Team

Table Tennis

Tuvalu Table Tennis Team

Tennis

Pacific Oceania Davis Cup Team; Pacific Oceania Fed Cup Team (Pacific Oceania teams represent a number of Pacific island countries)

Volleyball

Tuvalu Men's Volleyball Team; Tuvalu Women's Volleyball Team

INDIVIDUAL SPORTS

Tuvalu Athletics Team; Tuvalu Weight Lifting Team

NATIONAL HEROES OR PERSONIFICATIONS

Toaripi Lauti, the first prime minister of independent Tuvalu; Penitala Teo, the island group's first governor general

NATIONAL HOLIDAY/ INDEPENDENCE DAY

Independence Day, October 1

FESTIVALS/FAIRS

Tuvalu National Days, October 1–2

SIGNIFICANT EVENTS IN FORMATION OF NATIONAL IDENTITY

1000 B.C.E.   The first settlers are thought to have arrived from Tonga* and Samoa*.

1300 C.E.–1400 C.E.   A new wave of settlement populates the largest eight islands of the archipelago. The islands are called Tuvalu, meaning "eight standing together."

1568   A Spanish expedition sails through the islands.

18th century–19th century   Ships visit only infrequently due to a lack of anchorage at the coral-ringed atolls. In 1819, the British ship *Rebecca* visits the islands, which are named the Ellice Group for the ship's owner.

1862–1864   Slavers, known as blackbirders, raid the island and take over 400 captives to work in horrific conditions in the guano mines of Peru*. None of the kidnapped islanders ever returns.

1865   Missionaries settle in the islands, beginning the conversion of the population to the Protestant faith.

1892–1916   The islands become part of the British protectorate of the Ellice Islands, which is joined with the Gilbert Islands in 1916.

1943–1945   Thousands of American servicemen are stationed in the islands during World War II, leaving behind airstrips and other infrastructure.

1974–1978   Differences between the Ellice and Gilbert peoples leads to the separation of the two. The Ellice Islands become independent Tuvalu in 1978.

2000   The government negotiates the lease of its Internet domain name .tv for $50 million in royalties over a 12-year period.

2005–2009   Global climate change raises fears that the islands will become uninhabitable due to rising water levels in the Pacific.

UZBEKISTAN

OFFICIAL NAME

O'zbekiston Respublikasi (Uzbek); Republic of Uzbekistan (English)

POPULATION

27,536,100 (2009e)

INHABITANTS' NAME/NICKNAME

Uzbek(s), Uzbekistani(s)

LANGUAGE/LANGUAGES

Uzbek (official); Russian, Tajik, Kazak, Tatar, Karakalpak, others

RELIGION/RELIGIONS

Muslim (primarily Sunni), 88 percent; Orthodox Christian, 9 percent; other or no religion

NATIONAL FLAG

The flag is a horizontal tricolor of sky blue, white, and green, the stripes separated by thin red lines, charged with a white crescent moon and 12 small white stars on the blue stripe at the upper hoist. The blue represents the Turkic background of the majority of the Uzbek people, white symbolizes holy peace, and green is for Islam and nature. The thin red lines represent the power of life. The crescent represents the rebirth of the Uzbek nation, and the 12 stars represent the 12 principles that are the foundation of the Uzbek state.

COAT OF ARMS/SEAL

The coat of arms is a circle with a central scene with a *khumo*, wings outstretched, a symbol of happiness and the love of freedom. In the background, in the colors of the national flag, are a green valley, white rivers representing the Amu Darya and Syr Darya, and blue mountains before a rising sun. Above the scene is the star of Rub El Hizb, a symbol of Islam, the majority religion. On either side are bundles of wheat and cotton, the two major agricultural products, intertwined with ribbons striped in the national colors and, at the bottom, inscribed with the name of the county in Uzbek.

CAPITAL CITY
Tashkent

TYPE OF GOVERNMENT
Presidential republic

NATIONAL COLORS
Sly blue, white, and green

NATIONAL ANTHEM
The former Soviet anthem of Uzbekistan, with new lyrics, was adopted as the official anthem of newly independent Uzbekistan in 1992.

O'zbekiston Respublikasining Davlat Madhiyasi (Uzbek); National Anthem of the Republic of Uzbekistan (English)

Stand tall, my free land, happiness and
  salvation to the people,
You are a loving companion to your friends!
Flourish forever with learning and creativity,
May your glory shine as long as the world
  exists!

Chorus

These golden valleys—dear Uzbekistan,
The courageous spirit of your ancestors is
  with you!
When the great power of the people raged,
(You were) the country that charmed the
  world!

The faith of an openhearted Uzbek does not
  die out,
The young free generation is a strong wing
  for you!
Beacon of independence, guardian of peace,
Lover of truth, motherland, flourish forever!

Chorus

These golden valleys—dear Uzbekistan,
The courageous spirit of your ancestors is
  with you!

When the great power of the people raged,
(You were) the country that charmed the
  world!

CURRENCY
Uzbekistan som

INTERNET IDENTIFIER
.uz

VEHICLE IDENTIFICATION PLATES/STICKERS
UZ

PASSPORT
The passport cover has the name of the country in Uzbek (large letters) and English (smaller letters), the coat of arms, and the words *citizen's passport* in Uzbek and English.

AIRLINE
Uzbekistan Airways

NATIONAL FLOWER
Bodomgul (almond flower) (unofficial)

NATIONAL TREE
Chinara (plane tree) (unofficial)

NATIONAL PLANT
Cotton; wheat (shown on the coat of arms)

NATIONAL ANIMAL
Karakul sheep (unofficial)

NATIONAL BIRD
Khumo (an important creature in Uzbek mythology)

NATIONAL RESOURCES
Natural resources include natural gas, petroleum, coal, gold, uranium, silver, copper, lead and zinc, tungsten, and molybdenum. Richly endowed with minerals, the country

has a promising future but remains one of the poorest in Central Asia. Cotton is the major export. The economy is centrally planned on the former Soviet model.

FOODS

Plov, a versatile dish of browned rice cooked in broth with carrots and meat, is considered the national dish. Other specialties include *kifta shuvra,* a traditional soup with meatballs; *khuil norin,* beef soup with noodles; *manty,* small pastries filled with minced meat; *dimlama,* a stew of various vegetables; *zharkop,* a dish of lamb and vegetables; *lovia shavia,* a dish of meat with rice and beans; *kovurma,* stewed lamb with vegetables; and *samsa,* small bread rolls filled with chopped meat and onions.

SPORTS/SPORTS TEAMS

Association football (soccer), boxing, and wrestling are the most popular sports. Uzbekistan national teams participate in many sports at an international level.

TEAM SPORTS

Badminton

Uzbekistan Badminton Team

Baseball

Uzbekistan Baseball Team; Uzbekistan Softball Team

Basketball

Uzbekistan Basketball Team; Uzbekistan Women's Basketball Team

Football

Uzbekistan Football Team, nickname the White Wolves; Uzbekistan Women's Football Team, nickname the White Wolves; Uzbekistan Rugby Union Team; Uzbekistan Under-19 Football Team; Uzbekistan Women's Under-19 Football Team; Uzbekistan Women's Rugby Union Team; Uzbekistan Futsal Team

Handball

Uzbekistan Handball Team; Uzbekistan Women's Handball Team

Hockey

Uzbekistan Field Hockey Team

Table Tennis

Uzbekistan Table Tennis Team

Tennis

Uzbekistan Davis Cup Team; Uzbekistan Fed Cup Team

Volleyball

Uzbekistan Men's Volleyball Team; Uzbekistan Women's Volleyball Team

INDIVIDUAL SPORTS

Uzbekistan Amateur Boxing Team; Uzbekistan Archery Team; Uzbekistan Athletics Team; Uzbekistan Canoeing Team; Uzbekistan Cycling Team; Uzbekistan Equestrian Team; Uzbekistan Fencing Team; Uzbekistan Gymnastics Team; Uzbekistan Judo Team; Uzbekistan Karate Team; Uzbekistan Rowing Team; Uzbekistan Shooting Team; Uzbekistan Swim Team; Uzbekistan Tae Kwon Do Team; Uzbekistan Triathlon Team; Uzbekistan Weight Lifting Team; Uzbekistan Wrestling Team

WINTER SPORTS

Uzbekistan Alpine Ski Team; Uzbekistan Biathlon Team; Uzbekistan Skating Team

NATIONAL HEROES OR PERSONIFICATIONS

Abdullah Quaisi, a writer killed during the Stalinist purges of the 1930s; Ilyas Malayev, a poet and musician; Islam Karimov, the first president of independent Uzbekistan; Timur or Tamerlane, the conqueror of much of western Asia in the 15th century; Djamoli-dine Abdoujaparov, famed cyclist who participated in the Tour de France several times in the 1980s and 1990s

NATIONAL HOLIDAY/INDEPENDENCE DAY

Independence Day, September 1

FESTIVALS/FAIRS

Navrus (Uzbek New Year), March; Uzbek Food Festival, April; Silk and Spice Festival, May; Festival of Uzbek Plov, June; International Tourism Fair, October

SIGNIFICANT EVENTS IN FORMATION OF NATIONAL IDENTITY

Prehistory   The region has been populated since the second millennium B.C.E. Indigenous states Bactria and Sogdiana form.

327 B.C.E.   Alexander the Great conquers the region and marries Roxana, the daughter of a Bactrian chief.

100 B.C.E.–700 C.E.   The region is an important part of the overland trade routes known as the Great Silk Road, linking China* and the Middle East to Europe. Invading Arabs conquer the region and introduce Islam.

13th century–16th century   The Mongols invade the region. The successors of the Mongol empire are the Turks, who replace Iranians as the dominant culture in Central Asia.

18th century–19th century   The Uzbeks are divided between the independent emirates and khanates of Bukhara, Kokand, and Samarkand.

1865–1876   Russian conquest is centered on Tashkent, which becomes the center of the expanding Russian province of Turkestan.

1914–1917   Russian attempts to conscript Central Asians during World War I lead to a widespread uprising that continues until the Russian Revolution. A revolutionary government is created at Tashkent.

1918–1922   The new Soviet rulers depose the emir of Bukhara and the khans of the Uzbek states. Mosques are closed and Muslim clergy persecuted as part of the anti-religious stance of the new Soviet state.

1924   The Uzbek Soviet Socialist Republic is formed from traditional Uzbek territories. The new republic becomes a member state of the Soviet Union.

1930s–1940s   Many exiles from European Russia are sent to Central Asia. During the Stalinist purges before and after World War II, whole ethnic groups are deported to the region.

1950s–1980s   The emphasis on cotton production fed by vast irrigation projects severely harms the environment and dries up the Aral Sea.

1987–1989   Soviet leader Mikhail Gorbachev begins to reform Soviet life. Islam Karimov becomes head of the local communist party. Nationalism begins to resurface. Attacks on ethnic minorities shake the region.

1991   Uzbekistan declares independence during the collapse of the Soviet Union. Islam Karimov, the former communist leader, becomes the first president. Opposition groups and political parties are banned and harassed.

1999–2001   Radical Islamic groups set off a series of bombs and demand the resignation of the Uzbek leadership. Skirmishes increase between radical and security forces. Reports are published of widespread abuse of human rights.

2001–2005   Uzbekistan becomes an ally of the United States* in its fight against Islamic terrorism. Banned political parties are allowed to operate openly. Unrest and violence spread. An uprising in the east of the country is brutally put down, with many deaths.

2005–2009   Politicians, rights activists, and government critics are frequently jailed. Islam Karimov continues to win periodic, unfair elections, extending his term as president indefinitely.

VANUATU

OFFICIAL NAME

Ripablik blong Vanuatu (Bislama); République de Vanuatu (French); Republic of Vanuatu (English)

POPULATION

216,300 (2009e)

INHABITANTS' NAME/NICKNAME

ni-Vanuatu; Vanuatuan(s)

LANGUAGE/LANGUAGES

Bislama, English, French (all official); others

RELIGION/RELIGIONS

Presbyterian, 32 percent; Anglican, 13 percent; Roman Catholic, 13 percent; Seventh-day Adventist, 11 percent; indigenous beliefs, 6 percent; other or no religion

NATIONAL FLAG

The flag has two equal stripes of red over green with a black isosceles triangle at the hoist, all separated by a black-edged thin gold stripe. A boar's tusk enclosing two *namele* leaves, all in gold, is centered on the black triangle. The red symbolizes boar's blood and men, the green stands for the richness of the islands, and the black is for the ni-Vanuatu people. The gold stripes represent the Gospel going through the islands. The boar's tusk is a symbol of prosperity, and the leaves are a symbol of peace.

COAT OF ARMS/SEAL

The coat of arms features a Melanesian warrior armed with a spear in natural colors superimposed on a white boar's tusk and two crossed *namele* leaves. The warrior stands on brown earth, representing the islands, above a yellow scroll inscribed with the national motto in Bislama.

MOTTO

Long God yumi stanap (Bislama); We stand with God (English)

CAPITAL CITY

Port Vila

TYPE OF GOVERNMENT

Parliamentary republic

NATIONAL EMBLEM

Boar's tusk

NATIONAL COLORS

Green, black, and yellow

NATIONAL ANTHEM

The anthem was adopted in 1980, when Vanuatu gained independence from Britain and France*. It is written in Bislama, a hybrid language of indigenous dialects, Pidgin English, and French.

> **Yumi, Yumi, Yumi (We, We, We)**
> We are happy to proclaim
> We are the people of Vanuatu!
> God has given us this land;
> This gives us great cause for rejoicing.
> We are strong, we are free in this land;
> We are all brothers.
> We are happy to proclaim
> We are the people of Vanuatu!
> We have many traditions
> And we are finding new ways.
> Now we shall be one people,
> We shall be united forever.
> We are happy to proclaim
> We are the people of Vanuatu!
> We know there is much work to be done
> On all our islands.
> May God, our Father, help us!
> We are happy to proclaim
> We are the people of Vanuatu!

CURRENCY

Vanuatu vatu

INTERNET IDENTIFIER

.vu

VEHICLE IDENTIFICATION PLATES/STICKERS

VU

PASSPORT

The passport cover has the name of the country in Bislama, French, and English, the coat of arms, and the word *passport* in the three official languages.

AIRLINE

Air Vanuatu

NATIONAL FLOWER

Hibiscus (unofficial)

NATIONAL PLANT

Namele fern

NATIONAL ANIMAL

Boar (unofficial)

NATIONAL RESOURCES

Natural resources include manganese, hardwood forests, and fish. Mineral deposits are negligible; the country has no known petroleum deposits. Mostly subsistence farming, fishing, offshore financial services, and tourism, based on unspoiled island life, are the mainstays of the economy.

FOODS

Lap lap, a dish of grated yam, banana, or manioc covered in coconut cream and baked in an earth oven, is the national dish. Other specialties include *rousette,* a dish of flying fox (fruit bat) and vegetables; *nantou,* roast ground pigeon; coconut crab, a dish of fresh crab cooked in coconut milk; and *kava,* a drink made of the root of the pepper tree, which is the national drink.

SPORTS/SPORTS TEAMS

Association football (soccer), rugby, and cricket are popular sports. Vanuatu national teams participate in many sports at an international level.

TEAM SPORTS

Basketball

Vanuatu Basketball Team; Vanuatu Women's Basketball Team

Cricket

Vanuatu Cricket Team

Football

Vanuatu Football Team; Vanuatu Women's Football Team; Vanuatu Under-19 Football Team; Vanuatu Women's Under-19 Football Team; Vanuatu Rugby Union team; Vanuatu Futsal Team; Vanuatu Beach Soccer Team

Netball

Vanuatu Netball Team

Table Tennis

Vanuatu Table Tennis Team

Tennis

Pacific Oceania Fed Cup Team; Pacific Oceania Davis Cup Team (Pacific Oceania teams represent a number of Pacific island countries)

Volleyball

Vanuatu Men's Beach Volleyball Team; Vanuatu Women's Beach Volleyball Team; Vanuatu Men's Volleyball Team; Vanuatu Women's Volleyball Team

INDIVIDUAL SPORTS

Vanuatu Amateur Boxing Team; Vanuatu Archery Team; Vanuatu Athletics Team; Vanuatu Canoeing Team; Vanuatu Sailing Team; Vanuatu Tae Kwon Do Team; Vanuatu Weight Lifting Team

NATIONAL HEROES OR PERSONIFICATIONS

Father Walter Hayde Lini, the Anglican priest who served as the first prime minister from 1980 to 1991; Maxim Carlot Korman, the prime minister responsible for the nation's modernization in the 1990s

NATIONAL HOLIDAY/INDEPENDENCE DAY
Independence Day, July 30

FESTIVALS/FAIRS
Fete de la Francophonie, March; Naghol, April; Independence Day celebrations, July; Toka Festival, September

SIGNIFICANT EVENTS IN FORMATION OF NATIONAL IDENTITY

700 C.E.–1400 C.E. Multiple waves of colonizers, each speaking a distinct language, migrate to the islands.

1606 A Spanish expedition encounters the islands, naming them Terra Australis del Espiritu Santo. The name remains in Espiritu Santo, the name of the largest of the islands.

1768 The French, under Louis Antoine de Bougainville, visit the islands.

1774 British explorer Captain James Cook charts the islands and names them after the Hebrides Islands in Scotland*, calling them the New Hebrides.

19th century Blackbirders, or slavers, take thousands of ni-Vanuatu to work as slave labor on sugar and cotton plantations in Fiji* and Queensland.

1865–1887 European settlers, planters, and missionaries settle in the islands. France and the United Kingdom* establish a joint naval patrol to protect their citizens.

1906 The New Hebrides becomes a unique experiment in colonial administration, a joint British-French Condominium. Each power is responsible for its own citizens, but the indigenous peoples are a joint responsibility. Other nationalities choose under which laws they wish to live.

1935 Devastated by European diseases, the island population falls to an all-time low of just 45,000.

1938–1941 The John Frum cargo cult emerges, with believers waiting for their ancestors to return with goods, or "cargo," for them. Goods held by nonislanders are viewed as intercepted by the foreigners, leading to some violence.

1963 A political-cultural movement forms with demands for the return of the land to the ni-Vanuatu and a return to traditional ways.

1978 Self-government is introduced as a prelude to independence in 1980.

1980 Political leaders unilaterally declare Espiritu Santo independent. The movement is put down by troops from Papua New Guinea*. The New Hebrides become independent as Vanuatu. Father Walter Lini is the first prime minister.

2003–2009 Reforms of the tax and financial laws tighten controls on money laundering and end international criticism. Ethnic clashes between different island groups leave several dead. Democratic elections, held regularly since independence, become a democratic tradition.

VIETNAM

OFFICIAL NAME
Cộng hòa xã hội chủ nghĩa Việt Nam (Vietnamese); Socialist Republic of Vietnam (English)

POPULATION
86,235,300 (2009e)

INHABITANTS' NAME/NICKNAME
Vietnamese

LANGUAGE/LANGUAGES
Vietnamese (official); French, English, Chinese, Khmer, others

RELIGION/RELIGIONS
Buddhist, 85 percent; Roman Catholic, 7 percent; Hoa Hao, 1.5 percent; Cao Dai, 1 percent; Protestant, Muslim, other or no religion

NATIONAL FLAG

The flag, known as *cờ đỏ sao vàng,* the "red flag with yellow star," is a red field charged with a large, yellow, five-pointed star in the center. Red represents the blood of the country's martyrs, and yellow represents the color of the Vietnamese skin. The five points of the star represent intellectuals, peasants, workers, traders, and soldiers.

COAT OF ARMS/SEAL

The coat of arms is a stylized circle of red charged with a yellow, five-pointed star and surrounded by sheaves of wheat and a yellow cogwheel, representing agriculture and industry. A red banner is entwined with the wheat from the base, where it is inscribed in yellow letters with the name of the country in Vietnamese.

MOTTO

Độc lập—tự do—hạnh phúc (Vietnamese); Independence—Freedom—Happiness (English translation)

CAPITAL CITY

Hanoi

TYPE OF GOVERNMENT

Socialist republic

NATIONAL EMBLEM

Ho Chi Minh

NATIONAL COLORS

Red and yellow

NATIONAL ANTHEM

The anthem dates from the independence movement of the 1940s and was adopted by the provisional government in 1946.

Tien quan ça (Forward, Soldiers!)
Soldiers of Vietnam, forward!
With one single determination to save our
    fatherland,
Our hurried steps resound on the long and
    arduous road.
Our flag, red with the blood of victory, bears
    the spirit of the country.
The distant rumbling of the guns mingles with
    our marching song.
The path to glory is built by the bodies of our
    foes.
Overcoming all hardships, together we build
    our resistance bases.
Ceaselessly for the people's cause let us
    struggle,
Let us hasten to the battlefield!
Onward! All together advancing!
For one eternal Vietnam.

Soldiers of Vietnam, forward!
The gold star fluttering
Leading the people of our native land out of
    misery and suffering.
Let us join our efforts in the fight to build a
    new life.
Arise and break these chains.
For too long have we swallowed our hatred.
Be ready for all sacrifices and life will be
    radiant.
Ceaselessly for the people's cause, let us
    struggle,
Let us hasten to the battlefield!
Onward! All together advancing!
For one eternal Vietnam.

PATRON SAINT

Saint Joseph

CURRENCY

Vietnamese dong

INTERNET IDENTIFIER

.vn

VEHICLE IDENTIFICATION PLATES/STICKERS

VN

PASSPORT

The passport cover has the name of the country in Vietnamese and English, the coat of arms, and the word *passport* in Vietnamese and English.

AIRLINE
Vietnam Airlines

NATIONAL FLOWER
Yellow lotus

NATIONAL PLANT
Bamboo; rice

NATIONAL ANIMAL
Water buffalo

NATIONAL RESOURCES
National resources include phosphates, coal, manganese, bauxite, chromate, offshore oil and gas deposits, forests, and hydropower. Since 1986, when economic reforms were enacted, the economy has grown substantially. Manufacturing, information technology, and high-tech industries are now the economic mainstays. Tourism has also grown, based on the country's varied scenery, historic cities and monuments, sandy beaches, pleasant climate, and unique culture. Remittances from Vietnamese living outside the country are a source of foreign currency and investment.

FOODS
Pho, a dish of beef, beef broth, rice noodles, and vegetables, is considered the national dish. Other specialties include *banh mi thit,* a Vietnamese version of a baguette sandwich; *bo kho,* a dish of beef and vegetables; *ga nuong sa,* grilled chicken with lemongrass; *ca cuon,* a roll of fine pastry filled with fish and spring onions; *mam,* salted fish; *com chien duong chau,* a rice and chicken dish with mint; and *sup mang cua,* a bamboo and crab soup.

SPORTS/SPORTS TEAMS
Association football (soccer), badminton, and volleyball are popular sports. Vietnam national teams participate in many sports at an international level.

TEAM SPORTS

Badminton
Vietnam Badminton Team

Baseball
Vietnam Softball Team

Basketball
Vietnam Basketball Team; Vietnam Women's Basketball Team

Football
Vietnam Football Team, nickname Ngôi sao Vàng (the Golden Star); Vietnam Women's Football Team, nickname Ngôi sao Vàng (the Golden Star); Vietnam Under-19 Football Team, nickname Ngôi sao Vàng (the Golden Star); Vietnam Women's Under-19 Football Team, nickname Ngôi sao Vàng (the Golden Star); Vietnam Futsal Team

Kabaddi
Vietnam Kabaddi Team

Table Tennis
Vietnam Table Tennis Team

Tennis
Vietnam Davis Cup Team

Volleyball
Vietnam Men's Volleyball Team; Vietnam Women's Volleyball Team

INDIVIDUAL SPORTS
Vietnam Amateur Boxing Team; Vietnam Archery Team; Vietnam Athletics Team; Vietnam Canoeing Team; Vietnam Cycling Team; Vietnam Gymnastics Team; Vietnam Rowing Team; Vietnam Shooting Team; Vietnam Swim Team; Vietnam Tae Kwon Do Team; Vietnam Fencing Team; Vietnam Judo

Team; Vietnam Weight Lifting Team; Vietnam Wrestling Team

NATIONAL HEROES OR PERSONIFICATIONS

Trung Trac and Trung Nhi, sisters who led a revolt against Chinese rule in 40–43 C.E.; Ngo Quyen, who led the movement that regained the nation's independence from China in 938; Tran Hung Dao, the military leader responsible for the defeat of the invading Mongols in 1288; Emperor Gia Long, the unifier of Vietnam in the early 19th century; Phan Boi Chau, the first modern nationalist in the early 20th century; Ho Chi Minh, known as the father of the country

NATIONAL HOLIDAY/INDEPENDENCE DAY

Independence Day, September 2

FESTIVALS/FAIRS

Tet (Lunar New Year), January; Lim Festival, February; Cau Ngu Festival, January-Festival; Nui Ba Festival, February–March; Mid-Autumn Festival, September; Oc Om Boc Festival, October; Kate Festival, November–December

SIGNIFICANT EVENTS IN FORMATION OF NATIONAL IDENTITY

3000 B.C.E. The Lac civilization emerges in the Red River delta in northern Vietnam.

207 B.C.E.–939 C.E. The Chinese conquer and rule the region for over a thousand years.

11th century–14th century The establishment of the Ly dynasty ends a period of chaos and instability in present northern Vietnam. The south forms part of the Indianized state of Champa, which fights several wars of resistance against Vietnamese expansion.

1428–1757 A period of rapid population growth and expansion occurs at the expense of Champa, which is conquered in 1471. Vietnam absorbs Champa and expands into Khmer territory in the Mekong delta. French Catholic missionaries become active. Saigon is conquered in

the late 17th century. In 1757, Vietnam reaches its present borders.

1802 A decade of civil war and conflict between northern and southern territories ends with unification under Emperor Gia Long.

1858–1900 Persecution of Vietnamese Catholics is used as a pretext for a French invasion. Saigon falls to the invaders in 1861. Northern Vietnam is conquered in 1883.

1908–1930 The first nationalist organization forms. Nationalist sentiment grows under Phan Boi Chau, a writer and scholar, who adopts Marxism. An attempted uprising results in thousands imprisoned and hundreds dead.

1940–1954 The Japanese occupy the country during World War II. At the end of the war, the Viet Minh organization, led by Ho Chi Minh, announces the formation of the Democratic Republic of Vietnam, which is overthrown by the returning French forces. The First Indochina War begins as nationalists battle the French for control of the country.

1954 Unable to defeat the Viet Minh, the French agree to partition the country temporarily until 1956, leaving the north to the communist leader Ho Chi Minh.

1955 Encouraged by the United States*, the south is declared the Republic of Vietnam, popularly known as South Vietnam. A guerilla movement called the Viet Cong begins operations in the south against the new government. War with North Vietnam begins.

1963–1967 Political instability disrupts South Vietnam. The United States sends troops to fight the North Vietnamese and the local Viet Cong and begins bombing North Vietnam.

1967–1968 The number of U.S. troops reaches half a million. During the lunar new year truce, the North Vietnamese and the Viet Cong launch a surprise attack, the Tet Offensive. Although unsuccessful, the offensive convinces many Americans that the Vietnam War cannot be won.

1973–1976 An agreement is signed that calls for U.S. military withdrawal and a peaceful resolution between the two Vietnamese states. Fighting continues, and in 1975, the North Vietnamese take Saigon and the communist government unites north and south into one country.

1986–1995 The economic cost of unification leads to a major economic restructuring that allows a free market. The collapse of the Soviet Union spurs the liberalization movement. The United States lifts its trade embargo, and the countries restore diplomatic relations.

2006–2009 Younger leaders take charge of the government. Rapid economic growth begins to expand relative prosperity beyond the cities. A new middle class emerges. Democratic reforms are adopted.

WALLIS AND FUTUNA

OFFICIAL NAME
Territoire des Îles Wallis-et-Futuna (French); Territory of the Wallis and Futuna Islands (English)

POPULATION
15,600 (2009e); thousands of Wallisians live in New Caledonia* and French Polynesia*

INHABITANTS' NAME/NICKNAME
Wallisian(s); Uvean(s); Futunan(s)

LANGUAGE/LANGUAGES
French, Uvean (Wallisian), Futunan (all official); others

RELIGION/RELIGIONS
Roman Catholic, 98 percent; other or no religion

NATIONAL FLAG
The official flag is the French tricolor. The National Flag is a red field with four white isosceles triangles arranged in a square on the fly side of center. The French tricolor is a canton on the upper hoist. Red symbolizes courage, and white represents purity of ideals. The triangles signify the three indigenous kings and the French administra-tor. The French tricolor represents French sovereignty.

COAT OF ARMS/SEAL
The coat of arms is a red crest or shield bearing the same four isosceles triangles shown on the national flag in the lower right quadrant and the French tricolor in the upper left quadrant.

CAPITAL CITY
Mata-Utu

TYPE OF GOVERNMENT
Parliamentary democracy as a collectivity (territory) of the French Republic

NATIONAL EMBLEM
The kava bowl, which is used to honor chiefs and the existing hierarchy

NATIONAL COLORS
Red and white

NATIONAL ANTHEM
The territory has no official anthem. The French anthem "La Marseillaise" is the anthem of all French territories.

CURRENCY
CFP franc

INTERNET IDENTIFIER
.wf

VEHICLE IDENTIFICATION PLATES/STICKERS
F France (official); WF Wallis and Futuna (unofficial)

PASSPORT
Wallisians and Futunans are French citizens and travel on French passports.

NATIONAL ANIMAL
Dolphin (unofficial)

NATIONAL BIRD

Frigate bird (unofficial)

NATIONAL RESOURCES

Natural resources are negligible. The major resources are annual French subsidies, remittances from Wallisians living in New Caledonia and French Polynesia, and tourism. Agriculture and fishing are the main occupations.

FOODS

Roast suckling pig, cooked in an earth oven of hot rocks, is considered the national dish. It is often served with *fafai*, spinach cooked with coconut cream. Pigs and chickens are raised mainly for celebratory occasions. Other specialties include *poisson cru*, raw fish marinated in coconut cream and lime juice; *poe*, a pudding made of papaya, mango, and banana; and *fruit à pain fume*, smoked breadfruit. Kava, the national drink, served both ritually and secularly in Futuna, is made from the root of the pepper tree.

SPORTS/SPORTS TEAMS

Association football (soccer) is the most popular sport. Wallis and Futuna national teams participate in basketball, football, rugby union, and volleyball at an international level.

TEAM SPORTS

Basketball

Wallis and Futuna Basketball Team; Wallis and Futuna Women's Basketball Team

Football

Wallis and Futuna Football Team; Wallis and Futuna Rugby Union Team

Volleyball

Wallis and Futuna Men's Volleyball Team

NATIONAL HEROES OR PERSONIFICATIONS

King Tomasi Kulimoetoke II, who defied the French to save his grandson

NATIONAL HOLIDAY/INDEPENDENCE DAY

Bastille Day, July 14; Territory Day, July 29

FESTIVALS/FAIRS

Futuna Festival, November; Uvea Festival, March

SIGNIFICANT EVENTS IN FORMATION OF NATIONAL IDENTITY

1200 C.E.–1600 C.E. The Wallis Islands form part of the island empire of Tonga* until its decline in the 15th century. Contact between the islands ceases. Kingdoms are created on Wallis and Futuna.

17th century–18th century Dutch, British, and French expeditions visit the islands.

1837 French Catholic missionaries are the first Europeans to settle on the islands. Most of the population is eventually converted to Catholicism.

1842 The kings of the islands request French aid during a rebellion.

1887–1888 The queen of Uvea, on Wallis, signs a treaty establishing a French protectorate. The kings of Sigave and Alo, on Futuna and Alofi, also sign protectorate agreements.

1917 The three kingdoms are annexed and become the colony of Wallis and Futuna, under the authority of the French administration of New Caledonia.

1959–1961 The islanders vote to become a separate overseas territory in 1961.

1960s–1990s The islands come to depend on French financial subsidies. Overpopulation becomes a problem, with many moving to New Caledonia or Tahiti*.

2005 A crisis breaks out when King Tomasi Kulimoetoke II of Uvea faces being deposed after giving sanctuary to his grandson, who is accused of manslaughter. The king claimed his grandson's right to trial under island law rather than the French penal code.

2008   Tomasi Kulimoetoke dies and is replaced by Kapiliele Faupala, despite opposition from some royal clans.

2009   The effects of global warming, particularly a rise in sea levels, threaten the islands.

See also France

WEST PAPUA

OFFICIAL NAME
Special Autonomous Region of Papua

POPULATION
2,778,200 (2009e)

INHABITANTS' NAME/NICKNAME
West Papuan(s); Papuan(s)

LANGUAGE/LANGUAGES
Bahasa Indonesia (official); Papuan languages, English, Dutch, others

RELIGION/RELIGIONS
Protestant, 54 percent; Roman Catholic, 24 percent; Muslim, 21 percent; Buddhist, Hindu, other or no religion

NATIONAL FLAG
The flag, called the Morning Star, has 13 equal stripes of blue and white with a broad vertical red stripe at the hoist, charged with a single white, five-pointed star. The 13 stripes represent the 13 major tribes. The blue stripes stand for the country's diverse peoples and languages, and the six white stripes represent the island's six traditional divisions and future provinces. The red stripe stands for courage, political struggle, and the blood shed in the struggle for freedom. The star, the Morning Star, stands for hope for a new day and a new era.

COAT OF ARMS/SEAL
The coat of arms, the seal of the government-in-exile, is a shield of the national flag, with the red stripe and white star at the top and 13 vertical blue and white stripes before a *mambruk* with wings spread. Below is a banner with the name of the proposed country, West Papua. Above the shield, between the spread wings, is a banner with the national motto. The coat of arms adopted just before the Indonesian invasion consists of a central shield, a vertical version of the Morningstar flag, supported by two yellow and green birds of paradise holding a banner with the name of the country in their claws. The shield and birds are surrounded by two Papuan blue orchids plants.

MOTTO
One people—one soul

CAPITAL CITY
Jayapura (Indonesian); Port Numbai (Papuan)

TYPE OF GOVERNMENT
The region constitutes a special autonomous region with two Indonesian provinces, Papua and West Papua (Papua Barat). The West Papua government-in-exile has endorsed a presidential republic.

NATIONAL EMBLEM
The Morning Star flag

NATIONAL COLORS
Blue, white, and red

NATIONAL ANTHEM
The anthem was adopted in 1961 as the territory was preparing for independence. It was outlawed when Indonesia* took control in 1963 but was adopted in 2003 as the anthem of the autonomous region. No English translation is available.

Hai Tanahku Papua (Papuan); My Beloved Papua Land (English)

Hai tanah ku papoea,
Kau tanah lahirku,
Ku kasih akan dikau
sehingga adjalku.

Kukasih pasir putih
Dipantaimu senang
Dimana lautan biru
Berkilat dalam trang.

Kukasih gunung-gunung
Besar mulialah
Dan awan jang melajang
Keliling puntjaknja.

Kukasih dikau tanah
Jang dengan buahmu
Membajar keradjinan
Dan pekerdjaanku.

Kukasih bunji ombak
Jang pukul pantaimu
Njanjian jang selalu
Senangkan hatiku.

Kukasih hutan-hutan
Selimut tanahku
Kusuka mengembara
Dibawah naungmu.

Sjukur bagimu, tuhan,
Kau brikan tanahku
Bri aku radjin djuga
Sampaikan maksudMu.

CURRENCY

Indonesian rupiah

VEHICLE IDENTIFICATION PLATES/STICKERS

RI Indonesia (official); WPA West Papua (unofficial)

PASSPORT

West Papuans are Indonesian citizens and travel on Indonesian passports.

NATIONAL FLOWER

Bird of paradise (unofficial)

NATIONAL TREE

Merbau (unofficial)

NATIONAL BIRD

Mambruk

NATIONAL FISH

Talapia (tilapia) (unofficial)

NATIONAL RESOURCES

Natural resources include gold, copper, silver, natural gas, timber, oil, and fisheries. The world's largest open-cut mine, run by a U.S. company, is a major resource but with little benefit for the local population. Remittances from West Papuans living outside the region are a major source of foreign currency and investment.

FOODS

Mumu, a dish of pork, sweet potatoes, rice, and greens, is considered the national dish of the Papuans. Other local specialties include curried fish, a dish of fresh fish, pineapple, onions, garlic, and curry; fried sweet potatoes and bananas; chicken and greens in coconut milk; vegetables in coconut milk; sago grubs with peanut sauce; chicken on a stick; flying fox (fruit bat) with prunes and cream sauce; and *paua sup,* made of python, pork, onion, and chilies.

SPORTS/SPORTS TEAMS

Association football (soccer) is the most popular sport. The West Papua national team participates in football at an international level.

Football

West Papua Football Team, nickname Biru Putih (the Blue and Whites)

NATIONAL HEROES OR PERSONIFICATIONS

Jacob Hendrik Prai, pro-independence leader; Seth Jaferth Roemkorem, leader of the national movement; Moses Werror, head of the Revolutionary Council; Nicolaas Jouwe, leader of the national movement in the 1960s; Theys Eluay, national leader murdered in 2001; Nicholass Jouve, a leader of the independence movement

NATIONAL HOLIDAY/INDEPENDENCE DAY

National Day (Independence Day), December 1

FESTIVALS/FAIRS

Baliem Valley Festival, June; West Papua Festival (Netherlands*), July; Morning Star Festival, February

SIGNIFICANT EVENTS IN FORMATION OF NATIONAL IDENTITY

5000 B.C.E.–1500 C.E.   The early inhabitants settle into village patterns, each with its own culture and language. Indonesian and Asian seafarers, who trade with the indigenous peoples or take slaves from the coastal tribes, know of the large island.

1511–1600   The island is sighted by a Portuguese expedition. A Spanish expedition, in 1546, names the large island New Guinea for its resemblance to Spain's Guinea territory in Africa.

1606   A Dutch expedition reaches the island. Lacking the economic interest of the Indonesian islands, New Guinea is generally ignored.

1828–1900   The Dutch formally claim the southwestern region of the island. The island of New Guinea is formally divided between the Netherlands, the United Kingdom*, and Germany* in 1895.

1900   Missionaries convert much of the population to Christianity. Dutch control is limited to the coastal regions, and immigration from the overcrowded Indonesian islands is prohibited.

1942–1944   The invading Japanese take control of the territory. A brutal regime of forced labor and mistreatment leaves the West Papuans with an abiding hatred of all Asians, and the Dutch are welcomed on their return in 1945.

1949–1959   The Dutch reject claims by newly independent Indonesia and begin preparing West Papua for separate independence.

1959–1961   A Dutch plan for independence is created. The West Papuans adopt a national flag, anthem, and other trappings of statehood, including a national legislature.

1961–1963   Indonesia launches an invasion of the territory, and fighting with Dutch forces begins. West Papuan leaders declare the independence of West Papua on December 1, 1961, but it remains unrecognized. The United States brokers a compromise that places West Papua under United Nations control, with provisions for a plebiscite to decide the region's future. Ignoring the agreement, the United Nations turns the territory over to Indonesian control.

1965–1972   The betrayed West Papuans form a guerrilla liberation army to fight for independence. Fighting and Indonesian repression leave between 30,000 and 100,000 dead. The Indonesian government's transmigration policy leads to the settlement of 1.2 million Muslims from the overcrowded central islands.

1975   Separatist leaders issue the Seri Declaration, a second unilateral declaration of independence of the Republic of West Papua.

1990s   The separatist organization, the Free Papua Movement, gains greater support due to anger over the actions of an American mining company, Freeport-McMoRan, which is accused of massive pollution and of supporting the human-rights abuses committed by the Indonesian military. The Indonesian government, as in East Timor*, gives its backing to prointegration militias, leading to even more violence.

2000   Nationalist leaders demand that the West Papuans be allowed to vote in the plebiscite promised by the United Nations in the early 1960s.

2001 The province is granted limited autonomy. In spite of autonomy guarantees, the province is split into two new provinces in 2003.

2005–2009 The struggle to gain the promised independence continues to be the focus of life in the territory. The Indonesian military occupation, although less brutal than in previous decades, remains a fact of life for most West Papuans.

See also Indonesia

2

Central and South America

The symbols adopted by the various nations of Central and South America are often holdovers from the colonial period, when Spain* and Portugal* controlled the vast majority of the territory in the region. When the colonial powers lost their possessions in the early 19th century, European symbolism remained in the often operatic national anthems, the coats of arms, and other national symbols. Argentina*, the first to win recognized independence, adopted a color scheme of blue and white, which, along with the red, white, and blue of the French and American revolutions, greatly influenced many of the new flags and coats of arms adopted in the region. The colors yellow, blue, and red, adopted by the newly independent nation of New Granada were retained when that country split into Ecuador*, Colombia*, and Venezuela*. Some symbols, such as national foods, music, dances, and other cultural symbols, remain fairly uniform across a vast region stretching from Mexico to the southern tip of South America, part of the colonial legacy. The exceptions are the Portuguese-influenced Brazil* and the small regions where British, French, or Dutch influence remains paramount.

Two of the territories included in this section, French Guiana* and Falkland Islands*, are not independent nations but are dependent territories with their own identities and symbols. The other nonindependent nations, Santa Cruz and Zulia, are undergoing a popular movements for greater independence

from increasingly radical governments, including the recognition of their distinct national symbols.

ARGENTINA

OFFICIAL NAME
República Argentina (Spanish); Argentine Republic (English)

POPULATION
40,820,000 (2009e)

INHABITANTS' NAME/NICKNAME
Argentinean(s); Argentine(s)

LANGUAGE/LANGUAGES
Spanish (official); Italian, English, German, French, Portuguese, others

RELIGION/RELIGIONS
Roman Catholic, 70 percent; Protestant, 2 percent; Jewish, 2 percent; Muslim, other or no religion

NATIONAL FLAG
The flag consists of three horizontal stripes of pale blue, white, and pale blue bearing a centered gold sun with a human face, the Sun of May. The popular interpretation of the flag is that it represents the sky, clouds, and sun. Others believe that the blue symbolizes the clothing of the Virgin Mary and the white represents silver (the name Argentina comes from the Latin word for silver, *argentums*),

Other theories state that the colors are based on those of the House of Bourbon or that they are derived from the Rio de la Plata (River of Silver) that flows through the country.

COAT OF ARMS/SEAL

At the top is the famous sun symbol of Argentina, the golden-yellow Sun of May, also found on the flag of Argentina. The rising sun symbolizes the rising of Argentina. In the center ellipse are two shaking hands that symbolize the unity of the various provinces of Argentina. The hands come together to hold a pike, which represents power and willingness to defend the freedom that is symbolized by the Phrygian cap, or liberty cap, on the top of the pike. The blue and white colors are symbols of the Argentine people and are the same colors of the flag. The blue half of the ellipse represents the sky, and the white represents the Rio de la Plata. The hands are flesh-colored and represent friendship, peace, union, and brotherhood; the pike is the brown of wood, and the Phrygian cap is red, like the traditional French cap.

MOTTO

En unión y libertad (Spanish); In union and freedom (English)

CAPITAL CITY

Buenos Aires

TYPE OF GOVERNMENT

Federal presidential republic

NATIONAL EMBLEM

Sun of May

NATIONAL COLORS

White and sky blue

NATIONAL ANTHEM

The anthem, adopted soon after independence in 1810, has undergone many modifications. In a presidential decree in 1900, it was shortened to just the first and last verses of the nine verses in use at the time.

Marcha de La Patria (Spanish); March of the Fatherland (English)

Mortals! Hear the sacred cry:
"Freedom, freedom, freedom!"
Hear the noise of broken chains,
see the noble equality enthroned.
The United Provinces of the South
have now opened their very honorable throne.
And the free people of the world reply:
"We salute the great people of Argentina!"
"We salute the great people of Argentina!"
And the free people of the world reply:
"We salute the great people of Argentina!"

Chorus

May the laurels be eternal
that we knew how to win,
that we knew how to win.
Let us live crowned with glory
. . . or swear to die gloriously!
Or swear to die gloriously!
Or swear to die gloriously!

PATRON SAINT

Our Lady of Lujan (unofficial); Francis Solano; Immaculate Conception of Mary; Laura Vicuna

CURRENCY

Argentine peso

INTERNET IDENTIFIER

.ar

VEHICLE IDENTIFICATION PLATES/ STICKERS

RA

PASSPORT

The cover has the words Mercosur and República Argentina, the coat of arms, and the Spanish word for passport, *pasaporte*. A thin line encloses the information.

AIRLINES

Aerolineas Argentinas (Argentine Airlines); Austral Airlines; Lan Argentina

NATIONAL FLOWER

Ceibo

NATIONAL TREE

Jacaranda

NATIONAL ANIMAL

Cougar (unofficial); *yaguareté* (jaguar)

NATIONAL BIRD

Hornero

NATIONAL RESOURCES

Natural resources include the fertile plains of the pampas and abundant mineral wealth, including lead, zinc, tin, copper, iron ore, manganese, petroleum, and uranium. Other resources include sophisticated cities, a distinct culture combining Latin and European elements, and many natural attractions that support a very important tourist industry.

FOODS

Asado (barbecue); empanadas, stuffed pastries of meat, cheese, or fish; and *lorco,* a mixture of corn, meat, bacon, onion, and gourd, are considered national dishes. Other specialties include pizza and pasta, brought to Argentina by Italian immigrants; *chimichurri,* a spicy sauce made of peppers, capers, and spices; *sopa de lentijas,* lentil soup; *chipas,* cheese bread; *crillo de pollo,* a stew of chicken, potatoes, and corn; *dulce de leche,* condensed milk with vanilla and sugar; *milhoja,* a dessert; and maté, an invigorating green tea adopted from the indigenous peoples that is considered Argentina's national drink.

SPORTS/SPORTS TEAMS

Association football (soccer) is a national passion. Rugby union and basketball are also very popular. The national sport, as defined by an Argentine law of 1953, is *pato,* a game played on horseback that combines elements of polo and basketball. Argentina national teams participate in many sports at an international level.

TEAM SPORTS

Badminton

Argentina Badminton Team

Baseball

Argentina Baseball Team; Argentina Softball Team

Basketball

Argentina Basketball Team; Argentina Wheelchair Basketball Team; Argentina Women's Basketball Team; Argentina Under-21 Basketball Team; Argentina Under-19 Basketball Team

Cricket

Argentina Cricket Team; Argentina Women's Cricket Team

Football

Argentina Football Team, nickname Albicelestes (the White and Sky-Blues) or Los Gauchos (the Gauchos); Argentina Women's Football Team, nickname Albicelestes (the White and Sky-Blues); Argentina Under-20 Football Team, nickname Albicelestes (the White and Sky-Blues); Argentina Under-19 Football Team; Argentina Women's Under-19 Football Team; Argentina Rugby Union Team, nickname Los Pumas; Argentina Rugby League Team; Argentina A Rugby Union Team; Argentina Rugby Union Team (Sevens), nickname Argentina Seven or Argentina 7s; Argentina Women's Rugby Union Team (Sevens), nickname Argentina Sevens or Argentina 7s; Argentina Australian-Rules Football Team, nickname Las Aguilas (the Eagles); Argentina Wheelchair Rugby Team;

Argentina American Football Team; Argentina Beach Soccer Team; Argentina Futsal Team

Handball

Argentina Handball Team

Hockey

Argentina Field Hockey Team, nickname Los Leones (the Lions); Argentina Women's Field Hockey Team, nickname Las Leonas (the Lionesses); Argentina Ice Hockey Team

Korfball

Argentina Korfball Team

Lacrosse

Argentina Lacrosse Team

Netball

Argentina Netball Team

Polo

Argentina Polo Team

Racing

Argentina Speedway Team

Table Tennis

Argentina Table Tennis Team

Tennis

Argentina Davis Cup Team; Argentina Fed Cup Team

Volleyball

Argentina Men's Volleyball Team; Argentina Women's Volleyball Team; Argentina Fistball Team; Argentina Men's Beach Volleyball Team

INDIVIDUAL SPORTS

Argentina Aikido Team; Argentina Amateur Boxing Team; Argentina Archery Team; Argentina Athletics Team; Argentina Canoeing Team; Argentina Chess Team; Argentina Cycling Team; Argentina Equestrian Team; Argentina Fencing Team; Argentina Gymnastics Team; Argentina Judo Team; Argentina Karate Team; Argentina Modern Pentathlon Team; Argentina Rowing Team; Argentina Sailing Team; Argentina Shooting Team; Argentina Swim Team; Argentina Tae Kwon Do Team; Argentina Triathlon Team; Argentina Weight Lifting Team; Argentina Wrestling Team

WINTER SPORTS

Argentina Alpine Ski Team; Argentina Bandy Team; Argentina Biathlon Team; Argentina Bobsleigh and Tobogganing Team; Argentina Ice Hockey Team; Argentina Luge Team; Argentina Skating Team

NATIONAL HEROES OR PERSONIFICATIONS

The gaucho is the personification of Argentina.

National heroes include Christopher Columbus, the first European to visit the New World; José de San Martin, military leader of the war for independence; Juan Perón, populist dictator in the 1940s, whose influence is still very strong in Argentine politics; Eva Perón (Evita), wife of Juan Perón and one of the icons of popular culture in Argentina

NATIONAL HOLIDAY/INDEPENDENCE DAY

Independence Day, July 9

FESTIVALS/FAIRS

Bue Music Festival, October–November; Moonpark Music Festival; Pepsi Music Festival, September–October; Buenos Aires Book Fair, April; La Falda National Tango and Milonga Festival, July; Gaucho Festival, November; International Rural Exhibition, July–August

SIGNIFICANT EVENTS IN FORMATION OF NATIONAL IDENTITY

1000 B.C.E.–1480 C.E. Amerindian tribes settle the region in prehistoric times. The Guarani people develop an agricultural society in the northeast, while the Pampas and Patagonia are dominated by nomadic cultures.

1480 Troops of the Inca Empire, under the rule of Pachacutec, launch an invasion of northwestern Argentina, which is added to the imperial region called Collasuyu. Inca influence spreads to other areas of present Argentina.

1516–1776 Europeans explore the region. A Spanish colony is established on the site of present Buenos Aires in 1580. The Viceroyalty of the Rio de la Plata is created in 1776.

1806–1815 Dissatisfaction with Spanish rule increases following the independence of the United States* from the United Kingdom*. On May 25, 1810, following confirmation of rumors about the overthrow of the Spanish king by Napoleon of France*, the citizens of Buenos Aires stage the May Revolution and establish a separatist government. Two nations emerge in what is now Argentina: the United Provinces of South America in 1810 and the Liga Federal in 1815.

1816–1820 The United Provinces of the Rio Plata declare their independence from Spain. Eventually, Bolivia*, Paraguay*, and Uruguay* go their own way, and the area that remains becomes Argentina. The Liga Federal is crushed and incorporated into the new state in 1820.

1820–1930 The country's population and culture is subsequently heavily influenced by mass immigration from Europe, particularly from Italy* and Spain. Argentina is one of the wealthiest and most advanced societies in the world, mostly due to exports of agricultural products.

1939–1978 After World War II, an era of Peronist authoritarian rule and interference in subsequent governments is followed by a military junta that takes power in 1976. The military government devastates the country, which is already floundering after several decades of poor government and mismanagement. The Dirty War, noted for its brutal methods, mass disappearances, and universal lack of human rights, sinks the Argentine nation into the darkest period of its history.

1983–2006 Democracy returns in 1983 and persists despite numerous challenges, the most formidable of which is a severe economic crisis in 2001–02 that leads to violent public protests and the resignation of several interim presidents. The economy recovers strongly after bottoming out in 2002. The government renegotiates its public debt in 2005 and pays off its remaining obligations to the International Monetary Fund in early 2006.

2007–2008 The election of the wife of the outgoing president in December 2007 begins a period of faltering economy and political conflicts. Spiraling oil prices and growing poverty lead to several violent confrontations between trade unionists and security forces. Dissatisfied consumers also stage mass protests against rapidly rising prices and a lack of basic goods.

2009 The government declares a state of emergency to combat the worst drought in decades. Farmers threaten to halt livestock and grain sales to protest new agricultural export taxes.

BELIZE

OFFICIAL NAME
Belize

POPULATION
303,800 (2009e)

INHABITANTS' NAME/NICKNAME
Belizean(s)

LANGUAGE/LANGUAGES
English (official); Spanish, Creole, Mayan dialects, Garifuna, German, others

RELIGION/RELIGIONS
Roman Catholic, 50 percent; Pentecostal, 7.5 percent; Anglican, 5.5 percent; Seventh-day

Adventist, 5 percent; Mennonite, 4 percent; Methodist, 3.5 percent; other or no religion

NATIONAL FLAG

The flag has a blue field with narrow red stripes at the top and bottom, bearing a centered white disk with 50 olive leaves along its inner periphery. This represents the year 1950, when British Honduras (Belize's former name) began its quest for independence from the United Kingdom*. When Belize became independent in 1981, the two red stripes were added to the previous flag. In the center of the white disk is a coat of arms divided in three sections. The left field holds an oar and a sledgehammer, the right contains a saw and an ax, and the bottom has a sailing ship. Above the coat of arms is a mahogany tree, and below the coat of arms is Belize's motto in Latin. To the left of the coat of arms, a mulatto man holds an ax. On the right side, a black man holds an oar. The flag of Belize is unique, as it contains 12 colors, three more than any other national flag.

COAT OF ARMS/SEAL

The shield of the coat of arms is divided into three sections by a vertical line and an inverted V. The base section bears a ship in full sail on waves of the sea. The two upper sections show tools of the timber industry in Belize: a paddle and a squaring axe in the right section and a saw and a beating axe in the left section. Supporting the shield are two woodcutters, a mulatto man on the right holding a beating axe over his shoulder in his right hand, and a black man on the left holding a paddle over his shoulder in his left hand. Above the shield rises a mahogany tree. Below the shield is the motto scroll. A wreath of leaves encircles the coat of arms.

MOTTO

Sub umbra florero (Latin); I flourish in the shade (English)

CAPITAL CITY

Belmopan

TYPE OF GOVERNMENT

Parliamentary democracy

NATIONAL EMBLEM

Mahogany tree

NATIONAL COLORS

Red, blue, and white

NATIONAL ANTHEM

The anthem was written in 1963 by a Belizean who fought with the British during World War II. It was adopted at independence in 1981, but there has been some debate about its suitability due to its militaristic imagery and references that are opposed by women's groups, such as "Our manhood we pledge to thy liberty."

Land of the Free

O, land of the free by the Carib Sea,
Our manhood we pledge to thy liberty!
No tyrants here linger, despots must flee
This tranquil haven of democracy.
The blood of our sires, which hallows the sod,
Brought freedom from slavery oppression's rod,
By the might of truth and the grace of God,
No longer shall we be hewers of wood.

Chorus (repeated after second verse)

Arise! ye sons of the Baymen's clan,
Put on your armor, clear the land!
Drive back the tyrants, let despots flee—
Land of the free by the Carib Sea!

Nature has blessed thee with wealth untold,
O'er mountains and valleys where prairies
    roll;
Our fathers, the Baymen, valiant and bold
Drove back the invader; this heritage hold
From proud Rio Hondo to old Sarstoon,
Through coral isle, over blue lagoon;
Keep watch with the angels, the stars and
    moon;
For freedom comes tomorrow's noon.

PATRON SAINT

Saint Peter

CURRENCY

Belize dollar

INTERNET IDENTIFIER

.bz

VEHICLE IDENTIFICATION PLATES/ STICKERS

BH

PASSPORT

The passport cover has the initials CC for Caribbean Community, the coat of arms, the name of the country, and the word *passport.*

AIRLINE

Maya Island Air MIA

NATIONAL FLOWER

Black orchid

NATIONAL TREE

Mahogany tree

NATIONAL ANIMAL

Tapir (mountain cow); hawksbill turtle (unofficial)

NATIONAL BIRD

Keel-billed toucan

NATIONAL FISH

Nassau grouper (unofficial)

NATIONAL RESOURCES

Natural resources include potential arable land, timber, fish, potential petroleum, and hydropower. Mayan ruins, underwater reefs (including a UNESCO World Heritage site), sandy beaches, a pleasant climate, and a friendly population support a tourist industry that is growing in importance. The small, essentially private-enterprise economy is based on agriculture, primarily sugar, bananas, and citrus for export. Recent discoveries of underground oil have spurred the growth of the country's untapped mining and manufacturing capabilities.

FOODS

Kriol rice-and-beans, rice and haricot beans cooked in coconut milk, is considered the national dish. Other specialties are fry jack, a fried bread served with almost every meal; baked chicken Belize-style; chicken stew made with red achiote paste; fried plantains; potato salad; and Belize scrambled eggs, made with dried tomatoes, avocados, and salsa.

SPORTS/SPORTS TEAMS

Association football (soccer) is the most popular sport. Basketball and cricket are also very popular. Belize national teams participate in many sports at an international level.

TEAM SPORTS

Baseball

Belize Men's Softball Team; Belize Women's Softball Team

Basketball

Belize Basketball Team; Belize Women's Basketball Team; Belize Under-17 Basketball Team

Cricket

Belize Cricket Team

Football

Belize Football Team, nickname the Jaguars; Belize Women's Football Team, nickname the Jaguars; Belize Under-17 Football Team; Belize Under-16 Football Team

Volleyball

Belize Men's Volleyball Team; Belize Women's Volleyball Team

INDIVIDUAL SPORTS

Belize Amateur Boxing Team; Belize Athletics Team; Belize Canoeing Team; Belize Cycling Team; Belize Judo Team; Belize Shooting Team; Belize Tae Kwon Do Team; Belize Triathlon Team; Belize Weight Lifting Team

NATIONAL HEROES OR PERSONIFICATIONS

Philip Goldson, newspaper editor and independence leader; George Cadle Price, independence leader and first prime minister of Belize; Manuel Esquivel, a former prime minister

NATIONAL HOLIDAY/INDEPENDENCE DAY

National Day, September 10; Independence Day, September 21

FESTIVALS/FAIRS

International Costa Maya Festival, August; Saint George's Cay Day Festival, September; Independence Day Festival, September; Baron Bliss Day, March 9

SIGNIFICANT EVENTS IN FORMATION OF NATIONAL IDENTITY

1500 B.C.E.–900 C.E. The Maya civilization flourishes in Belize, leaving behind many artifacts and ruins. The complete collapse of the Maya empire leaves the people of the region to survive as subsistence farmers and fishermen.

1638–1700 European settlement begins with British Jews, privateers and pirates, and shipwrecked English seamen. The origin of the name Belize is still disputed. Some believe it derives from the Spanish pronunciation of the surname of the famous pirate Peter Wallace, who establishes the first European settlement in Belize in 1638. Others believe that the name comes from the Maya *belix,* meaning "muddy water," as applied to the Belize River.

18th century The early settlement on the Bay of Honduras grows from a few houses located at Belize Town and Saint George's Cay into a de facto colony of the United Kingdom during the late 18th century. The area was originally claimed by Spain as part of Honduras but is mostly ignored by the Spanish colonial authorities. Many of the early English settlers are drawn by the region's large logwood and mahogany forests. After many conflicts between the English and Spanish, war breaks out in 1796, and a Spanish expedition is sent to drive the English from the region. The Battle of Saint George's Cay in 1798 is won by a handful of local woodmen and fishermen against a larger Spanish force. Modern Belize honors the victors with celebrations in September, Saint George's Cay Day and National Day, both commemorating the victory over the Spanish.

1836–1862 In 1836, following the independence of the Central American countries from Spanish rule, the British claim the right to administer the ethnically and linguistically distinct region known as British Honduras. The region is formally declared a colony in 1862.

1900–1929 The economy of British Honduras remains based on the logging of mahogany until the early 20th century. Export crops of citrus, sugar cane, bananas, and tropical fruits come to dominate the economy by the 1920s. Settlers from neighboring Spanish-speaking countries, Jamaica*, and other Caribbean islands add to the population of the tiny colony.

1930s The Great Depression of the 1930s devastates the colony as demand for timber plummets. The effects of widespread unemployment and hardship are worsened by a devastating hurricane in 1931. Local perceptions of the government relief efforts as inadequate and unorganized are aggravated by its refusal to legalize trade unions or to introduce a minimum wage. Demonstrations and riots in 1934 mark the beginning of the independence movement.

1961–1970 Hurricane Hattie sweeps through Belize in 1961, devastating the coastal region, including the capital, Belize City. British colonial authorities decide to move the seat of government inland, and a new city, Belmopan, is designed and built. In 1970, government offices begin transferring to the new city in the heart of the country.

1964–1981 British Honduras becomes a self-governing colony in 1964 and is renamed Belize on June 1, 1973. Nationalist leader George Price leads the country to full independence on September 21, 1981, after delays caused by the territorial claims of neighboring countries, particularly Guatemala*, which refuses to formally recognize the new country at independence. Guatemala has claimed all or parts of Belize since colonial times. The claim is occasionally reflected in maps that show Belize as Guatemala's 23rd province. The territorial dispute remains unresolved, despite mediation attempts by the United Kingdom, various heads of government in the Caribbean, the Organization of American States, and even the United States.

2005–2007 Unrest sweeps the country in 2005, leading to protests and demonstrations against government plans for tax increases. A more buoyant economy in 2006 and 2007 calms people's fears and allows for new elections. The Organization of American States recommends that border disputes with Guatemala be referred to the International Court of Justice.

2008–2009 On February 8, 2008, Dean Barrow is sworn in as Belize's first black prime minister, demonstrating the rarity of racial tensions in the small, multiethnic country. The government tightens laws in an effort to protect the country's famed offshore reefs and the ruins of Mayan cities and religious sites.

BOLIVIA

OFFICIAL NAME
República de Bolivia (Spanish); Bulibya Republika (Quechua); Wullwya Suyu (Aymara); Republic of Bolivia (English)

POPULATION
10,348,300 (2009e)

INHABITANTS' NAME/NICKNAME
Bolivian(s)

LANGUAGE/LANGUAGES
Spanish, Quechua, Aymara (all official); Portuguese, others

RELIGION/RELIGIONS
Roman Catholic (official), 90–95 percent; Protestant, 4–5 percent; other or no religion

NATIONAL FLAG
The flag is a horizontal tricolor of red, yellow, and green. The red stands for the blood of the Bolivian patriots and the bravery of Bolivia's soldiers, the yellow represents the country's mineral wealth, and the green stands for the fertility of the land.

COAT OF ARMS/SEAL
The coat of arms of Bolivia has an oval border, the upper part yellow with the caption "República Boliviana" in red and the lower part blue with 10 five-pointed gold stars, one for each department, including the lost maritime department. In the center are an Andean llama or alpaca, a small Andean house, a palm tree, a yellow sun, Mount Potosí, a prairie, and a sheaf of wheat. The background is white on the upper half and green on the lower part.

MOTTO
¡La unión es la fuerza! (Spanish); Unity is strength! (English)

CAPITAL CITY
Sucre (constitutional, judicial); La Paz (administrative)

TYPE OF GOVERNMENT
Presidential republic

NATIONAL EMBLEM
Cerro de Potosi (Mount Potosí) (the Mountain of Silver); the llama

NATIONAL COLORS
Red, yellow, and green

NATIONAL ANTHEM
The composer of the music to the Bolivian anthem was an Italian, which explains its similarity to Italian operatic pieces.

Canción Patriótica (Spanish); Patriotic Song (English)

Bolivians, a favorable destiny
Has crowned our vows and longings;
This land is free,
Your servile state has ended.
The martial turmoil of yesterday
And the horrible clamor of war
Are followed today, in harmonious
    contrast,
By sweet hymns of peace and unity.
(repeat previous two lines)

Chorus

We have kept the lofty name of our country
In glorious splendor,
And on its altars we once more swear
To die, rather than live as slaves.
(repeat three times)
This innocent and beautiful land,
Which owes its name to Bolivar,
Is the happy homeland where men
Enjoy the benefits of good fortune and
    peace.
For the sons of the great Bolivar
Have sworn, thousands upon thousands
    of times,
To die rather than see the country's
Majestic flag humiliated.
(repeat previous two lines)

Chorus

Eternal praise to the brave warriors
Whose heroic valor and firmness
Conquered the glories that now
A happy Bolivia begins to enjoy!
Let their names, in marble and in bronze,
Transmit to remote ages
And in resounding song repeat the call:
Freedom! Freedom! Freedom!
(repeat previous two lines)

Chorus

PATRON SAINT

Saint Francis Solano; Our Lady of Capucdana; Our Lady of Mount Carmel; Sacred Heart of Jesus; Virgin de la Candelaria; Virgin of Copacabana

CURRENCY

Bolivian boliviano

INTERNET IDENTIFIER

.bo

VEHICLE IDENTIFICATION PLATES/ STICKERS

BOL

PASSPORT

The passport cover has the name *Comunidad Andina* (Andean Community), the name of the country in Spanish, the coat of arms, and the word for passport in Spanish, English, and French.

AIRLINE

Boliviana de Aviación BOA

NATIONAL FLOWER

Cantuta (Kantuta)

NATIONAL TREE

Palm, *artocarpus* (breadfruit) (unofficial)

NATIONAL ANIMAL

Llama

NATIONAL BIRD

Andean condor

NATIONAL RESOURCES

Natural resources include tin, natural gas, petroleum, zinc, tungsten, antimony, silver, iron, lead, gold, timber, and hydropower. Cultural resources include ancient ruins, indigenous Andean cultures, and colonial cities.

FOODS

Humitas, cornmeal tortillas filled with potatoes, pureed corn, onions, cheese, and other ingredients, are considered a national dish. *Picante de pollo,* deep-fried chicken with fried potatoes, rice, and a hot pepper salad, and *salteñas*, pastry filled with minced meat, peas, olives, and raisins, are also considered national dishes. Other specialties include *chairo paceño*, a stew of beef, lamb, and vegetables; *fritanga*, a spicy pork and egg stew; *majao*, a dish of meat and rice; and *lechon al horno*, roast suckling pig, usually served at the New Year.

SPORTS/SPORTS TEAMS

Association football (soccer) is the most popular sport, while the indoor variety, called futsal or *fulbito* in Bolivia, is also very popular. Bolivia national teams participate in many sports at an international level.

TEAM SPORTS

Baseball

Bolivia Baseball Team; Bolivia Softball Team

Basketball

Bolivia Basketball Team; Bolivia Women's Basketball Team

Football

Bolivia Football Ream, nickname La Verde (the Green One); Bolivia Women's Football Team, nickname La Verde; Bolivia Futsal Team

Hockey

Bolivia Field Hockey Team

Racing

Bolivia Speedway Team

Table Tennis

Bolivia Table Tennis Team

Tennis

Bolivia Davis Cup Team; Bolivia Fed Cup Team

Volleyball

Bolivia Men's Volleyball Team; Bolivia Women's Volleyball Team

INDIVIDUAL SPORTS

Bolivia Amateur Boxing Team; Bolivia Athletics Team; Bolivia Canoeing Team; Bolivia Chess Team; Bolivia Cycling Team; Bolivia Equestrian Team; Bolivia Fencing Team; Bolivia Gymnastics Team; Bolivia Judo Team; Bolivia Modern Pentathlon Team; Bolivia Rowing Team; Bolivia Shooting Team; Bolivia Swim Team; Bolivia Triathlon Team; Bolivia Weight Lifting Team; Bolivia Wrestling Team

NATIONAL HEROES OR PERSONIFICATIONS

Simón Bolivar, one of the leaders of the independence movement in South America, a form of whose name was adopted as the name of the country; Pedro Domingo Murillo, the first martyr of Bolivian independence in 1810; Andrés de Santa Cruz, the self-styled Napoleon of the Andes, who dominated early Bolivia; Ismael Móntes, the only Bolivian leader identified in Bolivian history as the "great president"; Evo Morales, the current president and the first indigenous president of the country

NATIONAL HOLIDAY/INDEPENDENCE DAY

Independence Day, August 6

FESTIVALS/FAIRS

The best known of the various festivals in the country is the Carnaval de Oruro, which was among the first 19 Masterpieces of the Oral and Intangible Heritage of Humanity, as acknowledged by UNESCO in May 2001.

SIGNIFICANT EVENTS IN FORMATION OF NATIONAL IDENTITY

2000 B.C.E.–1500 C.E. The territory now known as Bolivia is the home of advanced civilizations that eventually came under the rule of the Incas.

The area's ruined cities, irrigation systems, and water canals are evidence of advanced engineering and state organization.

1524–1700 The Spanish conquest of the Inca Empire ends the advance of that empire, and the highlands are brought under Spanish rule. Modern Bolivia is known as Upper Peru or Charcas and is under the authority of the Spanish viceroy of Lima. Local Spanish authority is vested in the Audiencia de Charcas, centered on the city of Chuquisaca (La Plata—the modern city of Sucre).

17th century–18th century Silver from the Potosí region produces much of the Spanish empire's wealth. A steady stream of enslaved native people serves as the labor force in the silver mines. A Spanish oligarchy rules over a large indigenous population in the mountains to the east of the territory, while in the eastern plains, there is more ethnic mixing and a large mestizo population develops.

1809 As Spanish royal authority weakens during the Napoleonic wars, sentiment against colonial rule grows. Inspired by the American Revolution, the various Spanish colonies throw off Spanish rule. The territory of Bolivia declares its independence in 1809.

1825–1835 Following the declaration of independence, instability and violent struggle keep the country in turmoil until the declaration of the Bolivian republic on August 6, 1825. As during the colonial era, the minority of European origin continues to control the country, while the majority of the population lives in abject poverty. Most of the indigenous people continue to live much as they had for centuries, speaking their own languages and living as their ancestors had.

1836–1842 Bolivia and Peru* briefly form a confederation in 1836, but following a war with Chile* and Argentina*, the confederation is dissolved. The Peruvians invade Bolivia in an attempt to reunify the two countries. The war continues until an unstable peace is negotiated in 1842.

1842–1883 Political and economic instability continues through the middle decades of the 19th century. The country's weakness is demonstrated during the War of the Pacific (1879–83) and other conflicts, during which it loses more than half its national territory to neighboring countries.

1890s–1920s An increase in the world price of silver brings about a period of relative prosperity and political stability in the late 19th century.

1932–1952 Bolivia's defeat by neighboring Paraguay* in the Chaco War marks a turning point in the country's history. Various revolutionary movements emerge, adding to the country's chronic instability. Following a successful 1952 revolution, political reform is finally introduced, with a sweeping land reform, the introduction of universal suffrage, rural education, and the nationalization of the country's largest tin mines.

1950s A succession of weak national governments allows public disorder and military interference in the country's government.

1960s–1980s The following decades are marked by coups, countercoups, and caretaker governments. Governments are known for narcotics trafficking, economic mismanagement, and abuses of the indigenous population, trade unions, and critics of government excesses.

1990s Social protests, growing schisms between the eastern plains and the highlands, and a decline in cocoa production further damage the country's fragile structures.

2002–2005 In 2002, a cocoa advocate and indigenous peasant leader, Evo Morales, becomes the first indigenous president in the history of Bolivia.

2005–2006 Morales begins by nationalizing the country's natural resources, particularly the important natural gas production. His preference for the indigenous population of the highlands further alienates the eastern provinces, particularly the wealthiest and most economically advanced, Santa Cruz*.

1995–2008 Bolivia's nine departments receive greater autonomy under the Administrative Decentralization law of 1995. In 2008, the eastern provinces, led by Santa Cruz, vote for autonomy from the central government. The Morales government moves Bolivia into close political alignment with the more radical governments of Latin America, including Cuba*, Venezuela*, and Nicaragua*.

2009 A new constitution gives greater rights to the indigenous majority concentrated in the western highlands, although it is not supported by the people of the lowland provinces in the east.

BRAZIL

OFFICIAL NAME

República Federativa do Brasil (Portuguese); Federative Republic of Brazil (English)

POPULATION

192,049,600 (2009e)

INHABITANTS' NAME/NICKNAME

Brazilian(s)

LANGUAGE/LANGUAGES

Portuguese (official); Spanish, German, Italian, Japanese, English, indigenous languages, others

RELIGION/RELIGIONS

Roman Catholic, 74 percent; Protestant, 16 percent; spiritualist, 1.5 percent; other or no religion

NATIONAL FLAG

The flag has a green field with a large yellow rhombus centered bearing a blue disk with the Southern Cross constellation of 27 stars behind a white band inscribed with the national motto. Brazil's flag is one of the few national flags without one of the blood and war colors, red and black. The green represents the forests, yellow stands for the country's mineral wealth, and the blue disk or globe represents the sky over Rio de Janiero on November 15, 1889 when the republic was proclaimed. The stars represent the member states of the Brazilian federation.

COAT OF ARMS/SEAL

The coat of arms is a round shield composed of a sky-blue field containing five silver stars arranged in the form of the Southern Cross, with the border of the field outlined in gold and charged with silver stars equal to the stars in the national flag. The shield is placed on a star divided into 10 pieces, alternating green and gold, bordered by two stripes, the inner red and the outer gold. Below is the hilt of a sword on crossed branches of coffee and tobacco. Below the shield complex is a blue banner bearing the name of the country and the date November 15, 1889.

MOTTO

Ordem e progresso (Portuguese); Order and Progress (English)

CAPITAL CITY

Brasilia

TYPE OF GOVERNMENT

Presidential federal republic

NATIONAL EMBLEM

Christ the Redeemer Statue in Rio de Janeiro; Carnival in Rio de Janeiro; *Pão de Açúcar* (Sugarloaf Mountain)

NATIONAL COLORS

Green and yellow

NATIONAL ANTHEM

Brazil's national anthem was originally composed in 1822, the year when Brazil won independence from Portugal. One hundred years later, in 1922, the present lyrics were adopted.

Hino Nacional Brasileiro (Portuguese); Brazilian National Anthem (English)

The Ypiranga's placid banks heard
The resounding shouts of a heroic people.
And the sun of freedom, in bright rays,

Shone at this moment in the homeland's
skies.
As the promise of this equality
Was secured by our strong arms,
In your bosom, O Freedom,
We are ready to die.

O beloved, idolized homeland, hail, hail!
Brazil, a vivid dream, a lively ray
Of love and hope settles on the earth,
As in your beautiful sky, smiling and limpid,
The image of the Southern Cross shines
resplendent.
A giant by nature, you are beautiful,
Strong, an intrepid colossus,
And your future mirrors this grandeur.

Chorus:
O land we adore, among a thousand others
You are the beloved one.
You are the gentle mother of the sons of this
land,
Beloved homeland, Brazil!

Eternally laid in a splendid cradle,
To the sound of the sea and the light from the
depths of the sky,
Brazil, you gleam, *fleuron* of the Americas,
Illuminated by the sun of the New World.
Your smiling, lovely fields have more flowers
Than the most attractive land elsewhere,
Our forests have more life,
Our life in your bosom more love.

O beloved, idolized homeland, hail, hail!
Brazil, may you have as eternal symbol
The starry banner you display,
And may the green laurel of this pennant
speak
Of peace in the future and glory in the past.
But if you raise a strong cudgel in the name of
justice,
You will see that a son of yours does not run
from a fight,
Nor does one who adores you fear death.

Chorus

PATRON SAINT
Blessed Virgin Mary; Saint Peter of Alcantara

CURRENCY
Brazilian real

INTERNET IDENTIFIER
.br

VEHICLE IDENTIFICATION PLATES/STICKERS
BR

PASSPORT
The passport cover has the name of the regional group, Mercosur; the name of the country in Portuguese; the coat of arms; and the word *passport* in Portuguese.

AIRLINES
Varig, TAM

NATIONAL FLOWER
Tabelua flower

NATIONAL TREE
Tabebula (*Ipê-amarelo*)

NATIONAL ANIMAL
Jaguar (unofficial)

NATIONAL BIRD
Sabiá-Iaranjeira (Rufous-bellied thrush)

NATIONAL RESOURCES
Natural resources include bauxite, gold, iron ore, manganese, nickel, phosphates, platinum, tin, uranium, petroleum, hydropower, and timber, as well as a large labor pool and well-developed agricultural, manufacturing, mining, and service sectors. Brazil's natural attractions, fascinating cities, vibrant culture, sandy beaches, and pleasant climate support an important tourist industry.

FOODS
Brazil's most famous dish—often considered the national dish, although it originated in

the southeast around Rio de Janeiro—is *feijoada,* a stew of black beans and various meats. Other specialties include *bigadeiro,* a chocolate nut candy; *farofa,* fried cassava; *molho de pimienta malagueta,* a spicy chili sauce served with meat; *feijoada de peixe,* a fish and bean stew; and *moqueca de camaro,* a stew made of shrimp and vegetables.

SPORTS/SPORTS TEAMS

Association football (soccer) is the most popular sport, with other football games and basketball also very popular. Capoeira, a type of martial arts developed in the northeastern states, was defined by law as a national sport in 1972. Brazil national teams participate in many sports at an international level.

TEAM SPORTS

Badminton
Brazil Badminton Team

Baseball
Brazil Baseball Team; Brazil Softball Team

Basketball
Brazil Basketball Team; Brazil Women's Basketball Team; Brazil Wheelchair Basketball Team; Brazil Women's Wheelchair Basketball Team; Brazil Under-21 Basketball Team; Brazil Under-19 Basketball Team

Cricket
Brazil Cricket Team

Curling
Brazil Curling Team

Football
Brazil Football Team, nickname A Seleção (the Selection or the Team) or Canarinhos (Little Canaries) or Seleção Canarinho (the Canary Team) or La Verde Amarella (the Green and Yellows); Brazil Women's Football Team, nickname A Seleção (the Selection or the Team), As Canarinhas (the Canaries), Auriverde (the Green and Yellow), the Samba Queens; Brazil Under-20 Football Team, nickname A Seleção (the Selection or the Team); Brazil Women's Under-19 Football Team; Brazil Rugby Union Team, nickname Vitória-régia; Brazil Rugby Union Team; Brazil Women's Rugby Union Team; Brazil Futsal Team; Brazil Beach Soccer Team; Brazil Wheelchair Rugby Team; Brazil American Football Team; Brazil Beach Soccer Team; Brazil Rugby Union Team (Sevens), nickname Brazil Sevens or Brazil 7s; Brazil Women's Rugby Union Team (Sevens), nickname Brazil Sevens or Brazil 7s

Handball
Brazil Handball Team; Brazil Women's Handball Team; Brazil Beach Handball Team; Brazil Women's Beach Handball Team

Hockey
Brazil Ice Hockey Team; Brazil Field Hockey Team

Kabaddi
Brazil Kabaddi Team

Korfball
Brazil Korfball Team

Polo
Brazil Polo Team

Racing
A1 Team Brazil; Brazil Speedway Team

Table Tennis
Brazil Table Tennis Team

Tennis
Brazil Davis Cup Team; Brazil Fed Cup Team

Volleyball

Brazil Men's Volleyball Team; Brazil Women's Volleyball Team; Brazil Fistball Team; Brazil Men's Beach Volleyball Team; Brazil Women's Beach Volleyball Team

Water Polo

Brazil Water Polo Team; Brazil Women's Water Polo Team

INDIVIDUAL SPORTS

Brazil Aikido Team; Brazil Amateur Boxing Team; Brazil Archery Team; Brazil Athletics Team; Brazil Canoeing Team; Brazil Chess Team; Brazil Cycling Team; Brazil Equestrian Team; Brazil Fencing Team; Brazil Gymnastics Team; Brazil Judo Team; Brazil Karate Team; Brazil Modern Pentathlon Team; Brazil Rowing Team; Brazil Sailing Team; Brazil Shooting Team; Brazil Swim Team; Brazil Tae Kwon Do Team; Brazil Triathlon Team; Brazil Weight Lifting Team; Brazil Wrestling Team

WINTER SPORTS

Brazil Alpine Ski Team; Brazil Biathlon Team; Brazil Curling Team; Brazil Ice Hockey Team; Brazil Luge Team; Brazil Skating Team

NATIONAL HEROES OR PERSONIFICATIONS

The *Efígie da República* (Effigy of the Republic) is a national personification of Brazil, symbolizing the republic. The effigy is a representation of a young woman wearing a crown of bay laurel leaves in Roman style.

National heroes include Joaquim José da Silva Xavier, also known as Tiradentes, who led an unsuccessful uprising against Portuguese rule in 1789; José Bonifacio de Andrada e Silva, called the father of Brazilian independence; Emperor Dom Pedro II, who voluntarily stepped down in 1889 so that Brazil could become a republic; Deodoro Fonseca, the first president of the republic; and Joaquim Nabuco, a champion of the abolition of slavery.

NATIONAL HOLIDAY/INDEPENDENCE DAY

Independence Day, September 7

FESTIVALS/FAIRS

Carnival, four days preceding Ash Wednesday; Festas Juninas (June Festivals), a series of popular festivals with religious origins, the feasts of Saint Anthony (June 13), Saint John (June 24), and Saint Peter (June 29); New Year's Eve, December 31, when thousands of followers of Afro-Brazilian religions celebrate on beaches to honor Yemanjá, goddess of the sea

SIGNIFICANT EVENTS IN FORMATION OF NATIONAL IDENTITY

1000 B.C.E.–1500 C.E. Most of the tribal peoples live by hunting or by slash and burn agriculture, although cultures vary greatly across the vast region.

1500–1501 Pedro Álvares Cabral claims the new land for the Kingdom of Portugal and calls it Ilha de Santa Cruz, Island of the True Cross, thinking he is on an island. Italian explorer Amerigo Vespucci, in 1501, sailing for the Portuguese, returns to Europe with a cargo of hard, reddish wood similar to an East Indian variety called *pau braxil*, brazilwood, then popular in Europe for making cabinets and violin bows. Brazilwood, the first product to be exploited by the Portuguese, is the origin of the country's name.

16th century Diseases devastate the indigenous population. The survivors in the areas settled by the Europeans gradually mix with the local population.

1600–1700 Sugar quickly becomes the leading export, requiring the importation of large numbers of African slaves.

18th century During the 18th century, private explorers who call themselves the Bandeirantes open gold and diamond mines in the interior.

1789–1800 Some popular movements supporting independence emerge against the abusive taxes established by the metropolis, such as the Tiradentes rebellion in 1789.

1808–1821 The Portuguese court, fleeing from Napoleon's troops, arrives in a large fleet escorted by British war ships. Long after the end of the Napoleonic Wars, in 1821, the king returns to Portugal, leaving his heir-apparent as regent of the Kingdom of Brazil.

1822–1889 One year after assuming the throne, Pedro I announces Brazil's secession from the Portuguese Empire and the creation of the Empire of Brazil. His reign is marked by numerous revolts. At the end of his reign, he presides over the abolition of slavery in 1888. In 1889, he is ousted, and Brazil becomes a republic.

1930 A military junta takes control of the country.

1960s A new capital, Brasilia, is constructed, and excess population from the coastal regions is encouraged to move inland as part of a huge development scheme.

1985–1999 A return to civilian rule fails to end the endemic corruption and mismanagement that stifles growth and feeds unrest.

2002–2009 The election of Luiz Inácio Lula da Silva begins a vast program of social change while managing to keep the economy moving ahead. Reducing poverty, reducing unemployment, and ending dependence on external resources, such as oil, make Lula one of South America's most popular politicians.

CHILE

OFFICIAL NAME
República de Chile (Spanish); Republic of Chile (English)

POPULATION
17,012,900 (2009e)

INHABITANTS' NAME/NICKNAME
Chilean(s)

LANGUAGE/LANGUAGES
Spanish (official); Mapudungun, German, English, Arabic, others

RELIGION/RELIGIONS
Roman Catholic, 70 percent; Protestant/Evangelical, 16 percent; Jehovah's Witness, 1 percent; other or no religion

NATIONAL FLAG
The flag is a white over red bicolor with a blue square on the upper hoist bearing a white five-pointed star. The star represents a guide to progress and honor, blue symbolizes the sky, white is for the snow-covered Andes, and red stands for the blood spilled to achieve independence.

COAT OF ARMS/SEAL
The coat of arms consists of a central shield divided horizontally, the top blue and the bottom red. A five-pointed white star is in the center of the shield. The shield is supported on one side by a condor, the most significant bird of prey from the Andes, and on the other by a *huemul*, the most singular and rare mammal of the Chilean territory. Both animals wear the navy's golden crown, symbol of the heroic deeds of the Chilean Navy in the Pacific Ocean. A three-feathered crest crowns the shield, each feather bearing one of the national colors of blue, white, and red. This crest is a symbol of distinction former presidents of the republic used to wear on their hats. Beneath the shield, on the elaborate pedestal, is a white band with the country's national motto.

MOTTO
Por la razón o la fuerza (Spanish); By reason or force/By right or might (English)

CAPITAL CITY
Santiago

TYPE OF GOVERNMENT

Democratic republic

NATIONAL EMBLEM

Andes Mountains, which divide Chile from the rest of South America

NATIONAL COLORS

Blue, white, and red

NATIONAL ANTHEM

The anthem dates from the 19th century and has undergone several changes. The latest addition, during the Pinochet government, was a verse extolling Chile's army. It was common to remain silent during this verse as an act of protest. The verse was removed when democracy was restored in 1990.

Himno Nacional de Chile (Spanish); National Hymn of Chile (English)

Pure, Chile, is your blue sky;
Pure breezes flow across you as well.
And your flower-embroidered field
Is a happy copy of Eden.
Majestic is the snow-capped mountain
That was given as a bastion by the Lord
That was given as a bastion by the Lord,
And the sea that quietly washes your shores
Promises you future splendor
And the sea that quietly washes your shores
Promises you future splendor.

Chorus

Sweet fatherland, accept the vows
That were given by Chile at your altars:
Either you be the tomb of the free
Or the refuge against oppression

PATRON SAINT

Virgin of Carmen

CURRENCY

Chilean peso

INTERNET IDENTIFIER

.cl

VEHICLE IDENTIFICATION PLATES/STICKERS

RCH

PASSPORT

The passport cover has the name of the country in Spanish, the coat of arms, and the Spanish word for passport, *pasaporte.*

AIRLINES

Lan Airlines; Sky Airline

NATIONAL FLOWER

Copihue

NATIONAL TREE

Arucaria araucana (Chilean pine)

NATIONAL ANIMAL

Huemul (white-tailed deer)

NATIONAL BIRD

Andean condor

NATIONAL RESOURCES

Natural resources include copper, timber, iron ore, nitrates, precious metals, molybdenum, and hydropower. Copper is one of the country's most important resources. The Andes Mountains, colonial cities, winter sports, and varied scenery support an important tourist industry.

FOODS

Cazuela, a casserole meal of chicken or beef, a potato, a piece of pumpkin, and a rich stock obtained from boiling the ingredients, is the national dish. Empanadas, meat-filled pastries, are another national dish, along with *porotos Granados,* a mixture of beans, corn, and squash. Other specialties include *tortilla de acietuna,* an omelet of eggs and olives; *sopaipillas,* a type of sweet flatbread made of squash dipped in a molasses-based sauce; *sopa de lentejas,* a lentil and sausage soup; *chancho a la Chilena,* pork loin Chilean-style; and *pollo arvejado,* a chicken stew with peas and tomatoes.

SPORTS/SPORTS TEAMS

The most popular sports are association football (soccer) and Chilean rodeo. Chilean rodeo was declared the national sport in 1962. Chile national teams participate in many sports at an international level.

TEAM SPORTS

Badminton
Chile Badminton Team

Baseball
Chile Baseball Team; Chile Softball Team

Basketball
Chile Basketball Team; Chile Women's Basketball Team; Chile Wheelchair Basketball Team

Cricket
Chile Cricket Team

Football
Chile Football Team, nicknamed La Roja (the Red); Chile Women's Football Team, nickname La Roja (the Red); Chile Under-20 Football Team, nickname La Rojita (the Little Red); Chile Under-17 Football Team, nickname La Rojita (the Little Red); Chile Women's Under-19 Football Team, nickname La Riojita; Chile Rugby Union Team, nickname Los Cóndores (the Condors); Chile Australian-Rules Football Team; Chile Futsal Team; Chile Women's Touch Football Team

Golf
Chile Men's Pitch and Putt Team; Chile Women's Pitch and Putt Team

Hockey
Chile Field Hockey Team; Chile Women's Field Hockey Team

Polo
Chile Polo Team

Racing
Chile Speedway Team

Table Tennis
Chile Table Tennis Team

Tennis
Chile Davis Cup Team; Chile Fed Cup Team

Volleyball
Chile Men's Volleyball Team; Chile Women's Volleyball Team; Chile Fistball Team

INDIVIDUAL SPORTS

Chile Aikido Team; Chile Amateur Boxing Team; Chile Archery Team; Chile Athletics Team; Chile Canoeing Team; Chile Cycling Team; Chile Equestrian Team; Chile Fencing Team; Chile Gymnastics Team; Chile Judo Team; Chile Modern Pentathlon Team; Chile Rowing Team; Chile Sailing Team; Chile Shooting Team; Chile Swim Team; Chile Tae Kwon Do Team; Chile Triathlon Team; Chile Weight Lifting Team; Chile Wrestling Team

WINTER SPORTS

Chile Alpine Ski Team; Chile Biathlon Team

NATIONAL HEROES OR PERSONIFICATIONS

The *huaso,* the Chilean cowboy, dressed Seville-style with a flat-topped hat, colorful *poncho,* and shiny high-heeled boots with large spurs, is the national personification. Another important personification is the *roto,* a poorly educated and poorly clothed lower-class Chilean with a great sense of humor, known for his courage and wit. He represents the humble Chileans who fought against Spanish rule and later against the Peruvians and Bolivians. Doña Juanita, a typical countrywoman, is another personification of the Chilean nation.

José de San Martin, the liberator of Chile during the war for independence in the early 18th century, is the most important national hero; Bernardo O'Higgins—the hero of Irish origin—of the fight for independence in the early 19th century; Salvador Allende, the leftist president overthrown in a coup in 1973; Michelle Bachelet, elected as Chile's first woman president in 2006

NATIONAL HOLIDAY/INDEPENDENCE DAY

Independence Day/National Day, September 12

FESTIVALS/FAIRS

National Day Celebration, September

SIGNIFICANT EVENTS IN FORMATION OF NATIONAL IDENTITY

12th century–15th century The native Mapuche people, under constant pressure from the Incas, develop a warrior culture. They halt the southern expansion of the Incas, defeating several invasion attempts between 1448 and 1482.

1520–1535 Ferdinand Magellan discovers the southern passage around South America. A Spanish expedition from Peru* moves south seeking gold in 1535.

1553 A massive Mapuche attack results in the destruction of many of the colony's principal settlements. The attack begins a long series of conflicts known as the Mapuche Wars.

18th century Cut off at the north by forbidding deserts, at the south by the Mapuche, at the east by the high Andes Mountains, and at the west by the sea, the Chileans developed one of the most centralized, homogeneous colonies in Spanish America.

1808–1818 Napoleon's usurpation of the Spanish throne begins Chile's drive for independence. Chile is declared an autonomous republic in 1810, but fighting between Chilean and Spanish forces continues until the royalists are defeated in 1818.

19th century Independence does little to change Chilean society, with its colonial social structure, great-family politics, and powerful Roman Catholic Church.

1870–1881 In 1880, the Chileans again move against the Mapuche, calling upon the force of the entire national army. Unable to hold out against such a military force, the Mapuche are finally defeated in 1881 after 300 years of warfare.

1884–1891 War with Peru and Bolivia* ends with Chilean victory and control of territory taken from both, including Bolivia's only outlet to the sea. Civil war breaks out between conservatives and liberals, bringing about a new political system, a parliamentary-style democracy.

1921–1932 A growing middle class and industrial expansion lead to the election of reformist political leaders, but a coup in 1924 sets off a period of instability.

1970 A narrowly won election, finally decided in the Chilean Congress, gives the presidency to Salvador Allende Gossens, a Marxist intent on liberalizing Chile.

1971–1973 Inflation reaches astronomical heights and strikes paralyze the country. A U.S.-backed military coup overthrows Allende. A new military government led by Augusto Pinochet is installed.

1973–1980 Pinochet's brutal regime organizes mass arrests and executions. Thousands flee the country. A new constitution installs Pinochet as president.

1980–1990 The Pinochet government moves Chile away from nationalized industries and adopts a free market.

1990–2006 Pinochet steps down but remains the commander in chief of the Chilean Army until he retires in 1998. When Pinochet dies in 2006, about 300 criminal charges are pending against him.

2006 The Chileans elect their first woman president, Michelle Bachelet Jeria, a socialist.

2008–2009 Peru files a suit with the International Court of Justice in a bid to settle a long-standing territorial dispute with Chile. The Chileans rebuff Bolivian President Evo Morales' reactivated claims to the Atacama region, ceded to Chile in 1884, offering instead unrestricted access to Chilean ports in the region.

COLOMBIA

OFFICIAL NAME

República de Colombia (Spanish); Republic of Colombia (English)

POPULATION

44,9803,500 (2009e)

INHABITANTS' NAME/NICKNAME

Colombian(s)

LANGUAGE/LANGUAGES

Spanish (official); English, indigenous languages, others

RELIGION/RELIGIONS

Roman Catholic, 90 percent; Protestant, Jewish, other or no religion

NATIONAL FLAG

A horizontal tricolor of yellow, dark blue, and red; the yellow stripe is twice the width of the lower two stripes. The yellow represents the fertility of the land, the blue represents the seas on Colombia's coasts, and the red represents the blood spilled by the heroes who won Colombia's independence.

COAT OF ARMS/SEAL

The coat of arms consists of a shield with numerous national symbols. Perched on the top of the shield is an Andean condor holding an olive crown, symbolizing freedom. A scroll just below the condor has the national motto in black on yellow. The national flag is draped on each side of the shield, which is divided into three parts. In the bottom are ships, symbolizing Colombia's maritime past

and its present economy, and the Isthmus of Panama, which was part of Colombia until 1903. A Phrygian hat of red on a field of platinum, a traditional symbol of liberty and freedom, is the middle section. The top contains a field of blue with a pomegranate, the symbol of the Viceroyalty of New Granada, or colonial Colombia. Two cornucopias, one with tropical fruits and the other with gold and silver coins, representing agriculture and mineral wealth, flank the pomegranate.

MOTTO

Libertad y orden (Spanish); Liberty and Order (English)

CAPITAL CITY

Bogotá

TYPE OF GOVERNMENT

Presidential republic

NATIONAL EMBLEM

Andean condor

NATIONAL COLORS

Yellow, blue, and red

NATIONAL ANTHEM

Although the anthem was composed in 1887, it was not officially adopted until 1920, and an official transcription was made only in 1946.

Oh, Gloria Inmarcesible (Spanish); Oh, Unfading Glory (English)

O unfading glory!
O immortal joy!
In furrows of pain
Good is already germinating.

The horrible night has ended,
sublime liberty
spreads the dawn
of its invincible light.
The whole of humanity,
crying in its chains,

understands the words
of the One who died on the cross.

"Independence!" cries
the American world;
bathed in the blood of its heroes
the land of Columbus.
Still, this one great principle,
"The king is not sovereign,"
resounds, and those who suffer
praise its passion.

PATRON SAINT

Saint Louis Bertrán; Our Lady of Chiquinquira; Our Lady of the Rosary; Saint Peter Claver

CURRENCY

Colombian peso

INTERNET IDENTIFIER

.co

VEHICLE IDENTIFICATION PLATES/ STICKERS

COL

PASSPORT

The passport cover has the name of the Andean Community in Spanish, a small coat of arms, the name of the country in Spanish, and the Spanish word for passport in large letters above the words, in smaller letters, for passport in English and French.

AIRLINE

Avianca

NATIONAL FLOWER

Cattleya trinae orchid

NATIONAL TREE

Quindio wax palm

NATIONAL BIRD

Andean condor

NATIONAL RESOURCES

Natural resources include petroleum, natural gas, coal, iron ore, nickel, gold, copper, emeralds, and hydropower. Colombia is rich in minerals and energy resources. It has the largest coal reserves in Latin America and is second to Brazil in hydroelectric potential. Kidnappings and violence have hurt what could be a buoyant tourist industry built on historic cities, varied scenery, sandy beaches, and a pleasant climate.

FOODS

Arepas, cornmeal patties similar to tortillas, and *sancocho,* a stew of meats and vegetables, are considered the national dishes. *Fitanga,* a type of barbecue with grilled beef, chicken, ribs, and sausages served with small potatoes and *arepas,* is also very popular throughout Colombia. Other specialties include *posta en frutas secas,* a beef and dried fruit stew; *patacones,* green plantain chips; *pastelitos,* small pastries filled with minced pork; *sabalo guisado con coco,* shad fillets cooked in coconut milk; *sopa de crema de coco,* coconut cream soup; and *cuajado de camarones,* a shrimp and potato omelet.

SPORTS/SPORTS TEAMS

Association football (soccer) is the country's most popular sport, but *tejo,* which consists of throwing a metallic disk through the air and making it hit a target, was declared the national sport in 2000. Colombia national teams participate in many sports at an international level.

TEAM SPORTS

Badminton

Colombia Badminton Team

Baseball

Colombia Baseball Team; Colombia Softball Team

Basketball

Colombia Basketball Team; Colombia Women's Basketball Team; Colombia Wheelchair Basketball Team

Football

Colombia Football Team, nickname Los Cafeteros (the Coffee Makers); Colombia Women's Football Team, nickname Las Cafeteras (the Coffee Makers); Colombia Under-20 Football Team; Colombia Under-17 Football Team; Colombia Women's Under-19 Football Team; Colombia Futsal Team; Colombia Rugby Union Team; Colombia Wheelchair Rugby Team

Hockey

Colombia Field Hockey Team

Racing

Colombia Speedway Team

Table Tennis

Colombia Table Tennis Team

Tennis

Colombia Davis Cup Team; Colombia Fed Cup Team

Volleyball

Colombia Men's Volleyball Team; Colombia Women's Volleyball Team

INDIVIDUAL SPORTS

Colombia Amateur Boxing Team; Colombia Archery Team; Colombia Athletics Team; Colombia Cycling Team; Colombia Canoeing Team; Colombia Equestrian Team; Colombia Fencing Team; Colombia Gymnastics Team; Colombia Judo Team; Colombia Modern Pentathlon Team; Colombia Rowing Team; Colombia Sailing Team; Colombia Shooting Team; Colombia Swim Team; Colombia Tae Kwon Do Team; Colombia Triathlon Team; Colombia Weight Lifting Team; Colombia Wrestling Team

NATIONAL HEROES OR PERSONIFICATIONS

Juan Valdez, a fictional character created in 1959, is the embodiment of a typical Colombian coffee farmer.

National heroes include Simón Bolivar, independence leader; Manuela Beltrán, who organized a peasant revolt against excessive taxation in 1780; Francisco de Paula Santander, a leader of the war for independence and first president of independent Colombia; José María Córdova, a military leader in the independence war; and Gabriel García Márquez, Nobel Prize winner and father of Colombian literature.

NATIONAL HOLIDAY/INDEPENDENCE DAY

Independence Day, July 20

FESTIVALS/FAIRS

Carnival, with the second-longest carnival parade, after Rio de Janeiro, in Barranquilla; Carnaval de Bogotá (Bogotá Carnival), August; Rock al Parque (Rock in the Park), October, the second-largest rock festival in Latin America; Feria de las Flores, August

SIGNIFICANT EVENTS IN FORMATION OF NATIONAL IDENTITY

First millennium B.C.E.–16th century C.E. The *zipa*, or chief, of the Muisca people in the highlands traditionally covers his body in gold and offers treasures to the *Guatavita* goddess in the middle of a sacred lake. This old Muisca tradition becomes the origin of the El Dorado legend.

1498–1538 Christopher Columbus sails along the coast in 1502. Spanish conquistadores begin the conquest of the Caribbean region in 1508, crossing to the Pacific in 1513.

1550–1610 Finding that the indigenous people make poor slaves, the Spanish begin importing African slaves to work in mines and on plantations.

The Spanish Inquisition is established in Cartagena de Indias.

1717–1779 The Viceroyalty of New Granada is created.

1780 Manuela Beltrán organizes and leads a peasant revolt against excess taxation.

1810–1816 During the Napoleonic Wars in Europe, the king of Spain* is overthrown, beginning a movement for independence in New Granada.

1819 Simón Bolivar and other independence leaders meet to create Greater Colombia, encompassing modern-day Colombia, Venezuela*, Ecuador*, and Panama*. Greater Colombia partially fulfills Bolivar's dream of one great federal state in South America.

1830 Internal political and territorial divisions characterize the first years of the new state. In 1830, Venezuela and Ecuador secede.

1858 A new constitution legalizes a federal republic made up of autonomous states. Regionalist groups demand greater self-government.

1886–1903 Internal divisions remain between the two political forces, occasionally erupting into very bloody civil wars, such as the Thousand Days War in 1899–1902. This instability allows the United States*, then involved in the construction of the Panama Canal, to support the separation and independence of Panama in 1903.

1948–1953 The assassination of the liberal candidate for president of Colombia in 1948 begins the bloody conflict known as *La Violencia* (the Violence). Rioting leads to bitter fighting that engulfs the entire country. Between 1948 and 1953, an estimated 180,000 Colombians are killed in the Violence.

1953–1964 Social and political problems continue, and guerilla groups are formally created, including the Revolutionary Armed Forces of Colombia, known as FARC.

1970s–1980s Powerful drug cartels emerge in the late 1970s. They exert political, economic, and social influence on Colombia. Many Colombians leave for other countries, particularly the United States.

1991–2005 The country is plagued by the effects of the drug trade and the cartels; guerilla insurgencies, such as FARC; and paramilitary groups representing a variety of political and economic groupings.

2007–2008 By the end of 2007, an estimated 1.8 million Colombians—some claim much higher numbers—are refugees or are internally displaced due to the country's endemic violence. Several high-profile victories over the FARC, the largest and oldest of the guerilla movements in South America, leads to the liberation of a number of captives held by the group, some for a number of years.

2008–2009 The sudden collapse of several pyramid investment schemes triggers violent protests among the country's poorest sectors.

COSTA RICA

Official Name
República de Costa Rica (Spanish); Republic of Costa Rica (English)

Population
4,548,600 (2009e)

Inhabitants' Name/Nickname
Costa Rican(s); Tico(s)/Tica(s)

Language/Languages
Spanish (official); English, indigenous languages, others

Religion/Religions
Roman Catholic, 76 percent; Evangelical, 14 percent; Jewish, other or no religion

National Flag
The national flag has horizontal stripes of blue, white, red, white, and blue, with proportions of 1:1:2:1:1. On hoist side of the red stripe is a white disk bearing the coat of arms. The blue stands for the sky, opportunities, idealism, and perseverance.

The white stands for peace, wisdom, and happiness. The red represents the blood spilled by martyrs in defense of the country, as well as the warmth and generosity of the people.

COAT OF ARMS/SEAL

The coat of arms consists of a shield showing seven stars, one for each province; three volcanoes, representing the country's three mountain ranges; and two merchant ships. There is a rising sun at the horizon between the blue sky and the blue ocean. On the sides of the shield are small golden beads representing coffee, traditionally the largest export. Above the shield is a blue banner with the words *America Central*.

MOTTO

Vivan siempre el trabajo y la paz (Spanish); May work and peace live forever (English)

The unofficial motto is *Pura vida*, conveying the state of happiness, tranquility, and peace that political stability and freedom bring to Costa Ricans.

CAPITAL CITY

San José

TYPE OF GOVERNMENT

Democratic republic

NATIONAL EMBLEM

Decorated ox-cart, a symbol of work

NATIONAL COLORS

Red, blue, and white

NATIONAL ANTHEM

The melody of the national anthem was composed in 1852, to be played for the first foreign diplomats accredited as representatives in Costa Rica. The lyrics were written in 1903 but were not declared official until 1949.

Noble Patria, Tu Hermosa Bandera (Spanish) Noble Homeland, Your Beautiful Flag (English)

Noble homeland, your beautiful flag
Express for us your life:
Under the limpid blue of your skies,
Peace reigns, white and pure.

In the tenacious battle of fruitful toil,
That brings a glow to men's faces,
Your sons, simple farm hands,
Gained eternal renown, esteem and honor,
Gained eternal renown, esteem and honor.

Hail, gentle country!
Hail, loving mother!
If anyone should attempt to besmirch your glory,
You will see your people, valiant and virile,
Exchange their rustic tools for weapons.

Hail, O homeland! Your prodigal soil
Gives us sweet sustenance and shelter.
Under the limpid blue of your sky,
May peaceful labor ever continue.

PATRON SAINT

Our Lady of the Angels

CURRENCY

Costa Rican colón

INTERNET IDENTIFIER

.cr

VEHICLE IDENTIFICATION PLATES/ STICKERS

CR

PASSPORT

The passport cover has the name of the country in Spanish in large letters above the words *America Central* in smaller letters, the coat of arms, and the word *passport* in both Spanish, in large letters, and English, in smaller letters.

AIRLINE

TACA International Airlines, a grouping of five national airlines of Central America

NATIONAL FLOWER

Cattleya skinneri orchid

NATIONAL TREE

Guanacaste

NATIONAL ANIMAL

White-tailed deer

NATIONAL BIRD

Yigüirro (clay-colored robin)

NATIONAL RESOURCES

Natural resources include hydropower and arable land, but mineral wealth is negligible. Sandy beaches, famed natural parks, historic cities, and a pleasant climate support an important tourist industry. Ecotourism is particularly important. A well-educated population and a reputation for stability and good governance have drawn in many foreign companies making electronics, computers, and software.

FOODS

Gallo pinto, a mixture of rice and black beans fried together with onion and pepper and spices such as cilantro, is the national dish. Other specialties include *sopa de verduras y arroz,* a soup of beef, vegetables, and yellow rice; *el vinagre chilera,* a dish of bananas, chilies, carrots, onions, sweet peppers, cauliflower, and green beans; tamales, minced meat and onions rolled in cornmeal dough and cooked in banana leaves; *ensalada palmito,* a hearts of palm salad; *ceviche,* raw fish marinated in lemon, lime, and coconut milk; and *sopa de pejibaye,* palm fruit soup.

SPORTS/SPORTS TEAMS

Association football (soccer) is the most popular sport in Costa Rica. Basketball and baseball are also very popular. Costa Rica national teams participate in many sports at an international level.

TEAM SPORTS

Badminton

Costa Rica Badminton Team

Baseball

Costa Rica Baseball Team; Costa Rica Softball Team

Basketball

Costa Rica Basketball Team; Costa Rica Women's Basketball Team; Costa Rica Wheelchair Basketball Team

Football

Costa Rica Football Team, nicknames Los Ticos, Tricolor, or La Sele (the Selection or the Team); Costa Rica Rugby Union Team, nickname Los Ticos; Costa Rica Beach Soccer Team; Costa Rica American Football Team; Costa Rica Futsal Team; Costa Rica Women's Under-19 Football Team, nickname Las Ticas

Hockey

Costa Rica Field Hockey Team

Racing

Costa Rice Speedway Team

Table Tennis

Costa Rica Table Tennis Team

Tennis

Costa Rica Davis Cup Team; Costa Rica Fed Cup Team

Volleyball

Costa Rica Men's Volleyball Team; Costa Rica Women's Volleyball Team

INDIVIDUAL SPORTS

Costa Rica Amateur Boxing Team; Costa Rica Athletics Team; Costa Rica Archery Team; Costa Rica Canoeing Team; Costa Rica Cycling Team; Costa Rica Equestrian Team; Costa Rica Fencing Team; Costa Rica Gymnastics Team; Costa Rica Judo Team; Costa Rica Modern Pentathlon Team; Costa Rica Rowing Team; Costa Rica Shooting Team; Costa Rica Swim Team; Costa Rica Tae Kwon Do Team; Costa Rica Triathlon Team; Costa Rica Weight Lifting Team; Costa Rica Wrestling Team

WINTER SPORTS

Costa Rica Biathlon Team

NATIONAL HEROES OR PERSONIFICATIONS

Juan Vásquez de Coronado, the first governor who led the settlement of the temperate central valleys; Juan Mora Fernandez, the country's first chief of state in 1824; Juan Santamaria, the martyred drummer boy from the campaign against the filibusters from the United States*; José Figueres Ferrer, the political leader who abolished the army in 1949

NATIONAL HOLIDAY/INDEPENDENCE DAY

Independence Day, September 15

SIGNIFICANT EVENTS IN FORMATION OF NATIONAL IDENTITY

1000 B.C.E. The indigenous peoples are mostly small tribal groups engaged in farming, fishing, and hunting. High mountains and swampy lowlands impede the migration of the more advanced civilizations of Mesoamerica.

1502–1522 Christopher Columbus arrives on the east coast. European settlement begins in 1522. The Spanish optimistically call the region the Rich Coast, but, finding little gold or other valuables, the settlers soon turn to agriculture. Diseases and violence eliminate the majority of the indigenous peoples.

1562 Juan Vásquez de Coronado arrives as governor. He treats the surviving Indians more humanely and moves the existing Spanish settlers into the central valley, with its abundant land and temperate climate.

17th century–18th century The region's isolation, the lack of a large indigenous labor force or imported slaves, and the distance from the seat of local government in Guatemala* helped evolve a society unique in Central America. Working their own lands and with little intermarriage with other groups, the people remained European in culture. An egalitarian tradition survives the introduction of banana and coffee cultivation and the subsequent prosperity.

1821–1838 The Central American provinces, inspired by Mexico*, declare independence from Spain*. A Central American federation fails, and Costa Rica becomes an independent republic. Juan Mora Fernandez, the country's first president in 1824, begins a period of political stability and good government. He also encourages the cultivation of coffee, giving free land grants to would-be coffee growers.

1856–1859 William Walker, an American filibuster, begins incursions in Central America. When he crosses into Costa Rica after taking control of Nicaragua*, the Costa Ricans rally to defeat Walker and his followers.

1898 The first truly free and fair elections are held.

1948–1953 A civil war, the bloodiest violence in Costa Rican history, erupts and lasts for 44 days, leaving 2,000 dead and many more injured. José Figueres Ferrer takes control of the country, abolishes the army, and establishes democratic government.

1855–1986 The country's dependence on coffee and bananas brings a severe economic crisis.

Oscar Arias Sanchez, elected to the presidency in 1986, helps to bring peace to Central America and initiates reforms in the country.

1986–2000 Peaceful changes of government under a functioning democratic system set Costa Rica apart from the unstable and often undemocratic nations of Central America.

2008–2009 Democratic changes of government remain the norm, unlike in most of Central America. Once a largely agricultural society, Costa Rica becomes a center of high technology and ecotourism. The Costa Ricans enjoy the highest standard of living in Central America and are proud of their prosperity, their lack of armed forces, and their democratic traditions.

ECUADOR

OFFICIAL NAME

República del Ecuador (Spanish); Republic of Ecuador (English)

POPULATION

13,835,600 (2009e)

INHABITANTS' NAME/NICKNAME

Ecuadorian(s)

LANGUAGE/LANGUAGES

Spanish (official); Quechua, other Amerindian languages, others

RELIGION/RELIGIONS

Roman Catholic, 95 percent; Protestant, Evangelical, animist, other or no religion

NATIONAL FLAG

The flag consists of three horizontal stripes of yellow, blue, and red, the yellow twice the width of the other stripes. The coat of arms is centered on the flag, overlapping the blue and yellow stripes. The yellow stands for the abundance and fertility of the crops and land, the blue stands for the sea and sky, and the red stands for the blood spilled by soldiers and martyrs of the independence battles.

COAT OF ARMS/SEAL

In the background of the oval shield is the volcano Chimborazo, while the river originating from its base represents the Guayas. Together, they symbolize the beauty and wealth of the coastal regions and the highlands. The ship on the river is named *Guayas* as well. In 1841, it was built in Guayaquil and was the first seaworthy steamship built on the South American west coast. Instead of a mast, it features a Caduceus, representing trade and economy. Above, a golden sun is surrounded by the astrological signs for Aries, Taurus, Gemini, and Cancer, representing the months March through July to symbolize the duration of the March Revolution of 1845. The condor on top of the shield stretches its wings to symbolize the power, greatness, and strength of Ecuador. The shield is flanked by four flags of Ecuador. The laurel on the left represents the glory of the republic. The palm leaf on the right is a symbol for peace. The fasces below the shield represents republican dignity.

CAPITAL CITY

Quito

TYPE OF GOVERNMENT

Presidential republic

NATIONAL EMBLEM

Mount Chimborazo

NATIONAL COLORS

Yellow, blue, and red

NATIONAL ANTHEM

The lyrics were written in 1865, although the anthem was composed earlier.

Salve, Oh Patria (Latin); We Salute You, Our Homeland (English)

Chorus

O homeland, we greet you a thousand times!
Glory be to you, glory be to you!
Your breast, your breast overflows,
Joy and peace from your breast overflow.
And your face, your radiant face,
We contemplate its brightness more than the
    sun,
And your face, your radiant face,
We contemplate its brightness more than the
    sun.

The worthy sons of the soil
Who magnificently adorned Pichincha,
They always declared you as their sovereign
    lady
And shed their blood for you.
God observed and accepted that sacrifice,
And this blood was the prolific seed
Of other heroes who amazed the world,
And in turn, of thousands arising around
    you.
Arising in thousands around you,
Arising in thousands around you.

PATRON SAINT

Most Pure Heart of Mary; Our Lady of Quinche; Sacred Heart of Jesus

CURRENCY

U.S. dollar; Ecuadorian centavo coins

INTERNET IDENTIFIER

.ec

VEHICLE IDENTIFICATION PLATES/STICKERS

EC

PASSPORT

The passport cover has *Comunidad Andina* (Andean Community) and the name of the country in Spanish, the coat of arms, and the word *passport* in Spanish and English.

AIRLINES

Lan Ecuador; AeorGal

NATIONAL FLOWER

Rose (official); white nun orchid (unofficial)

NATIONAL ANIMAL

Galapagos tortoise; Galapagos marine iguana (both unofficial)

NATIONAL BIRD

Andean condor

NATIONAL FISH

Andean catfish (unofficial)

NATIONAL RESOURCES

Natural resources include petroleum, fish, timber, hydropower, and arable land. The country's substantial petroleum reserves are its most valuable resource. The large Ecuadorian Diaspora, partly due to the economic crash in 1999, living mostly in the United States* and Spain*, is a valuable source of foreign currency and investment.

FOODS

Fanesca, a soup made during Lent with milk and 12 types of bean (i.e., green beans, lima beans, lupini beans, fava beans, etc.) and usually served with codfish, is considered the most typically Ecuadorian dish. Empanadas, pastries filled with meat, cheese, or fish, are also very popular. Popular specialties include *ceviche de camarones,* marinated shrimps; *locro,* potato soup; *seco de chancho,* a pork stew with vegetables; *llapingachos,* potato cakes; *pudin de choclo,* corn soufflé; *pristinos,* pumpkin fritters; and *torta de zapallo,* pumpkin cake.

SPORTS/SPORTS TEAMS

The most popular sport is association football (soccer). Tennis is also very popular in the big cities. Basketball and *ecuavolley*, a three-person version of volleyball, are also popular sports. Ecuador national teams participate in many sports at an international level

TEAM SPORTS

Badminton
Ecuador Badminton Team

Baseball
Ecuador Baseball Team; Ecuador Softball Team

Basketball
Ecuador Basketball Team; Ecuador Women's Basketball Team; Ecuador Wheelchair Basketball Team

Football
Ecuador Football Team, nickname La Tri (the Tricolor) or Los Amarillos (the Yellows); Ecuador Women's Football Team, nickname La Tri (the Tricolor); Ecuador Futsal Team

Hockey
Ecuador Field Hockey Team

Table Tennis
Ecuador Table Tennis Team

Tennis
Ecuador Davis Cup Team; Ecuador Fed Cup Team

Volleyball
Ecuador Men's Volleyball Team; Ecuador Women's Volleyball Team

INDIVIDUAL SPORTS
Ecuador Amateur Boxing Team; Ecuador Archery Team; Ecuador Athletics Team; Ecuador Canoeing Team; Ecuador Cycling Team; Ecuador Equestrian Team; Ecuador Fencing Team; Ecuador Judo Team; Ecuador Modern Pentathlon Team; Ecuador Rowing Team; Ecuador Sailing Team; Ecuador Shooting Team; Ecuador Swim Team; Ecuador Tae Kwon Do Team; Ecuador Triathlon Team; Ecuador Weight Lifting Team; Ecuador Wrestling Team

NATIONAL HEROES OR PERSONIFICATIONS
Francisco Javier Eugenio de Santa Cruz y Espejo, who inspired the independence movement from Spain; Simón Bolivar, who achieved independence for Ecuador in 1822; José de Sucre, a leader of the independence movement in the early 19th century; José Maria Velasco Ibarra, four time president and political leader of the 20th century

NATIONAL HOLIDAY/INDEPENDENCE DAY
Independence Day, August 10

FESTIVALS/FAIRS
Carnival, February–March; Semana Santa (Holy Week or Easter Week), variable dates; Mama Negra Festival, November

SIGNIFICANT EVENTS IN FORMATION OF NATIONAL IDENTITY
3500 B.C.E.–1453 C.E. Many indigenous civilizations emerge. The region comes under the authority of the vast Inca Empire.

1525–1530 The Inca Empire is divided, with a northern capital at Quito and a southern capital at Cuzco, in present Peru*. The southern portion is conquered, and a unified kingdom has its capital at Quito. The civil war facilitates the Spanish conquest of the empire.

1532–1534 The Spanish conquistadores move north and take control of Quito, building a settlement on the city's ruins in 1534. The indigenous population is devastated by disease and slavery during the first decades of Spanish rule.

17th century–18th century The Spanish-speaking elite rules the region from the Spanish administration at Quito. The indigenous peoples are relegated to a peasant existence or to work on Spanish ranches and farms.

1809–1822 The first call for independence begins among the coastal Spanish settlers, weary of Spanish taxes and inspired by the revolution in the United States. Ecuador gains independence from Spain.

1822–1830 Ecuador joins Simón Bolivar's Republic of Grand Colombia, only to withdraw and become a separate republic.

1830 Instability, rivalries between regions, and a rapid succession of rulers impede progress. With the support of the Roman Catholic Church, the country is finally unified in the 1860s.

1895–1925 A liberal revolution reduces the power of the clergy and the wealthy landowners. The victorious group of liberals governs the country until 1925.

1930s–1940s Another period of instability begins under populist politicians. Ecuador and Peru go to war over control of territory in the Amazon Basin. Peru takes the disputed territory in 1941.

1950s–1970s Popular unrest and economic recession lead to a return of populist politics and military interference in the political life of the country. Military governments rule the country until a return to democracy in 1978.

1990s Decades of mismanagement and a massive foreign debt since the 1970s make the country nearly ungovernable.

1996–2000 The three democratically elected presidents fail to finish their terms. An economic crisis forces thousands to leave in search of work in other countries, particularly the United States and Spain. Ecuadorians become Spain's largest immigrant group.

2006 Presidential elections return Rafael Correa, who emulates earlier populist leaders.

2007 Allegations of Ecuador's support and aid to rebel groups in Colombia* raise tensions in the region. Ecuador's key ally, Venezuela*, gives support during dispute with Colombia.

2008 An estimated 250,000 Colombians in the country, as refugees from the violence in their home country, become a grave economic and political problem.

2009 The leftist government of Ecuador announces that it will default on billions of dollars in "illegitimate" debt.

EL SALVADOR

Official Name

República de El Salvador (Spanish); Republic of El Salvador (English)

Population

6,123,900 (2009e)

Inhabitants' Name/Nickname

Salvadorean(s)

Language/Languages

Spanish (official); Caliche (a local Spanish dialect), Nahua (an Amerindian language), others

Religion/Religions

Roman Catholic, 70 percent; Protestant, 20 percent; other or no religion

National Flag

The flag has horizontal stripes of blue, white, and blue with the national coat of arms centered on the white. The blue and white are based on the colors of the original flag of the Federal Republic of Central America.

Coat of Arms/Seal

The coat of arms consists of a triangle in which five volcanoes rise out of the sea. The volcanoes symbolize the five members of the Federal Republic of Central America. Above the triangle is a red Phrygian cap on a staff in front of a rising sun and the date September 15, 1821, El Salvador's independence day. Over the sun is a rainbow. Behind the triangle are five flags, and below is a scroll with the national motto. A laurel garland that is divided into 14 parts, representing the country's 14 departments, surrounds the triangle and flags.

Motto

Dios, unión, libertad (Spanish); God, Union, Liberty (English)

Capital City

San Salvador

Type of Government

Presidential republic

National Emblem

San Vicente volcano

National Colors

Blue and white

National Anthem

The anthem was adopted in 1879 but did not receive official recognition until 1953.

> **Himno Nacional de El Salvador (Spanish);**
> **National Anthem of El Salvador (English)**
>
> **Chorus**
>
> Let us salute the motherland,
> Proud to be called her children.
> To her well-being let us swear
> Boldly and unceasingly to devote our lives.
> (*repeat*)
> Devote our lives! (*repeat 4 times*)
>
> Of peace enjoyed in perfect happiness,
> El Salvador has always nobly dreamed.
> To achieve this has been her eternal
>   proposition,
> To keep it, her greatest glory.
> With inviolable faith, she eagerly follows
> The way of progress
> In order to fulfill her high destiny
> And achieve a happy future.
> A stern barrier protects her
> Against the clash of vile disloyalty,

> Ever since the day when her lofty banner,
> In letters of blood, wrote "Freedom,"
> Wrote "Freedom," wrote "Freedom."
>
> Freedom is her dogma and her guide;
> A thousand times she has defended it,
> And as many times has she repelled
> The hateful power of atrocious tyranny.
> Her history has been bloody and sad,
> Yet at the same time sublime and brilliant,
> A source of legitimate glory
> And a great lesson in Spartan pride.
> Her innate bravery shall not waver:
> In every man there is an immortal hero
> Who knows how to maintain the level
> Of the proverbial valor of old.
>
> All are self-denying and faithful
> To the tradition of warlike ardor
> With which they have always reaped fame
> By saving the motherland's honor.
> To respect the rights of others
> And base her actions on right and justice
> Is for her, without infamous intrigue,
> The constant and most firm ambition.
> And in following this line she persists,
> Dedicating her tenacious efforts
> In giving hard battle for battle;
> Her happiness is found in peace.

Patron Saint

El Salvador del Mundo (Savior of the World); Our Lady of Peace

Currency

U.S. dollar (formerly the colón)

Vehicle Identification Plates/ Stickers

ES

Passport

The passport cover has the name of the region and the country, Central America and the Republic of El Salvador, in Spanish, a map of Central America with El Salvador highlighted, the coat of arms, and the Spanish word for passport, *pasaporte*.

AIRLINE

TACA International Airlines, a grouping of five national airlines of Central America

NATIONAL FLOWER

Flor de izote

NATIONAL TREE

Maquilishuat

NATIONAL ANIMAL

Collared anteater (unofficial)

NATIONAL BIRD

Torogoz

NATIONAL RESOURCES

Natural resources include hydropower, geothermal power, petroleum, and arable land. Tourism is growing, based on the country's natural attractions, such as volcanoes, historic cities, and sandy beaches. The many Salvadoreans living outside the country are a valuable asset and a source of foreign currency.

FOODS

Pupusa, the national dish, originated with the indigenous Pipils. *Pupusas* are thick, handmade corn or rice tortillas filled with one or more ingredients, such as cheese, ground pork, refried beans, squash, or other vegetables. *Yuca frita,* deep-fried cassava root served with *curido,* a relish of pickled cabbage, onion, and carrot, and pork rinds or fried sardines, is also very popular. Other national specialties include *pollo encebollado,* chicken simmered with onions; *salpicón,* shredded beef with tomatoes, chilies, and cilantro; *ceviche de camarones,* shrimp marinated in lime juice; and *arroz de leche,* rice pudding.

SPORTS/SPORTS TEAMS

Association football (soccer) is the most popular sport in El Salvador. Other popular sports are basketball, baseball, and boxing. El Salvador national teams participate in many sports at an international level

TEAM SPORTS

Badminton

El Salvador Badminton Team

Baseball

El Salvador Baseball Team; El Salvador Softball Team

Basketball

El Salvador Basketball Team; El Salvador Women's Basketball Team; El Salvador Wheelchair Basketball Team

Football

El Salvador Football Team, nicknames La Selecta, Selección Cuscatleca, Cuscatlecos, La Azul (the Blue), or Guanacos; El Salvador Women's Football Team, nickname La Selecta, Selección Cuscatleca, Cuscatlecos, or La Azul (the Blue); El Salvador Under-23 Football Team; El Salvador Beach Soccer Team; El Salvador Futsal Team; El Salvador Women's Under-19 Football Team

Hockey

El Salvador Field Hockey Team

Racing

El Salvador Speedway Team

Table Tennis

El Salvador Table Tennis Team

Tennis

El Salvador Davis Cup Team; El Salvador Fed Cup Team

Volleyball

El Salvador Men's Volleyball Team; El Salvador Women's Volleyball Team

INDIVIDUAL SPORTS

El Salvador Amateur Boxing Team; El Salvador Archery Team; El Salvador Athletics Team; El Salvador Canoeing Team; El Salvador Cycling Team; El Salvador Equestrian Team; El Salvador Fencing Team; El Salvador Gymnastics Team; El Salvador Judo Team; El Salvador Modern Pentathlon Team; El Salvador Rowing Team; El Salvador Sailing Team; El Salvador Shooting Team; El Salvador Swim Team; El Salvador Tae Kwon Do Team; El Salvador Triathlon Team; El Salvador Weight Lifting Team; El Salvador Wrestling Team

NATIONAL HEROES OR PERSONIFICATIONS

Atlacatl, the Pipil leader who led the resistance to the Spanish invasion; José Matías Delgado, a priest, doctor, and independence leader known as *el padre de la patria salvadoreña* (father of the Salvadorean homeland); Manuel José Arce, president of the Federal Republic of Central America in the 1820s; Farabundo Martí, revolutionary leader of the a rebellion of indigenous *campasinos* in the early 1930s

NATIONAL HOLIDAY/INDEPENDENCE DAY

Independence Day, September 15

FESTIVALS/FAIRS

August Festival, August; Semana Santa (Holy Week), March–April; Queen of Peace Festival, November

SIGNIFICANT EVENTS IN FORMATION OF NATIONAL IDENTITY

1000 B.C.E.–1400 C.E. The region is divided into three indigenous states controlled by the Pipils, the Lencas, and the Chortis Maya. The Pipil are one of the few indigenous groups in Mesoamerica to abolish human sacrifice; otherwise, the cultures are similar to those of the Aztecs and Maya.

1524–1525 A Spanish expedition from Guatemala* is defeated and forced to retreat. The Spanish return and bring the region under the control of Spanish Guatemala. The region is called El Salvador, for one of the names of God, the Savior of the World.

1785 The Intendencia of San Salvador is created, although the region remains subordinate to the colonial government in Guatemala.

1810–1811 The French invasion of Spain* loosens colonial control. The ideas of the French Revolution support the idea of independence from Spain. The colonial elites are interested in controlling the territory without interference from far-away Spain. The insurrections beings when a priest, José Delgado, rings the bells of La Merced Church in San Salvador.

1811–1822 A decade of fighting, factionalism, and confusion lead to independence and union with Mexico*.

1823 The Central American provinces withdraw from Mexico and form the Federal Republic of Central America.

1838–1872 The federation is dissolved, and El Salvador becomes an independent republic. The early history of the country is marked by frequent revolutions and instability.

1872–1898 El Salvador champions attempts to establish a new Central American federation. El Salvador, Honduras*, and Nicaragua* form the Greater Republic of Central America, but a revolution in El Salvador ends the project.

1898–1932 The cultivation of coffee creates a small oligarchy of wealthy families that control the government, the military, and the economy. A peasant uprising ends with approximately 30,000 dead, commonly referred to as *La Matanza* (the Massacre).

1932–1991 Efforts to reform the feudal system are resisted by the elite and marked by massacres and atrocities carried out by the military. Civil war breaks out in 1980, partly due to the elite's efforts to stop reforms. The United States* becomes involved in the conflict, which is seen as an anti-communist campaign. The war is characterized by brutality and mass abuse of human rights.

1991–1992 The civil war ends with a peace accord that brings the military under civilian control and allows former guerillas to form political parties.

1992–2008 Free elections, a growing economy, and the return of tens of thousands of refugees begin a period of unprecedented peace and prosperity.

2009 A former leftist guerilla group turned political party wins presidential elections.

FALKLAND ISLANDS

OFFICIAL NAME

Falkland Islands (English); Islas Malvinas (Spanish/Argentine claims)

POPULATION

3,600 (2009e)

INHABITANTS' NAME/NICKNAME

Falkland Islander(s); Islander(s); Kelper(s)

LANGUAGE/LANGUAGES

English (official); Spanish

RELIGION/RELIGIONS

Christian (Church of England, Roman Catholic, United Free Church, Lutheran, others)

NATIONAL FLAG

The flag is a dark blue field with the Union Jack as a canton on the upper hoist and the coat of arms centered on the fly. From 1948 to 1999, the coat of arms was centered on a white disk. The coat of arms is now larger, symbolizing the self-government of the Falkland Islands.

COAT OF ARMS/SEAL

The coat of arms consists of a blue shield with a white ram standing on green grass over white wavy lines behind a Tudor-style ship. Below is a banner with the motto of the Falkland Islands. The ram represents the island's main historical economic activity, sheep farming. The blue of the shield stands for the sky over the island, while the blue and white wavy lines represent the sea. The green grass represents the tussock grass the covers the islands. The ship represents the *Desire,* the first ship to visit the islands in 1592, and the reason for the island's motto.

MOTTO

Desire the Right

CAPITAL CITY

Stanley

TYPE OF GOVERNMENT

Parliamentary democracy as a British overseas territory

NATIONAL EMBLEM

White ram

NATIONAL COLORS

Red and black

NATIONAL ANTHEM

The anthem was written in the 1930s and became very popular as an unofficial song of the islands. The official anthem is the anthem of the United Kingdom* and its associated territories, "God Save the Queen."

Song of the Falklands (unofficial)

In my heart there's a call for the isles far away
Where the wind from the Horn often wanders
  at play.
Where the kelp moves and swells to the wind
  and the tide
And penguins troop down from the lonely
  hillside.

Those isles of the sea are calling to me
The smell of the campfire a dear memory.
Though far I may roam, some day I'll come
  home
To the islands, the Falklands, the isles of the
  sea.

There's a camp house down yonder I'm long-
ing to see,
Though it's no gilded palace it's there I would
be.
Just to be there again I would race o'er the
foam,
For that lone house so far is my own home
sweet home.

Those isles of the sea are calling to me
The smell of the campfire a dear memory.
And though I would roam, I'll gladly go
home
To the islands, the Falklands, the isles of the
sea.

Now we're off to the Falklands, so wild and
so free,
Where there's tussock and kelp and the red
diddle-dee,
And the wild rugged beauty that thrills more
than me
Is bred in the bones on the isles of the sea.

Those isles of the sea are calling to me
The smell of the campfire a dear memory.
Though far I may roam, one day I'll go home
To the islands, the Falklands, the isles of the
sea.

CURRENCY

Falkland pound

INTERNET IDENTIFIER

.fk

VEHICLE IDENTIFICATION PLATES/ STICKERS

GB Great Britain (official); FK Falkland Islands
(unofficial)

PASSPORT

Falkland Islanders are British citizens and
travel on British passports.

AIRLINE

FIGAS Falkland Islands Government Air
Service

NATIONAL FLOWER

Pale maiden

NATIONAL PLANT

Tussock grass

NATIONAL ANIMAL

Sheep; sea lion (unofficial)

NATIONAL BIRD

Rockhopper penguin (unofficial)

NATIONAL FISH

Killer whale (unofficial)

NATIONAL RESOURCES

Natural resources include fish, squid, wildlife, calcified seaweed, and sphagnum moss.
Sheep farming is historically the main economic activity, but fishing has now surpassed
sheep farming as a major source of revenue.
Potentially large oil reserves hold the promise of future prosperity. Tourism is a growing
asset, with over 30,000 visitors a year.

FOODS

British-style dishes are the most popular in
the islands. Traditional dishes include lamb
chops with potatoes, meat puddings, and
fish and chips. Other specialties are meat
pies; boiled sausages made of mutton, garlic,
and tomato paste; leg of lamb; and smoked
lamb.

SPORTS/SPORTS TEAMS

A number of sports are practiced in the islands. The most popular are association football (soccer) and cricket. Falkland Islands
national teams participate in many sports at
an international level.

TEAM SPORTS

Badminton

Falkland Islands Badminton Team

Basketball

Falkland Islands Basketball Team; Falkland Islands Women's Basketball Team

Cricket

Falkland Islands Cricket Team

Football

Falkland Islands Football Team, nickname the Oilers

NATIONAL HEROES OR PERSONIFICATIONS

John Davis, captain of the *Desire*, the first European ship to visit the islands in 1592; Simon Weston, a hero of the Falklands War; Terry Peck, a member of the Falklands Islands Defense Force and a hero of the Falklands War; Margaret Thatcher, the prime minister of the United Kingdom who is credited with liberating the Falklands after seven weeks of Argentine occupation in 1982

NATIONAL HOLIDAY/INDEPENDENCE DAY

Liberation Day, June 14

FESTIVALS/FAIRS

Liberation Day Festival, June; Stanley Sports Festival, December

SIGNIFICANT EVENTS IN FORMATION OF NATIONAL IDENTITY

1592   The English ship *Desire* under sea captain John Davis is believed to be the first ship to visit the uninhabited islands.

1748   The British claim to the island is disputed by Spain* under the terms of the Treaty of Tordesillas that in 1494 divided the continent of South America between Spain and Portugal*.

1765–1770   The British establish a settlement at Port Egmont in 1765.

1816   Argentina takes over Spain's territorial claim to the islands after independence from the Spanish crown.

1828–1831   The Argentine occupation of the uninhabited islands begins with the foundation of a permanent settlement and a penal colony.

1833–1870   The United Kingdom sends two naval vessels to reassert British sovereignty. The British allows those already on the island to remain. The Royal Navy builds a base at Stanley. The introduction of the hardy Cheviot breed of sheep makes sheep farming the dominant form of agriculture.

1880s–1911   The first telephone lines are established to connect the islands' several settlements. A wireless telegraphy station is established that enables telegrams to be sent to mainland Uruguay*.

1939–1945   Stanley becomes an important port for the British naval squadron in the South Atlantic. The famous sea battle between British ships and the German *Graf Spee* is launched from the islands.

1964–1968   Argentina begins diplomatic efforts to win control of the islands through the United Nations. The islanders reject a British proposal to discuss sovereignty as long as the islanders' wishes are respected.

1970s   Tensions between Argentina and the United Kingdom increase in 1975–1976.

1982   The military junta that rules Argentina during the so-called Dirty War seeks to divert public attention by ordering an invasion of the Falkland Islands. The British respond with an expeditionary force that lands on the islands seven weeks after the occupation. The Falklands War ends the Argentine occupation, and soon after, the junta is overthrown in Buenos Aires.

1983–1989   Falkland Islanders are granted British citizenship. The military presence in the islands is increased, and new facilities are constructed in Stanley. The islands become self-governing through a local legislature. Argentines are again allowed to visit the islands, often to visit the graves of those killed in the war.

1998   Argentina, under a democratically elected government, reiterates its territorial claim, but only through peaceful means.

1998–2004 Attempts are made to diversify the local economy away from sheep farming. Economically viable reserves of petroleum are explored.

2005 A permanent memorial to the Argentine war dead is dedicated. Argentine harassment of shipping in Falkland waters continues.

2007–2009 Argentina renews its sovereignty claim and renounces agreements over joint exploitation of the petroleum reserves found in island waters. The British government rejects Argentine requests for sovereignty talks.

See also United Kingdom

FRENCH GUIANA

OFFICIAL NAME
Guyane Française (French); French Guiana (English); Région Guyane (French); Guiana Region (English)
   Guyane (French); Guiana (English)

POPULATION
220,800 (2009e)

INHABITANTS' NAME/NICKNAME
Guianese; Guyanese

LANGUAGE/LANGUAGES
French (official); Portuguese, Spanish, Creole, Chinese, Hmong, others

RELIGION/RELIGIONS
Roman Catholic, indigenous beliefs, Baha'i, other or no religion

NATIONAL FLAG
The French tricolor of blue, white, and red is the official flag. The flag of the nationalists is a bicolor of yellow over green divided diagonally from upper hoist to lower fly, with a centered red five-pointed star. The green stands for the rainforest and fertility, the yellow stands for the sun that shines on the land, and the red star is for the people and independence.

COAT OF ARMS/SEAL
The official seal of the region is a blue over green design bearing a single gold star above a stylized canoe on red waves with the words *Guyane* (above) and *La Région* (below). The nationalists use a shield bearing the same design as their flag.

CAPITAL CITY
Cayenne (French); Cajenna (Creole)

TYPE OF GOVERNMENT
An overseas department and region of France governed as a metropolitan region with little self-government

NATIONAL EMBLEM
Devil's Island (former penal colony)

NATIONAL COLORS
Red, yellow, and green

PATRON SAINT
Saint Sauveur (the dioceses of Cayenne)

CURRENCY
Euro

INTERNET IDENTIFIER
.gf

VEHICLE IDENTIFICATION PLATES/STICKERS
F France (official); GF French Guiana (unofficial)

PASSPORT
The Guianese are French citizens and travel on French passports.

AIRLINE
Air Guyane

NATIONAL RESOURCES

Natural resources include gold, timber, and fish. The region's sandy beaches, pleasant climate, historic penal colonies, and scenery support a growing tourist industry. French Guiana is heavily dependent on France for subsidies and goods. The European Space Center at Kourou is a major national resource and accounts for 25 percent of the gross domestic product of the territory.

FOODS

Bouillon d'aoura, a dish of smoked eel, crab, prawns, chicken, and vegetables served with *aoura,* the fruit of the savanna tree, is considered the national specialty. Other typical dishes include *poulet creole,* chicken cooked in coconut milk; *crab matoutou,* a dish of crab and rice; *feroce,* a dish of marinated salt cod and avocados; fricassee, a chicken curry dish with coconut; and *migan,* a dish of breadfruit and salt cod.

SPORTS/SPORTS TEAMS

Association football (soccer) is the territory's most popular game. Basketball is also widely played. French Guiana national teams participate in basketball and football at the international level.

TEAM SPORTS

Basketball

French Guiana Basketball Team; French Guiana Women's Basketball Team

Football

French Guiana Football Team

Volleyball

French Guiana Men's Volleyball Team; French Guiana Women's Volleyball Team

NATIONAL HEROES OR PERSONIFICATIONS

Henri Charrière, an famous escaped French convict imprisoned in the region from 1933 to 1945 and the inspiration for the film *Papillon;* Alfred Dreyfus, a French military officer of Jewish background whose trial and conviction on baseless charges of treason began a life sentence on Devil's Island before his exoneration and release

NATIONAL HOLIDAY/INDEPENDENCE DAY

Bastille Day, July 14; Abolition of Slavery, June 10

FESTIVALS/FAIRS

Mardi Gras, February–March; Cayenne Festival, October 15; Bastille Day, July

SIGNIFICANT EVENTS IN FORMATION OF NATIONAL IDENTITY

1450 C.E. The region is inhabited by a number of Amerindian peoples.

1498 Christopher Columbus' visit, on his third voyage to the New World, is the first recorded visit by Europeans.

1604 France* attempts to settle the territory but is forced to abandon the settlement when the Portuguese threaten, viewing French colonization as a violation of the 1494 Treaty of Tordesillas that divided South America between Spain* and Portugal*.

1643 French colonizers return and establish a settlement at Cayenne and some small plantations. The second attempt is abandoned following attacks by the indigenous peoples.

1664 The French again attempt to colonize the Cayenne region, with some success. A second settlement is established.

1763 The Treaty of Paris deprives France of almost all its colonies in the Americas, except French Guiana and a handful of Caribbean islands. Thousands of settlers are sent to the colony, many lured there by stories of plentiful gold. Instead, they face hostile tribes and tropical diseases. Less than two years later, only a few hundred survive.

1789–1795 During the French Revolution, the colony begins to be used as a penal colony for discredited revolutionaries and other enemies of the new French republic.

1815 African slaves are imported as plantations spread along the more disease-free rivers.

1848 France abolishes slavery, and many ex-slaves flee into the rainforest to set up communities similar to those they had known in Africa. Known as Maroons, they form a string of villages hidden from the Europeans.

1850 Indians, Malays, and Chinese begin to arrive in the colony. Brought in as plantation labor, they quickly set up shops in Cayenne and other villages.

1852–1930 The first shiploads of chained prisoners arrive from France. Political prisoners are imprisoned on the Salut Islands, and other prisons are used for solitary confinements. The camps become famous for brutality and the short lifespan of the prisoners.

1930–1946 The territory of Inini, consisting of most of the interior, is created. It is later abolished and the territory reunited with French Guiana, which becomes an overseas department of France.

1951 The last of the infamous penal colonies is closed.

1964 Kourou is chosen as a launch site for rockets, due to its location close to the equator. The space center is constructed, becoming an important economic asset to the colony.

1970s Hmong and Lao refugees from Laos* are settled in the territory. The first stirring of a local autonomy movement spread across the region.

1990–2000 A nationalist movement grows out of the autonomy movement, with demands for greater self-government or outright independence. Widespread demonstrations lead to violence in 1996–97 and in 2000.

2000–2009 Nationalist agitation continues to disrupt the territory. A territorial dispute with Suriname* again threatens good relations with the neighboring republic.

See also France

GUATEMALA

OFFICIAL NAME

República de Guatemala (Spanish); Republic of Guatemala (English)

POPULATION

13,010,800 (2009e)

INHABITANTS' NAME/NICKNAME

Guatemalan(s)

LANGUAGE/LANGUAGES

Spanish (official); 23 Amerindian languages recognized as national languages where they are spoken; English, others

RELIGION/RELIGIONS

Roman Catholic, 60 percent; Protestant, 33 percent; traditional Maya religion, 2 percent; other or no religion

NATIONAL FLAG

The flag has three equal vertical stripes of sky blue, white, and sky blue bearing the coat of arms centered on the white. The blue, white, blue design symbolizes Guatemala's position between two oceans. The blue also represents honor and the sky over Guatemala. The white represents peace and purity.

COAT OF ARMS/SEAL

The coat of arms comprises a wreath of olive branches, the symbol for victory, around an arrangement of the Resplendent Quetzal, a bird that symbolizes liberty, and a scroll with the Spanish words for Liberty and September 15, 1821, the date of Central American independence from Spain. Behind the scroll are two crossed rifles, representing Guatemala's willingness to defend itself by force if needed, and two crossed swords, representing honor.

NICKNAME

El pais de la eterna primavera (Spanish); Land of eternal spring (English)

MOTTO

Libre Creza Fecundo (Spanish); Grow Free and Fertile (English)

CAPITAL CITY

Guatemala City

TYPE OF GOVERNMENT

Presidential republic

NATIONAL EMBLEM

Quetzal

NATIONAL COLORS

Blue and white

NATIONAL ANTHEM

The anthem was first performed in 1897. The lyrics were changed in 1934 to eliminate the earlier militant and bloody context.

Himno Nacional de Guatemala (Spanish)/ Guatemala National Anthem (English)

Fortunate Guatemala! May your altars
Never be profaned by cruel men.
May there never be slaves, who submit to
  their yoke,
Or tyrants who deride you.
If tomorrow your sacred soil
Should be threatened by foreign invasion,
Your fair flag, flying freely in the wind,
Will call to you: Conquer or die.

Chorus

Your fair flag, flying freely in the wind,
Will call to you: Conquer or die;
For your people, with heart and soul,
Would prefer death to slavery.

From your old and hard chains
You forged, with an ire-driven hand,
The plow that fertilizes the soil
And the sword that saves honor.

Our fathers fought one day,
Lit up in patriotic burning
And they were able, without bloody clash,
To place you on a throne of love.

Chorus

And they were able, without bloody clash,
To place you on a throne of love,
That our nation, in energetic assent,
Gave life to the ideal redeemer.

Your emblem shows a piece of the sky
In which a cloud gets its whiteness
Wretched is he who dares in madness
stain your colors

Well, your brave and proud sons
who admire the peace within
will never avoid the rough battles
if they are to defend their land and their
  home.

Chorus

They will never avoid the rough battles
if they are to defend their land and their home
that honor is the idea that reigns over their
  souls
and the altar of the mother country their altar

Lying in the magnificent Andes
with two oceans at hearing distance
under the wing of seeds and gold
you become entranced with the beautiful
  quetzal

Native bird that lives in your seal
protector that protects your soil
hopefully he will fly high
more than the condor and the royal eagle!

Chorus

Hopefully he will fly high
more than the condor and the royal eagle
and in his wings, raise up to the sky:
Guatemala, your immortal name!

PATRON SAINT

Saint James the Greater; Our Lady of the Rosary

CURRENCY

Guatemalan quetzal

INTERNET IDENTIFIER

.gt

VEHICLE IDENTIFICATION PLATES/ STICKERS

GCA

PASSPORT

The passport cover has the name of the country in Spanish and English, the coat of arms, and the word *passport* in Spanish and English.

AIRLINE

TACA International Airlines, a group of five Central American national airlines

NATIONAL FLOWER

White nun orchid

NATIONAL TREE

Cieba

NATIONAL BIRD

Quetzal

NATIONAL RESOURCES

Natural resources include petroleum, nickel, rare woods, fish, chicle, and hydropower. The important tourist industry depends on the country's many ancient ruins, Spanish colonial architecture, beautiful scenery, sandy beaches, and a pleasant climate. Remittances from Guatemalans living in the United States* now constitute the largest source of foreign income, larger than the combined income from tourism and exports.

FOODS

National dishes include *kac ic,* a soup made of turkey and seasoned with *samat,* an herb that grows only in the Alta Verapaz region; *flan de naranja,* orange-flavored egg custard; and guacamole, a sauce or dip made of avocados. Tamales of many varieties are considered a national food, made of dough derived from corn, potatoes, or rice filled with meat, fruits, or nuts and then wrapped in leaves or husks for cooking. Other specialties include *arroz con pollo,* a rice dish with chicken; and *sopa de plantanos,* a soup made of plantains.

SPORTS/SPORTS TEAMS

Association football (soccer) is the most popular sport in Guatemala. Basketball is also popular, as is a game inherited from the Mayas called *pok-a-tok.* Guatemala national teams participate in many sports at an international level.

TEAM SPORTS

Badminton

Guatemala Badminton Team

Baseball

Guatemala Baseball Team; Guatemala Softball Team

Basketball

Guatemala Basketball Team; Guatemala Women's Basketball Team; Guatemala Wheelchair Basketball Team

Football

Guatemala Football Team, nickname El Azul y Blanco (the Blue and White) or Los Chapines; Guatemala Women's Football Team, nickname El Azul y Blanco (the Blue and White); Guatemala American Football Team; Guatemala Futsal Team; Guatemala Under-19 Football Team; Guatemala Women's Under-19 Football Team

Hockey

Guatemala Field Hockey Team

Racing

Guatemala Speedway Team

Table Tennis

Guatemala Table Tennis Team

Tennis

Guatemala Davis Cup Team; Guatemala Fed Cup Team

Volleyball

Guatemala Men's Volleyball Team; Guatemala Women's Volleyball Team

INDIVIDUAL SPORTS

Guatemala Amateur Boxing Team; Guatemala Athletics Team; Guatemala Archery Team; Guatemala Canoeing Team; Guatemala Equestrian Team; Guatemala Fencing Team; Guatemala Gymnastics Team; Guatemala Judo Team; Guatemala Karate Team; Guatemala Modern Pentathlon Team; Guatemala Rowing Team; Guatemala Sailing Team; Guatemala Shooting Team; Guatemala Swim Team; Guatemala Tae Kwon Do Team; Guatemala Triathlon Team; Guatemala Weight Lifting Team; Guatemala Wrestling Team

NATIONAL HEROES OR PERSONIFICATIONS

Quiché leader Tecún Umán, Guatemala's national hero, faced an army of Spanish conquistadores in the battle of Pinal in 1534. According to the legend, although he had no armor, Tecún Umán fought for the people when they were about to lose their freedom to the conquistadors; Justo Rufino Barrios, president of Guatemala in the mid-19th century, known for his reforms and liberalizing administration; Juan José Arévalo, elected president in 1944 in the first fair and democration election in the country's history

NATIONAL HOLIDAY/INDEPENDENCE DAY

Independence Day, September 15

FESTIVALS/FAIRS

Lent/Easter processions

SIGNIFICANT EVENTS IN FORMATION OF NATIONAL IDENTITY

2000 B.C.E.–250 C.E.   The Maya culture develops as a sophisticated and advanced civilization. Great pyramids are raised, cities emerge, trade is organized, and farming is extended to new areas.

250–900   The Mayan Empire expands, founding new cities that develop as independent city-states. At the empire's height, it is wealthy, sophisticated, and in contact with other cultures in Mesoamerica. The empire declines for unknown reasons and many cities are abandoned.

1518   The Spanish begin expeditions to the region. European diseases devastate the indigenous peoples.

1523–1527   Spanish forces under Pedro de Alvarado finally defeat the local nations. Alvarado, know for his cruelty to the indigenous peoples, is made governor of Guatemala.

1541–1776   Guatemala lacks the riches of Mexico* or Peru* and so is considered less important by Spain*. The region's exports are mostly agricultural. The Captaincy-general of Guatemala governs present Chiapas, Guatemala, El Salvador*, Nicaragua*, Costa Rica* and Honduras*.

1806   The French depose the Spanish king during the Napoleonic Wars in Europe.

1821   The Captaincy-general of Guatemala is proclaimed independent of Spain and is incorporated into newly independent Mexico. All the provinces except Chiapas soon separate from Mexico to form the Central American Federation.

1838–1840   The federation dissolves in civil war.

1871–1945   A liberal revolution begins to modernize the country. Coffee becomes the most important export crop.

1950s–1960s   The Cold War starts, and the United States begins directly supporting Guatemala's army with training, weapons and money. Military governments continue to rule Guatemala for long periods, mostly supported by the United States.

1970s   Guerillas gain support, while the army systematically abuses the poor and those suspected of supporting them. Massacres of indigenous peoples are reported.

1980s A scorched-earth policy against any region suspected of aiding the rebels sends thousands of refugees fleeing into Mexico. Hundreds of Mayan villages are destroyed.

1990 The Guatemalan government recognizes the independence of Belize* but continues to claim the country as national territory.

1996–1999 The Guatemalan Civil War ends. Over a million people are refugees, tens of thousands are dead, and over 90 percent of atrocities committed during the conflict are blamed on the military and government paramilitary groups.

2000–2008 After the peace accords, Guatemala has several successive democratic elections. Territorial claims in Belize, the burden of the still-displaced refugees, and the drain of thousands of impoverished Guatemalans leaving the country continue to undermine stability and progress. Guatemala's murder rate is one of the highest in the world.

2009 In September 2009, the government declares a "state of public calamity" in response to increasing malnutrition that threatens over 400,000 families in the country.

GUYANA

OFFICIAL NAME
Cooperative Republic of Guyana

POPULATION
753,400 (2009e)

INHABITANTS' NAME/NICKNAME
Guyanese

LANGUAGE/LANGUAGES
English (official); Guyanese Creole, Hindi, Urdu, others

RELIGION/RELIGIONS
Christian, 50 percent; Hindu, 37 percent; Muslim, 10 percent; Baha'i, other or no religion

NATIONAL FLAG
The flag, known as the Golden Arrowhead Flag, consists of five colors—green, gold, red, black, and white—arranged in overlapping triangles with their bases to the hoist. Green symbolizes agriculture and forests, white is for rivers and water, gold is for mineral wealth, black is for endurance, and red is for zeal and dynamism.

COAT OF ARMS/SEAL
The coat of arms consists of a central shield decorated with a water lily, three blue wavy lines representing the three major rivers, and the national bird. Above the shield is an Amerindian headdress, symbolizing the country's indigenous peoples. Two diamonds on each side of the headdress represent the mining industry. Below the headdress is a helmet. Two jaguars support the shield, and below is a banner with the country's national motto.

MOTTO
One people, one nation, one destiny

CAPITAL CITY
Georgetown

TYPE OF GOVERNMENT
Republic

NATIONAL COLORS
Green, white, and yellow

NATIONAL ANTHEM
The anthem, the result of a public competition one month before independence, was adopted in 1966.

Dear Land of Guyana, of Rivers and Plains

Dear land of Guyana, of rivers and plains,
Made rich by the sunshine, and lush by the
    rains,
Set gem-like and fair, between mountains and
    sea,
Your children salute you, dear land of the
    free.

Green land of Guyana, our heroes of yore,
Both bondsmen and free, laid their bones on
    your shore.

This soil so they hallowed, and from them are we,
All sons of one mother, Guyana the free.

Great land of Guyana, diverse though our strains,
We are born of their sacrifice, heirs of their pains.
And ours is the glory their eyes did not see,
One land of six peoples, united and free.

Dear land of Guyana, to you will we give,
Our homage, our service, each day that we live.
God guard you, Great Mother, and make us to be
More worthy of our heritage, land of the free.

CURRENCY

Guyanese dollar

INTERNET IDENTIFIER

.gy

VEHICLE IDENTIFICATION PLATES/STICKERS

GUY

PASSPORT

The passport cover has initials CC, Caribbean Community, and the name of the country in English, the coat of arms, and the word *passport*.

AIRLINE

TravelSpan

NATIONAL FLOWER

Victoria Regia water lily

NATIONAL PLANT

Sugarcane, rice

NATIONAL ANIMAL

Jaguar

NATIONAL BIRD

Hoatzin (Canje pheasant)

NATIONAL FISH

Arapaima (unofficial)

NATIONAL RESOURCES

Natural resources include bauxite, gold, diamonds, hardwood timber, shrimp, and fish. Agriculture and mining are the two most important industries. The country's sandy beaches, pleasant climate, varied cultures, and colonial towns could be the basis of a thriving tourist industry.

FOODS

The food reflects the ethnic makeup of the country and its colonial history and includes dishes from the Africans and creoles, East Indians, Amerindians, Chinese, Portuguese, and Europeans (mostly British). Pepperpot, a meat dish of Amerindian origin flavored with cinnamon, hot peppers, and *cassareep*, a sauce made from cassava root, is considered the national dish. Local specialties include cookup rice, a rice dish with various vegetables accompanied by chicken, beef, or fish; *metemgie,* a thick coconut-based soup with dumplings; *foo-foo,* plantain cakes; and Portuguese garlic pork.

SPORTS/SPORTS TEAMS

Association football (soccer) is the country's most popular sport. Traditional sports, such as wrestling and athletics, and cricket, the legacy of the British, are also very popular. Guyana national teams participate in many sports at an international level.

TEAM SPORTS

Badminton

Guyana Badminton Team

Basketball

Guyana Basketball Team

Cricket

Guyana Cricket Team; West Indies Cricket Team, nickname the Windies (West Indies teams represent a number of English-speaking Caribbean countries)

Football

Guyana Football Team, nickname the Golden Jaguars; Guyana Women's Football Team, nickname the Golden Jaguars; Guyana Rugby Union Team; Guyana Women's Rugby Union Team; Guyana Futsal Team; West Indies Rugby League Team, nickname the Wahoos (West Indies teams represent a number of English-speaking Caribbean countries

Hockey

Guyana Field Hockey Team

Netball

Guyana Netball Team

Table Tennis

Guyana Table Tennis Team

Volleyball

Guyana Men's Volleyball Team; Guyana Women's Volleyball Team

INDIVIDUAL SPORTS

Guyana Amateur Boxing Team; Guyana Athletics Team; Guyana Canoeing Team; Guyana Cycling Team; Guyana Judo Team; Guyana Karate Team; Guyana Shooting Team; Guyana Swim Team; Guyana Tae Kwon Do Team; Guyana Weight Lifting Team; Guyana Wrestling Team

NATIONAL HEROES OR PERSONIFICATIONS

Cuffy, the leader of the Berbice Slave Rebellion in 1763; Reverend John Smith, a missionary arrested and tried for inciting the slaves to rebel in 1823, who was sentenced to be executed but died as a result of prison conditions; Cheddi Jagan, a leading politician of the transition to independence and the first president of the country; Linden Forbes Burnham, leader of one of the major political parties, prime minister from 1964 to 1908 and president from 1980 to 1985

NATIONAL HOLIDAY/INDEPENDENCE DAY

Independence Day, May 26; Mashramani-Republic Day, February 23

FESTIVALS/FAIRS

Divali Festival (Festival of Lights), variable dates; Eid al-Adha, variable dates; Easter, March–April; Mashramani Festival, February

SIGNIFICANT EVENTS IN FORMATION OF NATIONAL IDENTITY

2000 B.C.E.–1500 C.E. Arawak peoples along the coast and Caribs in the interior inhabit the region. The name of the region, Guyana, probably comes from an Arawak word *wai ana*, meaning "land of many waters."

1499–1500 The coast is visited by Spanish sailors.

1595–1598 El Dorado, the fabled land of riches linked to the exploits of Sir Walter Raleigh, who explores the coast in 1595, stimulates exploration. The Dutch begin to explore the region in 1598.

1616–1627 Three Dutch colonies are established, Essequibo, Berbice, and Demerara.

18th century Plantations worked by African slaves are created in the coastal sections. In 1763, a slave named Cuffy leads a widespread slave revolt. Many slaves escape into the interior to live as their ancestors had in Africa.

1796–1815 During the Napoleonic Wars, the British and Dutch fight for control of the colonies. The three colonies are officially ceded to the United Kingdom* and are combined to form British Guiana.

1823–1834 A slave revolt in Demerara results in the trial and execution of 33 slaves and the trial and conviction of John Smith, a missionary accused of inciting the revolt. Slavery is abolished.

1834 The freed slaves refuse to work for wages, and many scatter into the interior. Indentured laborers are imported from India*, Portugal*, and China*. Many of the laborers stay in British Guiana.

1897 After the discovery of gold in the region close to the Venezuelan border, determination of the exact boundaries of the colony is turned over to arbitration, which finds in Britain's favor, with 94 percent of the disputed region, covering most of the colony, confirmed as British territory.

1917 The practice of importing labor is ended. Many Afro-Guyanese urbanize, while the large Indian population remains rural.

1953–1961 Two political blocks representing the Afro-Guyanese and the Indo-Guyanese contest the first elections for a local legislature. British colonial authorities, hoping to thwart the drive to independence, incite violence between the region's two largest ethnic groups. Serious riots destroy a large part of Georgetown.

1961–1966 Strikes, instability, and interference by foreign governments mark the period known as the Disturbances. Guyana becomes an independent republic under a socialist government.

1978 An agricultural commune called Jonestown is the scene of a mass suicide of its members, mostly American followers of leader Jim Jones.

1985 State socialism, press censorship, and one-party rule come to an end.

1999 An Indo-Guyanese is elected president, reversing decades of Afro-Guyanese domination.

2001 Venezuela* reiterates its old claim to three-quarters of Guyana's territory. Potentially oil-rich waters are disputed by Guyana and Suriname*.

2006 The first nonviolent elections are held in more than 20 years.

2008–2009 National electoral authorities conduct a voter re-registration exercise to produce a new and accepted voter list. Guyana seeks arbitration to resolve the outstanding territorial claims with Venezuela and Suriname.

HONDURAS

OFFICIAL NAME
República de Honduras (Spanish); Republic of Honduras (English)

POPULATION
7,822,800 (2009e)

INHABITANTS' NAME/NICKNAME
Honduran(s); Catrucho(s)

LANGUAGE/LANGUAGES
Spanish (official); Amerindian languages, English, others

RELIGION/RELIGIONS
Roman Catholic, 97 percent; Protestant, other or no religion

NATIONAL FLAG
The flag has equal horizontal stripes of blue, white, and blue bearing five five-pointed blue stars on the white stripe. The two blue stripes represent the Pacific Ocean and the Caribbean Sea. The white stripe represents the land between the ocean and the sea and the peace and prosperity of the people. The five blue stars represent the five countries of the former Federal Republic of Central America.

COAT OF ARMS/SEAL
The coat of arms has a central oval crest with a central Masonic die and a border that features the name of the country and the national motto in Spanish, topped with a cornucopia and a quiver of arrows. The crest is flanked by deciduous trees and a limestone cliff with oak and pine trees, a mine, and agricultural land.

MOTTO

Libre, soberana, e independente (Spanish);
Free, sovereign, and independent (English)

CAPITAL CITY

Tegucigalpa

TYPE OF GOVERNMENT

Constitutional republic

NATIONAL COLORS

Blue and white

NATIONAL ANTHEM

The anthem was written in the 19th century
and was officially adopted in 1915.

Tu Bandera Es un Lampo de Cielo (Spanish); Your Flag Is a Heavenly Light (English)

Chorus

Your flag is a splendor of sky
Crossed with a band of snow;
And there can be seen, in its sacred depths,
Five pale blue stars.
In your emblem, which a rough sea
With its wild waves protects,
Behind the bare summit of a volcano,
A star brightly shines.

Like an Indian maiden you have been
  sleeping,
Lulled by the resonant song of your seas,
When, set in your golden valleys,
The bold navigator found you;
And on seeing, enraptured, your beauty,
And feeling your enchantment,
He dedicated a kiss of love to the blue hem
of your splendid mantle.

Chorus

To guard this sacred emblem
We shall march, O fatherland, to our death;
Our death will be honored
If we die thinking of your love.
Having defended your holy flag,
And shrouded in its glorious folds,
Many, Honduras, shall die for you,
But shall fall in honor.

PATRON SAINT

Our Lady of Suyapa

CURRENCY

Honduras lempira

INTERNET IDENTIFIER

.hn

VEHICLE IDENTIFICATION PLATES/ STICKERS

HN

PASSPORT

A black cover with the name of the country
in Spanish, the coat of arms, and the word
passport in Spanish and English.

AIRLINE

TACA International Airlines, which groups
together five Central American national
airlines

NATIONAL FLOWER

Rhyncholaelia orchid; rose (unofficial; official until 1969)

NATIONAL TREE

Honduran pine

NATIONAL ANIMAL

White-tailed deer

NATIONAL BIRD

Scarlet macaw

NATIONAL RESOURCES

Natural resources include timber, gold, silver, copper, lead, zinc, iron ore, antimony,
coal, fish, and hydropower. Sandy beaches,
a pleasant climate, historic cities, and a
friendly population support a small but
growing tourist industry. Remittances from
Hondurans living in the United States* and

elsewhere are a major asset and a source of foreign currency.

FOODS

Baleada, a thick corn tortilla filled with mashed fried beans, cheese, and other ingredients; *carne asada,* thin cuts of marinated beef grilled over charcoal; and tamales, steam-cooked corn dough often stuffed with meat or sweets, are considered the national dishes. Other national specialties include *nacatamales,* corn cakes filled with meat and vegetables and steamed in banana leaves; *plátanos fritos,* fried plantains; and *pollo con chili,* a spicy chicken dish.

SPORTS/SPORTS TEAMS

Association football (soccer) is the most popular sport in Honduras. Basketball and baseball are also very popular. Honduras national teams participate in many sports at an international level.

TEAM SPORTS

Badminton

Honduras Badminton Team

Baseball

Honduras Baseball Team; Honduras Softball Team

Basketball

Honduras Basketball Team; Honduras Women's Basketball Team

Football

Football Team, nicknames Los Catrachos, La Bicolor, La Seleccion (the Team), La H, or Garra Catracha; Honduras Women's Football Team, nickname Las Catrachas; Honduras Under-20 Football Team; Honduras American Football Team; Honduras Futsal Team

Hockey

Honduras National Field Hockey Team

Table Tennis

Honduras Table Tennis Team

Tennis

Honduras Davis Cup Team; Honduras Fed Cup Team

Volleyball

Honduras Men's Volleyball Team; Honduras Women's Volleyball Team

INDIVIDUAL SPORTS

Honduras Amateur Boxing Team; Honduras Archery Team; Honduras Athletics Team; Honduras Canoeing Team; Honduras Cycling Team; Honduras Equestrian Team; Honduras Fencing Team; Honduras Gymnastics Team; Honduras Judo Team; Honduras Karate Team; Honduras Rowing Team; Honduras Shooting Team; Honduras Swim Team; Honduras Tae Kwon Do Team; Honduras Triathlon Team; Honduras Weight Lifting Team; Honduras Wrestling Team

NATIONAL HEROES OR PERSONIFICATIONS

Lempira, the leader of an indigenous uprising in the late 16th century who is honored by the name of the Honduran currency; Francisco Morazán, who led the fight for independence from Spain and resisted the breakup of the Central American federation; Marco Aurelio Soto, a liberal president of the mid-19th century and the founder of the national library; Juan Manuel Gálvez, the president from 1949 to 1954, honored for building a system of roads to connect all parts of the country and for greatly expanding the economy and enacting labor laws

NATIONAL HOLIDAY/INDEPENDENCE DAY

Independence Day, September 15

FESTIVALS/FAIRS

Semana Santa (Holy Week), the week before Easter; La Ceiba Carnival, February–March;

Feria Juniana, June; Day of the Americas, April.

SIGNIFICANT EVENTS IN FORMATION OF NATIONAL IDENTITY

10,000 B.C.E.–3500 B.C.E. Early settlers migrate to the region from present Mexico*. Agriculture, particularly corn cultivation, is introduced.

2000 B.C.E.–250 C.E. The Maya culture develops as a sophisticated and advanced civilization. Great pyramids are built, cities are established, trade is organized, and farming is extended to new areas.

250–900 The Mayan Empire expands, founding new cities that develop as independent city-states. At the empire's height, it is wealthy and sophisticated. In the west, the people are influenced by contact with other cultures in Mesoamerica. The Mayan empire declines for unknown reasons, and many cities are abandoned.

900–1518 Smaller Mayan kingdoms preserve the culture but never equal the empire's earlier achievements or power. Spanish expeditions penetrate the region. European diseases devastate the indigenous peoples.

1502–1536 Christopher Columbus, on his fourth and final expedition to the New World, reaches the Bay Islands off the coast. Honduras becomes part of the Spanish Empire and is administered through Guatemala*. Spanish forces defeat the indigenous resistance.

17th century–18th century Spanish immigrants establish plantations, farms, and mines worked by indigenous forced labor. A population of mixed Spanish and indigenous strains becomes the largest part of the population.

1821–1838 Honduras declares independence from Spain* and becomes part of Mexico. In 1823, the Central American states form the Federal Republic of Central America, which disintegrates in 1838. As a result, Honduras becomes a separate republic.

1860 American soldiers of fortune, called filibusters, attempt to convert Central America into a U.S. colony. Led by William Walker, they invade Honduras but are defeated, and Walker is executed.

1911–1955 U.S. fruit companies dominate Honduran politics, able to choose presidents and topple governments. Instability and poverty are widespread.

1969 Tensions build when Honduras blames the large number of illegal immigrants from El Salvador* for the poor state of the economy. Following a preliminary to the football World Cup, tensions escalate. Troops from El Salvador invade Honduras, beginning the short Football War. Tensions between the two countries remain to the present day.

1970s Military governments and coups interspersed with elections mark the decade until elections in 1980 initiate a new civilian government in 1982.

1980s The United States establishes a large military presence in Honduras to support the illegally funded opposition to the leftist government of Nicaragua*.

1992 The border dispute between Honduras and El Salvador is settled.

1998 Hurricane Mitch causes massive and widespread loss of life and damage.

2005 Hondurans vote in the seventh consecutive democratic election. Honduras signs a free-trade agreement with the United States.

2008 Honduras remains one of the 10 poorest countries in the Western Hemisphere, with about half the population living below the poverty line. Honduran society remains rife with economic inequality. Over 50 percent of the population is under the age of 19, with endemic poverty, chronic unemployment, and limited prospects pushing many into youth gangs that often control the poorer districts of many towns and cities.

2009 In June 2009, President Manuel Zelaya is overthrown in a coup, which pleased most Hondurans but led to widespread condemnation in world opinion. Zelaya's ouster comes after he attempts to emulate Hugo Chavez in Venezuela* and holds a referendum that would allow him to stay in office beyond January 2010. International demands for his return further divides public opinion in the country.

NICARAGUA

OFFICIAL NAME
República de Nicaragua (Spanish); Republic of Nicaragua (English)

POPULATION
5,811,200 (2009e)

INHABITANTS' NAME/NICKNAME
Nicaraguan(s); Pinolero(s)/Pinolera(s)

LANGUAGE/LANGUAGES
Spanish (official); English, Miskito, others

RELIGION/RELIGIONS
Roman Catholic, 72 percent; Evangelical, 16 percent; Moravian, 1.5 percent; other or no religion

NATIONAL FLAG
The flag has three equal horizontal stripes of blue, white, and blue, with the national coat of arms centered on the white. The colors are derived from the flag of the Federal Republic of Central America that gained independence from Spain in 1821, colors originally taken from the flag of Argentina*.

COAT OF ARMS/SEAL
The coat of arms consists of a central triangle depicting a blue sea around five volcanoes, a Phrygian cap on a pole against a pale blue sky and a rainbow. Around the triangle in a circle is the name of the country above and America Central (Central America) below. The triangle signifies equality, the rainbow signifies peace, the Phrygian cap symbolizes liberty, and the five volcanoes express the union and brotherhood of all five Central American countries.

CAPITAL CITY
Managua

TYPE OF GOVERNMENT
Presidential republic

NATIONAL EMBLEM
The Momotombo volcano that rises above the capital city, Managua

NATIONAL COLORS
Blue and white

NATIONAL ANTHEM
The anthem is based on a liturgical hymn of the 18th century brought to Nicaragua from Spain*. The lyrics were written and adopted in 1939.

> **Salve a Ti, Nicaragua (Spanish); Hail to Thee, Nicaragua (English)**
>
> Hail to thee, Nicaragua! On thy land roars the voice of the cannon no more, nor does the blood of brothers now stain thy glorious bicolor banner.
> Let peace shine beautiful in thy sky, and nothing dim thine immortal glory, for work is thy well-earned laurel and honor is thy triumphal emblem!

PATRON SAINT
Saint James the Greater

CURRENCY
Nicaraguan córdoba

INTERNET IDENTIFIER
.ni

VEHICLE IDENTIFICATION PLATES/STICKERS
NIC

PASSPORT

The passport cover has the name of the country in Spanish, the coat of arms, and the word *passport* in Spanish and English.

AIRLINE

TACA International Airlines, a grouping of five Central American national airlines

NATIONAL FLOWER

Sacuanjoche (May flower); frangipani (*Plumeria alba*)

NATIONAL TREE

Madroño

NATIONAL BIRD

Guardabarranco (turquoise-browed motmot)

NATIONAL RESOURCES

Natural resources include gold, silver, copper, tungsten, lead, zinc, timber, arable land, and fish. Nicaragua is primarily an agricultural country, but light industry, tourism, banking, mining, fisheries, and general commerce are expanding. Remittances from Nicaraguans living outside the country are an important source of foreign currency and investment.

FOODS

Gallo pinto is the national dish, a mixture of red beans and rice, often served with meat or fish. Other national specialties include *nacatamal*, cornmeal dough filled with pork or chicken, rice, tomatoes, onions, sweet peppers, and spices, then wrapped in plantain leaves and boiled; *indio viejo*, shredded meat with onions, garlic, sweet peppers, and tomato; *sopa de albondigas*, meatball soup; *rosquillas*, biscuits made of cornmeal and cheese; and *rondon*, from the Bluefields area on the east coast, a dish of turtle meat, fish, or pork, sweet peppers, chilies, bananas, yucca, and spices.

SPORTS/SPORTS TEAMS

Baseball is the most popular sport and is considered the national sport. Boxing is also very popular. Nicaragua national teams participate in many sports at an international level.

TEAM SPORTS

Baseball

Nicaragua Baseball Team; Nicaragua Women's Softball Team; Nicaragua Softball Team

Basketball

Nicaragua Basketball Team; Nicaragua Women's Basketball Team

Football

Nicaragua Football Team, nicknames La Azul y Blanco (the Blue and White), Los Pinoleros (the Nicaraguans), or Albiazules; Nicaragua Women's Football Team, nicknames La Azul y Blanco (the Blue and White), Las Pinoleras (the Nicaraguans); Nicaragua Under-19 Football Team; Nicaragua Under-19 Football Team; Nicaragua Women's Under-19 Football Team; Nicaragua Futsal Team

Racing

Nicaragua Speedway Team

Table Tennis

Nicaragua Table Tennis Team

Tennis

Nicaragua Davis Cup Team; Nicaragua Fed Cup Team

Volleyball

Nicaragua Men's Volleyball Team; Nicaragua Women's Volleyball Team

INDIVIDUAL SPORTS

Nicaragua Amateur Boxing Team; Nicaragua Athletics Team; Nicaragua Canoeing Team;

Nicaragua Cycling Team; Nicaragua Fencing Team; Nicaragua Judo Team; Nicaragua Karate Team: Nicaragua Rowing Team; Nicaragua Shooting Team; Nicaragua Swim Team; Nicaragua Tae Kwon Do Team; Nicaragua Weight Lifting Team; Nicaragua Wrestling Team

NATIONAL HEROES OR PERSONIFICATIONS

Augusto César Sandino, revolutionary leader in the 1930s and the inspiration of modern Nicaragua; Dora Maria Téllez, a historian and revolutionary leader; Ajax Delgado, a student activist murdered during the Somoza dictatorship in the 1950s; Tomás Borge Martinez, revolutionary leader; Benjamin Zeledón, leader of the resistance to American occupation in 1912

NATIONAL HOLIDAY/INDEPENDENCE DAY

Independence Day, September 15

FESTIVALS/FAIRS

Palo de Mayo Festival, May; Santo Domingo Festival, August; Santiago Festival, July; La Gritería, December; La Purísima, December.

SIGNIFICANT EVENTS IN FORMATION OF NATIONAL IDENTITY

4000 B.C.E. Ancient Amerindian peoples occupy the region, which becomes a crossroads between the Mesoamerican and Andean cultural regions.

1500 C.E.–1502 C.E. Western Nicaragua is organized into several small kingdoms influenced by the Maya people to the north. Most of the population is made up of farmers living in towns. The Caribbean coast is populated by less sedentary tribes. Christopher Columbus reaches the Caribbean coast.

1520–1800 The first Spanish explorers sack the richer tribes of the highlands for gold and jewels until driven out by indigenous warriors resisting Spanish brutality. Permanent settlements are established by the Spanish. Forced conversions to Catholicism, slavery, and diseases devastate the population, which drops from an estimated 1 million to just a few tens of thousands in the first century of Spanish rule.

1821–1838 Nicaragua and the other Central American colonies declare independence as the Federal Republic of Central America. Nicaragua becomes a separate republic.

1855–1865 Nicaraguan conservatives, under pressure from liberalizing elements, hire an American filibuster, or adventurer, William Walker, who arrives at the head of a small army. He takes control of Nicaragua and seeks annexation to the United States*, which is rejected. He is overthrown and is executed.

1907–1925 The United States begins to interfere in Nicaraguan affairs after two American mercenaries are shot on government orders. U.S. forces occupy the country and impose a puppet government, which grants the United States the right to build a canal across Nicaraguan territory. Guerrilla war breaks out. U.S. troops are withdrawn, leaving the country in civil war, but soon return to restore order.

1925–1936 Augusto Sandino leads a guerrilla army against the conservatives and the U.S. forces. The Americans evacuate the country but bankroll the dictatorship of Anastasio Somoza. The brutal Somoza dynasty rules Nicaragua for over 43 years.

1972–1979 A devastating earthquake destroys Managua during an economic crisis. Anti-Somoza guerrillas, the Sandinista National Liberation Front (FSLN), launch a war against the Somoza dictatorship. Somoza resigns and flees to the United States.

1979–1985 The Sandinista government implements many social programs, with gains in literacy, health care, education and, land reform. The U.S. administration begins funding the Contra War to undermine the leftist Sandinistas. The war costs over 60,000 lives and devastates the country. The Iran-Contra affair, in direct violation of U.S. laws, involves illegal funds to the Contra soldiers.

1990–2008 A more moderate government brings an end to the civil war but also revokes many of the social programs and land distribution of the Sandinista era. The Sandinista candidate, Daniel Ortega, the ex-president from the 1980s, returns to office. The parliament approves a new bill that bans abortion, including in cases when the mother's life is at risk. The government fosters closer ties to the more radical leftist governments of Latin America, particularly Cuba* and Venezuela*.

PANAMA

OFFICIAL NAME
República de Panamá (Spanish); Republic of Panama (English)

POPULATION
3,465,100 (2009e)

INHABITANTS' NAME/NICKNAME
Panamanian(s)

LANGUAGE/LANGUAGES
Spanish (official); English, others

RELIGION/RELIGIONS
Roman Catholic, 79 percent; Protestant, 12 percent; Baha'i, Buddhist, Greek Orthodox, Jewish, Hindu, other or no religion

NATIONAL FLAG
The flag consists of a divided rectangle of four quadrants; the upper hoist is white with a five-pointed blue star; the upper fly is red; the lower hoist is blue; and the lower fly is white with a red five-pointed star. The blue and red stand for the two rival political parties, and white symbolizes the peace in which they operate.

COAT OF ARMS/SEAL
The coat of arms consists of a centered shield or crest. The center section of the shield depicts the Isthmus of Panama. The top left has a field of silver with a crossed sword and a rifle. The other has a red field with crossed mining tools. The lower part of the shield is also divided with a blue field showing a cornucopia and a white field with a gold flying coin. Around the shield are two draped national flags. Above the shield are nine gold stars and a brown eagle holding a banner in its beak, inscribed with the national motto. The whole rests on a green field representing the country's abundant vegetation.

MOTTO
Pro mundi beneficio (Latin); For the benefit of the world (English)

CAPITAL CITY
Panama City

TYPE OF GOVERNMENT
Republic

NATIONAL EMBLEM
The Panama Canal

NATIONAL COLORS
Red and white

NATIONAL ANTHEM
The anthem was performed at independence in 1903 to celebrate the Panama Canal and was adopted as the national anthem in 1925.

Himno Istemño (Spanish); Isthmus Hymn (English)

At last we reached victory
In the joyous field of the union;
With ardent fires of glory
A new nation is alight.
It is necessary to cover with a veil
The past times of Calvary and cross;
Let now the blue skies be adorned with
The splendid light of the concord.

Progress now caresses your path.
To the rhythm of a sublime song,
You see both your seas roar at your feet
Giving you a path to your noble mission.

Chorus

In your soil covered with flowers
To the kisses of the warm earth,
Warrior roars have ceased;
Only fraternal love reigns.

Ahead the shovel and pick,
At work without any more delay,
and we will be as such at work and gala
of this fruitful world of Columbus.

PATRON SAINT

Immaculate Conception; Immaculate Heart of Mary; Mary of La Antigua

CURRENCY

Panamanian balboa; U.S. dollar

INTERNET IDENTIFIER

.pa

VEHICLE IDENTIFICATION PLATES/STICKERS

PA

PASSPORT

The passport cover has the name of the country in Spanish, the coat of arms, and the word *passport* in Spanish.

AIRLINE

Copa Airlines

NATIONAL FLOWER

La flor del espiritu santo (Holy Spirit orchid)

NATIONAL TREE

Panama tree

NATIONAL BIRD

Harpy eagle

NATIONAL RESOURCES

Natural resources include copper, mahogany forests, shrimp, and hydropower. Panama's dollarized economy rests primarily on a well-developed services sector that includes operation of the Panama Canal, banking, the Colon Free Zone, insurance, container ports, flagship registry, and tourism.

FOODS

Sancocho, a stew of meat and vegetables, is considered the national dish. National specialties include *ceviche*, fish marinated in lime juice, onions, and peppers; *patacones de plátano*, fried plantains; tamales, minced meat wrapped in corn flour dough and then banana leaves for cooking; empanadas, small pastries filled with meat, chicken, fish, or cheese; *tamal de olla*, a pork or chicken dish with cornmeal dumplings, vegetables, olives, and raisins; and *carimañola*, a torpedo-shaped yucca fritter stuffed with seasoned meat and fried.

SPORTS/SPORTS TEAMS

Association football (soccer) and baseball are the most popular sports. Panama national teams participate in many sports at an international level.

TEAM SPORTS

Badminton

Panama Badminton Team

Baseball

Panama Baseball Team; Panama Softball Team

Basketball

Panama Basketball Team; Panama Women's Basketball Team

Football

Panama Football Team, nicknames La Marea Roja (the Red Tide) or Los Canaleros (the Canal Boys); Panama Women's Football Team, nicknames La Marea Roja (the Red Tide) or Las Canaleras (the Canal Girls);

Panama Under-20 Football Team; Panama Women's Under-19 Football Team; Panama Rugby Union Team; Panama Futsal Team

Handball

Panama Handball Team

Hockey

Panama Field Hockey Team

Racing

Panama Speedway Team

Table Tennis

Panama Table Tennis Team

Tennis

Panama Davis Cup Team; Panama Fed Cup Team

Volleyball

Panama Men's Volleyball Team; Panama Women's Volleyball Team

INDIVIDUAL SPORTS

Panama Archery Team; Panama Amateur Boxing Team; Panama Athletics Team; Panama Canoeing Team; Panama Cycling Team; Panama Equestrian Team; Panama Fencing Team; Panama Gymnastics Team; Panama Judo Team; Panama Modern Pentathlon Team; Panama Rowing Team; Panama Shooting Team; Panama Swim Team; Panama Tae Kwon Do Team; Panama Triathlon Team; Panama Weight Lifting Team; Panama Wrestling Team

NATIONAL HEROES OR PERSONIFICATIONS

Vasco Nunez de Balboa, the first European to encounter the Pacific Ocean on the west coast of the American continent; Tomás de Herrera, the leader of the republican movement in the 19th century; Justo Arosemana, leader of the national movement in the 19th century; Omar Torrijos Herrera, who successfully ne-

gotiated the Panama Canal treaties with the United States in 1979

NATIONAL HOLIDAY/INDEPENDENCE DAY

Independence Day, November 3

FESTIVALS/FAIRS

Panama Jazz Festival, January–February; Casco Viejo Performing Arts Festival, March–April; 1,000 Polleras Festival, September; Black Christ Festival, October.

SIGNIFICANT EVENTS IN FORMATION OF NATIONAL IDENTITY

2000 B.C.E.–1500 C.E. The region is settled by various tribal groups. Influences from both Mesoamerica and the Andean cultural region lead to the creation of advanced cultures.

1502–1514 Spanish mariners and explorers visit the isthmus region. Vasco Nunez de Balboa crosses to the west coast to claim the entire Pacific Ocean for Spain. A flotilla of Spanish settlers arrives. Typhoid and other European diseases devastate the indigenous population.

1530–1650 Panama, guarding the Isthmus of Panama, becomes an important strategic and economic center. Treasure galleons from Manila or Peru* transship their cargos across the narrow spit of land to ships waiting on the east coast. The few indigenous people to survive the many diseases, massacres, and slavery flee into the forests. Slaves imported from Africa replace them.

1698 Scotland* attempts to establish a colony at Darien, but it fails, leaving the Spanish in control of the entire region.

1717 Panama forms part of the Viceroyalty of New Granada, along with present Colombia*, Ecuador*, and Venezuela*.

1810 The overthrow of the Spanish king by Napoleon begins the separation of the American colonies from Spain*.

1815–1821 Simón Bolivar excludes Panama from his planned republic in northern South America. The first printing press arrives in the colony. Panama's attempts to follow other Spanish colonies to independence from Spain divide the colony, which ultimately joins Colombia.

1840 Nationalists declare the independence of the Free State of the Isthmus but are put down by Colombian troops.

1850s–1880s The United States is involved in the building of the first railway across the isthmus. France* makes a failed attempt to build a canal to link the Atlantic and the Pacific.

1902–1903 The United States urges and supports Panamanian separatists. Separation from Colombia and independence are proclaimed. The United States receives the right to construct a canal and to control it for nearly a century.

1904–1915 The United States builds the Panama Canal that finally links the two great oceans. Panama becomes a United States protectorate and is controlled by a commercial oligarchy.

1939 The protectorate status is ended.

1950s–1960s The military begins to challenge the oligarchy's control of Panama. Rioting breaks out against U.S. control of the canal. The government remains an unstable succession of coalitions and coups.

1979 Omar Torrijos signs treaties with the United States that begin the process of transferring control of the canal to Panama.

1980–1989 General Manuel Noriega creates a military dictatorship accused of drug trafficking. Noriega runs for president, then annuls the results when the opposition candidate wins. The United States invades Panama, and Noriega is overthrown.

1989–2008 The democratically elected president takes office and begins to rebuild democracy in Panama. Subsequent governments curb the power of the military, support government transparency, and attempt to end official corruption. Economic growth will be bolstered by the Panama Canal expansion project that begins in 2007 and is expected be completed by 2014. Former president Manuel Noriega is released from a Florida prison in September 2008.

2009 Panama becomes a major banking and investment center in the Americas. The global economic slowdown threatens the country's new prosperity.

PARAGUAY

OFFICIAL NAME

República del Paraguay (Spanish); Tetã Paraguái (Guarani); Republic of Paraguay (English)

POPULATION

6,543,700 (2009e)

INHABITANTS' NAME/NICKNAME

Paraguayan(s)

LANGUAGE/LANGUAGES

Spanish, Guarani (official); Portuguese, others

RELIGION/RELIGIONS

Roman Catholic, 89 percent; Protestant, 7 percent; other or no religion

NATIONAL FLAG

The flag is a horizontal tricolor of red, white, and blue, with the national coat of arms centered on the white; on the reverse side is the seal of the national treasury. The red, white and blue come from the French tricolor, which became a symbol of liberty in the Spanish colonies.

COAT OF ARMS/SEAL

The coat of arms is a circle with a central blue disk charged with a yellow five-pointed star. A green olive branch on one side and a green palm branch on the other surround the disk. Around the wreath is a red circle inscribed with the name of the country in yellow, and around the red is a white circle with a black outline.

MOTTO

Paz y justicia (Spanish); Peace and Justice (English)

CAPITAL CITY
Asunción

TYPE OF GOVERNMENT
Constitutional republic

NATIONAL COLORS
Red, white, and blue

NATIONAL ANTHEM
The anthem was adopted in 1846, but was only declared the official national anthem in 1934. The coat of arms has been changed a number of times so that the description of the emblem in the national anthem refers to a 19th-century version.

Paraguayos, Républica o Muerte! (Spanish); Paraguayans, the Republic or Death! (English)

For three centuries a reign oppressed
The unhappy peoples of America,
But one day, their anger aroused, they said:
"An end to this!" and broke the reign.
Our forefathers, fighting magnificently,
Displayed their martial glory,
And when the august diadem was shattered,
They raised the triumphal cap of liberty.

Chorus

Paraguayans, republic or death!
It was our strength that gave us our final
  liberty.
Neither tyrants nor slaves can continue,
Where unity and equality reign,
Where unity and equality reign.

A new Rome, the fatherland shall proudly
  display
Two leaders of name and valor
Who, rivals, like Romulus and Remus
Divided government and power.
Long years, during which Phoebus in the
  clouds
Saw darken the pearl of the south,
Today a grand hero appears
Raising up again her glory and virtue . . .

Chorus

Europe and the world salute her with
  applause
And also acclaim
Invincible bastion of heroism,
Magnificent Eden of riches.
(But) when discord rumbled all around
Which fatally devoured other peoples,
Paraguayans, the sacred ground
Was covered by an angel with its wings.

Chorus

Oh, how pure, of laurel girded
Sweet Fatherland, in this manner you show
  yourself.
In your ensign one sees the colors
Of sapphire, diamond, and ruby.
In your coat of arms, which the sun
  illuminates,
Under the cap, one sees the lion.
Double image of the strong and the free,
And of glories, the memory and crest.

Chorus

From the tomb of vile feudalism
The national deity rises free;
Oppressors, bend your knees!
Compatriots, intone the hymn!
Sound the cry, "Republic or death"!
Our breasts exhale it with faith,
And the mountains repeat its echoes
Like giants arising.

Chorus

Our fatherland defends liberty and justice;
Tyrants: Listen!
The laws in its sacred charter
Will sustain its heroism in the fight.
Against the world, if the world opposes it,
If the world dares to insult her security,
Battling to avenge we shall know her
Or die embracing her.

Chorus

Arise, O people, your splendid sword
That strikes with sparkles of God,
There is no middle ground between free or
  slave

And an abyss divides the two.
In the gentle breezes the hymn resounds,
Repeating with triumphal echo:
For the free, renowned glory!
For the fatherland, immortal laurel!

PATRON SAINT

Our Lady of the Assumption; Our Lady of Lujan; San Blas

CURRENCY

Paraguayan guarani

INTERNET IDENTIFIER

.py

VEHICLE IDENTIFICATION PLATES/ STICKERS

PY

PASSPORT

The passport cover has the name of the regional group, Mercosur, the name of the country in Spanish and Guarani, the coat of arms, and the word *passport* in Spanish and Guarani.

AIRLINES

TAM Airlines; Regional

NATIONAL ANIMAL

Yacare (crocodile)

NATIONAL BIRD

Guyra campana (bare-throated bellbird)

NATIONAL FISH

Surubí (Paraguay catfish; unofficial)

NATIONAL RESOURCES

Natural resources include hydropower, timber, iron ore, manganese, and limestone. Landlocked Paraguay has a market economy marked by a large informal sector, including the activities of thousands of microenterprises and urban street vendors. Because of the importance of the informal sector, accurate economic measures are difficult to obtain. Tourism, supported by historic cities, colonial monuments, and a unique culture, is of growing importance.

FOODS

Sopa paraguaya, a soup of mashed corn, cheese, milk, and onions, is considered the national dish. Other national specialties include *chipa,* a bagel-like corn bread flavored with egg and cheese; *soo-yosopy,* a soup of cornmeal and ground beef; *ensalada de palmitos,* a salad of lettuce and hearts of palm; *boribori,* beef soup with dumplings; *so'o ku'i,* a casserole of beef and rice; and *milanesa,* a breaded and fried thin beef steak.

SPORTS/SPORTS TEAMS

Association football (soccer) is the most popular sport. Paraguay national teams participate in many sports at an international level.

TEAM SPORTS

Basketball

Paraguay Basketball Team; Paraguay Women's Basketball Team

Football

Paraguay Football Team, nicknames the Guaranis, La Garra Guarani, or La Albirroja (the White and Red); Paraguay Women's Football Team, nickname La Albirroja (the White and Red); Paraguay Rugby Union Team, nickname Los Yacarés (the Alligators); Paraguay Women's Rugby Union Team, nickname Las Yacarés (the Alligators); Paraguay Futsal Team; Paraguay Beach Soccer Team; Paraguay Futsal Team

Handball

Paraguay Handball Team

Hockey
Paraguay Field Hockey Team

Racing
Paraguay Speedway Team

Table Tennis
Paraguay Table Tennis Team

Tennis
Paraguay Davis Cup Team; Paraguay Fed Cup Team

Volleyball
Paraguay Men's Volleyball Team; Paraguay Women's Volleyball Team

INDIVIDUAL SPORTS
Paraguay Aikido Team; Paraguay Amateur Boxing Team; Paraguay Archery Team; Paraguay Athletics Team; Paraguay Cycling Team; Paraguay Equestrian Team; Paraguay Fencing Team; Paraguay Gymnastics Team; Paraguay Judo Team; Paraguay Karate Team: Paraguay Modern Pentathlon Team; Paraguay Rowing Team; Paraguay Sailing Team; Paraguay Shooting Team; Paraguay Swim Team; Paraguay Tae Kwon Do Team; Paraguay Triathlon Team; Paraguay Weight Lifting Team; Paraguay Wrestling Team

NATIONAL HEROES OR PERSONIFICATIONS
José Gaspar Rodríguez de Francia, first leader of independent Paraguay in the 19th century; Francisco Solano Lopez, the president of Paraguay who died defending the country during the War of the Triple Alliance; José Félix Estigarribia, military leader during the Chaco War and later president of Paraguay; Luis Alberto de Paraná, considered Paraguay's national singer

NATIONAL HOLIDAY/INDEPENDENCE DAY
Independence Day, May 15

FESTIVALS/FAIRS
Carnival, February–March: Cerro Corá, March; San Juan Festival, June; Festival del Nanduti, July; Festival of San Juan, June; Alarcitas Handicrafts Fair, May

SIGNIFICANT EVENTS IN FORMATION OF NATIONAL IDENTITY

1000 C.E. Seminomadic Guarani tribes are avoided by neighboring peoples because of their fierce warrior tradition. They practice a mythical polytheistic religion, which would later blend with Christianity.

1537 Spanish explorers move up the Paraguay River to found a settlement at Asunción, which becomes a center for settlement of the plains region.

1540–1700 The region forms part of the Spanish territory of Río de Plata, governed from Buenos Aires. Spanish adventurers and prospectors take Guarani wives, beginning the distinct Paraguayan nationality. Over the next decades, pure Guaranis disappear as diseases and forced labor ravage the population. Jesuits arrive in 1550 to undertake a major mission-building project.

1720 Guarani warriors from the Jesuit missions defeat a revolt by the prosperous elite against the colonial government.

1810–1811 The Spanish monarchy is overthrown by Napoleon in Europe giving the Spanish colonies an opportunity. Local leaders declare Paraguay independent of Spain*.

1862 Argentina*, Brazil*, and Uruguay*, known as the Trible Alliance, declare war on Paraguay, which is accused of undermining regional stability. The Paraguayans, led by President Francisco Solano Lopez, are finally defeated, and the president is killed in 1870. The war leaves only 10 percent of the male population of the country alive.

1878 U.S. President Rutherford B. Hayes is called upon to arbitrate a dispute between Paraguay and Argentina over the Chaco, a grasslands region the size of Colorado. He rules in favor of Paraguay and becomes a national hero.

1928–1938 Clashes with Bolivian troops in the Chaco region lead to the Chaco War for access to the Paraguay River and, therefore, to the Atlantic Ocean. The Paraguayans are victorious, and the disputed region becomes part of the national territory.

1947–1951 The Colorado Party comes to power. A failed military revolt leaves over 8,000 people dead. Alfredo Stroessner is chosen as head of the army.

1954–1989 Stroessner becomes dictator and rules the country for 35 years. His rule is marked by brutality, nepotism, and corruption, but his anticommunist stance wins support from the United States*. He is overthrown in a military coup in 1989.

1991 Paraguay and other southern countries of South America form a common market known as Mercosur.

1993–1998 The country holds its first elections in 50 years. A democratic system is established. In 1998, the country is listed by Freedom House as having one of the murkiest political systems in the world.

2000–2009 Political unrest and instability continue to disrupt the country. The Paraguayans celebrate their heritage. Although little trace is left of the original Guarani culture, the language survives and is spoken by about 90 percent of the population as a second national language.

PERU

OFFICIAL NAME
República del Perú (Spanish); Republic of Peru (English)

POPULATION
28,649,200 (2009e)

INHABITANTS' NAME/NICKNAME
Peruvian(s)

LANGUAGE/LANGUAGES
Spanish (official); Quechua, Aymara, and other indigenous languages are recognized as co-official languages in areas where they predominate.

RELIGION/RELIGIONS
Roman Catholic, 81 percent; Protestant, 3 percent; others or no religion

NATIONAL FLAG
The flag has three equal vertical stripes of red, white, and red. The colors symbolize the Incas and their lasting impact on Peru. Red and white were also the colors of José de San Martin, known in Peru as "the Liberator." The official state flag has the national coat of arms centered on the white stripe.

COAT OF ARMS/SEAL
The coat of arms has a central crest divided into three parts. The top left depicts a vicuña on a pale blue field, the top right depicts a cinchona tree on white, and the lower half depicts a gold cornucopia spilling gold coins on a red background. Above the crest is a green wreath of holm oak known as the Civic Crown. Four national flags are draped behind the crest. The vicuña represents the fauna of Peru; the cinchona tree, the source of quinine, represents the flora; and the cornucopia represents the mineral wealth of the country.

CAPITAL CITY
Lima

TYPE OF GOVERNMENT
Presidential republic

NATIONAL EMBLEM
Machu Picchu, the lost city of the Incas

NATIONAL COLORS
Red and white

NATIONAL ANTHEM
The anthem was chosen from the entrants to a national contest soon after independence in 1821.

**Somos Libres, Seámosio Siempre (Spanish);
We are Free, May We Always Be So (English)**

Chorus

We are free, may we always be so,
and let the sun rather deny its light
Than allow us to break the solemn vow
which the motherland elevated to the eternal.

For a long time the oppressed Peruvian
dragged the ominous chain;
sentenced to a cruel servitude
for a long time in silence he moaned.
But as soon as the sacred cry of
"Liberty!" was heard on its coasts,
he shook off the indolence of slavery,
he raised the humiliated neck.

Already the roar of rough chains
that we had heard for three centuries of
  horror
from the free, at the sacred cry
that the world heard astonished, ceased.
Everywhere the inflamed San Martin
"Liberty," "Liberty" pronounced;
and the Andes, rocking their base,
announced it as well, in unison.

With its influence the peoples woke up,
and like lighting ran the opinion;
from the Isthmus to Tierra del Fuego,
and from Tierra del Fuego to the icy region.
Everyone vowed to break the link
that nature denied to both worlds,
and break the scepter that Spain
had laid, proud, on both.

Lima fulfilled this solemn promise,
and, severe, her anger showed
by throwing out the powerless tyrant,
who had been trying to extend his oppression.
On her endeavor the shackles cracked,
and the furrows that she had repaired in
  herself
stirred up her hatred and vengeance,
inherited from her Inca and lord.

Countrymen, may we see her a slave no more.
If for three centuries she moaned, humiliated,
forever may we vow that she be free,
maintaining her own splendor.

Our arms, until today unarmed,
be they always readying the cannon,
that some day the beaches of Iberia
will feel the horror of its roar.

On its summit may the Andes sustain
the two-color flag or standard,
may it announce to the centuries the effort
that gave us being free forever.
Under its shadow may we live calmly
and, at the sun's birth over its summits,
may we renew the great oath
we rendered to the God of Jacob.

PATRON SAINT

Saint Joseph; Saint Rose of Lima

CURRENCY

Peruvian nuevo sol

INTERNET IDENTIFIER

.pe

**VEHICLE IDENTIFICATION PLATES/
STICKERS**

PE

PASSPORT

The passport cover has name of the regional group, Andean Community, in Spanish, the name of the country in Spanish, the coat of arms, and the word *passport* in Spanish and English.

AIRLINES

Air Perú; TACA Peru; LanPeru

NATIONAL FLOWER

Cantuta

NATIONAL TREE

Cinchona

NATIONAL ANIMAL

Vicuña

NATIONAL BIRD

Rupicola (Andean cock-of-the-rock)

NATIONAL RESOURCES

Natural resources include copper, silver, gold, petroleum, timber, fish, iron ore, coal, phosphate, potash, hydropower, and natural gas. The service sector now accounts for more than half the Peruvian economy. Historic cities, ancient monuments, unique cultures, sandy beaches, and a pleasant climate support a thriving tourist industry. Remittances from Peruvians living outside the country are an important source of foreign currency and investment.

FOODS

Ceviche, fresh fish marinated in lemon or lime juice and hot chili pepper, served with fried corn, sweet potatoes, and onions and flavored with coriander, is considered the national dish. National specialties include *chupe de camarones,* a chowder of shrimp, milk, eggs, potatoes, and peppers; *causa rellena,* potato cakes filled with minced chicken, avocado, or crabmeat; *humitas,* boiled cornmeal dumplings filled with minced or shredded meat and wrapped in banana leaves for cooking; *anticuchos,* skewered cubes of meat cooked over charcoal; and *mazamorra morada,* a dessert made of purple corn, sweet potato, dried fruits, cinnamon, and cloves.

SPORTS/SPORTS TEAMS

Association football (soccer) is the most popular sport. Martial arts sports, such as tae kwon do, are also popular. Peru national teams participate in many sports at a national level.

TEAM SPORTS

Badminton

Peru Badminton Team

Baseball

Peru Baseball Team; Peru Softball Team

Basketball

Peru Basketball Team; Peru Women's Basketball Team

Cricket

Peru Cricket Team

Football

Peru Football Team, nickname La Blanquirroja or La Rojiblanca (the White and Red or the Red and White); Peru Women's Football Team, nickname La Blanquirroja or La Rojiblanca (the White and Red or the Red and White); Peru Under-17 Football Team, nickname Jotitas; Peru Women's Under-19 Football Team; Peru Rugby Union Team, nickname Los Tumis; Peru Women's Rugby Union Team: Peru Rugby Union Team (Sevens), nickname Peru Sevens or 7s; Peru Beach Soccer Team

Hockey

Peru Field Hockey Team

Racing

Peru Speedway Team

Table Tennis

Peru Table Tennis Team

Tennis

Peru Fed Cup Team; Peru Davis Cup Team

Volleyball

Peru Men's Volleyball Team; Peru Women's Volleyball Team

INDIVIDUAL SPORTS

Peru Amateur Boxing Team; Peru Archery Team; Peru Athletics Team; Peru Cycling Team; Peru Equestrian Team; Peru Fencing Team; Peru Gymnastics Team; Peru Judo Team; Peru Karate Team: Peru Modern Pentathlon Team; Peru Rowing Team; Peru

Sailing Team; Peru Shooting Team; Peru Swim Team; Peru Tae Kwon Do Team; Peru Triathlon Team; Peru Weight Lifting Team; Peru Wrestling Team

National Heroes or Personifications

Chalán, referring to the rider of a Peruvian paso horse, is used as a personification of Peru, as is Patría, meaning motherland.

Atahualpa, the last emperor of the Inca Empire, executed by the Spanish conquerors; Túpac Amaru, the last Inca ruler executed by the Spanish conquerors; Túpac Amaru II, leader of an uprising against Spanish rule in 1780; José de San Martin, called the Liberator, who led the independence movement in Spanish America; Simón Bolivar, leader of the struggle for independence from Spain*; Miguel Grau, a naval hero in the war with Chile* in the late 19th century

National Holiday/Independence Day

Independence Day, July 28

Festivals/Fairs

Festival of the Negritos, December–January; Carnival, February–March; Grape Festival, March; Festival of the Crosses, May; Ndo Edn Dari Festival, June; Quillabamba Festival, July; Exposur Fair, August; International Spring Festival, September–October

Significant Events in Formation of National Identity

3000 b.c.e.–1800 b.c.e. Complex societies emerge and flourish, with large cities, temple compounds, roads, and other constructions.

13th century–16th century The last of the great indigenous civilizations, the Incas, becomes a great empire, the largest in pre-Columbian America, stretching from present Colombia* into Argentina*. The society is based on agriculture, using advanced irrigation and terracing. Husbandry and fishing are also important.

1520–1532 Drawn by rumors of gold, the Spanish equip an expedition led by Francisco Pizarro. The expedition arrives during a civil war and conquers the empire. The last emperor, known as the Inca, is executed. Peru becomes a Spanish colony, with Lima designated the capital of Spanish America. Diseases, slavery, and brutality devastate the indigenous population.

1780 The indigenous peoples, suppressed and mistreated, rebel against Spanish rule led by a descendent of the Incas, Túpac Amaru II.

1810–1826 The Spanish kings is overthrown by Napoleon, beginning the disintegration of the Spanish Empire. José de San Martin invades Peru to defeat the Spanish forces in 1820. Peru is declared an independent republic in 1821.

1879 Disputes over coastal provinces lead to war with Chile and Bolivia* in the War of the Pacific. Chilean forces occupy Lima following the Peruvian defeat. Peru loses the provinces of Tacna, Arica, and Tarapacá.

1911 The lost city of the Incas, Machu Picchu, is discovered.

1929 Chile returns the province of Tacna to Peruvian control.

1948–1960 A military coup overthrows the government. Free elections are allowed in 1956. In 1960, the indigenous population finally returns to the estimated 12 million people residing in the region under Inca rule.

1975–1980 Quechua, the language of the Inca, is made an official language, along with Spanish. A new constitution ensures that freely elected governments will govern Peru.

1983 A weather phenomenon called El Niño causes widespread flooding in some provinces and drought in others, severely disrupting the country.

1998 Peru and Ecuador* sign a treaty that resolves their 57-year border dispute.

2000 Alberto Fujimori, president since 1990, is forced to resign over accusations of authoritarianism, corruption, and human-rights abuses. He flees the country for Japan*. A new government attempts to end official corruption.

2002–2009 Explorers find the remains of Inca towns lost for more than four centuries. Despite economic advances in recent years, over half the population still lives in poverty.

SANTA CRUZ

OFFICIAL NAME
Departamento de Santa Cruz de la Sierra (Spanish); Department of Santa Cruz de la Sierra (English). Santa Cruz declared autonomy and established an autonomous government in 2008.

POPULATION
2,675,900 (2009e)

INHABITANTS' NAME/NICKNAME
Cruceño/Cruceña; Camba(s)

LANGUAGE/LANGUAGES
Spanish, Guarani (both official); Portuguese, others

RELIGION/RELIGIONS
Roman Catholic, Protestant, others

NATIONAL FLAG
The official departmental flag and the flag of Cruceño nationalism has three equal horizontal stripes of green, white, and green. The flag is based on the colors of a regional movement that appeared in 1864. It was resurrected in 1980 as the flag of the antigovernment movement and was adopted as the official flag of the department.

COAT OF ARMS/SEAL
The coat of arms is a crest or shield divided into quarters by a red cross, symbolizing the predominance of the church. The first quadrant depicts three palm trees, the second a tree in natural colors, the third two crossed red crosses and the fourth a lion. Above the shield is a gold crown, symbolizing the sovereignty of Santa Cruz.

MOTTO
¡Arriba cruceños, hagamos historia! (Spanish); Stand up, Cruceños, let's make history! (English)

CAPITAL CITY
Santa Cruz de la Sierra

TYPE OF GOVERNMENT
Departmental government within Bolivia

NATIONAL EMBLEM
Red colonial cross (on the coat of arms)

NATIONAL COLORS
Green and white

NATIONAL ANTHEM
The anthem is the official anthem of the Department of Santa Cruz and has become the unofficial anthem of the autonomy movement. An English translation is not available.

> **Bajo el Cielo Más Puro de América (Spanish); Under the Clearest Sky in the Americas (English)**
>
> Bajo el cielo más puro de América
> y en la tierra de Ñuflo de Chávez,
> ¡Libertad! van trinando las aves
> de su veste ostentando el primor.
>
> De las flores el mundo galano,
> su ambrosía perfumada ofreciendo,
> ¡Libertad, libertad! van diciendo
> en efluvios de paz y de amor.
>
> **Coro (Chorus)**
>
> La España grandiosa,
> con hado benigno,
> aquí plantó el signo
> de la Redención.

Y surgió a su sombra
un pueblo eminente,
de límpida frente,
de leal corazón.

De entusiasmo y de fe rebosante,
venga el hombre y repita ese coro,
que en el suelo del "árbol del oro"
siempre libre y feliz ha de ser.

Que Natura, en transportes de Diosa,
abrir quiso con pródiga mano
en el suelo oriental boliviano
sus mil fuentes de gloria y poder.

Siempre libres, cruceños, seamos,
cual lo son nuestras aves y flores,
y sepamos vencer los rigores
del que intente a la Patria oprimir.

Nuestro nombre, en tal hora, con sangre
en la historia dejemos inscrito,
repitiendo de Warnes el grito:
"¡A vencer o con gloria morir!"

PATRON SAINT
Sacred Heart of Jesus

CURRENCY
Bolivian boliviano

INTERNET IDENTIFIER
.bo Bolivia

VEHICLE IDENTIFICATION PLATES/ STICKERS
BO Bolivia (official); SC Santa Cruz (unofficial)

PASSPORT
Cruceños are Bolivian citizens and travel on Bolivian passports.

AIRLINE
AeroSur

NATIONAL FLOWER
Amazon water lily (unofficial)

NATIONAL TREE
Urunday (unofficial)

NATIONAL ANIMAL
Oso perezoso (three-toed tree sloth) (unofficial)

NATIONAL BIRD
Toco toucan (unofficial)

NATIONAL RESOURCES
Natural resources include natural gas, iron, magnesium, and arable land. Forests, agriculture and animal husbandry, and cattle ranching are the main industries; others are timber, mining, and exploration for oil and natural gas. Tourism has not been promoted as actively as in western Andean Bolivia, which is surprising, given an array of attractions, the pleasant climate, and the hospitality of the Cruceños, who are playfully known as *cambas* (a Guarani word meaning "friend").

FOODS
Typical dishes include *picante de pollo*, chicken in a spicy sauce served with rice and yucca; *majao*, a rice dish with dried meat, duck, or chicken; *lorco de gallina*, a rice-based chowder of vegetables and chicken spiced with onions, garlic, and oregano and eaten with a piece of boiled yucca; *sopa de mani*, a soup with a base of crushed and boiled peanuts; *masaco*, mashed plantains with *charqui*, a dried meat similar to jerky; *cuñape*, a type of bread made with yucca flour and cheese; *patasca*, a soup of pork and maize; small pastries called *zonzo*, small pastries filled with cheese and yucca; and empanadas (filled pastries) of cheese, rice, or meats. Typical drinks include *mocochinchi*, a refreshment made of sun dried peaches boiled with honey and cloves; *somó*, a drink made of white corn; and *chichi*, a nonalcoholic drink made of white corn and cinnamon.

Sports/Sports Teams

Association football (soccer) is the most popular sport in the region. Santa Cruz participates in football at a regional level.

Team Sports

Football

Club Deportivo Oriente Petrolero, nickname Refineros or Alviverdes, is considered the national football team.

National Heroes or Personifications

Ñuflo de Chávez, the founder of Santa Cruz in 1561; Antonio Vicente Seoane, leader of independent Santa Cruz in 1809; Antonio Suarez, military leader of the independence movement in the early 19th century

National Holiday/Independence Day

Efemerides de Santa Cruz, September 24

Festivals/Fairs

Carnival, February–March; Efemerides de Santa Cruz, September 24; Santa Cruz Festival, May

Significant Events in Formation of National Identity

1500 C.E. The region is sparsely settled by indigenous Guarani people, mostly farmers and hunters.

1521 Spanish explorers cross the region, but, finding little of interest, such as gold or silver, leave the area to the Guarani.

1561 Spanish colonists moving north from Paraguay* settle the region.

1776–1782 The Spanish authorities separate Santa Cruz from the ethnically distinct Andean region and add it to the Viceroyalty of La Plata, centered on Buenos Aires. It is organized as a separate province in 1782.

1809–1811 News of the overthrow of the Spanish monarchy by Napoleon initiates an open rebellion, one of the first in Latin America. Rebel leaders declare Santa Cruz an independent republic.

1825 The Cruceños join with the highlanders in the Andes to fight the Spanish. A new republic, named after Símon Bolivar, incorporates Santa Cruz.

1892–1921 Cultural and economic differences lead to Cruceño rebellions in 1892 and 1904 that are put down by troops sent from the highlands. The rebellion resumes in 1920, and independence is again proclaimed.

1935 During the Chaco War between Bolivia and Paraguay, the Cruceños again rebel and attempt to create a separate republic.

1950s The isolated region is connected to Brazil and its ports by a new Brazilian railroad that extends to Santa Cruz.

1995 Tensions between the poorer and less developed highlands and Santa Cruz, the country's most developed region, spur the growth of nationalism once again.

1995–2007 Demands for economic and political autonomy lead to violence and confrontations between the local leaders and the leftist government of Evo Morales.

2008 A referendum is held in Santa Cruz. Called illegal by the Bolivian government, it shows overwhelming support for autonomy. The other plains departments soon follow with their own referendums. A national referendum on a new constitution proposed by Evo Morales that would benefit the poorer western half of Bolivia is soundly defeated in the region but passes with the support of the indigenous population of the western highlands.

2009 Polls show support growing for a complete break with the Bolivian government and its support base in the western part of Bolivia. Many pro-independence groups support the idea of a separate republic in Los Llanos (the Plains), which would include the eastern provinces of Santa Cruz, Tarija, Beni, and Pando.

See also Bolivia

SURINAME

OFFICIAL NAME
Republiek Suriname (Dutch); Republic of Suriname (English)

POPULATION
518,600 (2009e)

INHABITANTS' NAME/NICKNAME
Surinamese

LANGUAGE/LANGUAGES
Dutch (official); English. In addition, Sranan Tongo, Hindi, Hindustani, Javanese, Hakka Cantonese, Boni, Saramaccan, Paramakan, Nyuka, Kwinti, Matawai, Cariban, Arawakan, Aluku, and Kalina are recognized regional languages.

RELIGION/RELIGIONS
Hindu, 27 percent; Protestant, 25 percent; Roman Catholic, 23 percent; Muslim, 20 percent; others or no religion

NATIONAL FLAG
The flag has five horizontal stripes of green (double width), white, red (quadruple width), white, and green (double width). The center red stripe is charged with a single large, yellow, five-pointed star, which represents the unity of all the country's ethnic groups. The yellow stands for a golden future, the red for progress and love, the green for hope and fertility, and the white for peace and justice.

COAT OF ARMS/SEAL
The coat of arms consists of a central oval divided vertically with a sailing ship on the left representing Suriname's history and a palm tree on the right representing the present and justice for all. In the center is a small green diamond with a yellow five-pointed star, representing the five continents that are the origins of Suriname's people. The oval is supported by two Amerindians in traditional dress holding bows. Below is a red banner with the country's motto in Latin.

MOTTO
Justitia—Pietas—Fides (Latin); Justice—Duty—Loyalty

CAPITAL CITY
Paramaribo

TYPE OF GOVERNMENT
Parliamentary republic

NATIONAL EMBLEM
A patchwork quilt, representing the many ethnic, religious, and national groups in Suriname

NATIONAL COLORS
Green and white

NATIONAL ANTHEM
The anthem was composed and written in the late 19th century with Dutch lyrics. Sranan Tongo lyrics were written before the anthem was adopted at independence in 1959. It now has two verses, the first in Dutch and the second in Sranan Tongo.

God Zij Met Ons Suriname! (Dutch); God Be With Our Suriname (English)

God be with our Suriname
May he elevate our lovely homeland
No matter how we came together
We are dedicated to its soil
Working we keep in mind
Justice and truth will set free
All that's good to do
Will give value to our land

Rise countrymen, rise
The soil of Suriname is calling you.
Wherever our ancestors came from
We should take care of our country.
We are not afraid to fight
God is our leader

Our whole life until our death,
We will fight for Suriname.

CURRENCY

Surinamese dollar

INTERNET IDENTIFIER

.sr

VEHICLE IDENTIFICATION PLATES/ STICKERS

SME

PASSPORT

The passport cover has the initials CC, Caribbean Community; the Dutch word for passport, *paspoort*; a thin horizontal line; the coat of arms; another thin horizontal line; and the name of the country in Dutch.

AIRLINE

Surinam Airways

NATIONAL FLOWER

Popokai tongo (parakeet flower)

NATIONAL TREE

Suriname cherry (unofficial)

NATIONAL RESOURCES

Natural resources include timber, hydropower, fish, kaolin, shrimp, bauxite, gold, and small amounts of nickel, copper, platinum, and iron ore. The economy of Suriname is dominated by the bauxite industry. Other main export products include rice and bananas. The small tourist industry is beginning to grow as the country's attractions become better known. Remittances from Surinamese living in the Netherlands* are a major source of foreign currency and investment.

FOODS

Moksi meti, various meats served on rice, is considered the national dish. Other local specialties include *rijsttafel,* of Indonesian origin, a combination of rice and many small meat and vegetable side dishes; *pom,* a Creole dish of chicken with ground taro; *pastei,* chicken pie with various vegetables; *roti,* a type of savory crepe or pancake filled with curried chicken and potatoes; *bravu,* a Creole soup made of okra; *saoto ajam,* a soup of Indonesian origin; and *pinda soup en tom tom,* a soup of Creole origin.

SPORTS/SPORTS TEAMS

Association football (soccer) is the most popular sport. Suriname national teams participate in many sports at an international level.

TEAM SPORTS

Badminton

Suriname Badminton Team

Basketball

Suriname Basketball Team; Suriname Women's Basketball Team

Cricket

Suriname Cricket Team

Football

Suriname Football Team nickname A-Selektie (the Team); Suriname Women's Football Team nickname A-Selektie (the Team); Suriname Futsal Team; Suriname Under-19 Football Team: Surinam Women's Under-19 Football Team

Korfball

Suriname Korfball Team

Table Tennis

Suriname Table Tennis Team

Tennis

Suriname Davis Cup Team; Suriname Fed Cup Team

Volleyball

Suriname Men's Volleyball Team; Suriname Women's Volleyball Team

INDIVIDUAL SPORTS

Suriname Amateur Boxing Team; Suriname Archery Team; Suriname Athletics Team; Suriname Canoeing Team; Suriname Judo Team; Suriname Shooting Team; Suriname Swim Team; Suriname Tae Kwon Do Team; Suriname Triathlon Team; Suriname Wrestling Team

NATIONAL HEROES OR PERSONIFICATIONS

Johan Ferrier, the first president of independent Suriname; Henck Arron, a leader of the independence movement

NATIONAL HOLIDAY/INDEPENDENCE DAY

Independence Day, November 25

FESTIVALS/FAIRS

Revolution Day celebrations, February; Phagwah (Hindu New Year), March; Independence Day celebration, November; Suriname Jazz Festival, October

SIGNIFICANT EVENTS IN FORMATION OF NATIONAL IDENTITY

1000 C.E. The region is inhabited by the Surinen, whose name would later be given to the country.

1498 Christopher Columbus sights the coast.

16th century The Surinen are driven from the territory by the arrival of aggressive Caribs. European exploration begins with Dutch, French, Spanish, and English expeditions.

1602–1667 The Dutch establish settlements on the coast. English planters and their slaves carve out coffee and sugar plantations in the interior. The English portion is ceded to Dutch rule in exchange for New Amsterdam, later called New York.

1863 Slavery is abolished. Indentured labor is imported from India*, Java, and China* to work the plantations.

1916 Bauxite mining begins and gradually becomes the major export.

1954 Suriname is granted full autonomy.

1975–1980 The country becomes an independent republic. More than a third of the total population immigrates to the Netherlands, due to economic hardships and political instability.

1980–1982 Military coups and ethnic tensions disrupt life in the country.

1986 An uprising by Creoles, the descendants of African slaves, intent on restoring order forces the closure of the bauxite mines.

2004–2008 A tribunal is created to rule on the border dispute with neighboring Guyana*. The United Nations tribunal divides the region, potentially oil-rich, between the two countries.

2009 Oil explorations begin in the potentially oil-rich maritime region of Suriname.

URUGUAY

OFFICIAL NAME

República Oriental del Uruguay (Spanish); Eastern Republic of Uruguay (English)

POPULATION

3.478,200 (2009e)

INHABITANTS' NAME/NICKNAME

Uruguayan(s); Orientale(s) (Easterner(s)); Charrúa(s)

LANGUAGE/LANGUAGES

Spanish (official); Italian, German, others

RELIGION/RELIGIONS

Roman Catholic, 66 percent; Protestant, 2 percent; Jewish, 1 percent; other or no religion

NATIONAL FLAG

The flag has nine equal horizontal stripes of white and blue with a square white canton on the upper hoist charged with the Sun of May,

Abkhazia

Aceh

Afghanistan

Åland Islands

Albania

Algeria

Ambazania

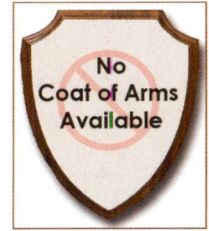

American Samoa

Andorra

Angola

Anguilla

Antigua and Barbuda

Argentina

Armenia

Aruba

Australia

Austria

Azerbaijan

Azores

Bahamas

Bahrain

Bangladesh

Barbados

Bashkortostan

Bavaria

Belarus

Belgium

Belize

Benin

Bermuda

Bhutan

Bolivia

Bosnia and Herzegovina

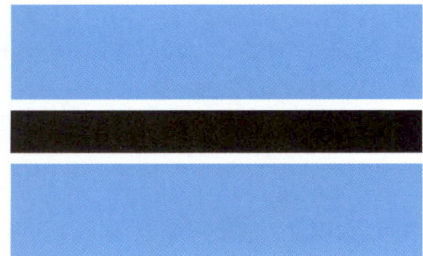

Botswana

Bougainville

Brazil

British Virgin Islands

Brittany

Brunei

Bulgaria

Burkina Faso

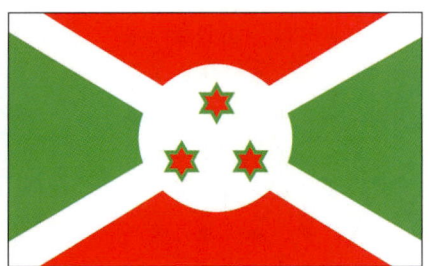

Burundi

Cabinda

Cambodia

Cameroon

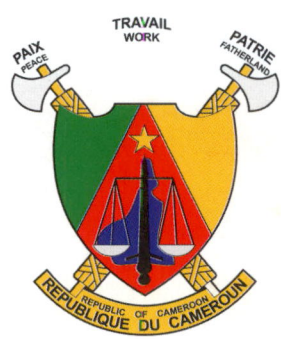

Canada

Canary Islands

Cape Verde

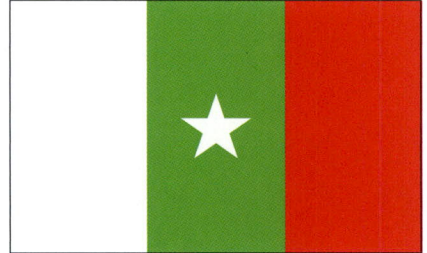

Casamance

Catalonia

Cayman Islands

Central African Republic

Chad

Chechnya

Chile

China

Colombia

Comoros

Congo, Democratic Republic

Congo, Republic

Cook Islands

Cornwall

Corsica

Costa Rica

Côte d'Ivoire

Croatia

Cuba

Curaçao

Cyprus

Czech Republic

Denmark

Djibouti

Dominica

Dominican Republic

East Timor

East Turkestan

Ecuador

Egypt

El Salvador

Equatorial Guinea

Eritrea

Estonia

Ethiopia

Euskal Herria

Falkland Islands

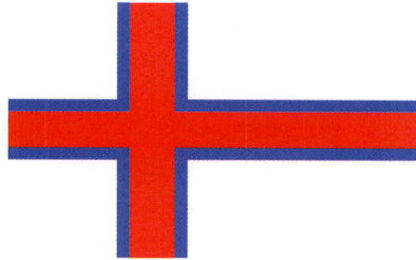

Faroe Islands

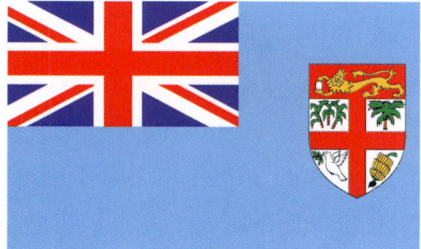

Fiji

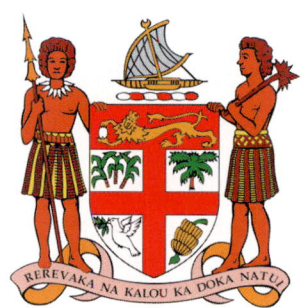

Finland

Flanders

France

French Guiana

French Polynesia

Gabon

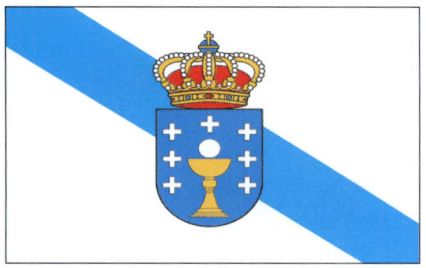

Galicia

Gambia

Georgia

Germany

Ghana

Gibraltar

Greece

Greenland

Grenada

Guadeloupe

Guam

Guatemala

Guernsey

Guinea

Guinea-Bissau

Guyana

Haiti

Honduras

Hong Kong

Hungary

Iceland

India

Indonesia

Iran

Iraq

Ireland

Isle of Man

Israel

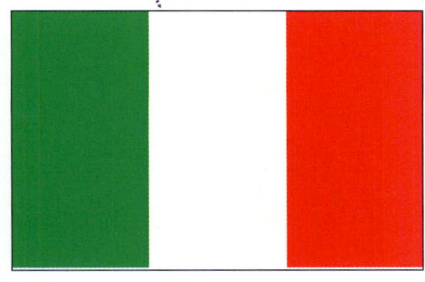

Italy

Jamaica

Japan

Jersey

Jordan

Kashmir

Katanga

Kazakhstan

Kenya

Kiribati

Korea, North

Korea, South

Kosovo

Kurdistan

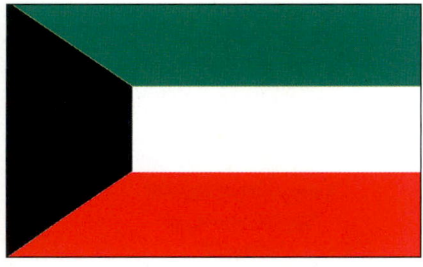

Kuwait

Kyrgyzstan

Laos

Latvia

Lebanon

Lesotho

Liberia

Libya

Liechtenstein

Lithuania

Luxembourg

Macau

Macedonia

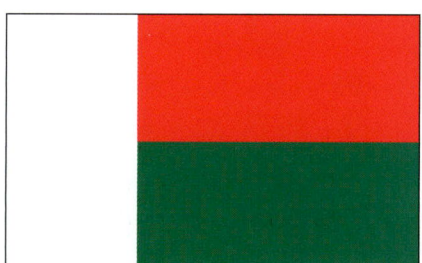

Madagascar

which has 16 rays, alternating triangular and wavy. The nine stripes represent the nine original counties incorporated into Uruguay.

COAT OF ARMS/SEAL

The coat of arms has a central oval divided into quarters and crowned by a rising Sun of May, symbolizing the rising of the Uruguayan nation. The upper left quadrant shows a scale on a blue background, symbolizing equality and justice. The upper right contains Montevideo Hill, with its fortress at the summit, representing strength, on a silver background. The lower left quadrant shows a galloping black horse, symbolizing liberty, on a silver field. The lower right depicts an ox, symbolizing abundance, on a blue background. The oval is surrounded by two olive branches, representing peace.

MOTTO

Libertad o muerte (Spanish); Freedom or Death (English)

CAPITAL CITY

Montevideo

TYPE OF GOVERNMENT

Presidential republic

NATIONAL EMBLEM

Sun of May; gaucho

NATIONAL COLORS

Sky blue and white

NATIONAL ANTHEM

The anthem was adopted in 1845 and is one of the longest national anthems in its formal version.

> ¡Orientales, la Patria o la Tumba! (Spanish); Uruguayans, Our Country or the Grave! (English)
>
> **Chorus**
>
> Uruguayans, our country or the grave!
> Freedom, or with glory to die.

Uruguayans, our country or the grave!
Freedom, or with glory to die.
This is the vow that our souls take
And which we know how, courageously, to
    fulfill,
This is the vow that our souls take
And which we know how, courageously, to
    fulfill,
Know how to fulfill,
This is the vow that our souls take
And which we know how, courageously, to
    fulfill,
Know how to fulfill!
Know how to fulfill!
Know how to fulfill!

Freedom, freedom, Uruguayans,
This cry saved our country,
Inflaming its brave men
With enthusiasm in fierce battles.
Freedom, freedom, eastern landsmen,
This cry saved our country,
Inflaming its brave men
With enthusiasm in fierce battles.
We merited the glory of this sacred gift.
Let tyrants tremble!
Let tyrants tremble!
Let tyrants tremble!

Chorus

PATRON SAINTS

Blessed Virgin Mary; Our Lady of Lujan; Saint Philip; Saint James the Apostle

CURRENCY

Uruguayan peso

INTERNET IDENTIFIER

.uy

VEHICLE IDENTIFICATION PLATES/ STICKERS

ROU

PASSPORT

The passport cover has the name of the regional group, Mercosur, the name of the country in Spanish, the coat of arms, and the word *passport* in Spanish, *pasaporte*.

AIRLINE
PLUNA (Primeras Líneas Uruguayas de Navigación Aérea)

NATIONAL FLOWER
Ceibo

NATIONAL TREE
Yellow poinciana; *ombu* (unofficial)

NATIONAL BIRD
Terotero (southern lapwing)

NATIONAL RESOURCES
Natural resources include arable land, hydropower, some minor minerals, and fisheries. The economy is largely based on agriculture. Tourism is an important resource, based on historic cities and monuments, sandy beaches, a pleasant climate, and the Uruguayan culture. According to international surveys, Uruguay is the least corrupt and most open in its politics and labor conditions among the countries of South America.

FOODS
Asado, various cuts of meat cooked over charcoal, is considered the national dish. *Chivito,* a sandwich of thinly sliced steak, bacon, ham, mushrooms, olives, tomatoes, and cheese, served on a sesame seed bun, is also considered a national dish. Other specialties include *casuela,* a stew usually containing *mondongo* (tripe); empanadas, small pastries filled with minced meat, onions, and raisins; *pascualina,* a baked pastry filled with spinach, onion, eggs, and cheese; *milanesa,* thinly sliced steak breaded and fried; and *camarones al ajillo,* fresh shrimp sautéed with garlic and parsley.

SPORTS/SPORTS TEAMS
Association football (soccer), rugby, and basketball are the most popular sports. Uruguay national teams participate in many sports at an international level.

TEAM SPORTS
Badminton
Uruguay Badminton Team

Baseball
Uruguay Softball Team

Basketball
Uruguay Basketball Team; Uruguay Wheelchair Basketball Team

Cricket
Uruguay Cricket Team

Football
Uruguay Football Team, nicknames Charrúas, La Celeste Olimpica (the Olympic Sky Blue), or La Celeste (the Sky Blue); Uruguay Women's Football Team, La Celeste (the Sky Blue), or Charrúas; Uruguay Rugby Union Team, nickname Los Teros (after the bird, *tertero*); Uruguay American Football Team; Uruguay Beach Soccer Team; Uruguay Futsal Team

Handball
Uruguay Handball Team; Uruguay Women's Handball Team; Uruguay Beach Handball Team; Uruguay Women's Beach Handball Team

Hockey
Uruguay Field Hockey Team

Racing
Uruguay Speedway Team

Table Tennis
Uruguay Table Tennis Team

Tennis

Uruguay Davis Cup Team; Uruguay Fed Cup Team

Volleyball

Uruguay Men's Volleyball Team; Uruguay Women's Volleyball Team; Uruguay Fistball Team

INDIVIDUAL SPORTS

Uruguay Aikido Team; Uruguay Amateur Boxing Team; Uruguay Archery Team; Uruguay Athletics Team; Uruguay Cycling Team; Uruguay Equestrian Team; Uruguay Fencing Team; Uruguay Gymnastics Team; Uruguay Judo Team; Uruguay Karate Team; Uruguay Modern Pentathlon Team; Uruguay Rowing Team; Uruguay Sailing Team; Uruguay Shooting Team; Uruguay Swim Team; Uruguay Tae Kwon Do Team; Uruguay Triathlon Team; Uruguay Weight Lifting Team; Uruguay Wrestling Team

NATIONAL HEROES OR PERSONIFICATIONS

José Gervasio Artigas, considered the father of Uruguayan independence; Juan Antonio Lavalleja, leader of the uprising that led to independence in 1828; José Enrique Rodó, writer who fostered the idea of the superiority of Latin American culture

NATIONAL HOLIDAY/INDEPENDENCE DAY

Independence Day, August 25

FESTIVALS/FAIRS

Lemanja (Festival of the Goddess of the Sea), February; Las Llamadas (Carnival), February–March; Festival of Gaucho Culture, March; Tango Festival, June

SIGNIFICANT EVENTS IN FORMATION OF NATIONAL IDENTITY

1000 C.E. The area is inhabited by various tribes of native American hunter-gatherers, the best known being the Charrúa, a small tribe driven south by the Guarani of Paraguay.

1516–1536 Spanish expedition sails up the Río de la Plata. Colonists establish the first European settlement.

16th century–17th century The lack of gold or silver discourages interest in the region. The region is included in territory controlled by Portugal*.

1726 The Spanish settle at Montevideo and take Uruguay from the Portuguese. The indigenous people are killed or perish from European diseases.

1776 The territory becomes part of the Viceroyalty of La Plata, governed from Buenos Aires. Uruguay is called the Eastern Province because of its situation on the eastern bank of Río de la Plata.

1808–1820 A rebellion begins when news arrives of the overthrow of the Spanish monarchy by Napoleon Bonaparte. The Uruguayans fight off invasions from Argentina* and Brazil*.

1828 Argentina and Brazil renounce claims to the region, which becomes independent as the Eastern Republic of Uruguay.

1838–1865 A long civil war between conservatives and liberals disrupts the country.

1903–1915 Political and social reforms make Uruguay the most progressive state in Latin America. Women are enfranchised and a welfare state established. The church is removed from any official role, and the death penalty is abolished.

1933–1959 Growing instability leads to a coup and military rule. Dictatorship becomes the normal form of government.

1962–1980 The Tupamaros, a leftist guerrilla group, becomes active. The terror campaign lasts until 1973, when the military again seizes power and initiates a period of extreme repression. Uruguay becomes known as the "torture chamber of Latin America."

1984–1985 Violent protests break out against repression and a deteriorating economy. A new democratic government is elected.

2000 A commission begins investigating the fate of people who disappeared during the years of military dictatorship.

2006–2008 The leaders of the former military dictatorship are arrested in connection with murders in the 1970s. Uruguay's buoyant economy allows the country to pay off larger foreign debts.

2009 A slowing world economy leads to economic hardship and a sharp rise in unemployment.

VENEZUELA

OFFICIAL NAME
República Bolivariana de Venezuela (Spanish); Bolivarian Republic of Venezuela (English)

POPULATION
28,202,900 (2009e)

INHABITANTS' NAME/NICKNAME
Venezuelan(s)

LANGUAGE/LANGUAGES
Spanish (official); indigenous languages, Portuguese, English, others

RELIGION/RELIGIONS
Roman Catholic, 96 percent; Protestant, 2 percent; other or no religion

NATIONAL FLAG
The flag is a horizontal tricolor of yellow, blue, and red charged with a semicircle of small, white, five-pointed stars on the blue stripe and the coat of arms on the yellow at the upper hoist. Yellow represents the wealth of the land, blue represents courage, and red symbolizes independence.

COAT OF ARMS/SEAL
The coat of arms has a central crest or shield divided into three sections, two quarters above and half below. The upper right quadrant shows gold wheat on a red field, representing the union of 20 states and the wealth of the nation. The upper left quadrant depicts a sword, a saber, and three lances, superimposed on two national flags tied by a branch of laurel on a yellow field, representing military triumph. The lower half shows a white horse running free, symbolizing independence and freedom. Above the shield are two crossed cornucopias pouring out wealth. An olive branch and a palm frond support the shield, tied at the bottom by a banner, in national colors, that is inscribed, in gold letters, with *"19 Abril 1810; 20 Febrero 1859; Independencia; Federación; República de Venezuela"*

MOTTO
Dios y federación (Spanish); God and Federation (English)

CAPITAL CITY
Caracas

TYPE OF GOVERNMENT
Federal presidential republic

NATIONAL EMBLEM
Angel Falls

NATIONAL COLORS
Vinotinto (burgundy) and white

NATIONAL ANTHEM
The anthem dates from the war of independence in the early 19th century. It is sometimes referred to as the "Venezuelan Marseillaise."

> **Gloria al Bravo Pueblo (Spanish); Glory to the Brave Nation (English)**
>
> **Chorus**
>
> Glory to the brave nation
> That shook off the yoke,
> Respecting law, virtue and honor.

"Off with the chains! Off with the chains!"
Cried the Lord, cried the Lord,
And the poor man in his hovel
Implored freedom.
At this holy name, there trembled
The vile selfishness that had triumphed,
The vile selfishness that had triumphed.

Chorus

Let's cry out aloud:
"Down with oppression!"
Faithful countrymen, your strength
Lies in your unity;
And from the heavens
The supreme Creator
Breathed a sublime spirit
Into the nation.

Chorus

United by bonds
Made by heaven,
All America exists
As a nation;
And if tyranny
Raises its voice,
Follow the example
Given by Caracas.

PATRON SAINT

Our Lady of Coromoto

CURRENCY

Venezuelan bolivar fuerte

INTERNET IDENTIFIER

.ve

VEHICLE IDENTIFICATION PLATES/ STICKERS

YV

PASSPORT

The passport cover has the name of the country in Spanish, the coat of arms, the word *passport* in Spanish and English, and the standard biometric symbol.

AIRLINES

Conviasa; Santa Bárbara Airlines SBA

NATIONAL FLOWER

Flor de Mayo (May flower orchid)

NATIONAL TREE

Araguaney

NATIONAL ANIMAL

White horse

NATIONAL BIRD

Turpial

NATIONAL FISH

Tarpon (unofficial)

NATIONAL RESOURCES

Natural resources include petroleum, natural gas, iron ore, gold, bauxite, other minerals, hydropower, and diamonds. Venezuela has some of the largest oil and natural gas reserves in the world, yet 32 percent of the population lacks adequate sanitation, only 3 percent of sewage is treated, and 17 percent of Venezuelans lack access to potable water. Tourism is an important resource, although it has declined in recent years due to international tensions.

FOODS

Pabellón criollo, a dish of rice, black beans, and shredded beef, is considered the national dish. *Hallaca,* a dish of beef, pork, chicken, capers, raisins, and olives wrapped in cornmeal dough and plantain leaves, then steamed or boiled, is another typical dish. Other national dishes include *arepas,* cornmeal flatbreads similar to tortillas; *parrilla criolla,* marinated beef cooked over charcoal; *hervido,* a soup of beef, chicken, or fish with vegetables; empanadas, small pastries filled with minced meat; and *pasticho,* a type of lasagna.

SPORTS/SPORTS TEAMS

Baseball and association football (soccer) are the most popular sports. Venezuela national teams participate in many sports at an international level.

TEAM SPORTS

Baseball

Venezuela Baseball Team; Venezuela Softball Team

Basketball

Venezuela Women's Basketball Team; Venezuela Basketball Team; Venezuela Wheelchair Basketball Team; Venezuela Women's Wheelchair Basketball Team

Football

Venezuela Football Team, nickname La Vinotinto (the Wine-Colored or the Burgundy); Venezuela Women's Football Team, nickname La Vinotinto (the Wine-Colored or the Burgundy); Venezuela Rugby Union Team nickname Las Orquideas (the Orchids); Venezuela Beach Soccer Team; Venezuela Futsal Team

Hockey

Venezuela Field Hockey Team

Racing

Venezuela Speedway Team

Table Tennis

Venezuela Table Tennis Team

Tennis

Venezuela Davis Cup Team; Venezuela Fed Cup Team

Volleyball

Venezuela Men's Volleyball Team; Venezuela Men's Beach Volleyball Team; Women's Volleyball Team

INDIVIDUAL SPORTS

Venezuela Amateur Boxing Team; Venezuela Archery Team; Venezuela Athletics Team; Venezuela Canoeing Team; Venezuela Cycling Team; Venezuela Equestrian Team; Venezuela Fencing Team; Venezuela Gymnastics Team: Venezuela Judo Team; Venezuela Karate Team: Venezuela Modern Pentathlon Team; Venezuela Rowing Team; Venezuela Sailing Team; Venezuela Shooting Team; Venezuela Swim Team; Venezuela Tae Kwon Do Team; Venezuela Triathlon Team; Venezuela Weight Lifting Team; Venezuela Wrestling Team

WINTER SPORTS

Venezuela Luge Team

NATIONAL HEROES OR PERSONIFICATIONS

Simón Bolivar, the leader of the independence movement; Francisco de Miranda, the publisher of the country's first newspaper and a nationalist politician; Simón Rodríguez, the leading prerevolutionary liberal scholar; Juan Vicente González, known as the father of Venezuelan literature; Antonio Guzman Blanco, the modernizer of Venezuela in the late 19th century

NATIONAL HOLIDAY/INDEPENDENCE DAY

Independence Day, July 5

FESTIVALS/FAIRS

Carnival, February–March; Semana Santa (Holy Week), March–April; El Hatillo Music Festival, October; Valencia Fair, November; Independence Day celebration, July

SIGNIFICANT EVENTS IN FORMATION OF NATIONAL IDENTITY

1000 B.C.E.–1450 B.C.E. The region is inhabited by various indigenous tribes, such as the Mariches, descendants of the Caribes, Arawaks, and Chibchas, living as farmers or hunters along the coast, in the mountains, and along the Orinoco River.

1498–1499 Christopher Columbus visits the coastal region, claiming it for Spain*. A second expedition, led by Amerigo Vespucci, observes villages built over water and calls the region Venezuola, or Little Venice.

1521 Spanish colonization begins on the coast. Mines and plantations are established, first with indigenous people enslaved by the Spanish, and later with imported African slaves. Many of the indigenous groups perish from European diseases or the systematic destruction of entire tribes.

1749 The first rebellion protests arbitrary and oppressive Spanish rule.

1810–1811 Napoleon's overthrow of the Spanish monarchy in Europe sparks a revolution against Spanish rule. Led by Simón Bolivar, Gran Colombia, which combines Colombia*, Ecuador*, and Venezuela, is declared independent.

1829–1830 Regional differences lead to Venezuela's secession from Gran Colombia as a separate republic, under a succession of dictators.

1870–1888 Antonio Guzman Blanco attracts foreign investment, modernizes infrastructure, and develops agriculture. Education is extended beyond the upper classes.

1902 The Venezuelan government defaults on international loans and, as a result, British, Italian, and German warships blockade its ports.

1908–1935 Oil is discovered, and production begins during the dictatorship of Juan Vicente Gomez.

1947–1948 President Romulo Gallegos becomes Venezuela's first elected leader but is overthrown within eight months by a military coup.

1958–1964 Leftist Romulo Betancourt wins the presidential election. The first peaceful transfer of power takes place following elections in 1964.

1970–1990 Dependent on international oil prices, Venezuela swings between periods of high prices and a booming economy and periods of low world prices with cuts in government spending, leading to unrest and violence.

1992 Many people are killed in an attempted coup led by Hugo Chavez, who is jailed for two years before being pardoned.

1998–1999 Hugo Chavez is elected president. Severe flooding kills thousands of people.

2000 Chavez is reelected and becomes the first foreign head of state to visit Saddam Hussein in Iraq after the end of the 1991 Gulf War.

2002 Amid a crisis in the national oil company and a widespread strike, the military high command demands that Chavez resign. Chavez is briefly overthrown, and a new transitional government, hastily recognized by the United States*, is installed. Chavez returns to office after the collapse of the interim government.

2003–2004 The political opposition delivers a petition signed by more than 3 million Venezuelans demanding a referendum on Chavez's rule, but the petition is rejected on technical faults. A second petition is presented with 3.4 million signatures. Clashes break out between the opposition and Chavez supporters. Chavez wins the referendum.

2005–2006 The Chavez government begins to break up large estates, part of a land reform package promised to Chavez's poor supporters. Chavez wins a third term as president.

2007 The Chavez government nationalizes key industries, including energy and telecommunications companies. A popular television channel and a number of radio stations that openly criticize Chavez are closed down. Voters narrowly reject proposals to extend Chavez's powers and accelerate his socialist program.

2008 Revelations that the Chavez government finances and supports the FARC rebels in neighboring Colombia lead to increased tensions in the region. Several high-profile captives are released by the FARC, possibly at the urging of Venezuela's president. Venezuela has some of the world's largest proven oil deposits, as well as large amounts of coal, bauxite, iron ore, and gold, but most Venezuelans continue to live in poverty, despite the so-called socialist revolution of Hugo Chavez.

2009 Chavez, while on a visit to Moscow in mid-2009, announces that Venezuela will recognize the independence of Abkhazia* and South Ossetia*, becoming the third nation to do so after Russia* and Nicaragua*. Tens of thousands march in Caracas to protest a new education law that would include teaching political indoctrination. The government threatens to close 29 more radio stations critical of the Chavez government.

ZULIA

Official Name

Estado Zulia (Spanish); Zulia State (English); Pais Zuliano (nationalist name in Spanish); Nation of Zulia (English)

Population

4,085,400 (2009e)

Inhabitants' Name/Nickname

Zulian(s)

Language/Languages

Spanish (official); Wayúunaiki, Bari, Yukpa, Portuguese, English, others

Religion/Religions

Roman Catholic, 94 percent; Protestant, 3 percent; other or no religion

National Flag

The flag is a horizontal bicolor of blue over black with a centered golden sun and a white bolt of lightning. The blue stands for the waters of Lake Maracaibo, the Gulf of Venezuela, and the region's various rivers. Black represents Zulia's oil wealth. The sun stands for the warmth of the Zulians, hospitality, and wealth. The lightning represents the Catarumbo ray, the Zulian guide to the future.

Coat of Arms/Seal

The coat of arms has a central crest or shield divided into three sections, two quarters above and half below. The upper right quadrant shows a red field divided by golden lightning, the ray of Catarumbo. The upper left quadrant shows a red castle on a yellow field, representing the San Carlos fort, which guards the entrance to Lake Maracaibo and symbolizes the strength of the Zulians, and the lower half shows a white sailing ship on a blue field, representing Zulia's historic ties to the sea and to navigation on Lake Maracaibo. The crest is supported by a palm frond and a banana leaf, symbolizing the fertility of the region. Under the crest are the dates August 24, 1499, the day when Alonso de Ojeda claimed the region for Spain*, and January 28, 1821, the date Zulia proclaimed its independence from Spain.

Motto

El Zulia sigue ganando (Spanish); Zulia continues to gain (English)

Capital City

Maracaibo

Type of Government

A state of the federal republic of Venezuela*, with a local government heavily appointed by the central government

National Emblem

Urdaneta Bridge, the "bridge over the lake"

National Colors

Blue and black

National Anthem

The anthem was written and composed in 1909, the result of a campaign by the Zulian government. It still contains elements of the region's traditional abhorrence of the central government in Caracas. No English translation is available.

Himno de Zulia (Spanish); Riding the Waves (English)

Chorus

Sobre palmas y lauros de oro
yergue el Zulia su limpio blasón;
y flamea en su plaustro sonoros
del progreso el radiante pendón.

I

La luz con el relámpago
tenaz del catatumbo,
del nauta fija el rumbo,
cual límpido farol;
el alba de los trópicos,
la hoguera que deslumbra
cuando al zénit se encumbra
la cuadriga del sol
no emulan de tus glorias
el fúlgido arrebol

II

En la defensa olímpica
de los nativos fueros
tus hijos, sus aceros
llevaron al confín;
ciñendo lauros múltiples
los viste, con arrobo,
del Lago a Carabobo,
del Ávila a Junín;
y en Tarqui y Ayacucho
vibraron su clarín.

III

Erguido como Júpiter,
la diestra en alto armada,
fulgurante la mirada
de rabia y de rencor;
las veces que los sátrapas
quisieron tu mancilla:
mirarte de rodilla
sin prez y sin honor
cayó sobre sus frentes
tu rayo vengador.

IV

Y luego que la cólera
de tu justicia calmas,
va en pos de nuevas palmas
tu espíritu vivaz;

en aulas de areópagos,
cabildos y liceos;
te brindan sus trofeos
el numen de la paz;
y vese en blanca aureola
resplandecer tu faz.

V

En tu carroza alígera
que tiran diez corceles,
de cantos y laureles
guirnaldas mil se ven.
Allí del arte el símbolo
del sabio la corona,
de Temis y Pomona
la espada y el lairén.
La enseña del trabajo
y el lábaro del bien.

VI

Jamás, jamás, los déspotas
o la invasión taimada,
la oliva por la espada
te obliguen a trocar;
y sigas a la cúspide;
triunfante como eres,
rumores de talleres
oyendo sin cesar
en vez de los clarines
y el parche militar.

PATRON SAINT

Our Lady of Chiquinquirá

CURRENCY

Venezuelan bolivar fuerte

INTERNET IDENTIFIER

.ve Venezuela (official); .zu Zulia (unofficial)

VEHICLE IDENTIFICATION PLATES/ STICKERS

ZU

PASSPORT

Zulians are Venezuelan citizens and travel on Venezuelan passports.

AIRLINE

Venezolana Airlines

NATIONAL FLOWER

Cayena (hibiscus)

NATIONAL TREE

Cocotero (coconut palm)

NATIONAL ANIMAL

Capybara (unofficial)

NATIONAL BIRD

Pelican; violaceous trogon (unofficial)

NATIONAL FISH

Chivo (big-scale goatfish) (unofficial)

NATIONAL RESOURCES

Natural resources include petroleum, natural gas, iron ore, gold, bauxite, other minerals, hydropower, and diamonds. Venezuela has some of the largest oil and natural gas reserves in the world, yet 32 percent of the population lacks adequate sanitation, only 3 percent of sewage is treated, and 17 percent lack access to potable water. Tourism is an important resource, although it has declined in recent years due to international tensions.

FOODS

Chivo en coco, goatfish cooked with fresh coconut and yucca, is considered the national dish. Other typical dishes include *casuela marinara,* a casserole of mixed seafood; *mojito de coco,* a dry stew of goatfish and spices; *escabeche costeño,* lightly fried fish marinated in a vinegar mixture; *arroz con palomito,* a rice dish with hearts of palm; *bolos pelones,* balls of *platano* and yucca flour served with a spiced tomato sauce; *arroz de coco,* a rice dish with coconut, sugar, and spices; and *huevos de chimbo,* a dessert made of egg yolks, sugar, vanilla, and rum.

SPORTS/SPORTS TEAMS

Baseball and association football (soccer) are the most popular sports. Zulia national teams participate in baseball and football at an international level.

TEAM SPORTS

Baseball

Zulia Baseball Team, nickname Las Aguilas de Zulia (the Zulian Eagles) or El Equipo Petrolero (the Petroleum Team)

Football

Zulia Football Club (FC Zulia) is considered the national team of Zulia

NATIONAL HEROES OR PERSONIFICATIONS

Princess Zulia, the mythical daughter of the leader of a tribal federation that fought the Spanish conquest, is the personification of Zulia.

National heroes include Simón Bolivar, the leader of the independence movement; Francisco de Miranda, the publisher of Venezuela's first newspaper and a nationalist politician; and Rafael Urdaneta, a military leader in the wars for liberation from Spain*.

NATIONAL HOLIDAY/INDEPENDENCE DAY

Zulia National Day (Día de la Zulianidad), January 28

FESTIVALS/FAIRS

Carnival, February–March; Semana Santa (Holy Week), March–April; El Moján y Caja Seca, 27 January; Festival of La Chinita, July; Festival of Our Lady of Chiquinquirá, November 18

SIGNIFICANT EVENTS IN FORMATION OF NATIONAL IDENTITY

1000 B.C.E.–1450 C.E. The region is inhabited by various indigenous tribes living as farmers, fishermen, or hunters along the coast and around Lake Maracaibo.

1498–1499 Christopher Columbus visits the coastal region, claiming it for Spain. A second expedition, led by Amerigo Vespucci, observes villages built over water on Lake Maracaibo and calls the region Venezuola, or Little Venice.

1521–1650 Spanish colonization begins on the coast. Mines and plantations are established, first with indigenous people enslaved by the Spanish, and later with imported African slaves. Many of the indigenous groups perish from European diseases or the systematic destruction of entire tribes.

1676 Zulia forms a large province of Spanish America, often known as Espiritu Santo de Maracaibo. The region, far from the centers of power in Caracas and Bogota, remains an agricultural backwater.

1789 Zulia's territory is extended to include the present Venezuelan states of Zulia, Apure, Barinas, Táchira, Mérida, and Trujillo.

1810–1811 Napoleon's overthrow of the Spanish monarchy in Europe sparks a revolution against Spanish rule. Led by Simón Bolivar, Gran Colombia, which combines Colombia*, Ecuador*, Zulia, and Venezuela, is declared independent although most of the region remains under Spanish control.

1821 Zulia remains under Spanish military occupation and is more closely integrated with neighboring Colombia than with Venezuela. Zulia is declared an independent and sovereign republic on January 28, 1821.

1824 Ten years after the independence of Gran Colombia, Zulia becomes part of Venezuela when it withdraws from the Gran Colombia federation in 1824.

1825–1900 Venezuela, mostly under military rule or dictatorships, remains backward and undeveloped. The central government mostly ignores the far western region of Zulia. The region attempts to separate from Venezuela in 1863 but is reincorporated into the country in 1868.

1899 The present boundaries of the state are established following the creation of several separate states from the territory of the former province.

1902 The Venezuelan government defaults on international loans and, as a result, British, Italian, and German warships blockade its ports.

1908–1935 Oil is discovered in Lake Maracaibo and production begins. The region grows rapidly.

1947–1964 President Romulo Gallegos becomes Venezuela's first elected leader but is overthrown within eight months by a military coup. Under resulting military governments, Zulian sentiment is suppressed and Venezuelan patriotism is paramount. The first peaceful transfer of presidential power in Venezuela takes place following elections in 1964.

1970–1990 Dependent on international oil prices, Venezuela swings between periods of high prices and a booming economy and periods of low world prices with cuts in government spending, leading to unrest and violence, particularly in oil-rich Zulia. Nationalism begins to gain support, with calls for economic and administrative autonomy.

1992–1999 Many people are killed in an attempted coup led by Hugo Chavez, who is jailed for two years before being pardoned.

2000 The leading Zulian politician, Manuel Rosales, the governor of Zulia, forms a new political party, Un Nuevo Tiempo, to oppose the excesses of the Chavez government. Several Zulian leaders put together a plan for Zulian autonomy and local control of resources, including the oil reserves under Lake Maracaibo.

2002 Amid a crisis in the national oil company and a widespread strike, the military high command demands that Chavez resign. Chavez is briefly overthrown, and a new transitional government is installed. Chavez returns to office after the collapse of the interim government.

2003–2004 Clashes break out between the opposition and Chavez supporters. Chavez wins a referendum on limiting his power. Manuel Rosales is reelected as governor of Zulia.

2005–2006 The Chavez government begins to break up large estates, part of a land reform package promised to Chavez's poor supporters. In the 2006 elections, Manual Rosales opposes Chavez, representing a broad coalition of political parties and organizations. Chavez wins a third term as president.

2007 The Chavez government nationalizes key industries, including energy and telecommunications companies. A popular television channel that openly criticizes Chavez is closed down. Voters narrowly reject proposals to extend Chavez's powers and accelerate his socialist program.

2008 Revelations that the Chavez government finances and supports the FARC rebels in neighboring Colombia lead to increased tensions in the region. Many Zulians leave the country, often to live in the United States*, a country demonized by the Chavez regime. Rosales is charged with corruption, charges that many see as politically motivated.

2009 Zulia has some of the world's largest deposits of oil, abundant and fertile land, and the resources of the sea and Lake Maracaibo, but most continue to live in poverty, despite the so-called socialist revolution of Chavez, Venezuela's president. Rosales, faced with a long prison term, flees the country. In April 2009, it is reported that he has been granted political asylum in Peru*. Nationalists demand the same when Hugo Chavez, on a visit to Moscow, announces Venezuelan recognition of the independence of the breakaway republics of Abkhazia* and South Ossetia*.

Europe

The symbols that represent the European nations are the basis of much of the national symbolism in the modern world. The idea of symbols, in colors, flags, and other representations, mostly originated with the European colonial occupation of much of the rest of the world between the 15th and early 20th centuries. The internal colonization of Europe, which largely preceded world colonization, brought many nations under the rule of more powerful neighbors. These oppressed nations often adopted the colors and symbols of culturally and linguistically related independent nations; thus, Russia's white, blue, and red became the national colors of such diverse nations as Bulgaria, Serbia, Croatia, Slovenia, Slovakia, and the Czech Republic. Most of the inspiration for the colors, flags, and other symbols adopted by the non-Slavic nations derives from ancient traditions. As in many parts of the world, there are great similarities among Europe's national foods, music, and dance. National symbols have long played a leading role in the many wars that periodically convulsed Europe, and they continue to claim the loyalty of many Europeans, a reverence that is lacking in most other parts of the world.

Many of the nonindependent nations of Europe are also included. The majority of these territories are self-governing and possess distinct cultures and national symbols. Many of these territories are actively seeking greater self-government and recognition of their distinct cultures and histories, including their own often ancient national symbols.

ABKHAZIA

OFFICIAL NAME

Apkhazeti (Georgian); Apsny Ahntkarra (Abkhaz); Republic of Abkhazia (English)

POPULATION

180,000–220,000 (2009e)

INHABITANTS' NAME/NICKNAME

Abkhaz; Abkhazian(s)

LANGUAGE/LANGUAGES

Abkhaz, Russian (official); Georgian, Armenian, Greek, others

RELIGION/RELIGIONS

Christian (Russian Orthodox, Georgian Orthodox, Armenian Orthodox), 75 percent; Muslim, 10 percent; other or no religion

NATIONAL FLAG

The flag was created in 1991, based on the banner of the medieval Abkhazian kingdom. In the red canton, the open right hand represents Abkhaz nationhood. Seven is a number sacred to the Abkhaz, and seven green and white stripes represent the tolerance that allows Christianity and Islam to exist side by side. According to a popular, though erroneous, belief, the seven stripes of the Abkhazian flag correspond to the seven historical regions of the country—Sadzen, Bzyp, Gumaa, Abzhywa, Samurzaqan, Dal-Tsabal, and Pskhuy-Aibga.

COAT OF ARMS/SEAL

The coat of arms of Abkhazia is a shield divided vertically into white and green. On this are placed several devices outlined in gold: At the base is an eight-pointed star, and in the upper part of both the white and the green field are set two eight-pointed stars. At the centre of the shield is a horseman, flying on the fabulous steed called Arash and shooting an arrow towards the stars. This scene is from the heroic Abkhaz epic *Narts*. Green symbolizes youth and life, while white symbolizes spirituality. The stars represent the sun, as well as the union of East and West in Abkhazia.

CAPITAL CITY

Sukhumi (called Akua in the Abkhaz language)

TYPE OF GOVERNMENT

Internationally unrecognized but de facto independent presidential republic

NATIONAL EMBLEM

A horseman flying on the mythical steed Arash and shooting arrows toward the stars as depicted on the coat of arms; the white hand of freedom and five stars on a red background

NATIONAL COLORS

White and green

NATIONAL ANTHEM

The Abkhaz anthem, "Aiaaira" (Abkhaz) or "Victory" (English), is used by the nationalist government of Abkhazia. The anthem is instrumental only.

PATRON SAINT

Saint Simon

CURRENCY

Russian ruble

VEHICLE IDENTIFICATION PLATES/ STICKERS

ABH (unofficial)

PASSPORT

Most Abkhazians are considered Russian citizens and use Russian passports, although Abkhazia has begun to issue passports to some of its citizens.

AIRLINE

Abkhazia Airlines

NATIONAL FLOWER

Mimosa (unofficial)

NATIONAL TREE

Mandarin orange (unofficial)

NATIONAL ANIMAL

Ram (unofficial)

NATIONAL BIRD

Golden eagle (unofficial)

NATIONAL RESOURCES

With sandy beaches, a pleasant climate, and interesting scenery, tourism is the primary industry. Other national resources include tea, tobacco, fruits, and potential hydropower and coal development.

FOODS

Lobio, a dish of kidney beans, tomatoes, and onions, is considered the national dish of Abkhazia. Other ingredients, often lamb or beef, are frequently served with *lobio*. *Achma*, a flat, cheese-filled bread, is also considered an Abkhazian national dish. Other specialties include *kharcho*, a soup of chicken and vegetables; *khakapuli,* a dish of lamb with damson plums and onions; *shashlik*, skewered meats cooked over charcoal; *khinkali,* a type of mutton dumpling; *tabaka,* fried chicken with a sweet-and-sour sauce; and *mchadi,* a roll made of cornmeal.

Sports/Sports Teams

Association football (soccer) remains the most popular sport, even though Abkhazia is barred from most international tournaments. When permitted, the Abkhazia national team participates in football at an international level.

Team Sports

Football

Abkhazia Football Team

National Heroes or Personifications

Vladislav Ardzinba, the man who led Abkhazia to independence in 1992 as its first president; Sergei Bagapsh, president of Abkhazia since 2005, honored for successfully negotiating diplomatic recognition by Russia*

National Holiday/Independence Day

Independence Day, July 23; Saint Simon's Day, May 23

Significant Events in Formation of National Identity

Ninth–sixth centuries B.C.E. Abkhazia forms part of the ancient kingdom of Colchis.

First century B.C.E. Greeks establish ports and trading posts in the region. One of these ports, Dioscurias, stands at the site of present Sukhumi.

767 C.E. The Kingdom of Abkhazia is established. Centuries of invasions and wars turn the Abkhaz into a warrior people.

1325 The Principality of Abkhazia is established but is later incorporated into the medieval Georgian kingdom.

1578 Invading Turks incorporate Abkhazia into the Ottoman Empire. The Turk's religion, Islam, soon spreads through the Caucasus region.

1810–1842 The Russians, expanding into Ottoman territory from the north, take control of Sukhumi in 1810. The remainder of Abkhazia is acquired piecemeal between 1829 and 1842.

1859–1864 Continuing conflicts between the Caucasian peoples and the Russian colonizers lead to a widespread war, which ends in 1864 with the incorporation of Abkhazia and other Caucasian territories into the Russian Empire.

1864–1900 Large numbers of Muslim Abkhazians, estimated at 60 percent of the population at the time, or some 250,000 people, emigrate, are deported, or are forced to flee to Muslim territory in the Ottoman Empire. The depopulated districts in Abkhazia are opened to immigration by Christians, mostly Georgians, Armenians, and Russians.

1918 The coming of the Russian Revolution and the overthrow of the Russian Empire allow the Abkhazians to declare their homeland an independent republic on March 8, 1918. The infant Abkhaz republic is overrun by Georgian troops and incorporated into the newly proclaimed Georgian republic on April 19, 1918.

1921 The invasion of the Caucasus by the Red Army allows the Abkhazians to again break free of Georgian control. A separate Abkhazian Soviet Socialist Republic is proclaimed in March 1921. In December of the same year, the new Soviet authorities incorporate Abkhazia into the new Georgian Soviet Socialist Republic.

1921–1930 Soviet leader Joseph Stalin, a Georgian, restricts use of the Abkhazian language and culture and in 1930 decrees that Abkhazia's status be downgraded to that of an autonomous republic within Georgia.

1930–1953 Soviet authorities ban the Abkhazian language and decree Georgian and Russian as the region's official languages. Georgian names and culture are pressed on the Abkhazian population. This heavy-handed repression eases somewhat with Stalin's death in 1953.

1990–1991 The increasing instability and disintegration of the Soviet Union in the 1990s allows Abkhazian nationalism to once again surface. In 1990, the leaders of the autonomous republic declare Abkhazia an autonomous state following

Georgia's declaration of sovereignty. Georgia declares its independence in 1991 as the Soviet Union disintegrates. The Abkhazians refuse to acknowledge Georgian authority in their homeland.

1990s In 1992, the Abkhazian parliament approves a new law reestablishing the 1925 constitution of a sovereign Abkhazian state. Georgian troops invade, setting off a bitter war in the region. Tens of thousands of ethnic Georgians flee or are driven from the republic during the fighting. By the end of 1992, the Abkhazians, allegedly with Russian aid, control much of the Abkhazian republic. Independence is formally proclaimed on September 30, 1993. A military truce and cease-fire are established that continue today.

2005 The Georgian government offers Abkhazia a high degree of autonomy and possible federal structure within the borders and jurisdiction of Georgia, but the offer is rejected.

2008 Fighting erupts in Georgia between Georgian forces and separatist South Ossetians. Russian forces move from Abkhazia and South Ossetia* into Georgia until they are halted by Russian and Georgian agreement to a cease-fire brokered by the European Union. Russia* announces that it will extend formal diplomatic recognition to the Republic of Abkhazia. Nicaragua* becomes the second government to recognize the republic.

2009 Russia invests heavily in Abkhazia in an effort to shore up support for continued resistance to Georgian overtures. In July 2009, the UN monitors leave the region following Russia's veto of an extension to their mandate. Hugo Chavez, on a visit to Moscow, announces Venezuelan recognition of Abkhazian independence in September.

See also Georgia

ÅLAND ISLANDS

OFFICIAL NAME
Landskapet Åland (Swedish), Ahvenanmaan Maakunta (Finnish); Åland Islands/Aland Islands/Aland (English)

POPULATION
29,100 (2009e)

INHABITANTS' NAME/NICKNAME
Ålander(s); Åland Islander(s); Alandian(s)

LANGUAGE/LANGUAGES
Swedish (official); Ålandish (Swedish dialect spoken in the islands), Finnish, English

RELIGION/RELIGIONS
Protestant, mainly Lutheran 95 percent, Orthodox, Roman Catholic, other or no religion

NATIONAL FLAG
The flag is a blue field bearing a red Scandinavian cross outlined in yellow. The blue and yellow symbolize the Alanders' historic ties to Sweden. The red cross stands for their relationship with Finland, red being one of the colors used in Finland in the early 20th century.

COAT OF ARMS/SEAL
The coat of arms consists of a blue shield under a golden crown with red, blue and white jewels and white pearls. The shield bears a golden roe deer. The blue and gold symbolize the islands' ties to Sweden and the Swedish language and culture, and the crown stands for Finnish sovereignty.

MOTTO
Islands of Peace

CAPITAL CITY
Mariehamn

TYPE OF GOVERNMENT
Parliamentary democracy as an self-governing province of Finland*

NATIONAL EMBLEM
Harbor seal

NATIONAL COLORS
Blue, yellow, and red

NATIONAL ANTHEM

The anthem dates from the early 20th century and was adopted by groups seeking autonomy within the Russian Empire. It was officially adopted as the anthem of the autonomous Alander state in 1922.

Ålänningens sång (Swedish); Song of the Ålander (English)

The land of a thousand islands and skerries,
Born from deep beneath the waves
Åland, our Åland, our home it is
Thee we long to meet
Ancient graves beneath the birches
Tells of our thousand year history
We will never forget the land of our Fathers
No matter where we will go
No matter where we will go
Lovely is our Åland when bays and straits
Become blue in the bright days of spring
It's delightful to wander in forest and grove
In the flowered fields of our shores.
Midsummer pole to evening red sky
Is raised by willing hands
Farther out in the skerry fisher village
Beacons are lit by the young
Beacons are lit by the young
Lovely is our Åland when the froth of waves
Is whirling against the mighty precipice
When the church folks steer beneath the stars
Over the icy depths of the sea
Even when storm roars, in the cottages' peace
The song of the spinning wheel is sung
The memory of loving childhood is
Happily praised by the sons
Happily praised by the sons
Never have Alandian women and men
Let the honor of their tribe down
Warfare threatened us, but victoriously yet
We carry the heritage of freedom
Loudly shall it sound, our Swedish language
Spoken with an urging voice
Enlighten our path like a sea mark of flames
Show us where we belong
Show us where we belong

PATRON SAINT

Saint Olof

CURRENCY

Euro. Prior to adopting the Euro Åland had its own currency, the Åland Mark. The Swedish krona is also in use on the islands.

INTERNET IDENTIFIER

.ax

VEHICLE IDENTIFICATION PLATES/ STICKERS

FIN Finland (official); AX Åland (unofficial)

PASSPORT

The Alanders are Finnish citizens and travel on Finnish passports.

AIRLINE

Air Åland

NATIONAL FLOWER

Gullviva (cowslip)

NATIONAL TREE

Aland pine (Scots pine) (unofficial)

NATIONAL ANIMAL

Roe deer; harbor seal (unofficial)

NATIONAL BIRD

Arctic tern

NATIONAL RESOURCES

The geographic situation of the islands, astride the entrance to the Gulf of Finland and the entrance to Stockholm harbor, give them great strategic importance. Shipping and trade dominate the island economy, while tourism, fishing, farming, and the technology industry are also important.

FOODS

The national dish is *Ålandspannkaka*, known as the Åland Pancake, a cake made of rice or semolina flour served with berry jam and whipped cream. Other specialties include

Åland svärtbrot, a soft and moist bread that is slightly sweet; *havtorns marmelad,* sea buckthorn berry jam; fish dishes are an important part of the traditional cuisine and remain very popular.

SPORTS/SPORTS TEAMS

Association football is the most popular sport. Sailing, bandy, weight lifting, shooting and other traditional sports are also very popular. The Åland football team participates at an international level.

TEAM SPORTS

Football

Åland Football Team, nickname saarelaiset (the Islanders)

NATIONAL HEROES OR PERSONIFICATIONS

Haddon Sunblom, famed Åland-American artist who created the images of Santa Claus for Coca-Cola and other products and publications in the 1950s; Warner Sallman, artist who painted the famous Head of Christ in 1941; Göte Sundberg, the president of the Åland government who negotiated Åland's entry into the EU following two referenda on the islands' accession.

NATIONAL HOLIDAY/INDEPENDENCE DAY

Åland National Day, June 9; Demilitarization Day, March 30

FESTIVALS/FAIRS

Åland Country Festival, June; The Viking Market, July; Rockoff Music Festival, July; Åland Harvest Festival, August; Walpurgis, April

SIGNIFICANT EVENTS IN FORMATION OF NATIONAL IDENTITY

4000 B.C.E.–1000 C.E. The islands are inhabited by several early cultures that leave stone monuments across the region.

600 C.E.–900 C.E. Vikings settle the islands, which are used as gathering points for raids around the Baltic Sea. Christianity first appears in the islands.

12th century–15th century The Swedish kingdom expands to conquer the coast of present-day Finland and the Åland Islands. In 1154, the Swedes launch a military and religious crusade to conquer and Christianize the region. The conquered islands become Swedish in language and culture. Danes, Swedes, Germans, and Russians control the strategic islands for various lengths of time.

16th century The strategically important archipelago is contested by Sweden* and Russia* in a series of wars that sweep northern Europe. Russia seizes the islands in 1714, resulting in the flight of the majority of the population to mainland Sweden. The islands are returned to Swedish rule in 1721.

1809 The Åland Islands, along with Swedish Finland, are ceded to Russia and become part of the Russian-ruled Grand Duchy of Finland.

1856 At the end of the Crimean War, the defeated Russians are obliged to destroy the military fortifications in the islands, which are then demilitarized under the terms of the peace treaty with France* and the United Kingdom*.

19th century The Alanders, oppressed by the Russian bureaucracy, look beyond their islands in order to survive. A large Alander merchant fleet dominates the Australian-European grain trade and engenders a tradition of self-reliance and independence that remains to the present.

1880–1917 Opposition to heavy-handed Russian rule fans nationalist sentiment and demands for self-determination.

1914 Russia refortifies the islands at the outbreak of World War I.

1917 Finland declares independence from the collapsing Russian Empire, claiming Åland as part of their national territory. The Alanders reject the Finnish claims, declare autonomy, and prepare to join their islands to nearby Sweden.

1920–1921 Sweden and Finland come close to war over the issue of the Swedish-speaking islands. The conflict is referred to the new League of Nations, which recommends full self-government and cultural autonomy under Finnish sovereignty. Åland is declared politically neutral and is again demilitarized.

1947 At the end of World War II, the last of the great Alander sailing ships are laid up and Alander domination of the international grain trade ends.

1951–1952 Under Soviet pressure the Finnish government renounces the 1921 treaty but at the same time grants the islands even greater autonomy, retaining responsibility for international relations, defense, and some monetary policies only.

1960s–1980s Emigration, mostly to Sweden, reduces the region's population. Åland is given separate representation as a distinct Scandinavian nation in the Nordic Council. Tourism, including the sale of special Alander duty-free goods on ferries crossing the Baltic Sea, become important to the economy. The population stabilizes as the islands, by the 1980s, attain one of the highest per capita incomes in Scandinavia. In 1984, Åland begin to issue its own postage stamps and coins.

1993 A new autonomy statue gives the Alanders nearly full independence as an autonomous state freely associated with Finland.

1994 Alander negotiators win concessions on the continued sale of duty-free goods, which are eliminated in other parts of the European Union. They are also granted control over property sales to foreigners and voting rights following Finland's entry into the Union.

2000–2009 The majority of the Alanders are content with Finland's benevolent and liberal sovereignty over their islands, however a significant number support the idea of an independent Åland republic as the sixth Nordic country in Scandinavia. The pro-independence political party, Future of Åland, receives 6.5 percent of the vote in the Alander parliamentary elections in 2003. The figure grows to 8.1 percent in 2007

and according to polls taken in 2009 support for independence within the European Union is around 20 percent.

See also Finland

ALBANIA

OFFICIAL NAME
Republika e Shqipërisë (Albanian); Republic of Albania (English)

POPULATION
3,612,000 (2009e)

INHABITANTS' NAME/NICKNAME
Albanian(s)

LANGUAGE/LANGUAGES
Albanian is spoken in two distinct dialects, Tosk in the south and Geg in the north. The language used for official purposes is based on the Tosk dialect. Other languages include Greek, Vlach, Romani, and others.

RELIGION/RELIGIONS
Muslim, 70 percent; Albanian Orthodox, 20 percent; Roman Catholic, 10 percent; other or no religion

NATIONAL FLAG
The flag, known as *flamur e Skënderbeut* (Skanderbeg's flag), is a black, double-headed eagle on a red field. The open-winged eagle symbolizes the historical defiance of the Albanian highlanders to foreign conquest. The color red stands for the blood the Albanians have shed over the centuries while fighting for their freedom.

COAT OF ARMS/SEAL
The coat of arms has the same black eagle on red as the flag, but with a gold outline and a golden helmet, Skanderbeg's helmet, above the eagle.

MOTTO

Ti shqipëri më ep nder më ep emrin shqipëtar (Albanian); Albanians place their faith in Albania (English)

CAPITAL CITY

Tirana (Tiranë)

TYPE OF GOVERNMENT

Parliamentary republic

NATIONAL EMBLEM

Skanderbeg's eagle

NATIONAL COLORS

Red and black

NATIONAL ANTHEM

The anthem dates from Albanian independence in 1912 and has remained through the governmental changes of republics, kingdom, communist/Marxist state, and the modern democratic nation.

Hymni I Flamurit (Albanian); Hymn to the Flag (English)

United around the flag,
With one desire and one goal,
Let us pledge our word of honor
To fight for our salvation.

Chorus

Only he who is a born traitor
Averts from the struggle.
He who is brave is not daunted,
But falls—a martyr to the cause.

With arms in hand we shall remain,
To guard our fatherland round about
Our rights we will not bequeath,
Enemies have no place here.

Chorus

For the Lord Himself has said,
Those nations vanish from the earth,
But Albania shall live on,
Because for her, it is for her that we fight.

PATRON SAINT

Mother of Good Counsel (Our Lady of Shkodra)

CURRENCY

Albanian lek

INTERNET IDENTIFIER

.al

VEHICLE IDENTIFICATION PLATES/ STICKERS

AL

PASSPORT

The passport cover has the name of the country in Albanian and English, the coat of arms, and the word *passport* in French and English.

AIRLINES

Albanian Airlines; BelleAir

NATIONAL FLOWER

Albanian pasque-flower

NATIONAL TREE

Olive

NATIONAL ANIMAL

Eagle

NATIONAL RESOURCES

Natural resources include petroleum, natural gas, coal, bauxite, chromite, copper, iron ore, nickel, salt, timber, and hydropower. Other resources include sandy beaches, a pleasant climate, interesting scenery, ancient cities, and historical monuments.

FOODS

Fergese, a mixture of vegetables or meat and vegetables with feta cheese, is considered the national dish. Other specialties include *byrek ose lakror,* a type of vegetable pie; *tavë kosi,* baked lamb with yogurt (also considered an national dish); *jani me fasule,* bean soup; *gjellë me arra të ellit,* a chicken dish with walnuts; and *mish qingiji me barbunja,* sliced veal with large lima beans,

Sports/Sports Teams

Association football (soccer) is the most popular sport in Albania. *Bola* or ladder golf is considered the national sport. Albania national teams participate in many sports at an international level.

Team Sports

Badminton

Albania Badminton Team

Basketball

Albania Basketball Team; Women's Basketball Team

Football

Albania Football Team, nickname Kuq-E-Zinjtë (the Red and Blacks); Albania Women's Football Team, nickname Kuq-E-Zinjtë (the Red and Blacks); Albania Under-21 Football Team; Albania Futsal Team

Table Tennis

Albania Table Tennis Team

Volleyball

Albania Men's Volleyball Team; Albania Women's Volleyball Team; Albania Fistball Team

Individual Sports

Albania Amateur Boxing Team; Albania Archery Team; Albania Athletics Team; Albania Canoeing Team; Albania Chess Team; Albanian Cycling Team; Albania Equestrian Team; Albania Gymnastics Team; Albania Judo Team; Albania Rowing Team; Albania Shooting Team; Albania Swim Team; Albania Tae Kwon Do Team; Albania Weight Lifting Team; Albania Wrestling Team

National Heroes or Personifications

Mother Albania, a 12-meter statue located at the National Martyrs Cemetery in Tirana, is the personification of Albania; Scanderbeg, the national hero, is also considered a personification of the people of Albania.

Gjergj Kastrioti Skanderbeg, a local noble who led the Albanian resistance to Ottoman rule in the 15th century, is Albania's national hero. Mother Theresa of Calcutta, winner of the 1979 Nobel Peace Prize, has been adopted as an unofficial patron of Albania.

National Holiday/Independence Day

Independence Day, November 28

Festivals/Fairs

Durres Dance Festival, April; Tirana Film Festival, April

Significant Events in Formation of National Identity

200 B.C.E.–395 C.E. Cities and towns develop in the region as part of the Greek civilization. Illyria comes under Roman rule as the province of Illyricum. Following the division of the Roman Empire, modern Albania remains under Byzantine rule but is ecclesiastically subordinate to Rome.

Fourth century–seventh century C.E. The Illyrian lands are overrun by various invaders, including Goths, Huns, Avars, Croats, Serbs, and Bulgars.

732 The Illyrian people are subordinated to the patriarchate of Constantinople by the Byzantine emperor, Leo.

12th century–14th century During the Middle Ages, Albania forms, at various times, a part of the Bulgarian and Serbian states. The region is increasingly called Albania after the Albanoi, one of the Illyrian tribes.

1384–1389 The Ottoman invasion of Albanian territory begins in 1384 when the Albanian ruler of Durrës invites Ottoman forces to intervene against a local rival; subsequently, many Albanian clans pay tribute and swear loyalty to the Ottomans. In 1389, at Kosovo Polje, most of the clans join a Serbian-led Balkan army that is crushed by the Ottomans.

1433–1468 Giergi Kastrioti, known as Skanderbeg, leads a successful resistance against the invading Ottomans. After his death, resistance continues, but Ottoman rule is finally imposed.

17th century–18th century The majority of the Albanian population converts or is forced to convert to Islam under Turkish rule. Some Albanian converts find careers in the Ottoman Empire's government and military.

1822 The Albanian leader, Ali Pasha of Tepelenë, is assassinated by Ottoman agents for his support of an autonomous Albanian state.

1861 The first school known to teach in the Albanian language opens in Shkodër.

1912–1928 Albania emerges as a separate nation following the Balkan Wars that accompany the end of Ottoman rule in the early 20th century. Independence from Ottoman rule is declared on November 28, 1912. Various armies occupy parts of Albania from 1912 until the independence proclamation is finally recognized in 1921. In 1928, Albania becomes a kingdom.

1938–1943 Albania becomes a de facto protectorate of fascist Italy* in 1938. From April 1939 to September 1943, Albania is ruled by fascist Italy.

1943–1945 Germans occupy the country in late 1943 and remain until the end of World War II.

1946–1989 After the Second World War, local communists take power and proclaim the People's Republic of Albania. The country remains backward and isolated under a communist dynasty,

1990–1993 The overthrow of communist rule is followed by elections and the creation of the Republic of Albania. The opening of the economy, particularly to tourism, brings increasing prosperity.

1997 Albanians vote against the restoration of the monarchy. Serious disturbances spread across the country. Thousands flee to Italy.

1998–1999 Thousands of ethnic Albanians flee into Albania after civil war erupts in neighboring Kosovo* between its ethnic Albanian majority and Serbian security forces. The bombing of Yugoslavia by the North Atlantic Treaty Organization (NATO) leads to more Kosovar refugees.

2002–2003 Albania becomes a potential candidate for membership in the European Union as its democratic system is stabilized and its economy is transformed into a free, market-oriented system. An association agreement between Albania and the EU is signed.

2008 Albanian-populated Kosovo declares independence from Serbia on February 17, with Albania the first nation to extend official recognition. On July 9, Albania is accepted as a NATO member state.

2009 After decades of dictatorial rule, wars, chaos, and poverty, the country is finally beginning to progress economically, although Albania remains one of the poorest countries in Europe.

ANDORRA

OFFICIAL NAME
Principat d'Andorra (Catalan); Principality of Andorra (English)

NICKNAME
The Pyrenean Country

POPULATION
72,400 (2009e)

INHABITANTS' NAME/NICKNAME
Andorran(s)

LANGUAGE/LANGUAGES
Catalan (official); Spanish, French, others

RELIGION/RELIGIONS
Roman Catholic, 89 percent; Protestant, Jewish, other or no religion

NATIONAL FLAG
The flag is a vertical tricolor of blue, yellow, and red, often with the coat of arms centered

on the yellow stripe. The design is based on the French flag, as are the colors red and blue. Yellow and red represent Spain* and the neighboring region of Catalonia*.

COAT OF ARMS/SEAL

The Andorran coat of arms is a shield divided into four parts, representing the Bishopric of Urgell and Catalonia in Spain, and Foix and Bearn in France*.

MOTTO

Virtus unita fortior (Latin); Strength united is stronger (English)

CAPITAL CITY

Andorra la Vella

TYPE OF GOVERNMENT

Co-principality and parliamentary democracy (since 1993) that retains as joint chiefs of state two co-princes, the president of France and the Roman Catholic bishop of La Seu d'Urgell in the neighboring Spanish region of Catalonia. Responsibility for defending Andorra rests with Spain and France. Andorra has no military force.

NATIONAL EMBLEM

The Pyrenees Mountains that cradle the country

NATIONAL COLORS

Blue, yellow, and red

NATIONAL ANTHEM

The anthem presents Andorra's history in a first-person narrative. It was officially adopted in 1914, on the feast day of the Virgin of Meritxell.

El Gran Carlemany (Catalan); The Great Charlemagne (English)

The great Charlemagne, my father, liberated me from the Saracens,
And from heaven he gave me life of Meritxell, the great mother.

I was born a princess, a maiden neutral between two nations.
I am the only remaining daughter of the Carolingian empire
Believing and free for eleven centuries, believing and free I will be.
The laws of the land be my tutors, and princes my defenders!
And princes my defenders!

PATRON SAINT

Virgin of Meritxell

CURRENCY

Andorra uses the Euro, which replaced the official currencies in Spain and France in 2001. As of 2009, Andorra is in negotiations with the European Union over the minting of Andorran Euro coins.

INTERNET IDENTIFIER

.ad

VEHICLE IDENTIFICATION PLATES/STICKERS

AND

PASSPORT

The passport cover has the name Andorra over the country's coat of arms and the word passport in Catalan, *passaport*.

NATIONAL FLOWER

Grandalla (Andorra daffodil)

NATIONAL TREE

Pyrenean willow (unofficial)

NATIONAL ANIMAL

Pyrenees mountain goat

NATIONAL RESOURCES

With few natural resources, Andorra relies on tourism based on its mountain scenery, summer and winter resorts, and duty-free shopping. Andorra is also a financial center and a tax haven.

FOODS

Escudella, a stew of chicken, sausage, and meatballs, is considered the national dish. *Xai*, or roasted lamb, is also a national tradition. Other specialties include *truita amb pernil*, mountain trout stuffed with Serrano ham; *butifarra amb mongetes*, pork sausages with sautéed white beans; *truita am ceba i patata*, an omelet of onion and potatoes; *palatilla*, roast leg of lamb with potatoes and vegetables; and *llentias*, lentils prepared with tomatoes, onion, potatoes, and spicy sausage.

SPORTS/SPORTS TEAMS

Alpine skiing is the national sport of Andorra, while football and rugby are also very popular. Andorra national teams participate in many sports at an international level.

TEAM SPORTS

Basketball

Andorra Basketball Team; Andorra Women's Basketball Team

Football

Andorra Football Team, nickname Els Tricolors (the Tricolors); Andorra Women's Football Team, nickname Els Tricolors (the Tricolors); Andorra Under-21 Football Team; Andorra Under-19 Football Team; Andorra Under-17 Football Team; Andorra Futsal Team; Andorra Rugby Union Team, nickname Els Isards; Andorra Australian-Rules Football Team; Andorra Rugby Union Team (Sevens), nickname Andorra Sevens or Andorra 7s; Andorra Women's Rugby Union Team (Sevens), nickname Andorra Sevens or Andorra 7s; Federatió Andorrana de Fútbol (Andorran Football Federation)

Golf

Andorra Men's Pitch and Putt Team

Hockey

Andorra Ice Hockey Team; Andorra Field Hockey Team

Racing

Andorra Speedway Team

Table Tennis

Andorra Table Tennis Team

Tennis

Andorra Davis Cup Team

Volleyball

Andorra Men's Volleyball Team; Andorra Women's Volleyball Team

INDIVIDUAL SPORTS

Andorra Amateur Boxing Team; Andorra Athletics Team; Andorra Canoeing Team; Andorra Chess Team; Andorra Cycling Team; Andorra Equestrian Team; Andorra Gymnastics Team; Andorra Judo Team; Andorra Sailing Team; Andorra Shooting Team; Andorra Swim Team; Andorra Tae Kwon Do Team; Andorra Triathlon Team

WINTER SPORTS

Andorra Alpine Ski Team; Andorra Biathlon Team; Andorra Curling Team; Andorra Ice Hockey Team; Andorra Luge Team; Andorra Skating Team

NATIONAL HEROES OR PERSONIFICATIONS

The 1,200 Andorran soldiers who fought on the Allied side during World War II are the country's national heroes and are honored each year on September 8.

NATIONAL HOLIDAY/INDEPENDENCE DAY

National Day (Our Lady of Meritxell Day), September 8

FESTIVALS/FAIRS

Winter Music Festival, variable dates; National Festival of Mare de Deu Meritxell, September

SIGNIFICANT EVENTS IN FORMATION OF NATIONAL IDENTITY

Ninth century Charlemagne grants a charter to the people of the Andorran valleys in the Pyrenees in return for their aid in fighting the invading Moors. The authority for the territory passes to the local counts of Urgell and eventually to the bishop of the diocese of Urgell.

11th century Fearing military conquest by neighboring lords, the Bishop of Urgell places himself under the Lord of Caboet, a Catalan nobleman. Later, the Count of Foix becomes heir to the Caboet title through marriage, and a dispute over Andorra arises between the French count of Foix and the Catalan bishop of Urgell.

1278 The dispute over Andorra is resolved with sovereignty being shared between the two local authorities. In France, the title would eventually be transferred to the French head of state.

1278–1993 For 715 years, from 1278 to 1993, Andorrans live under a unique co-principality, ruled by French and Spanish leaders (from 1607 onward, the French chief of state and the Spanish bishop of Urgell). The end, in 1993, of the historic overlordship of Spain and France is celebrated on March 14.

1812–1815 The First French Republic annexes Catalonia and divides it into four departments. Andorra is also annexed and becomes part of Catalonia. At the end of the Napoleonic wars, Andorra's territory and sovereignty are restored.

1936–1940 A French detachment is garrisoned in Andorra to prevent influences of the Spanish Civil War and Franco's Spain.

1939–1945 During World War II, Andorra remains neutral and serves as an important smuggling route between Vichy France and Spain. Most Andorrans support the Allies, and 1,200 young men volunteer to fight with the Free French forces.

1946–1976 Long isolated and impoverished, Andorra is a thriving duty-free shopping center for French and Spanish shoppers beset by high taxes and post-war shortages. Tourism becomes a major industry in the small, mountainous state.

1993 The feudal system is modified, with the titular heads of state retained, but the government is transformed into a parliamentary democracy.

1993–2009 Andorra remains outside the European Union but enjoys a special relationship, such as being treated as an EU member for trade in manufactured goods, including no tariffs, and as a non-EU state for agricultural products. In 2008, the prosperous nation has the world's longest life expectancy, at 83.5 years, although Andorrans are a minority in their own country, being outnumbered by Spaniards, Portuguese, French, and others resident in the principality.

ARMENIA

OFFICIAL NAME

Hayastani Hanrapetutyun (Armenian); Republic of Armenia (English); Hayastan (Armenian); Armenia (English)

POPULATION

3,460,000 (2009e)

INHABITANTS' NAME/NICKNAME

Armenian(s)

LANGUAGE/LANGUAGES

Armenian (official); Yezidi, Russian, others

RELIGION/RELIGIONS

Armenian Apostolic, 93 percent; Yezidi, 1.5 percent; Roman Catholic (Armenian Catholic), Protestant, other or no religion

NATIONAL FLAG

The flag is a horizontal tricolor of red, blue, and orange. Red symbolizes the Armenian Highland, the Armenian people's continued struggle for survival, maintenance of the Christian faith, Armenia's independence, and freedom. Blue symbolizes the will of the people of Armenia to live beneath peaceful skies. Orange symbolizes the creative talent and hardworking nature of the people of Armenia.

COAT OF ARMS/SEAL

The coat of arms of the Republic of Armenia depicts, in the center on a shield, Mount Ararat with Noah's ark and the coats of arms of the four kingdoms of historical Armenia. A lion and an eagle support the shield, while a sword, a branch, a sheaf, a chain, and a ribbon are portrayed under the shield.

MOTTO

Mek arg, met mshakowyt (Armenian); One nation, one culture (English)

CAPITAL CITY

Yerevan

TYPE OF GOVERNMENT

Unitary republic

NATIONAL EMBLEM

Mount Ararat

NATIONAL COLORS

Red, blue, and orange

NATIONAL ANTHEM

The anthem is based on a 19th century poem composed in Istanbul, with some words changed to reflect the freedom and independence Armenia achieved in 1991. In 2006, the authorities began a search for a new anthem, as the present song was meant only as a temporary anthem.

> **Mer Hayrenik (Armenian); Our Fatherland (English)**
>
> Our fatherland, free and independent,
> That has lived for centuries
> His children are now calling
> Free independent Armenia.
>
> Here brother, for you a flag,
> That I made with my hands
> At nights I did not sleep,
> I washed it with tears.
>
> Look at it, in three colors
> It is our gifted symbol.

> Let it shine against the enemy.
> Let Armenia always be glorious.
>
> Everywhere death is the same
> Man will only die but once
> But fortunate is he
> Who dies for the freedom of his nation.

PATRON SAINT

Saint Gregory the Illuminator

CURRENCY

Armenian dram

INTERNET IDENTIFIER

.am

VEHICLE IDENTIFICATION PLATES/STICKERS

ARM

PASSPORT

The passport cover has the name of the country in Armenian, the coat of arms, the word *passport* in Armenian, and at the bottom, the name of the country and the word *passport* in English.

AIRLINE

Armavia

NATIONAL FLOWER

Armenian gladiolus (unofficial)

NATIONAL ANIMAL

Lion (a creature from Armenian mythology)

NATIONAL BIRD

Golden eagle

NATIONAL RESOURCES

Natural resources include small deposits of gold, copper, molybdenum, zinc, and bauxite. Tourism is especially important, due to the large number of Armenians living in other countries. The Armenian Diaspora is a very important national resource, as it provides vital support and investment.

FOODS

Lavash, also known as Armenian cracker bread, is considered a national dish, as are *khorovats,* a type of kebab, and *moussaka,* a baked dish of spiced lamb and eggplant, and *harissa,* a mixture of stewed chicken and cracked wheat. Other specialties include *vospapur,* a soup of lentils and spinach; *azokod abour,* eggplant and chickpea soup; *juki kebab,* skewered marinated chicken cooked over charcoal; *missov dziran,* lamb cooked with apricots; *missov sekhi dolma,* melon stuffed with minced meat and onion; *dolma,* grape leaves stuffed with minced meat; and *pakhlava,* a layered pastry with honey and walnuts.

SPORTS/SPORTS TEAMS

Association football (soccer) is the national sport, but traditional sports, such as wrestling and boxing, are also very popular. Armenia national teams participate in many sports at an international level.

TEAM SPORTS

Badminton

Armenia Badminton Team

Baseball

Armenia Baseball Team; Armenia Softball Team

Basketball

Armenia Basketball Team; Armenia Women's Basketball Team

Football

Armenia Football Team, nickname Ararat or the Highlanders; Women's Football Team, nickname Ararat or the Highlanders; Armenia Under-21 Football Team nickname Little Ararat; Armenia Rugby Union Team; Armenia Futsal Team

Handball

Armenia Handball Team; Armenia Women's Handball Team

Hockey

Armenia Ice Hockey Team; Armenia Field Hockey Team; Armenia Bandy Team

Korfball

Armenia Korfball Team

Table Tennis

Armenia Table Tennis Team

Tennis

Armenia Davis Cup Team; Armenia Fed Cup Team

Volleyball

Armenia Men's Volleyball Team; Armenia Women's Volleyball Team

INDIVIDUAL SPORTS

Armenia Amateur Boxing Team; Armenia Athletics Team; Armenia Archery Team; Armenia Canoeing Team; Armenia Chess Team; Armenia Cycling Team; Armenia Equestrian Team; Armenia Fencing Team; Armenia Gymnastics Team; Armenia Judo Team; Armenia Modern Pentathlon Team; Armenia Rowing Team; Armenia Sailing Team; Armenia Shooting Team; Armenia Swim Team; Armenia Weight Lifting Team; Armenia Wrestling Team

WINTER SPORTS

Armenia Alpine Ski Team; Armenia Bandy Team; Armenia Biathlon Team; Armenia Luge Team; Armenia Skating Team

NATIONAL HEROES OR PERSONIFICATIONS

Mayr Hayastan (Mother Armenia) is the personification of Armenia. A statue of Mother Armenia is located in Victory Park overlooking the Armenian capital. The monumental statue replaced an earlier statue of Joseph Stalin set up on the same pedestal in 1967. The statue symbolizes peace through strength and is dedicated to the heroic females of Armenian history.

National heros include Andranik Ozanian, a military leader and politician during the first republic in the early 20th century; Vazgen I, the Catholicos of the Armenian Apostolic Church during the collapse of the Soviet Union and the recovery of Armenian independence; Charles Aznavour, born to Armenian refugee parents in Paris, one of the 20th century's greatest entertainers; Monte Melkonian, a soldier and hero of the independence movement and the Nagorno-Karabakh war in the 1990s

NATIONAL HOLIDAY/INDEPENDENCE DAY

Independence Day, September 21

FESTIVALS/FAIRS

Golden Apricot International Film Festival, July; Independence Day Celebrations, September; Vardavar, an ancient festival that combines paganism with nationalism, variable dates (98 days after Easter each year)

SIGNIFICANT EVENTS IN FORMATION OF NATIONAL IDENTITY

10,000 B.C.E.–1000 B.C.E. Armenia is a highland country surrounded by Biblical mountains, particularly Ararat, upon which, according to Judeo-Christian theology, Noah's Ark came to rest after the great flood. In the Bronze Age, several ancient states control the region, adding their characteristics to the ethnogenesis of the Armenians.

600 B.C.E.–301 C.E. Around 600 B.C.E., the Kingdom of Armenia is established. Yerevan, the modern capital of Armenia, is founded in 782 B.C.E. The kingdom lives a golden age under Tigranes the Great in the first century B.C.E., becoming one of the most powerful kingdoms of the time. Armenia prides itself on being the first nation to formally adopt Christianity, traditionally in 301 C.E.

400–1500 Throughout its long history, Armenia enjoys periods of independence intermingled with periods of autonomy within contemporary empires or as a subject nation to more powerful neighbors. The country's strategic location between Europe and Asia leaves it open to invasions by Assyrians, Greeks, Romans, Byzantines, Arabs, Mongols, Persians, Turks, and Russians.

1500s The Turkish Ottoman Empire and the neighboring Persian Empire divide historical Armenia between them. The Armenians, as Christians living in Muslim states, are subjected to special taxes, restrictions, and often persecution.

1813–1828 The Russian Empire incorporates Eastern Armenia from territories taken piecemeal from Persia. The Russians, fellow Christians, are often welcomed as liberators by the Armenian populations.

1850–1896 Under Ottoman rule, the Armenians of Western Armenia are granted considerable autonomy; however, as Christians living in a Muslim empire they face pervasive discrimination. When activists begin pushing for more rights, the Turkish sultan responds by ordering state-sponsored massacres between 1894 and 1896, resulting in an estimated death toll of between 80,000 and 300,000 people. The Hamidian massacres, as they are known, earn Sultan 'Abdu'l-Hamid II the infamous nicknames the Red Sultan and the Bloody Sultan.

1914–1918 During World War I, the Armenians in the Turkish portion of Armenia again come under suspicion for supporting the Turks' Christian enemies. The Ottoman government institutes a policy of forced resettlement, coupled with other harsh practices, that results in an estimated 1–1.5 million Armenian deaths, called the Armenian Holocaust. Survivors flee to many parts of the world, laying the basis of the large Armenian Diaspora. Muslim Turks and Kurds later settle depopulated Western Armenia.

1918–1930 Eastern or Russian Armenia declares its independence in 1918, but it is conquered by the Soviet Red Army in 1920. Soviet leader Joseph Stalin assigns the Armenian-populated region of Nagorno-Karabakh to Soviet Azerbaijan*, over Armenian protests.

1930–1953 Stalin is distrustful of the Armenians and their contacts with the diaspora in the West. Repeated purges devastate intellectual circles and the Armenian leadership. Stalin's death in 1953 somewhat eases the repression.

1986–1988 During the Gorbachev reforms in the Soviet Union, the Armenians of Nagorno-Karabakh in Azerbaijan demand reunification with Armenia. Peaceful protests in Yerevan supporting the Karabakh Armenians are met by anti-Armenian violence in Azerbaijan. Fighting between Armenians and Azerbaijanis breaks out in Nagorno-Karabakh.

1991–1994 The struggle escalates after both countries attain independence with the collapse of the Soviet Union. By May 1994, when a cease-fire takes hold, Armenian forces hold not only Nagorno-Karabakh but also a significant portion of Azerbaijan proper. The economies of both sides are hurt by their inability to make substantial progress toward a peaceful resolution. Turkey* imposes an economic blockade on Armenia and closes the common border because of the Armenian separatists' control of Nagorno-Karabakh and surrounding areas in Azerbaijan.

1994–2008 The ongoing conflict with Azerbaijan harms the economy, and economic blockades by Azerbaijan and Turkey continue to curb development. Parliament adopts a bill allowing dual citizenship, creating a simple mechanism for the naturalization of Armenia's very large diaspora, estimated at around 6 million. Significant progress is made in 2008, when presidential elections are judged largely democratic by international observers. The Turkish president visits Armenia, the first time a Turkish official has visited the country.

2009 The Armenian nation, according to Armenian tradition, includes not only those Armenians living in the republic, but also the large and dispersed Armenian population known as the Armenian Diaspora. The people of the diaspora have become the prime supporters of Armenian democracy and the largest investors in the country. In August 2009, the governments of Armenia and Turkey announce their intention to establish diplomatic relations.

AUSTRIA

OFFICIAL NAME

Republik Oesterreich (German); Republic of Austria (English)

POPULATION

8,332,400 (2009e)

INHABITANTS' NAME/NICKNAME

Austrian(s)

LANGUAGE/LANGUAGES

German (official); Turkish, Serbian, Croatian (official in Burgenland), Slovene (official in Carinthia), Hungarian (official in Burgenland), others

RELIGION/RELIGIONS

Roman Catholic, 73 percent; Protestant, 5 percent; Muslim, 4.5 percent; Jewish, other or no religion

NATIONAL FLAG

The flag has three equal horizontal stripes of red, white, and red. According to legend, the flag was created by Duke Leopold while he was fighting the Crusades. After a battle, his white battledress was completely drenched in blood, but when he removed his wide belt, the white cloth underneath was untouched. He was so taken with the sight that he adopted the colors and stripes as his banner. The flag is possibly the oldest national flag design in the world.

COAT OF ARMS/SEAL

The coat of arms has the Austrian black eagle with a shield of the national colors centered. The eagle's claws hold a golden sickle and a golden hammer. The broken iron chain between its claws symbolizes Austria's liberation from Nazism and was added after World War II.

CAPITAL CITY
Vienna

TYPE OF GOVERNMENT
Federal parliamentary republic

NATIONAL EMBLEM
Austrian black eagle

NATIONAL COLORS
Red and white

NATIONAL ANTHEM
Following the end of World War II, the Austrian Federal Government held a competition for a new anthem to replace the anthem associated with the Nazi regime.

> **Land der Berge, Land am Strome (German); Land of Mountains, Land on the River (English)**
>
> Land of mountains, land on the stream,
> Land of fields, land of cathedrals,
> Land of hammers, with a rich future,
> You are home to great sons,
> A people blessed by their sense of beauty,
> Highly praised Austria,
> Highly praised Austria!
>
> Strongly feuded for, fiercely hard-fought for,
> You are in the centre of the Continent
> Like a strong heart,
> Since the early days of the ancestors you have
> Borne the burden of a high mission,
> Much-tried Austria,
> Much-tried Austria
>
> Into the new times,
> See us striding, courageous, free, and faithful,
> Assiduous and full of hope,
> Unified, in fraternal chorus, let us
> Pledge allegiance to you, our country,
> Much beloved Austria,
> Much beloved Austria

PATRON SAINT
Saint Joseph, Saint Maurice, Saint Coloman, Saint Leopold the Good, Saint Florian

CURRENCY
Euro

INTERNET IDENTIFIER
.at

VEHICLE IDENTIFICATION PLATES/ STICKERS
A

PASSPORT
The passport cover has the name of the European Union over the name of the Republic of Austria in German, the coat of arms, the German word for passport, *reisepass*, and the standard biometric symbol.

AIRLINES
Austrian Airlines; Lauda Airlines

NATIONAL FLOWER
Gentian (official); edelweiss (unofficial)

NATIONAL ANIMAL
Mountain goat (unofficial)

NATIONAL BIRD
Barn swallow

NATIONAL RESOURCES
Natural resources include oil, coal, lignite, timber, iron ore, copper, zinc, antimony, magnetite, tungsten, graphite, salt, and hydropower. Beautiful mountain scenery, the River Danube, historic cities, and a unique culture make tourism an important industry.

FOODS
Wiener schnitzel, thinly sliced veal, breaded and fried, is considered a national dish. Other national dishes include *tafelspitz,* boiled beef, Viennese style; *kaiserschmarrn,* a caramelized pancake with raisins; *knödel,* a dumpling casserole; Sachertorte, a distinc-

tive chocolate cake; *apfelstrudel*, a pastry made with apples; *gewürzte schweinsrippchen*, braised spicy spareribs; *erdäpfel salat*, potato salad; *Salzburger nockerin*, a special pastry from the Salzburg region; and *vanillekipferl*, a small pastry made with hazelnuts or almonds and vanilla.

SPORTS/SPORTS TEAMS

Alpine skiing is the national and most popular sport, followed closely by association football (soccer). Austria national teams participate in many sports at an international level.

TEAM SPORTS

Badminton

Australia Badminton Team

Baseball

Austria Baseball Team; Austria Softball Team

Basketball

Austria Basketball Team; Austria Women's Basketball Team; Austria Wheelchair Basketball Team

Cricket

Austria Cricket Team

Football

Austria Football Team, nickname Wunderteam (Wonder Team); Austria Women's Football Team, nickname Wunderteam (Wonder Team); Austria Under-21 Football Team; Austria Women's Under-19 Football Team; Austria Rugby Union Team; Austria Women's Rugby Union Team; Austria Rugby League Team; Austria Australian-Rules Football Team, nickname the Kangaroos; Austria Wheelchair Rugby Team; Austria American Football Team; Austria Beach Soccer Team; Austria Futsal Team

Handball

Austria Handball Team; Austria Women's Handball Team; Austria Beach Handball Team; Austria Women's Beach Handball Team

Hockey

Austria Field Hockey Team; Austria Ice Hockey Team; Austria Junior Ice Hockey Team; Austria Women's Ice Hockey Team

Racing

A1 Team Austria; Austria Speedway Team

Table Tennis

Austria Table Tennis Team;

Tennis

Austria Davis Cup Team; Austria Fed Cup Team

Volleyball

Austria Fistball Team; Austria Men's Beach Volleyball Team; Austria Women's Beach Volleyball Team; Austria Men's Volleyball Team; Austria Women's Volleyball Team

INDIVIDUAL SPORTS

Austria Amateur Boxing Team; Austria Athletics Team; Austria Archery Team, nickname Team Austria; Austria Canoeing Team; Austria Chess Team; Austria Cycling Team; Austria Equestrian Team; Austria Fencing Team; Austria Gymnastics Team; Austria Judo Team; Austria Karate Team; Austria Modern Pentathlon Team; Austria Rowing Team; Austria Sailing Team; Austria Shooting Team; Austria Swim Team; Austria Tae Kwon Do Team; Austria Triathlon Team; Austria Weight Lifting Team; Austria Wrestling Team

WINTER SPORTS

Austria Alpine Ski Team; Austria Biathlon Team; Austria Bobsleigh and Tobogganing

Team; Austria Curling Team; Austria Luge Team; Austria Ice Hockey Team; Austria Junior Ice Hockey Team; Austria Women's Ice Hockey Team; Austria Skating Team

NATIONAL HEROES OR PERSONIFICATIONS

Austria, the 19th century allegory, symbolizes the modern federal Austrian state.

Archduke Maximillian, first ruler of the Habsburg Austria during its period of expansion in the 16th century; Maria Theresa, empress of Austria in the 18th century; Francis I, first hereditary emperor of Austria

NATIONAL HOLIDAY/INDEPENDENCE DAY

National Day, October 26

FESTIVALS/FAIRS

Fasching (Carnival), February–March; Corpus Christi, spring; Vienna Festival Weeks, May–June; Viennale, Vienna Film Festival, October; Salzburg Festival, July–August

SIGNIFICANT EVENTS IN FORMATION OF NATIONAL IDENTITY

500 B.C.E.–16 B.C.E.   In the pre-Roman period, various Celtic tribes occupy central Europe. The Celtic kingdom of Noricum is claimed by the Roman Empire. After the Roman conquest, Noricum becomes a Roman province.

395 C.E.–788 C.E.   The fall of the Roman Empire opens the way to invasions by Bavarians, Slavs, and Avars. Charlemagne conquers the region in 788 and encourages conversion to Christianity and colonization by Christians to offset the pagan majority.

976–996   As part of Eastern Francia, the core areas of present Austria pass to the house of Babenberg.

996–1192   The following centuries are characterized by the settlement of the Babenberg holdings. In 1156, central Austria is elevated to the status of a duchy, and in 1192, the Babenbergs acquire the neighboring Duchy of Styria.

1278–1526   The region then comes under the rule of the Hapsburgs, who extend their rule to neighboring territories in the 15th and 16th centuries. The Habsburg holdings, through conquest or marriage, eventually extend across Europe. The Hapsburgs rule in the Low Countries and Spain* and its colonies, and acquire Bohemia and the part of Hungary* not occupied by the Ottoman Turks in 1526.

1526–1740   A series of wars against the Turks culminates in 1683 with the successful defense of Vienna.

1815   Austria is part of the allied forces that invade France in 1814 and emerges from the Napoleonic Wars as one of the three dominant powers in Europe, along with Russia* and Prussia.

1804–1867   Austria is declared the Empire of Austria in 1804 and in 1867 is transformed into the dual monarchy of Austria-Hungary.

1867–1914   The joint rule of the empire by the Austrians and Hungarians becomes increasingly difficult in the age of emerging nationalist movements. Czech, Romanian, Italian, Serbian, and many other ethnic groups grow restive under the domination of the two core nationalities.

1914–1918   A Serbian nationalist in Sarajevo assassinates Archduke Franz Ferdinand in 1914, and World War I begins. The non-Austrian peoples of the defeated empire declare the independence of their own states. Austria, separated from Hungary, is accepted by the Allies as representative of the majority of the German-speaking peoples of the empire. In 1918, Austria is declared a republic but is forbidden to unite with Germany.

1934   The Austrian Civil War in February 1934 allows the fascists to gain power.

1934–1945   A resurgent Germany claims German-speaking Austria as part of the Third Reich, and on March 12, 1938, German troops march into Vienna. Austrians, most often willingly, serve on all fronts as part of the German military during World War II.

1945–1955   The Allies divide Austria, like Germany, into four occupation zones; as with Berlin, the four major Allied armies also control Vienna. Finally, Austria concludes a state treaty and regains its full independence in 1955.

1955–1990 Austria's constitution declares the country to be strictly neutral in the ongoing Cold War. In spite of sharing a border with the countries behind the so-called Iron Curtain on the east, Austria's post-war economic recovery allows for the creation of a democratic, stable, and affluent society.

1995 Austria joins the European Union in 1995 but retains its strict neutrality and forbids the stationing of foreign troops on its soil.

2006–2009 Immigration to Austria, mostly from Turkey and the former Socialist states of Eastern Europe, becomes a leading issue for the Austrian people. Beginning in 2006, some Austrian states introduce standardized tests for new citizens to ensure their German language ability, their cultural knowledge, and, accordingly, their ability to integrate into the greater Austrian society. The adhesion of the neighboring, formerly Socialist states to the European Union has allowed the Austrians to renew old ties to the east. Austrians once again see themselves as part of the central core of Europe, rather than part of the Cold War frontier between East and West.

AZERBAIJAN

OFFICIAL NAME
Azerbaycan Respublikasi (Azerbaijani); Republic of Azerbaijan (English)

POPULATION
8,841,600 (2009e)

INHABITANTS' NAME/NICKNAME
Azerbaijani(s); Azeri(s)

LANGUAGE/LANGUAGES
Azerbaijani (Azeri) (official); Lezgi, Russian, Armenian, others

RELIGION/RELIGIONS
Muslim, 93 percent (80% Shia, 20% Sunni), Russian Orthodox, 2.5 percent; other or no religion

NATIONAL FLAG
The flag is a horizontal tricolor of pale blue, red, and green with a white crescent moon and eight-pointed star centered on the red. The eight points of the star stand for the eight branches of the Turkic people. The blue stripe symbolizes Azerbaijan's Turkish heritage, the green stands for Islam, and the red symbolizes progress.

COAT OF ARMS/SEAL
The coat of arms is a fire symbol centered on an eight-pointed white star outlined in gold and superimposed on three circles of blue, red, and green, the colors of the national flag. The fire stands for the traditional Azeri nickname, the Land of Eternal Fire.

CAPITAL CITY
Baku

TYPE OF GOVERNMENT
Secular unitary republic

NATIONAL EMBLEM
Red fire symbol, an ancient symbol of the Azerbaijanis

NATIONAL COLORS
Pale blue, red, and green

NATIONAL ANTHEM
The Azerbaijani anthem was originally created during the country's brief period of independence in 1918–1921. After the breakup of the Soviet Union, the anthem of the first Azerbaijani republic was adopted for the newly independent state.

Azerbaijan Marsi (Azerbaijani); March of Azerbaijan (English)

Azerbaijan, Azerbaijan!
You are the country of heroes!
We will die so that you might be alive!
We will shed our blood to defend you!
Long live the three-colored banner!
Thousands of people sacrificed their lives
You're become the field of battles.
Every soldier fighting for you,
Has become a hero.
We pray for your prosperity,
We sacrifice our lives to you
Our sincere love to you,
Comes from the bottom of our hearts.
To defend your honor,
To hoist your banner,
All the young people are ready.
Glorious motherland,
Azerbaijan, Azerbaijan!

CURRENCY

Azerbaijani manat

INTERNET IDENTIFIER

.az

VEHICLE IDENTIFICATION PLATES/STICKERS

AZ

PASSPORT

The passport cover has the name of the country in Azerbaijani, the coat of arms, and the Azerbaijani word for passport.

AIRLINE

Azerbaijan Airlines AZAL

NATIONAL FLOWER

Khunjilit (crocus) (unofficial)

NATIONAL TREE

Iberian oak (on the coat of arms)

NATIONAL ANIMAL

Gazelle (unofficial)

NATIONAL BIRD

Pheasant (unofficial)

NATIONAL FISH

Beluga sturgeon (unofficial)

NATIONAL RESOURCES

Natural resources include petroleum, natural gas, iron ore, nonferrous metals, and bauxite. Petroleum reserves are large and hold the promise of prosperity. Caspian Sea caviar is one of Azerbaijan's most prestigious exports. Tourism is minimal, but the country's historic cities, exotic culture, and Caspian Sea beaches could support a thriving tourist industry.

FOODS

Kebab, Caspian sturgeon served with a tart sour plum sauce, is considered the national dish. Other national specialties include *dushara*, a mutton soup with onions, mint, and grape vinegar; *yarpag dolmasi*, grape leaves stuffed with minced mutton and rice; *gutab*, a dish of mixed greens, spring onions, and wheat flour; *pilaff*, a rice dish with mutton, raisins, dried apricots, chestnuts, and onions; and *baklava*, a dessert of layered pastry with walnuts and honey.

SPORTS/SPORTS TEAMS

Association football (soccer) is the most popular sport in the country. Azerbaijan national teams participate in many sports at an international level.

TEAM SPORTS

Badminton

Azerbaijan Badminton Team

Baseball

Azerbaijan Softball Team

Basketball

Azerbaijan Basketball Team; Azerbaijan Women's Basketball Team

Football

Azerbaijan Football Team, nickname Azeri or Odlar Yurdu (Country of Fire); Azerbaijan Women's Football Team, nickname Azeri or Oldar Yurdu (Country of Fire); Azerbaijan Rugby Union Team; Azerbaijan Futsal Team

Handball

Azerbaijan Handball Team; Azerbaijan Women's Handball Team

Hockey

Azerbaijan Ice Hockey Team; Azerbaijan Field Hockey Team

Table Tennis

Azerbaijan Table Tennis Team

Tennis

Azerbaijan Davis Cup Team; Azerbaijan Fed Cup Team

Volleyball

Azerbaijan Men's Volleyball Team; Azerbaijan Women's Volleyball Team

Water Polo

Azerbaijan Water Polo Team

INDIVIDUAL SPORTS

Azerbaijan Aikido Team; Azerbaijan Amateur Boxing Team; Azerbaijan Archery Team; Azerbaijan Athletics Team; Azerbaijan Bodybuilding Team; Azerbaijan Canoeing Team; Azerbaijan Chess Team; Azerbaijan Cycling Team; Azerbaijan Equestrian Team; Azerbaijan Fencing Team; Azerbaijan Gymnastics Team; Azerbaijan Judo Team; Azerbaijan Karate Team; Azerbaijan Modern Pentathlon Team; Azerbaijan Rowing Team; Azerbaijan Sailing Team; Azerbaijan Shooting Team; Azerbaijan Sumo Team; Azerbaijan Swim Team; Azerbaijan Tae Kwon Do Team; Azerbaijan Weight Lifting Team; Azerbaijan Wrestling Team

WINTER SPORTS

Azerbaijan Ice Hockey Team; Azerbaijan Skating Team

NATIONAL HEROES OR PERSONIFICATIONS

Koroghlu, a mythical hero who stole from the rich to give to the poor, is the personification of Azerbaijan.

Heydar Aliyev, a former Soviet leader who became independent Azerbaijan's first president in 1991; Khaqani Shirvani, a 12th-century lyric poet considered the father of Azeri literature; Mammed Amin Rasulzade, a leader of the first republic in 1918–1920; Ali-Agha Shiklinski, a military commander of the Azeri forces during the first republic 1918–1920

NATIONAL HOLIDAY/INDEPENDENCE DAY

Founding Day (Independence Day), May 28

FESTIVALS/FAIRS

International Baku Jazz Festival: Ramazan Bayram, follows the month of fasting in October; Noruz; Zoroastrian New Year celebration, March–April

SIGNIFICANT EVENTS IN FORMATION OF NATIONAL IDENTITY

Bronze Age Evidence of early human habitation has been found in several caves in Azerbaijan. Jugs of dry wine found in early tombs testify to wine making in the region in the late Bronze Age.

5500 B.C.E. The Zoroastrian religion, believed by some to have originated in Azerbaijan, spreads throughout the Caucasus.

Ninth century–seventh century B.C.E. Most of Azerbaijan becomes part of ancient Media, which is centered in what is now Iranian Azerbaijan.

Sixth century–fourth century B.C.E. Media, including Azerbaijan, is incorporated into the Persian Empire.

Fourth century B.C.E. Overrun by the Greeks of Alexander the Great, the region gains new ties with the West.

First century B.C.E.**–eighth century** C.E. The Caucasian Albanians, the original inhabitants of the region, create a separate kingdom in the first century B.C.E. The Caucasian Albanian king Urnayr adopts Christianity as the state religion in the fourth century. The country remains a Christian state until the eighth century.

667 C.E. Invading Arabs defeat both the Persians and Byzantines to take control of most of the southern Caucasus. Islam, the Arab religion, gradually spreads through the tribes of the region.

8th century–11th century The decline of the Arab Caliphate leaves the region open to conquest. Various dynasties hold sway for periods of time until the Turkic peoples from Central Asia occupy the region. The Turkic language becomes the major language of the region.

16th century By the early 16th century, the rulers have imposed Persia's Shia form of Islam on the formerly Sunni Muslim population.

1813–1828 The Russian Empire, pushing its borders south into the Caucasus, takes control of northern Azerbaijan.

1914–1936 World War I brings the collapse of the Russian Empire and allows the subject peoples to declare their homelands independent nations. Azerbaijan briefly joins Armenia* and Georgia* in a short-lived federation but withdraws and declares separate independence in May 1918. The Azerbaijan Democratic Republic becomes the first Muslim republic in the world but lasts only two years before falling to the advancing Russian Red Army. Azerbaijan becomes a separate union republic of the Soviet Union in 1936.

1940–1945 Azerbaijan supplies much of the oil and gas for the Soviet Union's war against Germany during World War II.

1950–1990 The Cold War leads to much oppression in the Soviet Union. Intellectuals, artists, teachers, and others are persecuted. The Muslim religion, although tolerated, is severely restricted, particularly the important pilgrimage to Mecca and other observances.

1988–1991 The politics of glasnost, initiated by Mikhail Gorbachev, leads to civil unrest and ethnic strife. The region of Nagorno-Karabakh, disputed by Armenia and Azerbaijan, becomes a nationalist focus in both countries. The disintegration of the Soviet Union allows the country's leaders to declare complete independence on October 18, 1991.

1991–1994 The Nagorno-Karabakh War with Armenia overshadows the early years of independence. By the time a cease-fire is negotiated in 1994, Azerbaijan has lost to Armenian control between 14 percent and 16 percent of its national territory, including all of Nagorno-Karabakh.

1993–2009 The election of the former Soviet era leader, Heydar Aliyev, finally begins a period of reconstruction and recuperation. Production from several of Azerbaijan's oil fields begins to inject much-needed hard currency into the Azerbaijani economy. The formerly small middle class begins to expand, importing styles and technology from Europe and North America. Despite widespread fraud and corruption, the Aliyev dynasty continues with the election of Heydar's son, Ilham Aliyev, in 2003. Under the Aliyevs, the country maintains close ties to Europe and the West and remains a secular state relatively free of the radical religion prevalent in neighboring Iran and other parts of the Muslim World. Armenia and Azerbaijan sign a joint agreement aimed at intensifying their efforts to resolve the long-standing dispute over the territory of Nagorno-Karabakh.

AZORES

OFFICIAL NAME
Região Autónoma dos Açores (Portuguese); Azores Autonomous Region (English)

POPULATION
246,800 (2009e)

INHABITANTS' NAME/NICKNAME
Azorean(s)

LANGUAGE/LANGUAGES

Portuguese (official); Azorean (the language of daily life), English, others

RELIGION/RELIGIONS

Roman Catholic, 91 percent, Protestant, Jewish, other or no religion

NATIONAL FLAG

The Azores flag, based on the nationalist flag of the 1970s, consists of a bicolor of dark blue and white, the blue, at the hoist, making up two fifths of the flag's area. Over the division, and extending horizontally to about half of the flag's total width is a golden goshawk, wings spread under an arch of nine golden stars, extending from one wingtip to the other. On the upper hoist is a white shield bearing five blue eschuteons, each charged with a saltire of five golden castles. The goshawk, *açor* in Portuguese, is the name given the local buzzards by early explorers. It came to symbolize the islands. The nine stars stand for the nine islands in the archipelago. The shield on the upper hoist symbolizes the islands' ties to mainland Portugal*. The blue stands for the sea and the white for purity of purpose.

COAT OF ARMS/SEAL

The coat of arms has a central shield with a central blue goshawk surrounded by a border of red bearing nine gold stars. Above the shield is a heraldic gold helmet lined with red, surmounted by a wreath and mantling of silver and blue, below another blue goshawk decorated with the same nine gold stars. The shield is supported by two black bulls, collared and chained in gold, holding flagpoles bearing historical flags with traditional symbols, a Portuguese cross and a dove. Below is a gold banner bearing the national motto.

CAPITAL CITY

Ponta Delgada (some government functions are located in other island cities)

TYPE OF GOVERNMENT

Parliamentary democracy as an autonomous region of Portugal*

NATIONAL EMBLEM

Goshawk

NATIONAL COLORS

Blue and white

NATIONAL ANTHEM

The anthem, based on a traditional song, was adopted in 1979 as part of the creation of separate symbols for the autonomous country of the Azores.

Hino dos Açores (Portuguese); Hymn of the Azores (English)

Faith and firmness gave birth
In the splendor of a new chant
The Azores are our assurance

Of tracing the glory of a people
Ahead! In communion,
For our Autonomy.
Liberty, justice and reason
Are lit up in the lightning
Of the Flag that guides us
Ahead! Fight, Battle
For the immortal past
Seed in future the light
Of a triumphant people
Of a destiny achieved with pride
To pick more fruit and flowers
Because this is the sacred way
Of the stars that crown the Azores.
Ahead, Azoreans!
For peace in the united land.
We take large flights,
So that branches of deserved victory
Flower better.
Ahead! Fight, Battle
For the immortal past,
Seed in future the light,
Of a triumphant people.

PATRON SAINT

Santo Cristo dos Milagres (Christ of Miracles)

CURRENCY

Euro

INTERNET IDENTIFIER

.pt Portugal

VEHICLE IDENTIFICATION PLATES/
STICKERS

P Portugal (official); AZO Azores (unofficial)

PASSPORT

Azoreans are Portuguese citizens and travel on Portuguese passports.

NATIONAL FLOWER

Hydrangea (unofficial)

NATIONAL TREE

Azorean juniper (unofficial)

NATIONAL PLANT

Azorean heather (unofficial)

NATIONAL ANIMAL

Wild rabbit (unofficial)

NATIONAL BIRD

Goshawk (unofficial)

NATIONAL FISH

Common trout (brown trout) (unofficial)

NATIONAL RESOURCES

The fertile islands support an important dairy industry with cheese, dried milk and other dairy products as the islands' principal exports. Farming and animal husbandry are also important industries as is fishing in the deep Atlantic Ocean that surrounds the Azores. The local scenery, unique Azorean culture, the many festivals and the historical sites and monuments sustain an important tourist industry.

FOODS

The Azorean national dish is *Sopa de courves,* a stew of potatoes, onions, collard greens, savoy cabbage or kale, often served with cubes of pork or slices of local sausage, *chouriço.* Another soup, *Sopa de Espírito Santo,* made of beef, pork, chicken, onion, garlic, and dry bread, is also considered a national dish. Other traditional dishes include *Bacalhau à la ménagère,* a dish of salt cod, potatoes, and onions in a sauce made of milk and flour; *Alcatra,* roast beef cooked in a clay pot; *Torresmos,* a dish of pork, red wine, hot pepper, cloves, and orange juice; *Pudim flam,* a custard dessert, is considered a national dessert as is *Massa Sovada,* a dessert called Sweetloaf in English.

SPORTS/SPORTS TEAMS

Association football is the most popular sport. Traditional sports such as athletics, wrestling, and sailing are also very popular. The Azores national team participates in football at an international level.

TEAM SPORTS

Football

Azores Football Team

NATIONAL HEROES OR PERSONIFICATIONS

Gonçalo Velho Cabral, the first navigator to discover the uninhabited islands and leader of the colonists who settled the islands in the 15th century; Jácome de Bruges, the Flemish leader who organized the Flemish colonists in 1450; Vasco Gil Sodré, with his family settled the island of Graciosa in the 15th century; Antonio, Prior of Crato, the claimant to the Portuguese throne who lived in the Azores during the period of Spanish rule in Portugal; Diogo de Teive, the discoverer of the last two of the uninhabited islands, Flores and Corvo.

NATIONAL HOLIDAY/INDEPENDENCE DAY

Azores Day, June 1; Republic Day, October 17

FESTIVALS/FAIRS

Holy Ghost Festivals, at different times on each island from May to September; Festival of Senhor Santo Cristo dos Milagres (Christ of Miracles), May; Carnival, February-March; Festa das Vindimas (Wine Harvest Festival), September

SIGNIFICANT EVENTS IN FORMATION OF NATIONAL IDENTITY

1432 Gonçalo Velho Cabral, sailing for Portugal, sites the island of Santa Maria.

1439 The first known document to confirm the existence of the Azores is written, although only mentioning seven of the islands. The Azores become Portugal's first overseas colony. The first colonists arrive in the islands from overcrowded Europe.

1450–1452 The island of Terceira is granted to Jacome de Bruges as a site for Flemish colonization. The last of the islands, Flores and Corvo, are discovered.

1466–1474 Alfonso V gives the islands to the Duchess Isabella of Burgundy as a gift. The islands are later militarized to block a Burgundian bid to gain control.

1580–1640 The Azores, along with other Portuguese possession are occupied and incorporated into Spain*. An English expedition attempts to take the islands in 1587.

1820 Civil war in Portugal also divides the Azores, where liberal groups defeat the conservatives to establish a firm base for the Portuguese Council of Regency.

1886 The first stamps specifically for use in the Azores are issued.

1836–1976 The islands are divided into three districts. American and Canadian whalers use the islands as a base, beginning a long tradition of emigration of Azoreans to the east coast of the United States* and Canada*. Later Azorean immigration moves to Brazil and other areas of the Americas.

1910–1919 The Portuguese monarchy is overthrown and a republic proclaimed. The first hydroplane to cross the Atlantic stops in the islands for refueling and rest.

1943–1945 The dictator of neutral Portugal, Antonio la Salazar, agrees to bar German ships and submarines and leases facilities to the British during World War II. American troops arrive in the islands in 1944 where they construct Lajes Field, the first airfield in the islands.

1974–1976 Revolution in Portugal ends the Salazar dictatorship and Portugal's remaining colonies are quickly granted independence, igniting Azorean demands for independence as Portugal's first overseas colony. A leftist government is installed in Lisbon, which frightens many Azoreans and greatly increases support for independence. A more moderate government takes over and grants autonomy to the islands in 1976, which satisfies most Azoreans.

1986 Portugal becomes part of the European Community, later known as the European Union (EU). The Azores, because of their special autonomy and geographic isolation are accorded special regulations.

1990–2000 Increased prosperity and the financial benefits of EU membership reverse the historic tradition of emigration with many Azoreans returning to live in the islands.

1999–2009 Macau*, the last official Portuguese colony, is relinquished to Chinese sovereignty in 1999 with some nationalists reiterating their desire for the decolonization of their islands. The Azores, along with Portugal, adopt the Euro, although prices quickly rise, fanning resentment and demands for more development funds.

See also Portugal

BASHKORTOSTAN

OFFICIAL NAME
Republika Baŝkortostan (transliteration from Russian); Başqortostan Respublikahy (transliteration from Bashkort); Republic of Bashkortostan (English)

POPULATION
4,211,500 (2009e)

INHABITANTS' NAME/NICKNAME
Bashkort(s); Bashkir(s); Bashkirian(s)

LANGUAGE/LANGUAGES
Bashkort, Russian (both official); Tatar, Chuvash, Mari, Ukrainian, others

RELIGION/RELIGIONS
Sunni Muslim, 54 percent; Russian Orthodox, 43 percent; Armenian Orthodox, Roman Catholic, Protestant, other or no religion

NATIONAL FLAG
The flag consists of three equal horizontal stripes of pale blue, white, and green bearing a stylized *kurai* flower with seven petals in gold centered on the white field. The *kurai*, Bashkortostan's national flower, is a symbol of friendship and represents the seven divisions of the Bashkort nation and the unity of the nation. The blue stripe represents the sky and the integrity, clarity, and good will of the Bashkort people, the white represents peace, and the green stands for freedom, eternal life and the Islamic religion.

COAT OF ARMS/SEAL
The coat of arms is mostly in gold, yellow, and white, showing a large circle with a traditional Bashkort design surrounding the Salavat Yulaev monument of a horseman in front of a rising sun and fourteen sheaves of golden wheat. Below the horseman are a green *kurai* flower and a banner in the colors of the national flag, bearing the name of the country in the Cyrillic alphabet. The horseman represents the nomadic history and animal husbandry of the Bashkorts, the wheat represents the fertility of their homeland, and the *kurai* represents the seven original tribes of the Bashkort nation.

CAPITAL CITY
Ufa

TYPE OF GOVERNMENT
Semipresidential democracy as a member republic of the Russian Federation

NATIONAL EMBLEM
Kurai flower

NATIONAL COLORS
Blue, white, and green

NATIONAL ANTHEM
The anthem was tentatively adopted in 1993 and became the official anthem of the republic in 2008. It is designated as one of Bashkortostan's national symbols. It has both Bashkort and Russian translations. An English translation was not available.

Başqortostan Respublikahsınıñ Dült Gimnı (transliteration from Bashkort); National Anthem of the Republic of Bashkortostan (English) (Russian version)

First verse

Bashkortostan, Otchizna dorogaya,
Ty dlya nas svyashchennaya zemlya.
S Urala solntse vskhodit, ozaryaya
Nashi gory, reki i polya.

Chorus

Slav'sya, nash Bashkortostan!
Sud'boy narodu ty dlya schast'ya dan!
S Rossiyey my yediny—i vsegda
Protsvetay, Bashkortostan!

Second verse

Bashkortostan—ty nasha chest' i slava.
Dobroy voley, druzhboy ty silyon.
I styag tvoy reyet gordo, velichavo—
On svobodoy, bratstvom okrylyon.

Chorus

Slav'sya, nash Bashkortostan!
Sud'boy narodu ty dlya schast'ya dan!
S Rossiyey my yediny—i vsegda
Protsvetay, Bashkortostan!

Third verse

Respublika, siyay zvezdoy prekrasnoy,
Ty likuy v svershen'yakh i trudakh!
Rodnoy ochag pust' nikogda ne gasnet,
Pust' vedut nas pesni skvoz' goda.

Chorus

Slav'sya, nash Bashkortostan!
Sud'boy narodu ty dlya schast'ya dan!
S Rossiyey my yediny—i vsegda
Protsvetay, Bashkortostan!

PATRON SAINT

The Holy Resurrection

CURRENCY

Russian ruble

INTERNET IDENTIFIER

.ru Russia

VEHICLE IDENTIFICATION PLATES/STICKERS

RU Russia* (official); BA Bashkortostan (unofficial)

PASSPORT

The Bashkorts are Russian citizens and travel on Russian passports.

AIRLINE

Air Bashkortostan

NATIONAL FLOWER

Kurai (official); purple thistle (unofficial)

NATIONAL TREE

Birch tree (unofficial)

NATIONAL ANIMAL

Steppe wolf (unofficial); batyr dog (unofficial)

NATIONAL RESOURCES

Bashkortostan has an abundance of mineral resources, including crude oil reserves, natural gas, coal, ferrous metals, manganese, chromite, iron ore, lead, tungsten, and other minerals. Oil extraction and refining are the major industries. The republic is also rich in forest products, with over a third of the republic covered in forests. Agriculture is also an important resource.

FOODS

Toukmas is the national dish, made of wheat noodles with the addition of various meats and vegetables; *itle asi,* a traditional dish of baked horsemeat served with *lapsha,* a local bread, is also considered a national dish. *Pelmeni,* small meat-filled pastries traditionally served with garlic vinegar or sour cream and black pepper, is another very popular traditional dish. Other traditional foods include a type of stew or gruel called *öyrä* and a mare's milk cheese called *qurot.*

SPORTS/SPORTS TEAMS

Hockey is the major sport. Salavat Yulaev Ufa is the local hockey team, one of the most successful in Russia. Wrestling is a traditional sport and remains very popular. Bashkortostan teams compete at a national level in football and hockey.

TEAM SPORTS

Football

Bashinformsvyaz-Dynamo Ufa Football Team. The team is considered the national team and carries the national colors and symbols

WINTER SPORTS

Ice Hockey

Salavat Yulaev Ufa Hockey Team

NATIONAL HEROES OR PERSONIFICATIONS

Salavat Yulaev, national hero of Bashkortostan; Batyr, a legendary folk hero, a man of great strength and valor (depicted on the Bashkortostan coat of arms); Zeki Velidi Togan, a leader of the Bashkort national movement during the Russian Revolution and civil war, 1917–1920. He later led the anti-Soviet forces before fleeing to live in Turkey*. His writings on the culture and history of the Turkic peoples have been translated into many languages.

NATIONAL HOLIDAY/INDEPENDENCE DAY

National Day, June 12

FESTIVALS/FAIRS

Sabantuy Festival, June; Rudolph Nuryev International Ballet Festival, October; Ural Mongo Festival, May

SIGNIFICANT EVENTS IN FORMATION OF NATIONAL IDENTITY

9th–10th centuries C.E.   Bashkorts are mentioned in historical records as nomadic herders in the southern Ural Mountains.

13th century   The Mongols and Turkic peoples of the Golden Horde overrun the region, bringing the Bashkorts into the vast Mongol empire.

14th century   The Khanate of Kazan takes control of the region when Mongol power wanes.

1552   Ivan the Terrible, leading the Russian invasion of the region, conquers the khanate and imposes Russian rule on the Bashkorts.

1708–1711   The Bashkorts rebel and attack the Russian colonies established in their homeland.

1773–1774   A widespread rebellion, led by Yemelyan Pugachev and Salavat Yulaev, is supported by the majority of the Bashkorts. Follow-

ing their defeat and due to the frequency of revolts in the region, the Bashkort smiths are forbidden to practice their craft, which includes the fabrication of weapons.

18th century–19th century   A large influx of Tatars, Russians, and other national groups greatly reduces the Bashkort majority in their homeland. Most Bashkorts are forced to give up their nomadic existence as herders to settle in agricultural villages.

1861–1890   The abolition of serfdom in the Russian Empire brings a renewed influx of land-hungry colonists to the region. Bashkort resentment of the colonization leads to the growth of nationalism and demands for the return of stolen lands.

1905   Bashkort troops join the abortive 1905 revolution.

1917   The Russian Revolution spreads across the vast empire. Bashkort nationalists organize and demand autonomy for Bashkortostan within a new, democratic Russia. As the empire collapses, the Bashkort leaders attempt to secede and set up an independent Bashkort republic.

1918–1919   Bolshevik forces take control of the region. Bashkortostan, called Bashkiria, is established as the first autonomous republic within the newly proclaimed Soviet Russian federation.

1930–1939   The Bashkort lands are collectivized, with herds and farms becoming the property of the Soviet state.

1939–1943   During World War II, many factories and populations threatened by the Fascist invasion of the Soviet Union are transferred to the region. Oil production becomes important to the war effort.

1970s   Suppressed for over half a century, Bashkort culture begins to revive.

1980s   The liberalization of Soviet society allows the rebirth of Bashkort nationalist sentiment, based on the newly revived culture.

1991   The dissolution of the Soviet Union allows the Bashkort people to openly support demands for autonomy or even separate independence, based on their homeland's oil and natural gas.

1992–1994 The Bashkort government declares the autonomy of the republic. Persuaded by a newly democratic Russian government, the Bashkort leadership renounces its goal of separate independence while negotiating a series of treaties between Bashkortostan and Russia that allows for a large amount of the revenue from its mineral wealth to remain in the republic and permits the republic to enter into agreements with foreign governments directly.

2001–2002 The president of the republic, Murtaza Rakhimov, announces that any Russian attempt to tamper with the power-sharing agreements would lead to an irreparable breach between Bashkortostan and Russia. The influx of ethnic Bashkorts from other regions of the former Soviet Union increases their numbers in the republic.

2007 The republic celebrates the 450th anniversary of its formal incorporation into Russia.

2009 The Bashkort parliament sends a proposal to the Russian government outlining the renewal of the sovereignty agreements of the 1990s, but replacing the word *sovereignty* with the words *state structure,* which would acknowledge Bashkortostan as a sovereign state voluntarily tied to the Russian Federation.

BAVARIA

OFFICIAL NAME

Freistaat Bayern (German); Free State of Bavaria (English)

POPULATION

12,511,500 (2009e)

INHABITANTS' NAME/NICKNAME

Bavarian(s)

LANGUAGE/LANGUAGES

Standard German (official); Austro-Bavarian, Swabian, Franconian, English, French, others

RELIGION/RELIGIONS

Roman Catholic, 68 percent; Protestant, 26 percent; Muslim, 3 percent, other or no religion

NATIONAL FLAG

Bavaria has two official flags, the traditional national flag of a lozenge pattern of pale blue and white, and the less-often used state flag, a horizontal bicolor of white over pale blue. Although designs often differ, the lozenge flag must have at least 21 lozenges and the top right lozenge must be white. The colors are historically associated with the Wittelsbach dynasty that ruled Bavaria up to World War I. The blue and white also represent Bavaria's lakes and sky.

COAT OF ARMS/SEAL

The coat of arms consists of a centered crest or shield divided into four quadrants. The first quadrant, on the upper left, is a golden lion on a black background, representing the Upper Palatinate. The second quadrant, on the upper right, shows the "Franconian Rake," a serrated red over white, representing Middle and Lower Franconia. The third quadrant, on the lower left, shows the "Blue Panther" of Bavaria on a white background. The fourth quadrant shows the three lions of Swabia. Over the juncture of the four quadrants is the lesser coat of arms of Bavaria, a white and blue lozenge pattern. The crest is crowned with a jeweled golden crown representing the sovereignty of the Bavarian people. Two golden lions support the crest.

CAPITAL CITY

Munich

TYPE OF GOVERNMENT

Autonomous member state of the Federal Republic of Germany*

NATIONAL EMBLEM

Neuschwanstein Castle

NATIONAL COLORS

White and pale blue

NATIONAL ANTHEM

The anthem was written in 1835 and first performed in 1860. In 1946 a third stanza replaced the King's Stanza that was removed following the overthrow of the monarchy in 1918 but the third stanza was again removed in 1980.

> **Bayernhymne (German); Hymn of Bavaria (English)**
>
> God be with you, land of the Bavarians,
> German soil, fatherland!
> Over your wide area
> Rest His merciful hand!
> He shall protect your meadows,
> Shield the buildings of your towns
> And preserve you the colors
> of His sky, white and blue!
> God be with you, people of Bavaria,
> that we, to our fathers' worth,
> fixed in harmony and peace
> build our own fortunes!
> That with bonds of German brotherhood
> Everyone may see us united
> And the old splendor stands the test
> our Banner, white and blue!

PATRON SAINT

Saint Boniface; Saint Hedwig of Andechs; Saint Killian; Saint Sebald

CURRENCY

Euro

INTERNET IDENTIFIER

.de Germany (official); .by Bavaria (unofficial)

VEHICLE IDENTIFICATION PLATES/ STICKERS

D Germany (official); BY Bavaria (unofficial)

PASSPORT

Bavarians are German citizens and travel on German passports.

NATIONAL FLOWER

Chamomile (official); alpine snowbell (unofficial)

NATIONAL BIRD

Spotted nutcracker (unofficial)

NATIONAL RESOURCES

Natural resources include sand and gravel, natural stone, clay, silica, and kaolin. Bavaria has overcome a lack of natural resources to become one of Europe's strongest economies and the 18th largest economy in the world. Natural scenery, including the Bavarian Alps, historic cities, castles, and other monuments support a flourishing tourist industry.

FOODS

Bavarian cuisine is closely related to the cuisines of neighboring Austria* and the Czech Republic*. *Knödel*, various types of noodles, usually served with pork or vegetables, is considered the national dish. Other regional specialties include *dampfnudel*, a type of dumpling served with vegetables, salad, potato soup, or mushrooms; *surbraten*, roasted cured pork; *tellerfleisch*, boiled beef served with potatoes and apple compote (known as *tafelspitz* in Austria); *reiberdatschi*, potato pancakes; *schupfnudel*, a type of noodle made of grain or potato; *fleischpfianzerl*, round, flat meatballs served with sauce or potatoes. Bavarian beer is world famous and is considered the national drink.

SPORTS/SPORTS TEAMS

Association football is the most popular sport in Bavaria. Winter sports are also very popular, particular skiing and sledding. Bavaria national team participates in football at an international level.

TEAM SPORTS

Football

Bavaria Football Team, nickname Die Bayern (the Bavarians); Bavaria Women's Football Team, nickname Die Bayern (the Bavarians); Bavaria Futsal Team

NATIONAL HEROES OR PERSONIFICATIONS

Bavaria, dressed in traditional Greek or Roman robes, is the traditional personification of Bavaria.

National heroes include Maximilian II Emanuel, Duke of Bavaria and Prince-elector of the Holy Roman Empire, famed for his triumphs over the Turks in the Balkans; Maximilian Josef Garnerin, Count von Montgelas, the Bavarian minister who oversaw Bavaria's conversion to a kingdom in 1806; Kurt Eisner, the leader of the Bavarian revolution and the first premier of the Republic of Bavaria in 1918–1919; Joseph Alois Ratzinger, Pope Benedict XVI, the Bavarian cardinal who became pope in 2005

NATIONAL HOLIDAY/INDEPENDENCE DAY

National Day, also known as the Day of German Unification, November 3

FESTIVALS/FAIRS

Summer Festival, July-August; Gäudoben Folk Festival, August; Oktoberfest, September-October; Jewish Cultural Days, November; Christmas Markets in Würzburg, Nuremberg, and Munich, November-December; Tollwood Festival, December.

SIGNIFICANT EVENTS IN FORMATION OF NATIONAL IDENTITY

Second century B.C.E.–first century C.E. Celtic tribes inhabit the region, which is conquered just before the beginning of the Christian era.

Fifth century Germanic tribes overrun the last Roman outposts and settle across the region. The Bavarian tribe comes under the domination of the powerful Franks.

Sixth century Bavaria forms one of the stem duchies of the German peoples, serving as a frontier defense against incursions by Slavic peoples to the east.

696 Rupert, the bishop of Worms, comes to Bavaria at the invitation of Durk Theodo I. He founds monasteries and works to convert the pagan Bavarians to Christianity.

7th–12th centuries Bavaria continues to expand, becoming one of the most important of the German-speaking states. The Wittelsbach dynasty is established in 1180 as dukes. Bavaria's boundaries vary greatly as the duchy expanded or lost territory due to wars or alliances.

13th century Bavaria becomes the most powerful state in southern Germany but is later partitioned among various heirs.

16th century The Protestant Reformation is opposed by the majority of the staunchly Roman Catholic Bavarians, who fight in the Thirty Years War on the side of the Roman Catholic alliance.

1779 The War of the Bavarian Succession prevents powerful Austria* from annexing much of Bavaria's national territory.

1825–1918 The Wittelsbach kings, known for extravagant living and architectural fantasies, are increasingly out of touch with the Bavarian people. Bavaria joins the other German states during World War I and suffers defeat. The monarchy is overthrown and an independent Bavarian republic is proclaimed under Kurt Eisner.

1918–1919 Eisner's assassination leads to chaos and a coup by communist forces that proclaim a Soviet republic in Bavaria. German troops depose the communists and establish a state government firmly under the control of pan-German nationalists.

1919–1923 Bavarian nationalists, communists, socialists, and other political groups vie for power in the state. In 1923, monarchists attempt to restore the kingdom but are preempted by a small, radical group, the Nationalist Socialist Party in the so-called Beerhall Putsch. Adolf Hitler, for his part in the failed coup, spends five years in prison, where he writes *Mein Kumft,* his plan for world domination.

1932–1933 The National Socialists, known as Nazis, become the largest political party in all the German states except Bavaria, which is dominated by the nationalist Bavarian People's Party. The state government is overthrown and a Nazi government installed.

1939–1945 Bavarians are initially enthusiastic as war begins in Europe but soon suffer heavy bombing and shortages. In 1945, following Germany's surrender, a resurgent nationalist movement attempts to win Allied support for a separate Bavarian republic.

1946–1970 Under American military occupation, Bavaria, the poorest of the German states, becomes one of the most advanced as industries and people fleeing communist eastern Germany settle in the state. Bavaria is one of the leading states of the German economic miracle of the 1950s and 1960s.

1990–1995 European integration and German unification rekindle dormant Bavarian nationalism.

2000–2007 Bavarian leaders press for greater Bavarian participation as a distinct political entity in the European Union (EU).

2009 A small nationalist movement continues to advocate the "European option" for Bavaria, which would make Bavaria an independent member at the heart of the expanded EU.

See also Germany

BELARUS

OFFICIAL NAME
Respublika Belarus (Belarusian); Republic of Belarus (English)

POPULATION
9,687,500 (2009e)

INHABITANTS' NAME/NICKNAME
Belarusian(s)

LANGUAGE/LANGUAGES
Belarusian, Russian (both official); Polish, Lithuanian, others

RELIGION/RELIGIONS
Eastern Orthodox, 80 percent; Roman Catholic, 11 percent; Protestant, Jewish, Muslim, other or no religion

NATIONAL FLAG
The flag is modeled on the flag of the former Byelorussian Soviet Socialist Republic, with two horizontal stripes, red on the upper two-thirds and green on the lower third. A vertical strip at the hoist is decorated with traditional patterns. Red symbolizes the glorious past, green symbolizes the future, and the decorative stripe stands for the nation's rich cultural heritage, its spiritual continuity, and the unity of its people.

COAT OF ARMS/SEAL
The national emblem, which replaced the historical Pahonia arms in a questionable 1995 referendum, features a ribbon in the colors of the national flag, an outline of the map of Belarus, wheat ears, and a red star. The new emblem is an allusion to the seal used by the former Byelorussian Soviet Socialist Republic from 1950.

CAPITAL CITY
Minsk

TYPE OF GOVERNMENT
Presidential republic

NATIONAL EMBLEM
The historic emblem of Belarus and Belarusians (suppressed by the present government)

is the Pahonia, a white knight on a white charger against a red background.

NATIONAL COLORS

Red and white; under the present government, the old Soviet colors of red and green are used.

NATIONAL ANTHEM

The last Soviet Republic to adopt an official anthem, except for the Russian Soviet Federated Socialist Republic (RSFSR), which never had an anthem, Belarus adopted an instrumental anthem in 1955, which was retained following independence in 1991. In 1992, lyrics were finally added to the anthem.

My, Belarusy (Belarusian); We Belarusians (English)

We are Belarusians, peaceful people,
Our heart is to our native land,
We maintain generous friendship and gain our
  powers
Within the industrious, free family.

Refrain

Glory to the bright name of our land,
Glory to the fraternal union of our peoples!
Our beloved mother-Motherland,
Long you live and flourish, Belarus!
Together with brothers, with fortitude, during
  centuries
We guarded our native thresholds,
In struggles for freedom, in struggles for fate,
We have been gaining our banner of victories.

Refrain

The friendship of peoples (which is) the
  power of peoples
Is our venerable, sunny path
You soar up proudly, into the bright heights,
The banner of victory, the banner of joy!

PATRON SAINT

Saint George

CURRENCY

Belarusian rouble

INTERNET IDENTIFIER

.by

VEHICLE IDENTIFICATION PLATES/ STICKERS

BY

PASSPORT

The passport cover has the name of the country in Belarusian, Russian, and English, the coat of arms, and the word *passport* in the same three languages.

AIRLINE

Belavia Belarusian Airlines

NATIONAL FLOWER

Wild blue flax

NATIONAL TREE

Birch (unofficial)

NATIONAL ANIMAL

Wisent (Belarusian bison)

NATIONAL BIRD

Black stork

NATIONAL RESOURCES

Natural resources include forests, peat deposits, small quantities of oil and natural gas, granite, dolomitic limestone, marl, chalk, sand, gravel, and clay. Despite abundant resources, Belarus remains one of Europe's poorest countries due to the political situation in the country. The impact has mostly been in the form of international economic and political sanctions against the country or its leadership.

FOODS

Draniki, thick pancakes of shredded potatoes, eggs, and onion, often stuffed with mushrooms, and *babka,* another potato dish, are considered the national dishes. The potato became so common in the 19th century that it came to be considered the core of Belarus national cuisine. Other specialties include *aladdzi,* thin pumpkin pancakes; *klocki,* a pastry made of potatoes stuffed with minced pork and onions; *machanka,* a pork stew; and *piernik,* a dessert cake.

SPORTS/SPORTS TEAMS

A winter sport, biathlon, is the most popular sport, followed by association football (soccer) and ice hockey. Belarus national teams participate in many sports at an international level.

TEAM SPORTS

Badminton

Belarus Badminton Team

Baseball

Belarus Baseball Team; Belarus Softball Team

Basketball

Belarus Basketball Team; Belarus Women's Basketball Team

Football

Belarus Football Team; Belarus Women's Football Team; Belarus Under-21 Football Team; Belarus American Football Team; Belarus Futsal Team; Belarus Women's Under-19 Football Team

Handball

Belarus Handball Team; Belarus Women's Handball Team; Belarus Beach Handball Team

Hockey

Belarus Men's Ice Hockey Team; Belarus Junior Ice Hockey Team; Belarus Bandy Team; Belarus Field Hockey Team

Racing

Belarus Speedway Team

Table Tennis

Belarus Table Tennis Team

Tennis

Belarus Davis Cup Team; Belarus Fed Cup Team

Volleyball

Belarus Men's Volleyball Team; Belarus Women's Volleyball Team; Belarus Fistball Team

INDIVIDUAL SPORTS

Belarus Amateur Boxing Team; Belarus Archery Team; Belarus Athletics Team; Belarus Cycling Team; Belarus Canoeing Team; Belarus Chess Team; Belarus Equestrian Team; Belarus Fencing Team; Belarus Judo Team; Belarus Modern Pentathlon Team; Belarus Rowing Team; Belarus Sailing Team; Belarus Shooting Team; Belarus Swim Team; Belarus Tae Kwon Do Team; Belarus Triathlon Team; Belarus Weight Lifting Team; Belarus Wrestling Team

WINTER SPORTS

Belarus Bandy Team; Belarus Biathlon Team; Belarus Curling Team; Belarus Junior Ice Hockey Team; Belarus Men's Ice Hockey Team; Belarus Luge Team; Belarus Skating Team

NATIONAL HEROES OR PERSONIFICATIONS

Kastus Kalinouski, the national hero of the revolt of 1863; Tadeusz Kosciuszko, a national hero in Belarus, Poland*, and in the

United States*, where he fought with the rebels against the British Army in the Revolutionary War

NATIONAL HOLIDAY/INDEPENDENCE DAY

Independence Day, July 3 (commemorates the liberation of Minsk from German troops during World War II; independence from the Soviet Union was proclaimed on August 25, 1991)

FESTIVALS/FAIRS

National Festival of Belarusian Song and Poetry, June; Festival of National Cultures, June

SIGNIFICANT EVENTS IN FORMATION OF NATIONAL IDENTITY

Sixth century C.E.   Eastern Slavs settle the region of present Belarus between the sixth and 12th centuries C.E.

9th century–10th century   The Eastern Slav tribes soon come under the influence of the Varangians, traders and adventurers of Scandinavian origin. The early Slav state of Kievan Rus' is dominated by the Varangians, who bring most of the Eastern Slavs under their rule. Development as a separate people begins in the 10th century, when the Slavs of the northwestern region begin referring to themselves as Belarusy, "white Rus," after the distinctive white clothing worn in the region.

13th century   Parts of Kievan Rus' are swallowed up by the expanding Grand Duchy of Lithuania.

1386–1410   The Lithuanian state is beset by enemies on all sides, particularly the Teutonic Knights from the west. One of the major battles is fought by Lithuanians and Belarusians against the invading Teutonic Knights at Grunwald in 1410.

1569–1700   The merger of Poland* and Lithuania* brings considerable Polish linguistic and cultural influence to Belarus. The Old Russian dialects of the Belarusian peasants, under heavy Polish cultural influence, emerge as the modern Belarusian language in the 19th century.

1795   The Lithuanian-Polish federation collapses in 1795 under pressure from expanding neighbors. The lands of the federation, including Belarus, are divided between Russia*, Prussia, and Austria*.

1917–1918   The Russian Revolution frees the Belarusians of Russian domination. They form the short-lived Belarusian People's Republic, which is proclaimed independent on March 18, 1918.

1919–1922   War between the new Soviet Union and newly independent Poland leave the Belarusian territories divided between the two countries in 1921.

1930s   In the Soviet zone, forced collectivization leads to the death by starvation of between 3 percent and 5 percent of the Belarusian population. The Soviet purges further devastate the remaining cultural and national leadership. The Belarusians in Poland, although free of the fear and panic of the Soviet purges, are also deprived of their rights and language.

1939   The Soviet annexation of eastern Poland brings all the Belarusians under Soviet rule in an enlarged Belarusian Soviet Socialist Republic.

1940–1971   The Belarusian territories suffer the heaviest losses in Europe during and after the Second World War. An estimated quarter of the pre-war population perishes, including the large Jewish population. Many die in a post-war uprising against returning Soviet rule and in the purges that accompany the reimposition of the Soviet system.

1950s   A policy of Sovietization is instituted to protect the Belarusians from the influences of the West.

1986   The Belarusians present a petition detailing the loss of their traditional culture. The event has been referred to by historians as the cultural Chernobyl of the era, affecting Belarus nearly as much as the nuclear meltdown that spread nuclear fallout over much of Belarus earlier that same year.

1990–1991   The collapse of the Soviet Union is followed by the declaration of independence as Belarus.

1991–1993 A more liberal leadership chooses as Belarus' national symbols the historical white, red, and white flag and the Pahonia shield as its coat of arms at independence in 1991.

1994–1995 Dubious elections bring neo-Stalinists to power. The old Soviet symbols are resurrected, and a quasi-dictatorship begins.

2005 Belarusian nationalists, democrats, and dissidents of various political ideologies firmly oppose a planned union with Russia, which they claim will spell the end of the Belarusian nation.

2008–2009 Belarus is the poorest country in Europe, and its government is the most tyrannical. Human-rights violations and actions against nongovernmental organizations, independent journalists, and opposition politicians and groups, as well as its oppression of national minorities, have been repeatedly condemned by other nations. The Council of Europe has barred Belarus from membership since 1997 for undemocratic elections and voting irregularities.

BELGIUM

OFFICIAL NAME
Koninkrijk België (Flemish); Royaume de Belgique (Walloon/French); Königreich Belgien (German); Kingdom of Belgium (English)

POPULATION
10,618,400 (2009e)

INHABITANTS' NAME/NICKNAME
Belgian

LANGUAGE/LANGUAGES
Flemish (Dutch), French, German (all official); Turkish, Arabic, others

RELIGION/RELIGIONS
Roman Catholic, 75 percent; Protestant, 10 percent; Muslim, other or no religion

NATIONAL FLAG
The flag is a vertical tricolor of black, yellow, and red. The colors of the flag are those of the Duchy of Brabant. When riots broke out during the Belgian revolution against Dutch rule in the 1830s, a civil guard was formed under the colors of Brabant, and the colors were later adopted as the national colors.

COAT OF ARMS/SEAL
A small and a large coat of arms are in use. In the smaller coat of arms, a black shield shows the Golden Lion of Brabant with red claws. The shield bears the royal crown, and beneath the shield is a red banner with the national motto in French. Behind the shield are two crossed scepters, which represent the king as sovereign (lion scepter) and the supreme judge (oath-hand scepter). The shield is adorned with a chain of office with the Great Cross of the Leopold Order.

MOTTO
Eendracht maakt macht (Flemish/Dutch); *L'union fait la force* (Walloon/French); Strength through Unity (English)

CAPITAL CITY
Brussels

TYPE OF GOVERNMENT
Federal constitutional monarchy and bicameral parliamentary democracy

NATIONAL EMBLEM
Belgian lion

NATIONAL COLORS
Black, yellow, and red

NATIONAL ANTHEM
Popular tradition has the anthem being written by some young people in a café in Brussels in 1830. In 1860, the anti-Dutch lyrics were softened, and the present form of the anthem was adopted. There are official versions in French, Flemish (Dutch), and German.

La Brabançonne (French); The Song of Brabant (English)

Noble Belgium—for ever a dear land
We give you our hearts and our arms.
By the pure blood split for you, our
  Fatherland,
We swear with one cry—You will live!
You will live, always great and beautiful,
And your invincible unity
Will have as your invincible unity
Will have as your immortal emblem
For King, Justice and Liberty!
Will have as your immortal emblem
For King, Justice and Liberty!
For King, Justice and Liberty!
For King, Justice and Liberty!

PATRON SAINT

Saint Joseph

CURRENCY

Euro

INTERNET IDENTIFIER

.be

VEHICLE IDENTIFICATION PLATES

B

PASSPORT

The passport cover has the name of the European Union in the three official languages, Flemish Dutch, French, and German, across the top; the Kingdom of Belgium, again in the three official languages; the coat of arms; the word *passport* in the same three languages; and the standard biometric symbol.

AIRLINES

Brussels Airlines; JetairFly

NATIONAL FLOWER

Red poppy

NATIONAL ANIMAL

Belgian lion

NATIONAL BIRD

Common kestrel

NATIONAL RESOURCES

Natural resources include construction materials, silica sand, and carbonates. Belgium's location at the heart of Europe's most highly industrialized region helps make it one of the world's 10 largest trading nations.

FOODS

The national dishes are steak and French-fried potatoes (invented in Belgium) with salad and fried mussels with French-fried potatoes. Other specialties include *galettes,* thin, crispy waffles; *waterzooi,* a stew of chicken and vegetables, *et-su-put,* pork roast with potatoes, carrots, and cabbage; *chicons au gratin,* rolled ham and endive covered with white sauce and sprinkled cheese and baked; *potée paysanne,* a soup of pork, potatoes, and vegetables; *bloed worst,* blood sausage; and *pom koek,* a type of cake made of coffee, honey, and spices.

SPORTS/SPORTS TEAMS

Association football (soccer) is the most popular sport in Belgium. Tennis, cycling, basketball, volleyball, and athletics are also popular sports. Belgium national teams participate in many sports at an international level.

TEAM SPORTS

Badminton

Belgium Badminton Team

Baseball

Belgium Baseball Team; Belgium Softball Team

Basketball

Belgium Basketball Team; Belgium Women's Basketball Team; Belgium Wheelchair Basketball Team

Cricket

Belgium Cricket Team

Football

Belgium Football Team, nickname Rode Duivels/Diables Rouges (the Red Devils); Belgium Women's Football Team, nickname Rode Duivels/Diables Rouges (the Red Devils); Belgium Under-21 Football Team; Belgium Youth Football Team; Belgium Rugby Union team; Belgium Women's Rugby Union Team; Belgium Wheelchair Rugby Team; Belgium Australian-Rules Football Team; Belgium American Football Team; Belgium Beach Soccer Team; Belgium Futsal Team; Belgium Touch Football Team; Belgium Women's Touch Football Team

Handball

Belgium Handball Team

Hockey

Belgium Field Hockey Team; Belgium Women's Field Hockey Team; Belgium Ice Hockey Team; Belgium Junior Ice Hockey Team; Belgium Women's Ice Hockey Team

Korfball

Belgium Korfball Team

Racing

Belgium Speedway Team

Table Tennis

Belgium Table Tennis Team

Tennis

Belgium Davis Cup Team; Belgium Fed Cup Team

Volleyball

Belgium Men's Volleyball Team; Belgium Women's Volleyball Team; Belgium Beach Volleyball Team; Belgium Women's Beach Volleyball Team

INDIVIDUAL SPORTS

Belgium Aikido Team; Belgium Amateur Boxing Team; Belgium Archery Team; Belgium Athletics Team; Belgium Canoeing Team; Belgium Chess Team; Belgium Cycling Team; Belgium Equestrian Team; Belgium Fencing Team; Belgium Gymnastics Team; Belgium Judo Team; Belgium Rowing Team; Belgium Sailing Team; Belgium Shooting Team; Belgium Swim Team; Belgium Tae Kwon Do Team; Belgium Triathlon Team; Belgium Weight Lifting Team; Belgium Wrestling Team

WINTER SPORTS

Belgium Alpine Ski Team; Belgium Biathlon Team; Belgium Bobsleigh and Tobogganing Team; Belgium Curling Team; Belgium Ice Hockey Team; Belgium Women's Ice Hockey Team; Belgium Junior Ice Hockey Team; Belgium Luge Team; Belgium Skating Team

NATIONAL HEROES OR PERSONIFICATIONS

Maurice Maeterlinck, playwright and Nobel laureate; Edward de Smedt, the inventor of modern road asphalt in 1870; Lambert Quetelet, famed mathematician; King Leopold I, the first ruler of independent Belgium in 1831

NATIONAL HOLIDAY/INDEPENDENCE DAY

Ascension to the Throne of King Leopold I, July 21

FESTIVALS/FAIRS

Carnival in Binche, February (declared a UNESCO World Heritage Event); Ommegang Festival, Brussels, July; Procession of the Holy Blood, Bruges, May; Ghent Festival, July

SIGNIFICANT EVENTS IN FORMATION OF NATIONAL IDENTITY

First century B.C.E.–fourth century C.E. Originally occupied by Celtic tribes, the region comes under Roman rule in the first century B.C.E.

Fifth century The region is included in the Frankish kingdom, later Charlemagne's Holy Roman Empire.

1568–1797 The Netherlands*, including most of modern Belgium, are ruled successively by the Spanish and the Austrian Hapsburgs and are the scene of various European wars in the 17th and 18th centuries.

1815 The Allied nations, at the end of the Napoleonic Wars, agree to the reunification of the former Austrian Netherlands and the former Dutch Republic in the United Kingdom of the Netherlands.

1815–1839 The union of the northern and southern Low Countries lasts only 15 years. Political and religious differences lead the southern provinces to rebel.

1839–1914 French, the language of the nobility and the merchant classes, remains the sole official language. The small country, in the late 1800s, becomes a colonial power, with territories in Africa many times larger than its own national territory.

1914–1918 Due to the hundreds of thousands of casualties sustained during World War I, Flanders* becomes immortalized in the poem "Flanders Fields." The poppies that grow and spread across the former battlefields become Belgium's national flower and a symbol of the human cost of war.

1940–1945 Heavy fighting in World War II again devastates parts of the country until the German withdrawal in 1945.

1946–1960 Belgium becomes a champion of greater European cooperation as its own politics become increasingly divided along linguistic lines. Belgium renounces its traditional neutrality to join the North Atlantic Treaty Organization, headquartered at Brussels, and forms the Benelux group of nations with neighboring Luxembourg* and the Netherlands. In 1951, Belgium becomes one of the founding members of the European Coal and Steel Community, the nucleus of the later European Union.

1962–1967 The Flemish resurgence that began after the Second World War is accompanied by a corresponding political shift of power to the northern Flemish provinces. Always a numerical majority in Belgium, the Flemings had lived as second-class citizens, forced to speak French and mainly excluded from government and industry.

The so-called linguistic wars between the Flemish and the French-speaking Walloons make successive Belgian governments very unstable.

1970s–1980s Polarized between the two linguistic and cultural communities, the Belgian government seeks constitutional reform to combat the increasing scrutiny of Belgian unity. Political reforms establish autonomous states of Flanders and Wallonia* and later make Brussels a third autonomous region.

2007–2009 The Belgian state, comprising three fully autonomous regions, remains responsible for foreign relations, monetary policy, and defense. Flemish demands for even more autonomy are opposed by the majority of the Walloons. The debate often leaves Belgium without a functioning government for long periods of time. After the 2007 elections, nine months of hotly contested negotiations between the Flemish and Walloon political parties finally end and a new government is installed on March 20, 2008. Decisions on further state reforms are postponed and remain a matter of considerable debate.

BOSNIA AND HERZEGOVINA

Official Name

Bosna i Hercegovina (Bosnian/Croatian); Босна и Хероцеговина (Serbian); Bosnia and Herzegovina (English)

Population

3,887,900 (2009e)

Inhabitants' Name/Nickname

Bosnian(s); Bosnian Croat(s); Bosnian Serb(s)

Language/Languages

Bosnian, Croatian, Serbian (all official); Albanian, Romani, others

RELIGION/RELIGIONS

Muslim, 40 percent; Serbian Orthodox, 31 percent; Roman Catholic, 15 percent; other or no religion

NATIONAL FLAG

The flag has medium blue field bearing a yellow isosceles triangle, the point reaching the lower edge, above a row of seven whole and two half white stars and a broad blue band on the fly. The three points of the triangle represent the three major nationalities. The stars represent Europe, as do the colors of blue and yellow, the colors of the flag of the European Union.

COAT OF ARMS/SEAL

The coat of arms follows the design of the country's national flag. A shield bears the colors of the flag, yellow in the upper right corner over a larger blue field at the lower left bearing the diagonal row of white stars.

CAPITAL CITY

Sarajevo

TYPE OF GOVERNMENT

Emerging parliamentary democracy, with a rotating, tripartite presidency divided between predominantly Serb, Croatian, and Bosnian political parties

NATIONAL EMBLEM

Stari Most bridge in Mostar: Deliberately destroyed during the Bosnian War, it has been rebuilt and is now a UNESCO World Heritage Site.

NATIONAL COLORS

Blue and white

NATIONAL ANTHEM

A new anthem was adopted in February 1998 in an attempt to create an anthem acceptable to the country's three major nationalities. The instrumental anthem is called "Intermeco" (Bosnian/Croatian) or "Intermezzo" (English).

PATRON SAINT

Saint Gregory of Nazianzus

CURRENCY

Convertible mark

INTERNET IDENTIFIER

.ba

VEHICLE IDENTIFICATION PLATES

BIH

PASSPORT

The passport cover has the name of the country in the Cyrillic alphabet and in English, the coat of arms, and the word *passport* in Bosnian, Croatian, Serbian, and English.

AIRLINE

BH Airlines

NATIONAL FLOWER

White lily (unofficial)

NATIONAL RESOURCES

Natural resources include coal, iron ore, bauxite, copper, lead, zinc, chromite, cobalt, manganese, nickel, clay, gypsum, salt, sand, forests, and hydropower. Historic cities, mountain scenery, winter sports (Sarajevo staged the 1984 Winter Olympics), geographic location, and a fascinating blend of cultures have the potential to support a flourishing tourist industry.

FOODS

Bosnian cuisine is balanced between Western and Eastern traditions. *Cevapi,* grilled, minced meats grilled or stewed with spices, is popular throughout Bosnia and Herzegovina and is considered the national dish. *Bosanski lonac,* a casserole of layered meat and vegetables, is another national dish. Other specialties include *burek*, a type of filled pastry; *jasprak*, grape leaves stuffed with minced meat; *chevap*, a stew of beef, tomatoes, onions, and vegetables; and *musaks*, a dish of layered potatoes and meat with sauce. Plum or apple *rakia* (brandy) is considered the national drink.

SPORTS/SPORTS TEAMS

Association football (soccer) is the most popular sport in Bosnia and Herzegovina. Other sports, such as basketball, volleyball, and handball, are also very popular. Bosnia and Herzegovina national teams participate in many sports at an international level.

TEAM SPORTS

Badminton

Bosnia and Herzegovina Badminton Team

Basketball

Bosnia and Herzegovina Basketball Team; Bosnia and Herzegovina Women's Basketball Team; Bosnia and Herzegovina Wheelchair Basketball Team

Football

Bosnia and Herzegovina Football Team, nickname Plavo Žuti or Žuto Plavi (the Blue and Whites); Bosnia and Herzegovina Women's Football Team, nickname Plavo Žuti or Žuto Plavi (the Blue and Whites); Bosnia and Herzegovina Under-21 Football Team; Bosnia and Herzegovina Under-19 Football Team; Bosnia and Herzegovina Under-17 Football Team; Bosnia and Herzegovina Futsal Team; Bosnia and Herzegovina Rugby Union Team; Bosnia and Herzegovina Women's Rugby Union Team

Handball

Bosnia and Herzegovina Handball Team; Bosnia and Herzegovina Women's Handball Team

Hockey

Bosnia and Herzegovina Ice Hockey Team; Bosnia and Herzegovina Junior Ice Hockey Team; Bosnia and Herzegovina Field Hockey Team

Korfball

Bosnia and Herzegovina Korfball Team

Racing

Bosnia and Herzegovina Speedway Team

Table Tennis

Bosnia and Herzegovina Table Tennis Team

Tennis

Bosnia and Herzegovina Davis Cup Team; Bosnia and Herzegovina Fed Cup Team

Volleyball

Bosnia and Herzegovina Men's Volleyball Team; Bosnia and Herzegovina Women's Volleyball Team

INDIVIDUAL SPORTS

Bosnia and Herzegovina Amateur Boxing Team; Bosnia and Herzegovina Athletics Team; Bosnia and Herzegovina Canoeing Team; Bosnia and Herzegovina Chess Team, Bosnia and Herzegovina Cycling Team; Bosnia and Herzegovina Judo Team; Bosnia and Herzegovina Shooting Team; Bosnia and Herzegovina Tae Kwon Do Team; Bosnia and Herzegovina Triathlon Team; Bosnia and Herzegovina Weight Lifting Team; Bosnia and Herzegovina Wrestling Team

WINTER SPORTS

Bosnia and Herzegovina Alpine Ski Team; Bosnia and Herzegovina Biathlon Team; Bosnia and Herzegovina Ice Hockey Team; Bosnia and Herzegovina Junior Ice Hockey Team; Bosnia and Herzegovina Luge Team; Bosnia and Herzegovina Skating Team

NATIONAL HEROES OR PERSONIFICATIONS

Husein-kapetan Gradaščević, a Bosnian general who fought for Bosnian autonomy in the Ottoman Empire; Mehmed Spaho, a leading Bosnian Muslim leader in the early part of the 20th century; Alija Izetbegović, political activist, Bosnian nationalist, and first president of independent Bosnia and Herzegovina

NATIONAL HOLIDAY/INDEPENDENCE DAY

National Day, November 25

FESTIVALS/FAIRS

Bascarsija Nights, July; Cultural Summer of Zvornik, August; Festival Prijateljstva, July; Sarajevo Winter Festival, February; Sarajevo film festival, August; MESS International Theater Festival, October; Jazzfest Sarajevo, November

SIGNIFICANT EVENTS IN FORMATION OF NATIONAL IDENTITY

Fourth century–third century B.C.E. Celtic migrations in the fourth and third centuries B.C.E. displace many Illyrian tribes from their former lands, but some Celtic and Illyrian tribes mix.

Second century B.C.E.–third century C.E. Conflict between the Illyrians and Romans starts in 229 B.C.E., but Rome is unable to complete its annexation of the region until 9 C.E.

100 C.E.–455 C.E. Following the split of the empire between 337 and 395, the western regions become part of the Western Roman Empire.

Sixth century–seventh century The Slavs settle in what is now Bosnia and Herzegovina and in other parts of the Balkans.

9th century–12th century The neighboring principalities of Croatia* and Serbia* split the Bosnian territories in the ninth and 10th centuries, but by the 12th century, the region is contested by the Kingdom of Hungary* and the Byzantine Empire, while Bosnia briefly emerges as an independent state under local rule.

15th century–16th century Ottoman encroachments pose a major threat to the Christian Balkan states. After decades of political and social instability, Bosnia falls to the Ottomans in 1463.

17th century Ottoman conquests and expansion end Bosnia's position as a frontier province. A period of stability and prosperity begins. Many Bosnian Muslims join the Ottoman administration and military.

1800–1850 Bosnian aristocrats' opposition to Ottoman efforts to modernize culminates in an intimately unsuccessful revolt in 1831. Other revolts are mostly stamped out by 1850.

1875–1878 A widespread peasant revolt in 1875 draws in neighboring provinces and eventually leading European military powers. By the terms of the Treaty of Berlin, the province is placed under Austrian administration.

1878–1914 The decision to formally annex the province to the Austro-Hungarian Empire in 1908 is one of the reasons a Bosnian Serb nationalist, Gavrilo Princip, assassinates the heir to the Austro-Hungarian throne in Sarajevo on June 28, 1914, the opening shot of World War I.

1914–1918 In 1918, the region is incorporated into the new South Slav Kingdom of Serbs, Croats, and Slovenes. The establishment of the Kingdom of Yugoslavia in 1929 is accompanied by a redrawing of internal boundaries that completely eliminates any trace of the former Bosnia.

1939–1941 The creation of a separate Croatian state within Yugoslavia in 1939 leads to a partition of Bosnia between Croatia and Serbia.

1941–1945 Once the kingdom of Yugoslavia is conquered by Nazi forces, all of Bosnia is ceded to the newly created Independent State of Croatia. Fascist Croatian rule over Bosnia leads to widespread persecution of the large numbers of Jewish, Serbian, and Gypsy civilians. Many Serbs join the Chetnik forces, at first allied with the Germans, but later turning against them. Others join other groups fighting the Fascists, including Yugoslav communists under the leadership of Josip Broz Tito.

1943–1946 The former communist partisans of Josip Broz Tito take control of Yugoslavia. Bosnia and Herzegovina is made a separate republic in the new federation.

1946–1989 Bosnia and Herzegovina prospers as part of the Yugoslav federation. Ethnic relations, as part of the multiethnic federation, are generally good. On Tito's death in 1980, an increasingly nationalist climate overtakes Yugoslavia. The collapse of communism in 1989 looses nationalist sentiments and begins the breakup of Yugoslavia.

1990–1992 Croatia and Slovenia* declare independence, placing Bosnia and Herzegovina in a difficult position. A referendum on independence, boycotted by Bosnian Serbs, leads to a declaration of independence.

1992–1993 When the Yugoslav army withdraws, many of the Serb soldiers form their own army and quickly overrun much of the republic's territory. Fighting also breaks out between Bosnian Muslims and the Croatians in Herzegovina. Ethnic cleansing, concentration camps, mass rapes, the destruction of mosques and other religious sites, and other atrocities accompany the heavy fighting. In Srebrenica, in 1995, Radovan Karadzic, the president of Republika Srpska, oversees the massacre of over 8,000 Bosnian Muslim men and boys.

1994–1995 The Dayton Accord ends the fighting. Over 100,000 have been killed and nearly 2 million driven from their homes or displaced by the fighting. The accords create a Bosnian-Croat federation in a political union with the Bosnian Serb state, the Republika Srpska.

1996–2006 Orderly elections take place. In 2004, the European Union takes over NATO peacekeeping in the country. Elections in 2006 reinforce the ethnic tensions still evident a decade after the end of the war.

2008 Radovan Karadzic, the Bosnian Serb leader during the 1990s Bosnian War, is captured in Belgrade and charged with genocide, deportation, persecution, and other crimes against non-Serb civilians.

2009 The country continues to recover from the devastating three-year war that accompanied the breakup of Yugoslavia in the early 1990s. In spite of growing prosperity and democratic elections, the country remains unstable, largely due to the unwillingness of the Serbs in the north and east to share a country with the Bosnians and Croats.

BRITTANY

OFFICIAL NAME

Breizh (Breton); Bretagne (French); Brittany (English)

NICKNAME

Coastal regions: Armor (Breton); Country of the Sea (English). Interior: Argoat (Breton); Country of the Woods (English)

POPULATION

4,381,400 (2009e)

INHABITANTS' NAME/NICKNAME

Breton(s)

LANGUAGE/LANGUAGES

French (official); Breton, Gallo, English, others

RELIGION/RELIGIONS

The Bretons are predominately Roman Catholic, though they are less religious than their French neighbors: Roman Catholic, 88 percent; Protestant, Muslim, other or no religion

NATIONAL FLAG

The flag, known as *Gwenn-ha-du* (the White and Black), consists of nine black and white horizontal stripes bearing a white canton on the upper hoist with 11 black ermines (the national symbol). Prohibited for many years by the French state, which did not support any reference to Brittany, the Breton flag could be hoisted without obstacle or reprisal only beginning in the middle of the 1960s. The nine horizontal stripes represent the traditional districts of Brittany. The five black stripes represent the French dioceses, and the four white stripes represent the Breton-speaking dioceses. The ermine canton on the hoist represents the former independent Duchy of Brittany.

COAT OF ARMS/SEAL

The coat of arms is a white shield bearing 23 black ermines, based on the medieval arms of the Duchy of Brittany.

MOTTO

Potius mori quam foedari (Latin); *Kentoc'h mervel eget bezañ saotret* (Breton); Better death than dishonor (English)

CAPITAL CITY

Rennes (Roazhon)

TYPE OF GOVERNMENT

Regional government of France* (80% of historic Brittany); the other 20 percent; including the historic capital, Nantes, was separated to form part of the Pays-de-la-Loire region

NATIONAL EMBLEM

Ermine

NATIONAL COLORS

White and black

NATIONAL ANTHEM

As part of France, the official anthem is "La Marseillaise." The Breton anthem is based on the anthem of Wales*. The lyrics were written in 1897 and officially adopted in 1903.

> **Bro Gozh ma Zadoù (Breton); Ancient Land of My Fathers (English)**
>
> The ancient land of my fathers is dear to me,
> Land of poets and singers, famous men of
>   renown;
> Her brave warriors, very splendid patriots,
> For freedom shed their blood.
> Nation [or country], Nation, I am true to my
>   Nation.
> While the sea [is] a wall to the pure, most
>   loved land,
> O may the old language [*sc.* Brezgibeg]
>   endure.
> Old beloved Brittany, paradise of the bard,

> Every valley, every cliff, to me is beautiful.
> Through patriotic feeling, so charming is the
>   murmur
> Of her brooks, rivers, to me.
> If the enemy oppresses my land under his
>   foot,
> The old language of the Bretons is as alive as
>   ever.
> The muse is not hindered by the hideous hand
>   of treason,
> Nor [is] the melodious music of my country.

PATRON SAINT

Saint Anne, the mother of the Virgin Mary; Saint Ivo of Kermartin

CURRENCY

Euro

INTERNET IDENTIFIER

.bzh (unofficial). The possibility of authorizing the .bzh domain for Brittany was discussed at the ICANN conference in July 2008.

VEHICLE IDENTIFICATION PLATES

BZH (unofficial)

PASSPORT

Bretons are French citizens and travel on French passports.

AIRLINE

Brit Air

NATIONAL FLOWER

Hydrangea (unofficial)

NATIONAL TREE

Chestnut (unofficial)

NATIONAL ANIMAL

Stoat

NATIONAL BIRD

Egret (unofficial)

NATIONAL RESOURCES

Natural resources include granite, slate, kaolin, and timber. Brittany's unique culture, historic cities, quaint villages, and rugged coastline support a vibrant tourist industry.

FOODS

Very thin, wide pancakes made from buckwheat flour are eaten with ham, eggs, and other savory fillings. They are usually called *galetes,* except in the western districts, where they are called *krampouezh.* Thin crêpes made from wheat flour, often served with fruit compotes, are eaten for dessert. Other pastries, such as *kouign amann* ("butter cake" in Breton), made from bread dough, butter, and sugar; *far,* a sort of sweet Yorkshire pudding; and clafoutis with prunes, are traditional Breton dishes. Surrounded by the sea, Brittany offers a wide range of fresh seafood and fish, especially mussels and oysters. Among the seafood specialties is *cotriade,* often considered a national dish.

SPORTS/SPORTS TEAMS

Association football (soccer) is the most popular sport in Brittany. Traditional sports, such as Breton wrestling, are still practiced. The Brittany national team participates in football, Gaelic football, and beach soccer at an international level.

TEAM SPORTS

Football

Brittany Football Team, nickname the Black Devils; Brittany Women's Football Team, nickname the Black Devils; Brittany Gaelic Football Team; Brittany Beach Soccer Team

NATIONAL HEROES OR PERSONIFICATIONS

Peter Abelard, medieval Breton poet and philosopher; Jules Verne, the famed writer of 19th century science fiction; Nominoë, the first duke of independent Brittany who initiated a great flowering of medieval Breton culture; Raffig Tullou, an artist and sculptor devoted to the restoration of Brittany's Celtic heritage; Anjela Duval, a noted poet and defender of the Breton language

NATIONAL HOLIDAY/INDEPENDENCE DAY

(Unofficial) Saint Anne's Day, July 26; Saint Ivo of Kermatin Day, May 19

FESTIVALS/FAIRS

Annual Celtic Nations Festival, October; Fest Noz, music and cultural festivals held in summer throughout Brittany; the *pardons,* local religious festivals, various dates

SIGNIFICANT EVENTS IN FORMATION OF NATIONAL IDENTITY

Third century C.E.–sixth century C.E. Celtic peoples, fleeing the overcrowding of the British lands and the later Saxon invasion of Britain as Roman rule collapses, settle the long peninsula just south of the British mainland. Progressively, the Breton language replaces Latin as the language of the region.

600 C.E.–845 C.E. The Franks, after overrunning most of modern France, attempt to force the Bretons to submit, but without success. The French army is decisively defeated at Ballon in 845.

845–1341 The duchy of Brittany becomes a powerful medieval state, repeatedly fending off advances by the rival French and English. The ermine is introduced as Brittany's heraldic symbol during a long period of peace and prosperity that ends with the Breton War of Succession in 1341.

1341–1364 France and England back rival claimants to the Breton throne during the civil war that ravages Brittany. The war lasts 24 years, finally ending in 1364 with the victory of the Montfort family and its English supporters.

1365–1460 The accession of the Montforts to the throne ushers in a period of power and prosperity, the so-called Golden Age of Brittany. As an independent state, Brittany advances the arts, trade, and building. A university is founded at Nantes in 1460.

1487 The French again invade Brittany in 1487 but are stopped at Nantes. The French return and defeat the Bretons in 1488. The Breton defeat begins the end of independent Brittany. The peace treaty states that the duke's daughter, Anne, the heiress of the dukedom, can marry only with the consent of the French king.

1491–1532 On the death of her father, Anne, now the Duchess of Brittany, is forced to marry Charles, the king of France, in 1491and later his successor, Louis, in 1499. When Anne dies in 1514, her daughter is also forced to marry the king of France, adding weight to French claims on the duchy. A treaty of Everlasting Union is signed in 1532. Presented as a union of two sovereign states, the treaty confirms the incorporation of Brittany into the French kingdom.

1789–1792 The French Revolution deprives the Bretons of the last vestiges of their former independence. The duchy is divided into five departments, and Breton names are changed to French. The Chouan Rebellion erupts across the peninsula, and French troops again devastate many areas while quelling the uprising.

1815–1932 The French Republic deprives Brittany of economic development and bans the use of the Breton language. The Bretons become a rural, backward people, mostly farmers and fishermen, while the region's cities become increasingly French in language and culture. The first sign of the revival of the Breton culture and language is the 1932 bombing of the monument in Rennes representing the Treaty of Everlasting Union.

1941–1946 Some Bretons collaborate with the Nazis in an effort to win independence for Brittany, which leads to the discredit of the nationalist movement in the post-war period and nearly two decades of silence about the Breton language and culture.

1950s Use of the Breton language is strongly discouraged by the French state, and it is often looked down upon in schools and churches. Breton school children are punished for speaking their own language on school grounds. Many Bretons are forced to leave the region because of a lack of jobs and opportunities.

1960s A resurgence of interest in their past, their language, and their culture begins a renewed Breton nationalist movement. Contacts with other Celtic nations in Ireland*, Scotland*, Cornwall*, Wales*, and the Isle of Man* reinforce the Celtic culture.

1970s–1980s In 1976, figures show that for the first time in the 20th century, more Bretons are returning to than leaving the region. The Diwan movement begins with a system of Breton-language schools in an effort to stem the loss of the language. The separation of the Nantes region from Brittany becomes the focus of nationalist anger. Separatist violence increases in the late 1970s, but by the mid-1980s, most nationalist groups renounce violence. In 1987, the French government finally allows bilingual road signs and advertising.

1992 The Council of Europe passes the European charter of regional and minority languages, but the French government refuses to sign it and passes a constitutional amendment making French the only legal language in the republic.

1999 The first Breton television station begins transmitting, without French government approval or financial aid.

2000s Brittany has not been granted devolved powers such as those granted to other distinct European peoples. Regional politics remain the focus of Breton nationalism, with repeated demands for the reunification of historical Brittany into a single administrative region.

2001 The General Council of Loire-Atlantique Department officially calls for the incorporation of the department and its capital, Nantes, into the Brittany region, thus ending the partition of the historical territory of Brittany.

2009 The first-ever debate on the topic of unrecognized regional languages takes place in the French parliament. The clause "Regional languages are part of France's heritage" is made part of France's constitution following a vote in the senate. Breton leaders call on France to ratify the European Charter on Regional and Minority Languages. Street demonstrations, particularly in

Nantes, continue to demand the reunification of Brittany.

See also France

BULGARIA

OFFICIAL NAME

Republika Bulgariya (transliteration from Bulgarian); Republic of Bulgaria (English)

POPULATION

7,651,900 (2009e)

INHABITANTS' NAME/NICKNAME

Bulgarian(s); Bulgar(s)

LANGUAGE/LANGUAGES

Bulgarian (official); Turkish, Romany, Armenian, others

RELIGION/RELIGIONS

Bulgarian Orthodox, 82 percent; Muslim, 12 percent; Jewish, other or no religion

NATIONAL FLAG

A horizontal tricolor of white, green, and red, the flag was originally based on that of Russia, the only independent Slav state in the early 19th century. The red and white of the Russian flag were retained, but the blue was changed to green, which represents the freedom of the Bulgarian people.

COAT OF ARMS/SEAL

The coat of arms of the Republic of Bulgaria is a golden crowned lion, standing on his hind legs, on a dark red shield. The shield has a crown with five crosses and another cross above the crown, representing the former monarchy and Christianity. Two golden crowned lions, standing on their hind legs facing the shield, hold it. They stand on two crossed oak branches with acorns. Under the shield is a white band in the colors of the flag inscribed with the national motto.

MOTTO

Suedinenieto pravi silata (Bulgarian transliteration from Cyrillic); Unity Makes Strength (English)

CAPITAL CITY

Sofia

TYPE OF GOVERNMENT

Parliamentary democracy

NATIONAL EMBLEM

Crowned rampant lion

NATIONAL COLORS

White, green, and red

NATIONAL ANTHEM

The anthem dates from 1885 and the Serbo-Bulgarian War. A third verse, added by the communist government, praised Socialism and Bulgaria's allegiance to Moscow. The third verse was removed following the fall of the communist government in the early 1990s.

> **Mila Rodino (transliteration from Cyrillic); Dear Motherland (English)**
>
> Proudly rise the Balkan peaks,
> At their feet Blue Danube flows;
> Over Thrace the sun is shining,
> Pirin looms in purple glow.
>
> **Chorus**
>
> Oh, dear native land,
> Earthly paradise!
> For your loveliness, your beauty
> Ah, they are boundless
>
> Uncounted fighters fell
> For our beloved nation,
> Mother, give us manly strength
> Their path to continue.

PATRON SAINT

Sveti Ivan Rilski (Bulgarian); Saint John of Rila (English)

CURRENCY

Bulgarian lev

INTERNET IDENTIFIER

.bg

VEHICLE IDENTIFICATION PLATES

BG

PASSPORT

The passport cover has *European Union* in Bulgarian (using the Cyrillic alphabet) and English, the name of the country in Bulgarian and English, the coat of arms, the word *passport* in Bulgarian and English, and, at the bottom, the biometric standard symbol.

AIRLINES

Bulgaria Air

NATIONAL FLOWER

Rose (Bulgaria produces half the world's rose oil)

NATIONAL TREE

Oak (unofficial). The Granit oak, in the village of Granit, is one of the oldest trees in Europe, estimated to be about 1,650 years old.

NATIONAL ANIMAL

Lion (a mythical creature introduced to European heraldry from the Middle East)

NATIONAL BIRD

Painted stork (unofficial)

NATIONAL RESOURCES

Natural resources include bauxite, copper, lead, zinc, coal, gold, timber, arable land, and hydropower. Bulgaria is rich in nonmetalliferous minerals, such as rock salt, kaolin, gypsum, and marble. Winter ski resorts, summer resorts on the Black Sea, spas, historic cities and monuments, and prices well below those of most of Europe have allowed a rapid growth in tourism to over 7 million visitors a year. Remittances from Bulgarians living outside the country are a source of foreign currency and investment.

FOODS

Banitsa, a popular pastry filled with eggs and cheese, pumpkin, rice, spinach, or leeks, is considered the national dish. *Sarma,* grape or cabbage leaves stuffed with minced meat, is another national dish. Other national specialties include *shopska,* a salad of tomatoes, cucumbers, onion, peppers, and *sirene,* a white brine cheese; *kavarma kebap,* a dish of sliced beef with a sauce of garlic and wine, also considered a national dish; *tarator,* a cold yogurt and cucumber soup; *moussaka,* a dish of minced meat and eggs; *sirene po shopski,* a dish of vegetables and cheese; and *gyuveche,* a baked meat and vegetable dish with cheese. *Ayryan,* a nonalcoholic yogurt drink, is also a national tradition.

SPORTS/SPORTS TEAMS

Association football (soccer) is by far the most popular sport in Bulgaria. Volleyball and traditional sports, such as wrestling and athletics, are also very popular. Bulgarian national teams compete in many sports at the international level.

TEAM SPORTS

Badminton

Bulgaria Badminton Team

Baseball

Bulgaria Baseball Team; Bulgaria Softball Team

Basketball

Bulgaria Basketball Team; Bulgaria Women's Basketball Team

Cricket

Bulgaria Cricket Team

Football

Football Team, nickname Lavovete (the Lions) or the Tricolors; Bulgaria Under-21 Football Team; Bulgaria Under-19 Football Team; Bulgaria Rugby Union Team; Bulgaria Beach Soccer Team; Bulgaria Futsal Team

Handball

Bulgaria Handball Team; Bulgaria Women's Handball Team; Bulgaria Beach Handball Team; Bulgaria Women's Beach Handball Team

Hockey

Bulgaria Ice Hockey Team; Bulgaria Junior Ice Hockey Team; Bulgaria Field Hockey Team

Korfball

Bulgaria Korfball Team

Racing

Bulgaria Speedway Team

Table Tennis

Bulgaria Table Tennis Team

Tennis

Bulgaria Davis Cup Team; Bulgaria Fed Cup Team

Volleyball

Bulgaria Men's Volleyball Team; Bulgaria Women's Volleyball Team; Bulgaria Men's Beach Volleyball Team; Bulgaria Women's Beach Volleyball Team

INDIVIDUAL SPORTS

Bulgaria Aikido Team; Bulgaria Amateur Boxing Team; Bulgaria Archery Team; Bulgaria Athletics Team; Bulgaria Canoeing Team; Bulgaria Chess Team; Bulgaria Cycling Team; Bulgaria Equestrian Team; Bulgaria Fencing Team; Bulgaria Gymnastics Team; Bulgaria Judo Team; Bulgaria Modern Pentathlon Team; Bulgaria Rowing Team; Bulgaria Sailing Team; Bulgaria Shooting Team; Bulgaria Swim Team; Bulgaria Tae Kwon Do Team; Bulgaria Triathlon Team; Bulgaria Weight Lifting Team; Bulgaria Wrestling Team

WINTER SPORTS

Bulgaria Alpine Ski Team; Bulgaria Biathlon Team; Bulgaria Curling Team; Bulgaria Ice Hockey Team; Bulgaria Junior Ice Hockey Team; Bulgaria Luge Team; Bulgaria Skating Team

NATIONAL HEROES OR PERSONIFICATIONS

Bay Ganyo (also transliterated as Baj Ganjo or Bai Ganio) is a fictional character created by author Aleko Konstantinov in the late 19th century. Bay Ganyo is considered an exemplary image of an antihero—egoistic, ignorant, and uneducated. Mother Balgaria appears with her lion, sometimes together with the personification of Rumelia. Vasil Levski was one of the key figures in the Bulgarian liberation movement under Ottoman Turkey in the 19th century.

NATIONAL HOLIDAY/INDEPENDENCE DAY

Liberation Day, March 3

FESTIVALS/FAIRS

International Festival of Koukers (Mummers) and Masquerade Games, January; International Folk Festival, August; Rose Festival in Kazanlak, spring

SIGNIFICANT EVENTS IN FORMATION OF NATIONAL IDENTITY

500 B.C.E.   The Thracians live in many tribal groups until King Teres unites most of them around 500 B.C.E.

188 B.C.E.–45 C.E. The Romans invade the Balkans, and warfare continues until the final Roman conquest in 45 C.E.

First century–fifth century The Thracian identity is gradually lost as the population becomes Roman citizens.

Sixth century The Slavs, as part of the great Slav migrations, take control of the region and assimilate what remains of the Thracian population.

679–718 The Bulgars, originally from Central Asia, cross the Danube and conquer the region. A peace treaty with the Byzantine Empire and the establishment of a new capital south of the Danube mark the beginning of the First Bulgarian Empire.

Ninth century–10th century Boris I adopts Orthodox Christianity. In the ninth century, the Cyrillic alphabet is created by monks in Bulgaria.

1018 The Byzantines, led by Basil II, known as Basil the Bulgar-slayer, destroys the Bulgarian state and incorporates Bulgaria into the Byzantine Empire.

11th century–12th century Hungarian incursions are defeated by the Byzantines, but in 1185, Bulgaria attains independence and is later established as the Second Bulgarian Empire.

13th century–14th century The Empire expands to conquer most of the Balkan region by 1280. Bulgaria becomes a vassal state of the Ottoman Empire.

15th century–19th century Ottoman rule devastates the Bulgarian population and most of the people's cultural relics. In order to prevent rebellions, the Turkish authorities destroy most of the medieval fortresses and fortified churches.

1878–1908 Russia forces Ottoman Turkey to give Bulgaria its independence following the Russian victory in the Russo-Turkish War. The Bulgarian principality proclaims itself an independent kingdom in 1908.

1912–1913 Bulgaria takes part in the Balkan Wars over territory claimed as Bulgarian in Ottoman Macedonia.

1939–1945 Following the instability and coups of the 1930s, Bulgaria allies with the Axis Powers during World War II and occupies territories it claims in Greece* and Yugoslavia. Bulgaria refuses to hand over its Jewish citizens and becomes one of only three European nations to save their Jewish populations. In 1944, the Soviet army enters Bulgaria and a communist government is installed.

1946–1978 The people's republic is established in 1946 and becomes one of the Soviet Union's staunchest allies. Brutal assimilation policies drive many ethnic Turks to leave for Turkey*.

1989–1991 In 1989, communist leaders are overthrown and a new constitution creates a democratic republic with a capitalist economic system. Economic difficulties and a tide of corruption compel over 800,000 Bulgarians, including many professionals, to emigrate.

2001 Simeon II, the son of the last czar, Boris III, and the former head of state as czar during World War II, wins a narrow victory in democratic elections for parliament.

2004–2008 Bulgaria, once known for its slavish adherence to Moscow's wishes, joins the North Atlantic Treaty Organization in 2004. On January 1, 2007, Bulgaria becomes a full member state of the European Union. The European Commission suspends regional aid worth hundreds of millions of euros after reports criticize the Bulgarian government for its failure to tackle widespread corruption and organized crime.

2009 A gas dispute between Russia* and Ukraine* cuts supplies to Bulgaria, resulting in a severe energy shortage during some of the coldest weeks of the year.

CANARY ISLANDS

OFFICIAL NAME

Comunidad Autónoma de Canarias (Spanish); Autonomous Community of the Canary Islands (English)

POPULATION

2,101,300 (2009e)

Inhabitants' Name/Nickname

Canarian(s); Canary Islander(s); Guanche(s)

Language/Languages

Spanish (official); Arabic, German, English, others

Religion/Religions

Roman Catholic, 89 percent, Protestant, Muslim, other or no religion

National Flag

The flag has three vertical stripes of white, blue, and yellow bearing the coat of arms centered on the blue. The colors are derived from the nationalist flag of the 1960s, which combined the blue and white of Santa Cruz with the blue and yellow of Las Palmas. The nationalist flag has the same three stripes but bears a ring of seven green stars centered on the blue stripe.

Coat of Arms/Seal

The Coat of arms has a central sky blue shield bearing seven gray islands that represent the sky over the islands and the seven islands of the archipelago. The shield is crowned with a gold and red crown under a banner bearing the word "Oceano" and is supported by two brown dogs, representing the wild dogs that prompted the Romans to call Grand Canary Island the *Insularia Canaria* or Island of Dogs.

Capital City

The Canary Islands have two official capitals, Las Palmas de Gran Canaria and Santa Cruz de Tenerife.

Type of Government

Parliamentary democracy as an autonomous region of Spain*

National Emblem

Presa Canario (Canarian dog)

National Colors

Blue, white, and yellow

National Anthem

The anthem is based on part of the composition *Cantos Canarios* (Canarian Songs), written and composed by Teobaldo Power and Lugo Vina in the mid-19th century.

Arrorró (Spanish); Lullaby (English)

I am the shade of an almond tree,
I am volcano, saltpeter and lava.
Distributed in seven islands
The pulse of my soul beats.
I am history and future,
A heart that illuminates the dawn
Over our islands that are set
For sailing towards hope.
Fighters in nobility
Defend the bright pillar
Of freedom.
This is our beloved soil:
My Canary Islands.
As a single one
To be together
Dreams the dream of peace
On the wide sea.

Patron Saint

Virgin of Candelaria

Currency

Euro

Internet Identifier

.es Spain

Vehicle Identification Plates/Stickers

E Spain (official); IC Canary Islands (unofficial)

Passport

Canarians are Spanish citizens and travel on Spanish passports.

AIRLINE

Binter Canarias

NATIONAL FLOWER

Almond blossom (official); Tiede daisy (unofficial)

NATIONAL TREE

Canary pine (unofficial)

NATIONAL PLANT

Canary wallflower (unofficial)

NATIONAL ANIMAL

Presa canario (Canarian dog) (unofficial)

NATIONAL BIRD

Canary (unofficial)

NATIONAL FISH

Spotted eagle ray (unofficial)

NATIONAL RESOURCES

The Canary Islands have few natural resources other than arable land. The economy is based on tourism—which accounts for about a third of the total—construction, and agriculture. The islands are outside the European Union customs territory, though politically within the EU. Goods subject to Spanish customs and excise duties and Value Added Tax (VAT), such as tobacco, clothing, or electronic goods, are significantly less expensive than mainland Spain. A pleasant climate, a unique culture, sandy beaches, and dramatic scenery sustain the important tourist industry.

FOODS

Papas arrugadas, made of boiled potatoes served with chicken and usually covered in *mojo* sauce, is considered the national dish. *Mojo,* which can be orange, red, or green depending on the ingredients, is a vegetable sauce mixed with garlic. It is served through-out the islands. Other Canarian specialties include *Ropa Vieja,* a dish of chicken and beef mixed with potatoes and garbanzos; *Potaje* is the Canarian name for a number of local stews; *Sancocho,* a stew of salt fish, potatoes, and sweet potatoes served with roasted corn bread

SPORTS/SPORTS TEAMS

Association football (soccer) is the most popular sport in the islands. Traditional sports such as wrestling, swimming, and diving also remain popular. Surfing, introduced by tourists in the 1970s, is also a popular sport.

TEAM SPORTS

Football

Canary Islands Football Team

NATIONAL HEROES OR PERSONIFICATIONS

Jean de Bétencourt, the leader of the first colony established in the islands in 1402; Alonso Fernández de Lugo, the soldier responsible for the final defeat of the Guanches and the conquest of Gran Canaria and Tenerife in 1496; Tomas Borges Toledo, the founder of the island's important commercial fishing industry.

NATIONAL HOLIDAY/INDEPENDENCE DAY

Día de Las Canarias (Canary Islands National Day), May 30

FESTIVALS/FAIRS

Carnival, February-March; Corpus Cristi, June; Almond Blossom Festival, February; Horse Market/Agricultural Fair, May 1; Fiesta del Carmen, July; Fiesta del Charco, September; Santa Lucia Fiesta, December

SIGNIFICANT EVENTS IN FORMATION OF NATIONAL IDENTITY

40 B.C.E.–1000 C.E.   The islands are explored by an expedition from the nearby African coast. Known

as the Fortunate Isles, they were populated by a tall, fair people possibly related to the Berbers of North Africa. The Romans call Gran Canaria the Island of Dogs after the island's fierce breed of dogs, *canis* in the Latin language. The name was later applied to the entire archipelago as Canary. Arab traders establish small posts for trading with the Guanche tribes.

1000–1344 The islands existence is mostly forgotten during Europe's Dark Ages. Portuguese explorers encounter the islands, which they claim for Portugal* in 1341. A papal bull later awards the islands to Spain.

15th century Colonists from impoverished Andalucia, newly conquered from the Muslims in southern Spain, are settled in the islands to reinforce Spain's territorial claim. The Guanches are finally defeated in 1496 and are eliminated or absorbed by the colonial population and completely disappear.

16th century Christopher Columbus uses the islands to resupply his expeditions to the New World. The islands, designated as two separate colonies, become important stations on the sea routes between Spain and the Americas.

19th century–1920 The Spanish government neglects the islands following the independence of most of Spain's American colonies. The islanders develop a strong tradition of self-reliance and independence in their isolated colonies. Nationalist agitation in the early 20th century focuses on ending their humiliating colonial status.

1927 The islands are formally incorporated into the Spanish state. The islands remain divided as two provinces but full provincial status does little to alleviate centuries of neglect and underdevelopment.

1932–1936 Francisco Franco, a young officer sent to the islands in 1932, greatly resents his posting to the remote and unimportant outpost. He uses the islands as the first base in his Nationalist revolt, which eventually engulfs Spain in a long and bloody civil war.

1950s The spread of education and the growth of nationalism in nearby Morocco* stimulates the growth of Canarian nationalism. Tourism brings much needed development and income.

1960s As nationalist fervor sweeps much of Africa, many Canarians support the idea of an independent Canarian state like the new states emerging across the rest of Africa.

1977 A separatist bomb at Las Palmas Airport on Gran Canaria forces a Pan American 747 enroute from Los Angeles and New York to divert to overcrowded Los Rodeos Airport on Tenerife. A runway collision between the American jet and a Dutch 747 results in the deaths of 583 people, the worst disaster in world aviation history. The catastrophe horrifies the Canarians and causes a dramatic loss of support for the nationalists held responsible for the disaster.

1982–1983 The Organization of African Unity (OAU)* declares the islands an African territory still under foreign colonization. The islands are granted autonomy as a region of the newly democratic Spanish kingdom.

1990s The Canarians become more assertive and less willing to accept decisions made in faraway councils. Protection of their unique culture and fragile environment, both increasingly threatened by over-construction and mass tourism, become major issues.

2000–2009 The continuing growth of tourism and the construction of holiday apartments, hotels, and other tourist amenities seriously threatens the ecology of the islands. Demands for a sustainable growth plan and an end to uncontrolled building fan a resurgent national movement and lead to the growth of organizations dedicated to the protection of the island culture and environment.

See also Spain

CATALONIA

OFFICIAL NAME

Comunitat Autònoma de Catalunya (Catalan), Comunidad Autónoma de Cataluña (Spanish); Comunitat Autonòna de Catalonha (Aranese/Occitan); Autonomous Region of Catalonia (English)

POPULATION

7,411,500 (2009e)

INHABITANTS' NAME/NICKNAME

Catalan(s)

LANGUAGE/LANGUAGES

Catalan, Spanish, Aranese/Occitan (all official); English, French, German, Arabic, others

RELIGION/RELIGIONS

Predominately Roman Catholic; Protestant, Muslim, other or no religion

NATIONAL FLAG

La Senyera, as the Catalans call their flag, is one of the oldest banners in Europe: a yellow field bearing four horizontal red stripes that divide the flag into nine equal horizontal stripes of yellow and red. According to Catalan tradition, the flag dates from the ninth century, when the four red bars were drawn, as an act of gratitude, on the yellow shield of Wilfred I, count of Barcelona, by King Charles the Bald's fingers drenched in the blood of Wilfred's wounds prior to his death during the siege of Barcelona by the Moors in 897.

COAT OF ARMS/SEAL

The coat of arms is a shield bearing the same yellow and red stripes as the flag, except shown vertically, below a red and gold crown. It is based originally on the familiar arms of the counts of Barcelona. The emblem, one of the oldest in Europe, dates from 1150.

CAPITAL CITY

Barcelona

TYPE OF GOVERNMENT

Parliamentary democracy as an autonomous regional government within the Spanish kingdom

NATIONAL EMBLEM

Les Quatre Barres: four red stripes on a field of yellow; Sagrada Família cathedral

NATIONAL COLORS

Yellow and red

NATIONAL ANTHEM

The anthem originated in the late 19th century, and the present lyrics date from 1899. It was declared the Catalan national anthem by a special act of the Catalan Parliament on February 25, 1993.

Els Segadors (Catalan); The Reapers (English)

Catalonia triumphant
Will once again be rich and bountiful,
Drive them back, these people
So conceited and so arrogant. A good blow
  with the sickle,

A good blow with the sickle,
Defenders of the land!
A good blow with the sickle!
Now is the time, reapers,
Now is the time to be alert.
For when another June comes,
Let us sharpen our tools well. A good blow
  with the sickle,

A good blow with the sickle,
Defenders of the land!
A good blow with the sickle!
Let the enemy tremble
On seeing our banner.
Just as we cut down golden stalks of wheat,
When the time is right, we can hack chains.

A good blow with the sickle,
A good blow with the sickle,
Defenders of the land!
A good blow with the sickle!

PATRON SAINT

Sant Jordi (Saint George); Virgin of Montserrat

CURRENCY

Euro

INTERNET IDENTIFIER

.cat

VEHICLE IDENTIFICATION PLATES/ STICKERS

E Spain* (official); CAT Catalonia (unofficial)

PASSPORT

Catalans are Spanish or French citizens and use Spanish or French passports

NATIONAL FLOWER

Martagon lily (unofficial)

NATIONAL ANIMAL

Catalan donkey (unofficial)

NATIONAL BIRD

Night heron (unofficial)

NATIONAL RESOURCES

Catalonia is a country of limited natural resources. It owes its prosperity to its strategic location. With a perfect soil and temperature for wine culture, it produces quantities of wines and *cavas* (sparkling white wines). Fresh fruits and vegetables, pork and other meat products, and manufacturing are also important. Sandy beaches, a pleasant climate, historic cities, a unique culture, and easy access from all over Europe support an extremely important tourist industry.

FOODS

Catalan-style paella, a rice dish with seafood, is considered a national tradition. *Escudella i carn d'olla,* a stew of beef, sausage, chicken, potatoes, and vegetables, cooked in an earthenware pot, is another national favorite. Other national specialties include *bacallà* (salt cod), served in many different ways; *butifarra amb mongetes,* pork sausages with sautéed white beans; *llentias,* lentils prepared with onions, potatoes, and sausage; and *crema catalana,* a type of flan, the national dessert.

SPORTS/SPORTS TEAMS

Association football (soccer) is the most popular sport, followed by basketball and other forms of football. Catalan national teams compete in many sports at an international level.

TEAM SPORTS

Football

Catalonia Football Team, nickname La Selecció (the Team); Catalonia Futsal Team; Catalonia Australian-Rules Football Team; Catalonia Women's Australian-Rules Football Team; Catalonia Rugby Union Team; Catalonia Women's Rugby Union Team

Golf

Catalonia Pitch and Putt Team

Hockey

Catalonia Ice Hockey Team

Korfball

Catalonia Korfball Team

WINTER SPORTS

Catalonia Ice Hockey Team

NATIONAL HEROES OR PERSONIFICATIONS

Francesc Macià, nationalist leader during the 1930s; Louis Companys, president of the Catalan Republic in the 1930s; Antoni Gaudi, famed architect of Catalonia's golden age before the Spanish Civil War; Josep de Moragues i Mas, a military leader who died defending Catalonia against a Spanish invasion in 1714–1715; Jordi Pujol, the nationalist leader and first president of autonomous Catalonia in the 1980s

NATIONAL HOLIDAY/INDEPENDENCE DAY

La Diada (National Day of Catalonia), September 11

FESTIVALS/FAIRS

Dia de Sant Jordi (Saint George's Day), April 23; Carnival, February–March

SIGNIFICANT EVENTS IN FORMATION OF NATIONAL IDENTITY

600 B.C.E.–218 B.C.E. Greeks colonize Catalonia's Mediterranean coast. Carthaginians briefly take control of the Greek colonies, but following the Carthaginian defeat, Catalonia, along with the rest of Iberia (then called Hispania), becomes part of the Roman Empire.

Fifth century C.E. The region flourishes under Roman rule. Tarraco (Tarragona) is one of the major Roman ports in the western Mediterranean. The collapse of Roman power is followed by invasions by tribal peoples from outside the empire, including the Goths, who settle the region, calling it Gothalonia, later changed to Catalonia.

711–795 Moors conquer Catalonia. After the defeat of the Moors by the Franks at Tours in 732, Frankish forces move south to drive the Moors from Catalonia in 795.

801 Catalonia is organized by Charlemagne as the Spanish March, part of a defensive barrier between the Moorish territories and the Frankish kingdom. Catalonia becomes an independent state, the County of Barcelona.

1137–14th century Catalonia and Aragon are joined through marriage. The Catalans create a Mediterranean empire with colonies as far east as the Balkan Peninsula. Moving south, the Catalans conquer the Moors in Valencia and the Balearic Islands in the 13th and 14th centuries.

15th century The extinction of the male line of the counts of Barcelona weakens the Catalan position in the kingdom. The Aragonese seek to reassert control, leading to civil war from 1460 to 1472. The war's devastation marks the beginning of a long decline that accelerates following the merger of the kingdoms of Aragon and Castile in 1479.

16th century The Catalans struggle to preserve their ancient rights, their culture, and their language, all threatened by the centralization of the Spanish kingdom.

1640–1659 The Catalans rebel against Spanish rule during the Thirty Years War. The rebellion, from 1640 to 1659, ends with Catalan defeat. France* takes Rousillon (North Catalonia) and delimits the border between France and Spain at the Pyrenees.

1714–1716 During the War of the Spanish Succession, the Catalans again attempt to win independence from Spain. After a long siege, the Spanish conquer Barcelona and execute the Catalan leaders. The Catalans are deprived of their traditional privileges, and in 1716, the Catalan language is banned and Catalan culture is eradicated in the Spanish Empire.

1830s–1870s Catalan culture begins to revive with the spread of education and publishing. A Catalan rebellion in 1842 is followed by renewed repression, but by the 1870s, the revival is producing some of Europe's great artists, architects, and writers.

1902 At the turn of the 20th century, nationalism again gains support. The first openly nationalist organization forms in 1902.

1919–1934 The majority of the Catalans support some sort of autonomy or home rule based on their ancient privileges and the Catalan parliament, the Generalitat. In 1931, following a coup in Madrid, the Catalan leaders declare the autonomy of the Republic of Catalonia under President Louis Companys. In 1932, the Statute of Autonomy is adopted. Spanish troops end the republic and arrest the leaders.

1936 A new, leftist government in Madrid allows the restoration of Catalan autonomy, with its own language, flag, anthem, president, and parliament. To preserve their autonomy, most Catalans side with the antifascist Loyalists during the Spanish Civil War.

1939 With German and Italian military aid, the Spanish fascists conquer Catalonia in 1939, ending the long civil war. Over 200,000 Catalans flee across the border into France. The fascist dictator, Francisco Franco, bans all manifestations of Catalan language or culture.

1975–1979 Franco's death and Spain's democratization allows Catalan culture to resurface. Spain grants Catalan autonomy. The language and culture quickly revive and replace the Castilian language and culture imposed during the years of dictatorship. Catalonia's second statute of autonomy, adopted in 1979, officially recognizes Catalonia as a nationality.

1986–1988 Spain enters the European Community, later called the European Union (EU), which changes the focus of Catalan nationalism to independence within the union. Catalan becomes an official language of the EU in 1988, as it is spoken by more Europeans than many official national languages.

1994 Negotiations begin between Catalan leaders and the Spanish government over the Catalan desire to take up the status the region enjoyed before 1714—independence under the Spanish king, but not subject to the Spanish government.

2006 Amendments to the statute of autonomy define Catalonia as a nation rather than a nationality. The changes are endorsed by a large percentage of voters in a referendum.

2008–2009 Polls show that a significant portion of the population, about 36 percent, supports full independence from Spain. Another 20 percent would prefer independence but would settle for greater autonomy and more rights within the Spanish state. In March 2009, over 10,000 people travel to Brussels to demonstrate in favor of a referendum on independence from Spain. An unofficial referendum on independence, held in a small town on the northern edge of metropolitan Barcelona, results in 91 percent voting for separate independence within the European Union (EU).

See also Spain

CHECHNYA

OFFICIAL NAME

Noxçiyn Respublika (Chechen); Chechenskaya Respublika (transliteration from Russian); Chechen Republic (English)
    Separatist: Noxçiyn Respublika Noxçiyçö (Chechen); Chechen Republic of Ichkeria (English)

POPULATION

1,114,500 (2009e)

INHABITANTS' NAME/NICKNAME

Chechen(s)

LANGUAGE/LANGUAGES

Chechen, Russian (official); Ingush, Bats, others

RELIGION/RELIGIONS

Mostly Sunni Muslim

NATIONAL FLAG

The official Chechen flag, the flag of the Russian republic, is composed of three horizontal bars of, from top to bottom, green, representing Islam; white; and red. Superimposed on them is a narrow vertical white band at the hoist side containing the national ornament, a design of four golden scroll shapes. This flag, introduced in 2004, is primarily used by the government of Chechnya, while the opposition forces, particularly those seeking independence, use the flag of the republic declared in 1992, a green field bearing narrow white, red, and white stripes near the bottom with the national emblem centered, a disk bearing nine stars, a gray wolf, and a full moon. The emblem is often omitted, as Islam forbids representations of animals.

COAT OF ARMS/SEAL

The official coat of arms of Chechenya, introduced in 2004, has three concentric circles of white, blue, and gold. The center white circle has an oil well and a minaret on each side of a red Chechen design. The middle blue circle has a wreath of gold leaves and a gold crescent moon and star on the upper part. The outer gold circle has a continuous blue design of a traditional Chechen motif.

grey wolf in the national emblem used by Chechen opposition forces is a symbol of pan-Turkish nationalists. But it is also a Chechen national symbol, which characterizes the Chechen character. The nine stars symbolize the nine *tukhums,* or clans, that gave birth to the Chechen nation. The wolf and the moon refer to the mythical origins of the Turan/Turkish peoples. The nine stars also recall the nine imams whose names are quoted in the *silsile,* the Chechen sacred writings.

CAPITAL CITY

Grozny

TYPE OF GOVERNMENT

Member republic of the Russian Federation under military occupation. The separatist government is a government-in-exile.

NATIONAL EMBLEM

Gray wolf

NATIONAL COLORS

Gray, green, and white

NATIONAL ANTHEM

The Chechen national anthem was adopted when the separatist regime declared independence in 1992. When the Russians retook the capital, they installed a Moscow-friendly regime with a new national anthem in 2004.

Death or Freedom

We were born at night when the she-wolf whelped,
In the morning, to lion's deafening roar, they named us.
In eagles' nests our mothers nursed us,
To tame wild bulls our fathers taught us.

Our mothers raised us to dedicate ourselves to our sacred Homeland,
And if our nation needs us we're ready to fight the oppressive hand.
We grew up free as eagles, princes of the mountains.
There is no threshold from which we will shy away.

Sooner will cliffs of granite begin to melt like molten lead,
Than any one of us shall lose our honor in life's struggles.
Sooner shall the Earth be swallowed up by the broiling sun,
Than we emerge from a trial in life without our honor!

Never to bow our heads to anyone, we give our sacred pledge,
To die or to live in freedom is our fate.
Our sisters heal our brothers' bloody wounds with their songs,
Lovers' eyes will supply the strength of arms.

If hunger weakens us, we'll gnaw on the roots of trees,
And if thirst debilitates us, we'll drink the dew from the grass.
For we were born at night when the she-wolf whelped.
We pledge our lives to God, nation, and Vainakh homeland.

CURRENCY

Russian rouble. The nationalist government planned to introduce a separate currency, the nahar, but the Russian invasion during the Second Chechen War ended the plan.

VEHICLE IDENTIFICATION PLATES/ STICKERS

RF Russian Federation (official); NRN Chechnya (unofficial)

PASSPORT

Chechens are officially Russian citizens and travel on Russian passports.

NATIONAL ANIMAL

Gray wolf (unofficial)

NATIONAL RESOURCES

Chechnya has substantial mineral and petroleum deposits, but because of the war, the economy has collapsed except for petroleum, which continues to be extracted, though at a lower level. Smuggling and bartering make up a significant part of the Chechen economy.

FOODS

Adzhabsanda, steamed mutton with vegetables, is considered a national dish. Lamb and mutton are the main sources of meat in the region. Other national specialties include *cirdingis,* a type of pasta served with meat and sauces; *galushki sbodnye,* a wheat pasta fried with bacon and served with sour cream; *shashlyk,* marinated skewered lamb cooked over charcoal; and *pilav,* a rice dish with mutton and vegetables.

SPORTS/SPORTS TEAMS

Association football (soccer) is the most popular sport. Traditional sports, particularly horse races and games played on horseback, are also very popular. The Chechnya national team participates in football at an international level.

TEAM SPORTS

Football

Chechnya Football Team

NATIONAL HEROES OR PERSONIFICATIONS

Sheikh Mansur, a Chechen leader of the 18th century; Iman Shamil, who led the Chechens and other Caucasian peoples in war against the invading Russians from 1834 to 1859; Dzhokhar Dudayev, who proclaimed Chechnya's independence in 1992

NATIONAL HOLIDAY/INDEPENDENCE DAY

Independence Day, November 1 (illegal under the Russian-imposed government)

FESTIVALS/FAIRS

Noah's Arc International Film Festival, summer

SIGNIFICANT EVENTS IN FORMATION OF NATIONAL IDENTITY

600 B.C.E.–7th century C.E. The ancestors of the Chechens, the ancient Sythian tribes, are known to inhabit the North Caucasus region. Living in the path of numerous invasions, the Chechens develop a warrior culture.

1241 Mongols invade the territory, which is devastated. The Chechens withdraw to mountain strongholds and fight the invaders for over 50 years.

1598–1785 Slavic Cossacks, exploring the region south of Russia*, reach the Terek River. The Chechens, converted to Islam through Turkish influence around 1650, continue to resist Russian encroachment. In 1785, Sheikh Mansur leads a holy war against the Russian invaders.

1818–1859 Grozny is founded as a Russian fort in Chechen territory. Led by Iman Shamil, the North Caucasian peoples fight a prolonged and bloody war against Russia that lasts from 1834 until the final defeat in 1859. Thousands of surviving Chechens are driven from the fertile lands into the rugged mountains. Cossacks and other Russian peoples settle their former territory.

1863–1877 Hatred of the Slavs is manifested in repeated revolts. In 1865, the Russian authorities brutally deport nearly 40,000 Chechens to Turkish territory.

1893–1905 The discovery of oil gives the region new importance. By 1900, the Grozny fields are the second greatest producers of oil in czarist Russia. The fields are the focus of severe Chechen rioting in 1905. In reprisal, thousands are exiled to the wastes of Siberia.

1914–1917 Openly sympathetic to Muslim Turkey* during World War I, the Chechens rejoice at news of the Russian Revolution in 1917. The Chechens mobilize to drive the Slavs from their homeland. They petition the new Russian provisional government for autonomy.

1917–1918 The Bolshevik coup ends Chechen hopes of autonomy in a democratic Russia. The North Caucasian peoples join in a separate republic called North Caucasia, which is declared independent in May 1918. Fighting breaks out between the Muslims and the Whites, the anti-Bolshevik Russian forces.

1920–1922 The Bolsheviks take control of the contested North Caucasus. A Chechen autonomous region is established in 1922.

1927–1940 The Soviet antireligious stance provokes a widespread revolt in 1927. Chechnya and neighboring Ingushetia are joined and become an autonomous republic in 1936. In 1937, to avoid future upheavals, the Soviet government kills or deports the entire Chechen religious and political leadership. Under new leaders, a serious revolt disrupts the region in 1939–1940.

1940–1945 A Nazi drive to seize the Grozny oil fields nearly succeeds in 1942. Many Chechens join the Nazis to fight the Soviets. Others join the Soviet military or fight in partisan groups. The Red Army drives the Nazis from the North Caucasus in 1943. Soviet leader Joseph Stalin accuses the entire Chechen nation of treason. The Chechens suffer a brutal deportation to Central Asia. Tens of thousands die of huger or mistreatment.

1957–1978 Officially rehabilitated, the Chechens are finally allowed to return to their homeland. Repression and persecution of their religion are part of periodic purges of the Chechen leadership. In 1978, two mosques are allowed to reopen, but religion remains tightly restricted.

1988–1990 The liberalization of Soviet life allows the Chechens to openly organize cultural and religious organizations. By 1990, an active pro-independence movement receives widespread support.

1991 The attempted Soviet coup against Mikhail Gorbachev in Moscow triggers a popular uprising in Chechnya. Nationalists take control of the local government and declare the territory independent of the crumbling Soviet empire. The Chechen nationalists reject the new status offered by the Russians, that of a member state of the Russian Federation.

1992–1997 Conflict between Chechen clans leads to near civil war. In 1994, Russian troops invade the breakaway republic in the First Chechen War. A treaty in 1997 effectively ends the war, but tensions continue.

1999 A series of bomb attacks in Russia are blamed on the Chechens. Russian military forces again invade, starting the Second Chechen War. Indiscriminate bombing reduces Grozny and other cities to rubble. Over 200,000 Chechen civilians flee the fighting to refugee camps in neighboring areas.

2000–2001 A Russian-backed Chechen government is organized against the widely supported nationalists. Following the destruction of the Twin Towers in New York on September 11, 2001, the Russian government portrays the Chechen conflict as a fight against Islamic terrorism.

2004–2008 A pro-Russian government is installed. Grozny and other areas in the Russian-held northern part of the republic are rebuilt. The nationalists, who control the south, continue to fight for an independent Chechnya. In August 2008, following Russia's announcement of recognition of Abkhazia* and South Ossetia* as independent states, Chechen leaders call on Russia to extend the same to Chechnya.

2009 Russian-backed Chechen government officials claim that the Chechen rebels have been virtually wiped out and that Russia's anti-rebel operations will soon come to an end. In July, a leading human rights campaigner is abducted and murdered, allegedly by agents of the Russian-backed Chechen government, which has often used violence to control anti-Russian dissidence.

See also Russia

CORNWALL

OFFICIAL NAME

Kernow (Cornish); County of Cornwall, Duchy of Cornwall (English)

POPULATION

535,700 (2009e)

INHABITANTS' NAME/NICKNAME

Cornish; Chough(s); Cornishmen

LANGUAGE/LANGUAGES

English (official); Cornish, others

RELIGION/RELIGIONS

Methodist, Anglican, Roman Catholic, other or no religion. The Methodist faith is closely identified with the Cornish culture.

NATIONAL FLAG

The flag, called *Kroaz Du* (Cornish) or Saint Pirin's Flag (English), is a black field bearing a centered white cross. According to Cornish tradition, Saint Pirin is supposed to have adopted the black and white after seeing molten tin spill out of the black copper ore in his fire, making him the discoverer of tin and the patron saint of tin miners. Tin, of course, had been in use for several centuries before the revelation.

COAT OF ARMS/SEAL

The traditional crest is a black shield with 15 golden bezants (coins) framed in blue and white topped with a black chough and supported by a Cornish fisherman and a Cornish tin miner. The bezants represent the ransom raised in Cornwall to rescue the Duke of Cornwall, captured by the Saracens during the Crusades.

MOTTO

Onen hag oll (Cornish); One and All (English)

CAPITAL CITY

Truro

TYPE OF GOVERNMENT

County government of England/separate Duchy of Cornwall

NATIONAL EMBLEM

Tin mines

NATIONAL COLORS

Black and white

NATIONAL ANTHEM

The anthem of Cornwall is the song of a Cornish hero and is the unofficial anthem. As part of England, the official anthem is that of England and the United Kingdom, "God Save the Queen."

Trelawny

A good sword and a trusty hand!
A merry heart and true!
King James's men shall understand
What Cornish lads can do!
And have they fixed the where and when?
And shall Trelawny die?
Here's twenty thousand Cornish men
Will know the reason why!

And shall Trelawny live?
And shall Trelawny die?
Here's twenty thousand Cornish men
Will know the reason why!

Out spake their Captain brave and bold:
A merry wight was he:
If London Tower were Michael's hold,
We'd set Trelawny free!
We'll cross the Tamar, land to land:
The Severn is no stay:
With "one and all," and hand in hand;
And who shall bid us nay?

And when we come to London Wall,
A pleasant sight to view,
Come forth! Come forth! Ye cowards all:
Here's men as good as you.
Trelawny he's in keep and hold;
Trelawny he may die:
But twenty thousand Cornish bold
Will know the reason why!

PATRON SAINT

Saint Pirin

CURRENCY

British pound

INTERNET IDENTIFIER

.ker (unofficial)

VEHICLE IDENTIFICATION PLATES/ STICKERS

GB Great Britain (official); KER Cornwall (unofficial)

PASSPORT

The Cornish people are British citizens and travel on British passports.

NATIONAL FLOWER

Cornish heath (county flower)

NATIONAL TREE

Oak (unofficial)

NATIONAL BIRD

Chough (unofficial)

NATIONAL RESOURCES

Cornwall is one of the poorest areas in the United Kingdom, with few natural resources other than tin and fish. Cornwall's unique culture, spectacular landscape, and mild climate make it a popular tourist destination, with over 5 million visitors a year. In recent years, the Eden Project near Saint Austell has been a major financial success, drawing one in eight of Cornwall's visitors. Mining of tin and copper was historically the most important industry, but today, the derelict mine workings survive only as a World Heritage Site.

FOODS

Cornish pasties, a savory dish of beef, onion, and potatoes or other fillings wrapped in light pastry dough, is considered the national dish. Cornish clotted cream, the product of the region's famed dairies, is probably the most famous export. Other national dishes include *cowl bysk,* a stew of crab or lobster, tomatoes, bacon, onion, garlic, and seasonings; Cornish under-roast, a dish of beef and kidneys, potatoes, and onions; salt pork with pease pudding, a dish of pork, onions, turnip, carrots, celery, leeks, and mustard served with split peas cooked with onion and bacon; and crab pie, a pastry filled with crab, artichokes, hard-boiled eggs, white grapes, and clotted cream.

SPORTS/SPORTS TEAMS

Rugby union, thought to have originated at Rugby School in Cornwall, is the most popular sport, although association football (soccer) and traditional Cornish wrestling are also very popular. A national Olympic committee has been organized to send a Cornish team to the 2012 Olympics in London. Cornwall national teams participate in football and rugby union at an international level.

TEAM SPORTS

Football

Cornwall Football Team; Cornwall Rugby Union Team nickname Trelawny's Army

NATIONAL HEROES OR PERSONIFICATIONS

Sir Johnathan Trelawny, who defied King James II in 1687–1688 and is immortalized in the Cornish anthem; Bolster, whose stride spanned six miles and who fell in love with Saint Agnes, only to be betrayed; Jack the Giant Killer, an important figure from Cornish mythology; John Couch Adams, the astronomer credited with the discovery of the planet Neptune; Mary Bryant, who defied the English who deported her to Botany Bay by surviving and eventually returning to her beloved Cornwall; Robert Stephen Hawker, the creator of the Cornish national anthem; Alfred Wallis of St. Ives, who began painting in his 70s and became one of the most famous of painters of the primitive style in the 20th century

NATIONAL HOLIDAY/INDEPENDENCE DAY

Saint Pirin's Day, March 5

FESTIVALS/FAIRS

Inter Celtic Festival, October; Furry Dance, May 8; 'Obby 'Oss Festival, May 1; Royal Cornwall Show, June; Mazey Day Festival, mid-summer; Helston Flora Dance, May

SIGNIFICANT EVENTS IN FORMATION OF NATIONAL IDENTITY

2500 B.C.E. Ancient people inhabit the region. Trade in tin and copper begins, bringing bronze tools and gold ornaments in exchange.

First century B.C.E. Brythonic Celts migrate to the island of Britain from the European mainland.

55 C.E.–411 C.E. Romans conquer Britain. Most of the Celts of Britain assimilate into Roman culture, becoming an urban, sophisticated population. The Celts of Cornwall, called *Conovii*, "hill dwellers," are mostly cut off from Roman influence by natural barriers and a lack of safe ports. When the Romans abandon Britain, invading Saxons overrun Britain. Romanized Celts flee to the western peninsulas, Cornwall, and Wales* and across the narrow channel to settle Brittany* on the mainland.

Eighth century Celtic Dumonia, later known as Devon, falls to the Anglo-Saxons, isolating the Celts of Cornwall beyond the Tamar River. Early medieval Cornwall becomes closely associated with the Arthurian legend.

936 Cornwall's tin mines sustain the area's independence until the invasion of the Anglo-Saxons under King Athelstan. Cornwall is the last part of England to submit to the Anglo-Saxons.

1066–1337 The Norman invasion of England is vigorously resisted in Cornwall. In recognition of its separate history and character, Cornwall is made a separate duchy.

14th century–17th century The region's long isolation aids the survival of the Cornish language and culture, although English becomes the language of daily life in the 17th century.

18th century Traditionally, the Cornish are devout Catholics, but in the 18th century, they convert in mass to the new Methodist sect, which becomes closely associated with Cornish culture.

1860–1900 Tin mining, closely tied to the local culture and a mainstay of the Cornish economy, collapses in 1866. Thousands of destitute families, an estimated 13 percent of the Cornish population, emigrate to Canada*, the United States*, Australia*, New Zealand*, the Caribbean, and South Africa*, The Cornish language dies out in the 1890s.

1920s A renewed interest in their lost Celtic language prompts a modest revival of the traditional Cornish culture.

1939–1945 The Second World War allows the reopening of many of the region's mines as Britain's access to colonial resources disappears.

1951 Mebyon Kernow (Sons of Cornwall) is created as a political party to assert Cornwall's right to self-determination.

1960s Tourism replaces mining as the economic mainstay. Tourists, drawn to Cornwall's semitropical climate and unique culture, are called *emmets* for the insects they resemble as they swarm across the Cornish Peninsula. Ties to the other Celtic nations are renewed, spurring the growth of local nationalism and demands for recognition of the distinct Cornish culture.

1970s The Cornish national movement at first focuses on language and culture. New demands are put forward for special status within the United Kingdom equal to that of Scotland* and Wales. Britain's entry into the European Community adds another layer of government, with decisions being made in London or Brussels but not in Cornwall.

1980s Activists demand the teaching of Cornish in all county schools and the creation of a Cornish assembly to promote the interests of Cornwall.

1998–2002 The last active tin mine closes, leaving many Cornish feeling that they have lost a part of their history and culture. European Union mandates dealing with fishing further hurt the region's economy as resentment builds.

2003 Cornwall's first university opens.

2005 Cornwall is officially England's poorest county. Activists point to the autonomy that sustains the economies of Scotland and Wales as examples for Cornwall.

2007 The devolution campaign, to win greater autonomy and recognition of the Cornish land and culture, continues to thrive. The majority of the Cornish want to restore Cornwall's constitution based on the 1508 Royal Stannary Charter, which has never been abrogated. The Cornish claim that they have lived in Cornwall for over 3,000 years, and though support for full independence is very low, support for a distinct Cornish state within the United Kingdom is widespread.

2008–2009 Activists question the present constitutional status of Cornwall, referring to the Duchy of Cornwall and the parallel status as an English county. Militant activists demand a referendum on Cornwall's status, including the right to nationhood.

See also United Kingdom

CORSICA

OFFICIAL NAME

Collectivité Territoriale de Corse (French); Territorial Collectivity of Corsica (English)

POPULATION

286,500 (2009e)

INHABITANTS' NAME/NICKNAME

Corsican(s); Corso(s)

LANGUAGE/LANGUAGES

French (official); Corsu (Corsican)

RELIGION/RELIGIONS

Roman Catholic, Protestant, other or no religion

NATIONAL FLAG

The flag has a white field bearing a centered black Moor's head. In Corsican, the flag is called *a bandiera testa mora,* the Moor's Head Flag. The origin of the Moor's head has been the subject of speculation and legend. Some believe it began as a heraldic device, while others maintain that it represents the head of a defeated Muslim. Most historians attribute the symbol to the coat of arms of Aragon, rulers of the island in the Middle Ages.

COAT OF ARMS/SEAL

A white shield bearing the black Moor's head, the coat of arms is the traditional emblem of Corsica. The territorial collectivity has a different emblem, a very modern design of many parallel lines and an outline map of the islands.

CAPITAL CITY

Ajaccio; nationalists claim the city of Corte as the capital of the island

TYPE OF GOVERNMENT

A territorial collectivity of the French state with very limited powers of self-government

NATIONAL EMBLEM

A Testa di Moru (Moor's head)

NATIONAL COLORS

Blue and white

NATIONAL ANTHEM

The Corsican anthem dates from the brief period of independence in the early 18th century. It remains the unofficial anthem of Corsica, as France*, Europe's most centralized country, does not allow regions or territories to have separate official anthems. The official anthem is the anthem of France, "La Marseillaise."

> **Dio Vi Salvi, Regina (Corsican); Hymn to the Blessed Virgin (English) (unofficial)**
>
> May the Lord protect you, Queen
> And universal mother

By whose favor we are received
Into paradise.

You are the joy and the delight
Of the inconsolable
Of the tormented
The unique hope.

Welcome us poor sinners
Into your holy veil
And reveal your
Son to us.

PATRON SAINT
A Beatd'ssima (the Blessed Virgin Mary)

CURRENCY
Euro

INTERNET IDENTIFIER
.fr (official);.csc (unofficial)

VEHICLE IDENTIFICATION PLATES
F France (official); CSC Corsica (unofficial)

PASSPORT
Corsicans are French citizens and travel on French passports.

AIRLINE
Air Corsica CCM

NATIONAL FLOWER
L'albucciu (asphodel); *a filetta* (bracken)

NATIONAL TREE
Chestnut (unofficial)

NATIONAL ANIMAL
U cursinu (Corsican dog); *a muvra* (Corsican mouflon) (unofficial)

NATIONAL BIRD
Corsican nuthatch (unofficial)

NATIONAL FISH
U culombu (conch)

NATIONAL RESOURCES
Agriculture, sheep, olives, and tourism are the major resources. Tourism plays a major role in the island's economy, as the island's pleasant climate, sandy beaches, and beautiful mountains and coastlines make it a popular destination among the French and other Western Europeans. The island has not had the same level of intensive development as other parts of the Mediterranean and is thus relatively unspoiled.

FOODS
Prisuttu, a lean ham from acorn and chestnut-fed wild pigs, is considered the national food. *Figetelli,* a liver sausage, is also very popular, as is chestnut *pulenta.* Other specialties include *minestra,* a soup of vegetables, beans, potatoes and cabbage; *sciacci,* pastry turnovers filled with cheese; *beignets,* pastries made from chestnut flour; *cabri a la corse,* goat prepared with onions, carrots, tomatoes, wine, and chestnut flour; and *fiadone,* a cheese pie.

SPORTS/SPORTS TEAMS
Association football (soccer) is the most popular sport in Corsica. Another popular sport is volleyball, with a professional team in Ajaccio. The Corsica national team participates in football at an international level.

TEAM SPORTS
Football
Corsican Football Team

NATIONAL HEROES OR PERSONIFICATIONS
Pasquale Paoli, the leader of independent Corsica in the 18th century; Samperu Corsu, who led a nationalist revolt in the mid-16th century; Napoleon Bonaparte, born in Corsica a year after the island became French

NATIONAL HOLIDAY/INDEPENDENCE DAY
Corsica National Day, December 8

FESTIVALS/FAIRS

The Sea Festival (La Mer en Fête), March; Festival of Dreams ('Scen' è sonniu'), April; Street and Circus Arts Festival (Festival des arts de la rue et des arts du cirque), August; Festival of the Wind, November

SIGNIFICANT EVENTS IN FORMATION OF NATIONAL IDENTITY

556 B.C.E.–237 B.C.E. Greeks found the city of Aleria on the island they call Kumos. The Greeks are expelled by Carthaginians, who hold the island for several centuries.

237 B.C.E.–430 C.E. Romans take control of the island, which is colonized. The Latin language and culture replace earlier languages and influences.

430 C.E. With the decline of Roman power, the island is overrun by Vandals.

522–700 The island is recovered by the eastern Roman, or Byzantine, Empire, adding a new Greek influence to the culture. Christian missionaries begin to convert the islanders in the sixth century.

725–1047 The Byzantines are unable to hold the island against successive invasions from the mainland that plunder and ravage the coastal areas at will. The Corsicans abandon the coast and occupy the slopes of the mountains. The island falls to the Goths, is attacked by the Lombards, and eventually comes under the rule of the Germanic Franks. Under constant threat from the Muslims of North Africa from the 8th to the 12th centuries, the Franks cede Corsica to the Holy See. Pope Gregory VII gives the island to the maritime republic of Pisa.

1047–1347 The Pisans began to develop the island, but following a long and bloody war, they are expelled by the Genoans.

1347–1567 Genoese rule is brutal and unpopular. The French take control of the island, but following a rebellion led by Samperu Corso, the island is returned to Genoese control.

1729–1768 A decades-long rebellion begins. Led by Pasquale Paoli, the Corsicans win their independence, although the Genoese hold onto several ports on the island. During the 14 years of his rule, Paoli leads a revival of the Corsican culture, opens a Corsican university, represses vendettas, establishes a printing press, and creates a Corsican navy.

1768–1770 Unable to defeat the Corsicans, the Genoese sell the island to France, just in time for Corsica's most famous son, Napoleon Bonaparte, to be born a French citizen. French troops invade the island in overwhelming numbers. The new administration dissolves all Corsican institutions and forcibly closes the Corsican university.

1789–1815 The Corsicans rebel when news of the French Revolution reaches the island. Driving out the French officials, they request British assistance. A plebiscite organized in 1794 confirms Corsica's desire for union with the United Kingdom*. The Congress of Vienna, convened at the end of the Napoleonic Wars, returns the island to French control.

19th century A strong Bonapartist tradition and anti-Genoese feelings help to assure Corsican loyalty to France. The French language becomes predominant in the cities. As the island is neglected and underdeveloped, islanders find it necessary to leave for the French mainland to find work. Banditry, vendettas, and clan feuds continue to undermine the stability of the island's culture.

1920s Resentment of the need to leave their homeland to find work encourages nationalist sentiments to surface. The first autonomist organization is organized in 1927.

1940–1945 Italian troops occupy Corsica after the fall of France in World War II. A Corsican uprising, aided by the Free French, drives the Italians from the island in 1943.

1945 At the end of the war, the triumphant Corsicans, preparing for independence, are gravely disappointed by the reimposition of French rule.

1958–1980 The modern Corsican national movement stems from a failed uprising during France's colonial war in Algeria. Numerous nationalist groups form, supporting different forms of autonomy or outright independence. Some groups turn to terrorism, mostly targeting tourist installations owned by foreigners. Thousands of French citizens expelled from former colonies are settled on the island.

1980–1985 A Socialist victory in France brings negotiations with the nationalists, who demand the reopening of the Corsican university, closed since 1770; education in the Corsican language in all schools; and the teaching of a specifically Corsican history. The government grants additional powers of self-government in 1982. Unsatisfied with the French response, militant groups resume their activities.

1991–1995 The French Senate rejects a bill that would recognize Corsica as a separate nation. General frustration with the government's inability to meet even minimal demands gives the nationalists greater support. Polls show overwhelming support for some sort of autonomy, with one in three Corsicans supporting gradual independence within the European Union.

2001 Corsica becomes a territorial collectivity, which allows some autonomy and helps to end 25 years of separatist violence.

2003 A local referendum, aimed at disbanding the two departments that divide the island and leaving just the territorial collectivity with extended powers, is voted down by a narrow margin.

2008–2009 The nationalist movement suffers from factionalism and rivalries. The French government views the island as a nest of criminal gangs, which reinforces the policy of negotiations without compromise. In July, dozens of leading Corsican politicians and intellectuals sign a "manifesto for the right for the future of Corsica."

See also France

CROATIA

OFFICIAL NAME
Republika Hrvatska (Croatian); Republic of Croatia (English)

POPULATION
4,448,100 (2009e)

INHABITANTS' NAME/NICKNAME
Croatian(s); Croat(s)

LANGUAGE/LANGUAGES
Croatian (official); Serbian, Italian, Hungarian, others

RELIGION/RELIGIONS
Roman Catholic, 88 percent; Orthodox, 4 percent; Muslim, 1.5 percent; other or no religion

NATIONAL FLAG
The flag is a horizontal tricolor of red, white, and blue, with the national seal centered on the white but overlapping the red and blue stripes. Red, white, and blue are the traditional pan-Slavic colors originally used on the flag of Russia*.

COAT OF ARMS/SEAL
The coat of arms consists of a shield bearing the traditional *chequy,* called *šahovnica* by the Croatians, a chessboard design of red and white (13 red squares and 12 white squares arranged in a five-by-five pattern). The shield is surmounted by a crown of smaller shields that represent the five historical regions comprised by modern Croatia.

CAPITAL CITY
Zagreb

TYPE OF GOVERNMENT
Parliamentary republic

NATIONAL EMBLEM
Red and white chessboard pattern (*šahovnica*)

NATIONAL COLORS
Red, white, and blue

NATIONAL ANTHEM
The lyrics of the anthem were first printed as a poem in 1835, and the music was composed

in 1840. It was adopted as the official anthem of Croatia in 1972 and was retained when the country gained independence in 1990.

Lijepa naša Domovino (Croatian); Our Beautiful Homeland (English)

Our beautiful homeland,
Oh dear, heroic land,
Fatherland of ancient glory,
May you always be happy!
Dear, as much as you are glorious,
Only you are dear to us.
Dear, where your land is flat,
Dear, where it is mountainous.

Flow Sava, Drava flow,
Nor you, Danube, lose your power,
Azure sea, tell to the world
That a Croat loves his nation.
As long as sun warms his ploughed land,
As long as storms lash his oak trees,
As long as the grave hides his dead,
As long as his living heart beats!

PATRON SAINT

Saint Joseph

CURRENCY

Croatian kuna

INTERNET IDENTIFIER

.hr

VEHICLE IDENTIFICATION PLATES/ STICKERS

HR

PASSPORT

The passport cover has the name of the country in Croatian, English, and French, the coat of arms, and the word *passport*, also in Croatian, English and French.

AIRLINE

Croatia Airlines

NATIONAL FLOWER

Perunika (Iris croatica)

NATIONAL TREE

Beech (unofficial)

NATIONAL ANIMAL

Beech marten (unofficial)

NATIONAL RESOURCES

Natural resources include oil, some coal, bauxite, low-grade iron ore, calcium, gypsum, natural asphalt, silica, mica, clays, salt, and hydropower. A well-educated population and a stable, functioning market economy have attracted many foreign companies to Croatia. Tourism, based on the country's coastline on the Adriatic Sea, historic cities, and the proximity to the major population centers of Europe, supports a thriving tourist industry.

FOODS

Croatia is a country of regional cuisines. In the north, the traditional dishes are influenced by Austrian and Hungarian cooking, while along the Adriatic, the food more closely resembles Italian cooking. *Yota*, a stew of sauerkraut, smoked meats, and various seasonings, is traditionally a dish from the peninsula of Istria but is popular across the country. *Buzara*, a dish of shrimp prepared with oil, garlic, parsley, and wine, is also very popular, as is *novalja*, a dish of marinated fish and shellfish.

SPORTS/SPORTS TEAMS

Association football (soccer) is the country's most popular sport. Handball, water polo, and basketball are also very popular. Croatia national teams participate in many sports at an international level.

TEAM SPORTS

Badminton

Croatia Badminton Team

Baseball

Croatia Baseball Team; Croatia Softball Team

Basketball

Croatia Basketball Team; Croatia Women's National Basketball Team; Croatia Under-21 National Basketball Team; Croatia Wheelchair Basketball Team

Cricket

Croatia Cricket Team

Football

Croatia Football Team, nickname Vatreni (the Fiery Ones or the Blazers) or Kockasti (the Checkereds); Croatia Women's National Football Team, nickname Vatreni or Kockasti (the Checkereds); Croatia Under-21 Football Team; Croatia Rugby Union Team; Croatia Australian-Rules Football Team, nickname the Croatian Knights; Croatia American Football Team; Croatia Futsal Team; Croatia Women's Under-19 National Football Team

Handball

Croatia Handball Team; Croatia Women's National Handball Team; Croatia Beach Handball Team

Hockey

Croatia Field Hockey Team; Croatia Ice Hockey Team; Croatia Junior Ice Hockey Team

Racing

Croatia Speedway Team

Table Tennis

Croatia Table Tennis Team

Tennis

Croatia Davis Cup Team; Croatia Fed Cup Team

Volleyball

Croatia Men's National Volleyball Team; Croatia Women's National Volleyball Team; Croatia Beach Volleyball Team

Water Polo

Croatia Water Polo Team

INDIVIDUAL SPORTS

Croatia Amateur Boxing Team; Croatia Archery Team; Croatia Athletics Team; Croatia Canoeing Team; Croatia Cycling Team; Croatia Equestrian Team; Croatia Fencing Team; Croatia Gymnastics Team; Croatia Judo Team; Croatia Rowing Team; Croatia Sailing Team; Croatia Shooting Team; Croatia Swim Team; Croatia Tae Kwon Do Team; Croatia Triathlon Team; Croatia Weight Lifting Team; Croatia Wrestling Team

WINTER SPORTS

Croatia Alpine Ski Team; Croatia Biathlon Team; Croatia Curling Team; Croatia Ice Hockey Team; Croatia Junior Ice Hockey Team; Croatia Luge Team; Croatia Skating Team

NATIONAL HEROES OR PERSONIFICATIONS

Tomislav, the first Croatian king from 910 to 928; Matija Gubec, leader of the 1573 peasant revolt; Nikola Šubić Zrinski, a hero in the war against the Ottoman Turks in a siege in 1566; Franjo Tudman, the first president of modern Croatia

NATIONAL HOLIDAY/INDEPENDENCE DAY

Independence Day, October 8

FESTIVALS/FAIRS

Tjedan suvremenog pleas (Dance Week), June; Dubrovnik Summer Festival; International Folklore Festival, July

SIGNIFICANT EVENTS IN FORMATION OF NATIONAL IDENTITY

168 B.C.E. The Romans conquer the region, which becomes an important part of the Roman Empire. Several Roman emperors and many other important Roman citizens are born or live in the area.

600 C.E.–925 C.E. The Croats settle in the Balkans and form two principalities in Dalmatia and Pannonia. The majority adopts Christianity in the ninth century. The two small states are joined into a kingdom in 925 under King Tomislav.

1102–1527 Croatia enters into a personal union with the Kingdom of Hungary*. In 1409, the coastal region of Dalmatia is ceded to Venice. Hungary and Croatia become part of the Hapsburg Empire.

1592–1593 Ottoman Turks invade the region but are eventually repulsed.

1797–1815 The fall of the Venetian Republic opens a dispute over Venetian territory in the eastern Adriatic. Eventually, the Hapsburgs secure Dalmatia and Istria, which are joined to Austria*.

1848 The Croatians, fearing Hungarian encroachment, support Austria against Hungary's bid for independence. After the Hungarians are defeated, the Croatians are not rewarded but lose their autonomy.

1867–1868 The Dual Monarchy of Austria and Hungary is created. Croatian autonomy is restored.

1918 At the end of World War I, as defeated Austria-Hungary collapses, Croatia joins the other South Slav nations to form an autonomous state in the Kingdom of the Serbs, Croats, and Slovenes. An Italian army takes control of Istria and areas along the Croatian coast.

1921–1928 The kingdom is centralized in Belgrade, Croatian nationalism gains support against the Serbs' dream of a Greater Serbia* in place of the historical nations.

1929 The kingdom becomes a royal dictatorship under the name Kingdom of Yugoslavia. Underground nationalist movements proliferate, including the Ustaše movement, a fascist organization.

1934–1939 Radicals, including the Ustaše, assassinate King Aleksandar of Yugoslavia in Marseille. An autonomous Croatian state is created, including parts of Bosnia and Herzegovina* and Dubrovnik on the Adriatic coast.

1941–1945 The German invasion allows the Croatian fascists, the Ustaše, to come to power and create a separate Independent State of Croatia. Like the other fascist governments, Croatia adopts racial laws and establishes concentration camps for the "enemies" of the state: anti-fascist Croatians and ethnic Serbs, Jews, and Roma. Hundreds of thousands of people perish in Croatia's planned genocide. Many Croatians join the antifascist partisan units organized by the communists and dedicated to a socialist Yugoslavia.

1945 Croatia becomes a constituent republic of the communist Yugoslav federation led by Josip Broz Tito. Tito's tight control of the country is offset by economic gains and greater prosperity.

1970–1971 Students organize demonstrations for greater civil liberties and greater Croatian autonomy. The movement, called the Croatian Spring, is suppressed but leads to a new constitution that gives greater autonomy to the individual Yugoslav republics.

1980 Tito's death begins the slow implosion of the Yugoslav state. Ethnic, political, religious, and regional conflicts emerge.

1990–1991 Communism is overthrown, and the first free elections are held in Yugoslavia. Croatian nationalists, led by Franjo Tudman, win over the communists by a narrow margin in Croatia. Fighting between Croatians and members of Croatia's large Serbian minority expands to war between Serbia and Croatia. The Croatian government cuts all remaining ties to Yugoslavia and declares independence.

1991–2003 Croatia is involved in the war in neighboring Bosnia, which has a large Croatian minority. A desire to become normal Europeans becomes widespread. Democratic elections and notable economic expansion mark Croatia's postwar period.

2004–2009 Croatia becomes an official applicant for membership in the European Union. Negotiations begin on membership, which should result in membership in 2010 or 2011. Croatia becomes a member state of NATO, the North Atlantic Treaty Organization.

CYPRUS

OFFICIAL NAME

Kypriakí Dimokratía (transliteration from Greek); Kıbrıs Cumhuriyeti (Turkish); Republic of Cyprus (English)

NICKNAME

The Island of Aphrodite

POPULATION

795,700 (2009e)

INHABITANTS' NAME/NICKNAME

Cypriot(s); Greek Cypriot(s); Turkish Cypriot(s)

LANGUAGE/LANGUAGES

Greek, Turkish (official); English, Armenian, Arabic, others

RELIGION/RELIGIONS

Cypriot (Greek) Orthodox, 78 percent; Sunni Muslim, 18 percent; Roman Catholic (Maronite), Armenian Apostolic, other or no religion

NATIONAL FLAG

The flag is a white field with a map of the island in gold above two olive branches. The olive branches symbolize peace between the Greek Cypriots and the Turkish Cypriots. The map is a copper-yellow color, representing the island's large deposits of copper.

COAT OF ARMS/SEAL

The coat of arms has a central yellow-gold shield with the depiction of a white dove carrying an olive branch over *1960,* the year when Cyprus gained independence. The shield is surrounded by a garland of woven olive branches, representing the agriculture of the island and peace.

MOTTO

The Island of Aphrodite (unofficial)

CAPITAL CITY

Nicosia

TYPE OF GOVERNMENT

Republic

NATIONAL COLORS

Blue, yellow, and white

NATIONAL ANTHEM

No national anthem was adopted at independence in 1960. Since the separation of the Greek and Turkish communities and the proclamation of the Turkish Republic of Northern Cyprus*, the Greek Cypriots use the anthem of Greece*, "Imnos Eis Tin Eleftherian," and the Turkish community uses the Turkish anthem (see Northern Cyprus).

PATRON SAINT

Saint Barnabus the apostle; Saint Paul

CURRENCY

Cypriot pound

INTERNET IDENTIFIER

.cy

VEHICLE IDENTIFICATION PLATES/STICKERS

CY

PASSPORT

The passport cover has the words *European Union* in English, Greek and Turkish, the coat of arms, the word *passport* in the same three languages, and the standard biometric symbol.

AIRLINES

Cyprus Airlines; Eurocypria

NATIONAL FLOWER

Kyklamino (cyclamen)

NATIONAL TREE

Latzia (Cypriot oak)

NATIONAL ANIMAL

Mouffon, or mountain ram (unofficial)

NATIONAL BIRD

Turtle dove

NATIONAL FISH

Rainbow trout (unofficial)

NATIONAL RESOURCES

Natural resources include copper, pyrites, asbestos, gypsum, timber, salt, marble, and clay earth pigment.

FOODS

Loukanika, coriander-seasoned sausages soaked in red wine and then smoked, are popular across the island. *Souvla,* skewered meat cooked over charcoal; *halloumi,* an island cheese; *sheftalia,* a type of sausage; and *afelia,* marinated pork cooked in red wine, are considered national dishes. Greek-style *dolma,* grape leaves stuffed with minced meat and rice, are also very popular. *Stiphado,* beef or rabbit stew prepared as a casserole with onions, wine vinegar, and spices, and *ofto kleftiko,* chunks of lamb cooked in a sealed clay oven and seasoned with bay leaves, are traditional national dishes.

SPORTS/SPORTS TEAMS

Association football (soccer) is the most popular sport in Cyprus. Racing and basketball are also quite popular. Cyprus national teams participate in many sports at an international level.

TEAM SPORTS

Badminton

Cyprus Badminton Team

Baseball

Cyprus Baseball Team; Cyprus Softball Team

Basketball

Cyprus Basketball Team; Cyprus Women's Basketball Team

Cricket

Cyprus Cricket Team

Football

Cyprus Football Team, nickname Portokaloi; Cyprus Women's Football Team; Cyprus Under-21 Football Team; Cyprus Rugby Union Team, nickname Moufflons; Cyprus Futsal Team

Handball

Cyprus Handball Team; Cyprus Women's Handball Team; Cyprus Beach Handball Team; Cyprus Women's Beach Handball Team

Hockey

Cyprus Field Hockey Team

Korfball

Cyprus Korfball Team

Racing

Cyprus Speedway Team

Table Tennis

Cyprus Table Tennis Team

Tennis

Cyprus Davis Cup Team; Cyprus Fed Cup team

Volleyball

Cyprus Men's Volleyball Team; Cyprus Women's Volleyball Team; Cyprus Fistball Team; Cyprus Men's Beach Volleyball Team

INDIVIDUAL SPORTS

Cyprus Amateur Boxing Team; Cyprus Archery Team; Cyprus Athletics Team; Cyprus Canoeing Team; Cyprus Cycling Team; Cyprus Equestrian Team; Cyprus Fencing Team;

Cyprus Gymnastics Team; Cyprus Judo Team; Cyprus Karate Team; Cyprus Modern Pentathlon Team; Cyprus Sailing Team; Cyprus Shooting Team; Cyprus Swim Team; Cyprus Tae Kwon Do Team; Cyprus Triathlon Team; Cyprus Weight Lifting Team; Cyprus Wrestling Team

WINTER SPORTS

Cyprus Alpine Ski Team; Cyprus Biathlon Team; Cyprus Skating Team

NATIONAL HEROES OR PERSONIFICATIONS

Archbishop Makarios III, Greek Cypriot leader who led Cyprus to independence in 1960; Georgos Grivas, the leader of EOKA, the Greek Cypriot national organization in the 1950s; Stasinus, believed to be the author of an epic poem, the *Cypria,* written in the seventh century B.C.E.; Evagoras Karageorgis, modern musician and composer of Cypriot popular music; Kyriakos Charalambides, a writer and poet, often writing in the Greek-Cypriot dialect

NATIONAL HOLIDAY/INDEPENDENCE DAY

Independence Day, October 1

FESTIVALS/FAIRS

Limassol Carnival, February–March; Anthestiria (Flower Festival), May; Ancient Greek Drama Festival, July–August

SIGNIFICANT EVENTS IN FORMATION OF NATIONAL IDENTITY

Sixth millennium B.C.E.–334 B.C.E. Ancient cultures flourish on the island. Cities grow, and commerce with other nations develops. Cyprus becomes an independent kingdom around 669 B.C.E. Later invasions by Egyptians and Persians subjugate the Cypriots. A serious uprising against Persian rule is crushed.

321 B.C.E.–58 B.C.E. The Cypriot leaders side with the Ptolemaic rulers of Egypt* in the wars that follow the end of the empire of Alexander the Great. Under Ptolemaic rule, the island becomes Greek in language and culture.

58 B.C.E.–395 C.E. Rome takes control of Cyprus. According to Cypriot tradition, the apostle Paul converts the population to Christianity.

395 The collapse of Roman power brings Cyprus under the Eastern Roman, or Byzantine, Empire, the Greek-speaking successor to the Roman Empire in the east.

688–965 Arabs invade Cyprus. An agreement between the Arabs and the Byzantines creates a joint government, a condominium of both Arabs and Byzantines that rules the island for the next three centuries, despite constant warfare on the mainland.

12th century The island is conquered during the Crusades, is later sold to the Knights Templar, and is finally conquered by the Franks, who erect a separate Kingdom of Cyprus under the Lusignan dynasty. In 1196, the Latin Church is established, with persecutions of Orthodox Christians.

1489 Due to the looming threat posed by the expanding Ottoman Empire of the Turks, the Venetians take control of the island, ending the Lusignan kingdom.

1562–1571 The Greek Cypriots revolt and attempt to throw off Venetian rule. The Turks demand the cession of the island to the Ottoman Empire on dubious historical grounds. A Turkish invasion is finally successful, but thousands of Greek Cypriots and Venetians are massacred.

1571–1860 The Ottomans colonize the island with retired soldiers and their families. During the 17th century, the Turkish population grows rapidly, partly through conversion of Cypriot Greeks to Islam. Many Greek Cypriots support the Greek war of independence against the Turks in 1821, leading to severe reprisals. When Greece gains independence in 1829, many seek a union of Cyprus and Greece.

1869–1878 The construction of the Suez Canal brings British interest in the island, which is now strategically placed. The United Kingdom*, in exchange for support during the Russo-Turkish War of 1877, is given administrative control but not sovereignty over Cyprus.

1878–1914 The Greek Cypriots demand union with Greece, as happened with the Ionian Islands and Crete, but the demand is rejected by the new British rulers. The British annex Cyprus when war breaks out in Europe in 1914, with the Ottoman Turks allied with Germany*. Cyprus is made a British Crown Colony.

1920s Many Cypriot Turks, who suffer discrimination and persecution by their Greek neighbors, leave the island to settle on the Turkish mainland.

1955–1959 The Greek Cypriots continue to demand *enosis,* or union, with Greece. The Turkish Cypriots oppose the idea. The organization known as EOKA, led by George Grivas, turns to violence to force the British to allow the union.

1960–1974 In the face of Turkish Cypriot opposition to any ties to Greece, the British grant Cyprus independence as the Republic of Cyprus, with safeguards for both of the island communities. Fighting erupts, and a United Nations peacekeeping mission is dispatched to the island.

1974 A coup, backed by Greece, overthrows the government and attempts to unite Cyprus with Greece. The Turks invade and take control of the northern third of the island, as ethnic Greeks flee south and ethnic Turks move north to the area under Turkish control.

1975–1983 The de facto state of Northern Cyprus is proclaimed in the north under Turkish rule. The name is changed to the Turkish Republic of Northern Cyprus when the enclave is declared independent in 1983. Turkey* is the only country to grant the new republic diplomatic recognition.

1983–2004 Numerous negotiations fail to resolve the conflict on the divided island. In 2003, the European Union presents a plan to end the division and allow united Cyprus to join the union. The plan is accepted by the Turkish Cypriots but is rejected by the Greek Cypriots. Cyprus joins the European Union even though the Greek majority rejects the peace plan. The Turkish Cypriot north is excluded.

2008 Cyprus adopts the Euro, the currency of the European Union. In July 2008, the leaders of the Greek and Turkish communities in Cyprus announce negotiations toward a solution to the dispute that has divided the island for more than three decades. Crossings between the Greek and Turkish sectors open for the first time since 1964.

2009 Negotiations between Cypriot Greek and Turkish leaders continue. The Turkish leaders demand the end of the isolation of Northern Cyprus as a condition for negotiations.

CZECH REPUBLIC

OFFICIAL NAME
Česká republika (Czech); Czech Republic (English)

POPULATION
10,311,800 (2009e)

INHABITANTS' NAME/NICKNAME
Czech(s)

LANGUAGE/LANGUAGES
Czech (de facto official); Slovak, Polish, others

RELIGION/RELIGIONS
The Czech Republic, along with Estonia*, has one of the least religious populations in the European Union: agnostic, 59 percent; Roman Catholic, 27 percent; Protestant, 2.5 percent; other or no religion

NATIONAL FLAG
The flag is divided horizontally white over red with an equilateral blue triangle at the hoist. The colors are the red, blue, and white of the pan-Slavic movement of the 19th century. The flag is identical to that used by the former federation of Czechoslovakia, despite a resolution adopted at the breakup of the Czech Republic and Slovakia* that expressly forbade the use of the symbols of the former federation.

COAT OF ARMS/SEAL
The coat of arms is a shield or crest divided into four sections symbolizing the historical

regions of the country. The two-tailed white lions on red backgrounds represent Bohemia; the two eagles represent Moravia and Silesia.

MOTTO

Pravda vítězí (Czech); Truth Prevails (English)

CAPITAL CITY

Prague

TYPE OF GOVERNMENT

Republic

NATIONAL EMBLEM

The Czech Lion; Charles Bridge in Prague

NATIONAL COLORS

Red, blue, and white

NATIONAL ANTHEM

Kde Domov Můj? (Czech); Where Is My Home? (English)

Where is my home? Where is my home?
Waters roar across the meadows
Pinewoods rustle upon the cliff-rocks,
Bloom of spring shines in the orchard,
Paradise on Earth to see!
And that is the beautiful land,
The Czech land, my home!
The Czech land, my home!

Where is my home? Where is my home?
If, in the heavenly land, you have met
Tender souls in agile frames,
Of clear mind, vigorous and prospering,
And with strength that frustrates all defiance,
That is the glorious race of Czechs,
Among the Czechs (is) my home!
Among the Czechs, my home!

PATRON SAINT

Cyril and Methodius

CURRENCY

Czech koruna

INTERNET IDENTIFIER

.cz

VEHICLE IDENTIFICATION PLATES/ STICKERS

CZ

PASSPORT

The passport cover has the words *European Union,* the name of the country in Czech, the coat of arms, the Czech word for passport, and the standard biometric symbol.

AIRLINE

Czech Airlines CSA

NATIONAL FLOWER

Rose

NATIONAL TREE

Linden (unofficial)

NATIONAL ANIMAL

Lion (mythical creature introduced to Europe heraldry from the Middle East)

NATIONAL RESOURCES

Natural resources include hard coal, soft coal, kaolin, clay, graphite, and timber. The Czech economy has developed quickly since 1990, making the republic the first former Socialist country to be declared a developed country. Tourism remains an important resource, supported by historic cities and monuments, varied scenery, summer and winter sports, and a unique culture.

FOODS

Vepřová pečeně s knedlíky a se zelím, roast pork with dumplings and cabbage, is considered the national dish. *Svíčková na smetaně,* marinated beef sirloin with a thick sauce made of carrots, parsley, and cream and served with dumplings, is also considered a national dish. Other specialties include *haluski,* cabbage with potato dumplings; *verpovy gulas,* a stew of pork, tomatoes, and paprika; *knedlicky,* potato dumplings; *bosaky se rehm,* potato dumplings with sauerkraut; *leperice,* mashed potatoes with sauerkraut; *cmuda,* potato pancakes; and *kolaches,* a fried doughnut-like pastry.

SPORTS/SPORTS TEAMS

Association football (soccer) and ice hockey are the two most popular sports. Czech Republic national teams participate in many sports at an international level.

TEAM SPORTS

Badminton

Czech Republic Badminton Team

Baseball

Czech Republic Baseball Team; Czech Republic Softball Team

Basketball

Czech Republic Basketball Team; Czech Republic Women's Basketball Team; Czech Republic Wheelchair Basketball Team

Cricket

Czech Republic Cricket Team

Football

Czech Republic Football Team, nickname Lokomotiva (the Locomotive); Czech Republic Women's Football Team, nickname the Locomotive; Czech Republic Under-21 Football Team; Czech Republic Rugby League Team; Czech Republic Rugby Union Team; Czech Republic Women's Rugby Union Team; Czech Republic Australian-Rules Football Team, nickname the Czech Lions; Czech Republic Wheelchair Rugby Team; Czech Republic American Football Team; Czech Republic Beach Soccer Team;

Czech Republic Futsal Team; Czech Republic Rugby Union Team (Sevens), nickname Czech Sevens or Czech 7s; Czech Republic Women's Rugby Union Team (Sevens), nickname Czech Sevens or Czech 7s

Handball

Czech Republic Handball Team; Czech Republic Women's Handball Team

Hockey

Czech Republic Ice Hockey Team; Czech Republic Junior Ice Hockey Team; Czech Republic Women's Ice Hockey Team; Czech Republic Field Hockey Team

Korfball

Czech Republic Korfball Team

Lacrosse

Czech Republic Lacrosse Team; Czech Republic Women's Lacrosse Team

Racing

A1 Team Czech Republic; Czech Republic Speedway Team

Table Tennis

Czech Republic Table Tennis Team

Tennis

Czech Republic Davis Cup Tea; Czech Republic Fed Cup Team

Volleyball

Czech Republic Fistball Team; Czech Republic Beach Volleyball Team; Czech Republic Women's Beach Volleyball Team; Czech Republic Men's Volleyball Team; Czech Republic Women's Volleyball Team

INDIVIDUAL SPORTS

Czech Republic Aikido Team; Czech Republic Amateur Boxing Team; Czech Republic Archery Team; Czech Republic Athletics Team;

Czech Republic Canoeing Team; Czech Republic Cycling Team; Czech Republic Equestrian Team; Czech Republic Fencing Team; Czech Republic Gymnastics Team; Czech Republic Judo Team; Czech Republic Modern Pentathlon Team; Czech Republic Sailing Team; Czech Republic Shooting Team; Czech Republic Swim Team; Czech Republic Triathlon Team; Czech Republic Weight Lifting Team; Czech Republic Wrestling Team

WINTER SPORTS

Czech Republic Alpine Ski Team; Czech Republic Biathlon Team; Czech Republic Bobsleigh and Tobogganing Team; Czech Republic Curling Team; Czech Republic Ice Hockey Team; Czech Republic Junior Ice Hockey Team; Czech Republic Women's Ice Hockey Team; Czech Republic Luge Team; Czech Republic Skating Team

NATIONAL HEROES OR PERSONIFICATIONS

Jára Cimrman or Jára da Cimrman is a Czech fictional character. Although he was originally meant to be just a caricature of the Czech people, culture, and history, he became an immensely popular character of modern Czech folklore and a national hero.

Other national heroes include Thomas Masaryk, leader of the Czech national movement and the first president of Czechoslovakia; Edward Benes, a Czech leader during and after World War II; Vaclav Havel, a dissident playwright and first president of the Czech Republic in 1993; Antonin Dvorak, famed musician, composer, and supporter of Czech independence; Jan Huss, a religious thinker and reformer who was burned at the stake for his views on the Catholic religion in 1415

NATIONAL HOLIDAY/INDEPENDENCE DAY

Day of Establishment of Independent Czechoslovakia (Founding Day), October 28; Day of Czech Statehood, September 28

FESTIVALS/FAIRS

Karlovy Vary International Film Festival, August; Khamoro—World Roma Festival, May; Prague Spring Music Festival, May–June; Straznice Folklore Festival, June; Mozart Festival, September

SIGNIFICANT EVENTS IN FORMATION OF NATIONAL IDENTITY

Third century B.C.E.–sixth century C.E. Celtic tribes settle the region, followed by Germanic tribes. In the fifth century C.E., many Germanic tribes move westward out of Central Europe. Slav peoples from the Black Sea and Carpathian Mountains migrate west to settle the region.

Eighth century C.E.–ninth century Samo, a Frankish merchant, becomes the first ruler of the first known Slav state in Central Europe. The principality, called Great Moravia, is the center of a vibrant culture. Saints Cyril and Methodius, the creators of the Cyrillic alphabet, arrive in the principality in 863.

880–1198 Under the influence of Great Moravia, a small principality is created to the west, in Bohemia.

1348 Charles University is founded, the first university in Central Europe. The reign of Charles I begins a golden age of culture, art, and political power.

15th century The Hussite movement, a national and religious manifestation, develops as a counter to German influence. Religious wars and instability end the golden age.

1526–1648 Bohemia comes under Hapsburg rule through a personal union with Austria*. Moravia, also under Hapsburg rule, remains a separate territory.

1743–1815 Maria-Theresa is crowned queen in Prague. Social and political reforms remove the last vestiges of feudalism. The German language becomes the sole official language in 1749. The Czech language is relegated to the status of a peasant language.

1815–1848 A revival of the language and culture takes hold among the small educated class.

The Czech language is introduced in schools. Czech nationalism becomes a mass movement.

1867 The establishment of the dual monarchy gives Hungary* the same rights within the empire as Austria. Czechs demand the creation of a third Slav kingdom, but their demands are rejected.

1900 Stirred by immigrant Czechs in the United States* and Canada*, support for autonomy grows. Thomas Masaryk, joined by Milan Stefanik, the leader of the empire's Slovak population, leads a campaign for Czecho-Slovak independence.

1918 Czechoslovakia, a federation of the Czech and Slovak lands, is declared independent.

1938 The rise of Nazi Germany is supported by a majority of Czechoslovakia's large German-speaking minority.

1939 Germans annex the Czech lands, and Slovakia is declared independent as a German ally.

1945 The fall of Prague to the Allies marks the end of military operations and the end of World War II in Europe. Three million ethnic Germans are expelled from Czechoslovakia.

1946 Communists emerge as the strongest political group in elections. They seize the government in a coup, and Czechoslovakia becomes part of the Soviet Bloc during the Cold War.

1950s–1968 A period of harsh repression in the 1950s leads to calls for more freedom of expression. A program of liberal reforms called the Prague Spring ends with the Soviet invasion of the country in 1968.

1989 Huge demonstrations break out across the country as reforms in the Soviet Union bring an end to the communist era in Europe. The communist government resigns in what is called the Velvet Revolution, the overthrow of a communist government without bloodshed.

1993 Czechoslovakia is peacefully divided into two new republics, the Czech Republic and Slovakia, in the Velvet Divorce.

1999 The Czech Republic becomes a member of the North Atlantic Treaty Organization (NATO).

2004 The republic is accepted as a member state of the European Union (EU).

2006–2008 The Czech Republic is the first of the former communist countries to achieve the status of a developed country.

2009 Political chaos and economic hardships threaten to curtail the progress the country has enjoyed for over a decade.

DENMARK

OFFICIAL NAME
Kongeriget Danmark (Danish); Kingdom of Denmark (English)

POPULATION
5,502,300 (2009e)

INHABITANTS' NAME/NICKNAME
Danish; Dane(s)

LANGUAGE/LANGUAGES
Danish (official); English, German, others

RELIGION/RELIGIONS
Lutheran, 83 percent; other Protestant, Roman Catholic, Muslim, other or no religion

NATIONAL FLAG
The national flag of Denmark, the *Dannebrog,* has a red field with a white Scandinavian cross that extends to the edges of the flag. The *Dannebrog* is the oldest state flag in the world, dating back to the 14th century. Danish legend says the flag fell from the sky during a battle in Estonia* in 1219, bringing victory to the Danes. There are a number of theories as to the origin of the flag.

COAT OF ARMS/SEAL
There are two versions of the Danish coat of arms, the small one now called the National Coat of Arms and the large one now called

the Royal Coat of Arms. The National Coat of Arms consists of a gold shield with three crowned blue lions amid nine red hearts. Above the shield is a gold and red crown. The royal arms are a more elaborate version of the National Coat of Arms.

MOTTO

There is no national motto, but the royal motto is widely used: *Guds hjælp, folkets kærlighed, Danmarks styrke* (Danish); The help of God, the love of the people, the strength of Denmark (English).

CAPITAL CITY

Copenhagen

TYPE OF GOVERNMENT

Constitutional monarchy

NATIONAL EMBLEM

The Little Mermaid statue in Copenhagen harbor

NATIONAL COLORS

Red and white

NATIONAL ANTHEM

The anthem was adopted in 1844 and remains one of two official anthems. The other, "Kong Christian," is the royal anthem and has equal status as a national anthem.

Der Er Et Yndigt Land (Danish); There Is a Lovely Land (English)

I know a lovely land
With spreading, shady beeches
Near Baltic's salty strand;
Near Baltic's salty strand;
Its hills and valleys gently fall,
Its ancient name is Denmark,
And it is Freya's hall
And it is Freya's hall

There in the ancient days
The armored Vikings rested
Between their bloody frays

Between their bloody frays
Then they went forth the foe to face,
Now found in stone-set barrows,
Their final resting place
Their final resting place

This land is still as fair,
The sea is blue around it,
And peace is cherished there.
And peace is cherished there.
Strong men and noble women still
Uphold their country's honor
With faithfulness and skill
With faithfulness and skill

Praise King and Country with might
Bless every Dane at heart
For serving with no fright
For serving with no fright
The Viking kingdom for Danes is true
With fields and waving beeches
By a sea so blue
By a sea so blue

PATRON SAINT

Saint Anskar; Saint Canute

CURRENCY

Danish krone

VEHICLE IDENTIFICATION PLATES/ STICKERS

DK

PASSPORT

The passport cover has the name of the European Union and the name of the country in Danish, the coat of arms, the Danish word for passport, *pas*, and the standard biometric symbol.

AIRLINES

SAS Scandinavian Airlines System (joint national airline of Denmark, Norway* and Sweden*); Cimber Sterling Airlines

NATIONAL FLOWER

Red clover

NATIONAL TREE
Beech

NATIONAL ANIMAL
Squirrel (unofficial)

NATIONAL BIRD
Mute swan

NATIONAL RESOURCES
Natural resources include petroleum, natural gas, fish, salt, limestone, chalk, stone, gravel, and sand. A well-educated population is the basis for high-tech agriculture, a thriving export trade, and a variety of industries and services. The important tourist industry is built around historic cities, varied scenery, and a friendly people.

FOODS
Traditional Danish food includes *frikadeller,* fried meatballs, often served with potatoes and various sorts of gravy; and *karbonader/ krebinetter,* another type of fried meatballs, steaks, or other meats mostly eaten with potatoes, which used to be very popular in Denmark. Other specialties include *oksesteg i surfløde,* rump roast in sour cream; *dalvebryst med dildsauce,* lamb with dill sauce; *høne i ris,* chicken with rice; *stegt kylling,* roast chicken with white wine and cream; *torskeboller,* salted codfish balls; and *søtunge,* fillet of sole with tomatoes and wine. *Smørrebrød,* open-faced sandwiches on dark rye bread, are a national institution.

SPORTS/SPORTS TEAMS
The most popular sport in Denmark is association football (soccer). Sailing and other water sports are also popular pastimes. Indoor sports, such as badminton, handball, and gymnastics, are also popular. Denmark national teams participate in many sports at an international level.

TEAM SPORTS
Badminton
Denmark Badminton Team

Baseball
Denmark Baseball Team; Denmark Softball Team

Basketball
Denmark Basketball Team; Denmark Women's Basketball Team; Denmark Wheelchair Basketball Team

Cricket
Denmark Cricket Team; Denmark Women's Cricket Team

Football
Denmark Football Team, nickname Danish Dynamite or Olsen Banden (the Olsen Gang); Denmark Women's Football Team; Denmark Rugby Union Team; Denmark Women's Rugby Union Team; Denmark Australian-Rules Football Team, nickname the Vikings; Denmark Wheelchair Rugby Team; Denmark American Football Team; Denmark Futsal Team; Denmark Women's Under-19 Football Team

Handball
Denmark Handball Team; Denmark Women's Handball Team; Denmark Beach Handball Team; Denmark Women's Beach Handball Team

Hockey
Denmark Ice Hockey Team; Denmark Junior Ice Hockey Team; Denmark Women's Ice Hockey Team; Denmark Field Hockey Team

Golf
Denmark Pitch and Putt Team

Korfball
Denmark Korfball Team

Lacrosse

Denmark Lacrosse Team; Denmark Women's Lacrosse Team

Racing

Denmark Speedway Team

Table Tennis

Denmark Table Tennis Team

Tennis

Denmark Davis Cup Team; Denmark Fed Cup team

Volleyball

Denmark Fistball Team; Denmark Men's Beach Volleyball Team; Denmark Women's Beach Volleyball Team; Denmark Men's Volleyball Team; Denmark Women's Volleyball Team

INDIVIDUAL SPORTS

Denmark Amateur Boxing Team; Denmark Archery Team; Denmark Athletics Team; Denmark Canoeing Team; Denmark Cycling Team; Denmark Equestrian Team; Denmark Fencing Team; Denmark Gymnastics Team; Denmark Judo Team; Denmark Karate Team; Denmark Modern Pentathlon Team; Denmark Rowing Team; Denmark Sailing Team; Denmark Shooting Team; Denmark Tae Kwon Do Team; Denmark Triathlon Team; Denmark Weight Lifting Team; Denmark Wrestling Team

WINTER SPORTS

Denmark Alpine Ski Team; Denmark Biathlon Team; Denmark Curling Team; Denmark Ice Hockey Team; Denmark Junior Ice Hockey Team; Denmark Women's Ice Hockey Team; Denmark Luge Team; Denmark Skating Team

NATIONAL HEROES OR PERSONIFICATIONS

Holger Danske (Ogler the Dane) is the personification of the Danish people and culture.

Denmark's national hero is Hans Christian Andersen, the creator of the world's most loved fairy tales; Canute Lavard, a medieval prince who was later sainted; Valdemar I (Valdemar the Great), the ruler that extended Danish power to neighboring regions in the 12th century; Queen Margarete I, who united Denmark, Norway*, and Sweden* in the Kalmar Union in 1397

NATIONAL HOLIDAY/INDEPENDENCE DAY

Grundlovsdag, or Constitution Day, June 5, is generally considered the national day of the Danes, although no specific national holiday has been designated.

FESTIVALS/FAIRS

New Circus Festival, August; Aarhus Festival Week, August; Golden Days Festival, September; Copenhagen Jazz Festival, July

SIGNIFICANT EVENTS IN FORMATION OF NATIONAL IDENTITY

500 B.C.E.–400 C.E. Indigenous peoples move south to settle the region. Trade routes with Rome are established. The ancestors of the Danes become the dominant people and occupy the entire region.

Third century–eighth century C.E. The Danes remain a tribal people, living on farming and fishing. They gradually become a seafaring people, while building large defensive sites in Denmark. The first kings appear around the mid-eighth century. Ribe, the oldest town in Denmark, is founded around 700.

10th century–12th century The Danes become known as Vikings, and together with other Viking groups from across Scandinavia, they raid, colonize, and trade in all parts of Europe. The Danes are united and converted to Christianity by King Harald Bluetooth in 965. The Danish Vikings conquer and settle parts of England, the Danelaw, Ireland, and Normandy in modern France*. King Canute the Great unites Denmark, England, and Norway for several decades.

1397 Denmark, Sweden, and Norway are united in the Kalmar Union.

1523–1536 Sweden leaves the union, which is dissolved. The Protestant Reformation comes to Scandinavia. The Danes officially embrace Protestantism in 1536. Denmark and Norway are united.

1536–1645 During a century of rivalry and wars with Sweden, Denmark loses Scania and other areas now in southern Sweden.

18th century The Florissant Age, a golden age of commerce and culture, continues until the Napoleonic Wars in the early 19th century. Denmark acquires overseas colonies, including the Virgin Islands* in the Caribbean.

1849–1864 Denmark becomes a constitutional monarchy. War with Prussia ends in defeat and the loss of southern territories. The defeat leaves deep marks on the Danish national identity.

1918–1920 The Virgin Islands are sold to the United States*. Denmark remains neutral during the First World War.

1940–1945 Germany* violates Denmark's neutrality and occupies the country during the Second World War. The Danes, in heroic act of defiance, save their Jewish citizens by transporting them in fishing boats to neutral Sweden.

1946 Denmark abandons its long tradition of neutrality and is one of the founding members of the new United Nations and one of the original member states in the North Atlantic Treaty Organization (NATO).

1973 Denmark becomes a member state of the European Economic Community, later called the European Union (EU).

2000 The Danes reject adoption of the new European currency, the Euro.

2006–2009 Denmark is one of the most prosperous nations in Europe, with few international disputes other than fishing rights. The self-governing Danish territories, Greenland*, and the Faroe Islands*, press for greater autonomy.

ESTONIA

OFFICIAL NAME

Eesti Vabariik (Estonian); Republic of Estonia (English)

POPULATION

1,339,600 (2009e)

INHABITANTS' NAME/NICKNAME

Estonian(s)

LANGUAGE/LANGUAGES

Estonian (official); Russian, German, others. In the southern provinces, Võro and Seto are official in areas where they are spoken.

RELIGION/RELIGIONS

Estonia, along with the Czech Republic*, has one of the least religious populations in the European Union: Evangelical Lutheran, 14 percent; Orthodox, 13 percent; other Christian, 1.5 percent; other or no religion

NATIONAL FLAG

The flag, colloquially called the *sinimustvalge* or blue-black-white, is a horizontal tricolor of equal stripes of medium blue, black, and white. The blue stands for the sky over Estonia, the black for the soil of the homeland and the dark centuries in Estonia's history, and the white for hard work and the promise of a brighter future.

COAT OF ARMS/SEAL

The coat of arms is a golden shield with three blue lions surrounded by oak branches on each side. The lions date from the 13th century, when Denmark* ruled northern Estonia.

CAPITAL CITY

Tallinn

TYPE OF GOVERNMENT

Parliamentary democracy

NATIONAL EMBLEM

Pikk Hermann, the tower of Toompea Castle with the national flag that is raised each morning at sunrise

NATIONAL COLORS

Pale blue, black, and white

NATIONAL ANTHEM

**Mu Isamaa, Mu Õnn Ja Rõõm (Estonian);
My Fatherland, My Pride and Joy (English)**

My fatherland, my joy and pride,
How beautiful you are!
I shall not find such ever
In this huge wide world
Which would be so dear to me
As you, my fatherland!
You have given me birth
And raised me up; I shall thank you always
And remain faithful to you 'til death,
To me most beloved are you,
My precious fatherland!
May God watch over you,
My precious fatherland!
Let him be your defender
And provide bountiful blessings
For whatever you undertake
My precious fatherland!

PATRON SAINT

Saint Michael; Saint Catherine

CURRENCY

Estonian kroon (with plans to adopt the Euro in 2010)

INTERNET IDENTIFIER

.ee

VEHICLE IDENTIFICATION PLATES/ STICKERS

EST

PASSPORT

The passport cover has the words *European Union* and the short name of the country in Estonian, the coat of arms, the Estonian word for passport, *pass,* and the standard biometric symbol.

AIRLINE

Estonian Airlines

NATIONAL FLOWER

Blue cornflower

NATIONAL TREE

Oak (unofficial)

NATIONAL ANIMAL

Wolf (unofficial)

NATIONAL BIRD

Barn swallow

NATIONAL STONE

Limestone

NATIONAL RESOURCES

Estonia is generally resource-poor; natural resources include oil shale, peat, phosphorite, clay, limestone, sand, dolomite, arable land, and sea mud. Estonia's well-educated and highly skilled population and market-based economy are assets that have given the Estonians one of the highest per capita incomes in Eastern Europe. Tourism is another important asset, based on Estonia's proximity to major European population centers, historic cities, numerous castles, and scenic countryside.

FOODS

Rosolje, made of beets, meat, and herring with a vinaigrette sauce, is one of the country's national dishes. *Pirukas,* small pastries filled with meat, cabbage, or carrots are also very popular. *Silgusoust,* Baltic fish in a tart sauce; *mulgikapsad,* roast pork with sauerkraut and boiled potatoes; *suitsukala,* smoked fish; *verivorst,* a dish of blood sausage with barley; and *kama,* a dessert made of mixed cereals, are also considered national dishes.

SPORTS/SPORTS TEAMS

Association football (soccer) is the country's most popular sport. Traditional sports, such as athletics, weight lifting, wrestling, and skiing, are also very popular. Estonian national teams participate in many sports at international level.

TEAM SPORTS

Badminton

Estonia Badminton Team

Baseball

Estonia Baseball Team; Estonia Softball Team

Basketball

Estonia Basketball Team; Estonia Women's Basketball Team

Cricket

Estonia Cricket Team

Football

Estonia Football Team, nickname *Sinisärgid* (Blue shirts); Estonia Women's Football Team, nickname *Sinisärgid* (Blue shirts); Estonia Youth Football Team; Estonia Under-21 Football Team; Estonia Rugby Union Team; Estonia Rugby League Team; Estonia Beach Soccer Team; Estonia American Football Team; Estonia Futsal Team; Estonia Women's Under-19 Football Team

Handball

Estonia Handball Team

Hockey

Estonia Ice Hockey Team; Estonia Junior Ice Hockey Team; Estonia Field Hockey Team

Racing

Estonia Speedway Team

Table Tennis

Estonia Table Tennis Team

Tennis

Estonia Davis Cup Team; Estonia Fed Cup Team

Volleyball

Estonia Beach Volleyball Team; Estonia Men's Volleyball Team; Estonia Women's Volleyball Team

INDIVIDUAL SPORTS

Estonia Amateur Boxing Team; Estonia Archery Team; Estonia Athletics Team; Estonia Canoeing Team; Estonia Cycling Team; Estonia Equestrian Team; Estonia Fencing Team; Estonia Gymnastics Team; Estonia Judo Team; Estonia Karate Team; Estonia Modern Pentathlon Team; Estonia Rowing Team; Estonia Sailing Team; Estonia Shooting Team; Estonia Swim Team; Estonia Tae Kwon Do Team; Estonia Triathlon Team; Estonia Weight Lifting Team; Estonia Wrestling Team

WINTER SPORTS

Estonia Alpine Ski Team; Estonia Bandy Team; Estonia Biathlon Team; Estonia Curling Team; Estonia Ice Hockey Team; Estonia Junior Ice Hockey Team; Estonia Luge Team; Estonia Skating Team

NATIONAL HEROES OR PERSONIFICATIONS

The unofficial personification of Estonia is Mats Hobusega, a metaphor for the average Estonian. Mats is always with his horse, presenting a somewhat comical, self-deprecating view of Estonia's humble, agricultural history.

Other national heroes include Kalevipoeg, the hero of the great national epic of the same name; Carl Robert Jakobson, one of the leaders of the Estonian national reawakening in the second half of the 19th century; Konstantin Päts, the first president of independent Estonia, who was arrested and deported by the Soviets in 1940; and Jüri Uluots, prime minister of Estonia at the time of the Soviet invasion in 1940 and the leader of the government-in-exile; Andrus Veerpalu, two-time winter Olympics gold metalist

NATIONAL HOLIDAY/INDEPENDENCE DAY

Independence Day, February 24; Restoration (of independence), August 20

FESTIVALS/FAIRS

Laulupidu (Estonian Song Festival), once every five years in July; Black Nights Film Festival, November; Christmas Market Festival, December; Tallinn Food Fair, October–November

SIGNIFICANT EVENTS IN FORMATION OF NATIONAL IDENTITY

Fifth century C.E. Attacks by Vikings from nearby Scandinavia disrupt the region. Several Viking sagas tell of campaigns against the Estonians. A king or elder becomes the highest official as Estonia is divided into provinces.

1193–1208 Pope Celestine III calls for a crusade against the remaining pagans in northern Europe. German crusaders invade the Baltic and establish control of present Latvia*. From their bases in Latvia, the crusaders attack the Estonians to the north, which the Estonians fiercely resist.

1218–1220 The Danes attack and take control of northern Estonia.

1227 Estonia is divided between the German crusaders in the Livonian region in the south and the Danes in the north.

1228–1346 The Danes hold northern Estonia until 1346, when the region is sold to the Teutonic Knights. Germans settle as feudal lords on large estates worked by Estonian serfs.

1523–1525 The Reformation comes to Estonia through Germany*. The rapid conversion of the Baltic German-populated towns increases tensions with rural Estonians, who remain Roman Catholic until much later. The first book is published in the Estonian language.

1561–1625 During the Livonian War, northern Estonia comes under the rule of Sweden*.

1721 The Great Northern War ends with a Russian victory. The upper and merchant classes, the Baltic Germans, retain their culture, power, and positions under Russian rule.

1816–1819 Serfdom is abolished, allowing Estonian peasants to leave German estates. Most take up farming on the lands of the German manors. Schools, teaching in both German and Estonian, quickly raise the educational level of the peasantry.

1860–1880 The spread of education begins a great national reawakening among the Estonians. Estonian nationalism grows as an anti-German movement, inspired by the near-feudal subjugation. The Estonian national epic, *Kalevipoeg*, is published in 1862.

1881–1914 Czar Alexander III greatly reduces the privileges of the Baltic German aristocracy but also suppresses the activities of the Estonian cultural movement.

1917–1918 Revolution spreads across the Russian Empire during World War I. Estonian nationalists declare the independence of the country in 1918.

1918–1938 Estonia becomes a prosperous republic culturally allied to the Scandinavian countries.

1939–1941 Soviet troops invade neutral Estonia. The majority of the Baltic Germans are evacuated to Germany. Tens of thousands are deported to Siberia and Central Asia. Germany invades its Soviet ally and occupies Estonia.

1941–1953 The Soviets again occupy Estonia. Many more are deported. Over 100,000 Estonians reach the West before the Soviets close the escape routes. The Soviet authorities replace the 350,000 Estonians killed, deported, murdered in the Holocaust, or fled abroad since 1939 with "reliable" Slavs from Russia.

1960s The Estonians achieve the highest standard of living in the Soviet Union. The suppression of the Estonian culture rekindles Estonian nationalism

1987–1991 The liberalization of Soviet society opens the way for nationalists to demand the restoration of Estonia's independence. A 1991

referendum shows overwhelming support for independence. Estonians declare the restoration of their 1918 republic, beginning the rapid disintegration of the Soviet Union.

1992–1994 Estonia successfully reorients its culture and economy toward the West. The last Soviet troops withdraw from the republic on August 31.

2004 Estonia joins both the North Atlantic Treaty Organization (NATO) on March 29 and the European Union (EU) on May 1, ensuring its security as part of democratic Europe.

2008–2009 The large Russian-speaking minority and Estonian demands for a realignment of the boundary based on the 1920 treaty with Soviet Russia that would bring the now divided ethnic Seto people into Estonia continue to hinder better relations with neighboring Russia.

EUSKAL HERRIA

OFFICIAL NAME

Euskal Autonomia Erkidegoa (Basque); Comunidad Autónoma de País Vasco (Spanish) Basque Country Autonomous Region (English); Euskal Herria (Basque); País Vasco (Spanish); Pays Basque (French); Basque Country (English)

POPULATION

2,146,900 in the Basque Country Autonomous Region in Spain (2009e); the entire region known as Euskal Herria includes this region, the Foral Community of Navarre, and the French Basque Country, with a total population of 3,202,800 (2009e). The national symbols of Euskal Herria are recognized and used throughout the Basque areas of Spain and France.

INHABITANTS' NAME/NICKNAME

Basque(s)

LANGUAGE/LANGUAGES

Euskerra (Basque), Spanish (both official); French, others. Basque is not an official language in the French Basque Country.

RELIGION/RELIGIONS

Predominantly Roman Catholic, Protestant, other or no religion

NATIONAL FLAG

The flag, called *Ikurriña*, is a red field bearing a green cross diagonally behind a white cross. The flag is the official flag of the Basque Country Autonomous Region in Spain and also represents all Basques in the territory known as Euskal Herria, which includes territory in both Spain and France*. The red stands for the Basque people, the green represents the Oak of Guernica, the Basque national symbol, and the white cross symbolizes the Basque devotion to the Catholic religion.

COAT OF ARMS

The coat of arms of Euskal Herria is a shield divided into seven parts, each bearing the heraldic emblem of one of the seven territories that make up Euskal Herria. The seven territories are Araba, Bizkaia, and Gipuzkoa (Basque), Alava, Vizcaya, and Guipúzcoa (Spanish), which make up the autonomous region of the Basque Country, and Nafarroa (Navarra in Spanish), a separate autonomous region in Spain, and the French Basque country, made up of three regions, Lapurdi, Behe Nafarroa (Lower Navarre), and Zuberoa, called Labourd, Basse-Navarre, and Soule in French

MOTTO

Jaungoikoeta lege zaharrak (Basque); God and the old laws (English) (unofficial)

CAPITAL CITY

Gasteiz (Euskerra); Vitoria (Spanish)

TYPE OF GOVERNMENT

The Basque Country and Navarre form autonomous regions within the Spanish kingdom. The three territories of the French

Basque country form part of the French Department of Pyrenees-Atlantiques

NATIONAL EMBLEM

Gernikako Arbola (Tree of Guernica); the Ikurriña (the Basque flag)

NATIONAL COLORS

Red, white, and green

NATIONAL ANTHEM

The anthem dates from the turn of the twentieth century and was adopted as the official anthem of the first Basque government created during the Spanish Civil War. After 1939, the fascist dictatorship forbade its use, but with the establishment of Basque autonomy, it was again adopted by the autonomous region.

Eusko Abendaren Ereserkia (Eskerra); Anthem of Basque Ethnicity (English)

Up and up, Basque Country
glory and glory
to its Good Lord from above.
There is an oak tree in Biscay
old, strong, healthy
It as its law
On the tree we find
the holy cross
always on our top
Sing "Up. Basque Country"
glory and glory
to its Good Lord from above

PATRON SAINT

Saint Ignatius of Loyola

CURRENCY

Euro

INTERNET IDENTIFIER

.es Spain (official); .eh Euskal Herria (unofficial)

VEHICLE IDENTIFICATION PLATES/ STICKERS

E Spain (official); EH Euskal Herria (unofficial)

PASSPORT

The Basques in Spain are Spanish citizens and travel on Spanish passports. French Basques travel on French passports.

NATIONAL FLOWER

Rose (unofficial)

NATIONAL TREE

Oak or Tree of Guernica (unofficial)

NATIONAL RESOURCES

Natural resources include timber, arable land, fisheries, coal, and iron. The region is one of the wealthiest in Spain. Traditional industries, such as shipbuilding and steel, were centered on the region's coal and iron. The large Basque communities outside Europe are an important source of tourism and investment. The important tourist industry is focused on the region's sandy beaches, pleasant climate, historic cities, and such attractions as the Guggenheim Museum in Bilbao.

FOODS

Marmitako, a stew of fresh tuna and potatoes, is considered a national dish, as are *bacalao al la viscaina*, salt cod with tomato sauce, and *pintxos*, the wide variety of small seafood, meat, and vegetable dishes also known as tapas. Tapas were first served in Basque bars before spreading to other parts of Spain and France.

SPORTS/SPORTS TEAMS

Association football (soccer) is the most popular game in the Basque Country. Traditional sports, such as jai alai, called *pelota* in Spanish, are still very popular. The Euskal Herria national team participates in football and pelota (frontón) at an international level.

TEAM SPORTS

Football

Basque Football Team, nickname Euskal Herria

Pelota

Basque Pelota (Frontón) Team

NATIONAL HEROES OR PERSONIFICATIONS

Sancho II, called Sancho the Great, king of Navarre in the Middle Ages; José Antonio Aguirre, the leader of the Basque nationalists in the 1930s; Léopold Eyharts, the first Basque astronaut in space

NATIONAL HOLIDAY/INDEPENDENCE DAY

Aberri Eguna (National Day), celebrated on Easter Sunday

FESTIVALS/FAIRS

Annual Carnival; Semana Grande, August; Euskal Jaiak (Basque Week), September; Aste Nagusia, August; Tamborrada, January; Alarde, June

SIGNIFICANT EVENTS IN FORMATION OF NATIONAL IDENTITY

First century B.C.E. Romans move north into the region. The Roman chroniclers cite the Basques as a very difficult nation to subdue. The Romans mostly leave the Basque tribes to rule themselves under nominal Roman rule, probably the reason the Basque language survives while so many languages are replaced by the Romans' Latin.

Third century C.E.–fifth century C.E. Christianity is introduced and is slow to penetrate, but once the Basques embrace the new religion, they become fervent Christians. Barbarian invasions follow the fall of Roman power, but the Basques remain independent, defending their culture and language against all encroachments.

Eighth century Germanic Franks overrun most of the Basque Country.

824 The Basques expel the Franks and create the Kingdom of Navarre.

927 Invading Muslim Moors are stopped, and the Basques take the offensive, later playing a prominent role in the Christian reconquest of northern Spain.

1200–1530 The Castilians from central Spain conquer the Basque Country between 1200 and 1390. With the fall of Navarre in 1512, the Basques lose their last independent territory. Granted special rights, called the *fueros,* the Basques enjoy broad autonomy in exchange for personal loyalty to the Spanish kings.

1601–1789 The northern Basques, incorporated into the French kingdom, are granted limited autonomy that continues until the French Revolution in 1789.

1850s–1860s Basque resistance to attempts by the Spanish government to abrogate their ancient rights stimulates the growth of Basque nationalism, which begins to reverse centuries of assimilation.

1873–1876 During the Carlist Wars in Spain, the Basques resist the Spanish Republican forces. As punishment for their resistance, the *fueros* are abolished.

1920s–1930s Political turmoil in Spain strengthens Basque nationalism. Basque leaders declare the region autonomous of Spain in 1931, but the movement is soon ended by Spanish troops.

1936–1937 A new, leftist government in Spain grants autonomy at the outbreak of the Spanish Civil War. German bombers deliberately destroy the town of Guernica, immortalized by Pablo Picasso and the site of the Basque's sacred oak tree, in 1937. The fascists conquer the Basque Country, and all autonomy is officially ended. Thousands of Basques flee the collapse of their republic.

1950s–1960s Government-sponsored immigration from the poorer parts of Spain dilutes the Basque population. Persecution of the Basque language and culture produce a nationalist backlash with the creation of several nationalist organizations, including ETA (Basque Country and Freedom) that begins a violent campaign for Basque independence.

1975–1983 The death of fascist leader Francisco Franco and the election of a democratic government in Spain end the persecutions. The

Basque Country is given autonomy, while Navarre becomes a separate autonomous region within Spain.

1983–2000 The Basque terrorist group ETA continues its violent campaign to drive the Spanish, and the French, from the greater Basque Country with a long series of bomb attacks that leave many dead and injured, even though the vast majority of the Basques have rejected violence as the way to win independence.

2006–2007 The government of the Basque Country announces that Basque will become the first language of education, with Spanish taught several hours a week as a second language. The separatist organization ETA announces a "permanent ceasefire" in 2006 but resumes violence confrontations, including several bomb attacks and assassinations in 2007.

2008–2009 The Basque government prepares a nonbinding two-question referendum regarding Basque self-determination. According to the plan, a second, binding referendum would then determine the future of the Basques in Spain. One of the two questions covers negotiations to end the violent campaign by ETA, while the other asks citizens whether they agree to negotiations to reach a democratic agreement about the right of the Basques to decide their own future. Militants, while rejecting the violence of the terrorists, continue to demand the reunification of the various Basque territories into one European region.

See also Spain

FAROE ISLANDS

Official Name

Faerøerne (Danish); Føroya (Faroese); Faroe Islands (English)

Population

48,300 (2009e)

Inhabitants' Name/Nickname

Faroese

Language/Languages

Faroese, Danish (official); English, Norwegian, others

Religion/Religions

Faroese People's Church (Lutheran), 84 percent; Open Brethren, 10 percent; other or no religion

National Flag

The flag, called *Merkid,* is a white field with a red Scandinavian cross outlined in blue. The white represents the pure sky over the Faroes, as well as the foam of the waves breaking on its shores; the red and the blue are colors taken from traditional Faroese headdresses.

Coat of Arms/Seal

The coat of arms is a shield that depicts a *vedrur* (ram) on a blue shield. The emblem carries the same colors and symbolism as the national flag, with the addition of yellow on the hooves and horns.

Capital City

Thorshavn

Type of Government

Parliamentary democracy as an autonomous state of the Kingdom of Denmark*

National Emblem

White ram

National Colors

White and blue

National Anthem

The anthem was written and composed in the early 20th century. It is now the official anthem of the country.

> **Mitt Alfagra Land (Faroese); Faroe National Anthem (English)**
>
> My land, oh most beauteous, possession most dear,
> Thou drawest me to thee, embracing me near;

becalmed in the summer, in winter snow
  covered,
magnificent islands, by God named beloved.
The name which men gave thee when they
  thee discovered,
Oh, God bless thee, Faroes my land.

Bright gleam, which in summer makes hill-
  tops so fair;
rough gale, which in winter drives men to
  despair;
oh life-taking storm, oh conquest of soul,
all making sweet music uniting the whole.
Each hoping and trusting, inspiring us all,
to guard thee, O Faroes my land.

And therefore, I kneel down, to thee God, in
  prayer,
may peaceful my lot be, and do thou me
  spare,
my soul cleansed; in glory; I ask thee to bless,
when I raise my banner and venture the stress.
The sign of my task, be it lifted on high,
to guard thee, O Faroes my land.

PATRON SAINT
Saint Olav the Holy

CURRENCY
Faroese króna

INTERNET IDENTIFIER
.fo

VEHICLE IDENTIFICATION PLATES/STICKERS
FO (official); FØ (unofficial)

PASSPORT
The Faroese are Danish citizens and travel
on Danish passports.

AIRLINE
Atlantic Airways

NATIONAL FLOWER
Marsh marigold (unofficial)

NATIONAL TREE
Willow (unofficial)

NATIONAL ANIMAL
Sheep

NATIONAL BIRD
Faroese puffin; oystercatcher (unofficial)

NATIONAL RESOURCES
Natural resources include fisheries, whales,
hydropower, and possible oil and natural
gas. The islands' almost total dependence on
fishing may soon be offset by promising petroleum deposits found near the islands. The
large Faroese population living in Denmark
is a source of investment and remittances.

FOODS
Skerpikjøtm, wind-dried and well-aged mutton that is a bit like jerky, is a popular national dish. Other traditional foods are *ræst
kjøt,* semidried mutton, and *ræstur fiskur,*
matured fish. Another Faroese specialty is
grind og spik, pilot whale meat and blubber.

SPORTS/SPORTS TEAMS
Association football (soccer) is the most
popular sport in the country. Faroe Islands
national teams participate in many sports at
an international level.

TEAM SPORTS
Badminton
Faroe Islands Badminton Team

Basketball
Faroe Islands Basketball Team

Football
Faroe Islands Football Team; Faroe Islands
Women's Football Team; Faroe Islands
Rugby Union Team; Faroe Islands Women's
Rugby Union Team; Faroe Islands Under-21
Football Team

Table Tennis

Faroe Islands Table Tennis Team

Volleyball

Faroe Islands Men's Volleyball Team; Faroe Islands Women's Volleyball Team

INDIVIDUAL SPORTS

Faroe Islands Archery Team; Faroe Islands Judo Team; Faroe Islands Swim Team

NATIONAL HEROES OR PERSONIFICATIONS

Símun av Skardi, the poet who wrote the lyrics to the national anthem, teacher, and leader of the Faroese self-government movement in the early 20th century; Petur Alberg, songwriter who composed the national anthem; Dr. Jakob Jakobsen, a noted linguist and the "father of the Faroese language"

NATIONAL HOLIDAY/INDEPENDENCE DAY

Faroese National Day (Ólavsøka), July 29

FESTIVALS/FAIRS

Summartónar, July–August; Ólavsøka, the Saint Olav Festival, July

SIGNIFICANT EVENTS IN FORMATION OF NATIONAL IDENTITY

700 C.E.   Irish hermit monks come to the islands, which are inhabited by Celtic peoples.

8th century C.E.–10th century C.E.   Norwegian Vikings take control of the islands and colonize the region from mainland Scandinavia.

11th century   Christianity is introduced from Norway* and soon becomes the islands' religion. Norway retains control of the islands.

1380   Norway enters the Kalmar Union with Denmark and Sweden*, which gradually changes control of the islands from the Norwegians to the Danes.

1538   The Protestant Reformation reaches the Faroes, with the majority of the islanders adopting the Lutheran creed.

1814   The union of Denmark and Norway is dissolved, and Denmark retains control of the Faroes. The Danish government imposes a trade monopoly that forbids the Faroese to fish in their own waters.

1856   The Danish trade monopoly is abolished, and the Faroese develop a modern fishing fleet of their own.

1888   The defense and extension of the Faroese language against the domination of the Danish language marks the beginning of the Faroese cultural awakening.

1906   The cultural movement spawns a political faction and the foundation of separate political parties.

1940   After the Nazi invasion of Denmark, the islands are occupied by British troops.

1945–1946   The Faroe Islands revert to Danish rule at the end of the Second World War. Nationalists want to follow Iceland* and declare independence from Denmark, as the Icelanders do in 1944. A plebiscite on the question shows that a majority favor independence, which is declared on September 18, 1946. The inhabitants of one of the larger islands announce their desire to remain with Denmark, so the plebiscite is overruled as inconclusive. A second vote shows a slight plurality for retaining ties to Denmark.

1948   Continued agitation for greater autonomy results in an agreement granting a high degree of self-government.

1973   Fearing interference in the all-important fishing industry, the Faroese vote to stay out of the European Community when Denmark joins.

1990s   The fishing industry, suffering from mismanagement and overfishing, collapses. Recovery and diversification of the economy quickly follow. The discovery of oil promises to end the ups and downs of the fishing industry.

2001   Oil production begins in the islands.

2001–2009   The anticipated oil resources are not realized. Faroese proposals for full independence remain active, but many fear losing Denmark's financial guarantees.

See also Denmark

FINLAND

OFFICIAL NAME

Suomen Tasavalta (Finnish); Republic of Finland (English)

POPULATION

5,331,200 (2009e)

INHABITANTS' NAME/NICKNAME

Finn(s); Finnish

LANGUAGE/LANGUAGES

Finnish, Swedish (both official); Sami, Russian, others

RELIGION/RELIGIONS

Lutheran (Church of Finland), 82 percent; Orthodox, 1 percent; Roman Catholic, other or no religion

NATIONAL FLAG

The flag, called the *Siniristilippu* (blue cross flag), is a white field with a blue Scandinavian cross. Blue represents the country's many lakes and the sky; white represents snow and the white nights of the Finnish summer.

COAT OF ARMS/SEAL

The coat of arms consists of a red shield with a crowned golden lion brandishing a white sword with another white blade at the feet. Around the lion are scattered nine white roses. The emblem is derived from the original coat of arms of Finland under Swedish rule. The white roses represent the nine historical provinces.

MOTTO

Vapaa, vankka, vakaa (Finnish); Free, Strong, Stable (English) (unofficial)

CAPITAL CITY

Helsinki

TYPE OF GOVERNMENT

Semipresidential parliamentary democracy

NATIONAL EMBLEM

Golden Lion of Finland

NATIONAL COLORS

White and blue

NATIONAL ANTHEM

The song originated in the mid-19th century with Swedish lyrics. It was translated into Finnish and became the national anthem of Finland before independence in 1917. The anthem, although never officially legislated as such, has Finnish and Swedish versions of the lyrics.

> **Maame (Finnish); Vårt Land (Swedish); Our Land (English)**
>
> O our home country, Finland, the land where
>   we were born,
> sound high, you golden word!
> There is no valley, no mountain,
> no lake or shore more dear,
> than this northern home,
> the land of our fathers.
>
> There shall be time
> when you will burst
> into full blossom,
> then our love shall be roused
> by your glorious hope and joy,
> at last, your song, O motherland,
> will sound in higher tone!

PATRON SAINT

Saint Henry; Saint Urho

CURRENCY

Euro

INTERNET IDENTIFIER

.fi

VEHICLE IDENTIFICATION PLATES/STICKERS

FIN

PASSPORT

The passport cover has the name of the European Union in Finnish and Swedish, the coat of arms, the short name of the country in Finnish and Swedish, and the word *passport* in Finnish and Swedish.

AIRLINE

Finnair

NATIONAL FLOWER

Lily of the valley

NATIONAL TREE

Silver birch

NATIONAL ANIMAL

Brown bear; lion (mythical creature introduced to European heraldry from the Middle East)

NATIONAL BIRD

Whooper swan; Eurasian eagle-owl (unofficial)

NATIONAL FISH

Humpbacked perch

NATIONAL RESOURCES

Natural resources include timber, iron ore, copper, lead, zinc, chromite, nickel, limestone, copper, gold, and silver. Finland has an industrial economy based on abundant forest resources, capital investments, and high technology. The tourist industry is growing and has become an important asset.

FOODS

Lihapullat, Finnish meatballs traditionally served with *grabby,* boiled or mashed potatoes and lingonberry jam, is considered the national dish. *Kaalikääyleet,* cabbage rolls stuffed with minced meat, chopped cabbage, and rice and served with lingonberry jam, and *hernekeitto,* pea soup, are also traditional

dishes considered national dishes. Other specialties include *karjalanpaisti,* (Karelian hot pot), a stew of beef, pork, lamb or mutton, onions, and spices; *kainuulainen kalakeitto,* a fish soup with onions, potatoes, and allspice berries; *marjakiisseli,* a dessert made of lingonberries; and *poronkäristys,* sautéed reindeer meat.

SPORTS/SPORTS TEAMS

The country's most popular sports are association football (soccer) and ice hockey, which is considered a national sport. *Pesäpallo,* also called Finnish baseball, is a traditional national sport. Finland national teams participate in many sports at an international level.

TEAM SPORTS

Badminton

Finland Badminton Team

Baseball

Finland Baseball Team; Finland Softball Team

Basketball

Finland Basketball Team; Finland Women's Basketball Team

Cricket

Finland Cricket Team

Football

Finland Football Team, nickname Huuhkajat (the Eagle Owls or the Owls) or Sinivalkoiset; Finland Women's Football Team, nickname Huuhkajat (the Eagle Owls or the Owls); Finland Rugby Union Team; Finland Women's Rugby Union Team; Finland Australian Rules Football Team, nickname the Lions; Finland Under-21 Football Team; Finland Wheelchair Basketball Team; Finland Wheelchair Rugby Team; Finland American

Football Team; Finland Futsal Team; Finland Rugby Union Team (Sevens), nickname Finland Sevens or Finland 7s; Finland Women's Rugby Union Team (Sevens), nickname Finland Sevens or Finland 7s; Finland Women's Under-19 Football Team

Handball

Finland Handball Team; Finland Women's Handball Team

Hockey

Finland Men's Ice Hockey Team; Finland Women's Ice Hockey Team; Finland Junior Ice Hockey Team; Finland Field Hockey Team

Korfball

Finland Korfball Team

Lacrosse

Finland Lacrosse Team

Racing

Finland Speedway Team

Table Tennis

Finland Table Tennis Team

Tennis

Finland Davis Cup Team; Finland Fed Cup Team

Volleyball

Finland Men's Beach Volleyball Team; Finland Women's Beach Volleyball Team; Finland Men's Volleyball Team; Finland Women's Volleyball Team

INDIVIDUAL SPORTS

Finland Aikido Team; Finland Amateur Boxing Team; Finland Archery Team; Finland Athletics Team; Finland Canoeing Team; Finland Cycling Team; Finland Equestrian Team; Finland Fencing Team; Finland Gym-
nastics Team; Finland Judo Team; Finland Karate Team; Finland Modern Pentathlon Team; Finland Rowing Team; Finland Sailing Team; Finland Shooting Team; Team; Finland Swim Team; Finland Tae Kwon Do Team: Finland Triathlon Team; Finland Weight Lifting Team; Finland Wrestling Team

WINTER SPORTS

Finland Alpine Ski Team; Finland Bandy Team; Finland Biathlon Team; Finland Curling Team; Finland Men's Ice Hockey Team; Finland Women's Ice Hockey Team; Finland Junior Ice Hockey Team; Finland Luge Team; Finland Skating Team

NATIONAL HEROES OR PERSONIFICATIONS

Suomi-neito (Finnish Maiden) is the national personification. She is a barefoot young woman with blond hair and blue eyes, wearing a blue and white or all-white dress, often holding aloft the Finnish flag; Pekka Põder is the personification of the ordinary people.

Finland's national hero is Carl Gustaf Emil Mannerheim, a soldier and statesman who led the White forces to victory, ensuring Finland's independence, in 1918–1919 and later commander-in-chief of Finland's forces during the wars with the Soviet Union in 1940 and 1944; Elias Lönnrot, the author/compiler of the Finnish national epic, Kalevala; Risto Ryti, president during World War II who was later sentenced, at the insistence of the Soviet Union, to prison for allying Finland with Germany* against the Soviet Union, which had invaded Finland; Adolf Ehrnrooth, decorated hero of the wars against the Soviet Union 1939–1945

NATIONAL HOLIDAY/INDEPENDENCE DAY

Independence Day, December 6

FESTIVALS/FAIRS

Savonlinna Opera Festival, July–August; Kuhmo Chamber Music Festival, July; Helsinki Festival, August; Lahti Sibelius Festival, September; World Village Festival, May; Tampere Theatre Festival, August; Turku Jazz, March

SIGNIFICANT EVENTS IN FORMATION OF NATIONAL IDENTITY

3000 B.C.E.–2500 B.C.E. Agriculture is introduced and becomes an important part of the subsistence economy.

500 B.C.E.–1200 C.E. The early Finns maintain extensive contacts with other cultures in the region. Christianity gains support across the region. The Swedes attempt to conquer Finland in the 1150s.

13th century The first verifiable written documents record daily life in early Finland. The Second Swedish Crusade in 1249 and the Third Swedish Crusade in 1293, part of the long series of conflicts for territory and influence between Sweden and Novgorod, bring Finland and part of Karelia under Swedish rule.

1389 Denmark*, Norway*, and Sweden* are joined in the Kalmar Union, beginning a period of population growth and economic expansion in Finland.

1495–1497 A brutal war between Sweden and Russia* brings devastation and ruin to many parts of eastern Finland.

1521–1551 The Kalmar Union collapses and Sweden becomes a separate kingdom under Gustav Vasa. The Protestant Reformation comes to Finland through Sweden. Although the official language remains Swedish, the New Testament is translated into the Finnish language.

1561 The Finns suffer conscription, high taxes, and abuse that lead to the rebellion known as the Cudgel War of 1596–97, which is brutally suppressed. Agricultural settlements move north displacing the original Sami inhabitants.

1638–1655 Sweden founds a colony in the New World in present Pennsylvania-Delaware. At least half the colonists are of Finnish origin.

1697–1699 A famine brought on by poor harvests caused by climate change kills about a third of the Finnish population.

1700–1721 Russians occupy Finland during the Great Northern War. Russia annexes territory in the southeast.

1812 Russia conquers Swedish Finland, which is reunited with territory annexed to Russia in the 18th century to form the autonomous Grand Duchy of Finland.

1855–1893 The publication of the Finnish national epic, the Kalevala, a collection of traditional myths and legends, stirs Finnish nationalism. The Swedish-speaking upper classes join in promoting a sense of shared national culture. The Finnish language is accepted in local administration in 1863 and becomes an official language along with Swedish.

1899–1917 A new Russian government policy promotes the Russification of Finland. Russian becomes the state language, conscription is begun, and the formerly separate Finnish army is incorporated into the imperial army. The Finns resist with petitions, demonstrations, and strikes.

1917–1920 In the aftermath of the Russian Revolution, Finland is declared an independent state. As in Russia, a civil war breaks out between Whites and Reds. After the White victory, a democratic government is created.

1940–1944 Finland fights the Soviet Union in two separate wars in 1940 and in 1944. Finland manages to maintain its democratic government and independence, unlike the majority of countries bordering the Soviet Union. It is one of only three European countries to save their Jewish populations from the Holocaust.

1950–1991 Finland develops closer ties to the other Nordic countries and declares neutrality during the Cold War. The Finnish economy expands rapidly, bringing prosperity to every part of the country. Finland signs an association agreement with the European Free Trade Association in 1961 and becomes a full member in 1986. Finland constructs one of the most extensive welfare states in the world.

1994–1999 Finland abandons its historically strict neutrality and establishes ties to the North Atlantic Treaty Organization (NATO). The country joins the European Union and adopts the new European currency, the euro.

2005–2008 Finland is among the most stable countries in the world, based on a survey of social, economic, political and military indicators. Some Finns would like to press claims to territory now in Russia that traditionally formed part of Finland, but the Finnish government refuses to consider such a controversial stance.

2009 Stricter gun control is imposed following two mass shootings in 2007–2008.

See also Åland; Sápmi

FLANDERS

OFFICIAL NAME

Vlaamse Gewest (Flemish); Flemish Region (English)
    Vlaanderen (Flemish); Flanders (English)

POPULATION

6,091,500 (2009e); the Brussels-Capital Region, claimed by nationalist groups as part of Flanders, has a population of 1,033,800 (2009e)

INHABITANTS' NAME/NICKNAME

Fleming(s): Flemish

LANGUAGE/LANGUAGES

Flemish (Dutch) (official); French may be used for some administrative purposes in the Brussels area and in the areas bordering Wallonia.

RELIGION/RELIGIONS

Roman Catholic, 75 percent; Protestant, Orthodox, Muslim, Jewish, other or no religion

NATIONAL FLAG

The official flag of the Flanders Region is yellow with a black lion outlined in white and with red claws and tongue. A flag with a completely black lion outlined in white, without the red claws and tongue, is unofficial, although very popular in Flanders, particularly among Flemish nationalists, as the official version of the flag reflects the three colors of the Belgian flag, while a completely black lion is particularly Flemish.

COAT OF ARMS/SEAL

The Flemish most often use a yellow shield bearing the black lion of Flanders with either black claws and tongue (nationalist) or red claws and tongue (the Flemish Community). The official emblem of the Flemish Region is a stylized version of the Flemish Lion in gray, with five narrow yellow bars facing away from the lion.

MOTTO

Vlaanderen den leeuw (Flemish); Flanders the Lion (English)

CAPITAL CITY

Brussel (Flemish); Brussels (French)

TYPE OF GOVERNMENT

Parliamentary democracy as an autonomous region within the Kingdom of Belgium*

NATIONAL EMBLEM

Flemish Lion

NATIONAL COLORS

Yellow and black

NATIONAL ANTHEM

The anthem was written in 1847 and became the anthem of Flemish nationalism. It was adopted as the anthem of the Flemish Region of Belgium in 1973.

> **De Vlaamse Leeuw (Flemish); The Flemish Lion (English)**
>
> They will never tame him, the proud Flemish Lion,

Even if they threaten his freedom with fetters and with shouts.
They will never tame him, as long as a Fleming lives.
As long as the lion can claw, as long as he has teeth.

They will never tame him, as long as a Fleming lives.
As long as the lion can claw, as long as he has teeth.
Time devours cities, no thrones will ever last,
Armies may go under, but a people never dies.
The enemy comes marching in; surrounded by mortal danger
We laugh at his anger: the Flemish Lion is here!

For a thousand years now has he fought, for freedom, land and God,
And yet his strength is as youthful as ever.
Should anyone think him powerless, and taunt him with a kick,
Both menacing and fearsome will he rise.

Pity the mindless who, deceptive and full of treason,
Comes to pet the Flemish Lion and hit him faithlessly.
Not a single movement he does not see:
And if he feels offended, he will raise his manes and roar.

The sign of revenge has been given, he is tired of their bait;
With fire in the eye, in anger he jumps towards the enemy.
He tears, destroys, crushes, covers in blood and mud
And in victory grins over his enemy's trembling corpse.

PATRON SAINT

Saint Pharaildis

CURRENCY

Euro

INTERNET IDENTIFIER

.vl

VEHICLE IDENTIFICATION PLATES/ STICKERS

B Belgium (official); VL Flanders (unofficial)

PASSPORT

The Flemings are Belgian citizens and travel on Belgian passports.

AIRLINE

Vlaamse Luchttransportmaatschappij VLM

NATIONAL FLOWER

Red poppy (unofficial)

NATIONAL TREE

Tree of life (unofficial)

NATIONAL BIRD

Chaffinch (unofficial)

NATIONAL RESOURCES

Natural resources include fisheries, iron, construction materials, carbonates, and arable land. Antwerp, the second busiest port in Europe after Rotterdam, is a major asset and the center of an excellent network of ports, canals, highways and railways. Historic cities and proximity to many of Europe's largest population centers support a thriving tourist industry.

FOODS

Carbonade, stewed meat in a brown beer sauce, is very popular. *Waterzooi,* a type of chicken stew; *frieten,* fried potatoes; *paling-en-het groen,* eel in green herb sauce; and many dishes made with mussels are all considered national dishes. Another specialty is *hutespot,* a stew of vegetables, beans, potatoes, and sausages.

SPORTS/SPORTS TEAMS

Association football (soccer) is the most popular sport. Tennis, cycling, volleyball, and athletics are also popular sports. The Flanders national team participates in football at an international level.

TEAM SPORTS

Football

Flanders Football Team

NATIONAL HEROES OR PERSONIFICATIONS

Baldwin I, the first ruler of the County of Flanders; Jan Frans Willems, an activist for language equality in Belgium in the early 19th century; Jan Theodoor van Rijswijck, the People's Poet, a writer and Flemish activist in the early 19th century

NATIONAL HOLIDAY/INDEPENDENCE DAY

Flemish National Day, July 11

FESTIVALS/FAIRS

National Song Fest, Antwerp (annual); Flemish Movement visit to World War I battlefields, last Sunday of August (annual); Festival van Vlaanderen (Flanders Festival), September

SIGNIFICANT EVENTS IN FORMATION OF NATIONAL IDENTITY

57 B.C.E. Belgica, named for the Celtic Belgae tribe conquered by Julius Caesar, forms part of the Roman Empire.

Fourth century C.E. Invasions by Huns and Salic Franks drive the Latin-speaking population south to a line approximating the present linguistic division of Belgium.

Fifth century As part of the Frankish empire, the region is called Pagus Flandrensis. The name Flanders appears in the early eighth century.

814 The Frankish empire begins to collapse following Charlemagne's death. Baldwin Bras-de-Fer (Iron Arm) becomes the first count of Flanders in 862. Under a succession of able rulers, the basis is laid for later commercial greatness.

11th century–12th century The County of Flanders is a powerful European nation with territories now in Belgium, France*, and the Netherlands*.

The economy develops from an agricultural to a commercial economy based on trade and industry. The Flemish Renaissance is a golden age of art, literature, and music. In 1191, the direct line of Flemish counts dies out, and the counts of Hainault, in Wallonia*, become counts of Flanders, as well. French is the language of the towns and upper classes, while Flemish is spoken as a peasant dialect.

14th century France expands north, taking control of part of Flanders. The Battle of the Golden Spurs, in 1302, is a great Flemish victory against the French, who then recognize Flemish independence. The date of the battle, July 11, is now the Flemish national holiday.

15th century During another golden age of Flanders, Flemish commerce flourishes and Flemish art reaches its full flower. Protestant beliefs spread through the region, winning some converts.

1555–1584 Flanders passes to the Spanish Hapsburgs and become part of the Spanish Netherlands. Religious differences between the Protestant Dutch and the Roman Catholic Flemings lead to a serious division of the Low Countries until the two join in an anti-Spanish uprising in 1576. The Dutch win their independence, but Flanders is recovered by Spain*. The spoken form of Flemish diverges from Dutch.

1801–1815 Flanders becomes part of Napoleonic France. At the end of the Napoleonic Wars, the Low Countries are again reunited in the Kingdom of the Netherlands.

1830 The predominantly Roman Catholic southern provinces of Flanders and Wallonia rebel against Protestant Dutch rule and form the separate Kingdom of Belgium.

1830–1900 The new kingdom remains a French-speaking state, with the Flemish language relegated to the position of a peasant dialect. The language issue stimulates the growth of Flemish nationalism and an accompanying cultural revival. A sense of Flemish grievance grows throughout the 19th century.

1917–1918 A faction of the Flemish national movement, encouraged by the Germans during World War I, declares Flanders independent of

Belgium. The movement collapses with the German surrender.

1940–1945 German occupation authorities during World War II raise Flemish to the level of an official language alongside French, which lasts until the German defeat and the return of the exiled Belgian government.

1945–1962 The rapid post-war reconstruction favors formerly neglected Flanders and its increasingly important ports. By the early 1960s, Flanders has surpassed Wallonia as Belgium's predominant region. Material prosperity prompts calls for cultural and linguistic equality, with mass rallies across Flanders in 1961–62. Flemish is made an official language. Universities, banks, political parties, and other official institutions split along linguistic lines.

1977–1993 The Egmont Pact of 1977 creates autonomous governments in Flanders and Wallonia, and later in bilingual Brussels. Devolution of such areas as taxation, culture, and education follows. The status of Brussels, a French-speaking enclave surrounded by Flemish-speaking suburbs, remains a point of contention, as both communities claim the city as their own. The Belgian government is left with little more than responsibility for finance, foreign policy, and defense.

2003–2009 The increasing rift between the Flemish and the Walloons is reflected in the country's politics, as Belgium is left without a functioning government for months at a time.

See also Belgium

FRANCE

OFFICIAL NAME

République Française (French); French Republic (English)

POPULATION

64,473,900 (2009e)

INHABITANTS' NAME/NICKNAME

French

LANGUAGE/LANGUAGES

French (official); Breton, Alsatian, Corsican, Catalan, Basque, Flemish, Provençal (Occitan), Arabic, others

RELIGION/RELIGIONS

Roman Catholic, 85 percent; Muslim, 10 percent; Protestant, 2 percent; other or no religion

NATIONAL FLAG

The flag, known as the *drapeau tricolore,* the tricolor flag, is a vertical tricolor of blue, white, and red. The colors of the flag are associated with the ideals of the French Revolution. Blue represents liberty, white is for equality, and red stands for fraternity.

COAT OF ARMS/SEAL

The coat of arms has been a symbol of France since 1953, although it has no legal status as an official coat of arms. It consists of a wide shield with lion-head terminal bearing a monogram *RF,* standing for République Française (French Republic). An olive branch behind the shield symbolizes peace. An oak branch symbolizes wisdom. The fasces is a symbol associated with justice (from Roman axes).

MOTTO

Liberté, égalité, fraternité (French); Liberty, Equality, Fraternity (English)

CAPITAL CITY

Paris

TYPE OF GOVERNMENT

Unitary, semipresidential republic

NATIONAL EMBLEM

Eiffel Tower; Galic rooster; fleur de lis

NATIONAL COLORS

Blue, white, and red

National Anthem

The anthem was written during the French Revolution and became the marching song of the National Guard of Marseille. They were singing it when they marched into Paris, and the Parisians dubbed it the "La Marseillaise."

La Marseillaise

Arise, children of the fatherland
The day of glory has arrived
Against us tyranny's
Bloody standard is raised
Listen to the sound in the fields
The howling of these fearsome soldiers
They are coming into our midst
To cut the throats of your sons and consorts
To arms, citizens
Form you battalions
March, march
Let impure blood
Water our furrows
What do they want this horde of slaves
Of traitors and conspiratorial kings?
For whom these vile chains
These long-prepared irons?
Frenchmen, for us, ah! What outrage
What methods must be taken?
It is we they dare plan
To return to the old slavery!

What! These foreign cohorts!
They would make laws in our courts!
What! These mercenary phalanxes
Would cut down our warrior sons
Good Lord! By chained hands
Our brow would yield under the yoke
The vile despots would have themselves be
The masters of destiny

Tremble, tyrants and traitors
The shame of all good men
Tremble! Your parricidal schemes
Will receive their just reward
Against you we are all soldiers
If they fall, our young heroes
France will bear new ones
Ready to join the fight against you

Frenchmen, as magnanimous warriors
Bear or hold back your blows
Spare these sad victims
Who with regret are taking up arms
   against us
But not these bloody despots
These accomplices of Bouillé
All these tigers who pitilessly
Are ripping open their mothers' breasts

Sacred Love for the Fatherland
Lead and support our avenging arms
Liberty, cherished liberty
Join the struggle with your defenders
Under our flags, let victory
hasten to you virile (or manly) force
So that in death your enemies
See your triumph and our glory!

We shall enter into the pit
When our elders will no longer be there
There we shall find their ashes
And the mark of their virtues
We are much less jealous of surviving them
Than of sharing their coffins
We shall have the sublime pride
Of avenging or joining them

Patron Saint

Saint Louis IX

Currency

Euro

Internet Identifier

.fr

Vehicle Identification Plates/Stickers

F

Passport

The passport cover has the name of the European Union and the name of the country in French across the top, the coat of arms, the French word for passport, *passeport,* and the standard biometric symbol.

AIRLINES
Air France; XL Airways

NATIONAL FLOWER
Fleur-de-lis iris

NATIONAL TREE
Yew

NATIONAL ANIMAL
Gallic rooster

NATIONAL BIRD
Gallic rooster

NATIONAL RESOURCES
Natural resources include coal, iron ore, bauxite, zinc, uranium, antimony, arsenic, potash, feldspar, fluorspar, gypsum, timber, and fish. Although diverse, the natural resources of France are fairly limited in quantity. France's position at the heart of Western Europe is a geographic asset. The flourishing and economically important tourist industry is probably the world's most developed.

FOODS
Coq au vin, chicken cooked with wine and mushrooms; pot-au-feu, a boiled meal of beef, vegetables, and spices; and *confit de canard*, duck poached in its own fat, are three of the dishes considered national dishes. The baguette, the classic loaf of French bread; pot-au-feu; cassoulet, a dish of beans, chicken, and sausage from the south; and foie gras, duck liver pate, were declared part of the French cultural heritage by a new law in 2005. Regional specialties remain popular across the country.

SPORTS/SPORTS TEAMS
The country's most popular sports include association football (soccer), rugby union, rugby league, basketball, handball, and cycling. France national teams participate in many sports at an international level.

TEAM SPORTS

Badminton
France Badminton Team

Baseball
France Baseball Team; France Softball Team

Basketball
France Basketball Team, nickname Les Bleus (the Blues); France Women's Basketball Team, nickname Les Bleues (the Blues); France Under-21 Basketball Team; France Wheelchair Basketball Team

Cricket
France Cricket Team

Football
France Football Team, nickname Les Bleus (the Blues); France Women's Football Team, nickname Les Bleues (the Blues); Rugby League Team, nickname Les Tricolores or Les Chanteclairs (the Cockerels); France Women's Rugby League Team; France Rugby Union Team, nickname Les Bleus or Les Tricolors or Le Quinze de France; France Under-21 Football Team, nickname Les Bleuets (the Little Blues) or Espoirs; France B Football Team; France Rugby Union Team (Sevens), nickname France Sevens; France Australian-Rules Football Team: France Wheelchair Rugby Team; France American Football Team; France Beach Soccer Team; France Touch Football Team; France Women's Touch Football Team; France Rugby Union Team (Sevens), nickname France Sevens; France Women's Under-19 Football Team nickname Les Bleuettes (the Little Blues)

Golf
France Men's Pitch and Putt Team; France Women's Pitch and Putt Team

Handball

France Handball Team; France Women's Handball Team; France Beach Handball Team; France Women's Beach Handball Team

Hockey

France Ice Hockey Team; France Junior Ice Hockey Team; France Women's Ice Hockey Team; France Field Hockey Team

Kabaddi

France Kabaddi Team

Korfball

France Korfball Team

Racing

A1 Team France; France Speedway Team

Table Tennis

France Table Tennis Team

Tennis

France Davis Cup Team;

Volleyball

France Men's Volleyball Team; France Women's Volleyball Team; France Men's Beach Volleyball Team; France Women's Beach Volleyball Team

Water Polo

France Polo Team

INDIVIDUAL SPORTS

France Aikido Team; France Amateur Boxing Team; France Archery Team; France Athletics Team; France Canoeing Team; France Cycling Team; France Equestrian Team; France Fencing Team; France Judo Team; France Karate Team; France Modern Pentathlon Team; France Rowing Team; France Sailing Team; France Shooting Team; France Swim Team; France Tae Kwon Do Team; France Triathlon Team; France Weight Lifting Team; France Wrestling Team

WINTER SPORTS

France Alpine Ski Team; France Biathlon Team; France Bobsleigh and Tobogganing Team; France Curling Team; France Ice Hockey Team; France Junior Ice Hockey Team; France Women's Ice Hockey Team; France Luge Team; France Skating Team

NATIONAL HEROES OR PERSONIFICATIONS

Marianne is a symbol of the French Republic. She is an allegorical figure of liberty and the Republic and first appeared at the time of the French Revolution. The earliest representations of Marianne are of a woman wearing a Phrygian cap.

National heroes include Charles de Gaulle, leader of the Free French during the Second World War and the most important political figure in French history; Napoleon Bonaparte, the 19th century leader who made France Europe's leading power in the early 19th century; and Joan of Arc, the girl warrior who led French forces to victory over the English in the 15th century

NATIONAL HOLIDAY/INDEPENDENCE DAY

Bastille Day, July 14

FESTIVALS/FAIRS

Bastille Day (Fête Nationale), July; Cannes Film Festival, May; Nice Carnival, February–March; La Fête de la Musique, June

SIGNIFICANT EVENTS IN FORMATION OF NATIONAL IDENTITY

First century B.C.E.   Ancient Gaul, with approximately the same borders as modern France, the home of the Celtic Gauls, is conquered by Julius Caesar and incorporated into the Roman Empire.

Second century C.E.–**third century** C.E.   Christianity is introduced and becomes strongly entrenched.

Fourth century Germanic tribes invade as Roman power collapses. The Salic Franks, a Germanic tribe from beyond the Rhine, take control and give their name to the country as Francie, part of the vast Frankish empire.

498 The Franks' King Clovis converts to Christianity, which becomes the official religion of the kingdom.

843 The Frankish empire is divided at Charlemagne's death, separating France from the Germanic lands to the east.

987–1700 The Kingdom of France is created and, over centuries, through a series of wars and dynastic inheritances, reaches approximately its present boundaries. France reaches its height during the 17th century. It has the largest population in Europe and has tremendous influence over European politics, culture, and economy.

1789–1799 The French Revolution ends the French monarchy. The king is executed, along with thousands of aristocrats, their servants, and others deemed a danger to the revolution. After a series of government convulsions, Napoleon Bonaparte seizes control of the new republic.

1799–1815 Crowning himself as emperor, Napoleon leads his armies to conquer most of continental Europe, with members of his family appointed as monarchs of newly established kingdoms. At Napoleon's final defeat at Waterloo, the French monarchy is reestablished.

1815–1870 Periods of rule by the royals are interspersed with the declaration of the second and third republics.

1900–1914 France's colonial empire is second only to that of the United Kingdom*.

1914 France emerges victorious from the First World War and insists on imposing humiliating peace conditions on defeated Germany*.

1940–1945 The German invasion during the Second World War ends with France under German occupation. France is divided into a German occupation zone in the north and Vichy France, a fascist puppet regime, in the south.

1945–1954 Charles de Gaulle, the wartime French leader, establishes the Fourth Republic. France attempts to maintain control of its colonial empire but is forced out of Southeast Asia following a military defeat by nationalists.

1954–1962 Demands for independence in Algeria*, with its million European settlers, become a national trauma that nearly leads to civil war. The Fifth Republic is declared in 1958. France gives up, and Algeria becomes independent. The European colonists return to France.

1980–2000 France and Germany, after decades of war and tensions, cooperate to bring a lasting peace to Europe. Their cooperation proves central to the success and expansion of the European Union.

2005–2008 The French majority votes against the European Union constitution in 2005 but ratifies the successor treaty in 2008. Claims by neighboring countries and national movements in the country's remaining overseas territories are a continuing problem.

2009 The government unveils a set of stimulus packages to revitalize the sagging economy. Massive bonuses for executives of government-aided industries and firms are outlawed.

GALICIA

OFFICIAL NAME

Comunidade Autónoma de Galiza (Galician); Comunidad Autónoma de Galicia (Spanish); Autonomous Region of Galicia (English)

POPULATION

2,791,900 (2009e)

INHABITANTS' NAME/NICKNAME

Galician(s); Galego(s); Gallego(s)

LANGUAGE/LANGUAGES

Galician, Spanish (official); Portuguese, others

RELIGION/RELIGIONS

Roman Catholic, 91 percent; Protestant, 4 percent; Muslim, other or no religion

NATIONAL FLAG

A white field bearing a diagonal pale blue stripe upper hoist to lower fly with the Galician coat of arms centered. The colors, blue and white, come from the former maritime flag flown on ships carrying Galician emigrants to the Americas. The central shield is modeled on the flag of the 16th-century Kingdom of Galicia. The white and blue flag, without the coat of arms, is considered the national flag. The same flag, with the addition of a single centered red star, is the flag of Galician nationalism.

COAT OF ARMS/SEAL

The coat of arms consists of a blue shield or crest bearing the national emblem, a gold chalice and a silver host, surrounded by six silver crosses. Above the shield is a jeweled gold crown filled with red. The blue and white represent the national colors. The chalice symbolizes Galicia's ties to the historic Kingdom of Galicia, and the seven silver crosses represent the seven historic provinces of Galicia. The crown represents the sovereignty of Galicia.

CAPITAL CITY

Santiago de Compostela

TYPE OF GOVERNMENT

Parliamentary democracy as an autonomous region of Spain*

NATIONAL EMBLEM

Chalice and paten of Cebreiro (shown on the flag and coat of arms); A Pont Vella (Roman bridge at Ourense)

NATIONAL COLORS

White and pale blue

NATIONAL ANTHEM

The anthem is based on the Galician-language poem *Queixumes dos pinos,* written in 1886 by Eduardo Pondal. The music was composed in 1907. The song was adopted as the official anthem in 1977.

Os Pinos (Galician); The Pines (English)

What do the murmuring say
In the greenish coast
To the transparent beam
Of the placid moon place?
What do the high
Dark pine needle jagged tops say
With its well compassed
Measured grumble?
With your girdled greenness
And with benign stars
Limit of the green castroes
And courageous land,
Don't give to oblivion
Of outrage the hard effort;
Wake up from your dream
Home of Breogán.
The good and generous
Our voice understand,
And with determination they attend
Our harsh sound,
But only the ignoramus,
And wounded and hard,
Idiot and dark
Don't understand us, they do not.
The times are arrived
Of Age Bards,
That your indeterminacies
End they will put down;
Because where it wants, giant
Our voice proclaims
The redemption of the good
Nation of Breogán.

PATRON SAINT

Saint James the Apostle

CURRENCY

Euro

INTERNET IDENTIFIER

.es Spain (official); .gz Galicia (unofficial)

VEHICLE IDENTIFICATION PLATES/STICKERS

E Spain (official); GZ Galicia (unofficial)

PASSPORT

Galicians are Spanish citizens and travel on Spanish passports.

NATIONAL FLOWER

Ulex (gorse) (unofficial)

NATIONAL TREE

Chestnut (unofficial)

NATIONAL ANIMAL

Eurasian wolf (unofficial)

NATIONAL BIRD

Yellow-legged seagull (unofficial)

NATIONAL RESOURCES

Natural resources include fisheries, shellfish, timber, hydropower, and construction materials. The tradition of dividing land between heirs has made Galicia a checkerboard of small and often economically unsustainable holdings even though agriculture and fisheries are the mainstays of the economy. The western regions have the major population centers and the majority of the fisheries and manufacturing while agriculture remains the mainstay of the largely rural hinterland. However, the rise of tourism, sustainable forestry, and organic agriculture are bringing other possibilities to the Galician economy without compromising the preservation of the region's natural resources and the Galician culture.

FOODS

Galician cuisine often employs fish and shellfish. A local pastry, known as *empanadas*, filled with ground meat or fish, is considered the national dish. Other traditional specialties include *Caldo Galego*, a stew of potatoes and *grelos* (broccoli rabe), sometimes including fish or shellfish. *Lacón con grelos*, pork shoulder with spicy sausages and *grelos*, is also considered a national dish. *Centolla* is a local variety of crab, boiled quickly then opened and its innards mixed with mayonnaise or a spicy sauce, is typical of the coastal regions. *Pulpo Galego*, is a dish of boiled octopus cut into small pieces and served on a wooden plate with olive oil, sea salt, and ground red pepper. A classical dessert is *filloas*, crêpe-like pancakes made with flour, broth, sugar, and eggs. Famous almond cakes are a specialty of Santiago de Compostela.

SPORTS/SPORTS TEAMS

Association football (soccer) is the most popular sport. Futsal, a variety of indoor football (soccer), rowing, yachting, wrestling, and fishing are also popular sports. Galicia national teams participate in a number of sports at an international level.

TEAM SPORTS

Basketball

Galicia Basketball Team; Galicia Women's Basketball Team

Football

Galicia Football Team; Galicia Women's Football Team; Galicia Futsal Team; Galicia Rugby Union Team

INDIVIDUAL SPORTS

Galicia Rowing Team; Galicia Wrestling Team

NATIONAL HEROES OR PERSONIFICATIONS

Breogán, a mythical Celtic king of Galicia, is considered the personification of Galicia and the mythological father of the Galician nation.

Rosalía de Castro, a writer and poet in the Galician language in the mid- and late-19th century; Alfonso Rodríguez Castelao, a leader of the Galician cultural revival in the early 20th century; Xose Manuel Beiras, a leading Galician intellectual and one of the leaders of the Galician national movement; Manuel Fraga, one of the leading Spanish politicians spanning the Franco dictatorship and the later democratic transformation. He was president of Galicia from 1990 to 2005; Adolfo Dominguez, one of Spain's leading fashion designers and a proponent of Galician culture.

NATIONAL HOLIDAY/INDEPENDENCE DAY

Dia da Patria Galega (Galician Day or National Day) also known as Saint James the Apostle Day, July 25

FESTIVALS/FAIRS

Magosto, November; La Rapa de Bestas (the Taming of the Beasts), June-July; Carballiño (Octopus Festival), August; Viking Pilgrimage, August; Seafood Festival, October; Festival of Santiago, July

SIGNIFICANT EVENTS IN FORMATION OF NATIONAL IDENTITY

Fifth century B.C.E.–second century B.C.E. Celtic peoples known as Gallacci or Callaeci inhabit the region, often building massive stone monuments

137 B.C.E. The Celtic region is conquered by the Romans, who call it Gallaecia after the region's inhabitants. The Celts gradually adopt the Roman culture and the Latin language.

411 C.E.–584 C.E. The Germanic Suevi overrun Roman Galicia. The Suevi are in turn defeated by invading Germanic Visigoths in 584. Galicia becomes a Visicothic kingdom, often extending into neighboring parts of Spain and into modern Portugal*.

711–739 During the Moorish invasion of Spain, the Moors conquer Galicia but are unable to hold it when defeated by Aflonso I of Asturias.

9th century–10th century Viking raids on the coastal region force the Galicians to build a system of fortifications to stop attacks on the major ports and cities.

1063–1072 Galicia becomes a separate kingdom until forcibly incorporated into the stronger Kingdom of Castile of central Spain.

11th century–15th century Although often allowed considerable self-government, the Galicians remain isolated from the rest of Spain. They develop a unique medieval culture, using Celtic, Germanic, Latin, and Iberian elements. Galician becomes the foremost literary language of the Iberian Peninsula, known for its lyrical, poetic literature, the first to develop in a Romance language in the Christian Era.

1479 Galicia loses most of its remaining autonomy with the merger of the kingdoms of Castile and Aragon.

1640 A Galician attempt to separate from the Spanish kingdom is brutally crushed, beginning a long cultural and economic decline in the region.

18th century–19th century The Galician language remains a peasant dialect while the upper classes adopt the Spanish language and culture. A cultural revival, centered on the language, begins a renewal of the traditions, customs, and language. The cultural revival is based on the belief that Galicia must regain the mythical "golden age" of the medieval kingdom. Many Galicians leave the impoverished and underdeveloped region for the Spanish colonies in the Americas.

1931–1936 Galician leaders demand autonomy from Spain's new republican government. They quickly revive the Galician parliament, closed and forbidden since the early 19th century. The national revival is overtaken by the outbreak of civil war in Spain. Although Francisco Franco, the leader of the conservative rebels, is Galician, the majority of the Galicians join the antifascist forces opposing Franco.

1939–1975 At the end of the civil war, Franco punishes the Galicians for their opposition. The language is banned and the culture suppressed. Underground nationalist organizations form, some seeking democracy, others demanding autonomy or complete separation from fascist Spain. Nationalist demonstrations demanding self-government in the early 1970s lead to a reign of terror instituted by the elderly Franco, which ends only with his death in 1975.

1980 Galicia is granted major autonomy as part of the democratization of the Spanish kingdom.

By the late 1980s, around 90 percent again speak the Galician language. Ties to other Celtic nations in Europe fan the rebirth of the traditional Galician culture.

1998 An estimated 98 percent of the regional population uses Galician as the language of daily life. Spanish remains the language of the significant non-Galician population, mostly living in the larger cities.

2000–2009 Galicia remains one of the poorest regions of Spain. Galician identity focuses on gaining recognition as a distinct European nation and on improving the local economy although a minority continues to work for complete political separation from Spain and independence for Galicia within the protection of the European Union (EU).

See also Spain

GEORGIA

Official Name
Sakartvelo (transliteration from Georgian); Georgia (English)

Population
4,658,900 (2009e)

Inhabitants' Name/Nickname
Georgian(s)

Language/Languages
Georgian (official); Russian, Armenian, Azeri, Abkhaz, Ossetian, others

Religion/Religions
Georgian Orthodox, 84 percent; Muslim, 10 percent; Armenian Apostolic, 4 percent; Russian Orthodox, 2 percent; Roman Catholic, other or no religion

National Flag
The flag, known as the five-cross flag, is based on the historical flag of the country that was used between the 5th and 14th centuries. The design was adopted as the national flag in 2004. It consists of a white field with a centered red Saint George Cross with smaller red crosses on each of the four quadrants. The five crosses are said to represent the five holy wounds of Christ.

Coat of Arms/Seal
The coat of arms was adopted in 2004. It is partially based on the medieval arms of the Georgian royal house of Bagrationi. It contains a central red shield showing Saint George, Georgia's patron saint, slaying the dragon. The shield is supported by two golden lions and is surmounted with the royal crown of Georgia. Below the shield is a banner with the national motto in the Georgian language.

Motto
Dzala ertobashia (Georgian); Strength is in unity (English)

Capital City
Tbilisi

Type of Government
Semipresidential unitary republic

National Emblem
The *borjjgali*, an ancient symbol of the sun, is used on Georgian identity cards and passports, as well as currency.

National Colors
Red and white

National Anthem
The anthem was adopted after a popular revolt replaced the former government of Georgia in 2004.

Tavisupleba (Georgian); Freedom (English)

My icon is my motherland,
And the whole world is its icon-stand.
Bright mounts and valleys

Are shared with God
Today our freedom
Sings to the glory of future,
The dawn star rises up
And shines out between two seas.
Praise be to liberty,
Praise be to liberty!

PATRON SAINT

Saint George

CURRENCY

Georgian lari

INTERNET IDENTIFIER

.ge

VEHICLE IDENTIFICATION PLATES/ STICKERS

GE

PASSPORT

The passport has the name of the country in Georgian and English, the *borjgali*, an ancient symbol of the sun, and the word *passport* in Georgian and English.

AIRLINE

Georgian Airways

NATIONAL FLOWER

Rose (after the Rose Revolution of 2003)

NATIONAL TREE

Tree of life (unofficial)

NATIONAL ANIMAL

Lion; snow leopard (unofficial)

NATIONAL BIRD

Common pheasant

NATIONAL RESOURCES

Natural resources include forests, hydropower, manganese deposits, iron ore, copper, and minor coal and oil deposits. The coastal climate and soils allow for important tea and citrus growth. The country's ancient monuments, historical cities, unique and ancient cultures, and sandy beaches and pleasant climate along the Black Sea have the potential to support a thriving tourist industry. The sizable number of Georgians living outside the country is a source of remittances and investment.

FOODS

Khachapuri, Georgian cheese bread; *basturma*, marinated and spiced kebabs of lamb or pork; *chkmeruli*, chicken prepared with a garlic-walnut sauce, and *khinkali*, beef and pork dumplings, are considered national dishes. Other specialties include *chikhitrma*, a type of onion soup; *lobio mtsvanilit*, a dish of herbed kidney beans; *azelila*, egg salad; and *kotmis satsivi*, roast chicken with garlic walnut sauce.

SPORTS/SPORTS TEAMS

Association football (soccer) is Georgia's most popular sport. Traditional sports, such as wrestling and weight lifting, remain popular. Georgia national teams participate in many sports at international level.

TEAM SPORTS

Badminton

Georgia Badminton Team

Baseball

Georgia Baseball Team; Georgia Softball Team

Basketball

Georgia Basketball Team; Georgia Women's Basketball Team

Football

Georgia Football Team, nickname Jvarosnebi (the Crusaders); Georgia Women's Football

Team nickname Jvarosnebi (the Crusaders); Georgia Rugby League Team, nickname 13 Georgians; Georgia Rugby Union Team, nickname Lelos; Georgia Under-21 Football Team; Georgia Rugby Union (Sevens) Team, nickname Georgia Sevens or Georgia 7s; Georgia Futsal Team; Georgia Women's Under-19 Football Team

Hockey

Georgia Field Hockey Team

Korfball

Georgia Korfball Team

Table Tennis

Georgia Table Tennis Team

Tennis

Georgia Davis Cup Team; Georgia Fed Cup Team

Volleyball

Georgia Men's Beach Volleyball Team; Georgia Women's Beach Volleyball Team; Georgia Men's Volleyball Team; Georgia Woman's Volleyball Team

INDIVIDUAL SPORTS

Georgia Amateur Boxing Team; Georgia Archery Team; Georgia Athletics Team; Georgia Biathlon Team; Georgia Canoeing Team; Georgia Cycling Team; Georgia Equestrian Team; Georgia Fencing Team; Georgia Gymnastics Team; Georgia Judo Team; Georgia Karate Team; Georgia Modern Pentathlon Team; Georgia Swim Team; Georgia Rowing Team; Georgia Sailing Team; Georgia Shooting Team; Georgia Tae Kwon Do Team; Georgia Weight Lifting Team; Georgia Wrestling Team

WINTER SPORTS

Georgia Alpine Ski Team; Georgia Luge Team; Georgia Skating Team

NATIONAL HEROES OR PERSONIFICATIONS

Amirani, a noble hero analogous to Prometheus; Prince Kakutsa Cholokasvilli, the leader of the 1924 uprising against the Bolsheviks; Ilia Chavchavadze, leader of the national revival in the 1860s; King Heraclius II, who reunited the Georgian territories in the 18th century

NATIONAL HOLIDAY/INDEPENDENCE DAY

Independence Day, May 26

FESTIVALS/FAIRS

Assumption, August; Giorgoba/Saint George's Day, November; Tbilisoba National Film Festival, October

SIGNIFICANT EVENTS IN FORMATION OF NATIONAL IDENTITY

Third century B.C.E. Two major cultures develop in the region, Colchis in the west and Iberian in the east. In Greek mythology, Colchis is the location of the famed Golden Fleece sought by Jason and the Argonauts.

66 B.C.E.–500 C.E. Romans conquer the Caucasus region. Georgia remains a client kingdom of Rome for nearly four centuries. Christianity becomes the state religion in 330 C.E. Their Christian religion ties the people of Georgia to the Byzantine Empire.

500–645 The kingdom disintegrates into small feudal states. Muslim Arabs overrun the region.

813 The Bagrationi dynasty is established and rules over all or parts of Georgia for nearly 1,000 years.

12th century–1236 King David IV initiates the Georgian golden age. The Georgian renaissance is characterized by religious and ethnic tolerance and advances in literature, music, and political innovations.

1236–1747 Invading Mongols destroy the kingdom. Neighboring Persians and Ottoman Turks take parts of the fallen kingdom.

1747–1762 The Georgian territories are re-united under King Heraclius.

1783–1873 The Georgian kingdom of Kartii-Kakheti signs a treaty of protection with Russia*. In 1800, Georgia is incorporated into the Russian Empire. The western Georgian territories come under Russian rule between 1810 and 1873.

1917–1921 During the First World War, the Russian Revolution sweeps the empire, leading to civil war. Georgia is declared independent in 1918. Abkhazia* is incorporated into the new republic.

1921–1922 An uprising in Abkhazia is the pretext for a Soviet invasion. The Red Army takes control of the republic. A Soviet Georgian republic becomes a founding member of the Union of Soviet Socialist Republics.

1930s Joseph Stalin, an ethnic Georgian, is the head of state of the Soviet Union, but Georgia suffers the same repression as the other parts of the vast Soviet empire.

1960s Dissidents begin to talk of the restoration of the 1918 Georgian Republic, an idea that gains support during the 1960s. The movement is repeatedly undermined by arrests, persecution, and harassment.

1989 The liberalization of Soviet life under Mikhail Gorbachev allows limited expression of Georgian grievances. Soviet troops attack a peaceful demonstration, killing and injuring many people.

1990–1991 Dissidents lead a political movement dedicated to Georgian independence. The collapse of the Soviet Union in 1991 leads to the disintegration of the country. Georgia is declared an independent republic.

1991–1995 A coup attempt becomes a bitter civil war with widespread ethnic violence and fighting. Abkhazia and South Ossetia* declare their independence of Georgia.

2003–2004 A peaceful revolution, the Rose Revolution, brings a new, more democratic government to power. Relations with Russia deteriorate over Russian support for the breakaway republics.

2007 The last Russian troops leave Georgia. The European Union (EU) signs a free-trade agreement with Georgia and a visa facilitation agreement.

2008 Fighting breaks out between Ossetians and the Georgian military, prompting a full-scale attack on South Ossetia by the Georgian army. One day later, Russian troops cross into South Ossetia. Fighting spreads as the Russians invade Georgia. Russia recognizes the independence of Abkhazia and South Ossetia. Nicaragua* recognizes the independence of Abkhazia and South Ossetia.

2009 Georgia announces its departure from the Commonwealth of Independent Nations. Many Georgians support moves to join NATO and the EU. Venezuela announces its recognition of Abkhazia and South Ossetia.

See also Abkhazia; South Ossetia

GERMANY

OFFICIAL NAME
Bundesrepublik Deutschland (German); Federal Republic of Germany (English)

POPULATION
82,223,700 (2009e)

INHABITANTS' NAME/NICKNAME
German(s)

LANGUAGE/LANGUAGES
German (official); Danish, Low German, Sorbian, Romany, and Frisian (recognized and protected); Turkish, French, others

RELIGION/RELIGIONS
Protestant, 34 percent; Roman Catholic, 34 percent; Muslim, 4 percent; Jewish, other or no religion

NATIONAL FLAG
The flag is based on one used in 19th century Germany, a horizontal tricolor of black, red, and gold. The colors represent the freedom of Germany and the personal freedom of the German people.

COAT OF ARMS/SEAL

The coat of arms consists of a golden shield bearing a black eagle with a red beak and legs. The colors of the emblem reflect the national colors of the flag. It is the one of the oldest extant state symbols of Europe and one of the oldest insignia in the world. Its history as an emblem began even earlier. To the Germanic tribes, the eagle was the bird of the god.

MOTTO

Einigkeit und recht und freiheit (German); Unity and justice and freedom (English)

CAPITAL CITY

Berlin

TYPE OF GOVERNMENT

Parliamentary federal republic

NATIONAL EMBLEM

Iron cross; German eagle

NATIONAL COLORS

Red, black, and gold

NATIONAL ANTHEM

The text of the anthem was written in 1841 but not adopted until 1922, and it was first retained by the Nazis and later banned. It was resurrected as the national anthem of united Germany in 1991.

Das Lied Der Deutschen (German); The Song of the Germans (English)

Unity and justice and freedom
For the German fatherland;
For these let us all strive,
Brotherly with heart and hand.
Unity and justice and freedom
Are the pledge of happiness.
Flourish in this fortune's blessing,
Flourish, German fatherland.
Flourish in this fortune's blessing
Flourish, German fatherland!

PATRON SAINT

Saint Michael

CURRENCY

Euro

INTERNET IDENTIFIER

.de

VEHICLE IDENTIFICATION PLATES/ STICKERS

D

PASSPORT

The passport cover has the name of the European Union and the name of the country in German, the coat of arms, the word for passport in German, *reisepass*, and the standard biometric symbol.

AIRLINES

Lufthansa; Air Berlin; TUIfly

NATIONAL FLOWER

Cornflower (knapweed) (unofficial)

NATIONAL TREE

Oak (unofficial)

NATIONAL BIRD

German eagle (black eagle) (as depicted on the coat of arms)

NATIONAL RESOURCES

National resources include coal, lignite, natural gas, iron ore, copper, nickel, uranium, potash, salt, construction materials, timber, and arable land.

FOODS

Sauerbraten, meat marinated in vinegar, sugar, and spices, and sauerkraut, fermented shredded cabbage, are considered national dishes. Various sausages, called wursts, are also characteristic of German cuisine, particularly currywurst, bratwurst, and frankfurters. The many regional cuisines maintain their distinct traditions.

SPORTS/SPORTS TEAMS

Association football (soccer) is the national sport of Germany. Racing and rugby union are also popular, as are cycling and tennis and various winter sports. Germany national teams participate in many sports at international level.

TEAM SPORTS

Badminton

Germany Badminton Team

Baseball

Germany Baseball Team; Germany Softball Team

Basketball

Germany Basketball Team; Germany Women's Basketball Team; Germany Wheelchair Basketball Team; Germany Women's Wheelchair Basketball Team

Cricket

Germany Cricket Team

Football

Germany Football Team, nickname Die Nationalelf (the National Eleven) or Mannschaft (the Team); Germany Women's Football Team, nickname Die Nationalelf (the National Eleven); Germany Under-21 Football Team; Germany Under-20 Football Team; Germany Women's Under-19 Football Team; Germany Rugby Union Team; Germany Rugby League Team; Germany Women's Rugby League Team; Germany Youth Football Team; Germany Australian-Rules Football Team, nickname the Black Eagles; Germany Wheelchair Rugby Team; Germany American Football Team; Germany Beach Soccer Team; Germany Touch Foot-

ball Team; Germany Women's Touch Football Team; Germany Rugby Union Team (Sevens), nickname Germany Sevens or Germany 7s; Germany Women's Rugby Union Team (Sevens), nickname Germany Sevens or Germany 7s

Handball

Germany Handball Team; Germany Women's Handball Team; Germany Beach Handball Team; Germany Women's Beach Handball Team

Hockey

Germany Ice Hockey Team; Germany Women's Ice Hockey Team; Germany Junior Ice Hockey Team; Germany Field Hockey Team; Germany Women's Field Hockey Team

Kabaddi

Germany Kabaddi Team

Korfball

Germany Korfball Team

Lacrosse

Germany Lacrosse Team; Germany Women's Lacrosse Team; Germany Under-19 Lacrosse Team; Germany Women's Under-19 Lacrosse Team

Racing

A1 Team Germany; Germany Speedway Team

Table Tennis

Germany Table Tennis Team

Tennis

Germany Davis Cup Team; Germany Fed Cup Team

Volleyball

Germany Men's Volleyball Team; Germany Women's Volleyball Team; Germany Fistball Team; Germany Men's Beach Volleyball Team; Germany Women's Beach Volleyball Team

INDIVIDUAL SPORTS

Germany Aikido Team; Germany Amateur Boxing Team; Germany Archery Team; Germany Athletics Team; Germany Canoeing Team; Germany Cycling Team; Germany Equestrian Team; Germany Fencing Team; Germany Gymnastics Team; Germany Judo Team; Germany Karate Team; Germany Modern Pentathlon Team; Germany Rowing Team; Germany Sailing Team; Germany Shooting Team; Germany Swim Team; Germany Tae Kwon Do Team; Germany Triathlon Team; Germany Weight Lifting Team; Germany Wrestling Team

WINTER SPORTS

Germany Alpine Ski Team; Germany Biathlon Team; Germany Bobsleigh and Tobogganing Team; Germany Curling Team; Germany Luge Team; Germany Skating Team

NATIONAL HEROES OR PERSONIFICATIONS

Personifications of Germany include Germania, representing the German Nation, usually shown wielding Joyeuse, Charlemagne's personal sword; Otto Normalverbrauscher, the average guy; and Der Deutsch Michel, a simple man in knee breeches and a sleeping cap.

Arminius, a Celtic chieftain who defied the Roman Empire was the first national hero.,Others are Otto von Bismarck, who oversaw the unification of Germany; Konrad Adenauer, who oversaw Germany's postwar recovery; Helmut Kohl, chancellor during the reunification of Germany in 1990 and a firm supporter of greater European integration; Angela Merkel, the first woman chancellor of Germany, elected in 2005

NATIONAL HOLIDAY/INDEPENDENCE DAY

Unity Day, October 3

FESTIVALS/FAIRS

Berlin Film Festival, February; Oktoberfest, October; Christkindlesmarkt, the Christmas Market, December; Stuttgart Spring Festival, April; Bayreuth Festival, August; Bunte Republik Neustadt, June

SIGNIFICANT EVENTS IN FORMATION OF NATIONAL IDENTITY

First century B.C.E. Germanic tribes from Scandinavia and northern Germany begin expanding south, east, and west.

50 C.E.–9 C.E. Romans begin a series of invasions of the area they call Germania. In 9 C.E., tribal leader Arminius defeats three Roman legions. Germany, beyond the Rhine and the Danube, remains outside the Roman Empire.

Third century C.E. Large tribal groups emerge among the German tribes. Around 250 C.E., German tribes break through the Roman lines and the Danube frontier to infiltrate Roman territory.

Fifth century–ninth century The collapse of Roman power leads to invasions of former Roman provinces by German tribes. Germanic monarchies replace Roman power, particularly the Franks, who establish an empire spanning most of Western Europe.

843–1448 The division of the empire at Charlemagne's death into three parts is the birth of the German and French nations. Germany is divided into numerous small states within the Holy Roman Empire of the German Nation.

1517 Martin Luther publishes his "95 Theses," initiating the Protestant Reformation. The Lutheran creed became the official religion of many of the German states.

1618–1648 The Thirty Years' War results from religious conflicts. The war reduces the population of the German states by about 30 percent.

1740–1806 The rivalry between the two largest German states, Austria* and Prussia, dominates the German territories. The Holy Roman Empire is overrun and dissolved as a result of the Napoleonic Wars.

1814–1848 The German Confederation is founded. Nationalism becomes a significant force, reinforced by the ideals of the French Revolution. Revolutionaries in many German states adopt the colors of black, red, and gold as the colors of the revolutions of 1848 that were based on more liberal ideals.

1871–1884 Germany is unified as a modern nation-state with the creation of the German Empire. Beginning in 1884, Germany establishes several colonies outside Europe.

1914–1918 Germany joins Austria and Hungary* in World War I and suffers defeat by the Allies. Peace conditions dictated by France* are harsh and vengeful, leading to Germany's humiliation, poverty, and political instability.

1919–1933 The Great Depression exacerbates Germany's many problems. Political groups of many ideologies compete for power. Amid rising chaos, Adolf Hitler is named chancellor of Germany.

1933–1939 German economic expansion is fueled by rearmament of Germany's military.

1939–1945 The German invasion of Poland* initiates the Second World War. The murder of millions of Jews, Roma, Slavs, and others, know as the Holocaust, is official policy. Nearly 10 million Germans die in the war. Germany and its allies are defeated and surrender.

1949 The German occupation zones are united in the Federal Republic of Germany in the west and the German Democratic Republic in the eastern Russian occupation zone. Berlin remains divided by the Allies. The so-called Iron Curtain is established between democratic West Germany and communist East Germany.

1949–1961 West Germany recovers quickly and makes rapid economic advances known as the German miracle. East Germany, as a Soviet client state, stagnates under oppressive communist rule. The Berlin Wall is built by East Germany's government to hinder the large number of people fleeing to West Germany through divided Berlin.

1970s West Germany accepts the division of Germany, although tensions between the German

states continue. West Germany maintains close ties to the Western democracies.

1989–1990 The liberalization of life in the Soviet Union brings rapid changes to the Soviet client states in eastern and central Europe. The collapse of East Germany's totalitarian government opens the way for the fall of the Berlin Wall and the rapid reunification of the two Germanys in an expanded federal republic.

1990–2009 United Germany takes a leading role in the European Union and the North Atlantic Treaty Organization. The rebuilding of the new eastern states of the federation is undertaken as a national task. Germany becomes the world's third-largest economy and the largest in Europe.

See also Bavaria

GIBRALTAR

OFFICIAL NAME
Gibraltar

POPULATION
28,900 (2009e)

INHABITANTS' NAME/NICKNAME
Gibraltarian(s); Llanito(s); Gibo(s)

LANGUAGE/LANGUAGES
English (official); Llanito, Spanish, Italian, Portuguese, others

RELIGION/RELIGIONS
Roman Catholic, 78 percent; Anglican, 7 percent; Muslim, 4 percent; Jewish, 2 percent; Hindu, 1.5 percent; other or no religion

NATIONAL FLAG
The flag is a banner of the arms granted in 1502. The upper two thirds of the flag are white, and the lower third is red. A red castle is depicted on the white, with a gold key hanging into the red. The castle does not resemble any in Gibraltar but instead symbolizes the fortress of Gibraltar. The key rep-

resents Gibraltar's geographic position as the key to the Mediterranean.

COAT OF ARMS/SEAL

The coat of arms is a shield with same pattern as the flag, white over red with a red castle and gold key. Below the shield is a banner with the Latin words *Montis Insignia Calpe,* "Landmark Mount of Calpe," the historical name of the Rock of Gibraltar.

MOTTO

Nulli expugnabilis hosti (Latin); Conquered by no enemy (English)

CAPITAL CITY

Gibraltar

TYPE OF GOVERNMENT

Parliamentary democracy as a British Overseas Territory

NATIONAL EMBLEM

Rock of Gibraltar

NATIONAL COLORS

Red and white

NATIONAL ANTHEM

The Gibraltar Anthem was officially adopted in 1994 and is co-official with the British national anthem, "God Save the Queen."

Gibraltar Anthem

Gibraltar, Gibraltar, the rock on which
  I stand,
May you be forever free, Gibraltar, my own
  land.
Mighty pillar, rock of splendor, guardian of
  the sea,
Port of hope in times of need, rich in history.

Gibraltar, Gibraltar, the rock on which I
  stand,
May you be forever free, Gibraltar my own
  land.

God give grace to this our homeland; help us
  to live as one,
Strong in freedom, truth and justice, let this
  be our song:

Gibraltar, Gibraltar, the rock on which
  I stand,
May you be forever free—Gibraltar! Gibraltar! My own land!

PATRON SAINT

Saint Bernard of Clairvaux; Our Lady of Europe

CURRENCY

Gibraltar pound

INTERNET IDENTIFIER

.gi

VEHICLE IDENTIFICATION PLATES/STICKERS

GBZ

PASSPORT

The passport cover has the European Union in smaller letters, the United Kingdom of Great Britain and Northern Ireland in larger letters, the name Gibraltar, the coat of arms of the United Kingdom*, and the word *passport.*

NATIONAL FLOWER

Gibraltar candytuft (unofficial)

NATIONAL TREE

Nettle tree (unofficial)

NATIONAL ANIMAL

Barbary macaque

NATIONAL BIRD

Barbary partridge (unofficial)

NATIONAL FISH

Pink dentex (unofficial)

NATIONAL RESOURCES

The British military traditionally dominated the economy of Gibraltar. This has, however, diminished in the past 20 years and was estimated to account for only 7 percent of the local economy in 2008, compared to over 60 percent in 1984. Gibraltar has an extensive service-based economy, dominated by financial services and tourism. The Rock of Gibraltar and the port are the two most valuable resources.

FOODS

British food is widely available, but the national dishes owe more to Gibraltar's varied population and its proximity to Spain*: *calentita,* a type of thick pancake made of garbanzo flour that originated with Genoese immigrants, is considered the national dish. *Tortilla de espinacas,* a spinach omelet; *tortilla de patata,* potato omelet, and a quiche-like dish called *panissa.*

SPORTS/SPORTS TEAMS

Cricket is the most popular sport in Gibraltar. Association football (soccer) is also very popular. The Gibraltar Football Association applied for full membership in the Union of European Football Associations (UEFA) in 2007 but was turned down in a contentious decision. Gibraltar national teams participate in many sports at the international level.

TEAM SPORTS

Badminton

Gibraltar Badminton Team

Basketball

Gibraltar Basketball Team; Gibraltar Women's Basketball Team

Cricket

Gibraltar Cricket Team

Football

Gibraltar Football Team, nickname Gib or the Giblets; Gibraltar Women's Football Team, nickname the Giblets

Hockey

Gibraltar Field Hockey Team

Netball

Gibraltar Netball Team

Table Tennis

Gibraltar Table Tennis Team

Volleyball

Gibraltar Men's Volleyball Team; Gibraltar Women's Volleyball Team

INDIVIDUAL SPORTS

Gibraltar Amateur Boxing Team; Gibraltar Athletics Team; Gibraltar Rowing Team; Gibraltar Swim Team; Gibraltar Triathlon Team

NATIONAL HEROES OR PERSONIFICATIONS

Pedro de Herrera, who established the Rock as a safe bastion for Spanish Jews in 1474; Isabella of Castile, who granted Gibraltar's arms in 1502; Peter Caruana, the present chief minister of Gibraltar and a champion of Gibraltarian rights, reelected in 2007 to a fourth term

NATIONAL HOLIDAY/INDEPENDENCE DAY

National Day, September 10

FESTIVALS/FAIRS

International Chess Festival, January; Festival of the Three Kings, January

SIGNIFICANT EVENTS IN FORMATION OF NATIONAL IDENTITY

950 B.C.E. Phoenicians settle at the foot of the Rock. Later, Carthaginians and Romans establish

semipermanent settlements. The Rock is known as one of the Pillars of Hercules.

711 C.E. Moors crossing from North Africa capture the Rock. It serves as a southern defense post of the Muslim state of Al-Andalus.

1462–1502 The Christian Spaniards, during the conquest of Muslim Spain, capture the citadel. Queen Isabella of Castile officially annexes Gibraltar and grants the coat of arms that remains to the present.

1704–1713 During the European war known as the War of the Spanish Succession, British and Dutch troops capture Gibraltar. The Treaty of Utrecht confirms British possession of Gibraltar. Spain tries several times to recover Gibraltar, but without success.

1830–1930 Gibraltar becomes a British Crown Colony, in spite of continuing Spanish objections. The impregnable fortress becomes Britain's major base in the Mediterranean. Gibraltar develops as a flourishing trade center, attracting settlers from Italy*, Malta*, Portugal*, and other parts of the Mediterranean. The Spanish population dwindles, and the immigrant population, schooled in English, gradually emerges as a distinct Mediterranean people.

1939–1945 The citadel and naval base protect Allied shipping when the Second World War begins. Neutral Spain's dictator, Francisco Franco, resists Hitler's demand for a Spanish attack on Gibraltar.

1964 The British government grants autonomy, giving Gibraltar its own elected government and control of the booming economy. Spain continues to demand that the colony be returned to Spanish sovereignty.

1967 The British government agrees to a referendum, but only 44 votes favor Spain.

1969 A new legislative assembly is organized with wider powers of autonomy. In protest, Spain closes the border and forbids Spanish citizens to hold jobs in Gibraltar.

1970s The economy, long dependent on military spending, diversifies into banking, international trade, and tourism. Spain's return to democracy in 1975 greatly reduces tensions over Gibraltar.

1981–1985 The Gibraltarians are granted British citizenship. Spain reopens the border to foot traffic in 1983 and vehicle traffic in 1985, following a British threat to veto Spain's application to join the European Community.

1986–2000 Spain entry in the European Community secured, the Madrid government again raises the question of sovereignty over Gibraltar. The Gibraltarians again vote overwhelmingly against Spanish sovereignty.

2000 An agreement between the British and Spanish governments clarifies many outstanding matters concerning passports, driver's licenses, and provisions for greater police cooperation, but leaves the question of sovereignty unresolved.

2002 Gibraltarians again vote overwhelmingly to reject any "shared sovereignty" arrangements. The government of Gibraltar insists on equal participation in talks between the United Kingdom and Spain regarding Gibraltar.

2006–2009 Spain disapproves of British plans for greater autonomy for Gibraltar. Gibraltarians vote to confirm a new constitution giving Gibraltar more self-government. Spain continues to demand at least joint sovereignty over Gibraltar. The Gibraltarian economy booms while both Spain and the United Kingdom* grapple with the global economic crisis. Over 3,000 Spanish workers commute to Gibraltar to work each day.

See also United Kingdom

GREECE

OFFICIAL NAME

Ellinikí Dimokratía (transliteration from Greek); Hellenic Republic (English)

POPULATION

11,220,800 (2009e)

INHABITANTS' NAME/NICKNAME

Greek(s)

LANGUAGE/LANGUAGES

Greek (official); Macedonian, Arvantika, Vlach, Pomak Bulgarian, others

RELIGION/RELIGIONS

Greek Orthodox, 98 percent; Muslim, 1.5 percent; Roman Catholic, Protestant, other or no religion

NATIONAL FLAG

The flag consists of nine horizontal stripes, alternately blue and white, with a white cross on a blue canton on the upper hoist. The cross represents Greek Orthodoxy. The nine stripes represent the nine syllables of the Greek motto; to some, they also represent the nine Muses, the goddesses of the arts and civilization. The blue color is interpreted as symbolizing the blue sky and water, while the white represents white clouds and sea waves.

COAT OF ARMS/SEAL

The coat of arms has a central blue shield or crest with a white cross, totally surrounded by laurel branches. The interpretation of the colors is the same as for the flag.

MOTTO

Eleftheria i thanatos (transliteration from Greek); Freedom or Death (English)

CAPITAL CITY

Athens

TYPE OF GOVERNMENT

Parliamentary republic

NATIONAL EMBLEM

The Acropolis

NATIONAL COLORS

Blue and white

NATIONAL ANTHEM

The anthem was written and composed as a patriotic poem later set to music. It was not adopted as the official anthem until 1865.

Ímnos is tin Eleftherían (transliteration from Greek); Hymn to Liberty (English)

I shall always recognize you
By the dreadful sword you hold,
As the Earth, with searching vision,
You survey, with spirit bold.
'Twas the Greeks of old whose dying
Brought to birth our spirit free.
Now, with ancient valor rising,
Let us hail you, O Liberty!

PATRON SAINT

Saint Andrew the Apostle, Saint George, Saint Nicholas of Myra, the Virgin Mary; Saint Paul the Apostle (Roman Catholic)

CURRENCY

Euro

INTERNET IDENTIFIER

.gr

VEHICLE IDENTIFICATION PLATES/STICKERS

GR

PASSPORT

The passport cover has the name of the European Union and the name of the country in Greek, the coat of arms, and the Greek word for passport.

AIRLINES

Olympic Airways; Aegean Airlines

NATIONAL FLOWER

Bear's breech, violet (unofficial)

NATIONAL TREE

Laurel; olive (unofficial)

NATIONAL ANIMAL
Dolphin

NATIONAL BIRD
Athenian Owl

NATIONAL RESOURCES
Natural resources include lignite, petroleum, iron ore, bauxite, lead, zinc, nickel, magnesite, marble, salt, and hydropower potential. The important tourist industry is based on the country's magnificent ruins, ancient cities, unique culture, sandy beaches, many islands, and pleasant climate. Greeks living outside the country are an important source of investment.

FOODS
Greek cuisine incorporates fresh ingredients into a variety of local dishes, such as those considered national dishes: *moussaka,* a meat, eggplant, and cheese casserole; *stifado,* a meat stew with pearl onions, red wine, and cinnamon; spanakopita, savory or sweet stuffed phyllo dough; *fasolada,* a soup of white beans and vegetables; dolmas, grape leaves stuffed with meat and rice; souvlaki, skewered meats and vegetables grilled over an open fire; and *xorjatiki salata,* Greek salad.

SPORTS/SPORTS TEAMS
Association football (soccer) remains the most popular sport, but basketball and other sports are also gaining popularity. Greece national teams participate in many sports at international level.

TEAM SPORTS

Badminton
Greece Badminton Team

Baseball
Greece Baseball Team; Greece Softball Team

Basketball
Greece Basketball Team, nickname Official Cherished; Greece Women's Basketball Team; Greece Under-21 Basketball Team; Greece Wheelchair Basketball Team

Cricket
Greece Cricket Team

Football
Greece Football Team, nickname To Peiratiko (the Pirate Ship); Greece Women's Football Team nickname To Peiratiko (the Pirate Ship); Greece Rugby Union Team; Greece Rugby League Team, nickname the Titans; Greece Under-21 Football Team, nickname the Team of Hopes; Greece Under-19 Football Team; Greece Beach Soccer Team; Wheelchair Rugby Team; Greece American Football Team; Greece Futsal Team

Handball
Greece Handball Team; Greece Women's Handball Team; Greece Beach Handball Team; Greece Women's Beach Handball Team

Hockey
Greece Ice Hockey Team; Greece Field Hockey

Korfball
Greece Korfball Team

Racing
A1 Team Greece; Greece Speedway Team

Tennis
Greece Davis Cup Team; Greece Fed Cup Team

Volleyball
Greece Men's Volleyball Team; Greece Women's Volleyball Team; Greece Fistball Team;

Greece Men's Beach Volleyball Team; Greece Women's Beach Volleyball Team

Water Polo

Greece Men's Water Polo Team; Greece Women's Water Polo Team

INDIVIDUAL SPORTS

Greece Amateur Boxing Team; Greece Archery Team; Greece Athletics Team; Greece Canoeing Team; Greece Cycling Team; Greece Equestrian Team; Greece Fencing Team; Greece Gymnastics Team; Greece Judo Team; Greece Karate Team; Greece Modern Pentathlon Team; Greece Rowing Team; Greece Sailing Team; Greece Shooting Team; Greece Swim Team; Greece Tae Kwon Do Team; Greece Triathlon Team; Greece Weight Lifting Team; Greece Wrestling Team

WINTER SPORTS

Greece Alpine Ski Team; Greece Biathlon Team; Team; Greece Curling Team; Greece Ice Hockey Team; Greece Luge Team; Greece Skating Team

NATIONAL HEROES OR PERSONIFICATIONS

Athena is the personification of the Greek people, as seen in the painting *Greece Expiring on the Ruins of Missolonghi*. Eugéne Delacroix painted a second painting in support of the Greeks in their war of independence in 1827, showing a woman in Greek costume with her arms raised in a powerless gesture toward the horrible scene: the suicide of the Greeks, who chose to kill themselves and destroy their city rather than surrender to the Turks.

National heroes include Ioannis Kapodistrias, the assassinated first head of state of independent Greece in 1827; and Charilaos Trikoupis, who served as prime minister seven times and was responsible for curbing the excesses of the monarchy.

NATIONAL HOLIDAY/INDEPENDENCE DAY

Independence Day, March 25

FESTIVALS/FAIRS

Aprokrias, Greek Carnival, February; Greek National Anniversary, March; Navy Week, June; Herod Atticus Festival, July; Anhillos Wine Festival, September

SIGNIFICANT EVENTS IN FORMATION OF NATIONAL IDENTITY

2700 B.C.E.–1100 B.C.E. The Minoan civilization emerges in Crete. The advanced Mycenaean culture flourishes on the mainland.

776 B.C.E. The first Olympic games are staged. The rise of city-states initiates a golden age of culture. The city-states often war among themselves.

500 B.C.E.–448 B.C.E. The Persian Wars intrude on Greek civilization until the Persians are finally pushed back.

346 B.C.E.–323 B.C.E. Macedon, north of the Greek city-states, becomes a regional power. Alexander III of Macedon, called Alexander the Great, takes control of Greece and extends his empire into Africa and the Middle East and as far east as the Indian subcontinent.

187 B.C.E.–395 C.E. Greece declines to the point that Rome is able to conquer the region, incorporating much of Greek civilization into Roman life.

395 C.E. The division of the Roman Empire into east and west gives rise to the Greek Byzantine Empire in the east. Greek Byzantine civilization carries the Greek culture to Anatolia and the Middle East.

11th century–13th century The 11th through 13th centuries represent the golden age of Byzantine culture in the Greek-speaking Empire. Crusaders from Western Europe conquer Constantinople in 1204.

1453–1821 The conquest of the Byzantine Empire by invading Ottoman Turks brings Turkish rule to Greece. Under Turkish rule, the segregation of the peoples according to religion contributes to the ethnic cohesion of the various Greek-speaking Christian groups.

1821–1914 The Greeks rebel and declare independence. The war for independence ends in 1829, and Greece becomes a republic under Ioannis Kapodistrias. Following Kapodistrias' assassination, Greece becomes a monarchy. In series of wars with the Ottoman Empire, Greece seeks to enlarge its boundaries to include the Greek-speaking populations still under Turkish rule.

1918–1923 At the end of the First World War, Greece is awarded parts of Asia Minor from the defeated Ottomans, but the resurgent Turks attack and Greece loses the territory on the Anatolian mainland. Over a million Greeks are forced to leave the territory conquered by Turkey, and hundreds of thousands of Muslims leave Greece in an unprecedented population exchange.

1940–1949 First Italian and then German occupation leads to the deaths of thousands of Greeks during World War II. With the German withdrawal, civil war breaks out between pro-Western government forces and a large communist insurgency.

1950s–1974 Greek economic recovery, aided by the U.S. Marshall Plan, is called the Greek Miracle. The Greek military overthrows the government, and a military junta rules Greece. The monarchy is abolished, and Greece becomes involved in Cyprus*.

1975 Restoration of democracy brings stability and economic prosperity. Greece joins the European Community (later the European Union).

1975–2000 Tensions between Greece and Turkey* continue over Cyprus. Greece rejects the independence of Macedonia* over use of the name, which also refers to the northern portion of the Greek state.

2004–2009 Greece hosts a safe and very successful Olympic games. Greece and Turkey continue discussions to resolve complex maritime, air, and territorial disputes in the Aegean Sea. Greece blocks Macedonia's bid to join the North Atlantic Treaty Organization. Strikes, protests, and violence continue over government economic policies.

GUERNSEY

OFFICIAL NAME
Balliwick of Guernsey (English); Bailliage de Guernesey (French)

POPULATION
65,400 (2009e)

INHABITANTS' NAME/NICKNAME
Guernseian(s)

LANGUAGE/LANGUAGES
English, French (both official); Guernésiais, Sercquiais (recognized regional languages); others

RELIGION/RELIGIONS
Protestant, Roman Catholic, other or no religion

NATIONAL FLAG
The flag is a white field bearing a red cross of Saint George with a gold Norman cross within it. The white and red represent Guernsey's historic ties to England. The gold cross was added in 1985 to end confusion between the flag of Guernsey and that of England. The gold cross represents Duke William of Normandy.

COAT OF ARMS/SEAL
The coat of arms is a red shield with three gold lions surmounted by a small branch of leaves. It is very similar to the arms of Normandy, Jersey*, and England. The lions are known as the Norman Lions.

CAPITAL CITY
Saint Peter Port

TYPE OF GOVERNMENT
Parliamentary democracy as a British Crown Dependency

NATIONAL EMBLEM
Norman Lions

NATIONAL COLORS

Green and white

NATIONAL ANTHEM

The British anthem, "God Save the Queen," is the official anthem of Guernsey. The Guernsey anthem was written and composed in the early 20th century. It was unofficially adopted as the island's national anthem but serves as official when a distinct anthem is required.

Sarnia Cherie (*Guernésiais*); Dear Guernsey (English)

Sarnia; dear homeland, gem of the sea.
Island of beauty, my heart longs for thee.
Thy voice calls me ever, in waking, or sleep,
Till my soul cries with anguish, my eyes ache to weep.
In fancy I see thee, again as of yore,
Thy verdure-clad hills and thy wave-beaten shore.
Thy rock-sheltered bays, ah; of all thou art best,
I'm returning to greet thee, dear island of rest.

Chorus

Sarnia Cherie. Gem of the sea.
Home of my childhood, my heart longs for thee.
Thy voice calls me ever, forget thee I'll never,
Island of beauty. Sarnia Cherie.
I left thee in anger, I knew not thy worth.
Journeyed afar, to the ends of the earth.
Was told of far countries, the heav'n of the bold,
Where the soil gave up diamonds, silver and gold.
The sun always shone, and "race" took no part,
But thy cry always reached me, its pain wrenched my heart.
So I'm coming home, thou of all art the best.
Returning to greet thee, dear island of rest.

PATRON SAINT

Saint Samson of Dol

CURRENCY

Guernsey pound; British pound

INTERNET IDENTIFIER

.gg

VEHICLE IDENTIFICATION PLATES/ STICKERS

GBG

PASSPORT

Guernseians are British citizens and travel on British passports.

AIRLINE

Aurigny

NATIONAL FLOWER

Guernsey lily

NATIONAL ANIMAL

Golden Guernsey goat; Guernsey cow (unofficial)

NATIONAL FISH

Conger eel (unofficial)

NATIONAL RESOURCES

Natural resources, other than arable land and fisheries, are negligible. Light taxes and death duties make Guernsey a popular offshore banking center. Guernsey's proximity to important European population centers makes it a convenient site for several large European companies. Tourism is also an important resource.

FOODS

Fresh fish, lobster, and crabs form the basis of many Guernsey dishes. Traditional specialties include Guernsey *gâche*, a traditional dessert of a type of fruitcake, often served with cream, and Guernsey butter; Guernsey bean jar, a stew made of beans and pork;

ormer casserole, a stew of ormer abalones, carrots, shallots, and pork; and *gâche melée*, a dessert made of apples and cinnamon, is also considered a national dish.

SPORTS/SPORTS TEAMS

Association football (soccer) is the most popular sport. Traditional sports, such as softball, remain popular. Guernsey national teams participate in several sports at an international level.

TEAM SPORTS

Baseball

Guernsey Softball Team; Guernsey Women's Softball Team

Cricket

Guernsey Cricket Team

Football

Guernsey Football Team, nickname the Green Lions; Guernsey Women's Football Team, nickname the Green Lions; Guernsey Touch Football Team; Guernsey Women's Touch Football Team

Table Tennis

Guernsey Table Tennis Team

NATIONAL HEROES OR PERSONIFICATIONS

Victor Hugo, the famed French author self-exiled to Guernsey in the late 19th century; William, Duke of Normandy, the most famous ruler of the Duchy of Normandy, of which Guernsey and Jersey are the last remnants; Admiral James Saumarez, a hero of the Napoleonic wars in the early 19th century

NATIONAL HOLIDAY/INDEPENDENCE DAY

Liberation Day, May 9

FESTIVALS/FAIRS

Festival of the Sea (La Fête d' la Maïr, in Guernésiais), June; The Old Market (Lé Vlaer Marchi, in Guernésiais), July; Guernsey Live Festival, May; Springtime Guernsey, April; Floral Guernsey Festival, April; Tennerfest, October-November

SIGNIFICANT EVENTS IN FORMATION OF NATIONAL IDENTITY

Prehistory The islands are settled by Celts from the European mainland.

58 B.C.E. Julius Caesar conquers Gaul and takes control of the Celtic territories, including Guernsey.

395 C.E.–450 C.E. The fall of Roman power is followed by invasions of Franks moving into the former Roman provinces of Gaul.

Sixth century Christianity is introduced.

Ninth century Norseman, Vikings from Scandinavia, conquer the mainland region later known as Normandy and take control of the Channel Islands.

1066–1206 William, Duke of Normandy, and the Normans, descendants of the Vikings, cross the Channel to conquer England. Guernsey and the other Channel Islands are attached to the new Norman Kingdom of England. France* annexes Normandy, but the islands, known as the Norman Islands, remain under English rule.

1294 French raiders massacre much of the population.

14th century–18th century Guernsey retains its distinct Norman law, its Norman dialect, and its unique culture. The state is subject to the English and later British monarch, but not the English parliament. Feudal customs that disappear elsewhere remain a part of Guernsey life.

1835–1900 The office of governor is abolished and the duties are later transferred to a bailiff who presides over the Royal Court of Guernsey. The island becomes a popular Victorian resort.

1940–1945 During the Second World War, the Channel Islands are overrun by German troops, making them the only British territory to suffer occupation.

1960s Low taxes make Guernsey a major off-shore tax haven and banking center. In 1968, a commission considers the relationship of Guernsey with the British Crown. The islanders indicate that they prefer to remain a self-governing state, with the British government retaining responsibility for defense and foreign affairs.

1973 The United Kingdom* joins the European Community, later the European Union. Guernsey is not a member but negotiates associate status.

1980s Alarmed at the island's rapid population growth, Guernsey restricts immigration, with only a few self-supporting settlers allowed to move to the state each year.

1990s Several groups form to protect and encourage Guernsey's status and its distinct culture and dialects. A minority favors independence and separate membership in the European Union.

2000–2008 Guernsey declares an extension to its territorial waters over French objections, following the announcement that French claims to the islands had been revived. The territorial waters are believed to include areas with possibly substantial oil reserves.

2009 In spite of the global economic downturn, Guernsey moves up to 12th place in the world rankings of global financial centers. The most far-reaching study of the local language, Guernésiais or Dgernésiais, begins.

See also United Kingdom

HUNGARY

OFFICIAL NAME
Magyar Köztársaság (Hungarian); Republic of Hungary (English)

POPULATION
10,028,400 (2009e)

INHABITANTS' NAME/NICKNAME
Hungarian(s); Magyar(s)

LANGUAGE/LANGUAGES
Hungarian (Magyar) (official); German, Slovak, others

RELIGION/RELIGIONS
Catholic, 54 percent; Calvinist, 16 percent; Lutheran, 3 percent; Greek Catholic, 2.5 percent; other or no religion

NATIONAL FLAG
The flag is a horizontal tricolor of three equal stripes of red, white, and green. Red represents strength, white is for faithfulness, and green represents hope.

COAT OF ARMS/SEAL
The coat of arms is a shield or crest divided vertically. The left side has a red field charged with a silver double cross with its base in a small golden crown, which sits on three green hills. The right side is known as the Arpad stripes, four horizontal stripes of silver and four of red representing Hungary's four major rivers. Above the shield is depiction of the Crown of Saint Stephen.

MOTTO
The republic has no official motto. Historically, Hungary's motto was *Regnum mariae patronae hungariae* (Latin); Kingdom of Mary, patroness of Hungary (English).

CAPITAL CITY
Budapest

TYPE OF GOVERNMENT
Parliamentary republic

NATIONAL EMBLEM
Crown of Saint Stephen

NATIONAL COLORS
Red, white, and green

NATIONAL ANTHEM
The anthem, simply titled "Anthem" or "Hymn," is also known as *"Isten, áldd meg a Magyart"* in Hungarian and "God Bless the Hungarians" in English. The latter names are taken from the first line of the anthem.

Himnusz (Hungarian); Anthem (English)

God bless the Hungarians
With good cheer and prosperity.
Extend a protective arm
If they fight the enemy.
Torn by misfortune for long,
Give them happy years.
These people have expiated
The past and the future.

By thy help our fathers gained
Kárpát's proud and sacred height;
Here by thee a home obtained
Heirs of Bendegúz, the knight.
Where'er Danube's waters flow
And the streams of Tisza swell
Árpád's children, thou dost know,
Flourished and did prosper well.

For us let the golden grain
Grow upon the fields of Kún,
And let nectar's silver rain
Ripen grapes of Tokay soon.
Thou our flags hast planted o'er
Forts where once wild Turks held sway;
Proud Vienna suffered sore
From King Mátyás' dark array.

But, alas! for our misdeed,
Anger rose within thy breast,
And thy lightnings thou did'st speed
From thy thundering sky with zest.
Now the Mongol arrow flew
Over our devoted heads;
Or the Turkish yoke we knew,
Which a freeborn nation dreads.

O, how often has the voice
Sounded of wild Osman's hordes,
When in songs they did rejoice
O'er our heroes' captured swords!
Yea, how often rose thy sons,
My fair land, upon thy sod,
And thou gavest to these sons
Tombs within the breast they trod!

Though in caves pursued he lie,
Even then he fears attacks.
Coming forth the land to spy,
Even a home he finds he lacks.
Mountain, vale—go where he would,
Grief and sorrow all the same—

Underneath a sea of blood,
While above a sea of flame.

'Neath the fort, a ruin now,
Joy and pleasure erst were found,
Only groans and sighs, I trow,
In its limits now abound.
But no freedom's flowers return
From the spilt blood of the dead,
And the tears of slavery burn,
Which the eyes of orphans shed.

Pity, God, the Magyar, then,
Long by waves of danger tossed;
Help him by thy strong hand when
He on grief's sea may be lost.
Fate, who for so long did'st frown,
Bring him happy times and ways;
Atoning sorrow hath weighed down
All the sins of all his days.

PATRON SAINT

The Virgin Mary; Saint Stephen

CURRENCY

Hungarian forint

INTERNET IDENTIFIER

.hu

**VEHICLE IDENTIFICATION PLATES/
STICKERS**

H

PASSPORT

The cover has the name of the European Union and the name of the country in Hungarian, the coat of arms, the word *passport* in Hungarian, and the standard biometric symbol.

AIRLINE

Malév (Magyar Légiközlekedési Vállalat)

NATIONAL FLOWER

Tulip

NATIONAL TREE

Hungarian lilac (unofficial)

NATIONAL ANIMAL

Hungarian stag (unofficial)

NATIONAL BIRD

Turul (mythological bird) (unofficial)

NATIONAL RESOURCES

Natural resources include bauxite, coal, natural gas, fertile soils, arable land, and grazing land. A well-educated population and Hungary's position at the heart of the European Union have helped raise Hungary to the ranks of high-income countries. Tourism, based on Hungary's historic cities, monuments, and unique culture, is very important to the country.

FOODS

Gulyás, known as goulash in English, is Hungary's national dish. Other national specialties are *halázlé,* a spicy soup made of freshwater fish and paprika; *paprikás csirke,* chicken cooked with paprika; *rakott puliszka,* a layered cornmeal casserole; *spaetzel,* small dumplings or noodles; *halousky,* potato dumplings; and *gundel palascinta,* a thin pancake served with raisins, walnuts, lemon rind, chocolate sauce, and rum.

SPORTS/SPORTS TEAMS

Association football (soccer) is the most popular sport. Hungarians are known for their prowess at water sports, such as water polo, swimming and canoeing. Hungary national teams participate in many sports at an international level.

TEAM SPORTS

Badminton

Hungary Badminton Team

Baseball

Hungary Baseball Team; Hungary Softball Team

Basketball

Hungary Basketball Team; Hungary Women's Basketball Team

Football

Hungary Football Team, nickname Magical Magyars (name comes from the 1950s); Hungary Women's Football Team; Hungary Under-21 Football Team, nickname the Magyars; Hungary Under-19 Football Team; Hungary Women's Under-19 Football Team; Hungary Rugby Union Team; Hungary American Football Team; Hungary Beach Soccer Team; Hungary Futsal Team

Handball

Hungary Handball Team, nickname the Heroes of Kiel; Hungary Women's Handball Team; Hungary Beach Handball Team; Hungary Women's Beach Handball Team

Hockey

Hungary Ice Hockey Team; Hungary Women's Ice Hockey Team; Hungary Field Hockey Team

Korfball

Hungary Korfball Team

Racing

Hungary Speedway Team

Table Tennis

Hungary Table Tennis Team

Tennis

Hungary Davis Cup Team; Hungary Fed Cup Team

Volleyball

Hungary Fistball Team; Hungary Men's Volleyball Team; Hungary Women's Volleyball Team

Water Polo

Hungary Water Polo Team; Hungary Women's Water Polo Team

INDIVIDUAL SPORTS

Hungary Amateur Boxing Team; Hungary Archery Team; Hungary Athletics Team; Hungary Canoeing Team; Hungary Cycling Team; Hungary Equestrian Team; Hungary Fencing Team; Hungary Gymnastics Team; Hungary Judo Team; Hungary Karate Team; Hungary Modern Pentathlon Team; Hungary Rowing Team; Hungary Sailing Team; Hungary Shooting Team; Hungary Swim Team; Hungary Tae Kwon Do Team; Hungary Triathlon Team; Hungary Weight Lifting Team; Hungary Wrestling Team

WINTER SPORTS

Hungary Alpine Ski Team; Hungary Bandy Team; Hungary Biathlon Team; Hungary Curling Team; Hungary Ice Hockey Team; Hungary Women's Ice Hockey Team; Hungary Luge Team; Hungary Skating Team

NATIONAL HEROES OR PERSONIFICATIONS

Saint Stephen, first king of Hungary; János Hunyadi, a hero in the fight against the Ottoman Turks in the 15th century; János Damjanich, a major military leader during the Hungarian Revolt of 1848; Imre Nagy, prime minister of Hungary during the Hungarian Uprising in 1956, who was guaranteed safe passage out of the country but then arrested, tried in secret, and executed in 1958

NATIONAL HOLIDAY/INDEPENDENCE DAY

Saint Stephen's Day, August 20: National Day, October 23.

FESTIVALS/FAIRS

Budapest Spring Festival, March; Balathon Festival of Classical Music, May; Budapest Festival, September; Festival of Guilds, August

SIGNIFICANT EVENTS IN FORMATION OF NATIONAL IDENTITY

896 C.E. The newly unified Magyars under Prince Arpad settle the Carpathian Basin from their original home in present Russia*.

1000 Saint Stephen is crowned as the Christian king of Hungary. By 1006, the old religion has given way to Christianity throughout the kingdom.

1222 The Golden Bull, the first constitution in continental Europe, limits the king's power and gives nobles the right to resist the king's illegal acts.

1241–1286 The Mongol invasion overruns Hungary. When they retreat, a series of strong stone castles is constructed that helps to defeat a second Mongol invasion.

1526–1596 The Ottoman Turks defeat the Hungarians. The country is divided into three parts: the west, ruled by the Hapsburgs of Austria*; the center as independent Transylvania, often under Turkish control; and the east, including Budapest, ruled by Ottoman Turkey*.

1699 The Austrian Hapsburgs under Leopold I expel the Turks from Hungary. Hungary becomes part of the Austrian Empire as a kingdom.

1700 Hungarian replaces Latin as the official language. Economic reforms and limited political reforms are introduced. Tensions grow between Hungary and the central government of the Austrian Empire.

1848 The Hungarians attempt to overthrow the monarchy and create a republic.

1867 Hungary becomes an autonomous kingdom in partnership with Austria in the multicultural Austro-Hungarian Empire.

1918 At the end of the First World War, the defeated empire breaks up into small national states. Hungary, stripped of about half its territory, becomes a republic.

1919 Communists take over the republic under Bela Kun. Kun wages war on neighboring Romania* and Czechoslovakia in an effort to retake areas populated by ethnic Hungarians. Romanian troops invade and take Budapest.

1920   The peace treaty that ends the war officially gives historically Hungarian territory to neighboring states. Miklós Horthy takes power as the regent of the Hungarian kingdom.

1938   Hungary allies with Nazi Germany and is rewarded with some territory lost in 1920.

1941   Germany* invades the Soviet Union with Hungarian aid. The Hungarian army is mostly destroyed. Hungary declares war on the United Kingdom* and the United States*.

1944   The Hungarian Nazis depose Horthy and install a puppet regime. Hungary's Jews, until then protected by Horthy, are deported to Nazi death camps.

1945   The Soviet Red Army drives the Germans from Hungary. A new pro-Soviet government is formed.

1949   A new constitution makes Hungary a socialist state. Industries and agriculture are nationalized, and a wave of police terror begins.

1956–1958   Protesters demand the withdrawal of Soviet troops. Imre Nagy becomes prime minister and announces plans to withdraw Hungary from the Warsaw Pact and become a neutral state, like neighboring Austria. Soviet forces crush the uprising, and thousands are killed and many more flee to the West. Nagy is arrested, tried, and executed.

1960s   After several years of severe totalitarian rule, limited reforms are introduced. The economy is liberalized, and a modest prosperity begins to spread.

1989–1999   As communism begins to implode, the border with Austria is opened. Elections are held. Hungary withdraws from the Warsaw Pact, and Soviet forces withdraw from Hungary. In 1999, Hungary joins the North Atlantic Treaty Organization (NATO).

2001   The Hungarian parliament passes a controversial law entitling ethnic Hungarians living in other European countries to a special identity document allowing them to work, study, and claim health care in Hungary.

2004   Hungary joins the European Union (EU).

2006   Violent demonstrations in Budapest demand the resignation of the government, which is accused of lies during the most recent election. The demonstrations overshadow the 50th anniversary of the 1956 uprising.

2008   The position of some 5 million ethnic Hungarians living in neighboring countries remains a concern for the Hungarians, but as the EU widens its borders, ties among the ethnic Hungarians become easier.

2009   Hungary's ailing economy, rising unemployment, and political instability become grave problems as Europe feels the global economic slowdown.

ICELAND

OFFICIAL NAME

Lýðveldið Ísland (Icelandic); Republic of Iceland (English)

POPULATION

319,600 (2009e)

INHABITANTS' NAME/NICKNAME

Icelander(s)

LANGUAGE/LANGUAGES

Icelandic (de facto official); English, Nordic languages, German, others

RELIGION/RELIGIONS

Lutheran (National Church of Iceland), 82 percent; Roman Catholic, 2.5 percent; Reykjavik Free Church, 2 percent; Hafnarfjorour Free Church, 1.5 percent; other or no religion

NATIONAL FLAG

The flag has a blue field bearing a red Scandinavian cross outlined in white. The blue stands for the Atlantic Ocean that surrounds Iceland, white is for the ice and snow that cover the land, and red represents the fire produced by the island's volcanoes.

COAT OF ARMS/SEAL

The coat of arms has a central shield with a white cross on a blue field and a red cross centered in the white cross, which reflects the cross and colors of the national flag. The shield bearers are the four protectors of Iceland standing on volcanic rock. The bull (Griðungur) is the protector of southwestern Iceland, the eagle or griffin (Gammur) protects northwestern Iceland, the dragon (Dreki) the northeastern part and the Rock-giant (Bergrisi) is the protector of southeastern Iceland.

CAPITAL CITY

Reykjavik

TYPE OF GOVERNMENT

Parliamentary republic

NATIONAL COLORS

Blue and white

NATIONAL ANTHEM

The anthem was originally written and composed as a popular song before Icelandic independence in 1944. The first line of the song is sometimes used as the name.

Lofsöngur (Icelandic); Song of Praise (English)

Our country's God! Our country's God!
We worship thy name in its wonder sublime.
The suns of the heavens are set in thy crown
By thy legions, the ages of time!
With thee is each day as a thousand years,
Each thousand years, but a day.
Eternity's flow'r, with its homage of tears,
That reverently passes away.
Iceland's thousand years!
Eternity's flow'r, with its homage of tears,
That reverently passes away.

Our God, our God, we bow to thee,
Our spirits most fervent we place in thy care.
Lord, God of our fathers, from age unto age,
We are breathing our holiest prayer.
We pray and we thank thee a thousand years
For safely protected we stand;
We pray and we bring thee our homage of
  tears
Our destiny rests in thy hand.
Iceland's thousand years
The hoarfrost of morning that tinted those
  years,
Thy sun rising high, shall command!

Our country's God! Our country's God!
Our life is a feeble and quivering reed;
We perish, deprived of thy spirit and light
To redeem and uphold in our need.
Inspire us at morn with thy courage and love,
And lead through the days of our strife!
At evening send peace from thy heaven above,
And safeguard our nation through life.
Iceland's thousand years!
O, prosper our people, diminish our tears
And guide, in thy wisdom, through life!

PATRON SAINT

Saint Thorlac Thorhallsson

CURRENCY

Icelandic króna

INTERNET IDENTIFIER

.is

VEHICLE IDENTIFICATION PLATES/STICKERS

IS

PASSPORT

The passport cover has the name of the country in Icelandic, English, and French, the coat of arms, and the word *passport* in Icelandic, English, and French.

AIRLINE

Icelandair

NATIONAL FLOWER

Mountain avens

NATIONAL BIRD

Falcon

NATIONAL ANIMAL

Icelandic sheep (unofficial)

NATIONAL FISH

Cod (unofficial)

NATIONAL RESOURCES

Natural resources include fish, hydropower, geothermal power, and diatomite. Historically, Iceland's fish stocks were its major source of income. Over 99 percent of the country's electricity is produced from hydropower and geothermal energy.

FOODS

Hangikjöt, smoked lamb; *hardfiskur,* dried fish; *skyr,* a yogurt-like cheese; and *gravlax,* marinated salmon, are considered the national dishes. Other specialties include *lambaraefa,* a type of pâté made of lamb; *lifrarpylsa,* liver sausage; *lifrarbuff,* liver patties; *beinlausir fuglar,* lamb or beef cooked with bacon and mushrooms; *mjólkursoðinn lundi,* puffin in milk sauce; *ofnsteikfur fiskur,* fish casserole; *fiskisúpa,* fish soup; and *ávaxtagrautur,* stewed dried fruits. *Porramatur,* a selection of traditional foods served on special occasions, is an Icelandic tradition.

SPORTS/SPORTS TEAMS

Association football (soccer) is the most popular sport. Traditional sports, such as *glima,* a form of wrestling, and athletics, also remain popular. Iceland national teams participate in many sports at an international level.

TEAM SPORTS

Badminton

Iceland Badminton Team

Basketball

Iceland Basketball Team; Iceland Women's Basketball Team

Cricket

Iceland Cricket Team

Football

Iceland Football Team, nickname Strákanir Okkar; Iceland Women's Football Team; Iceland Under-21 Football Team; Iceland Under-19 Football Team; Iceland Women's Under-19 Football Team

Handball

Iceland Handball Team, nickname Strákanir Okkar; Iceland Women's Handball Team

Hockey

Iceland Ice Hockey Team; Iceland Junior Ice Hockey Team; Iceland Field Hockey Team

Racing

Iceland Speedway Team

Table Tennis

Iceland Table Tennis Team

Tennis

Iceland Davis Cup Team; Iceland Fed Cup Team

Volleyball

Iceland Fistball Team; Iceland Men's Volleyball Team; Iceland Women's Volleyball Team

INDIVIDUAL SPORTS

Iceland Amateur Boxing Team; Iceland Archery Team; Iceland Athletics Team; Iceland Equestrian Team; Iceland Fencing Team; Iceland Gymnastics Team; Iceland Judo Team; Iceland Karate Team; Iceland Rowing Team; Iceland Sailing Team; Iceland Shooting Team;

Iceland Swim Team; Iceland Tae Kwon Do Team; Iceland Weight Lifting Team; Iceland Wrestling Team

WINTER SPORTS

Iceland Alpine Ski Team; Iceland Curling Team; Iceland Ice Hockey Team; Iceland Junior Ice Hockey Team; Iceland Skating Team

NATIONAL HEROES OR PERSONIFICATIONS

Fjalikonan, the Lady of the Mountain, is the female personification of Iceland. She symbolizes what Icelanders consider to be genuine and purely Icelandic.

National heroes include Ingólfur Arnarson, the first permanent Nordic settler in Iceland in 874 C.E.; Leif Erikson, the Icelandic explorer noted for founding settlements in Greenland* and in present-day Canada*; Jón Sigurdsson, a leader of the 19th-century independence movement; and Sveinn Björnsson, first president of independent Iceland in 1944.

NATIONAL HOLIDAY/INDEPENDENCE DAY

National Day, June 17

FESTIVALS/FAIRS

Reykjavik Arts Festival, May; Icelandic Airwaves Music Festival, October; Reykjavik Jazz Festival, August

SIGNIFICANT EVENTS IN FORMATION OF NATIONAL IDENTITY

874 C.E. Ingólfur Arnarson, a Norwegian chief, establishes the first homestead on the island. Other emigrant settlers arrive, mostly Norsemen and their Irish slaves.

930 The Althing, the national parliament, is established around 930 as the political center of the Icelandic Free State.

1000 Christianity is adopted as the island's religion.

1262 The political system proves unable to cope with the increasing powers of Icelandic chieftains. Iceland comes under the crown of Norway.

1397 Norway*, Denmark*, and Sweden* are united in the Kalmar Union. Denmark becomes the predominant power.

1402–1495 The Black Death sweeps Iceland twice, each time killing about half the population.

16th century The Danish king imposes Lutheranism on his subjects, including Icelanders. The last Roman Catholic bishop in Iceland is beheaded in 1550.

17th century–18th century The Danes impose harsh trade restrictions excluding Icelanders from the Danish trade monopoly. Pirates often raid the coastal settlements.

1783 The Laki volcano erupts, devastating the island and killing over half of all livestock, leading to a famine that kills about a quarter of the population.

1814 Denmark and Norway become separate kingdoms. Iceland remains a Danish dependency. An independence movement emerges under the leadership of Jón Sigurdsson.

1874–1918 Denmark grants Iceland home rule. The Act of Union recognizes Iceland as a sovereign state under the Danish king.

1940–1944 The German occupation of Denmark during the Second World War severs links between the two countries. The British and later the Americans occupy Iceland. Following a plebiscite, Iceland is declared independent of Denmark.

1949–1951 Iceland becomes a member of the North Atlantic Treaty Organization. American bases are established on the island.

1970s Iceland extends its fishing limits, initiating a conflict with the United Kingdom* known as the Cod Wars.

1994 Membership in the European Economic Area helps to diversify and liberalize the economy.

2000–2007 Iceland becomes one of the world's most affluent countries, with high levels of economic and personal freedom.

2008–2009 Iceland's financial system nears collapse, forcing the government to adopt severe measures and apply for emergency financial aid. In July 2009, the Icelandic parliament votes 33 to 28 to apply for membership in the European Union (EU).

IRELAND

OFFICIAL NAME

Éire (Irish Gaelic); Ireland or Republic of Ireland (English)

POPULATION

4,424,600 (2009e)

INHABITANTS' NAME/NICKNAME

Irish

LANGUAGE/LANGUAGES

Irish Gaelic, English (official); others

RELIGION/RELIGIONS

Roman Catholic, 87 percent; Church of Ireland, 3 percent; other or no religion

NATIONAL FLAG

The flag is a vertical tricolor of green, white, and orange. The green represents the Gaelic tradition in Ireland, the orange represents the supporters of William of Orange, and the white symbolizes the lasting truce between the Greens and the Oranges.

COAT OF ARMS/SEAL

Ireland's arms are a golden Gaelic harp with silver strings on a shield of blue. The harp, known as the Brian Boru Harp, is Ireland's historical heraldic symbol. The blue, called Saint Patrick's Blue, is the color of Ireland's patron saint.

CAPITAL CITY

Dublin

TYPE OF GOVERNMENT

Parliamentary democracy

NATIONAL EMBLEM

Celtic harp, called the *clairseach* or the Brian Boru Harp (official); shamrock (unofficial)

NATIONAL COLORS

Green and white

NATIONAL ANTHEM

The anthem was written in 1907 and adopted as the national anthem in 1926. A movement is ongoing to replace the anthem, due to its militancy and anti-British tone.

Amhrán na bhFiann (Irish Gaelic); The Soldier's Song (English)

We'll sing a song, a soldier's song
With cheering rousing chorus
As round our blazing fires we throng
The starry heavens o'er us
Impatient for the coming fight
And as we await the morning's light
Here in the silence of the night
We'll chant a soldier's song

Chorus

Soldiers we are
Whose lives are pledged to Ireland
Some have come
From a land beyond the wave
Sworn to be free
No more our ancient Ireland
Shall shelter the despot or the slave
Tonight we man the *bhearna bhaoil*
In Erin's cause, come woe or weal
'Mid cannon's roar and rifles' peal
We'll chant a soldier's song

In valley green, on towering crag
Our fathers fought before us
And conquered 'neath the same old flag
That's proudly floating o'er us
We're children of a fighting race

That never yet has known disgrace
And as we march, the foe to face
We'll chant a soldier's song

Chorus

Soldiers we are
Whose lives are pledged to Ireland
Some have come
From a land beyond the wave
Sworn to be free
No more our ancient Ireland
Shall shelter the despot or the slave
Tonight we man the *bhearna bhaoil*
In Erin's cause, come woe or weal
'Mid cannon's roar and rifles' peal
We'll chant a soldier's song

Sons of the Gael! Men of the Pale!
The long-watched day is breaking
The serried ranks of Inisfail
Shall set the tyrant quaking
Our campfires now are burning low
See in the east a silv'ry glow
Out yonder waits the Saxon foe
So chant a soldier's song

Chorus

Soldiers we are
Whose lives are pledged to Ireland
Some have come
From a land beyond the wave
Sworn to be free
No more our ancient Ireland
Shall shelter the despot or the slave
Tonight we man the *bhearna bhaoil*
In Erin's cause, come woe or weal
'Mid cannon's roar and rifles' peal
We'll chant a soldier's song

Patron Saint

Saint Patrick; Saint Brigid of Kildare; Saint Columba

Currency

Euro

Internet Identifier

.ie

Vehicle Identification Plates/ Stickers

IRL

Passport

The passport cover has the name of the European Union in Gaelic and English, the name of the country in Gaelic and English, and the Brian Boru Harp.

Airlines

Aer Lingus; Ryanair

National Flower

Flax

National Tree

Sessile oak

National Plant

Shamrock (unofficial)

National Animal

Stag, Irish wolfhound, Irish setter (all unofficial)

National Fish

Coarse (unofficial)

National Resources

Natural resources include zinc, lead, natural gas, petroleum, copper dolomite, barite, limestone gypsum, peat, silver, fisheries, timber, and arable land. Ireland's well-educated population and proximity to major European population centers has transformed the economy of Ireland in recent years from an agricultural focus to one dependent on trade, industry, and investment. Historic cities and monuments, spectacular scenery, and an English-speaking population support a flourishing tourist industry. The Irish Diaspora is a valuable source of investment.

FOODS

National specialties include Dublin Bay prawns prepared in various ways; oysters served with dark beer and whole-wheat bread; Irish stew, a stew of lamb or beef with potatoes, onions, carrots, and garlic; colcannon, a mixture of cooked cabbage and mashed potatoes; and soufflé of carrageen, a variety of seaweed. Irish soda bread is also considered a national food.

SPORTS/SPORTS TEAMS

The most popular sports in Ireland are Gaelic football and hurling. Association football (soccer) and rugby are also very popular. Ireland national teams participate in many sports at an international level.

TEAM SPORTS

Badminton

Ireland Badminton Team

Baseball

Ireland Baseball Team; Ireland Softball Team

Basketball

Ireland Basketball Team; Ireland Women's Basketball Team; Ireland Wheelchair Basketball Team

Bowls

Ireland Bowls Team

Cricket

Ireland Cricket Team, nickname the Green and Whites or the Boys in Green; Ireland Women's Cricket Team, nickname the Green and Whites or the Girls in Green; Ireland Under-19 Cricket Team

Football

Ireland Football Team, nickname the Boys in Green; Ireland Women's Football Team, nickname the Girls in Green; Ireland Rugby Union Team (represents the island of Ireland, including Northern Ireland*), nickname the Green and Whites or the Boys in Green; Ireland Women's Rugby Union Team; Ireland Under-21 Football Team; Ireland Women's Under-19 Football Team; Ireland Rugby League Team; Ireland B Football Team; Ireland Schoolboy Rugby Union Team; Ireland American Football Team; Ireland Australian-Rules Football Team, nickname the Green Machine or the Warriors; Ireland InterRules Football Team; Ireland Wheelchair Rugby Team; Ireland American Football Team; Ireland Beach Soccer Team; Ireland Futsal Team; Ireland Rugby Union Team (Sevens), nickname Ireland Sevens or 7s

Golf

Ireland Men's Pitch and Putt Team

Handball

Ireland Handball Team; Ireland Women's Handball Team

Hockey

Ireland Ice Hockey Team; Ireland Field Hockey Team

Korfball

Ireland Korfball Team

Lacrosse

Ireland Lacrosse Team; Ireland Women's Lacrosse Team

Racing

A1 Team Ireland; Ireland Speedway Team

Table Tennis

Ireland Table Tennis Team

Tennis

Ireland Davis Cup Team; Ireland Fed Cup Team

Volleyball

Ireland Men's Volleyball Team; Ireland Women's Volleyball Team

INDIVIDUAL SPORTS

Ireland Aikido Team; Ireland Amateur Boxing Team; Ireland Archery Team; Ireland Athletics Team; Ireland Canoeing Team; Ireland Cycling Team; Ireland Equestrian Team; Ireland Fencing Team; Ireland Gymnastics Team; Ireland Judo Team; Ireland Karate Team; Ireland Modern Pentathlon Team; Ireland Rowing Team; Ireland Sailing Team; Ireland Shooting Team; Ireland Swim Team; Ireland Triathlon Team; Ireland Weight Lifting Team; Ireland Wrestling Team

WINTER SPORTS

Ireland Alpine Ski Team; Ireland Bandy Team; Ireland Biathlon Team; Ireland Curling Team; Ireland Ice Hockey Team; Ireland Luge Team; Ireland Skating Team

NATIONAL HEROES OR PERSONIFICATIONS

Erin, a romantic name for Ireland, represents the Irish people and spirit. Hibernia is the national personification of Ireland. Kathleen Ni Houlihan is a mythical symbol of Irish nationalism.

National heroes include Brian Boru, who unified Ireland in the 11th century; Éamon de Valera, a leader of the independence movement and later prime minister; Michael Collins, a leader of the Irish Revolution killed during the Irish Civil War in 1922; and Cathal Brugha, revolutionary leader and first head of state of free Ireland.

NATIONAL HOLIDAY/INDEPENDENCE DAY

Saint Patrick's Day, March 17

FESTIVALS/FAIRS

Annual Saint Patrick's Festival, March; The Clonmel Junction Festival, July; Kilkenny Arts Festival, August; Puck Fair; August; Festival of World Cultures, August; Rose of Tralee Festival, August; Lisdonvarna Matchmaking Festival, September

SIGNIFICANT EVENTS IN FORMATION OF NATIONAL IDENTITY

500 B.C.E. Celtic settlers from mainland Europe arrive in Ireland.

432 C.E.–563 C.E. Saint Patrick, once held as a slave on the island, returns to Ireland to convert the island to Christianity. A golden age of art and literature is led by Irish monasteries.

795–1014 Vikings begin to raid the Irish coasts. A Viking fortress is established on Dublin Bay in 852. The Vikings are defeated by Brian Boru, who unifies most of Ireland under his rule.

1167–1175 During a dynastic conflict, English aid is sought by one of the parties. England's King Henry II lands at Waterford and declares himself Lord of Ireland, beginning the Norman conquest of Ireland.

1297 The first representative parliament meets at Dublin.

1494–1600 Ireland's parliament is forbidden to pass laws without the prior consent of the English parliament. Ireland becomes a kingdom ruled by the English monarchs in 1542. Potatoes are introduced from the Americas and quickly become the major food crop of the islands.

1641–1647 The Irish rebel against English rule. Protestant England promises toleration of Catholicism.

1782–1829 Unrest sweeps Ireland, leading to the Irish Rebellion of 1798. Another rebellion breaks out in 1803. The Catholic Relief Act allows Catholics to sit in parliament.

1845–1865 Potato blight destroys two-thirds of Ireland's staple crop, leading to widespread famine. With little aid from the British government, thousands die of hunger, while others flee the country, including the notorious death ships carrying refugees to North America.

1916 During the First World War, Irish nationalists initiate the Easter Rising, the beginning of the Irish Revolution. The Protestant majority in the northern counties rejects Irish nationalism and fights to remain British.

1919–1923 The Irish parliament proclaims Ireland independent of the United Kingdom*, setting off the Irish War of Independence. Ireland is partitioned, and the Irish Free State becomes a sovereign nation incorporating the south and west of Ireland. Northern Ireland* remains under British rule, leading to civil war between those favoring independence of the southern counties and those opposed to the treaty that partitioned Ireland.

1937–1949 A new constitution replaces the free state with a republic simply called Ireland or Éire. The republic remains a member of the British Commonwealth until 1949. Emigration, high unemployment, and a lack of opportunities plague the republic.

1949–1973 The question of Northern Ireland and Irish desires for the reunification of the island remain a grave problem known as the Troubles. The Irish Republican Army (IRA) continues a terrorist campaign against British rule in the north. Ireland joins the European Economic Community.

1985–2002 The Irish Miracle transforms Ireland from one of the poorest to one of the richest countries in Europe. Referendums in the republic and Northern Ireland approve a peace agreement to end the Troubles.

2006 The government launches a strategy to establish a bilingual, Irish Gaelic– and English-speaking, country within two decades.

2007–2008 The end of the violence in Northern Ireland brings peace to the whole island. Closer ties are established between the republic and Northern Ireland. Ireland becomes the first country in western Europe to officially enter into recession with the onset of the global financial crisis.

2009 Protests and demonstrations continue against the government's handling of the financial crisis.

ISLE OF MAN

OFFICIAL NAME
Ellan Vannin (Manx); Isle of Man (English)

POPULATION
80,600 (2009e)

INHABITANTS' NAME/NICKNAME
Manx

LANGUAGE/LANGUAGES
Manx, English (official); others

RELIGION/RELIGIONS
Protestant (Anglican, Methodist, Baptist, Presbyterian, Quaker), 55 percent; Roman Catholic, 8 percent; other or no religion

NATIONAL FLAG
The flag is a red field with the triskelion, the Three Legs of Man, in white outlined in black at the center. The three legs are joined at the thigh and bent at the knee. The Manx flag is based on the coat of arms of the last recognized Norse king of the island, Magnus III. The triskelion has its roots in an early Celtic sun symbol.

COAT OF ARMS/SEAL
The coat of arms has a central red shield bearing the triskelion in white outlined in black. The supporters are a falcon and a raven. The falcon is used due to the historical importance of the bird in the island's history. The raven features in Manx legends. The crown over the shield represents the British monarch as the Lord of Man.

MOTTO
Quocunque jeceris stabit (Latin); Whichsoever way you throw it, it stands (English)

CAPITAL CITY
Douglas (Doolish)

TYPE OF GOVERNMENT

Parliamentary democracy as a British crown dependency; the Isle of Man is constitutional monarchy with the monarch of the United Kingdom* as the Lord of Man, but the country is not subject to the United Kingdom directly.

NATIONAL EMBLEM

Triskelion or Three Legs of Man

NATIONAL COLORS

Red and gold

NATIONAL ANTHEM

As a British Crown dependency, the royal anthem is "God Save the Queen." The anthem was adopted as the official national anthem in 2001, although it dates back to 1770.

**Arrane Ashoonagh Dy Vannin (Manx);
O Land of Our Birth (English)**

O land of our birth,
O gem of God's earth,
O Island so strong and so fair;
Built firm as Barrule,
Thy throne of home rule
Make us free as thy sweet mountain air.

When Orry, the Dane,
In Mannin did reign,
'Twas said he had come from above;
For wisdom from heav'n
To him had been giv'n
To rule us with justice and love.

Our fathers have told
How saints came of old,
Proclaiming the gospel of peace;
That sinful desires,
Like false Baal fires,
Must die ere our troubles can cease.

Ye sons of the soil,
In hardship and toil,
That ploughs both the land and the sea,
Take heart while you can,
And think of the man
Who toiled by the Lake Galilee.

When fierce tempests smote
That frail little boat,
They ceased at his gentle command;
Despite all our fear,
The Savior is near
To safeguard our dear fatherland.

Let storm winds rejoice,
And lift up their voice,
No danger our homes can befall;
Our green hills and rocks
Encircle our flocks,
And keep out the sea like a wall.

Our island, thus blest,
No foe can molest;
Our grain and our fish shall increase;
From battle and sword
Protecteth the Lord,
And crowneth our nation with peace.

Then let us rejoice
With heart, soul and voice,
And in the Lord's promise confide;
That each single hour
We trust in his power,
No evil our souls can betide.

PATRON SAINT

Saint Maughold

CURRENCY

Isle of Man pound (interchangeable with British pound); Isle of Man also issues its own coins

INTERNET IDENTIFIER

.im

VEHICLE IDENTIFICATION PLATES/ STICKERS

GBM Great Britain-Isle of Man (official); EV Ellan Vannin (Isle of Man in the Manx language) (unofficial)

PASSPORT

The Manx are British dependents and travel on British passports.

AIRLINE

Manx2

NATIONAL FLOWER

Cushag

NATIONAL TREE

Hawthorne

NATIONAL ANIMAL

Manx *loaghtan* sheep (unofficial)

NATIONAL BIRD

Peregrine falcon; Common raven

NATIONAL FISH

Basking shark (unofficial)

NATIONAL RESOURCES

Natural resources are negligible, but the island thrives on offshore banking, agriculture, manufacturing, and tourism. The Manx government promotes island locations for filmmakers by contributing to the production costs.

FOODS

The national dish of the Isle of Man is *priddhas an' herrin,* boiled potatoes and herring. Other national specialties include *bonnag arran oarn,* a bread made of barley flour; Manx broth, a soup of beef, vegetables, and pearl barley; Cheddar flapjacks, pancakes made with Cheddar cheese; herring pie, a pastry with fresh herring, onions, and cooking apples; *prinjeig,* a dish of chopped meat, potatoes, onions, and groats boiled in the stomach of a sheep; hot pot, a soup of beef, leeks, and onions; and *crusnos,* a custard dessert.

SPORTS/SPORTS TEAMS

Cricket is the most popular sport in the country, followed by association football (soccer).

Isle of Man national teams participate in many sports at an international level.

TEAM SPORTS

Basketball

Isle of Man Basketball Team; Isle of Man Women's Basketball Team

Cricket

Isle of Man Cricket Team

Football

Isle of Man Football Team; Isle of Man Women's Football Team; Isle of Man Rugby Union Team

Table Tennis

Isle of Man Table Tennis Team

INDIVIDUAL SPORTS

Isle of Man Men's Athletics Team; Isle of Man Cycling Team; Isle of Man Shooting Team; Isle of Man Swim Team; Isle of Man Tae Kwon Do Team

NATIONAL HEROES OR PERSONIFICATIONS

Manannân mac Lir, a Celtic sea god who could draw his misty cloak around the island to protect it from invaders, is the personification of the Celtic Manx people.

National heroes include Godred Crovan, the first Norse king of Man and the Isles; and Godred VI Magnuson, the last Norse king of the island in 1275; Illiam Dhone, the leader of the rebellion against English rule in the 17th century

NATIONAL HOLIDAY/INDEPENDENCE DAY

Tynwald Day, July 5

FESTIVALS/FAIRS

Isle of Man Bowling Festival, September; Mananan Opera Festival, September; Isle of Man International Jazz Festival, September; Isle of Women Festival, October; Manx Flower Festival, July; Big Wheel Blues Festival, May

SIGNIFICANT EVENTS IN FORMATION OF NATIONAL IDENTITY

1200 B.C.E.–700 B.C.E. Celts from mainland Europe settle the island. A distinctive island Celtic culture flourishes.

Fifth century C.E. Christianity comes to the island through Saint Maughold, originally converted to Christianity in Ireland* by Saint Patrick.

700 C.E. Around 700 C.E., Celts from Ireland settle the island, displacing or absorbing the earlier Celtic inhabitants.

800–990 Norse Vikings plunder the island. Between 850 and 990, a sizable Norse colonization occurs. The Manx parliament, the Tynwald, is established in 979.

1079–1275 Godred Crovan, the Norse-Gael ruler of Dublin conquers the island and becomes King of Mann and the Isles, nominally under the suzerainty of the kings of Norway*.

1290–1405 England's king grants Mann to Sir John Stanley for a feudal fee of rendering homage and two falcons to all future kings of England upon their coronations.

1651–1704 A Manx rebellion briefly overthrows the Stanleys during the English Civil War.

1720–1828 Smuggling becomes a way of life on the island. To stop the practice, the Parliament purchases the rights of the Lord of Mann in 1765.

1866 The Isle of Man is granted home rule.

1890 The Isle of Man becomes a favored Victorian resort.

1900–1950 A revival of Manx music, dance, and language leads to an overall cultural revival.

1914–1945 Internment camps for enemy aliens are erected on the island during both world wars.

1960s To offset a slump in tourism, the island is made a tax haven and a center of offshore banking. Manx nationalism becomes an important factor, with the creation of a nationalist political party and demands for protection of the culture and language and closer ties to other Celtic nations.

1992–1996 Greater recognition of the Manx culture results in schooling in the language, as well as a general reevaluation of the island's economy and its ties to the British Crown. Nationalists demand independence to end the veto the British Crown retains over Manx legislation and to allow the island to develop its financial industry further.

2000–2009 The continuing integration of Europe in the European Union presents some Manx groups the opportunity to look to the EU as the future of their small nation. A campaign begins to transfer sovereignty from the British Crown to the government of the EU.

See also United Kingdom

ITALY

OFFICIAL NAME

Repubblica Italiana (Italian); Italian Republic (English)

POPULATION

59,689,800 (2009e)

INHABITANTS' NAME/NICKNAME

Italian(s)

LANGUAGE/LANGUAGES

Italian (official); French, German, Sardinian, others. French is co-official in the Aosta Valley; German is co-official in Trentino Alto Adige/South Tyrol; Ladin is co-official in the province of Bolzaon/Bozen; Sardinian, Catalan and Corsican have special status in Sardinia*; and Albanian, Greek, Occitan, Friulan, and Slovenian are all officially recognized to different degrees.

RELIGION/RELIGIONS

Roman Catholic, 87 percent; Orthodox, Protestant, other or no religion

NATIONAL FLAG

The flag is a vertical tricolor of green, white, and red. Green represents the plains and hills of Italy, white represents the snowy Alps, and red stands for the blood of the heroes killed in the Italian wars of independence.

COAT OF ARMS/SEAL

The emblem comprises a white five-pointed star with a fine red border, superimposed on a cogwheel and surrounded by an olive branch and an oak branch. The green branches are tied together with a red banner bearing the name of the country in large white letters. The star, an ancient symbol, was a symbol of the Kingdom of Italy and is known as the *Stellone d'Italia,* the Great Star of Italy. The cogwheel refers to the Italian constitution's interpretation of a republic based on work. The olive and oak branches represent the strength and dignity of the Italian nation.

CAPITAL CITY

Rome

TYPE OF GOVERNMENT

Parliamentary republic

NATIONAL EMBLEM

The Coliseum of Rome

NATIONAL COLORS

Sky blue and white

NATIONAL ANTHEM

The anthem dates from 1847 and was provisionally adopted as the national anthem in 1947 but has never been officially adopted.

Il Canto Degli Italiani (Italian); The Song of the Italians (English)

Brothers of Italy,
Italy has awakened,
She has wreathed her head
With the helmet of Scipio.

Where is Victory?
She bows her head to you,
You, whom God created
As the slave of Rome.

Let us band together,
We are ready to die,
We are ready to die,
Italy has called us.

PATRON SAINT

Saint Francis of Assisi; Saint Catherine of Sienna

CURRENCY

Euro

INTERNET IDENTIFIER

.it

VEHICLE IDENTIFICATION PLATES/STICKERS

I

PASSPORT

The passport cover has the name of the European Union and the name of the country in Italian, the coat of arms, the Italian word for passport, *passporto,* and the standard biometric symbol.

AIRLINES

Alitalia; Air Italy; Eurofly

NATIONAL FLOWER

Poppy; white lily (both unofficial)

NATIONAL TREE

Oak; olive (depicted on the coat of arms)

NATIONAL ANIMAL

Italian wolf (unofficial)

NATIONAL RESOURCES

Natural resources include coal, mercury, zinc, potash, marble, barite, asbestos, pumice, fluorspar, feldspar, pyrite (sulfur), natural gas and crude oil reserves, fish, and arable land. Historic cities and monuments, superb scenery, sandy beaches, and a unique culture are the basis of a thriving tourist industry. The Italian Diaspora is the source of many tourists and of investment in the country.

FOODS

Pastas and pizza are the most international of Italian recipes, but there are many regional specialties, such as gnocchi, semolina or potato dumplings; *bagna caoda,* an anchovy dip served with vegetables; panettone, a Christmas cake from Lombardy with raisins and candied fruit; pesto, a sauce of fresh basil, pine nuts, and cheese from Liguria; and *Parmigiano,* the famed cheese of Emilia-Romagna. Other national specialties include minestrone, a vegetable soup with many varieties; *ciabatta,* a variety of Italian bread; *baccala,* salted cod served in many ways; and polenta, cornmeal porridge, which is especially popular in the north. Italy's many regional cuisines maintain their traditions.

SPORTS/SPORTS TEAMS

Association football (soccer) and basketball are the two most popular sports. Winter sports are popular in northern Italy. Italy national teams participate in many sports at an international level.

TEAM SPORTS

Badminton

Italy Badminton Team

Baseball

Italy Baseball Team; Italy Softball Team

Basketball

Italy Basketball Team, nickname Gli Azzurri (the Light Blues); Italy Women's Basketball Team, nickname Gli Azzurri (the Light Blues); Italy Wheelchair Basketball Team

Cricket

Italy Cricket Team

Football

Italy Football Team, nickname Gli Azzurri (the Blues) or Squadra Azzurra (the Blue Team); Italy Women's Football Team, nickname Azzurre (the Blues); Italy Rugby Union Team, nickname Azzurri (the Blues); Italy Women's Rugby Union Team, nickname Azzurre (the Blues); Italy Under-21 Football Team, nickname Azzurrini (the Little Blues); Italy Futsal Team; Italy A Rugby Union Team; Italy Beach Soccer Team; Italy Rugby League Team; Italy Rugby Union Team (Sevens), nickname Italy Sevens; Italy Women's Rugby Union Team (Sevens), nickname Italy Sevens or Italy 7s; Italy Under-19 Basketball Team; Italy Women's Under-19 Football Team; Italy American Football Team; Italy Touch Football Team; Italy Women's Touch Football Team

Golf

Italy Men's Pitch and Putt Team; Italy Women's Pitch and Putt Team

Handball

Italy Handball Team; Italy Women's Handball Team; Italy Beach Handball Team; Italy Women's Beach Handball Team

Hockey

Italy Ice Hockey Team; Italy Women's Ice Hockey Team; Italy Junior Ice Hockey Team; Italy Field Hockey Team

Korfball

Italy Korfball Team

Lacrosse

Italy Lacrosse Team

Racing

A1 Team Italy; Italy Speedway Team

Table Tennis

Italy Table Tennis Team

Tennis

Italy Davis Cup Team; Italy Fed Cup Team

Volleyball

Italy Men's Volleyball Team; Italy Women's Volleyball Team; Italy Fistball Team; Italy Men's Beach Volleyball Team; Italy Women's Beach Volleyball Team

Water Polo

Italy Water Polo Team; Italy Women's Water Polo Team

INDIVIDUAL SPORTS

Italy Aikido Team; Italy Amateur Boxing Team; Italy Archery Team; Italy Athletics Team; Italy Canoeing Team; Italy Cycling Team; Italy Equestrian Team; Italy Fencing Team; Italy Gymnastics Team; Italy Judo Team; Italy Karate Team; Italy Modern Pentathlon Team; Italy Rowing Team; Italy Sailing Team; Italy Shooting Team; Italy Swim Team; Italy Tae Kwon Do Team; Italy Triathlon Team; Italy Weight Lifting Team; Italy Wrestling Team

WINTER SPORTS

Italy Alpine Ski Team; Italy Bandy Team: Italy Bobsleigh and Tobogganing Team; Italy Biathlon Team; Italy Luge Team; Italy Skating Team

NATIONAL HEROES OR PERSONIFICATIONS

Italia Turrita is the personification of Italy. She is characterized by a crown of towers (*turrita* means "with towers").

National heroes include Giuseppe Garibaldi, the leader of the movement for the unification of Italy in the 19th century; and Camillo Benso, Conte de Cavour, a leading figure in the unification of Italy; Leonardo da Vinci, the most famous of the Renaissance artists and inventors; Enrico Fermi, a noted physicist who helped create the first nuclear reactor for reliable energy; Federico Fillini, the "father" of modern Italian cinema

NATIONAL HOLIDAY/INDEPENDENCE DAY

Republic Day, June 2

FESTIVALS/FAIRS

Carnival (Carnevale), February–March; Corpus Domini (religious processions on carpets of flowers), June; Sanremo Music Festival; Palio di Siena, July; Wine Festival, October

SIGNIFICANT EVENTS IN FORMATION OF NATIONAL IDENTITY

Eighth century B.C.E.–seventh century B.C.E Greek colonies are founded along the coasts, particularly in Sicily and the southern part of the peninsula. The area comes to be called Magna Graecia, or Greater Greece, for the density of Greek settlements. Rome is founded as an agricultural community.

Eighth century B.C.E.–first century C.E. Rome grows into a powerful state over the centuries, eventually encompassing the whole area around the Mediterranean Sea.

Second century C.E. The Roman Empires begins to decline and finally divides into two parts, the western and eastern Roman empires. The western part, overrun by Germanic tribes, collapses, leaving Italy divided into small, independent states and kingdoms.

Sixth century The Byzantine Empire, the eastern Roman Empire, recaptures most of Italy.

10th century Merchant republics emerge and grow rich on trade, particularly trade with the East.

14th century The Italian Renaissance, the rebirth of learning based on classical sources, begins in northern Italy and eventually spreads across Europe. Italy is divided into smaller city-states and territories. The Black Death strikes in 1348, killing one-third of the population.

15th century–17th century Competition between France* and Spain* for influence in Italy is offset by the power of Venice, with its growing empire. French invasions disrupt the northern states, while Spanish control of the south is extended. Austria* succeeds France and Spain as the most influential power in Italy. Northern Italy becomes economically advanced, while the south remains feudal and backward.

1796–1815 The Napoleonic Wars change the map of Italy and introduce the ideas of the French Revolution. Italian nationalism begins to stir, with calls for the unification of the Italian-speaking territories of Europe.

1848–1860 Giuseppe Garibaldi leads the national movement in the south, while the Kingdom of Piedmont-Sardinia expands in the north. As northern Italy industrializes and modernizes, the overpopulated south languishes. Millions of people immigrate to other parts of Europe and the Americas.

1860–1870 The Kingdom of Italy is proclaimed in 1861, with the Papal territories, except the Vatican*, incorporated in 1870.

1890–1913 Italy becomes a colonial power. Universal suffrage is introduced in 1913.

1914–1922 Italy joins the allies during the First World War and is rewarded with the Italian-speaking parts of the Austro-Hungarian Empire but fails to achieve its goals. Fascists emerge as a political power.

1936–1943 Benito Mussolini, the fascist leader, forms a dictatorship and enters the Second World War as an ally of Nazi Germany. The Allied invasion leads to the collapse of the fascist regime and Italian surrender. Germans occupy the north.

1946–1965 The Italian Republic is proclaimed. The American Marshall Plan helps revive the economy, which enjoys prolonged growth, particularly in northern Italy. The country becomes a member of the North Atlantic Treaty Organization and the European Economic Community. In the south, the Italian state faces the strength of entrenched criminal organizations.

1970s–1980s Chaotic politics and the strength of leftist parties in northern Italy lead to more moderate public life in the 1980s. Official corruption, particularly in the south, continues to disrupt the country.

1990s Italy faces massive government debt, extensive corruption, and organized crime. Changes of government are frequent.

2000–2008 Italy's long coastline and its developed economy entice tens of thousands of illegal immigrants from northern Africa and southeastern Europe.

2009 Economic problems continue as Italy deals with an economic recession as part of the global financial downturn.

See also Sardinia

JERSEY

OFFICIAL NAME
Bailiwick of Jersey (English); Bailliage de Jersey (French and Jèrriais)

POPULATION
90,400 (2009e)

INHABITANTS' NAME/NICKNAME
Jerseian(s)

LANGUAGE/LANGUAGES
English, French (both official); Jèrriais (recognized regional language); Portuguese, others

RELIGION/RELIGIONS
Anglican, Roman Catholic, Baptist, Congregational New Church, Methodist, Presbyterian, other or no religion

NATIONAL FLAG
The flag is white with a diagonal red cross extending to the corners of the flag; in the upper quadrant is the badge of Jersey, a red shield with the three leopards of Normandy

in yellow surmounted by a yellow Planta-genet crown, symbolizing the monarchy (Queen Elizabeth II, Duke of Normandy). The white and red symbolize Jersey's historic ties to England.

COAT OF ARMS/SEAL

The coat of arms is a red shield with three gold lions (traditionally called Norman leop-ards). The arms, granted by Edward I in 1279, are similar to the arms of Guernsey* and England and symbolize the British mon-arch's role as the Duke of Normandy.

CAPITAL CITY

Saint Helier

TYPE OF GOVERNMENT

Parliamentary democracy and constitutional monarchy as a British Crown dependency

NATIONAL EMBLEM

The three Norman lions

NATIONAL COLORS

Red and white

NATIONAL ANTHEM

The anthem with lyrics in French is also the unofficial anthem of the French region of Normandy. A new anthem was commis-sioned in 2007, called "Island Home," but it awaits official confirmation by the Jersey legislature. The Jersey anthem is official for occasions when a distinguishing anthem is re-quired; otherwise, the anthem of the United Kingdom*, "God Save the Queen," is the of-ficial anthem of Jersey.

Ma Normandie (French); My Normandy (English)

When everything is reborn in hope
And winter flees far from us,
Under the beautiful sky of our France,
When the sun returns gentler,

When nature has turned green again,
When the swallow has returned,
I like to see once more my Normandy,
It's the country where I saw the light of day.

I've seen the fields of Helvetia,
And its chalets and its glaciers,
I've seen the sky of Italy,
And Venice and its gondoliers.
Greeting each homeland,
I told myself that no stay
Is finer than my Normandy,
It's the country where I saw the light of day.

There comes a time of life,
When every dream must finish,
A time when the restful spirit
Needs to remember.
When my chilled muse
Makes its way back to the past,
I'll go see once more my Normandy,
It's the country where I saw the light of day.

PATRON SAINT

Saint Helier

CURRENCY

Jersey pound (notes and coins circulate along with the British pound)

INTERNET IDENTIFIER

.je

VEHICLE IDENTIFICATION PLATES/STICKERS

GBJ Great Britain (official); SJ Jersey (unof-ficial)

PASSPORT

Jerseians are British citizens and travel on British passports.

NATIONAL FLOWER

Jersey lily (unofficial)

NATIONAL ANIMAL

Jersey cow (unofficial)

NATIONAL FISH

Sea bass (unofficial)

NATIONAL RESOURCES

Other than limited arable land, Jersey's natural resources are negligible. Jersey's well-educated population and its proximity to large European markets sustain an affluent economy based on financial services, tourism, electronic commerce, and agriculture.

FOODS

Seafood has traditionally been important to the cuisine of Jersey, including mussels (locally called *moules*), oysters, lobster, crabs, *ormers* (small abalones), and conger eels. *Bourdélots,* apple dumplings, and black butter (*lé nièr beurre*), a dark, spicy spread prepared from apples, cider, and spices, are the national specialties. Other traditional dishes are cabbage loaf; Jersey wonders (*les mèrvelles*), fried snacks akin to doughnuts; *ortchie* soup, made of nettles; *les pais au fou,* a bean dish; and *vraic,* local buns.

SPORTS/SPORTS TEAMS

Cricket is the most popular sport, followed by association football (soccer). Jersey national teams participate in many sports at an international level.

TEAM SPORTS

Basketball

Jersey Basketball Team; Jersey Women's Basketball Team; Jersey Touch Football Team; Jersey Women's Touch Football Team

Cricket

Jersey Cricket Team

Football

Jersey Football Team, nickname the Reds; Jersey Women's Football Team, nickname the Reds. The football association is the Jersey Football Association.

Table Tennis

Jersey Table Tennis Team

NATIONAL HEROES OR PERSONIFICATIONS

Victor Hugo, the famous French writer who lived in Jersey in the mid-19th century; Albert Bedane, who sheltered an escaped Dutch Jew, a French flyer, and Russian slave laborers from the Nazi occupation of Jersey during the Second World War; Peter Crill, who organized an escape from German-occupied Jersey in two small boats and later became the bailiff; Alexander Coutanche, the bailiff and governor from 1935 to 1963, overseeing the modernization of the islands

NATIONAL HOLIDAY/INDEPENDENCE DAY

Liberation Day, May 9

FESTIVALS/FAIRS

Battle of the Flowers, August; Jersey International Film Festival, September; Jersey Seaside Festival, August; Gorey Fete de la Mer, August

SIGNIFICANT EVENTS IN FORMATION OF NATIONAL IDENTITY

50 B.C.E. The island is called Caesarea, named for Caesar, the conqueror of Gaul, although evidence of Roman occupation has not been found. The Celtic islanders adopt the Latin language and much of Latin culture from the Romans.

555 C.E. Christianity is introduced by Saint Helier, who is martyred on the island.

Eighth century Norsemen, Vikings from Scandinavia, take control of the islands and the mainland, which becomes known as Normandy.

933–1066 Jersey is annexed to the Duchy of Normandy and becomes part of the Kingdom of England when the Normans of William the Conqueror invade and conquer England.

1117–1360 The French conquer mainland Normandy, but the Channel Islands, made up of Jersey, Guernsey, and several smaller islands, are protected by English ships and remain part of Norman England. The French, after attempting to take control of the islands, recognize English sovereignty.

15th century–16th century The French again attempt to gain control of the strategic islands but are repelled. Jersey retains its Norman laws, language, and customs. Politically, the island is self-governing under the English monarch in his role as Duke of Normandy but is not subject to the English parliament.

1664 The English king rewards Sir George Carteret of Jersey for his loyalty with a grant of land in the New World, which Carteret calls New Jersey.

1789–1794 French refugees from the horrors of the French Revolution escape to the island, reinforcing the Latin culture. Their language, standard French, gradually replaces the local Norman dialect.

1880–1920 Jersey becomes a famous Victorian resort and retirement center. Liberal tax laws bring a new wave of settlement from the British mainland after the First World War.

1940 The Germans quickly overrun France* during the Second World War. Unable to defend Jersey, the British evacuate all troops and thousands of civilians but are unable to evacuate the whole island before the Germans occupy Jersey. The Channel Islands are the only British territory to suffer occupation during the War.

1940–1944 Under German rule, thousands are deported as forced labor to Germany*, and many suffer malnutrition and disease due to a lack of food.

1945–1955 Jersey quickly recovers. Offshore banking and financial services become the mainstays of the island's economy.

1958–1968 Jersey begins to issue its own stamps and currency. The British study Jersey's ties to the United Kingdom and find that most Jerseians prefer the status quo, with Britain responsible for defense and foreign affairs.

2000–2009 Jersey restricts the number of people allowed to settle on the island, as population growth is encroaching on green zones and causing a chronic housing shortage. Some groups advocate full independence for the island within the European Union.

See also United Kingdom

KOSOVO

OFFICIAL NAME
Republika e Kosovës (Albanian); Republika Kosovo (Serbian); Republic of Kosovo (English)

POPULATION
2,142,300 (2009e)

INHABITANTS' NAME/NICKNAME
Kosovar(s)

LANGUAGE/LANGUAGES
Albanian (Gheg dialect), Serbian (both official); Turkish, Gorani, Romani, Bosnian (recognized regional languages); English, others

RELIGION/RELIGIONS
Muslim, 90 percent; Serbian Orthodox, Roman Catholic, other or no religion

NATIONAL FLAG
The flag is a blue field with six white five-pointed stars in an arc above a golden map of Kosovo. The six stars represent Kosovo's six major ethnic groups. The colors blue and white are the colors of the European Union.

COAT OF ARMS/SEAL
The coat of arms is a shield with the blue field, six stars, and golden map of the national flag. The blue is outlined with a thin gold stripe.

CAPITAL CITY
Pristina

TYPE OF GOVERNMENT
Parliamentary republic

NATIONAL COLORS
Red and black

NATIONAL ANTHEM
The anthem, titled *"Hymni i Republikës së Kosovës Europa"* (Albanian) or "Anthem of the Republic of Kosovo" (English), was adopted in June 2008. It was chosen because it reflects the multiethnic character of Kosovo. The anthem is instrumental only. Lyrics may be added in the future.

CURRENCY
Euro; Serbian dinar in Serbian areas

INTERNET IDENTIFIER
.cs

VEHICLE IDENTIFICATION PLATES/STICKERS
KS or KOS (unofficial)

PASSPORT
The passport cover has the name of the country in Albanian, Serbian, and English, the coat of arms, and the word *passport* in Albanian, Serbian, and English.

AIRLINE
Air Prishtina

NATIONAL RESOURCES
National resources include nickel, lead, zinc, magnesium, lignite, kaolin, chrome, and bauxite. The many Kosovars living outside the country, particularly in Albania, are a major source of foreign currency and investment.

FOODS
National specialties include *fërgesë,* a dish of meat, liver, eggs, and tomatoes; *tavë kosi,* a dish of mutton and yogurt; shish kebab, skewered meat cooked over charcoal; and *oshaf,* a dessert of figs and sheep's milk cheese with honey and candied fruits. Other specialties include *byrek me perime,* vegetable pies; *turšija,* pickled vegetables, often stuffed with cheese, cabbage, or green tomatoes; *burek,* a pastry made of layered pancakes or crêpes; *mantija,* small pastries stuffed with ground meat and onions; *burjan,* a dish of rice, spinach, and lamb; *gjellë me arra,* veal or chicken with walnuts; *qofte të fërguara,* fried meatballs; and *halve,* a dessert of Turkish origin.

SPORTS/SPORTS TEAMS
Association football (soccer) is the most popular sport, along with other sports such as athletics and basketball. Kosovo national teams participate in many sports at an international level.

TEAM SPORTS
Basketball
Kosovo Basketball Team; Kosovo Women's Basketball Team

Football
Kosovo Football Team, nickname Kuqezinjët (Red and Blacks); Kosovo Women's Football Team, nickname Kuqezinjët (Red and Blacks); Kosovo Under-18 Football Team

Handball
Kosovo Handball Team

Table Tennis
Kosovo Table Tennis Team

INDIVIDUAL SPORTS
Kosovo Swim Team

NATIONAL HEROES OR PERSONIFICATIONS
Fadil Hoxha, a leader of the Kosovar partisans fighting the invaders during World

War II; Ibrahim Rugova, considered by some as the father of the nation, the leader of the independence movement in the 1980s and 1990s; Ramush Haradinaj, a former commander of the Kosovar guerila group; Mehmet Bislimi, a leader of the modern national movement; Hasan Prishtina, a nationalist leader in the early 20th century

NATIONAL HOLIDAY/INDEPENDENCE DAY
Independence Day, February 17

FESTIVALS/FAIRS
Dokufest (Festival of Documentaries and Short Films), August; Pristina Jazz Festival, November; International Students Film and Theater Festival, November

SIGNIFICANT EVENTS IN FORMATION OF NATIONAL IDENTITY

Fourth century B.C.E.–third century B.C.E. The Thraco-Illyrian tribe known as the Dardani occupies the region.

59 B.C.E. The region forms part of the Roman province of Illyricum.

Sixth century C.E.–seventh century C.E. Slavic migrations overrun much of the Balkans, pushing the indigenous peoples into the southern territories.

850 C.E. Kosovo forms part of the Bulgarian Empire. Christianity and Byzantine culture spread through the region.

11th century–14th century The Serbian principality of Rascia, which later forms part of the Serbian kingdom, conquers Kosovo. Kosovo becomes the center of Serbian resistance to Ottoman Turkish expansion in the Balkans and the spiritual center of the medieval Serbian state.

1389–1455 Ottoman forces defeat a coalition of Christian peoples at the Battle of Kosovo. The region becomes part of the Ottoman Empire.

1690 Thousands of Serbian Christians leave the region to settle in territory beyond Ottoman control. Others would leave the region during the 18th century.

1766 The position of the Christians deteriorates, with new taxes and other restrictions.

1864–1911 Kosovo becomes a separate Ottoman province. Albanian nationalism, the desire for a separate Albanian nation in the Balkans, spreads to Kosovo. An Albanian uprising begins in Pristina and spreads to Albania*.

1914–1918 Kosovo comes under occupation by the Central Powers until the Serbian military takes the region at the end of the First World War. Kosovo becomes part of the new Yugoslav kingdom.

1918–1940 Education in the Albanian language is forbidden, along with other restrictions on cultural and political life.

1941–1945 Yugoslavia is invaded by the Axis powers. Italians take control of Kosovo, which is joined to Italian-controlled Albania. At the end of the Second World War, despite Kosovar pleas, the region becomes part of the communist-controlled Yugoslav federation.

1945–1953 The Kosovar Albanians, unlike the other nationalities in the federation, are not allowed a separate state, but remain part of Serbia*. The Serbian authorities curtail Albanian culture and language. Attempts are made to force the Kosovars to declare themselves as ethnic Turks and leave Yugoslavia for Turkey*.

1960s–1980s Kosovo is granted limited autonomy. Due to a very high birthrate, the proportion of ethnic Albanians rises from 75 percent to 90 percent of the population. Ethnic tensions between Kosovars and Serbs lead to violence.

1989–1995 Kosovo's autonomy is curtailed. Kosovar Albanian separatism gains support. Yugoslavia disintegrates into several warring countries. Serbian control of Kosovo is tightened to prevent yet another separatist war in the region.

1996–2007 Kosovar guerilla fighters resist Serbian control, leading to war in the region. International intervention results in control of Kosovo by the United Nations. The international community is unable to agree on the disposition of the territory.

2008 Kosovo unilaterally declares independence on February 17 and is recognized by the United States* and most member states of the European Union. A number of nations, including Serbia, Spain*, and Russia*, refuse to recognize the newly independent state.

2009 The Spanish government announces that its troops are shortly to be withdrawn from the North Atlantic Treaty Organization (NATO) contingent in Kosovo.

LATVIA

OFFICIAL NAME
Latvijas Republika (Latvian); Republic of Latvia (English)

POPULATION
2,264,900 (2008e)

INHABITANTS' NAME/NICKNAME
Latvian(s)

LANGUAGE/LANGUAGES
Latvian (official); Russian, Lithuanian, others

RELIGION/RELIGIONS
Lutheran, Roman Catholic, Russian Orthodox, other or no religion

NATIONAL FLAG
The flag has three horizontal stripes of maroon, white (half the width of the maroon stripes), and maroon. The maroon color is described as symbolizing the Latvians' readiness to shed blood from their hearts for freedom and their willingness to defend their liberty. According to legend, the color comes from the blood of a Latvian leader wounded in battle that soaked the sheet he was wrapped in.

COAT OF ARMS/SEAL
The coat of arms consists of a central shield or crest divided into an upper half depicting a rising sun that symbolizes Latvian statehood and a lower half with two quadrants showing the arms of the historical regions of Western Latvia and Eastern Latvia. The three stars above the shield represent the three historical districts that make up the country, Vidzeme, Latgalia, and Curland-Semigalia. A red lion and a winged griffin support the shield.

MOTTO
Tēvzemei un brīvībai (Latvian); For fatherland and freedom (English)

CAPITAL CITY
Riga

TYPE OF GOVERNMENT
Parliamentary republic

NATIONAL EMBLEM
Brīvības pieminekja (the Freedom Monument)

NATIONAL COLORS
Maroon (dark red) and white

NATIONAL ANTHEM
The anthem was originally written while Latvia formed part of the Russian Empire, as a direct defiance of the czarist authorities. It was adopted by independent Latvia in 1918.

> **Dievs, Sveti Latviju! (Latvian); God Bless Latvia (English)**
>
> Bless Latvia, O God,
> Our verdant native sod,
> Where Baltic heroes trod,
> Keep her from harm!
> Bless Latvia, O God,
> Our verdant native sod,
> Where Baltic heroes trod,
> Keep her from harm!
>
> Our lovely daughters near,
> Our singing sons appear,
> May fortune smiling here
> Grace Latvia!

Our lovely daughters near,
Our singing sons appear,
May fortune smiling here
Grace Latvia!

PATRON SAINT
Saint John the Baptist

CURRENCY
Latvian lats

INTERNET IDENTIFIER
.lv

VEHICLE IDENTIFICATION PLATES/ STICKERS
LV

PASSPORT
The passport cover has the name of the European Union and the name of the country in Latvian, the coat of arms, the Latvian word for passport, *pase,* and the standard biometric symbol.

AIRLINE
Air Baltic

NATIONAL FLOWER
Pīpine (Latvian daisy)

NATIONAL TREE
Linden (lime), oak

NATIONAL BIRD
White wagtail

NATIONAL INSECT
Two-spot ladybug

NATIONAL RESOURCES
Natural resources include peat, limestone, dolomite, amber, hydropower, wood, and arable land.

FOODS
National dishes include *cotlettes,* meat patties; *piragi,* flaky pastry filled with bacon and onions; *skabu kapostu zupa,* Latvian cabbage soup; Alexander torte, cranberry- or raspberry-filled pastry strips; Black Balsam, a thick, black alcohol produced since the 17th century; Jänis cheese, caraway cheese; and *karbonäde,* breaded pork chops.

SPORTS/SPORTS TEAMS
Basketball is the most popular sport and is sometimes called the national sport. Association football (soccer) is also very popular. Latvia national teams participate in many sports at an international level.

TEAM SPORTS

Badminton
Latvia Badminton Team

Baseball
Latvia Baseball Team

Basketball
Latvia Basketball Team; Latvia Women's Basketball Team; Latvia Wheelchair Basketball Team

Cricket
Latvia Cricket Team

Football
Latvia Football Team; Latvia Women's Football Team; Latvia Under-21 Football Team; Latvia Rugby Union Team; Latvia Futsal Team; Latvia Rugby League Team; Latvia Women's Under-19 Football Team

Handball
Latvia Handball Team

Hockey
Latvia Ice Hockey Team; Latvia Junior Ice Hockey Team; Latvia Women's Ice Hockey Team; Latvia Field Hockey Team

Racing

Latvia Speedway Team

Table Tennis

Latvia Table Tennis Team

Tennis

Latvia Davis Cup Team; Latvia Fed Cup Team

Volleyball

Latvia Men's Volleyball Team; Latvia Women's Volleyball Team; Latvia Men's Beach Volleyball Team; Latvia Women's Beach Volleyball Team

INDIVIDUAL SPORTS

Latvia Amateur Boxing Team; Latvia Archery Team; Latvia Athletics Team; Latvia Canoeing Team; Latvia Cycling Team; Latvia Equestrian Team; Latvia Fencing Team; Latvia Gymnastics Team; Latvia Karate Team; Latvia Modern Pentathlon Team; Latvia Rowing Team; Latvia Sailing Team; Latvia Shooting Team; Latvia Swim Team; Latvia Tae Kwon Do Team; Latvia Triathlon Team; Latvia Weight Lifting Team; Latvia Wrestling Team

WINTER SPORTS

Latvia Alpine Ski Team; Latvia Bandy Team; Latvia Biathlon Team; Latvia Bobsleigh and Tobogganing Team; Latvia Curling Team; Latvia Ice Hockey Team; Latvia Junior Ice Hockey Team; Latvia Women's Ice Hockey Team; Latvia Luge Team; Latvia Skating Team

NATIONAL HEROES OR PERSONIFICATIONS

Krišjānis Barons, known as the father of the *dainas*, who gathered the Latvian folk songs and tales for publication in *Latvju Dainas* in the 19th century; Albert of Livonia, the founder of Riga in the 13th century; Kārlis Ulmanis, leader of the independence movement and later prime minister of Latvia; Wladyslaw Raginis, World War II military hero

NATIONAL HOLIDAY/INDEPENDENCE DAY

Independence Day, November 18

FESTIVALS/FAIRS

Jāņi (Summer Solstice Festival), June; Martini Festival, November; Winter Solstice Festival, December

SIGNIFICANT EVENTS IN FORMATION OF NATIONAL IDENTITY

8th century C.E.–12th century C.E. Baltic tribes inhabit the region. The name *Latvia* is derived from the Latgalians, one of four tribes that form the Latvian nation. The region is called the Amber Coast after its most valuable export.

1180–1211 Christian missionaries begin the conversion of the pagan Latvians, but Latvian resistance triggers a German crusade to forcibly convert the tribes to Christianity. A federation of feudal states called Livonia is created under German rule. The Latvians are reduced to a class of serfs on German manors.

1285 Riga joins the Hanseatic League, establishing cultural and trading ties with the rest of northern Europe.

1500s The Protestant Reformation reaches the Baltic region. The Livonian state collapses in the Livonian War (1558–1583), and Latvia comes under Polish-Lithuanian rule.

17th century–18th century Poland*, Sweden* and Russia* struggle for control of the eastern Baltic. Swedish rule from 1629 eases serfdom and sees the establishment of schools for the Latvian peasants. By the end of the 18th century, the Latvian lands form part of the Russian Empire.

1817–1897 The emancipation of the peasants frees the Latvians from serfdom on the Baltic German estates. A class of farmer-owners emerges, while other Latvians urbanize and develop a bourgeois class in the cities. The Young Latvians movement lays the ground for the later national movement. In the 1890s, a leftist revolutionary movement begins.

1905 The 1905 Russian Revolution initiates a strong nationalist movement.

1914–1918 Latvia is devastated in heavy fighting during World War I. The Russian Revolution overtakes czarist Russia, and Latvia is declared independent.

1939–1944 The Baltic Germans are evacuated to Germany*. Soviet troops invade and occupy the country. The Germans turn on their Soviet allies and invade the Soviet Union, quickly overrunning Latvia. Terrorized by Soviet deportations of thousands of Latvians, many join the Nazis' anticommunist crusade.

1945–1949 Over 130,000 Latvians flee the return of the Red Army. Another 100,000 to 120,000 are executed or deported. Ethnic Slavs are settled in the region. By 1949, the Latvian portion of the population has fallen from 75 percent in 1939 to just 56 percent.

1960s Massive settlement of ethnic Slavs in the region raises Latvian fears that their culture and language will disappear. Nationalist sentiment is reborn, in spite of harsh Soviet suppression.

1980s The limited liberalization of Soviet society in the late 1980s allows Latvian nationalism to become a strong force in the Latvian Soviet republic. Latvian is declared the state language; the flag, anthem, and coat of arms of independent Latvia of 1918–1940 are readopted.

1990–1991 The collapse of the Soviet Union allows Latvia to resume its former independence. The Latvian parliament is reopened, and elections are held.

1994–2000 The last Russian military units leave the country. Tensions grow between Latvia and Russia over the treatment of the large Russian minority settled in the region under Soviet rule.

2004–2008 Latvia becomes a member state of the North Atlantic Treaty Organization (NATO) and joins the European Union (EU), which helps to ensure Latvia's future security. Latvia has the EU's fastest-growing economy. Russia refuses to sign a boundary treaty, due to Latvian demands for territory lost under Soviet rule. Russia continues to demand better treatment for the large Russian minority in Latvia.

2009 Financial problems bring political instability as the ruling coalition collapses amid widespread discontent over economic measures. A new coalition government is sworn in but faces the same economic problems.

LIECHTENSTEIN

OFFICIAL NAME

Fürtentum Liechtenstein (German); Principality of Liechtenstein (English)

POPULATION

35,700 (2009e)

INHABITANTS' NAME/NICKNAME

Liechtensteiner(s); Liechter(s) (used locally)

LANGUAGE/LANGUAGES

German (official); Alemanic dialect is most widely spoken

RELIGION/RELIGIONS

Roman Catholic, 76 percent; Protestant, 7 percent; Muslim, 5 percent; other or no religion

NATIONAL FLAG

The flag is a horizontal bicolor of blue over red with a gold ducal crown on the blue near the hoist. The colors derive from the livery colors of the royal household in the 18th century. The ducal crown was added in 1937, after it was discovered at the 1936 Olympics that the flag's simple bicolor was the same as that of Haiti*.

COAT OF ARMS/SEAL

The coat of arms has a central shield or crest quartered, with a smaller crest of yellow over red superimposed. The quarters represent areas of Europe where Liechtenstein has been involved by conquest or marriage. The first quadrant represents Silesia, the second the arms of the Kuenring family, the third the Duchy of Troppau, and the fourth the arms of the Cirksena family. Above the shield are a ducal crown and a purple cloak that frames the shield in ermine.

MOTTO

Für gott, fürst, und vaterland (German); For God, prince, and fatherland (English)

CAPITAL CITY

Vaduz

TYPE OF GOVERNMENT

Parliamentary constitutional monarchy

NATIONAL EMBLEM

The Ducal Crown of Liechtenstein

NATIONAL COLORS

Blue and red

NATIONAL ANTHEM

The melody of the anthem is the same as that of the United Kingdom's "God Save the Queen."

Oben am Jungen Rhein (German); High Above the Young Rhine (English)

High above the young Rhine
Lies Liechtenstein, resting
On Alpine heights.
This beloved homeland,
This dear fatherland
Was chosen for us by
God's wise hand.
This beloved homeland,
This dear fatherland
Was chosen for us by
God's wise hand.

Long live Liechtenstein,
Blossoming on the young Rhine,
Happy and faithful!
Long live the prince of the land,
Long live our fatherland,

United by brotherly bonds and free.
Long live the prince of the land,
Long live our fatherland,
United by brotherly bonds and free.

PATRON SAINT

Saint Florin (Dioceses of Vaduz)

CURRENCY

Swiss franc

INTERNET IDENTIFIER

.li

VEHICLE IDENTIFICATION PLATES/ STICKERS

FL

PASSPORT

The passport cover has the name of the principality in German, the coat of arms, and the word *passport* in German.

NATIONAL RESOURCES

Natural resources include hydropower and arable land. A well-educated population and proximity to Europe's large population centers are resources the country has put to good use. Despite its small size, the principality has developed as a prosperous, highly industrialized, free-market economy with living standards comparable to its large European neighbors. Low business taxes— the maximum tax rate is 20 percent—and easy incorporation laws have induced many holding or letter-box companies to establish nominal offices in Liechtenstein.

FOODS

The national dish is *käseknöpflt,* small dumplings made with cheese. The national drink is *Vaduzer,* a red wine particular to the country. Other specialties include *leber mit polenta,* veal or beef liver with onions, speck, capers, lemon juice, and white wine served with polenta; and *groestl,* sliced and pan-fried potatoes and onions often served with meat.

Sports/Sports Teams

Association football (soccer) is the most popular sport, along with winter sports. Liechtenstein national teams participate in many sports at an international level.

Team Sports

Badminton

Liechtenstein Badminton Team

Basketball

Liechtenstein Basketball Team

Football

Liechtenstein Football Team; Liechtenstein Women's Football Team; Liechtenstein Under-21 Football Team

Handball

Liechtenstein Handball Team; Liechtenstein Women's Handball Team

Hockey

Liechtenstein Ice Hockey Team; Liechtenstein Women's Ice Hockey Team

Racing

Liechtenstein Speedway Team

Table Tennis

Liechtenstein Table Tennis Team

Tennis

Liechtenstein Davis Cup Team; Liechtenstein Fed Cup Team

Volleyball

Liechtenstein Men's Volleyball Team; Liechtenstein Women's Volleyball Team

Individual Sports

Liechtenstein Athletics Team; Liechtenstein Archery Team; Liechtenstein Cycling Team; Liechtenstein Equestrian Team; Liechtenstein Judo Team; Liechtenstein Karate Team; Liechtenstein Sailing Team; Liechtenstein Shooting Team; Liechtenstein Swim Team

Winter Sports

Liechtenstein Alpine Ski Team; Liechtenstein Biathlon Team; Liechtenstein Bobsleigh and Tobogganing Team; Liechtenstein Curling Team; Liechtenstein Ice Hockey Team; Liechtenstein Women's Ice Hockey Team; Liechtenstein Luge Team

National Heroes or Personifications

Anton Florian, the first prince of Liechtenstein in 1719; Johann I Josef, prince of Liechtenstein during the Napoleonic Wars; Franz Joseph, prince of Liechtenstein during World War II, who gave asylum to about 500 anti-Soviet Russians fighting with the German forces at the end of the war

National Holiday/Independence Day

Assumption Day, August 15

Festivals/Fairs

Vaduz Film Festival, January; National Day celebrations, August

Significant Events in Formation of National Identity

50 C.E.–400 C.E. The territory in the Rhine Valley and the mountains forms part of the Roman province of Raetia. Germanic Alemanni tribes settle the region as Rome withdraws.

1140 The Liechtenstein family has its seat at Liechtenstein Castle in Lower Austria. Over centuries, the family, through alliances and marriage, acquires lands in Moravia, Lower Austria, and Styria.

1342 The small county of Vaduz is formed.

17th century The Liechtensteins are raised to princely rank in the Holy Roman Empire under the Hapsburgs. The Liechtenstein family purchases the small territory of Schellenberg in 1699.

1719 The territories of Vaduz and Schellenberg are combined as a principality under Anton Florian of Liechtenstein as part of the Holy Roman Empire.

1806–1815 Liechtenstein joins Napoleon's Confederation of the Rhine and is recognized as a sovereign state. Liechtenstein retains it independent status at the end of the Napoleonic Wars.

1862–1868 A new constitution is adopted, making the principality a constitutional monarchy. The country disbands its army of 80 men and declares permanent neutrality, which is respected during both World Wars.

1919 Liechtenstein, long dependent on Austria*, turns to Switzerland* after the First World War. A new treaty cements closer diplomatic ties to the Swiss.

1938 Prince Franz I abdicates, citing age, but his treasured Jewish wife might have been the reason. Franz Joseph II becomes prince, the first to take up permanent residence in the principality.

1939–1945 At the end of World War II, the prince gives asylum to about 500 anti-Soviet Russian soldiers who had fought with Germany* during the war. They prove expensive to feed and house, but as others are repatriated and disappear into the Soviet gulag, the prince remains adamant. Finally, Argentina* agrees to take the refugees.

1946–1948 Poland* and Czechoslovakia, at the end of the war, confiscate the extensive Liechtenstein estates as German property, even though Liechtenstein remained neutral. The tiny state is very poor and survives as the prince sells off personal possessions for much-needed money.

1970 Liechtenstein modernizes and prospers.

1990 The principality joins the Council of Europe and the United Nations,

2003 A referendum gives Prince Hans-Adam, who had threatened to leave the country, more powers than any other European monarch.

2007–2008 The principality appoints two citizens of the United States* as honorary consuls, the first in the history of the principality.

2009 The government agrees to cooperate with other countries on tax matters as part of a tightening of financial laws in the popular tax haven.

LITHUANIA

OFFICIAL NAME

Lietuvos Respublika (Lithuanian); Republic of Lithuania (English)

POPULATION

3,351,300 (2009e)

INHABITANTS' NAME/NICKNAME

Lithuanian

LANGUAGE/LANGUAGES

Lithuanian (official); Russian, Polish, others

RELIGION/RELIGIONS

Roman Catholic, 79 percent; Russian Orthodox, 4 percent; Protestant, 2 percent; other or no religion

NATIONAL FLAG

The flag is a horizontal tricolor of yellow, green, and red. The yellow symbolizes the golden fields of Lithuania, the green is for its green countryside, and the red represents the blood that has been shed for Lithuania. The colors also symbolize traditional values, such as national pride and solidarity.

COAT OF ARMS/SEAL

The coat of arms is a red shield with the *Vytis* (the Chaser), a depiction of a white armor-clad night on horseback holding a silver sword with a gold hilt and a sky blue shield. The horse is white with sky blue trappings, saddle, and belts. The coat of arms is one of the oldest in Europe.

MOTTO

Tautos jéga vienybéje (Lithuanian); The strength of the nation lies in unity (English)

CAPITAL CITY

Vilnius

TYPE OF GOVERNMENT

Parliamentary republic

NATIONAL EMBLEM

Vytis (armor-clad white knight on horseback on a red field)

NATIONAL COLORS

Yellow, green, and red

NATIONAL ANTHEM

The anthem was first adopted by independent Lithuania in 1918 and was readopted at independence from the Soviet Union in 1991.

Tautiska Giesme (Lithuanian); The National Song (English)

Lithuania, our homeland
You're the land of heroes
From the past your sons
Are bailing strength

Let your children go
Only in the paths of virtue
Let them work for your benefit
And the good of people

Let the sun in Lithuania
Remove the darkness
Let both light and truth
Follow our steps

Let the love of Lithuania
Burn in our hearts
In the name of this Lithuania
Let the unity bloom

PATRON SAINT

Saint Casimir of Poland; Saint Cunegundes; Saint George; Saint John of Dukla; Saint John of Kanty

CURRENCY

Lithuanian iitas

INTERNET IDENTIFIER

.lt

VEHICLE IDENTIFICATION PLATES/ STICKERS

LT

PASSPORT

The passport cover has the name of the European Union and the name of the country in Lithuanian, the coat of arms, and the Lithuanian word for passport, *pasas.*

AIRLINE

Lithuanian Airlines LAL (flights suspended temporarily in January 2009)

NATIONAL FLOWER

Rue (herb of repentance)

NATIONAL TREE

Oak (unofficial)

NATIONAL ANIMAL

Horse (unofficial)

NATIONAL BIRD

Stork

NATIONAL STONE

Amber

NATIONAL RESOURCES

Natural resources include peat, arable land, and amber. A well-educated population and proximity to major European population centers in the European Union are major resources. The thriving tourist industry is based on the historic cities and monuments, the unique culture and the country's Soviet past.

FOODS

Lithuanian specialties include *skilandis,* smoked meat; *salti barsciai,* a special cold soup; *cepelinai,* dumplings made of grated potatoes stuffed with minced meat, considered the national dish; *vedarai,* potato sausage; *bulviniai blynai,* potato pancakes; *kugelis,* potato pudding; *koldunai,* dumplings; pierogi, dough shells stuffed with meat; and *blynai,* crepes filled with meat or vegetables.

SPORTS/SPORTS TEAMS

Basketball is the country's most popular sport, although association football (soccer) is also very popular. Lithuania national teams participate in many sports at an international level.

TEAM SPORTS

Badminton
Lithuania Badminton Team

Baseball
Lithuania Baseball Team; Lithuania Softball Team

Basketball
Lithuania Basketball Team; Lithuania Women's Basketball Team; Lithuania Wheelchair Basketball Team; Lithuania Under-21 Basketball Team; Lithuania Under-19 Basketball Team

Cricket
Lithuania Cricket Team

Football
Lithuania Football Team; Lithuania Women's Football Team; Lithuania Rugby Union Team; Lithuania Under-21 Football Team

Handball
Lithuania Handball Team; Lithuania Women's Handball Team

Hockey
Lithuania Ice Hockey Team; Lithuania Junior Ice Hockey Team; Lithuania Women's Ice Hockey Team; Lithuania Field Hockey Team

Racing
Lithuania Speedway Team

Tennis
Lithuania Davis Cup Team; Lithuania Fed Cup Team

Table Tennis
Lithuania Table Tennis Team

Volleyball
Lithuania Men's Volleyball Team; Lithuania Women's Volleyball Team; Lithuania Beach Volleyball Team

INDIVIDUAL SPORTS
Lithuania Amateur Boxing Team; Lithuania Archery Team; Lithuania Athletics Team; Lithuania Canoeing Team; Lithuania Cycling Team; Lithuania Equestrian Team; Lithuania Fencing Team; Lithuania Gymnastics Team; Lithuania Judo Team; Lithuania Karate Team: Lithuania Modern Pentathlon Team; Lithuania Rowing Team; Lithuania Sailing Team; Lithuania Shooting Team; Lithuania Swim Team; Lithuania Tae Kwon Do Team; Lithuania Triathlon Team; Lithuania Weight Lifting Team; Lithuania Wrestling Team

WINTER SPORTS
Lithuania Alpine Ski Team; Lithuania Bandy Team; Lithuania Biathlon Team; Lithuania Curling Team; Lithuania Ice Hockey Team; Lithuania Junior Ice Hockey Team; Lithuania Women's Ice Hockey Team; Lithuania Luge Team; Lithuania Skating Team

NATIONAL HEROES OR PERSONIFICATIONS
Mindaugas, the unifier of Lithuania and the first ruler; Vytautas the Great, a revered ruler of medieval Lithuania; Maironis, leader of the Lithuanian national revival in the late

19th and early 20th centuries; Jonas Basanavicius, leader of the national revival and signatory to the declaration of independence of 1918; Simonas Daukantas, initiator of the national rebirth in the early 19th century; Vincas Kudirka, a participant in the rebirth movement and the author of the national anthem

NATIONAL HOLIDAY/INDEPENDENCE DAY

Independence Day, February 16

FESTIVALS/FAIRS

Usgavenes Festival (Spring Festival), February; International Old World Music Festival, September; Vilnius Festival, July–August; Vocal Music Festival (Aria), September; International Festival of Dancesport, March; Kino Pavasaris (International Film Festival), May

SIGNIFICANT EVENTS IN FORMATION OF NATIONAL IDENTITY

2000 B.C.E. The Baltic tribes settle the region east of the Baltic Sea.

1009 C.E. Lithuania is first mentioned in European archives.

1236–1500 The Lithuanian lands are unified by Mindaugas, who becomes the ruler of the unified kingdom. By the end of the 14th century, Lithuania has become the largest country in Europe.

1385 Pressured by enemies, the country joins a union with neighboring Poland*, agreeing to accept Christianity for the Lithuanians.

1399 The Lithuanians lead a great European army against the Mongols and Turks of Tamerlane. The battle is inconclusive, but the invaders are so weakened that they withdraw from Europe.

1410 A great victory over invading Teutonic Knights leaves Lithuania the most powerful state in northeastern Europe.

1499–1569 War breaks out between the expanding Russians and the Polish-Lithuanian alliance and continues sporadically for over two decades. Poland and Lithuania formally unite in the Polish-Lithuanian Commonwealth.

1772–1831 The weakened commonwealth is dissolved in the partition of the state by Russia*, Prussia, and Austria*. Lithuania comes under the rule of czarist Russia. Serious Lithuanian uprisings against Russian rule occur in 1794 and 1830–31.

1850–1863 Under intense pressure to assimilate into Russian culture, the Lithuanians instead embrace Lithuanian nationalism. The abolition of serfdom frees many Lithuanians to join the Poles in the great rebellion of 1863. Restrictions on the language, printing, and the Catholic Church follow.

1915–1918 Germans occupy Lithuania when the First World War begins. Following the Russian Revolution in 1917, the Lithuanians organize and declare independence in 1918.

1918–1940 Poland takes control of Vilnius, so the Lithuanians make the second city, Kaunas, their capital. Territorial disputes with neighboring countries and the growing threat from Nazi Germany* disrupt the country in the 1930s.

1940 Soviet demands increase following the Soviet alliance with Nazi Germany. Soviet occupation ends with the annexation of Lithuania to the Soviet Union. Tens of thousands of Lithuanians are deported or executed before the Germans invade, and overrun Lithuania.

1944–1953 At the end of the war, the Soviets return, and thousands flee to displaced-persons camps across Europe. Deportations and the suppression of the Lithuanian culture begin again. From 1939 to 1945, Lithuania loses over 780,000 citizens to deportations, the war, and the Holocaust. The last of the thousands of resistance fighters is eliminated.

1955–1985 Lithuania languishes under Soviet rule. An underground nationalist movement is active, but nationalism is mostly kept alive among the large number of Lithuanians living outside the Soviet Union.

1987–1991 The Lithuanians organize as Soviet life is liberalized. Nationalist leaders proclaim the independence of Lithuania on March 11, 1990. The collapse of the Soviet Union in 1991 allows the country to reiterate its independence.

1991–2003 Lithuania begins to recover from decades of Soviet rule.

2004 The country is accepted as a full member of the North Atlantic Treaty Organization (NATO) and joins the European Union (EU), ensuring the future security of the republic.

2007–2009 The Lithuanian economy shows one of the fastest growth rates in the EU. The Russian enclave of Kaliningrad on Lithuania's western border is allowed a simplified transit system for Russians crossing Lithuania. The government bans displays of Soviet or Nazi symbols.

LUXEMBOURG

OFFICIAL NAME

Groussherzogtum Lëtzebuerg (Luxembourgish); Grand-Duché de Luxembourg (French); Grossherzogtum Luxemburg (German); Grand Duchy of Luxembourg (English)

INHABITANTS' NAME/NICKNAME

Luxembourger(s)

POPULATION

482,300 (2009e)

LANGUAGE/LANGUAGES

French, German, Luxembourgish (national language)

RELIGION/RELIGIONS

Roman Catholic, 87 percent; other or no religion

NATIONAL FLAG

The flag is a horizontal tricolor of red, white, and blue. The colors of the flag are derived from the coat of arms of the 13th century. The flag is very similar to that of the neighboring Netherlands*, but the shade of blue in the Luxembourg flag is lighter.

COAT OF ARMS/SEAL

The coat of arms has a central shield or crest of silver and blue stripes behind a red lion with a gold crown and tongue. Above the shield is a gold ducal crown, and at the sides, two golden lions support it. A red, ermined cape below another ducal crown encloses the arms.

MOTTO

Mir wëlle bleiwe wat mir sinn (Luxembourgish); We wish to remain what we are (English)

CAPITAL CITY

Luxembourg

TYPE OF GOVERNMENT

Parliamentary constitutional monarchy

NATIONAL EMBLEM

Red lion

NATIONAL COLORS

Red, white, and blue

NATIONAL ANTHEM

The country uses two anthems, the royal anthem and the national anthem that was adopted in 1864, below.

> **Ons Heemecht (Luxembourgish); Our Homeland (English)**
> Where the Alzette slowly flows,
> The Sura plays wild pranks,
> Where fragrant vineyards amply grow
> On the Mosella's banks;
> There lies the land for which we would
> Dare everything down here,
> Our own, our native land which ranks
> Deeply in our hearts.
> Our own, our native land which ranks
> Deeply in our hearts.
> O thou above whose powerful hand
> Makes states or lays them low,
> Protect this Luxembourger land

From foreign yoke and woe.
Your spirit of liberty bestow
On us now as of yore.
Let freedom's sun in glory glow
For now and evermore.
Let freedom's sun in glory glow
For now and evermore.

PATRON SAINT
Saint Willibrord

CURRENCY
Euro

INTERNET IDENTIFIER
.lu

VEHICLE IDENTIFICATION PLATES/ STICKERS
L

PASSPORT
The passport cover has the words *European Union* and the name of the country in French, the word *passport* in French, a large representation of the Luxembourg lion, a smaller depiction of the coat of arms, and the standard biometric symbol.

AIRLINE
Luxair

NATIONAL FLOWER
Rose (unofficial)

NATIONAL ANIMAL
Red lion (a mythical creature introduced to European heraldry from the Middle East and North Africa) (unofficial)

NATIONAL BIRD
Goldcrest (unofficial)

NATIONAL RESOURCES
Natural resources include iron ore (no longer exploited) and arable land. The country's well-educated population and its proximity to large European markets support a thriving financial and banking sector. Tourism is also an important resource.

FOODS
Luxembourg's national dishes reflect the influences of its larger neighbors: *carré de porc,* smoked pork with broad beans or sauerkraut; *cochon de lait en gelée,* jellied suckling pig; *jambon d'Ardennes,* famous smoked Ardennes ham; *gromprekichelcher,* spiced potato pancakes with chopped onion and parsley; *kachkéis,* cooked cheese, a soft cheese spread; and *quetschentart,* traditionally a plum tart, but also peach, cherry, or pear.

SPORTS/SPORTS TEAMS
Association football (soccer) is the most popular sport, although over 100,000 Luxembourgers belong to sports federations of all types.

TEAM SPORTS

Badminton
Luxembourg Badminton Team

Baseball
Luxembourg Baseball Team

Basketball
Luxembourg Basketball Team; Luxembourg Women's Basketball Team; Luxembourg Under-20 Basketball Team; Luxembourg Under-18 Basketball Team

Cricket
Luxembourg Cricket Team

Football
Luxembourg Football Team, nickname D'Roud Léiwen (the Red Lions); Luxembourg Women's Football Team; Luxembourg

Rugby Union Team, nickname Les Lions (the Lions); Luxembourg Women's Rugby Union Team, nickname Les Lions (the Lions); Luxembourg Under-21 Football Team; Luxembourg American Football Team

Handball

Luxembourg Handball Team; Luxembourg Women's Handball Team

Hockey

Luxembourg Ice Hockey Team; Luxembourg Junior Ice Hockey Team; Luxembourg Field Hockey Team

Korfball

Luxembourg Korfball Team

Racing

Luxembourg Speedway Team

Table Tennis

Luxembourg Table Tennis Team

Tennis

Luxembourg Fed Cup Team; Luxembourg Davis Cup Team

Volleyball

Luxembourg Men's Volleyball Team; Luxembourg Women's Volleyball Team; Luxembourg Men's Beach Volleyball Team; Luxembourg Women's Beach Volleyball Team

INDIVIDUAL SPORTS

Luxembourg Aikido Team; Luxembourg Amateur Boxing Team; Luxembourg Athletics Team; Luxembourg Archery Team; Luxembourg Canoeing Team; Luxembourg Cycling Team; Luxembourg Equestrian Team; Luxembourg Fencing Team; Luxembourg Gymnastics Team; Luxembourg Judo Team; Luxembourg Karate Team; Luxembourg Sailing Team; Luxembourg Shooting Team; Luxembourg Swim Team; Luxembourg Tae Kwon Do Team; Luxembourg Triathlon Team; Luxembourg Weight Lifting Team; Luxembourg Wrestling Team

WINTER SPORTS

Luxembourg Alpine Ski Team; Luxembourg Bobsleigh and Tobogganing Team; Luxembourg Curling Team; Luxembourg Ice Hockey Team; Luxembourg Junior Ice Hockey Team; Luxembourg Skating Team

NATIONAL HEROES OR PERSONIFICATIONS

Siegfried, Count of Ardennes, the founder of Luxembourg; Grand Duchess Charlotte, the ruler during World War II, became a symbol of national unity and whose broadcasts from London buoyed the unhappy Luxembourgers; William I, the first grand duke of Luxembourg in 1815.

NATIONAL HOLIDAY/INDEPENDENCE DAY

National Day, June 23

FESTIVALS/FAIRS

National Day celebrations, June; Schuebefouer, August; International Festival of Classical Music, June; International Theatre and Music Festival, July-August; Medieval Festival, August; Summer in the City, June-September; Zeltik Festival, March

SIGNIFICANT EVENTS IN FORMATION OF NATIONAL IDENTITY

600 B.C.E.–100 B.C.E.   Celtic peoples inhabit the region of present Luxembourg.

Fourth century C.E.–963 C.E.   Roman rule lasts until the fourth century C.E., when the region is overrun by Germanic tribes from the north and east. Christianity is introduced. The recorded history of Luxembourg begins with the acquisition of Luxembourg Castle by Siegfried, Count of Ardennes.

1437–1581   Luxembourg is sold to Philip the Good of Burgundy and later comes under Hapsburg rule as part of the Hapsburg Netherlands.

1581–1795 The territory of Luxembourg is divided between the Netherlands and the Hapsburg territories, which come under Spanish and then Austrian rule.

1794–1815 The French Revolution initiates a period of French rule that ends with the final defeat of Napoleon. Luxembourg remains divided, with the former Hapsburg territory established as the Grand Duchy of Luxembourg in personal union with the Netherlands.

1839–1867 Luxembourg loses additional territory. The Luxembourg Crisis of 1867, a diplomatic dispute between France* and Prussia over the status of Luxembourg, almost leads to war.

1890 A separate ruling house is established in the Grand Duchy, and the personal union under the Netherlands monarchy ends.

1940–1945 During the Second World War, the country is annexed to Germany* and the Luxembourgers are declared German citizens subject to conscription. Refusing to speak German, a passive resistance, and with French forbidden, many in wartime Luxembourg take up the Luxembourgish language, which leads to a post-war linguistic and cultural revival.

1949–1957 Neutrality, twice violated by invasions during both world wars, is abandoned, and Luxembourg becomes a founding member of the North Atlantic Treaty Organization (NATO) and joins the European Economic Community, later the EU.

1960–2000 The Luxembourgish language, a blend of Dutch, old German, and Frankish elements, becomes the primary language, although French remains the language of the civil service, law, and parliament and German is used for police cases and as the primary language of the press.

2000–2009 Luxembourgers enjoy a level of economic prosperity among the highest in Europe. The country is among the top three aid donors per capita in the world.

MACEDONIA

OFFICIAL NAME

Republika Makedonija (Macedonian); Republic of Macedonia (English)

The provisional designation used by the United Nations, the European Union, and the North Atlantic Treaty Organization is Former Yugoslav Republic of Macedonia (FYROM), due to Greece's objection to the name Macedonia, which is also used for the region of northern Greece that forms part of historic Macedonia.

POPULATION

2,101,500 (2009e)

INHABITANTS' NAME/NICKNAME

Macedonian(s)

LANGUAGE/LANGUAGES

Macedonian (official); Albanian (official in areas with at least 20% Albanian population); Turkish, Serbian, Romany, Aromanian, others

RELIGION/RELIGIONS

Macedonian Orthodox, 65 percent; Muslim, 33 percent; Macedonian Catholic, other or no religion

NATIONAL FLAG

The flag has a red field with a centered disk representing the sun and eight yellow rays extending from the disk to the edges of the red field. The red represents the blood spilled in the pursuit of independence, and the disk and rays represent the "new sun of liberty" mentioned in the Macedonian national anthem.

COAT OF ARMS/SEAL

The coat of arms is an oval with a mountain, lake, and sunrise depicted in the center, with garlands of wheat, tobacco, and poppy buds around the edge, representing the agriculture of the country, all held by a ribbon decorated with a traditional Macedonian design. Above the seal is a five-pointed red star, the symbol of communism.

MOTTO

Freedom or Death

CAPITAL CITY

Skopje

TYPE OF GOVERNMENT

Parliamentary republic

NATIONAL EMBLEM

Vergina sun, a stylized star with 16 rays

NATIONAL COLORS

Red and yellow

NATIONAL ANTHEM

The anthem was written and composed in 1943 and served as the anthem of the briefly independent Macedonian republic at the end of World War II. It was retained as the anthem of Macedonia as part of the Yugoslav federation and was selected as the anthem of independent Macedonia in 1991.

Denes nad Makedonija (Macedonian); Today over Macedonia (English)

Today over Macedonia,
the new sun of liberty rises.
The Macedonians fight,
for their own rights!
The Macedonians fight
for their own rights!

Now once again flies
the flag of the Krushevo Republic
Goce Delchev, Pitu Guli
Dame Gruev, Sandanski!
Goce Delchev, Pitu Guli
Dame Gruev, Sandanski!

The Macedonian forests sing
new songs and awakenings.
Macedonia is liberated
It lives in liberty!
Macedonia is liberated
It lives in liberty!

PATRON SAINT

Saint Clement of Ohrid

CURRENCY

Macedonian denar

INTERNET IDENTIFIER

.mk

VEHICLE IDENTIFICATION PLATES/STICKERS

MK

PASSPORT

The passport cover has the name of the country in Macedonian and English at the top and the word *passport*, in larger letters, in Macedonian and English.

AIRLINE

Macedonian Airlines MAT

NATIONAL FLOWER

Red poppy

NATIONAL TREE

Molika (Macedonian pine) (unofficial)

NATIONAL ANIMAL

Lion

NATIONAL RESOURCES

Natural resources include low-grade iron ore, copper, lead, zinc, chromite, manganese, nickel, tungsten, gold, silver, asbestos, gypsum, timber, and arable land. At independence in September 1991, Macedonia was the least developed of the Yugoslav republics. A Greek embargo over use of the name Macedonia and the 1991 flag hindered economic growth until 1996. The large Macedonian population outside the country is a valuable asset and a source of foreign currency and investment.

FOODS

National dishes include moussaka, eggplant and potatoes layered with minced meat and then baked; *gravce tavce,* a dish of beans and meat or sausages; *Ohrid* trout, fresh trout prepared with spices; kebab, skewered lamb cooked over charcoal; *kashkaval,* a local cheese; *pindzhur,* eggplant, tomatoes, and peppers cooked in a casserole; *sarma vo lozov list,* stewed pork and beef minced and wrapped in grape leaves; and *sutlijash,* a dessert rice pudding with cinnamon and toasted almonds.

SPORTS/SPORTS TEAMS

Association football (soccer) is the most popular sport. Basketball and handball are also quite popular. Macedonia national teams participate in many sports at an international level.

TEAM SPORTS

Badminton

Macedonia Badminton Team

Basketball

Macedonia Basketball Team: Macedonia Women's Basketball Team

Football

Macedonia Football Team, nickname, Crveni Lavovi (the Red Lions) or Crveno-Žolti (the Red-Yellows); Macedonia Women's Football Team, nickname Crveni Lavovi (the Red Lions) or Crveno-Žolti (the Red-Yellows); Macedonia Under-21 Football Team, nickname the Red Lions; Macedonia Futsal Team; Macedonia Women's Under-19 Football Team

Handball

Macedonia Handball Team; Macedonia Women's Handball Team; Macedonia Beach Handball Team; Macedonia Women's Beach Handball Team

Hockey

Macedonia Ice Hockey Team; Macedonia Field Hockey Team

Table Tennis

Macedonia Table Tennis Team

Tennis

Macedonia Davis Cup Team; Macedonia Fed Cup Team

Volleyball

Macedonia Men's Volleyball Team; Macedonia Women's Volleyball Team

INDIVIDUAL SPORTS

Macedonia Amateur Boxing Team; Macedonia Athletics Team; Macedonia Canoeing Team; Macedonia Cycling Team; Macedonia Equestrian Team; Macedonia Fencing Team; Macedonia Gymnastics Team; Macedonia Judo Team; Macedonia Karate Team; Macedonia Rowing Team; Macedonia Sailing Team; Macedonia Shooting Team; Macedonia Swim Team; Macedonia Tae Kwon Do Team; Macedonia Triathlon Team; Macedonia Wrestling Team

WINTER SPORTS

Macedonia Alpine Ski Team; Macedonia Biathlon Team; Macedonia Ice Hockey Team

NATIONAL HEROES OR PERSONIFICATIONS

Grigor Prichev, a noted 19th century writer; Krste Petkov Misirkov, a leader of the 19th century national movement and a collector of Macedonian folk songs; Goce Delchev, leader of the Macedonian national movement in the late 19th and early 20th centuries

NATIONAL HOLIDAY/INDEPENDENCE DAY

Independence Day, September 8; National Day (Day of the Republic), August 2

Festivals/Fairs

Ohrid Summer Festival, August; Struga Poetry Evenings (international poetry), March; Skopje Opera Evenings, May; International Cinematographers Film Festival, September–October; Skopje Jazz Festival, October

Significant Events in Formation of National Identity

336 B.C.E.–323 B.C.E. King Philip II unites the Macedonian kingdom. Philip's son, Alexander the Great, extends Macedonian power to a great empire encompassing the Balkans, Greece, Anatolia, and Persia and reaching into the Indian subcontinent and Central Asia.

146 B.C.E. Macedonia becomes a province of the Roman Empire divided into two parts, Macedonia Prima, in present northern Greece, and Macedonia Salutaris, the present Republic of Macedonia.

395 C.E. The Roman Empire splits into west and east, with the Greek Byzantine Empire centered on Constantinople, present Istanbul. Byzantine rule over Macedonia continues until the sixth century.

Sixth century Slavic tribes from the north overrun the region, assimilating some of the inhabitants but displacing many. The Byzantines attempt to incorporate the Slavs into Byzantine culture.

Eighth century–10th century Northern Macedonia becomes part of the Empire of Bulgaria*. Christianity is introduced, and the majority embraces the new religion.

14th century–15th century The Serbs take control of the Balkans. Macedonia remains part of the Empire of Serbia* until the Turkish Ottoman Empire conquers the Christian states of the Balkans.

1689–1800 The Macedonian Slavs rebel against harsh Turkish rule. The Albanians to the north and west often adopt the Turks' Islamic religion, opening a rift between them and the Orthodox Slavs, who have lost their ethnic identity. Instead, they consider themselves Bulgarians, Serbians, or Slavic-speaking Greeks.

1878 At the end of the Russo-Turkish War of 1878, a Bulgarian principality is created from Turkish territory in the Balkans, including most of present Macedonia.

1885 The idea of a separate Macedonian nationality arises from the conflict between Bulgaria, Greece, and Serbia over the Macedonian territories still under Turkish rule. The Macedonian Question becomes a serious European debate. A Macedonian national revival begins to spread across the region.

1897–1903 The Greco-Turkish War spurs the growth of Macedonian nationalism, led by Goce Delchev. The nationalists rebel and declare Macedonian independence, but a political compromise by the major European powers places the province back under Turkish rule.

1912–1913 The First and Second Balkan Wars are fought for control of Turkish territory in the Balkans, which is partitioned by the victors. Serbia annexes northern Vardar Macedonia, Greece takes Aegean Macedonia, and Bulgaria takes Pirin Macedonia.

1944–1946 The Germans occupy Serbia and other parts of Yugoslavia. The Macedonians declare Vardar Macedonia independent in 1944, but Macedonia becomes part of communist Yugoslavia in 1946.

1990–1991 The disintegration of Yugoslavia allows the Macedonians to declare the independence of the Republic of Macedonia. Greece objects to the use of the name, as it may represent claims on Aegean Macedonia. Tensions arise between the Macedonian Slavs and the large Albanian population in the republic.

1995–1996 The Greek government finally recognizes the country, but only under the name Former Yugoslav Republic of Macedonia. Greece's crippling trade and oil embargo is ended.

2001 The Albanians in the north and west rebel, setting off fighting with the Macedonian military. The North Atlantic Treaty Organization (NATO) intervenes, and an agreement is signed giving the Albanians greater rights.

2005 Macedonia is officially recognized as a European Union (EU) candidate under the name Former Yugoslav Republic of Macedonia.

2008 The NATO member states agree that Macedonia meets the criteria for membership, but an official invitation is not sent, due to Greece's continued objections to the name of the country.

2009 The Macedonian government applies to the International Court of Justice in the Hague for a ruling on its long-running dispute with Greece over the country's name.

MADEIRA

OFFICIAL NAME

Rigião Autónoma da Madeira (Portuguese); Madeira Autonomous Region (English)

POPULATION

244,400 (2009e)

INHABITANTS' NAME/NICKNAME

Madeiran(s)

LANGUAGE/LANGUAGES

Portuguese (official); Madeiran (the language of daily life), Spanish, English, others

RELIGION/RELIGIONS

Roman Catholic, 88 percent; Protestant, 4 percent; Muslim, other or no religion

NATIONAL FLAG

The flag has three equal vertical stripes of blue, gold, and blue with a red-bordered white Cross of Christ centered on the gold. Many people in the islands claim the flag, adopted in 1976, is based on the flag of the independence movement, which has the same three stripes but bears five blue shields, each with five white *guinas* (roundels), in the form of a centered cross.

COAT OF ARMS/SEAL

The coat of arms consists of a central shield or crest with the three stripes and the centered Cross of Christ of the flag. Above the shield is a gold crest that represents Portugal's Age of Discovery with Madeira the country's first overseas colony. Two Madeira monk seals support the shield. Below is a white banner with the national motto.

MOTTO

Das Ilhas, as Mais Belas e Livres (Portuguese); Of all Islands, the Most Beautiful and Free (English)

CAPITAL CITY

Funchal

TYPE OF GOVERNMENT

Parliamentary democracy as an autonomous region of Portugal*

NATIONAL EMBLEM

Red-bordered Cross of Christ

NATIONAL COLORS

Blue and yellow

NATIONAL ANTHEM

The official anthem is the Portuguese national anthem *A Portuguesa*. The anthem of Madeira is *Hino da Madeira,* which was officially adopted in 1980.

> **Hino de Madeira (Portuguese); Hymn of Madeira (English)**
>
> From the valley to the mountain and from the
>   sea to the highlands,
> Thy humble people, stoic and brave
> Amidst the hard stone plowed thine land,
> To cast, of the bread, the seed:
> Hero of the labor of the harsh mountain,
> Cast to the sea in enormous waves:
> The laurels of victory, in thy callous hands,
> Were the heritage bestowed to thine children.
> In this World beyond
> Madeira thy name continues
> In thy longing children
> That in distant lands
> Of thee are proud.

In this World beyond,
Madeira, we shall honor thy History
In the path of labor
We shall struggle
And achieve
Thine well being and glory.

PATRON SAINT

Saint Peter; Saint Mary, Mother of Jesus

CURRENCY

Euro

INTERNET IDENTIFIER

.pt Portugal (official)

VEHICLE IDENTIFICATION PLATES/STICKERS

P Portugal (official); MAD Madeira (unofficial)

PASSPORT

Madeirans are Portuguese citizens and travel on Portuguese passports.

NATIONAL FLOWER

Strelitzia (Bird of Paradise) (unofficial)

NATIONAL TREE

Dragon tree (unofficial)

NATIONAL ANIMAL

Monk seal

NATIONAL BIRD

Trocaz pidgeon (unofficial)

NATIONAL FISH

Gray Triggerfish (unofficial)

NATIONAL RESOURCES

Natural resources are limited. Madeira has arable land, but mostly relies on its island scenery, unique culture, and sandy beaches to support a flourishing tourist industry. Other islands products include tropical agricultural produce, the famous Madeira wines, and the traditional lace made by Madeiran women for many centuries.

FOODS

National dishes include *espada,* black scabbard fish served with banana; *espada de camarão,* scabbard fish with prawns and avocado; *bife de atum e milho frito,* fresh tuna steak served with another island specialty, fried corn (maize); *lulas,* squid served in many different ways; *caldeirada,* a fish soup with potatoes and local vegetables; *espetada,* skewered meat cooked over an open grill; *vinho e alho,* pickled pork cured in Madeira wine and garlic. *Gelaia de vinho Madeira,* is a desert made of Madeira wine, sugar, lemon, and gelatine, and *bolo de mel,* dark honey cake, are traditional desserts.

SPORTS/SPORTS TEAMS

Association football (soccer) is the most popular sport on the islands. Traditional sports such as swimming and sailing are also popular, as is handball, which is played throughout Madeira. Madeira national teams participate in football and handball at an international level.

TEAM SPORTS

Football

Madeira Football Team

Handball

Madeira Handball Team

NATIONAL HEROES OR PERSONIFICATIONS

The national personification is Autonomia, depicted as a young woman dressed in classical fashion. The personification was adopted when autonomy was granted in 1976.

João Gonçalves Zarco, Portuguese explorer who established the first settlements and was appointed the islands' first governor (captain); José Travassos Valdez, the governor who rallied the islands to hold out against a usurper to the Portuguese throne in the early 19th century; and Christopher Columbus (Cristóvão Colombo in Portuguese), the famed explorer married the governor of Porto Santo and lived for a time on the island.

NATIONAL HOLIDAY/INDEPENDENCE DAY

Madeira Day, July 1

FESTIVALS/FAIRS

Flower Festival (spring); Carnival, February-March; Porto Santo Columbus Marathon, March 1; National Day Festival, June-July; Funchal Festival, August; All Saints, October-November

SIGNIFICANT EVENTS IN FORMATION OF NATIONAL IDENTITY

1000 B.C.E.–400 C.E. The islands are known to the Romans as the Purple Islands, due to the frequent haze that surrounds them.

500 C.E.–1000 C.E. Knowledge of the islands is lost to all but legend during Europe's Dark Ages.

1351 The islands are depicted on an Italian map, possibly copied from much earlier Roman maps.

1418–1421 Portuguese explorer João Gonçalves Zarco sights Porto Santo after being blown off course while exploring the African coast. Colonists from mainland Portugal establish settlements on the islands, which become Portugal's first overseas colony.

1452–1755 The introduction of sugar cane requires large numbers of workers. Slaves captured or purchased in nearby Morocco* become the primary work force in the cane fields. The islands, lying on the trade routes between Europe, Africa, and the Americas, prosper as a way station. Vineyards begin producing wine for export to Europe. Agriculture and wine production decline rapidly following the abolition of slavery in 1755.

1850 Embroidery is introduced from England and becomes a major cottage industry employing thousands of Madeiran women.

1800–1920 Thousands of Madeirans leave the underdeveloped islands in search of a better life in the Americas and southern Africa. Some settle as far away as Hawaii, where they introduce a stringed musical instrument later known as the ukulele. Madeira becomes a fashionable resort for wealthy English travelers.

1950s–1960s Bananas for the European market replace sugar as the major agricultural product. Emigration continues to reduce Madeira's population by 2.5 to 3 percent each year.

1960–1974 Partly in response to the need to leave their beloved islands to find work, the Madeirans experience a cultural revival with new emphasis on their unique traditions and customs. The cultural revival evolves a strong nationalist streak. Nationalist organizations grow quickly following the leftist revolution in Portugal in 1974.

1975–1976 The leftist government in Lisbon grants independence to Portugal's remaining colonies, spurring the nationalist movement in Madeira to demand immediate independence for Portugal's first overseas colony. When a more moderate government comes to power in Portugal support for independence wanes. The new government, to placate nationalist demands, grants wide powers of self-government as an autonomous region.

1986–1990 Portugal's entry into the European Community aids the Madeiran economy, which receives European monetary subsidies. The slow loss of population begins to reverse as Madeirans return to their home islands.

1991–2000 During a heated debate over island finances, the governor of Madeira threatens to throw his government's support to the nationalists, who continue to work for the independence of Madeira and an end to what they call the region's semicolonial status. Funds from the European Union (EU) help to raise the living standards and to end Madeira's traditional isolation.

2000–2009 New Portuguese law makes advocating secession a grave offense. Nationalist organizations are banned although nationalism remains a potent force among the large Madeiran populations in Brazil* and South Africa*. Emigration again becomes necessary for young Madeirans looking for work. The population, which reached 253,000 in 1991, falls to under 245,000 in 2009.

See also Portugal

MALTA

OFFICIAL NAME
Repubblika ta' Malta (Maltese); Republic of Malta (English)

POPULATION
424,800 (2009e)

INHABITANTS' NAME/NICKNAME
Maltese

LANGUAGE/LANGUAGES
Maltese, English (official); Italian, others

RELIGION/RELIGIONS
Roman Catholic, 98 percent; others

NATIONAL FLAG
The flag is a vertical bicolor of white and red, with the George Cross, added in 1943, outlined in red on the white field at the upper hoist. Red and white are the traditional colors given the islanders by Count Roger of Sicily in 1091. The cross was awarded to the entire Maltese population for exceptional heroism during the Second World War.

COAT OF ARMS/SEAL
The coat of arms is a shield showing a heraldic representation of the national flag. Above the shield is a mural crown with eight turrets, although only five are visible, and a sally port centered, representing the fortifications of Malta. Around the shield are olive and palm branches, and below is a banner with the name of the country in Maltese.

CAPITAL CITY
Valletta

TYPE OF GOVERNMENT
Parliamentary republic

NATIONAL EMBLEM
Maltese cross

NATIONAL COLORS
Red and white

NATIONAL ANTHEM
The anthem was first performed in 1923, with lyrics by Dun Karm Psaila, Malta's national poet. It became the national anthem in 1945.

> **L'Innu Malti (Maltese); National Anthem of Malta (English)**
>
> This motherland so dear whose name we bear!
> Guard her, O Lord, as ever thou hast guarded!
> Keep her in mind, whom thou hast made so fair!
> May he who rules, for wisdom be regarded!
> In master mercy, strength in man increase!
> Confirm us all, in unity and peace!

PATRON SAINT
Saint Peter; Saint Paul the Apostle; Saint Agata; Saint George Preca, known as Dun Gorg, who was canonized in June 2007 as Malta's first official saint

CURRENCY
Euro

INTERNET IDENTIFIER
.mt

VEHICLE IDENTIFICATION PLATES/STICKERS
M

PASSPORT
The passport cover has the name of the European Union in Maltese, the short name of

the country, Malta, and the Maltese word for passport, *passaport*.

AIRLINE
Air Malta

NATIONAL FLOWER
Maltese rock centaury

NATIONAL TREE
Għargħar (tetraclinis); palm, olive (both unofficial)

NATIONAL ANIMAL
Kelb-tal Fenek dog (pharaoh hound); dolphin (unofficial)

NATIONAL BIRD
Blue rock thrush

NATIONAL FISH
Lampuka (dolphinfish) (unofficial)

NATIONAL RESOURCES
Natural resources include limestone, salt, and arable land, but the most important resources are the limestone quarries, a favorable geographic location, and a well-educated and productive population. Agriculture is limited by access to freshwater supplies. Tourism, supported by sandy beaches, a pleasant climate, historic cities and monuments, and a unique culture, is one of the thriving industries, along with banking and finance.

FOODS
Lampuki pie, a fish pastry made of dolphinfish; *fenek*, rabbit prepared in wine; *helwa tat-tork*, a dessert of crushed and whole almonds; *pastizzi*, pastries filled with cheese, egg, vegetables, meat, or fish; *bragoli*, parcels of mince, chopped eggs, breadcrumbs, and parsley wrapped in thin slices of beef and simmered in gravy; *ravjul*, raviolis stuffed with ricotta and parsley and served with a tomato sauce; and *aljotta*, fish soup with garlic, tomatoes, and rice, are all considered national dishes.

SPORTS/SPORTS TEAMS
Association football (soccer) is the most popular sport in Malta. Boccie, traditionally the country's national sport, and water polo are also very popular. Malta national teams participate in many sports at an international level.

TEAM SPORTS
Badminton
Malta Badminton Team

Baseball
Malta Baseball Team; Softball Team

Basketball
Malta Basketball Team

Cricket
Malta Cricket Team

Football
Malta Football Team, nickname Knights of Saint John; Malta Women's Football Team, nickname Ladies of Saint John; Malta Under-21 Football Team, nickname Knights of Saint John; Malta Rugby Union Team, nickname the Rams; Malta Rugby League Team, nickname the Knights; Malta Futsal Team

Handball
Malta Handball Team, nickname Il-Ħomor; Malta Women's Handball Team

Hockey
Malta Field Hockey Team

Netball
Malta Netball Team

Table Tennis
Malta Table Tennis Team

Tennis

Malta Davis Cup Team; Malta Fed Cup Team

Volleyball

Malta Men's Volleyball Team; Malta Women's Volleyball Team; Malta Fistball Team

INDIVIDUAL SPORTS

Malta Amateur Boxing Team; Malta Archery Team; Malta Athletics Team; Malta Canoeing Team; Malta Cycling Team; Malta Equestrian Team; Malta Fencing Team; Malta Gymnastics Team; Malta Judo Team; Malta Karate Team; Malta Modern Pentathlon Team; Malta Sailing Team; Malta Shooting Team; Malta Swim Team; Malta Tae Kwon Do Team; Malta Triathlon Team; Malta Weight Lifting Team; Malta Wrestling Team

NATIONAL HEROES OR PERSONIFICATIONS

Dun Mikiel Xerri, leader of a Maltese rebellion against oppressive French rule during the Napoleonic Wars; Dun Karm Psaila, Malta's national poet; Jean Parisot de la Valette, grand master of the Knights Hospitaller and defender of Malta during the Turkish siege in the 16th century, for whom Valetta is named; Dom Mintoff, nationalist politician and twice prime minister

NATIONAL HOLIDAY/INDEPENDENCE DAY

Independence Day, September 21

FESTIVALS/FAIRS

Malta International Airshow, September; Military Tatoo, November–December; Mediterranea Festival, October; Mnarja Festival, September; Maltese Carnival, February–March; Holy Week, February–March

SIGNIFICANT EVENTS IN FORMATION OF NATIONAL IDENTITY

3500 B.C.E.–2500 B.C.E. A Megalithic civilization builds temples and large freestanding structures in the islands.

700 B.C.E. Phoenicians colonize the islands, using them as an outpost for exploration and colonization of the Mediterranean.

400 B.C.E.–400 C.E. The most successful Phoenician colony, Carthage, takes control of the islands, but Carthage's rivalry with Rome leads to the destruction and Roman control of the islands in 218 B.C.E. Christianity is introduced.

870 Arabs from North Africa conquer the islands. Christians are tolerated, and citrus fruit and irrigation are introduced. The Arabs greatly influence the language of the Maltese, which is now a Semitic language with strong Latin influences written in the Latin alphabet.

1091–1283 The Normans of Sicily take the islands from the Arabs. Subsequent rulers include the Angevins, Hohenstaufens, and Aragonese, the last of whom creates the County of Malta in 1283.

1530–1565 Holy Roman Emperor Charles V of Spain* gives the islands to the Order of Knights of the Hospital of Saint John of Jerusalem, a military religious order now known as the Knights of Malta.. The knights withstand a long siege by the Turks in 1565, after which the islands are heavily fortified and the new city of Valetta is founded and named after Grand Master Jean de la Valette.

1798–1814 The rule of the knights ends with the capture of the islands by Napoleon during the expedition to Egypt*. The Maltese rebel and, with the help of a British fleet, defeat the French in 1800. British possession of Malta is formalized in 1814.

1930s Maltese and English become dual official languages, and the first grammar in Maltese is published in 1934.

1940–1947 The Maltese remain loyal to the United Kingdom* during the Second World War and sustain repeated heavy attacks by the Axis forces. Operation Pedestal Convoy arrives in Malta, saving the people of the island from starvation and surrender. For their bravery, the British monarch bestows the George Cross on the entire population.

1964–1980 Malta gains independence but remains part of the British Commonwealth. In 1974, Malta becomes a republic and, in 1980, declares neutrality during the Cold War. The last British troops leave the island in 1979.

1982–1988 Agatha Barbara becomes the third, and the first female, president of Malta. The first gathering of the Knights of Saint John in Malta since their departure in 1798 takes place in 1988.

2004–2008 Malta becomes a full member of the European Union (EU). On January 1, 2008, Malta, with a stable economy and support from other member states, adopts the European currency, the Euro.

2009 Europe's financial problems hurt Malta's financial sector and its burgeoning tourist industry.

MOLDOVA

OFFICIAL NAME
Republica Moldova (Moldovan); Republic of Moldova (English)

POPULATION
4,189,400 (2009e)

INHABITANTS' NAME/NICKNAME
Moldovan(s)

LANGUAGE/LANGUAGES
Moldovan (official); Russian, Ukrainian, Gagauz, others

RELIGION/RELIGIONS
Eastern Orthodox, 98 percent; Jewish, Protestant, other or no religion

NATIONAL FLAG
The flag is a vertical tricolor of blue, yellow, and red, with the national coat of arms centered on the yellow stripe. The colors and vertical design are taken from the flag of Romania*, which is ethnically and linguistically close to Moldova, and symbolize the two countries' common roots.

COAT OF ARMS/SEAL
The coat of arms has a central shield or crest divided horizontally, red over blue, charged with a stylized aurochs's head with an eight-pointed star between the horns and flanked by a five-petaled rose and a crescent, all in yellow. The shield is held by a golden eagle with a gold cross in its beak and holding a scepter and an olive branch. The aurochs represents the old province of Bessarabia.

MOTTO
Limba noastră-i o comoară (Moldovan); Our language is a treasure (English)

CAPITAL CITY
Chisinau

TYPE OF GOVERNMENT
Parliamentary republic

NATIONAL EMBLEM
Aurochs's head

NATIONAL COLORS
Red, yellow, and blue

NATIONAL ANTHEM
At independence in 1991, Moldova used the Romanian national anthem. A new anthem was adopted in 1994.

> **Limba Noastră (Moldovan); Our Language (English)**
>
> A treasure is our language that surges
> From deep shadows of the past,
> Chain of precious stones that scattered
> All over our ancient land.
>
> A burning flame is our language
> Amidst a people waking
> From a deathly sleep, no warning,
> Like the brave man of the stories.

Our language is the greenest leaf
Of the everlasting forests,
Gentle river Nistru's ripples
Hiding starlight bright and shining.

Our language is more than holy,
Words of homilies of old
Wept and sung perpetually
In the homesteads of our folks.

A treasure will spring up swiftly
From deep shadows of the past,
Chain of precious stones that scattered
All over our ancient land.

PATRON SAINT

Saint Paraskeva

CURRENCY

Moldovan leu

INTERNET IDENTIFIER

.md

VEHICLE IDENTIFICATION PLATES/ STICKERS

MD

PASSPORT

The passport cover has the name of the country in Moldovan, the coat of arms, and the Moldovan word for passport.

AIRLINE

Moldavian Airlines MDV

NATIONAL TREE

Oak

NATIONAL ANIMAL

Aurochs

NATIONAL BIRD

Golden eagle

NATIONAL RESOURCES

Natural resources include lignite, phosphorites, gypsum, arable land, and limestone.

The country has a favorable climate and good farmland but few minerals, so the economy depends heavily on agriculture. Remittances from Moldovans living outside the country are a major source of foreign currency and investment. Although the country has much to offer tourists, it remains relatively unknown.

FOODS

Sarmale, minced meat, rice, and vegetables wrapped in vine leaves or cabbage, is considered the national dish. *Borș,* a type of borscht made of fermented wheat bran, is also a national dish. Other specialties include *mititeyi,* small grilled sausages with onions and peppers; *mamaliga,* a thick maize pie that is served with feta cheese; *tocana,* pork stew often served with fruits or pickled melon; *ghiveci,* lamb stew; *sorpa,* a spicy soup made of lamb and vegetables from the Gagauz minority; and borscht, beet and beef soup. The national drink is white wine, as Moldova is a leading wine producer.

SPORTS/SPORTS TEAMS

Association football (soccer) and rugby union are the most popular sports. Moldova national teams participate in many sports at an international level.

TEAM SPORTS

Badminton

Moldova Badminton Team

Baseball

Moldova Baseball Team; Moldova Softball Team

Basketball

Moldova Basketball Team; Moldova Women's Basketball Team

Football

Moldova Football Team; Moldova Women's Football Team: Moldova Men's Under-19

Football Team: Moldova Women's Under-19 Football Team; Moldova Rugby Union Team; Moldova Futsal Team; Moldova Rugby League Team; Rugby Union Team (Sevens), nickname Moldova Sevens or Moldova 7s; Moldova Women's Rugby Union Team (Sevens), nickname Moldova Sevens or Moldova 7s; Moldova American Football Team

Handball
Moldova Handball Team

Hockey
Moldova Field Hockey Team

Table Tennis
Moldova Table Tennis Team

Tennis
Moldova Davis Cup Team; Moldova Fed Cup Team

Volleyball
Moldova Men's Volleyball Team; Moldova Women's Volleyball Team

INDIVIDUAL SPORTS
Moldova Amateur Boxing Team; Moldova Archery Team; Moldova Athletics Team; Moldova Canoeing Team; Moldova Cycling Team; Moldova Equestrian Team; Moldova Fencing Team; Moldova Gymnastics Team; Moldova Judo Team; Moldova Karate Team: Moldova Modern Pentathlon Team; Moldova Rowing Team; Moldova Sailing Team; Moldova Shooting Team; Moldova Swim Team; Moldova Tae Kwon Do Team; Moldova Triathlon Team; Moldova Weight Lifting Team; Moldova Wrestling Team

WINTER SPORTS
Moldova Alpine Ski Team; Moldova Biathlon Team; Moldova Luge Team

NATIONAL HEROES OR PERSONIFICATIONS
Prince Dimitrie Cantemir, the 18th century writer of the first geographic, ethnographic, and economic survey of the country; Stephen the Great, the medieval ruler of Moldavia, responsible for the consolidation of the state and the great flowering of medieval Moldovan culture; Ion Inculet, first and only president of independent Moldavia in 1917–1918; Mircea Snegur, the politician who led Moldova to independence in 1991 and was first president of the modern Moldovan republic; Petru Lucinshi, elected president in 1996 when he began to move the country politically closer to the European Union (EU); Vladimir Voronin, elected president in 2001 and 2005

NATIONAL HOLIDAY/INDEPENDENCE DAY
Independence Day, August 27

FESTIVALS/FAIRS
Festival Nufarul Alb (Water Lily), July-August; International Music Festival Faces of Friends, August; Wine Festival, October; Moldeco Fair, October-November; Moldagrotech Fair, October-November; Christmas Fair, December

SIGNIFICANT EVENTS IN FORMATION OF NATIONAL IDENTITY
107 C.E. The region, populated by a people known as the Getae, comes under the rule of the Roman Empire. Latin-speaking colonists settle the region, and the Roman culture and language become dominant.

250–270 Overrun by tribes from beyond Rome's borders, the Roman colonists withdraw south of the Danube River, leaving their Latin language as a legacy.

Seventh century The Slavic Bessi tribe settles the region during the Slav migrations and the area becomes known as Bessarabia. The territory forms part of the first great Slav state, Kievan Rus', in the ninth century, laying the basis of later Russian claims.

1242–1513 Invading Mongols ravage the region, which slowly recovers under the rule of Stephen the Great, who creates the first Moldavian state in 1369, covering modern Moldova, the Moldavia region of Rumania, and territory now in Ukraine. Ottoman Turkish rule begins in 1513.

1812–1818 Bessarabia comes under Russian rule. The overwhelmingly Romanian-speaking region is subjected to intense Russification, and the territory is opened to settlement by non-Romanians.

19th century The neighboring Romanians lay claim to the region on ethnic, linguistic, and historical grounds and promote Moldovan nationalism as an anti-Russian movement.

1900–1909 The Russian government seeks to channel unrest by enflaming the region's traditional anti-Semitism, leading to horrible pogroms, particularly the massacre in Chishinau's Jewish quarter in 1903. A widespread revolt begins in 1907 but is finally crushed in 1909.

1917–1918 The Russian Revolution leaves Moldova without an effective government. Nationalists proclaim the independence of the Moldavian Democratic Republic. Threatened by the advance of the Red Army, the legislature votes for union with Romania.

1918–1925 Moldova is virtually colonized by Romanian boyars, landlords given large estates by the Romanian government. The Soviets form a separate Moldovan autonomous state east of the Dniester with its capital at Tiraspol.

1940–1945 Soviet troops occupy Moldova, which is ceded to the Soviet Union by Romania. Thousands considered anticommunist, nationalist, or pro-Romanian are deported to labor camps in Siberia and Central Asia. The Romanians, with their German allies, retake the region in 1941, but at the end of World War II, it again comes under Soviet rule.

1945–1949 The Moldovan Soviet Socialist Republic, joined with the region east of the Dniester, becomes a member state of the Soviet Union. The Russian language is imposed, along with the Cyrillic alphabet for use with the Romanian language, called Moldovan by the Soviet authorities. Soviet policy is to separate the Moldovans from the Romanian language and culture. An estimated 800,000 Moldovans are deported between 1940 and 1949.

1964–1966 The Romanian government accuses the Soviet Union of manufacturing the Moldovan ethnic group out of a branch of the Romanian people.

1970s–1980s Soviet efforts to promote a separate Moldovan nationalism succeed too well, and nationalist sentiment spreads as a mass movement. Nationalism gains further support as the Soviet Union begins to lose power.

1990–1991 A nationalist government is formed, and thousands join demonstrations demanding use of the Latin alphabet and the replacement of Russian with Romanian, which alienates the heavily Slavic districts east of the Dniester. The Soviet Union collapses, and Moldova becomes independent under Mircea Snegur.

1991–1992 The Slavic majority east of the Dniester, fearing a Moldovan union with Romania, proclaims the independence of Transnistria*, and fighting breaks out between the Moldovans and the Russian 14th Army, still stationed in the region.

1993–2000 The Moldovan parliament narrowly defeats a proposal for union with Romania. Transnistria is given special status within Moldova but remains virtually independent.

2006 Serious economic problems lead to mass emigration of between 8 and 10 percent of the population from 1990 onward. Some units of the Russian 14th Army remain in Transnistria, where a referendum reaffirms the Slavs' desire to remain independent or to join Russia*.

2006–2009 Moldova remains one of the poorest countries in Europe, with a large debt, high unemployment, and many people continuing to leave to find work elsewhere.

MONACO

OFFICIAL NAME

Principauté de Monaco (French); Principality of Monaco (English)

POPULATION

32,700 (2009e)

INHABITANTS' NAME/NICKNAME

Monégasque; Monacan(s)

LANGUAGE/LANGUAGES

French (official); Italian, English, Monégasque, others

RELIGION/RELIGIONS

Roman Catholic, 90 percent; other or no religion

NATIONAL FLAG

The flag is a horizontal bicolor of red over white. The colors are derived from the heraldic colors of the House of Grimaldi, the ruling family of Monaco since 1297.

COAT OF ARMS/SEAL

The coat of arms has a central shield emblazoned in lozenges of red and white. The shield is supported by two monks holding swords, a reference to the conquest of Monaco in 1297, when Francois Grimaldi entered the city with soldiers dressed as monks who carried swords hidden under their cassocks. The green and gold jeweled collar around the shield represents the Order of Saint Charles. Above the shield are a prince's crown and a red ermined cape. Below the shield is the national motto in Latin.

MOTTO

Deo juvante (Latin); With God's Help (English)

CAPITAL CITY

Monaco

TYPE OF GOVERNMENT

Constitutional monarchy

NATIONAL EMBLEM

The casino in Monte Carlo

NATIONAL COLORS

Red and white

NATIONAL ANTHEM

The anthem was officially adopted in 1867, with new lyrics written in the Monégasque language in 1931.

> **A Marcia de Muneghu (Monégasque); The March of Monaco (English)**
>
> All the time, over our country,
> The same flag has been flying in the wind
> All the time, the colors red and white
> Have been the symbol of our liberty
> Great and small have always respected them.

PATRON SAINT

Sainte Dévote (Saint Devota or Donata)

CURRENCY

Euro; Monaco is not a member of the European Union, but it is very closely linked to it via a customs union with France*, and as such, the official currency is the euro. Monaco mints euro coins with special Monégasque features on the national side.

INTERNET IDENTIFIER

.mc

VEHICLE IDENTIFICATION PLATES/STICKERS

MC

PASSPORT

The passport cover has the name of the country in French, the coat of arms, and the French word for passport.

NATIONAL FLOWER

Carnation

NATIONAL RESOURCES

One of the country's main sources of income is tourism. Each year, millions of people visit the famed casino in Monte Carlo or stay in the principality for its scenery, culture, and pleasant climate. In 2001, a major new construction project extended the pier used by cruise ships in the main harbor. The principality has successfully diversified into financial services and small, high-value, non-polluting industries, such as cosmetics and precision instruments.

FOODS

National specialties include *barbagiuan,* a type of pastry filled with rice and pumpkin; *socca,* pancakes or crepes made of chickpea flour; *fougasse,* orange flower–water pastries decorated with nuts and aniseed; *stocafi,* salt cod cooked in tomato sauce; *gratin de fruits de mer,* a seafood dish; *tomates à la monégasque,* stuffed tomatoes; and *soupe au pistou,* a soup of vegetables and spices.

SPORTS/SPORTS TEAMS

Association football (soccer) is the most popular sport. Racing is also very popular. Monaco national teams participate in many sports at an international level.

TEAM SPORTS

Basketball

Monaco Basketball Team; Monaco Women's Basketball Team

Football

Monaco Football Team; Monaco Rugby Union Team

Hockey

Monaco Field Hockey Team

Racing

Monaco Speedway Team

Table Tennis

Monaco Table Tennis Team

Tennis

Monaco Davis Cup Team

Volleyball

Monaco Men's Volleyball Team; Monaco Women's Volleyball Team

INDIVIDUAL SPORTS

Monaco Aikido Team; Monaco Amateur Boxing Team; Monaco Archery Team; Monaco Athletics Team; Monaco Cycling Team; Monaco Equestrian Team; Monaco Fencing Team; Monaco Gymnastics Team; Monaco Judo Team; Monaco Karate Team; Monaco Modern Pentathlon Team; Monaco Rowing Team; Monaco Sailing Team; Monaco Shooting Team; Monaco Swim Team; Monaco Tae Kwon Do Team; Monaco Triathlon Team; Monaco Weight Lifting Team

WINTER SPORTS

Monaco Alpine Ski Team; Monaco Biathlon Team; Monaco Skating Team

NATIONAL HEROES OR PERSONIFICATIONS

François Grimaldi, first Grimaldi ruler of Monaco in 1297; Honoré II, first Prince of Monaco in the 17th century; Grace Kelly, an American film and stage actress and Princess of Monaco; Prince Rainier III, former ruler of Monaco

NATIONAL HOLIDAY/INDEPENDENCE DAY

National Day (Saint Rainier's Day), November 19, also known as Prince Rainier Day or Monaco National Festival

FESTIVALS/FAIRS

Monaco Grand Prix

SIGNIFICANT EVENTS IN FORMATION OF NATIONAL IDENTITY

Sixth century B.C.E.   The Greeks refer to the local Ligurians as Monoikos, a name that becomes associated with the fortresslike Rock of Monaco.

1215–1228 C.E.   The Genoese establish a colony on the site.

1297   François Grimaldi and his men capture the fortress disguised as monks. The Grimaldis establish the line of lords of Monaco.

1614–1662   Honoré II is the first ruler to be recognized as the sovereign Prince of Monaco. An alliance with France puts Monaco under French protection.

1793–1814   During the Napoleonic Wars, the principality is incorporated into France.

At the end of the Napoleonic Wars, Monaco becomes a protectorate for the Kingdom of Sardinia*.

1860–1861   The Italians cede the surrounding territory, including Nice, to France. Unrest in Menton and Roquebrune leads to the cession of the towns to France. The two towns, comprising 95 percent of Monaco's total area, become part of France in return for a payment of 4 million francs and a treaty recognizing Monaco's sovereignty.

1911–1918   A new constitution limits the powers of the ruling princes. At the end of the First World War, as part of the Treaty of Versailles, Monaco's international policy is aligned with French political, military, and economic interests.

1943–1949   The Italians, and then the Germans, occupy Monaco. The principality's Jewish citizens are deported, including René Blum, the creator of the famed Monte Carlo ballet, who would die in Auschwitz. Prince Rainier III becomes Prince of Monaco.

1956   Prince Rainier marries Grace Kelly, an American film and stage actress, bringing world attention to the tiny principality.

1962   A new constitution extends the vote to women and abolishes capital punishment.

1993   Monaco becomes a voting member of the United Nations.

2002   A new treaty between Monaco and France clarifies that even if there are no heirs to carry on the Grimaldi dynasty, the principality will remain an independent nation rather than revert to France, which retains responsibility for the principality's defense.

2005   Prince Rainier III dies and is succeeded by his son, Prince Albert II.

2007–2009   Monaco remains on a European list of uncooperative tax havens, due to the secrecy laws of its important banking and financial industry. The government announces that it is canceling plans to expand into the Mediterranean Sea through land reclamation, citing the international financial crisis and growing environmental concerns.

MONTENEGRO

OFFICIAL NAME

Crna Gora (Montenegrin); Montenegro (English)

POPULATION

678,800 (2009e)

INHABITANTS' NAME/NICKNAME

Montenegrin(s)

LANGUAGE/LANGUAGES

Montenegrin (official); Serbian, Bosnian, Albanian, Croatian, others

RELIGION/RELIGIONS

Orthodox Christian, 74 percent; Sunni Muslim, 17 percent; Roman Catholic, 3.5 percent; other or no religion

NATIONAL FLAG

The flag is a red field edged in gold bearing the coat of arms, a golden two-headed eagle, centered. The flag is designed after the historic flags of Montenegro.

COAT OF ARMS/SEAL

The coat of arms has a small centered shield of blue over green charged with a golden lion.

Supporting the shield is a golden two-headed eagle in flight below a golden crown. The eagle holds a scepter in one claw and an orb in the other. The eagle is the oldest symbol of Montenegro, dating from the 15th century.

MOTTO
Čojstvo i junaštvo (Montenegrin); Humanity and Bravery (English) (unofficial)

CAPITAL CITY
Podgorica

TYPE OF GOVERNMENT
Semipresidential republic

NATIONAL EMBLEM
Montenegrin eagle

NATIONAL COLORS
Red and gold

NATIONAL ANTHEM
The anthem was adopted in 2004, while Montenegro was still part of a federation with Serbia*. The song is a traditional folk song.

Oj, svijetla majska zoro (Montenegrin); Oh, Bright Dawn of May (English)

Oh, bright dawn of May
Our mother Montenegro
We are sons of your rocks
And keepers of your honesty

We love you, the rocky hills
And your awesome gorges
That never came to know
The chains of shameful slavery.

While our unity gives wings
To our Lovćen cause
Proud shall be, celebrated will be
Our dear homeland.

A river of our waves,
Jumping into two seas,
Will bear voice to the ocean,
That Montenegro is eternal.

PATRON SAINT
Saint George

CURRENCY
Euro

INTERNET IDENTIFIER
.me

VEHICLE IDENTIFICATION PLATES/STICKERS
MNE

PASSPORT
The passport cover has the name of the country in Montenegrin and English, the coat of arms, and the word *passport* in Montenegrin and English.

AIRLINE
Montenegro Airlines

NATIONAL ANIMAL
Lion (a mythical creature introduced to European heraldry from the Middle East and North Africa)

NATIONAL BIRD
Falcon; golden eagle

NATIONAL RESOURCES
National resources are limited, except for bauxite and hydroelectricity.

A large aluminum complex, the country's largest, has been privatized, and other industries are beginning. Tourism, supported by sandy beaches on the Adriatic Sea, a pleasant climate, mountain scenery, historic cities, and a unique culture, is becoming one of the most important resources. Remittances from Montenegrins living outside the country are an important source of foreign currency and investment.

FOODS

Popular dishes include *sarma,* minced meat and rice rolled into grape or cabbage leaves; *musaka,* eggplant, cheese, and minced meat layered and baked; *pilav,* a dish of rice with vegetables, meat, or fish; *meza,* a variety of appetizers; *corba od crnjaka,* black onion chowder; *kuvani brav,* a stew of lamb and vegetables; *japraci,* minced meat and rice wrapped in collard greens; and *kacamak,* polenta served with fresh salted cream.

SPORTS/SPORTS TEAMS

Association football (soccer) and basketball are the most popular sports. Montenegro national teams participate in many sports at an international level.

TEAM SPORTS

Badminton

Montenegro Badminton Team

Basketball

Montenegro Basketball Team; Montenegro Women's Basketball Team

Football

Montenegro Football Team, nickname Hrabri Sokoli (the Brave Falcons); Montenegro Women's Football Team, nickname Hrabri Sokoli (the Brave Falcons); Montenegro Under-21 Football Team, nickname Hrabri Sokoli (the Brave Falcons); Montenegro Under-19 Football Team, nickname Hrabri Sokoli (the Brave Falcons); Montenegro Under-17 Football Team, nickname Hrabri Sokoli (the Brave Falcons); Montenegro Futsal Team

Handball

Montenegro Handball Team; Montenegro Women's Handball Team

Hockey

Montenegro Field Hockey Team

Racing

Montenegro Speedway Team

Table Tennis

Montenegro Table Tennis Team

Tennis

Montenegro Davis Cup Team; Montenegro Fed Cup Team

Volleyball

Montenegro Men's Volleyball Team; Montenegro Women's Volleyball Team

Water Polo

Montenegro Men's Water Polo Team

INDIVIDUAL SPORTS

Montenegro Aikido Team; Montenegro Amateur Boxing Team; Montenegro Archery Team; Montenegro Athletics Team; Montenegro Canoeing Team; Montenegro Cycling Team; Montenegro Judo Team; Montenegro Karate Team: Montenegro Modern Pentathlon Team; Montenegro Shooting Team; Montenegro Tae Kwon Do Team; Montenegro Wrestling Team

WINTER SPORTS

Montenegro Alpine Ski Team; Montenegro Ice Hockey Team: Montenegro Luge Team

NATIONAL HEROES OR PERSONIFICATIONS

Danilo Petrovic Njegos, the founder of the Petrovic Njegos dynasty in the 18th century; Sava Petrovic Njegos, the ruler who fought to maintain Orthodox Christianity against the might of the Ottoman Turks; Petar II Petrovic Njegos, the 19th-century ruler considered the father of modern Montenegro identity; Milo Dukanovic, the politician who led Montenegro to independence in 1006

NATIONAL HOLIDAY/INDEPENDENCE DAY

Statehood Day, July 13; Independence Day, May 21

FESTIVALS/FAIRS

Vrela zima u brdima (Hot Winter in the Hills), February; Dan Svetog Tripuna, February; Mimosa Festival, February; Herceg Novi Theater Festival, April; Montenegro Fair, April; Budva Music Festival, June; International Fashion Fair, July; Mountain Flower Festival, July; Summer Carnival, August; Cetinje Biennale, August

SIGNIFICANT EVENTS IN FORMATION OF NATIONAL IDENTITY

300 B.C.E.–9 C.E.   Illyrian tribes occupy the region, which comes under Roman rule in 9 C.E.

Sixth century–seventh century C.E.   Slavs settle the region as part of the great Slav migrations. A small Slav state, known as Duklja, comes under the influence of the Byzantine Empire and the early Serbian states.

11th century–12th century   Duklja becomes fully independent under local dynasties until its conquest and incorporation into the medieval Serbian state of Raska. Venetians, in control of the coast, call the region Monte Negro, "Black Mountain," or Crna Gora in the local Slavic dialect.

1355   The Serbian Empire collapses, leaving the region, now known as Zeta, virtually independent. Turks of the Ottoman Empire conquer most of the Balkans, but the tiny state defeats Turkish attacks and remains independent. The Montenegrins develop a warrior society, with a culture distinct from that of Turkish-dominated Serbia.

1515   The Petrovich dynasty is established as both secular and religious leaders. Orthodox Christianity becomes the state religion.

1702–1703   During the reign of Prince-Bishop Danilo I, religious conflicts break out, leading to the Montenegrin Vespers, the massacre of converts to Islam by their Orthodox countrymen.

Danilo establishes a close alliance with Russia* that continues until the Russian Revolution.

1796–1799   The Montenegrins, with Russian help, defeat the invading Turks. Montenegro is recognized as an independent state by the Ottoman Empire.

1852–1878   Montenegro remains a theocracy until secular and religious duties are separated under Danilo II. In 1878, Montenegro is recognized as an independent state at the Congress of Berlin.

1910–1918   The principality becomes a kingdom under Nicholas I. The kingdom is overthrown by pro-Serbian groups, and Montenegro is integrated into the new kingdom later known as Yugoslavia.

1946   At the end of the Second World War, Montenegro becomes the smallest and poorest of the six republics of the communist Yugoslav federation.

1966–1967   A campaign to separate the historic Montenegrin Orthodox Church from the official Serbian church stimulates a rebirth of national sentiment.

1989–1991   The collapse of communism in Yugoslavia begins the disintegration of the federation. In free elections, pro-Serbian groups win, and Montenegro remains in a union with Serbia as the other Yugoslav republics become independent states.

1998–1999   The strident nationalist government of Serbia alienates many Montenegrins, stimulating new calls for independence. Serbia warns that Montenegro will not be allowed to leave peacefully.

2000   Pro-Western political parties win a majority.

2006–2008   A referendum shows that a majority favors independence, which is declared. A new, more moderate government in Serbia recognizes the new state. The government of Montenegro then recognizes the independence of Kosovo*, prompting protests from Serbia.

NETHERLANDS

OFFICIAL NAME

Koninkrijk der Nederlanden (Dutch); Kingdom of the Netherlands (English)

POPULATION

16,457,800 (2009e)

INHABITANTS' NAME/NICKNAME

Dutch

LANGUAGE/LANGUAGES

Dutch (official); West Frisian, Low Saxon (Nedersaksisch) (official regional languages); Limburgish, English, German, French, others

RELIGION/RELIGIONS

The Netherlands is highly secular, with 41 percent professing no religion: Roman Catholic, 31 percent; Dutch Reformed, 13 percent; Calvinist, 7 percent; Muslim, 6 percent; Hindu, other or no religion

NATIONAL FLAG

The flag is a horizontal tricolor of red, white, and blue. The original colors of the flag were orange, white, and blue, the colors of the Prince of Orange, who led the rebellion against Spanish rule in the 16th century. The orange dye proved unstable and often turned red with age, however, so the color red was adopted.

COAT OF ARMS/SEAL

The coat of arms has a central crest or shield with a blue field bearing a gold lion holding a sword and seven arrows, representing the original seven provinces of the Union of Utrecht. The shield is crowned with the Dutch royal crown above a crimson ermined cape. Two golden lions support the shield. Below the shield is a blue banner inscribed with the national motto in medieval French.

MOTTO

Je maintiendrai (Medieval French motto of Prince William of Orange); *Ik zal handhaven* (Dutch); I Shall Stand Fast, or I Shall Endure (English)

CAPITAL CITY

Amsterdam; the seat of government is The Hague

TYPE OF GOVERNMENT

Parliamentary constitutional monarchy

NATIONAL EMBLEM

Tulips; the color orange

NATIONAL COLORS

Orange, white, and blue

NATIONAL ANTHEM

The anthem is based on a rebel song written during the war for independence from Spain in the 16th century. It was adopted as the national anthem in 1932.

Het Wilhelmus, or Wilhelmus van Nassouwe (Dutch); The William, or William of Nassau (English)

William of Nassau, scion
Of an old Germanic line,
Dedicate undying
Faith to this land of mine.
A prince I am, undaunted,
Of Orange, ever free,
To the king of Spain I've granted
A lifelong loyalty.

I've ever tried to live in
The fear of God's command
And therefore I've been driven,
From people, home, and land,
But God, I trust, will rate me
His willing instrument
And one day reinstate me
Into my government.

Let no despair betray you,
My subjects true and good.

The Lord will surely stay you
Though now you are pursued.
He who would live devoutly
Must pray God day and night
To throw his power about me
As champion of your right.

Life and my all for others
I sacrificed, for you!
And my illustrious brothers
Proved their devotion too.
Count Adolf, more's the pity,
Fell in the Frisian fray,
And in the eternal city
Awaits the judgment day.

I, nobly born, descended
From an imperial stock.
An empire's prince, defended
Braving the battle's shock
Heroically and fearless
As pious Christian ought
With my life's blood the peerless
Gospel of God our Lord.

A shield and my reliance,
O God, thou ever wert.
I'll trust unto thy guidance.
O leave me not ungirt.
That I may stay a pious
Servant of thine for aye
And drive the plagues that try us
And tyranny away.

My God, I pray thee, save me
From all who do pursue
And threaten to enslave me,
Thy trusted servant true.
O Father, do not sanction
Their wicked, foul design,
Don't let them wash their hands in
This guiltless blood of mine.

O David, thou soughtest shelter
From King Saul's tyranny.
Even so I fled this welter
And many a lord with me.
But God the Lord did save me
From exile and its hell
And, in his mercy, gave him
A realm in Israel.

Fear not 't will rain sans ceasing
The clouds are bound to part.
I bide that sight so pleasing
Unto my princely heart,
Which is that I with honor
Encounter death in war,
And meet in heaven my Donor,
His faithful warrior.

Nothing so moves my pity
As seeing through these lands,
Field, village, town and city
Pillaged by roving hands.
O that the Spaniards rape thee,
My Netherlands so sweet,
The thought of that does grip me
Causing my heart to bleed.

Astride on steed of mettle
I've waited with my host
The tyrant's call to battle,
Who durst not do his boast.
For, near Maastricht ensconced,
He feared the force I wield.
My horsemen saw one bounce it
Bravely across the field.

Surely, if God had willed it,
When that fierce tempest blew,
My power would have stilled it,
Or turned its blast from you
But he who dwells in heaven,
Whence all our blessings flow,
For which aye praise be given,
Did not desire it so.

Steadfast my heart remaineth
In my adversity
My princely courage straineth
All nerves to live and be.
I've prayed the Lord my Master
With fervid heart and tense
To save me from disaster
And prove my innocence.

Alas! my flock. To sever
Is hard on us. Farewell.
Your Shepherd wakes, wherever
Dispersed you may dwell,
Pray God that he may ease you.
His Gospel be your cure.

Walk in the steps of Jesu
This life will not endure.

Unto the Lord his power
I do not confession make
That ne'er at any hour
Ill of the King I spake.
But unto God, the greatest
Of majesties I owe
Obedience first and latest,
For justice wills it so.

PATRON SAINT

Saint Bavo; Saint Plechelm; Saint Willibrord

CURRENCY

Euro

INTERNET IDENTIFIER

.nl

VEHICLE IDENTIFICATION PLATES/ STICKERS

NL

PASSPORT

The passport cover has the name of the European Union and the name of the country in Dutch, the word passport in Dutch, *paspoort,* the coat of arms, and the standard biometric symbol.

AIRLINES

KLM Royal Dutch Airlines; Martinair; Arkefly

NATIONAL FLOWER

Tulip (unofficial)

NATIONAL TREE

Elm (unofficial)

NATIONAL ANIMAL

Lion (on the coat of arms)

NATIONAL RESOURCES

Natural resources include salt, natural gas, petroleum, peat, limestone, sand and gravel, and arable land. The natural gas field in the north of the country is one of the largest in the world. The country's geographic situation near the major population centers of western Europe and its ports connected to the major rivers into central Europe are major resources. Tourism, based on the country's unique culture, historic cities, and varied scenery, is one of the most important industries.

FOODS

Stampot, potatoes mashed with other vegetables, such as sauerkraut, endive, or kale and onion, often served with bacon, and *hutspot,* mashed potatoes mixed with carrots and onions, are considered the national dishes. Other specialties include *bruine bonen soep,* brown pea soup; *broodjes,* Dutch sandwiches; *poffertjes,* pancakes served with butter and sugar; *matjes,* salted herring; *bitterballen,* deep fried meatballs; *hete bliksem,* boiled potatoes and green apples, served with syrup or diced speck; and *balkenbrij,* a type of liver meatloaf.

SPORTS/SPORTS TEAMS

Association football (soccer) and basketball are the popular sports. Netherlands national teams participate in many sports at an international level.

TEAM SPORTS

Badminton

Netherlands Badminton Team

Baseball

Netherlands Baseball Team; Netherlands Softball Team; Netherlands Women's Softball Team

Basketball

Netherlands Basketball Team; Netherlands Women's Basketball Team; Netherlands Wheelchair Basketball Team; Netherlands Women's Wheelchair Basketball Team

Cricket

Netherlands Cricket Team; Netherlands Women's Cricket Team

Football

Netherlands Football Team, nicknames Oranje, Clockwork Orange, Orange Crush, the Orangemen; Netherlands Women's Football Team, nickname Oranje; Netherlands Rugby Union Team; Netherlands Women's Rugby Union Team; Netherlands Rugby League Team; Netherlands Under-21 Football Team, nickname Jong Oranje (Young Orange); Netherlands Women's Under-19 Football Team; Netherlands Futsal Team; Netherlands Australian-Rules Football Team, nickname de Vliegende Hollanders (the Flying Dutchmen); Netherlands Wheelchair Rugby Team; Netherlands American Football Team; Netherlands Beach Soccer Team; Netherlands Rugby Union Team (Sevens), nickname Netherlands Sevens or Netherlands 7s; Netherlands Women's Rugby Union Team (Sevens), nickname Netherlands Sevens or Netherlands 7s

Golf

Netherlands Men's Pitch and Putt Team; Netherlands Women's Pitch and Putt Team

Handball

Netherlands Handball Team; Netherlands Women's Handball Team

Hockey

Netherlands Field Hockey Team; Netherlands Women's Field Hockey Team; Netherlands Ice Hockey Team; Netherlands Junior Ice Hockey Team; Netherlands Women's Ice Hockey Team

Korfball

Netherlands Korfball Team

Racing

A1 Team The Netherlands; Netherlands Speedway Team

Table Tennis

Netherlands Table Tennis Team

Tennis

Netherlands Davis Cup Team; Netherlands Fed Cup Team

Volleyball

Netherlands Men's Volleyball Team; Netherlands Women's Volleyball Team; Netherlands Men's Beach Volleyball Team; Netherlands Women's Beach Volleyball Team

Water Polo

Netherlands Men's Water Polo Team; Netherlands Women's Water Polo Team

INDIVIDUAL SPORTS

Netherlands Aikido Team; Netherlands Amateur Boxing Team; Netherlands Archery Team; Netherlands Athletics Team; Netherlands Canoeing Team; Netherlands Cycling Team; Netherlands Equestrian Team; Netherlands Fencing Team; Netherlands Gymnastics Team; Netherlands Judo Team; Netherlands Karate Team: Netherlands Modern Pentathlon Team; Netherlands Rowing Team; Netherlands Sailing Team; Netherlands Shooting Team; Netherlands Swim Team; Netherlands Tae Kwon Do Team; Netherlands Triathlon Team; Netherlands Weight Lifting Team; Netherlands Wrestling Team

WINTER SPORTS

Netherlands Alpine Ski Team; Netherlands Bandy Team: Netherlands Biathlon Team; Netherlands Bobsleigh and Tobogganing Team; Netherlands Curling Team; Netherlands Ice Hockey Team; Netherlands Junior Ice Hockey Team; Netherlands Women's Ice Hockey Team; Netherlands Luge Team; Netherlands Skating Team

NATIONAL HEROES OR PERSONIFICATIONS

Hans Brinker, a fictional character from the novel of the same name, is known outside the Netherlands as the personification of the Dutch culture. Jan Modaal or Jan *met de pet* (average Joe) is another personification of the average Dutch citizen.

National heroes include William I, Prince of Orange, the leader of the Dutch rebellion against Spanish rule in the 16th century; Philip de Montmorency, leader of the Dutch revolt in the 16th century; and Ann Frank, a Jewish Dutch Holocaust victim; Queen Juliana, the ruler during World War II who maintained a government-in-exile in London and broadcast messages of hope to the Dutch population under German occupation

NATIONAL HOLIDAY/INDEPENDENCE DAY

Queen's Birthday, April 30

FESTIVALS/FAIRS

Carnival, February–March; Spring Flower Show, March–May; Bloemencorso, April; Queen's Birthday celebrations, April; Art Amsterdam, May; Holland Arts Festival, May–June; North Sea Jazz Festival, July; Prinsengracht Canal Festival, August; Jordaan Festival, September

SIGNIFICANT EVENTS IN FORMATION OF NATIONAL IDENTITY

First century C.E. Parts of the region south of the Rhine are included in the Roman province of Gallia Belgica.

Fifth century The Salian Franks migrate to the region following the collapse of Roman authority.

12th century–15th century The Low Countries, roughly the present-day Netherlands, Belgium*, and Luxembourg*, are divided into various counties, duchies, and dioceses. The Dutch begin a golden age of art, literature, and music.

1477–1506 The 17 provinces of the Low Countries come under the rule of the Hapsburgs of Austria* and later of Spain*.

1511–1555 Dutch expeditions reach the East Indies, bringing the spice trade under Dutch control over the next century. The Protestant Reformation causes a religious upheaval as many in the Low Countries convert.

1578–1600 The northern provinces of the Low Countries embrace Calvinism. Roman Catholic public worship is outlawed and churches are confiscated. The seven northern provinces unite in the United Provinces, which is declared independent of Spain, setting off the Dutch Rebellion and a long war of independence.

17th century The Dutch East India Company is formed and becomes a powerful force in the Netherlands' new golden age of discovery, exploration, and trade. Henry Hudson visits the island he calls Manhattan. The Eighty Years' War with Spain ends in 1648.

1782 The Netherlands is the first country to officially recognize the new United States*.

1814 The Netherlands becomes a constitutional monarchy under Willem I of the House of Orange-Nassau.

1830 The largely Roman Catholic southern provinces rebel to become the Kingdom of Belgium.

1917 Despite official Dutch neutrality, the country is occupied by German troops during the First World War.

1930s The Enclosure Dike at the head of the Zuiderzee is completed, transforming the open sea into the Ijsselmeer and bringing more land into cultivation. The land below sea level and protected by dikes becomes about 65 percent of the country's total land area.

1940–1945 Nazi Germany* invades the Netherlands, which surrenders following the near-total destruction of the port of Rotterdam by Nazi bombers. Over 100,000 Jews are deported, including Ann Frank.

1948 The Benelux customs union with Belgium and Luxembourg takes effect, setting the stage for the eventual European Union.

1949–1980 Indonesia* becomes independent, and most of the other territories of the extensive Dutch Empire soon follow. The Netherlands joins the European Community as a founding member in 1958.

2001 The world's first same-sex marriage is officially recognized.

2004–2005 The assassination of a controversial film director sets off anti-Islamic riots and brings into question the country's famed tolerance.

2009 A court orders a right-wing politician to stand trial for inciting hatred against Muslims in a film linking radical Islamists' violence to the Qur'an.

NORTHERN CYPRUS

OFFICIAL NAME
Kuzey Kıbrıs Türk Cumhuriyeti (Turkish); Turkish Republic of Northern Cyprus (English)

POPULATION
269,400 (2009e)

INHABITANTS' NAME/NICKNAME
Northern Cypriot(s); Turkish Cypriot(s)

LANGUAGE/LANGUAGES
Turkish (official); Cypriot Turkish (de facto official); English, Greek, others

RELIGION/RELIGIONS
Sunni Muslim, 97 percent; other or no religion

NATIONAL FLAG
The flag has a white field with a large red crescent and five-pointed star and two red horizontal stripes at the top and bottom. The colors are taken from the Turkish flag, but reversed.

COAT OF ARMS/SEAL
The coat of arms has a central gold shield charged with a white dove carrying an olive branch in its beak. Above the shield are the date of independence, 1983, and a crescent moon and five-pointed white star. Around the shield is a garland of woven green and white olive leaves.

The color of the shield symbolizes the copper found on the island.

CAPITAL CITY
Lefkosa (Nicosia)

TYPE OF GOVERNMENT
Democratic republic

NATIONAL EMBLEM
A huge depiction of the national flag drawn into a mountainside that can be seen by satellites from space

NATIONAL COLORS
Red and white

NATIONAL ANTHEM
The republic uses the same anthem as Turkey*.

İstiklâl Marşı (Turkish); Independence March (English)

Fear not and be not dismayed, this crimson
  flag will never fade.
It is the last hearth that is burning for my
  nation,
And we know for sure that it will never fail.
It is my nation's star, shining forever,
It is my nation's star and it is mine.

Frown not, fair crescent, for I am ready to die
for you.
Smile now upon my heroic nation, leave this
anger,
Lest the blood shed for thee be unblessed.
Freedom is my nation's right,
Freedom for us who worship God and seek
what is right.

PATRON SAINT

Saint Barnabas the Apostle (patron saint of
Cyprus*)

CURRENCY

New Turkish lira

VEHICLE IDENTIFICATION PLATES/ STICKERS

CY Cyprus (official); KIB (unofficial)

PASSPORT

Northern Cypriots travel on Turkish
passports.

AIRLINE

Cyprus Turkish Airlines

NATIONAL RESOURCES

Natural resources are negligible, other than
small deposits of copper, trace metals, and
fish. The service sector is the major part of
the economy, along with tourism, agriculture, and light manufacturing. Economic
subsidies from Turkey and remittances from
Northern Cypriots living outside the country
are important sources of revenue.

FOODS

Most of Northern Cyprus cuisine reflects
the Turkish origins of the population. Island
specialties include *mezes,* a variety of small
dishes or hors d'oeuvres; *sis kebap,* beef or
chicken on a skewer cooked over charcoal;
seftali kebap, a type of sausage; *barbunya
pilaki,* a dish of beans, olive oil, and tomato

sauce; *pide,* a type of lamb pizza; *kapama,*
lamb prepared with onions and lettuce; and
koylu corbasi, peasant soup.

SPORTS/SPORTS TEAMS

Association football (soccer), basketball,
and handball are the most popular sports.
Northern Cyprus national teams participate
in these sports at an international level.

TEAM SPORTS

Basketball

Northern Cyprus Basketball Team; Northern
Cyprus Women's Basketball Team

Football

Northern Cyprus Football Team

Handball

Northern Cyprus Handball Team; Northern
Cyprus Women's Handball Team; North-
ern Cyprus National Beach Handball Team;
Northern Cyprus Women's Beach Handball
Team

NATIONAL HEROES OR PERSONIFICATIONS

Fazil Küçük, activist and politician; Rauf
Denktas, founder of the Turkish Republic
of Northern Cyprus; Kibrisli Mehmet Emin
Pasha, Cypriot-born Ottoman grand vizier
in the 19th century

NATIONAL HOLIDAY/INDEPENDENCE DAY

Peace and Freedom Day (Turkish Intervention), July 20; National Day, November 15

FESTIVALS/FAIRS

Bayram, variable dates; Kurban Bairam,
variable dates; National Festival, July; Bel-
lapais Music Festival, April–May

SIGNIFICANT EVENTS IN FORMATION OF NATIONAL IDENTITY

Sixth millennium B.C.E.–300 B.C.E.   Ancient cultures
flourish on the island. Cities grow and commerce

with other nations develops. Cyprus becomes an independent kingdom around 669 B.C.E. Later, invasions by Egyptians and Persians subjugate the island.

321 B.C.E.–58 B.C.E.   The Cypriot leaders side with the Ptolemaic rulers of Egypt* in the wars that follow the end of the empire of Alexander the Great. Under Ptolemaic rule, the island becomes Greek in language and culture.

58 B.C.E.   Romans occupy Cyprus. According to tradition, Paul of Tarsus converts the population to Christianity.

395 C.E.   The collapse of Roman power brings Cyprus under the Eastern Roman or Byzantine Empire, the Greek-speaking successor to the Roman Empire in the east.

688–965   Muslim Arabs invade Cyprus. An agreement between the Arabs and the Byzantines creates a joint government that rules the island for the next three centuries, despite constant warfare on the mainland.

12th century   The island is conquered during the Crusades, is later sold to the Knights Templar, and is then conquered by the Franks, who erect a separate Kingdom of Cyprus under the Lusignan dynasty.

1489   Under the looming threat posed by the expanding Ottoman Empire of the Turks, the Venetians take control of the island, ending the Lusignan kingdom.

1562–1571   The Greek Cypriots revolt and attempt to throw off Venetian rule. The Turks demand the cession of the island to the Ottoman Empire on dubious historical grounds. A Turkish invasion is finally successful, but thousands of Greek Cypriots and Venetians are massacred.

1571–1850   The Ottomans colonize the island with retired soldiers and their families. During the 17th century, the Turkish population grows rapidly, partly through conversion of Cypriot Greeks to Islam. When Greece* gains independence in 1829, many Greek Cypriots seek a union of Cyprus and Greece.

1869–1878   The construction of the Suez Canal brings British interest in the island, which is now strategically placed. The United Kingdom*, in exchange for support during the Russo-Turkish War of 1877, is given administrative control but not sovereignty over Cyprus.

1914   The Greek Cypriots demand union with Greece. The British annex Cyprus when war breaks out in Europe in 1914, with the Ottoman Turks allied with Germany*. Cyprus is made a British Crown Colony.

1920s–1940s   Many Cypriot Turks, who suffer discrimination and persecution by their Greek neighbors, leave the island to settle on the Turkish mainland or to live in the United Kingdom.

1955–1960   The Greek Cypriots continue to demand *enosis,* union with Greece. The Turkish Cypriots oppose the idea. The Greek Cypriot organization known as EOKA turns to violence to force the British to allow the union and often targets Turkish Cypriots. The British arm a paramilitary police force of Turkish Cypriots. Cyprus becomes an independent republic.

1963   The Cyprus government proposes constitutional changes to end power sharing between the two communities. Violence between Greeks and Turks erupts across the island. The Turkish Cypriots withdraw from the government.

1974   The military government of Greece backs a coup against the Cypriot government. Turkish troops invade the north part of the island, sending tens of thousands of Greek Cypriots fleeing south.

1989–2000   United Nations–sponsored peace talks continue intermittently.

1994   The European Union rules that most goods, including fruits and vegetables, are not eligible for preferential treatment if coming from Northern Cyprus.

2002–2004   A new United Nations plan would create a federation of two constituent states, presided over by a rotating presidency. Cyprus is invited to join the European Union (EU), provided the two communities agree to the plan. Twin referendums show endorsement by the Turkish Cypriots, but the plan is overwhelmingly rejected by the Greek Cypriots. The Greek Cypriots are allowed to join the EU even though they rejected the peace plan. The Turkish Cypriots are excluded.

2004–2009   Greek Cypriot and Turkish Cypriot leaders launch intensive talks aimed at ending the division of the island.

NORTHERN IRELAND

OFFICIAL NAME

Tualsceart Éireann (Irish); Norlin Airlann (Ulster Scots); Northern Ireland (English)

POPULATION

1,759,300 (2009e)

INHABITANTS' NAME/NICKNAME

Northern Irish

LANGUAGE/LANGUAGES

English (de facto); Irish, Ulster Scots, others

RELIGION/RELIGIONS

Protestant, 53 percent; Roman Catholic, 44 percent; others or no religion

NATIONAL FLAG

The official flag of the province is the Union Jack. There is no official national flag of Northern Ireland, following the Northern Ireland Constitution Act of 1973, nor any unofficial flag universally accepted in Northern Ireland. The use of various flags in Northern Ireland is contentious. The official flag from 1953 to 1973 was a white field with a centered red cross and a Tudor crown above a centered six-pointed white star charged with a red hand. The flag of Ulster, the traditional flag of the region, is a yellow field with a centered red cross and a centered white shield charged with a red hand.

COAT OF ARMS/SEAL

The former official coat of arms (before 1972) has a central shield of the arms of the flag supported by a British Lion holding a blue banner bearing a gold harp and crown and an Irish elk supporting a banner of the arms of the De Burg family, the earls of Ulster, the basis for the flag of Ulster.

CAPITAL CITY

Belfast

TYPE OF GOVERNMENT

Autonomous state within the United Kingdom*, a constitutional monarchy and a parliamentary democracy

NATIONAL EMBLEM

Flax flower; red hand of Ulster

NATIONAL COLORS

Green and white

NATIONAL ANTHEM

"God Save the Queen," the British anthem, is the official anthem of Northern Ireland. Londonderry Air, an instrumental song, is used as the national anthem at various official functions. The same tune with lyrics, called "Danny Boy," is also used as an unofficial anthem.

> **Londonderry Air/Danny Boy**
> Oh Danny Boy, the pipes, the pipes are calling
> From glen to glen, and down the
>   mountainside.
> The summer's gone, and all the roses falling.
> 'Tis you, 'tis you must go and I must bide.
> But come ye back when summer's in the
>   meadow
> Or when the valley's hushed and white with
>   snow,
> For I'll be here in sunshine or in shadow.
> Oh Danny Boy, oh Danny Boy, I love you so.
> But if you come, and all the flowers are dying
> And if I'm dead, as dead I might well be,
> Ye'll come and find the place where I am lying
> And kneel and say an Ave there for me.
> And I shall hear, though soft you tread above
>   me,

And o'er my grave shall warmer, sweeter be,
And if you bow and tell me that you love me,
Then I shall sleep in peace until you come
    to me.

PATRON SAINT

Saint Patrick (shared with Ireland*)

CURRENCY

Northern Ireland pound sterling

INTERNET IDENTIFIER

.ie (shared with Ireland)

VEHICLE IDENTIFICATION PLATES/STICKERS

GB Great Britain (official); NI Northern Ireland (unofficial)

PASSPORT

The Northern Irish are British citizens and travel on British passports.

NATIONAL FLOWER

Flax

NATIONAL ANIMAL

Irish elk

NATIONAL FISH

Northern pike (unofficial)

NATIONAL RESOURCES

Northern Ireland has traditionally had an industrial economy, most notably in shipbuilding, rope manufacture, and textiles, but most heavy industry has since been replaced by services, primarily in the public sector. Tourism also plays a big role in the local economy. More recently, the economy has benefited from major investment in high-tech industry by large multinational corporations attracted by government subsidies and the highly skilled workforce in Northern Ireland.

FOODS

Ulster fry is considered the national dish, a breakfast combination of eggs, sausages, ham, and soda *farl,* a unique bread baked on a grill, or potato bread. Other specialties include Ulster vegetable soup; Irish stew, a stew of mutton or lamb, potatoes, and vegetables; smoked cod pie, a pastry of potatoes, onions, smoked cod, and green peas; Armagh stuffed rabbit, baked rabbit with a stuffing of apples, onion, bread crumbs, and herbs; and colcannon, a mixture of mashed potatoes, cooked cabbage, and onion, often served with bacon.

SPORTS/SPORTS TEAMS

Association football (soccer), Gaelic football, and Rugby are popular sports. Northern Ireland national teams participate in many sports at an international level.

TEAM SPORTS

Basketball

Northern Ireland Basketball Team; Northern Ireland Women's Basketball Team

Cricket

Northern Ireland Cricket Team

Football

Northern Ireland Football Team, nickname the Green and White Army or Norn Iron; Northern Ireland Women's Football Team, nickname Norn Iron; Ulster Rugby Team; Northern Ireland B Football Team, nickname Green and White Army or Norn Iron; Ireland Rugby Union Team (represents the Republic of Ireland and Northern Ireland)

Netball

Northern Ireland Netball Team

Volleyball

Northern Ireland Men's Volleyball Team; Northern Ireland Women's Volleyball Team

INDIVIDUAL SPORTS
Northern Ireland Weight Lifting Team

NATIONAL HEROES OR PERSONIFICATIONS
Sir Edward Carson, a hero to the Ulster Scots, who consider him the founder of the state of Northern Ireland in 1912; Michael Collins, an Irish Catholic leader assassinated in the 1920s

NATIONAL HOLIDAY/INDEPENDENCE DAY
Saint Patrick's Day, March 17; Battle of the Boyne (Orangemen's Day), July

FESTIVALS/FAIRS
Belfast Festival, October–November; Coors Light Open House Festival, September; Banks of the Foyle Hallowe'en Carnival, October; Foyle Film Festival, December; City of Song Festival, September; Ulster Scots Festival, November

SIGNIFICANT EVENTS IN FORMATION OF NATIONAL IDENTITY
1170–1171 England first becomes involved in Irish affairs in a local dispute. The English invade Ireland. Ulster, the most northerly of the four Irish regions, is conquered by the English.

14th century–15th century The English conquest of Ireland is halted, and English possessions are abandoned, except a small region around Dublin called the Pale. Everything outside is considered uncivilized, giving rise to the expression "beyond the pale."

16th Century–17th century Protestant settlers from England and Scotland systematically colonize the Plantation of Ulster. The Irish Catholics are dispossessed of their lands and usually driven out.

1690 The Protestants of King William of Orange defeat the Catholic army of King James at the Battle of the Boyne, confirming English control of Ireland.

1700–1795 Protestant domination leads to discrimination and repression of the Irish Catholic majority in Ireland. To ensure continued Protestant rule, the Orange Order is created.

1801 Ireland is incorporated into the United Kingdom*.

1840s Thousands die during the potato famine, which is blamed on British government policies. The Ulster Scots remain strongly pro-British and anti-Catholic.

1912–1916 The Ulster Volunteer Force is organized by Sir Edward Carson as a bulwark against Catholic domination of the Protestant-majority six counties. The Easter Rising begins, an Irish rebellion against British rule that continues as a guerrilla war.

1920–1922 Ireland is partitioned, with the Protestant-majority counties remaining under British rule. Michael Collins, the Irish leader, is assassinated as civil war breaks out between home rule forces and the Irish Republican Army (IRA), which refuses to accept partition.

1939–1945 The Republic of Ireland remains neutral during the Second World War. Northern Ireland becomes an important military base and is heavily bombed.

1949 The Republic of Ireland severs all remaining ties to the United Kingdom. New constitutional guarantees are given the Northern Irish parliament at Stormont.

1956 The IRA launches a violent campaign in the border region.

1968 The civil rights movement begins the campaign for equal rights for Roman Catholics in Northern Ireland. Protestants demonstrate in response. Sectarian violence spreads, with attacks by both the IRA and Ulster Unionists, those who favor continued union with the United Kingdom.

1972–1973 The British government closes the Stormont Parliament and imposes direct rule in an effort to restore order. British troops occupy the region. Both Ireland and Northern Ireland become part of the European Community.

1975–1985 Atrocities, bombing of civilian targets, and further segregation leave Northern Ireland a virtual war zone, although the majority is not involved in the violence. The hard-line unionists oppose a British-Irish agreement for cross-border initiatives.

1994 The IRA announces a complete cease-fire, followed by a similar declaration by the Unionists, but the truce is quickly broken and the violence resumes.

1997–1998 For the first time in over 25 years, unionists and Irish nationalists meet to seek a solution to Northern Ireland's problems. A power-sharing agreement is reached, which is approved by 71 percent of the voters.

2001 The IRA disarms, allowing peace talks to go forward. The IRA declares an end to its long campaign to reunite Ireland.

2007–2009 Self-government is restored to the Stormont Parliament under a government with both Protestant and Catholic ministers. The Irish and British governments supply significant financial aid to support the new autonomous government and regional peace.

See also United Kingdom

NORWAY

OFFICIAL NAME

Kongeriket Norge (Norwegian—Bokmål); Kongeriket Noreg (Norwegian—Nynorsk); Kingdom of Norway (English)

POPULATION

4,789,700 (2009e)

INHABITANTS' NAME/NICKNAME

Norwegian(s)

LANGUAGE/LANGUAGES

Norwegian (Bokmål and Nynorsk dialects), Sami (all official); English, Swedish, Danish, others

RELIGION/RELIGIONS

Protestant, 88 percent; Roman Catholic, 1 percent; Muslim, others

NATIONAL FLAG

The flag has a red field divided by an indigo blue Scandinavian cross outlined in white that extends to the edges. The design and colors of the flag are associated with the states that ruled Norway at different times, Denmark* and Sweden*.

COAT OF ARMS/SEAL

The coat of arms, one of the oldest in Europe, consists of a red shield charged with a gold lion holding the martyr axe of Saint Olav. Above the shield is a red and gold crown representing the monarchy. The full version of the arms includes a red ermined cape draped from the crown around the shield.

MOTTO

Royal motto: *Alt for Norge* (Bokmål); *Alt for Noreg* (Nynorsk); All for Norway (English)

CAPITAL CITY

Oslo

TYPE OF GOVERNMENT

Constitutional monarchy and parliamentary democracy

NATIONAL EMBLEM

The fjords

NATIONAL COLORS

Red, white, and blue

NATIONAL ANTHEM

Norway has two official anthems, the national anthem and the royal anthem. The national anthem dates from 1859 and was performed for the first time in 1864.

Ja, vi eisker dette landet (Norwegian); Yes, We Love This Country (English)

Yes, we love this country
as it rises forth,
rugged, weathered, above the sea,

with those thousand homes.
Loving, loving it and thinking
about our father and mother
and the saga night that sends
dreams to our earth.
And the saga night that sends,
sends dreams to our earth.

Norseman, in house and cabin,
thank your great God!
It was his will to protect the country
although things looked dark.
While fathers fought
and mothers cried,
our Lord quietly opened the way
so that we won our rights.
Our Lord quietly opened the way
so that we won our rights.

Yes, we love this country
as it rises forth,
rugged and weathered, above the sea,
with those thousand homes.
And as our fathers' struggle has raised it
from distress to victory,
even we, when it is demanded,
for its peace will encamp.
Even we, when it is demanded,
for its peace will encamp.

PATRON SAINT

Saint Olav

CURRENCY

Norwegian krone

INTERNET IDENTIFIER

.no

VEHICLE IDENTIFICATION PLATES/STICKERS

N

PASSPORT

The passport cover has the coat of arms, the name of the country in Bokmål, Nynorsk, and English, the word *passport* in Norwegian and English, and the standard biometric symbol.

AIRLINES

SAS Scandinavian Airlines Service (shared with Denmark and Sweden); Norwegian

NATIONAL FLOWER

Heather

NATIONAL TREE

Norway spruce (unofficial)

NATIONAL ANIMAL

Lion (heraldry)

NATIONAL BIRD

White-throated dipper

NATIONAL RESOURCES

Natural resources include petroleum, natural gas, iron ore, copper, lead, zinc, titanium, pyrites, nickel, fish, timber, and hydropower. The petroleum industry is one of the country's most important. A well-educated population and proximity to Europe's large population centers have helped make Norway one of the most prosperous countries in the world. Tourism, supported by historic cities, varied scenery, outdoor sports, and the unique culture, is also very important.

FOODS

National specialties include *koldtbord,* "cold table," a generous buffet of smoked fish, fresh lobster, shrimp, and a variety of hot and cold dishes; *lutefisk,* dried fish; *fårikål,* a casserole of lamb and cabbage; *husmannsgryte,* a dish of rutabagas and sausage; *nøkkelost,* a quiche of eggs, bacon, and cheese; *dyrestek med viltsaus,* reindeer roast with game sauce of sour cream, cranberry preserves, and goat cheese; *fiskesuppe,* a fish chowder with vegetables; *fårikål,* a stew of lamb and cabbage; *fiskboller,* balls of minced fish, spices, and vegetables; *fiskekaker,* fish cakes; and *rømmegrøt,* sour cream porridge.

SPORTS/SPORTS TEAMS

Association football (soccer) is the most popular sport. Norway national teams participate in many sports at an international level.

TEAM SPORTS

Badminton

Norway Badminton Team

Baseball

Norway Baseball Team; Norway Softball Team

Basketball

Norway Basketball Team; Norway Women's Basketball Team

Cricket

Norway Cricket Team

Football

Norway Football Team; Norway Women's Football Team; Norway Under-21 Football Team; Norway Women's Under-19 Football Team; Norway Rugby Union Team; Norway Women's Rugby Union Team; Norway Wheelchair Rugby Team; Norway American Football Team; Norway Rugby League Team

Golf

Norway Men's Pitch and Putt Team; Norway Women's Pitch and Putt Team

Handball

Norway Handball Team; Norway Women's Handball Team; Norway Beach Handball Team; Norway Women's Beach Handball Team

Hockey

Norway Ice Hockey Team; Norway Junior Ice Hockey Team; Norway Women's Ice Hockey Team; Norway Field Hockey Team

Racing

Norway Speedway Team

Table Tennis

Norway Table Tennis Team

Tennis

Norway Davis Cup Team; Norway Fed Cup Team

Volleyball

Norway Men's Beach Volleyball Team; Norway Women's Beach Volleyball Team; Norway Men's Volleyball Team; Norway Women's Volleyball Team

INDIVIDUAL SPORTS

Norway Aikido Team; Norway Amateur Boxing Team; Norway Athletics Team; Norway Canoeing Team; Norway Cycling Team; Norway Equestrian Team; Norway Fencing Team; Norway Gymnastics Team; Norway Judo Team; Norway Karate Team; Norway Rowing Team; Norway Sailing Team; Norway Shooting Team; Norway Swim Team; Norway Tae Kwon Do Team; Norway Triathlon Team; Norway Weight Lifting Team; Norway Wrestling Team

WINTER SPORTS

Norway Alpine Ski Team; Norway Biathlon Team; Norway Bobsleigh and Tobogganing Team; Norway Curling Team; Norway Ice Hockey Team; Norway Junior Ice Hockey Team; Norway Women's Ice Hockey Team; Norway Luge Team; Norway Skating Team

NATIONAL HEROES OR PERSONIFICATIONS

Ola Nordmann is the name for the average Norwegian, representing the whole population. Nór is the legendary founder of Norway.

National heroes include Einar Gerhardsen, three-time prime minister who oversaw Norway's post-World War II recovery, referred to as *Landsfaderen,* the father of the nation; Fridtjof Nansen, an explorer and diplomat awarded the Nobel Peace Prize in 1922; Roald Amundsen, leader of the first expedition to reach the South Pole; and Gro Harlem Brundtland, former prime minister and an international leader in sustainable development.

NATIONAL HOLIDAY/INDEPENDENCE DAY

Constitution Day, May 17

FESTIVALS/FAIRS

Trondheim Chamber Music Festival, September; Saint Olav Festival, July; Arendal Greigfestival, February; Bergen International Festival, May-June; Norwegian Big Band Festival, August; Oslo Mela Festival, August

SIGNIFICANT EVENTS IN FORMATION OF NATIONAL IDENTITY

2000 B.C.E.–1200 B.C.E. Norway is invaded and settled by Gothic-German tribes.

800 C.E.–1050 C.E. During the Viking age, seafaring longboats set out to conquer other lands. Erik the Red leads settlers across the sea to Greenland* in 985. King Olav establishes Christianity as the region's major religion in 955. Vikings attack the expanding Franks and conquer Normandy, Sicily and other territories.

1350 Bubonic plague, called the Black Death, kills over half the population.

1397–1523 Norway, Sweden, and Denmark join the Kalmar Union under a single monarch. The union ends when Sweden assumes independence in 1523.

1536 Norway is proclaimed part of the Danish kingdom.

1814 Norway passes to Swedish rule. The Norwegians adopt a constitution and elect a king, but after a brief war, they accept rule by the Swedish king while retaining their own constitution.

1905 Norway declares its independence of Sweden. Prince Carl of Denmark becomes the country's first king in modern times.

1940–1949 German troops invade neutral Norway. The brutal German occupation continues until the end of World War II. The Norwegians are honored for their resistance to the Nazi occupation and for hiding and smuggling over half the Norwegian Jews into neutral Sweden. Norway relinquishes its historic neutrality to join the North Atlantic Treaty Organization (NATO), a military alliance of European and North American nations.

1960s Commercial quantities of oil and natural gas are discovered in Norway's territorial waters. The Norwegian economy advances rapidly.

1972 In a referendum on membership in the European Economic Community, later the European Union, the Norwegians vote against.

1994 In a second referendum on membership of the European Union (EU), the Norwegians again vote against membership.

2000–2009 Norway is one of the most prosperous nations in Europe. Sustainable development of its many natural resources remains a priority.

See also Sapmi

POLAND

OFFICIAL NAME

Rzeczpospolita Polska (Polish); Republic of Poland (English)

POPULATION

38,237,600 (2009e)

INHABITANTS' NAME/NICKNAME

Pole(s); Polish

LANGUAGE/LANGUAGES

Polish (official); Belarusian, Kashubian, Lithuanian, German, English, Russian, others

RELIGION/RELIGIONS

Roman Catholic, 89 percent; Orthodox, 1.5 percent; Protestant, other or no religion

NATIONAL FLAG

The flag is a horizontal bicolor of white over red. The colors are derived from the medieval

Polish-Lithuanian Commonwealth. Both nations' symbols are white on red.

COAT OF ARMS/SEAL

The coat of arms is a red shield charged with the *Orzeł Biały* (White Eagle) with a golden beak and talons and wearing a golden crown. The imagery comes from Poland's legendary founder, Lech, who saw a white eagle touched by a ray of sun so that the wings appeared tipped by gold. He decided to settle in that location and took the eagle as his emblem.

MOTTO

Bóg, honor, ojczyzna (Polish); God, Honor, Fatherland (English) (unofficial)

CAPITAL CITY

Warsaw

TYPE OF GOVERNMENT

Parliamentary republic

NATIONAL EMBLEM

White eagle (the Polish Eagle)

NATIONAL COLORS

Red and white

NATIONAL ANTHEM

The anthem originated with Polish soldiers fighting in Italy* in the late 18th century. It was adopted as the official anthem in 1927.

Mazurek Dabrowskiego (Polish); Dabrowski's Mazurka (English)

Poland has not died yet
So long as we still live
That which alien force has seized
We at sabrepoint shall retrieve

Chorus

March, march, Dąbrowski
To Poland from Italy
Let us now rejoin the nation
Under thy command

Cross the Vistula and Warta
And Poles we shall be
We've been shown by Bonaparte
Ways to victory

Chorus

Like Czarniecki to Poznan
Returned across the sea
To free our fatherland from chains
Fighting with the Swede

Germans, Muscovites will not rest
When, backsword in hand,
Concord will be our watchword
And the fatherland will be ours

Chorus

Father, in tears,
Says to his Basia
Just listen, it seems that our people
Are beating the drums

Chorus

All exclaim in unison
Enough of this bondage
We've got scythes from Racławice
God will give us Kościuszko

PATRON SAINT

Saint Casimir; Saint Florian; Saint Wojciech (Adalbert); Mary, Queen of Poland; Saint Stanislaus; Saint Stanislaus Kostka

CURRENCY

Polish złoty

INTERNET IDENTIFIER

.pl

VEHICLE IDENTIFICATION PLATES/ STICKERS

PL

PASSPORT

The passport cover has the name of the European Union and the name of the country in Polish, the coat of arms, the word *passport* in Polish, English, and French, and the standard biometric symbol.

AIRLINE
LOT Polish Airlines

NATIONAL FLOWER
Corn poppy

NATIONAL TREE
Weeping willow

NATIONAL ANIMAL
Bear

NATIONAL BIRD
White-tailed eagle

NATIONAL RESOURCES
Natural resources include coal, sulfur, copper, natural gas, silver, lead, salt, amber, and arable land. The country's well-educated population and its proximity to major European markets have generated impressive economic growth since 1990. Tourism, based on the country's historic cities, unique culture, varied scenery, and national monuments, is an important resource. Remittances from Poles living outside the country are an important source of foreign currency and investment. Structural funds from the European Union are a resource but will cease when Poland's development rises to European averages.

FOODS
Bigos, a stew of sauerkraut, various cuts of meat and sausages, tomatoes, honey, and mushrooms, is considered the national dish. Other typical dishes include *barszcz,* the Polish version of borscht soup, made of beets; pierogi, small pastries filled with farmer's cheese, potatoes, and fried onions, or other ingredients, such as ground meat, mushrooms, or sweet fruit fillings; *kotlet schabowy,* breaded veal cutlet; *golonka,* pork knuckles cooked with vegetables; *kolduny,* meat dumplings; *zrazy,* stuffed slices of beef;

and *kabanos,* long, thick sausages. Vodka, in many flavors, is the national drink.

SPORTS/SPORTS TEAMS
Association football (soccer) is the country's most popular sport. Athletics, basketball, and boxing are other popular sports. Poland national teams participate in many sports at an international level.

TEAM SPORTS

Badminton
Poland Badminton Team

Baseball
Poland Baseball Team; Poland Softball Team

Basketball
Poland Basketball Team; Poland Women's Basketball Team; Poland Wheelchair Basketball Team

Cricket
Poland Cricket Team

Football
Poland Football Team, nickname Bialo-czerwoni (the White and Red) or Orly (the Eagles); Women's Football Team, nickname Bialo-czerwoni (the White and Red) or Orly (the Eagles); Poland Rugby Union Team; Poland Under-21 Football Team, nickname Bialo-czerwoni (the White and Red) or Orly (The Eagles); Poland Under-20 Football Team, nickname Bialo-czerwoni (the White and Red) or Orly (the Eagles); Poland Under-19 Football Team, nickname Bialo-czerwoni (the White and Red) or Orly (the Eagles); Poland Women's Under-19 Football Team, nickname Bialo-czerwoni (the White and Red) or Orly (the Eagles); Poland Wheelchair Rugby Team; Poland American Football Team; Poland Beach Soccer Team; Poland Futsal Team

Handball

Poland Handball Team, nickname Bialoczerwoni (the White and Red); Poland Women's Handball Team, nickname Bialoczerwoni (the White and Red)

Hockey

Poland Ice Hockey Team; Poland Junior Ice Hockey Team; Poland Field Hockey Team

Korfball

Poland Korfball Team

Racing

Poland Speedway Team

Table Tennis

Poland Table Tennis Team

Tennis

Poland Davis Cup Team; Poland Fed Cup Team

Volleyball

Poland Men's Beach Volleyball Team; Poland Women's Beach Volleyball Team; Poland Men's Volleyball Team; Poland Women's Volleyball Team; Poland Fistball Team

INDIVIDUAL SPORTS

Poland Aikido Team; Poland Amateur Boxing Team; Poland Archery Team; Poland Athletics Team; Poland Canoeing Team; Poland Cycling Team; Poland Equestrian Team; Fencing Team; Poland Judo Team; Poland Karate Team; Poland Modern Pentathlon Team; Poland Rowing Team; Poland Sailing Team; Poland Shooting Team; Poland Swim Team; Poland Tae Kwon Do Team; Poland Triathlon Team; Poland Weight Lifting Team; Poland Wrestling Team

WINTER SPORTS

Poland Alpine Ski Team; Poland Bandy Team: Poland Biathlon Team; Poland Bob-sleigh and Tobogganing Team; Poland Curling Team; Poland Ice Hockey Team; Poland Junior Ice Hockey Team; Poland Luge Team; Poland Skating Team

NATIONAL HEROES OR PERSONIFICATIONS

Polonia, the name of Poland in Latin and many Romance languages, is used as the personification of modern Poland.

National heroes include Adam Mickiewicz, a 19th century poet considered Poland's national poet; Tadeusz Kosciuszko, leader of the 1794 uprising against Russian rule and earlier a hero of the American Revolutionary War; Kazimierz Pulaski, military leader who fought against Russian domination and later served and died in the American Revolutionary War; Pope John Paul II, leader of the Roman Catholic resurgence in Poland under communist rule and leader of the world's Roman Catholics until his death in 2005; Wladyslaw Sikorski, leader of Poland's World War II government-in-exile.

NATIONAL HOLIDAY/INDEPENDENCE DAY

Constitution Day, May 3

FESTIVALS/FAIRS

Shanties Festival, February; International Contemporary Music Festival, February; Juwenalia, May; Festival of Polish Song, June; Mozart Festival, June; Jewish Cultural Festival, June; International Street Festival, July; Warsaw Film Festival, October

SIGNIFICANT EVENTS IN FORMATION OF NATIONAL IDENTITY

450 C.E.–500 C.E. Slavs migrating to the region from the east displace the earlier inhabitants.

9th century–10th century The Vistula Union forms as a confederation of Slavic tribes. Poland adopts Christianity in 966.

1182 The first parliament, the Sejm, is created.

1569 The Lublin Union establishes the Polish-Lithuanian Commonwealth. A golden age of literature, music, and culture begins as the commonwealth expands its borders to become the largest country in Europe.

1648–1654 The Khmelnytskyi Uprising, a Cossack rebellion in Ukraine*, spreads to Poland and Lithuania*, bringing an end to the golden age. War with Russia hastens the country's decline.

1772–1795 The first partition of Poland occurs as neighboring countries take territory from the weakened commonwealth. Another war with Russia leads to the second partition. Tadeusz Kosciuszko leads a rebellion against the imposition of Russian rule. The third partition erases Poland from the map as Russia, Prussia, and Austria* divide the remaining territory.

1918–1921 At the end of the First World War, Poland is resurrected as an independent republic. The new republic defeats the Red Army in the Polish-Soviet War.

1939–1945 Nazi Germany* invades Poland, initiating the Second World War. The Soviet Union invades from the east, and the defeated country is split between the two totalitarian allies. Poland loses over 6 million citizens, including nearly all of its formerly large Jewish population.

1945–1947 At the end of the war, Soviet troops stay to install a communist government. Several million Poles move from territory ceded to the Soviet Union in the east into territory taken from Germany in the west.

1980–1990 Labor unrest in the worker's state begins the Solidarity movement that soon becomes a political force. In 1989, Solidarity triumphs in parliamentary elections and leader Lech Walesa wins the 1990 presidential election. The collapse of communism in Poland begins the end of the Soviet Empire in Eastern Europe and Russia.

1999–2004 The democratic republic joins the North Atlantic Treaty Organization (NATO) and the European Union (EU).

2004–2009 Poland's economic growth begins to reduce high unemployment and inequities in the distribution of wealth. The country takes an active part in European and world affairs. The world financial crisis leads to renewed problems and rising unemployment.

PORTUGAL

OFFICIAL NAME

República Portuguesa (Portuguese); Portuguese Republic (English)

POPULATION

10,698,300 (2009e)

INHABITANTS' NAME/NICKNAME

Portuguese

LANGUAGE/LANGUAGES

Portuguese (official); Mirandese (recognized regional language); Spanish, others

RELIGION/RELIGIONS

Roman Catholic, 84 percent; Protestant, Jewish, other or no religion

NATIONAL FLAG

The flag is a vertical bicolor with unequal stripes of green, a third of the total, at the hoist and red, two thirds of the total, on the fly. The small version of the coat of arms is centered over the boundary between the two colors, at equal distances from the upper and lower edges. The green represents the hope of the nation, and the red represents the blood of those who died defending it.

COAT OF ARMS/SEAL

The coat of arms has a central white shield charged with five *quinas*, or escutcheons, in the form of a cross representing the five Moorish ships defeated by the King of Portugal. The edge of the shield has a red border with seven gold castles, representing the Moorish strongholds taken by Portugal during the reconquest. Around the shield is an armillary sphere, a navigation instrument of the 15th century. Below are banners of green and red. Around the sphere is golden foliage.

CAPITAL CITY

Lisbon

TYPE OF GOVERNMENT

Parliamentary republic

NATIONAL EMBLEM

Galo de Barcelos (Portuguese rooster)

NATIONAL COLORS

Red and green

NATIONAL ANTHEM

The anthem was originally a protest song. The new republican government adopted it after the overthrow of the monarchy in 1911.

A Portuguesa (Portuguese); The Portuguese Song (English)

Heroes of the sea, noble people,
Brave and immortal nation,
Give rise today, once more
To the splendor of Portugal!
Amidst the mists of memory,
Oh Fatherland, the voice is felt
Of your noble forefathers,
That shall lead you to victory!

Chorus

To arms, to arms!
Over the land, over the sea,
To arms, to arms!
To fight for the Fatherland!
Against the cannons, we march, we march!

Hoist the unconquerable flag,
In the living light of your sky!
Europe cries out to the world entire:
Portugal has not perished
Kiss the soil jolly of yours
The ocean, roaring of love,
And your winning arm
Gave new worlds to the world!

Chorus

Salute the sun that rises
Over a smiling future;
Let the echo of an offense
Be the sign for resurrection.
Rays of that strong dawn
Are as mother kisses,
That keep us, sustain us,
Against the injuries of fate.

PATRON SAINT

Our Lady of the Immaculate Conception; Our Lady of Fatima; Saint Anthony of Padua; Saint Francis Borgia; Archangel Gabriel; Saint George

CURRENCY

Euro

INTERNET IDENTIFIER

.pt

VEHICLE IDENTIFICATION PLATES/ STICKERS

P

PASSPORT

The passport cover has the coat of arms beside the Portuguese names for the European Union (EU) (small letters) and Portugal (large letters) and the Portuguese word for passport; below is the EU's circle of stars, the standard biometric symbol, and a larger depiction of the foliage that surrounds the coat of arms.

AIRLINES

TAP Portugal; SATA International

NATIONAL FLOWER

Lavender

NATIONAL TREE

Olive

NATIONAL BIRD

Galo de Barcelos (Portuguese rooster)

NATIONAL FISH

Atlantic cod (unofficial)

NATIONAL RESOURCES

Natural resources include fish, forests (particularly cork), iron ore, copper, zinc, tin, tungsten, silver, gold, uranium, marble, clay, gypsum, salt, arable land, and hydropower. Business services have overtaken the traditional industries of textiles, clothing, footwear, cork, and wood products. Portugal's historic cities and monuments, sandy beaches, pleasant climate, varied scenery, and unique culture support a thriving tourist industry. As Portugal was once a country of emigrants, the Portuguese communities in many parts of the world are a source of remittances and investment. EU structural funds continue to be a valuable resource.

FOODS

Bacalhau, dried or salted cod, is considered the national dish. The Portuguese say that there are so many ways to prepare it that there is a recipe for each day of the year. Other national specialties include *sopa de marisco,* shellfish soup cooked and served with wine; *caldo verde,* a green soup made of kale; *caldeirada,* a stew of nine types of fish, onions, and tomatoes; *carne de porco à Alentejana,* a dish of cubed pork, clams, tomatoes, and onions; and *cozido à portuguesa,* a stew of different meats and vegetables. Portuguese wines, particularly port and Madeira, are known around the world.

SPORTS/SPORTS TEAMS

Association football (soccer) is the most popular sport. Rugby union and rugby sevens are also very popular. Portugal national teams participate in many sports at an international level.

TEAM SPORTS

Badminton

Portugal Badminton Team

Baseball

Portugal Baseball Team; Portugal Softball Team

Basketball

Portugal Basketball Team; Portugal Women's Basketball Team; Portugal Under-19 Basketball Team; Portugal Wheelchair Basketball Team

Cricket

Portugal Cricket Team

Football

Portugal Football Team, nickname Selecção das Quinas (Team of the Bezants or Team of the Shields); Portugal Women's Football Team, nickname Selecção das Quinas (Team of the Bezants or Team of the Shields); Portugal Rugby League Team; Portugal Rugby Union Team; Portugal Women's Rugby Union Team; Portugal Under-21 Football Team; Portugal Women's Under-19 Football Team; Portugal Rugby Union Team (Sevens), nickname Portugal Sevens or 7s; Portugal Women's Rugby Union Team (Sevens), nickname Portugal Sevens or Portugal 7s; Portugal Beach Soccer Team; Portugal Futsal Team; Portugal American Football

Handball

Portugal Handball Team; Portugal Women's Handball Team; Portugal Beach Handball Team; Portugal Women's Beach Handball Team

Hockey

Portugal Ice Hockey Team; Portugal Roller Hockey Team

Korfball

Portugal Korfball Team

Racing

Ai Team Portugal; Portugal Speedway Team

Table Tennis

Portugal Men's Table Tennis Team; Portugal Women's Table Tennis Team

Tennis

Portugal Davis Cup Team; Portugal Fed Cup Team

Volleyball

Portugal Men's Volleyball Team; Portugal Women's Volleyball Team; Portugal Men's Beach Volleyball Team; Portugal Women's Beach Volleyball Team

INDIVIDUAL SPORTS

Portugal Aikido Team; Portugal Amateur Boxing Team; Portugal Archery Team; Portugal Athletics Team; Portugal Canoeing Team; Portugal Cycling Team; Portugal Equestrian Team; Portugal Fencing Team; Portugal Gymnastics Team; Portugal Judo Team; Portugal Karate Team: Portugal Modern Pentathlon Team; Portugal Rowing Team; Portugal Sailing Team; Portugal Shooting Team; Portugal Swim Team; Portugal Tae Kwon Do Team; Portugal Triathlon Team; Portugal Weight Lifting Team; Portugal Wrestling Team

WINTER SPORTS

Portugal Biathlon Team; Portugal Field Hockey Team; Portugal Skating Team

NATIONAL HEROES OR PERSONIFICATIONS

Zé Povinho is a personification of the Portuguese working class; Eu Nacional, the national self, is a personification of the Portugal to come; Lusitania, from the Roman name for the region, is a personification of Portugal and the Portuguese; and República, an effigy of the republic, is a national personification symbolizing the republic.

National heroes include Vasco de Gama, a famed explorer and the commander of the first ships to sail directly from Europe to India*; Pedro Álvares Cabral, regarded as the European discoverer of Brazil*; Henry the Navigator, the prince responsible for the beginning of the European worldwide explorations; and Aristides de Souza Mendes, the Portuguese consul in Bordeaux during World War II, who defied his government by giving visas to over 30,000 people fleeing the Nazi terror.

NATIONAL HOLIDAY/INDEPENDENCE DAY

Portugal Day, June 10

FESTIVALS/FAIRS

Carnival, February–March; Holy Week (the week before Easter), March; Algarve Music Festival, May–June; Festas da Cidade (Lisbon City Festival), June; Festival dos Oceanos (Two Oceans Festival), August; Romaria da Nossa Senhora de Nazaré, September

SIGNIFICANT EVENTS IN FORMATION OF NATIONAL IDENTITY

3000 B.C.E.–1000 B.C.E. Tribal groups dominate the region.

1104 B.C.E.–258 B.C.E. Phoenicians colonize the coastal regions. The Phoenicians' most successful colony, Carthage, takes control.

15 B.C.E. The region, called Lusitania, becomes part of the Roman Empire.

416 C.E. The collapse of Roman power opens the way for invasions by Germanic peoples from northern Europe. The Visigoths conquer Lusitania and create a Christian kingdom.

711 Arab invaders, known as Moors, invade the Iberian Peninsula from North Africa. The Christians retreat north to parts of the peninsula outside Muslim rule.

868 During the *Reconquista,* as the Christians advance into Muslim-held territories from the north, nobles create the first county of Portugal.

1139–1272 The Portuguese victory over the Moors at Ourique is traditionally considered the occasion when the county, then part of the Kingdom of Leon, becomes an independent kingdom. The last Moorish stronghold falls, ending Muslim rule in Portugal.

1373 The Portuguese kingdom makes an alliance with England, the oldest alliance still in existence in Europe.

1415–1500 A Portuguese fleet conquers Ceuta, a prosperous trade center on the coast of North Africa and the kingdom's first overseas colony. Explorers begin to sail farther from shore, encountering the Azores and Madeira, which are then colonized by settlers from the mainland. Other explorers, under Prince Henry the Navigator, sail around Africa and into the Indian Ocean. Vasco de Gama becomes the first European to sail directly to India. Pedro Álvares Cabral, en route to India, encounters Brazil and claims the land for Portugal.

1580–1640 Dynastic succession brings Portugal under Spanish rule.

1807–1822 Portugal is conquered by the French under Napoleon, causing chaos in the colonial possessions. Brazil declares its independence.

1910 A popular revolution ends the Portuguese monarchy.

1926 A military coup brings a fascist government to power.

1939–1949 Portugal remains neutral during the Second World War. The country becomes a founding member of the North Atlantic Treaty Organization (NATO).

1951 António de Oliveira Salazar becomes president of Portugal, maintaining the fascist government.

1954–1974 Liberation movements in the remaining African colonies disrupt the country. The Carnation Revolution brings an end to five decades of dictatorship. Most of the colonies become independent.

1986 Portugal joins the European Community, the later European Union (EU). Structural funds from the EU aid the country in creating a modern economy.

1999 The last Portuguese colony, Macau*, is returned to Chinese sovereignty.

2000–2009 The Portuguese parliament votes to bring the spelling of the Portuguese language more in line with Brazilian spellings. Although the country has one of the lowest per capita incomes in Western Europe, it rates high in lifestyle satisfaction and some ratings based on criteria other than economic.

See also Azores; Madeira

ROMANIA

OFFICIAL NAME
România (Romanian); Romania (English)

POPULATION
22,231,400 (2009e)

INHABITANTS' NAME/NICKNAME
Romanian(s)

LANGUAGE/LANGUAGES
Romanian (official); Hungarian, German, Romani, Croatian, Ukrainian, and Serbian (official at various local levels)

RELIGION/RELIGIONS
Romanian Orthodox, 85 percent; Roman Catholic, 5 percent; Protestant, 3.5 percent; other or no religion

NATIONAL FLAG
The flag is a vertical tricolor of equal stripes of blue, yellow, and red. The colors of the flag go back at least as far as the middle ages. Popular sentiment has the blue symbolizing the sky over the Romanian lands, the

yellow symbolizing the unity of the various branches of the Romanian people, and the red the blood sacrificed to achieve unity and freedom. The colors also represent the three historic regions of Wallachia, Moldavia, and Transylvania.

COAT OF ARMS/SEAL

The coat of arms is a blue field charged with a golden eagle holding a cross in its beak and a mace and sword in its claws. A central crest carries the heraldic emblems of the historic regions that make up the Romanian nation. The colors are those of the national flag.

CAPITAL CITY

Bucharest

TYPE OF GOVERNMENT

Unitary semipresidential republic

NATIONAL EMBLEM

Vlad III, known as Dracula; oak leaf

NATIONAL COLORS

Blue, yellow, and red

NATIONAL ANTHEM

The anthem is based on a popular protest song that emerged in the last days of the communist government. The new democratic government in 1990 adopted it.

Deşteaptă-te, Române (Romanian); Awaken, Romanian! (English)

Awaken thee, Romanian, shake off thy deadly slumber
The scourge of inauspicious barbarian tyrannies
And now or never to a bright horizon clamber
That shall to shame put all your enemies.

It's now or never to the world we readily proclaim
In our veins throbs Roman blood
And in our hearts forever we glorify a name
Resounding of battle, the name of gallant Trajan.

Do look, imperial shadows, Michael, Stephen, Corvinus
At the Romanian nation, your mighty progeny
With arms like steel and hearts of fire impetuous
It's either free or dead, that's what they all decree.

Priests, raise the cross, this Christian army's liberating
The word is freedom, no less sacred is the end
We'd rather die in battle, in elevated glory
Than live again enslaved on our ancestral land.

PATRON SAINT

Saint Nicetas; Saint Andrew

CURRENCY

Romanian leu; Romania hopes to adopt the euro in 2014

INTERNET IDENTIFIER

.ro

VEHICLE IDENTIFICATION PLATES/STICKERS

RO

PASSPORT

The passport cover has the name of the European Union, in Romanian; and the name of the country, Romania; the coat of arms; the Romanian word for passport, *pasaport*; and the standard biometric symbol.

AIRLINE

Romanian Air Transport TAROM

NATIONAL FLOWER

Dog rose

NATIONAL TREE

Oak (unofficial)

NATIONAL ANIMAL

Lynx

NATIONAL BIRD

Golden eagle

NATIONAL RESOURCES

Natural resources include declining petroleum reserves, timber, natural gas, coal, iron ore, salt, arable land, and hydropower. Tourism, based on the country's varied scenery; historic cities and monuments, such as Dracula's Castle; and unique culture are the basis of a rapidly growing tourist industry. Romania's economic gains have only recently started to spur creation of a middle class and to address Romania's widespread poverty. Corruption and red tape continue to handicap the business environment. Remittances from Romanians living and working in other parts of the European Union (EU) and EU structural funds are important resources.

FOODS

Mamaliga, a thick cornmeal mush that is historically a peasant food, is now considered a national dish. Other typical dishes include *mititei,* grilled minced meat rolls filled with garlic and spices; *shkembe chorba,* beef or pork stomach soup; *placinta,* small pastries filled with meat or vegetables; *perisoare,* meatball soup; *cozonac,* a sweet bread prepared for holidays; *fasole cu cârnati,* beans with sausages or *afumătură* (smoked meat); *tochitura,* a type of stew with several regional varieties; and *ardel umpluti,* green bell peppers stuffed with meat and rice with a tomato sauce.

SPORTS/SPORTS TEAMS

Association football (soccer) is the most popular sport. Other popular sports include handball, basketball and, athletics, and gymnastics. Romania national teams participate in many sports at an international level.

TEAM SPORTS

Badminton

Romania Badminton Team

Baseball

Romania Baseball Team; Romania Softball Team

Basketball

Romania Basketball Team; Romania Women's Basketball Team

Football

Romania Football Team, nickname Tricolorii (the Tricolors); Romania Women's Football Team, nickname Tricolorii (the Tricolors); Romania Under-21 Football Team; Romania Rugby Union Team, nickname Stejani (the Oaks); Romania Women's Rugby Union Team, nickname Stejani (the Oaks); Romania American Football Team; Romania Beach Soccer Team; Romania Futsal Team; Romania Rugby Union Team (Sevens), nickname Romania Sevens or Romania 7s; Romania Women's Rugby Union Team (Sevens), nickname Romania Sevens or Romania 7s

Handball

Romania Handball Team; Romania Women's Handball Team

Hockey

Romania Ice Hockey Team; Romania Junior Ice Hockey Team; Romania Women's Ice Hockey Team; Romania Field Hockey Team

Korfball

Romania Korfball Team

Racing

Romania Speedway Team

Table Tennis

Romania Table Tennis Team

Tennis

Romania Davis Cup Team; Romania Fed Cup Team; Romania Tennis Team

Volleyball

Romania Men's Volleyball Team; Romania Women's Volleyball Team

INDIVIDUAL SPORTS

Romania Amateur Boxing Team; Romania Archery Team; Romania Athletics Team; Romania Canoeing Team; Romania Cycling Team; Romania Equestrian Team; Romania Fencing Team; Romania Gymnastics Team; Romania Judo Team; Romania Karate Team: Romania Modern Pentathlon Team; Romania Rowing Team; Romania Sailing Team; Romania Shooting Team; Romania Swim Team; Romania Tae Kwon Do Team; Romania Triathlon Team; Romania Weight Lifting Team; Romania Wrestling Team

WINTER SPORTS

Romania Alpine Ski Team; Romania Biathlon Team; Romania Bobsleigh and Tobogganing Team; Romania Ice Hockey Team; Romania Junior Ice Hockey Team; Romania Women's Ice Hockey Team; Romania Luge Team; Romania Skating Team

NATIONAL HEROES OR PERSONIFICATIONS

Romania is the female personification of the Romanian nation.

National heroes include Vlad III, called Vlad Tepes or Vlad the Impaler, known as Dracula, a patriot known for his use of extreme methods in opposing Turkish invaders; Stephen III of Moldavia (Saint Stephen the Great), a ruler of medieval Moldavia who resisted invasions by Hungarians, Poles, and Ottoman Turks; Alexander John Cuza, the first ruler of the United Principalities of Wallachia and Moldavia; Michael the Brave, the first ruler to unite the three Romanian principalities in the late 16th century; Constantin Brâncoveanu, Prince of Wallachia, who was imprisoned and beheaded with his four sons by the Ottoman Turks in the early 18th century; and Ecaterina Teodoroiu, a Romanian woman who personified Romania when she fought and died in World War I.

NATIONAL HOLIDAY/INDEPENDENCE DAY

Unification Day, December 1

FESTIVALS/FAIRS

Sighişoara Medieval Festival, July; George Enescu Festival, September in alternate years; Traditional Crafts Fair, June; Medieval Days Festival, July; Folk Art Festival, August; Wine Festival, October; Christmas Traditions Festival, December

SIGNIFICANT EVENTS IN FORMATION OF NATIONAL IDENTITY

513 B.C.E. The first mention is made of Dacians inhabiting the region in the writing of the Roman Herodotus.

86 B.C.E.–74 B.C.E. The Dacian kingdom is at its height of power and expansion. The first encounter occurs between the Dacians and the expanding Roman Empire.

101 C.E.–106 C.E. The Romans invade and finally defeat the Dacians. Dacia becomes a Roman province.

271–600 The Romans withdraw to south of the Danube, leaving the Romanized population to the mercy of invading tribes. The Roman language survives in the region.

10th century The first Romanian state emerges.

1054 After the Great Schism between the Church of Rome and Constantinople, Romania retains ties to the Orthodox faith under the authority of the Patriarch of Constantinople.

1288 According to tradition, the first diet (parliament) of Transylvania meets.

1369 Ottoman Turks make their first raids into Romanian territory.

1428 Vlad III, called Vlad Tepes or Vlad the Impaler, becomes Prince of Wallachia.

1703–1711 War against the Hapsburgs ends in defeat and the loss of Transylvania to Austria* and Hungary*.

1859–1861 Alexander John Cuza is elected prince of both Moldavia and Wallachia, achieving a de facto union of the two principalities. The union is declared, and Romania becomes a unified nation.

1916–1920 Romania joins the Allies during World War I, which ends with the unification of Romania and Transylvania, including a large Hungarian minority. Romania becomes a kingdom.

1930s A fascist Iron Guard movement emerges.

1938 King Carol II establishes a dictatorship in an effort to restore order. A Nazi pact returns part of Transylvania to Hungarian rule.

1940–1947 Romania joins the Axis during World War II in an effort to recover territory taken by Hungary and the Soviet Union. Defeated but reunited, Romania becomes a Soviet satellite state under a communist government.

1965–1989 Nicolae Ceausescu becomes Romanian Communist Party leader. Ceausescu maintains a firm grip on Romania while attempting to distance himself from the Soviet Union. Mismanagement, cronyism, and corruption lead to food shortages and widespread power cuts.

1989 A national uprising overthrows Ceausescu, who is executed along with his wife. Violence leaves hundreds dead.

1990 Free elections are held, and a new government begins to apply much-needed reforms.

2001 The government approves a law aimed at returning property taken from its original owners under communist rule.

2004 The government admits Romanian complicity in the Holocaust deaths of hundreds of thousands of Jews and other Romanians during World War II.

2007–2009 Romania joins the European Union (EU). The EU calls on Romania to do more to combat corruption and threatens to withhold farm subsidies if the government does not reform its agricultural policies. Romania hopes to adopt the European currency, the euro, in 2014.

RUSSIA

OFFICIAL NAME

Rossiyskaya Federatsiya (Russian); Russian Federation (English)

POPULATION

141,987,400 (2009e)

INHABITANTS' NAME/NICKNAME

Russian(s)

LANGUAGE/LANGUAGES

Russian (official); 27 other languages are co-official in various member republics and regions.

RELIGION/RELIGIONS

Russian Orthodox, 15–20 percent; Muslim, 10–15 percent; Jewish, Roman Catholic, Protestant, Buddhist, other or no religion

NATIONAL FLAG

The flag is a horizontal tricolor of white, blue, and red. The colors became the pan-Slav colors used in many flags by Europe's Slavic nations. There are several theories as to the origin of the colors. One states that they stem from the coat of arms of the Grand Duchy of Moscow, another that they are taken from the robes of the Virgin Mary, Russia's patron protectress. Another theory is that the colors stand for the three East Slav nations, Belarus*, Ukraine*, and Russia.

COAT OF ARMS/SEAL

The coat of arms is a crest or shield of red charged with the Russian two-headed eagle behind a smaller shield depicting Saint George slaying the dragon. The symbols go back to the medieval Grand Duchy of Moscow and possibly further back in history.

CAPITAL CITY

Moscow

TYPE OF GOVERNMENT

Federal semipresidential republic

NATIONAL EMBLEMS

Russian Eagle (two-headed eagle); Mother Russia (the Motherland Calls) statue at Volgograd (128 feet taller than the Statue of Liberty)

NATIONAL COLORS

White, blue, and red

NATIONAL ANTHEM

The former anthem, adopted in 1990, had no lyrics, so a new anthem was adopted in 2000, based on the anthem of the former Soviet Union with new lyrics to fit the melody.

Gosudarstvenny Gimn Rossiyskoy Federatsii (transliteration from Russian); Hymn of the Russian Federation (English)

Russia—our sacred stronghold,
Russia—our beloved country.
A mighty will, a great glory
Are your inheritance for all time!

Chorus

Be glorious, our free Motherland,
Ancient union of brotherly peoples,
Ancestor given wisdom of the people!
Be glorious, country! We take pride in you!

From the southern seas to the polar region
Spread our forests and our fields.
You are one in the world! You are one of a
  kind,
Native land protected by God!

Chorus

A broad expanse for dreams and for lives
Is opened to us by the coming years
Our faith in our Motherland gives us
  strength.
So it was, so it is, and so it will always be!

PATRON SAINT

The Virgin Mary, the holy protectress of Russia; Saint Nicholas; Saint Andrew; Saint George; Saint Alexander Nevsky

CURRENCY

Russian ruble

INTERNET IDENTIFIER

.ru

VEHICLE IDENTIFICATION PLATES/ STICKERS

RUS

PASSPORT

The passport cover has the name of the country in Russian and English, the coat of arms, the word *passport* in Russian and English, and the standard biometric symbol.

AIRLINES

Aeroflot; Rossiya; Transaero; Ural Airlines

NATIONAL FLOWER

Chamomile

NATIONAL TREE

Birch

NATIONAL ANIMAL

Bear

NATIONAL BIRD

Golden eagle

NATIONAL RESOURCES

Natural resources are numerous and varied, including major deposits of oil, natural gas, coal, and many strategic minerals, timber, fish and arable land. Formidable obstacles of climate, terrain, and distance hinder exploitation of natural resources, however. From 1990, poverty has declined steadily and the middle class has continued to expand. Tourism, supported by varied scenery, historical cities and monuments, varied cultures and the growth of cruise lines visiting the country's Baltic and Black sea ports, is becoming an important industry.

FOODS

The best-known of Russia's national dishes is borscht, a soup of beets, beef broth, onions, and sour cream. Caviar with sour cream and vodka is also considered a national dish. Other national specialties include blintzes, a type of crepe served in a variety of ways; *pelmeni,* small pastries of unleavened dough filled with minced meat, potato, vegetables, or other ingredients; pierogis, boiled dumplings with meat fillings; *shashlyk,* skewered grilled meats; *kasha,* a porridge made of buckwheat, oats or semolina usually eaten at breakfast; *okroshka,* a cold soup made with *kvas,* a fermented broth of black or rye bread; *ukha,* a hot fish soup; and *kotlety,* small meatballs.

SPORTS/SPORTS TEAMS

Association football (soccer), ice hockey, and basketball are the most popular sports. Russia national teams participate in many sports at an international level.

TEAM SPORTS

Badminton
Russia Badminton Team

Baseball
Russia Baseball Team; Russia Softball Team

Basketball
Russia Basketball Team; Russia Women's Basketball Team; Russia Wheelchair Basketball Team

Cricket
Russia Cricket Team

Football
Russia Men's Football Team, nickname the Bears; Russia Women's Football Team nickname the Bears; Russia Under-21 Football Team; Russia Women's Under-19 Football Team; Rugby Union Team, nickname the Bears; Russia Women's Rugby Union Team, nickname the Bears; Russia Rugby League Team, nickname the Bears; Russia American Football Team; Russia Beach Soccer Team; Russia Rugby Union Team (Sevens), nickname Russia Sevens or Russia 7s; Russia Women's Rugby Union Team (Sevens), nickname Russia Sevens or Russia 7s; Russia Futsal Team

Handball
Russia Handball Team; Russia Women's Handball Team; Russia Beach Handball Team; Russia Women's Beach Handball Team; Russia Beach Handball Team; Russia Women's Beach Handball Team

Hockey
Russia Ice Hockey Team; Russia Women's Ice Hockey Team; Russia Junior Ice Hockey Team; Russia Field Hockey Team

Kabaddi
Russia Kabaddi Team

Korfball
Russia Korfball Team

Racing
A1 Team Russia; Russia Speedway Team

Table Tennis
Russia Table Tennis Team

Tennis
Russia Fed Cup Team; Russia Davis Cup Team

Volleyball
Russia Men's Volleyball Team; Russia Women's Volleyball Team; Russia Men's Beach Volleyball Team; Russia Women's Beach Volleyball Team

Water Polo
Russia Water Polo Team; Russia Women's Water Polo Team

INDIVIDUAL SPORTS

Russia Aikido Team; Russia Amateur Boxing Team; Russia Archery Team; Russia Athletics Team; Russia Canoeing Team; Russia Cycling Team; Russia Equestrian Team; Russia Fencing Team; Russia Gymnastics Team; Russia Judo Team; Russia Karate Team: Russia Modern Pentathlon Team; Russia Rowing Team; Russia Sailing Team; Russia Shooting Team; Russia Swim Team; Russia Tae Kwon Do Team; Russia Triathlon Team; Russia Weight Lifting Team; Russia Wrestling Team

WINTER SPORTS

Russia Alpine Ski Team; Russia Bandy Team; Russia Women's Bandy Team; Russia Biathlon Team; Russia Bobsleigh and Tobogganing Team; Russia Curling Team; Russia Ice Hockey Team; Russia Women's Ice Hockey Team; Russia Junior Ice Hockey Team; Russia Luge Team; Russia Skating Team

NATIONAL HEROES OR PERSONIFICATIONS

Mother Russia, known as Mother Motherland during the Soviet period, is a personification of Russia. The bear, the national animal, is often used to personify Russia.

National heroes include Czar Peter the Great, who modernized Russia in the early 18th century; Marshall Illarionovich Kutuzov, the military leader who repelled Napoleon's attack in the early 19th century; Marshall Georgi Zhukov, military leader of World War II; Mikhail Gorbachev, Soviet leader who began the end of communism in Russia; Vladimir Lenin, leader of the movement that overthrew the monarchy in 1917; Joseph Stalin, dictator of the Soviet Union, known for his strong leadership and many excesses; and Yuri Gagarin, the first man to go into space in 1961.

NATIONAL HOLIDAY/INDEPENDENCE DAY

Russia Day, June 12

FESTIVALS/FAIRS

Christmas Festival Saint Petersburg, January; Farewell to the Russian Winter, February–March; Saint Petersburg Music Spring, April; White Nights International Festival of Popular Music, June; Stars of the White Nights (Classical) Festival, May–June; Victory Day celebrations, May; Easter Festival, March–April

SIGNIFICANT EVENTS IN FORMATION OF NATIONAL IDENTITY

862 C.E.–882 C.E. Rurik, a semilegendary Scandinavian leader, establishes a settlement at Novgorod around 862 as the capital of the Varangian Viking kingdom called Rus'. The capital is moved to Kiev, giving the growing kingdom a new name, Kievan Rus'.

988 Vladimir, the ruler of Kievan Rus', destroys the pagan idols in Kiev and urges the inhabitants to baptize themselves in the Dnieper River.

1236–1263 Alexander Nevsky becomes Grand Prince of the trading Republic of Novgorod and leads Slavic resistance to Swedish and German invaders.

1237–1478 The Mongols invade Kievan Rus', leaving a large number of districts virtually depopulated and in ruins. The Mongol Golden Horde continues to oversee politics in the Russian principalities. Russia stops paying annual tribute to the Golden Horde. Novgorod is brought under Moscow's rule. Serfdom, virtual slavery, becomes widely practiced.

16th century–17th century Russia expands its borders in all directions through conquest or alliances. Wars with Sweden*, Poland*, Lithuania*, and other European states add to the expanding empire.

18th century Czar Peter I expands the empire to the south following war with the Ottoman Empire. A new capital, nicknamed Russia's "Window on the West," is built at Saint Petersburg. A limited legislature is created. Wars with Sweden extend Russian rule to the Baltic. Catherine the Great takes the throne in 1725.

1809–1812 Finland* is taken from Sweden. The French under Napoleon invade Russia and reach Moscow. Napoleon is forced to retreat by the Russian winter, losing tens of thousands of soldiers.

1904–1905 The Russo-Japanese War ends with Russian defeat, the first time a European power is defeated in Asia. The Revolution of 1905 spreads, with demands for reforms in the feudal, backward empire.

1914–1921 Russia enters World War I. After three years of hardship and massive losses, a revolution begins that eventually overthrows the monarchy and establishes a communist dictatorship. Civil war between the Red Army of the new government and the Whites, or anticommunists, devastates the country.

1939 Leader Joseph Stalin endorses an alliance with Nazi Germany to separate the countries lying between the two powers into spheres of influence. Germany* and the Soviet Union invade Poland, setting off World War II.

1941–1946 Hitler turns on his Soviet ally and invades the Soviet Union. Up to 20 million Soviet citizens perish in the war. Soviet troops drive deep into Central Europe, setting up communist governments in the countries under Soviet occupation.

1950–1989 The Cold War, the undeclared rivalry between the West and the Soviet bloc, includes a nuclear standoff and proxy wars around the globe.

1980s Mikhail Gorbachev begins much-needed political and economic reforms that spiral out of control, leading to the disintegration of the Soviet Empire.

1990–1992 Communism is ended in the Soviet Union, which splinters into 15 new countries. The Russian Federation inherits the Soviet Union's international commitments.

2000–2008 Instability and successive confrontations with ethnic separatists, the international community, and factions within the country continue to mar Russia's growing prosperity.

2009 In a dispute with neighboring Ukraine, the Russian government stops gas supplies, which also disrupts gas deliveries to other parts of Europe. Gambling becomes so widespread that the government, in July 2009, bans casinos and gambling houses from all but the regions farthest from Moscow.

See also Chechnya; Tuva

SAN MARINO

OFFICIAL NAME
La Serenissima Repubblica de San Marino; (Italian); The Most Serene Republic of San Marino (English)

POPULATION
30,900 (2009e)

INHABITANTS' NAME/NICKNAME
Sammarinese; San Marinese

LANGUAGE/LANGUAGES
Italian (official)

RELIGION/RELIGIONS
Roman Catholic, 88 percent; Pentecostal, 2 percent; other or no religion

NATIONAL FLAG
The flag has two equal horizontal stripes of white over blue with the national coat of arms centered. The colors are the heraldic colors of the medieval state of San Marino.

COAT OF ARMS/SEAL
The coat of arms has a central gold frame around a blue field with three green mountains surmounted by three silver towers, each decorated with a silver ostrich feather. The towers symbolize the three citadels built on the three summits of Monte Titano. Above the frame is a gold crown symbolizing sovereignty. Around the frame are branches of oak and laurel, symbols of stability and the defense of liberty, and beneath is a white banner inscribed with the national motto.

MOTTO

Libertas (Latin); Liberty (English)

CAPITAL CITY

San Marino

TYPE OF GOVERNMENT

Parliamentary republic

NATIONAL EMBLEM

The Three Towers

NATIONAL COLORS

Pale blue and white

NATIONAL ANTHEM

The anthem is based on a 10th century chorale piece. There are no official lyrics, but the unofficial lyrics are quite popular.

Inno Nazionale della Repubblica (Italian); National Anthem of the Republic (English)

O ancient Republic
Honor to you, virtuous
Honor to you
(repeat)

Generous fidelity,
O virtuous one.
O Republic,

Honor and eternal life,
With the life
And glory of Italy
O Republic
Honor to you.

PATRON SAINT

Saint Martinus

CURRENCY

Euro

INTERNET IDENTIFIER

.sm

VEHICLE IDENTIFICATION PLATES/ STICKERS

RSM

PASSPORT

The passport cover has the name of the country in Italian, the coat of arms, and the Italian word for passport, *passaporto.*

NATIONAL FLOWER

Cyclamen

NATIONAL TREE

Laurel (unofficial)

NATIONAL RESOURCES

Natural resources are limited to building stone. The important tourist industry, banking, light manufacturing, and ceramics are the mainstays of the country, giving the Sammarinese a standard of living comparable to neighboring Italy.

FOODS

National dishes include *faggioli con le cotiche,* a Christmas soup of beans flavored with bacon; *pasta e cede,* a soup of noodles and chickpeas flavored with rosemary and garlic; *nidi di rondine,* called swallow's nest, a pasta dish with smoked ham, cheese, beef, and tomato sauce, covered in white sauce and baked; *passatelli al formaggio de fossa,* a pastry made of bread, cheese, eggs, nutmeg, and lemon rind; *coniglio farcito,* stuffed roasted rabbit; and *erbazzone,* a spinach dish with onions and cheese.

SPORTS/SPORTS TEAMS

Association football (soccer) and volleyball are popular sports. San Marino national teams participate in many sports at an international level.

TEAM SPORTS

Baseball

San Marino Baseball Team; San Marino Softball Team

Basketball

San Marino Basketball Team; San Marino Women's Basketball Team

Football

San Marino Football Team, nickname La Serenissima, the Big Club; San Marino Women's Football Team, nickname La Serenissima; San Marino Futsal Team; San Marino Rugby Union Team

Golf

San Marino Men's Pitch and Putt Team

Hockey

San Marino Field Hockey Team

Racing

San Marino Speedway Team

Table Tennis

San Marino Table Tennis Team

Tennis

San Marino Davis Cup Team; San Marino Fed Cup Team

Volleyball

San Marino Men's Volleyball Team; San Marino Women's Volleyball Team

INDIVIDUAL SPORTS

San Marino Amateur Boxing Team; San Marino Archery Team; San Marino Athletics Team; San Marino Cycling Team; San Marino Equestrian Team; San Marino Fencing Team; San Marino Gymnastics Team; San Marino Judo Team; San Marina Shooting Team; San Marino Swim Team San Marino Tae Kwon Do Team; San Marino Weight Lifting Team; San Marino Wrestling Team

WINTER SPORTS

San Marino Alpine Ski Team

NATIONAL HEROES OR PERSONIFICATIONS

Giuseppe Garibaldi, an Italian military and political leader of the 19th century whose statue stands in San Marino; Domenico Fattori, foreign minister of San Marino from 1860 to 1908, the man credited with resisting incorporation into Italy*

NATIONAL HOLIDAY/INDEPENDENCE DAY

San Marino Day, September 3

FESTIVALS/FAIRS

Liberation Day celebrations, February; National Day celebrations, April; San Marino Day/Republic Day celebrations, September; San Marino Formula One Grand Prix, April

SIGNIFICANT EVENTS IN FORMATION OF NATIONAL IDENTITY

301 C.E. According to tradition, a stonecutter named Marino is persecuted for his Christian beliefs. He flees to Monte Titano, where he constructs a small church, the basis for the city and state of San Marino.

Fifth century The mountain community organizes to resist control from outside its borders.

1631 San Marino's independence is recognized by the papacy.

1860–1870 During the upheavals of Italian unification, San Marino serves as a refuge for people persecuted for their support of unification. In honor of this, Giuseppe Garibaldi accepts the Sammarinese wish not to be incorporated into unified Italy.

1914–1945 San Marino joins Italy in declaring war on Austria* in 1915, but declares neutrality when Italy declares war on the Allies in 1945. American and British troops occupy the country in pursuit of retreating Germans but withdraw after a few weeks.

1945–1957 The country elects the world's first freely elected communist government, which governs the country until 1957.

1968 San Marino remains the world's smallest republic from 301 to 1968, when the small island nation of Nauru gains independence.

1988–1992 The country joins the Council of Europe and the United Nations.

2002–2009 San Marino agrees to greater banking transparency to help combat tax evasion by Italian investors. Although not a member state of the European Union (EU), San Marino maintains many ties to the union through Italy, including use of its currency, the euro.

SAPMI

OFFICIAL NAME

The Sápmi (Sami) or Sapmi or Samiland (English) region, divided between Norway, Sweden, Finland, and the Kola Peninsula of Russia, has no official name. Unofficially, it is commonly called Lapland or Lappland.

POPULATION

200,000 (2009e)

INHABITANTS' NAME/NICKNAME

Sami(s); Lap(s); Lapp(s); Laplander(s)

LANGUAGE/LANGUAGES

Sami languages (official in northern Norway and in some areas of Sweden and Finland); Norwegian, Swedish, Finnish, Russian

RELIGION/RELIGIONS

Lutheran, 90 percent; Russian Orthodox, other or no religion

NATIONAL FLAG

The Sami flag, recognized by all Samis, is a blue field with a broad red stripe at the hoist divided from the blue by narrow vertical stripes of green and yellow. A circle centered on the division is divided vertically, blue near the hoist and red on the fly. The colors are interpreted as red for fire, blue for water, yellow for air, and green for earth, with the circle representing the sun and the moon. Others claim the colors come from the traditional dress of many Sami groups.

COAT OF ARMS/SEAL

The *poppamies* of a *noltarumpu,* drawings on the head of a ceremonial drum, is considered the seal of the Sapmi region. Although many designs are used, the favored design is a magical cross in control of the four elements, known as *poppamies*. The coat of arms of Finnish Sapmi is a red, crowned shield bearing a depiction of Aigin, the Sapmi national hero; the coat of arms of Norwegian Sapmi is a black shield charged with a gold fortress; and the coat of arms of Swedish Sapmi is a white shield bearing a depiction of Aigin.

CAPITAL CITY

Kautokeino, called Guovdageaidnu by the Sami, in Norway (unofficial)

TYPE OF GOVERNMENT

The territory of Sapmi is divided between Norway, Sweden, Finland, and Russia. There are Sami parliaments in the Sami areas of Norway, Sweden, and Finland that give them broad powers of autonomy. On November 16, 2005, in Helsinki, a group of experts submitted a proposal for a Nordic Sami Convention to the annual joint meeting of the ministers responsible for Sami affairs in Finland, Norway, and Sweden and the presidents of the three Sami parliaments from the respective countries. This convention recognizes the Sami as one indigenous people residing across national borders in all three countries. A set of minimum standards is proposed for the rights of developing the Sami language, culture, livelihoods and society. The convention has not yet been ratified in the Nordic countries.

NATIONAL EMBLEM

Reindeer

NATIONAL COLORS

Blue, red, yellow, and green

NATIONAL ANTHEM

The anthem is based on a poem written by Isak Saba, which was published for the first time in 1906. It was adopted as the national anthem in 1986.

> **Sàmi soga lávlla (Sami); Song of the Sami People (English)**
>
> North under the Great Bear
> Sápmi shines,
> Ridge upon ridge,
> lake stretching into lake.
> Rocky cliffs, craggy peaks
> point to the sky.
> Streams laugh, woods whisper
> precipice drops, steely point
> descends to stormy sea.
>
> Frost bites hard in winter,
> blizzards chased by crazy winds.
> But we Sami love this
> with all our heart.
> Moonlight helps a traveler,
> soaring borealis adds to joy.
> Hoof steps, reindeer voices
> in the brush—
> over lake and tundra the sled glides on.
>
> When summer sun shines gold
> on wood, on sea, on shore,
> fishing boats glisten,
> rocking wavy seas.
> Sea birds sail a glittering harbor,
> on silver streams steersmen *yoiking*.
> Oars are shining,
> boat poles flashing
> from pools to rapids to falls.
>
> Sápmi blood, oh Sami—
> survivors of the
> killing bands, cheating merchants,
> wicked taxmen.
> Hail, resilient Sami!

> Hail, the root and branch of peace!
> No wars flared
> and spilled the blood of Sápmi's clan.
>
> Our ancestors withstood
> cruel aggression in the old days.
> Family members, again we must
> combat oppression!
> Children of the sun!
> No one subdues us
> if we keep our golden language,
> and hold our
> elders' words of wisdom:
> Sápmi for the Sami.

PATRON SAINT

Saint Nicholas (unofficial)

CURRENCY

Sami use the local currency of each country.

VEHICLE IDENTIFICATION PLATES/STICKERS

Officially, the plate/sticker of Norway, Sweden, Finland, or Russia is used. Unofficially, some Sami use SAP or SÁP.

PASSPORT

The Sami are citizens of Norway, Sweden, Finland, or Russia and travel on the passports of those countries.

NATIONAL FLOWER

Globe flower (official in Finnish Sapmi); mountain avens (official in Swedish Sapmi)

NATIONAL TREE

Mountain birch (Unofficial)

NATIONAL ANIMAL

Reindeer

NATIONAL BIRD

Lapland bunting (unofficial)

NATIONAL FISH

Muikku (unofficial)

NATIONAL RESOURCES

The area has abundant grazing land, although the cool climate limits its use. There are deposits of iron and coal, and hydroelectric power is being developed.

FOODS

Traditionally, the Sami diet has been based on local materials, like fish, game, reindeer, and berries. Because of the climate, the products of agriculture were rare, unlike in other parts of Sweden, Norway, and Finland. Reindeer is essential for Sami cuisine, but game, fish, and wild birds are also important. Smoking and drying has traditionally been used to preserve meat and fish. *Souvas*, a salted and smoked reindeer filet, is the region's oldest food tradition and is considered the national dish. Other traditional foods include *guossalipma*, pine tree soup; *reiska*, a flatbread made of barley; *veriohukaiset*, blood pancakes; and *poronkâristys*, sautéed reindeer with onions from Finnish Sapmi.

SPORTS/SPORTS TEAMS

Ice hockey and skiing are the traditional sports. Skis are a Sami invention. Association football (soccer) is now the most popular sport across the region.

TEAM SPORTS

Football

Sapmi Football Team; Sapmi Women's Football Team

NATIONAL HEROES OR PERSONIFICATIONS

Aigin, the hero of a thousand-year-old legend (depicted on the coats of arms of Finnish and Swedish Sapmi); Lars Levi Laestadius, credited with the conversion of the majority of the Sami to Lutheranism in the 19th century; Isak Mikal Saba, an early Sami politician, the first Sami parliamentarian, and the author of the Sami national anthem; Johan Thuuri, the writer of the first Sami novel in the national language; Elsa Laula Renberg, the organizer of the first international Sami conference in the early 20th century

NATIONAL HOLIDAY/INDEPENDENCE DAY

Sami National Day, February 6

FESTIVALS/FAIRS

Riddu Riddu, in Norway, an annual cultural festival, July; Fishing Festival, August; Midnight Sun Film Festival, September; Jutajaiset Folklore Festival, June

SIGNIFICANT EVENTS IN FORMATION OF NATIONAL IDENTITY

500 B.C.E. The inhabitants of the Scandinavian Peninsula are culturally related tribal peoples living in clans or extended families.

1st century C.E.–10th century C.E. The Sami are driven into the northern parts of the peninsula by successive waves of Slavic, Finnic, and Gothic immigrants.

1500–1600 The Sami, although conquered and taxed by the advancing Norwegians, Swedes, and Russians, remain nomadic or seminomadic fishermen, trappers, and herders. A rapid decrease in the reindeer herds forces many to settle along the fjords, the coasts, and the inland waterways.

1673 The Swedish king begins Swedish and Finnish settlement of the northern peninsula. The colonists take the most productive lands, forcing the Sami to retreat to the less accessible and less hospitable regions.

1721–1800 The eastern Sami come under the rule of the Russian Empire. Hunting by colonists drives the beaver to the brink of extinction. Farms and cattle herds disrupt the traditional Sami nomadic routes. The economic base of Sapmi slowly collapses as colonization increases.

1751–1826 The national boundaries are demarcated, officially dividing the Sami homeland.

1851–1852 Active Sami resistance to Norwegian and Swedish authority ends with some reforms that allow the Sami to retain many aspects of their traditional way of life.

1868   A massive colonization of the Kola Peninsula in Russia begins.

1905   Norway separates from the Swedish kingdom and becomes the country with the largest Sami population.

1919–1939   Soviet rule devastates the Kola Sami. By 1941, only about 2,000 remain of the pre-Soviet population of some 15,000. Forced assimilation in the Nordic countries also greatly damages the Sami culture.

1939–1945   The European war beings destruction and chaos to the Norwegian Sami, whose language has no word for war.

1945–1993   The Sami begin to organize. The Nordic Sami Council is founded in 1956, and the Nordic Sami Institute in 1973. Local legislatures, the Sami parliaments, are created in Finland in 1972, in Norway in 1989, and in Sweden in 1993. In 1983, Sami leaders declare the collective sovereignty of the Sami peoples across the northern region of Europe.

1997–1998   Norway's King Harald V officially apologizes to the Sami nation for the government's past abuses. A Swedish minister also apologizes officially in 1998.

2000–2009   The Sami, although they enjoy equal rights and status in the Nordic countries, continue to press for greater autonomy and recognition of their nation in the face of conflicts over land use and the threat to their culture from tourism, development pressure, and assimilation.

See also Finland, Norway, Sweden

SARDINIA

OFFICIAL NAME

Regione Autonoma Sardegna (Italian); Region Autonoma Sardinnya (Sardinian); Sardinia (English)

POPULATION

1,739,700 (2009e)

INHABITANTS' NAME OR NICKNAME

Sard(s); Sardinian(s)

LANGUAGE/LANGUAGES

Italian (official); Sardinian (recently approved for use in official documents); others

RELIGION/RELIGIONS

Roman Catholic, Protestant, Muslim, other or no religion

NATIONAL FLAG

The flag, called the *Bandiera dei Quattro Mori* or the Four Moors flag, has a white field with a centered red cross dividing it into four quadrants, each with a black Moor's head facing away from the hoist and wearing a white headband above the eyes. Traditionally, the flag dates from 1017, a gift from Pope Benedict to help the Sardinians under attack by the Muslim Saracens.

COAT OF ARMS/SEAL

The coat of arms, like the flag, is a white field divided by a red cross with four Moor's heads within an ornate golden frame. Below the frame is a green flower with a red center attached to a green banner inscribed with the name of the region in Italian.

CAPITAL CITY

Cagliari

TYPE OF GOVERNMENT

Representative democracy as an autonomous region of Italy

NATIONAL EMBLEM

Black Moor's head

NATIONAL ANTHEM

The anthem was the official anthem of the Kingdom of Sardinia. It has been resurrected as the anthem of the Sardinian people. No English translation is available.

Hymu Sardu Nationali (Sardinian); Inno
Sardo Nationali (Italian); Sard National
Anthem (English)

Refrain:

Conservet Deus su Re
Salvet su Regnu Sardu
Et gloria a s'istendardu
Concedat de' su Re.

1.

De fidos et fort'homines
Si figios nos vantamus,
Bene nos provaramus
Figios ipsoro, o Re.

2.

Semper in nois hat a essere
Sa fide immota e forte,
Ne in variare e' sorte
Hat a mudarsi, o Re.

3.

Si da unu bonu figiu
Su babbu no est negadu
Ne has a essere abjuradu
Tue mae da nois, o Re.

4.

Si figiu pîu sacrìficat
Totu a su babbu sou
Et totu omni sardu
Dispretiat pro su Re.

5.

Qui manchet in nois s'animu
Qui languat su valore
Pro forza o pro terrore
No hapas suspetu, o Re.

6.

Unu a omni chentu intrepidos
A ferru et a mitralia
In vallu et in muralia
Hamus andare, o Re.

7.

Solu in sa morte tzedere
Soliat su Sardu antigu
Né vivu a s'innimigu
Ceder'happ'ego o Re.

8.

De ti mustrare cuppidu
Sa fide sua, s'amore
Sas venas in ardore
Sentit su Sardu, o Re.

9.

Indica un'adversariu
E horrenda da' su coro
Iscoppiàrat s'ira ipsoro
A unu tou cinnu, o Re.

10.

Cumanda su chi piàgati
Si bene troppu duru
E nde sias tue seguru
Chi hat a esser factu, o Re.

11.

Sa forza qui tant'atteros
Podesit superare
Facheràt operare
Unu tou cinnu, o Re.

12.

Sa forza qui mirabile
Jà fuit a' su Romanu
E innante a' s'Africanu
Tue bideràs, o Re.

13.

Sos fidos fortes homines
Abbaida tue cuntentu
Qui hant a essere in omni eventu
Quales jà fuint, o Re.

PATRON SAINT

Saint Maurice

CURRENCY

Euro

INTERNET IDENTIFIER

.sar (unofficial)

**VEHICLE IDENTIFICATION
PLATES/STICKERS**

I Italy (official); SR Sardinia (unofficial)

PASSPORT

Sardinians are Italian citizens and travel on Italian passports.

AIRLINE

Meridiana

NATIONAL FLOWER

Borage (starflower) (unofficial)

NATIONAL ANIMAL

Mountain *arcosu* (Sardinian buck) (unofficial)

NATIONAL BIRD

Golden eagle (unofficial)

NATIONAL RESOURCES

Natural resources include copper, silver, lead, cassiterite, and iron. Historic cities and monuments, sandy beaches, a pleasant climate, and proximity to large European population centers support a thriving tourist industry. Mining remains important, along with newer industries based on services and information technology. Remittances from Sardinians living in other parts of Italy* are an important resource and a source of investment.

FOODS

Porceddu, suckling pig roasted on a spit with garlic and rosemary potatoes, is considered the national dish. Other specialties include *pane de musica,* a thin, crisp, circular flatbread; *panada,* a flaky pastry stuffed with minced meat or eel; *malloreddus,* small gnocchi, traditionally served with a spicy tomato sauce; *bottarga,* salted mullet or tuna roe pressed into a firm mass, then thinly sliced; *culingiones,* a type of ravioli filled with spinach and pecorino cheese; *sa fregula,* a tiny pasta similar to couscous; *pane carasau,* a thin, crisp flatbread; and *sradas,* a type of crepe or pancake served with orange-flavored honey.

SPORTS/SPORTS TEAMS

Sardinia football teams play at regional level. The national sailing team participates at an international level.

TEAM SPORTS

Football

Cagliari Calcio is the most popular football club and is considered the national representative; its nicknames are Rossoblu (Red-Blues) and Isolani (Islanders).

INDIVIDUAL SPORTS

Sardinia Sailing Team, nickname Team Sardegna

NATIONAL HEROES OR PERSONIFICATIONS

Fabrizio de André, a noted Sardinian songwriter; Grazia Deledda, who won the Nobel Prize for literature in 1926; Elanora de Arborea, a 14th-century judge and ruler; Giovanni Maria Angloy, a Sardinian patriot in the Sardinian Revolution of 1794–1796 against the feudal privileges and laws still existing on the island

FESTIVALS/FAIRS

Festival of Saint Efisio, May; Sartiglia, February–March; S'ardia, July; Chestnut Festival, October

SIGNIFICANT EVENTS IN FORMATION OF NATIONAL IDENTITY

1800 B.C.E.–1000 B.C.E. The Nuragic civilization flourishes on the islands.

800 B.C.E.–500 B.C.E. Phoenicians establish settlements on the coast. According to Greek legends, Carthaginians, led by a mariner named Sardo, colonize the island around 500 B.C.E.

238 B.C.E. Romans from mainland Italy occupy the island, which would remain Roman for 700 years.

456 C.E.–500 C.E. Vandals conquer the island, destroying the Roman cities. The island is reconquered by the Byzantines, who foster the spread of Christianity.

827–900 Muslims from North Africa begin raiding the coastal towns. By 900, the island is divided into four independent monarchies.

1323–1409 Forces of the Kingdom of Aragon conquer the northern part of the island. The population of the city of Algero is expelled and replaced by settlers from Catalonia*. The inhabitants still speak Catalan.

1479 Aragon and Castile merge to form the Kingdom of Spain*. Sardinia remains under Spanish rule for a total of 400 years, from 1323 to 1720.

1718 Sardinia is ceded to the rulers of Savoy and Piedmont on the northern Italian mainland. The combined kingdom takes the name Kingdom of Sardinia.

1794–1796 The Sards rebel against the Savoy rulers, demanding greater self-government and an end to the feudal laws and privileges still existing in Sardinia.

1848–1861 Revolution in the kingdom begins the unification of Italy. The Kingdom of Sardinia forms the basis for the enlarged Kingdom of Italy.

1870 The adoption of a Tuscan dialect as the official language of Italy is accompanied by the banning of regional languages, including Sardinian. The language deteriorates into a peasant dialect ignored by the Italian-speaking upper classes in the towns and cities.

1946 At the end of World War II, Italians vote to end the monarchy, and Italy becomes a republic.

1960 Young Sards begin to take an interest in the island's declining culture and language.

1980s–1990s Resentment of official neglect and the need to leave the island to find work leads to demonstrations and a violent series of bombings by militant activists.

2000–2009 Sardinia is one of two Italian regions whose inhabitants are recognized as a *popolo*, a distinct people by the Italian government. De-

spite advances, the island remains a neglected appendage of the Italian state. Poverty, banditry, and vendettas continue to disrupt island life. The movement for autonomy seeks greater local control to address economic and cultural issues.

See also Italy

SCANIA

OFFICIAL NAME
Skånelandskape (Swedish/Danish); Scanian Provinces (English); Skåneland (Swedish/Danish); Scania (English)

POPULATION
1,651,400 (2009e)

INHABITANTS' NAME/NICKNAME
Scanian(s)

LANGUAGE/LANGUAGES
Swedish (official): Scanian (claimed by many Scanians as a separate Scandinavian language), Danish, German, English, others

RELIGION/RELIGIONS
Protestant (mostly Lutheran), 88 percent; Roman Catholic, 2 percent; Muslim, Jewish, other or no religion

NATIONAL FLAG
The Scanian flag, known as "Den Skånska," is a red field charged with a yellow Scandinavian cross. The flag combines the red field of the Danish flag with the yellow cross of the Swedish flag to represent Scania's position as nation between the two Scandinavian neighbors. The unofficial flag of Bornholm, historically and linguistically part of Scania although under Danish sovereignty, is the same red field as the Scania flag charged with a green Scandinavian cross.

COAT OF ARMS/SEAL
The coat of arms is a yellow-gold shield bearing a red griffin's head with a blue tongue

and wearing a blue crown. The colors represent the two historic influences in the region, Denmark* and Sweden*.

CAPITAL CITY
Malmo

TYPE OF GOVERNMENT
Scania forms a cultural and historical region divided into the present Swedish provinces of Skåne, Halland, and Blekinge, and the Danish island of Bornholm to the southeast.

NATIONAL EMBLEM
Sofiero Castle

NATIONAL COLORS
Red and yellow

NATIONAL ANTHEM
The official anthem is the Swedish national anthem. The unofficial Scania anthem is Om himlen och Österlen (Of Heaven and Österlen), written and composed by Michael Saxell. The lyrics are not available in English.

Om himlen och Österlen (Swedish/Danish);
Of Heaven and Österlen (English)

Gudarna målar med färggranna vindar - en
   rödgul solnedgång
Jag sluter mina ögon och flyger genom luften
på min bostadsrättsbalkong
Jag har rest jorden runt och har lärt mig—
Ett träd är ett träd och en sten

är en sten Men nog är det lite närmre till himlen från Österlen
Jag kommer ihåg en kväll i Chicago i den farliga delen av stan
Jag satt på en bar med mitt ensamma hjärta
och snacka' med Joe, min kumpan
Det kändes som slutet var nära
och jag visste när timmen var sen
Om jag dör vill jag inte till himlen—jag vill
   hellre till Österlen
Det är där havet och fälten

bildar den vackraste scen
som gör att det verkar så nära
mellan himlen och Österlen
När vinden sjunger om natten på slätten här
   utanför
Då flyger molnen ikapp
med blåstens goda humör
När jag tittar ut från mitt fönster
är det tydligt i månens sken
att det är nog lite närmre till himlen från
   Österlen
Ja, det är nog lite närmre till himlen från
   Österlen

PATRON SAINT
Saint Lars (Saint Laurentius)

CURRENCY
Swedish krona

INTERNET IDENTIFIER
.se Sweden

VEHICLE IDENTIFICATION PLATES/STICKERS
S Sweden (official): SKN Scania (unofficial)

PASSPORT
The Scanians are Swedish or Danish citizens and travel on the passports of those countries.

NATIONAL FLOWER
Rhododendron (unofficial) (each of the Scanian provinces in Sweden has its own official flower)

NATIONAL TREE
Beech (unofficial) (each of the Scanian provinces in Sweden has its own official tree)

NATIONAL ANIMAL
Lynx (unofficial) (each of the Scanian provinces in Sweden has its own official animal)

NATIONAL BIRD
Scanian goose (barnacle goose) (unofficial)

NATIONAL RESOURCES

Natural resources include timber, iron ore, hydropower, arable land, and fisheries. The region's unique culture and history along with many historical cities, sites, and monuments supports an expanding tourist industry.

FOODS

Köttbullar, a type of meatball similar to Swedish meatballs but make with pork, are considered a national dish. Meatballs are often served with another national dish, *skansk potatis,* Scania creamed potatoes. Other regional specialties include *inlagd sill,* salted herring marinated in sugar, vinegar, and water; *kåldomar,* cabbage leaves stuffed with ground meat and rice; and *Appelkaka* (Scanian Apple Cake), made of fresh apples, cottage cheese, oats, and cream, is a traditional dessert.

SPORTS/SPORTS TEAMS

Association football (soccer) is the most popular sport. Athletics, rugby, and sailing are also popular as are cycling and tennis and various winter sports.

NATIONAL HEROES OR PERSONIFICATIONS

Beowulf, the hero of the early epic of unknown origin set in Scania, Denmark, and Sweden; Sweyn II, the Danish king responsible for making Scania the heartland of the Danish kingdom; King Magnus Eriksson of Norway, Sweden, and Scania, which was held as a third kingdom; Peder Winstrup, the 17th-century Bishop of Lund, spanning both Danish and Swedish sovereignty of the region; Sven Poulsen, the Scanian patriot who led the fight against Swedish conquest of Scania in the 17th century.

NATIONAL HOLIDAY/INDEPENDENCE DAY

Scania Day (Scania Flag Day), third Sunday in July

FESTIVALS/FAIRS

Skyltsöndag (Shop Window Sunday), November-December; Malmö Rainbow Festival, June; Östersjöfestivalen (Baltic Festival), July; Malmöfestivalen (Malmo Festival), August; Kivik Apple Market Festival, August; Wapurgis, April-May.

SIGNIFICANT EVENTS IN FORMATION OF NATIONAL IDENTITY

First century B.C.E.–third century C.E. Germanic tribes, often warring among themselves, create tribal kingdoms in the region.

380–770 A tribal chief, Alaric, claims the title "Rex Scaniae" or King of Scania. Between 380 and 770, 15 known kings rule in Scania. King Ivar Vidfammne, in the 700s, begins to extend the boundaries of his kingdom, becoming the first empire-builder in Scandinavia.

Eighth century–ninth century Scanian Vikings participate in expeditions that raid as far south as the Mediterranean Sea. King Canute of Denmark unites Denmark and Scania in 811. Scania forms the heartland of the early Danish kingdom.

1104 The town of Lund becomes a separate bishopric and the center of spread of Christianity in Scandinavia.

1331–1523 The Nordic union of Sweden, Norway, Scania, and Finland under Magnus Eriksson makes Scandinavia a major European power. The Union of Kalmar again unites the Scandinavian kingdoms from 1397 to 1523.

16th century–17th century Sweden covets Scania to form a natural coastal frontier and to end Denmark's control of the Kattegat, the narrow entrance from the North Sea to the Baltic Sea. Control of Scania, the so-called Skåne Question, dominates northern European politics. Sweden and Denmark are almost constantly at war in the early 17th century. Sweden conquers Halland in 1645 and the remaining Scanian provinces in 1658. Denmark regains control of the island of Bornholm following an uprising against Swedish rule.

1675–1679 The Scanians rise in rebellion against the Swedes when war resumes between

Sweden and Denmark. The defeated Scanians suffer harsh repraisals that leaves some districts nearly depopulated.

1709 The Danes again invade Scania but the majority of the Scanians remain loyal to Sweden or adopt a neutral stance.

1750–1800 Devastated by the long series of wars, Scania begins to recover economically. The Swedish language and culture are imposed on the region to further divide Scania from Denmark. The Scania region is divided among several provinces.

19th century To forestall Scanian unrest, the Swedish government relaxes cultural and linguistic restrictions. A cultural revival takes hold in the 1870s and 1880s, focusing on the modernization of the Scanian language and a newal of interest in Scanian folklore, crafts, and traditions.

1944–1944 The Danes, conquered and occupied by Nazi Germany, save their Jewish citizens with the help of the Scanian fishing fleets.

1967 The first modern Scania National Day, celebrated on July 16, 1967, is widely condemned in Sweden as treason or the outward signs of Scanian separatism.

1995–1999 Attempts to resurrect a separate Scania region within Sweden are resisted by the Swedish government. In 1999, two smaller provinces were allowed to join to form a reduced Scania region, but without the historic Scanian provinces of Halland and Blekinge.

2000 A 10-mile (16-km) bridge linking Copenhagen and Malmo creates a new combined metropolitan region of the two cities and their satellite cities, strengthening economic, linguistic, and cultural ties between the Danes and the Scanians.

2008–2009 The Swedish government begins a study of the reorganization of the country, including a region in the south to be known as South Sweden. Many Scanians rally to demand the resurrection of historic Scania as an administration region of Sweden. Others demand a new European cultural region that would also include Danish Bornholm.

SCOTLAND

Official Name
Scotland (English and Scots); Alba (Gaelic)

Population
5,212,300 (2009e)

Inhabitants' Name/Nickname
Scot(s); Scottish

Language/Languages
English (de facto); Scottish Gaelic, Scots (Lallans) (recognized regional languages); others

Religion/Religions
Church of Scotland (Presbyterian), 47 percent; Roman Catholic, 18 percent; Muslim, 1 percent; other or no religion

National Flag
The flag has a blue field crossed by a white *saltaire,* the Cross of Saint Andrew. According to legend a white *saltaire* appeared against the blue sky during a Scottish battle against invading Angles in 832 C.E. It has been the Scottish flag since that time. There is also a royal flag featuring a red lion on a gold field.

Coat of Arms/Seal
The royal coat of arms is a yellow shield with a centered red lion rampant within two narrow ornamental red stripes known as *tessure.* The royal flag is a depiction of the royal arms.

Motto
Nemo me impune lacessit (Latin); *Cha togar m' fhearg gun dioladh* (Gaelic); *Wha daur meddle wi me* (Scots); None provokes me with impunity (English)

Capital City
Edinburgh

TYPE OF GOVERNMENT

Autonomous parliamentary democracy and constitutional monarchy

NATIONAL EMBLEM

Scottish lion, thistle, bagpipes, tartan, kilt

NATIONAL COLORS

Blue and white

NATIONAL ANTHEM

The song, written by Roy Williamson for the popular folk group the Corries, was first used as a Scottish anthem in 1990 in response to an unexpected victory over the English football team and has since become widely accepted as the national anthem although it has not been officially adopted.

Flùr na h-Alba (Gaelic); Flower of Scotland (English)

O Flower of Scotland,
When will we see,
Your like again,
That fought and died for,
Your wee bit hill and glen,
And stood against him,
Proud Edward's Army,
And sent him homeward,
Tae think again.

The hills are bare now,
And autumn leaves lie thick and still,
O'er land that is lost now,
Which those so dearly held,
And stood against him,
Proud Edward's Army,
And sent him homeward,
Tae think again.

Those days are past now,
And in the past
They must remain,
But we can still rise now,
And be the nation again,
That stood against him,
Proud Edward's Army,
And sent him homeward,
Tae think again.

PATRON SAINT

Saint Andrew; Saint Margaret

CURRENCY

Scots pound sterling

INTERNET IDENTIFIER

.uk (official); .sco (unofficial)

VEHICLE IDENTIFICATION PLATES/ STICKERS

GB Great Britain (official): SCO Scotland (unofficial)

PASSPORT

The Scots are British citizens and travel on British passports.

NATIONAL FLOWER

Thistle; heather; Scottish bluebell (unofficial)

NATIONAL TREE

Scots pine

NATIONAL ANIMALS

Lion, unicorn (both mythical animals introduced to European heraldry from the Middle East and North Africa)

NATIONAL BIRD

Golden eagle

NATIONAL FISH

Brown trout (unofficial)

NATIONAL RESOURCES

Natural resources include petroleum, coal, fish, and minerals. The economy, once dependent on mining and fishing, is now a service-oriented economy built around financial services, electronics and high technology, and whiskey production.

FOODS

Haggis, a dish of lamb or mutton minced with onion, oatmeal, suet, and spices and boiled, is considered the national dish. Other national specialties include *cock-a-leekie,* a soup of leeks, potatoes, and chicken stock; *forar bridie,* a type of pastry filled with minced meat; *finnan haddie,* a dish made of dried or smoked haddock; smoked salmon; mince and tatties, a dish of minced meat and mashed potatoes; *potit heid,* head cheese; Scotch pie, a double-crust pastry filled with mutton or other meat; shortbread, a sweet pastry; Aberdeen angus, a type of beef; oatcakes, a traditional bread; and Arbroath smokie, smoked haddock. Dundee marmalade, a sour orange marmalade, is probably Scotland's most famous food product. Whiskey, called Whisky in Scotland, is one of the country's most famous exports and is considered the Scottish national drink.

SPORTS/SPORTS TEAMS

Rugby and association football (soccer) are the most popular sports. Scotland national teams participate in many sports at an international level.

TEAM SPORTS

Badminton
Scotland Badminton Team

Baseball
Scotland Baseball Team

Basketball
Scotland Basketball Team; Scotland Women's Basketball Team

Bowls
Scotland Bowls Team

Cricket
Scotland Cricket Team; Scotland Women's Cricket Team; Scotland Under-19 Cricket Team

Football
Scotland Football Team, nickname the Bravehearts; Scotland Women's Football Team, nickname the Bravehearts; Scotland Rugby Union Team; Scotland Rugby League Team; Scotland Women's Rugby Union Team; Scotland Rugby Union Team (Sevens), nickname Edinburgh Sevens; Scotland Women's Rugby Union Team (Sevens), nickname Scotland Sevens or Scotland 7s or Edinburgh 7s; Scotland B Football Team; Scotland Under-21 Football Team; Scotland Under-19 Football Team; Scotland Women's Under-19 Football Team; Scotland Under-17 Football Team; Scotland Under-20 Football Team; Scotland A Rugby Union Team; Scotland Under-21 Rugby Union Team; Scotland Under-19 Rugby Union Team; Scotland Club Scotland International Rugby Union Team; Scotland Futsal Team; Scotland Australian-Rules Football Team nickname the Puffins; Scotland Touch Football Team; Scotland Women's Touch Football Team

Handball
Scotland Handball Team

Hockey
Scotland Ice Hockey Team; Scotland Junior Ice Hockey Team; Scotland Women's Field Hockey Team; Scotland Men's Field Hockey Team

Korfball
Scotland Korfball Team

Lacrosse
Scotland Lacrosse Team; Scotland Women's Lacrosse Team; Scotland Under-19 Lacrosse Team; Scotland Women's Under-19 Lacrosse Team

Netball
Scotland Netball Team

Table Tennis

Scotland Table Tennis Team

Tennis

Scotland Tennis Team

Volleyball

Scotland Men's Volleyball Team; Scotland Women's Volleyball Team

INDIVIDUAL SPORTS

Scotland Aikido Team; Scotland Amateur Boxing Team; Scotland Cycling Team; Scotland Weight Lifting Team

WINTER SPORTS

Scotland Curling Team; Scotland Ice Hockey Team; Scotland Junior Ice Hockey Team

NATIONAL HEROES OR PERSONIFICATIONS

The Stone of Scone, also known as the Stone of Destiny, the ancient coronation stone of Scottish kings, and more recently of English and British monarchs, is the symbolic personification of the Scottish nation; Jock Tamson is a personification of Scotland as the father of all Scots.

National heroes include Robert Burns, considered the national poet; Robert de Brus (Robert Bruce or Robert the Bruce), a Scottish leader who defeated the invading English in the early 14th century; Rob Roy MacGregor, who inspired Sir Walter Scott to write about his exploits; and William Wallace, who led a national war of liberation in the late 13th century; Sean Connery, noted actor, spokesman for Scottish tourism, and outspoken supporter of Scottish autonomy

NATIONAL HOLIDAY/INDEPENDENCE DAY

Saint Andrew's Day, November 30

FESTIVALS/FAIRS

Edinburgh Festival, August; Highland Games, May–September; Hogmanay, December–January; Saint Andrew's Week, November; Cowalfest, October; Beltane Festival, May; Glasgow Fair, July; Braemar Gathering, September

SIGNIFICANT EVENTS IN FORMATION OF NATIONAL IDENTITY

1000 B.C.E. The region's inhabitants, called Picts, are a tribal people living in clans or extended families.

First century C.E. The Romans, unable to defeat the fierce tribesmen, finally build a defensive wall to divide Roman Britannia from the territory they called Caledonia.

Sixth century Christianity is introduced to the region. Celtic migrants, called Scots, settle the region from Ireland*.

Ninth century Vikings raid the coastal settlements. The union of the Picts and the Scots in 843 is considered the foundation of the Scottish kingdom.

1189 The English king recognizes Scotland's independence, but English claims begin a long and bitter struggle between the neighboring kingdoms.

1314 A smaller army of Scots, led by Robert de Brus (Robert Bruce or Robert the Bruce), defeats a larger invading English army to secure Scottish independence

16th century The Protestant Reformation, led by religious reformer John Knox, spreads across Scotland, except the Highlands, which remain Catholic.

1603 The long conflict with England ends when Scottish king James VI succeeds to the English throne, combining the two kingdoms in an uneasy dynastic union.

1707–1746 The Scots give up their separate parliament and become a part of the United Kingdom*. Many Scots, particularly in the Highlands, oppose the union, leading to several serious rebellions.

1872 The compulsory teaching of English in all Scottish schools threatens the survival of the

Gaelic language, mostly spoken in the Highlands, and Lowland Scots, the language of the Scottish majority.

1928 Centuries of grievances result in the creation of the Scottish National Party (SNP) to press for greater independence.

1949 After World War II, nationalism again resurfaces, with many prominent Scots signing the Scottish Covenant that binds its signatories to work for Scottish home rule.

1971 The SNP remains a fringe party until the discovery of oil off Scotland's coast. Nationalists of the SNP lead a campaign for local control of Scotland's natural resources and the restoration of the Scottish parliament.

1996 The Stone of Scone, also called the Stone of Destiny or the Coronation Stone, taken by English invaders in 1296, is finally returned to Scotland.

1997–2000 The Scottish parliament is recreated for the first time since 1707. The first legislature meets to discuss Scottish issues.

2007–2009 The Scottish government establishes a national conversation on constitutional issues and a number of options, including increased powers for the Scottish Parliament, federalism within Britain, or a referendum on independence. The nationalist SNP wins the largest number of seats in parliamentary elections.

See also United Kingdom

SERBIA

OFFICIAL NAME
Republika Srbija (Serbian); Republic of Serbia (English)

POPULATION
7,404,600 (2009e)

INHABITANTS' NAME/NICKNAME
Serbian(s); Serb(s)

LANGUAGE/LANGUAGES
Serbian (official); Hungarian, Bosniak (called Bosnian in neighboring Bosnia and Herzegovina*), Romany, Albanian, others. Hungarian, Romanian, Slovak, Ukrainian, and Croatian are all recognized as official languages in Vojvodina, the autonomous northern province.

RELIGION/RELIGIONS
Serbian Orthodox, 83 percent; Roman Catholic, 6 percent; Muslim, 3.5 percent; Protestant, 1.5 percent; other or no religion

NATIONAL FLAG
The flag is a horizontal tricolor of red, blue, and white charged with the national coat of arms to the hoist side of center on the blue stripe and overlapping the red and white stripes. The colors of the flag are the pan-Slav colors originally used in Russia*.

COAT OF ARMS/SEAL
The coat of arms, readopted in 2004, is the same as that adopted in 1882. It has a central red shield or crest with the white Serbian eagle between two golden fleurs-de-lis. The eagle holds a smaller red shield divided by a white cross with a silver firesteel in each quadrant. Above the shield is the golden crown of Serbia. The great arms show the same shield and crown below another golden crown and a red, ermined cape draped around the shield.

MOTTO
Samo sloga Srbina spasava (Serbian); Only unity saves the Serbs (Serbians)

CAPITAL CITY
Belgrade

Type of Government
Parliamentary republic

NATIONAL EMBLEM

Firesteels (symbol of Serbia since the 14th century)

NATIONAL COLORS

Red, Blue, and White

NATIONAL ANTHEM

The anthem, dating from its first adoption as the Serbian anthem in 1904, was again adopted as the official anthem in 2004.

Boze Pravde (Serbian); God of Justice (English)

God of Justice; thou who saved us
When in deepest bondage cast,
Hear thy Serbian children's voices,
Be our help as in the past.

With thy mighty hand sustain us,
Still our rugged pathway trace;
God, our hope; protect and cherish
Serbian country and Serbian race!

Bind in closest links our kindred
Teach the love that will not fail,
May the loathed fiend of discord
Never in our ranks prevail.

Let the golden fruits of union
Our young tree of freedom grace;
God, our master! guide and prosper
Serbian country and Serbian race.

Lord! Avert from us thy vengeance,
Thunder of thy dreaded ire;
Bless each Serbian town and hamlet,
Mountain, meadow, heart, and spire.

When our host goes forth to battle
Death or victory to embrace—
God of armies! be our leader
Strengthen then the Serbian race.

On our sepulchre of ages
Breaks the resurrection morn,
From the slough of direst slavery
Serbia anew is born.

Through five hundred years of durance
We have knelt before thy face,
All our kin, O God! deliver,
Thus entreats the Serbian race.

PATRON SAINT

Saint Sava; Saint Stephen

CURRENCY

Serbian dinar

INTERNET IDENTIFIER

.rs

VEHICLE IDENTIFICATION PLATES/STICKERS

RS

PASSPORT

The passport cover has the name of the country in Serbian, the coat of arms, the word *passport* in Serbian, and the standard biometric symbol.

AIRLINE

Jat Airways

NATIONAL FLOWER

Plum

NATIONAL TREE

Oak; Serbian spruce

NATIONAL ANIMAL

Wolf

NATIONAL BIRD

White eagle

NATIONAL RESOURCES

Natural resources include oil, gas, coal, iron ore, copper, zinc, antimony, chromite, gold, silver, magnesium, pyrite, limestone, marble, salt, and arable land.

FOODS

Pljeskavica, meat patties of mixed beef, lamb, or pork, grilled with onions and served on pita bread, is the national dish. Other typical dishes include *pihtije,* jellied pork or duck; *raznjici,* skewered meat cooked over charcoal; *cevapcici,* charcoal-grilled minced meat; *sarma,* grape leaves stuffed with minced meat and rice; *japrak,* cabbage leaves stuffed with meat, rice, and onions; *strukli,* a cheese ball stuffed with nuts and plums and then boiled; and *lokum,* a dessert of thin layers of pastry, nuts, and honey.

SPORTS/SPORTS TEAMS

Association football (soccer), basketball, and rugby are the most popular sports. In recent years, tennis has become popular. Serbia national teams participate in many sports at an international level.

TEAM SPORTS

Badminton

Serbia Badminton Team

Baseball

Serbia Baseball Team; Serbia Softball Team

Basketball

Serbia Basketball Team; Serbia Women's Basketball Team; Serbia Under-19 Basketball Team; Serbia Wheelchair Basketball Team

Football

Serbia Football Team, nickname Plavi (Blues) or Beli Orlovi (White Eagles); Serbia Women's Football Team, nickname White Eagles; Serbia Under-21 Football Team, nickname White Eagles; Serbia Rugby Union Team; Serbia Women's Rugby Union Team; Serbia Rugby League Team, nickname White Eagles; Serbia Under-19 Football Team, nickname Orlići (Young Eagles);

Serbia American Football Team; Serbia Futsal Team; Serbia Women's Under-19 Football Team

Handball

Serbia Handball Team; Serbia Women's Handball Team; Serbia Beach Handball Team; Serbia Women's Beach Handball Team

Hockey

Serbia Ice Hockey Team; Serbia Junior Ice Hockey Team; Serbia Field Hockey Team

Korfball

Serbia Korfball Team

Table Tennis

Serbia Table Tennis Team

Tennis

Serbia Davis Cup Team; Serbia Fed Cup Team

Volleyball

Serbia Men's Volleyball Team; Serbia Women's Volleyball Team; Serbia Men's Beach Volleyball Team

Water Polo

Serbia Water Polo Team

INDIVIDUAL SPORTS

Serbia Aikido Team; Serbia Amateur Boxing Team; Serbia Archery Team; Serbia Athletics Team; Serbia Cycling Team; Serbia Equestrian Team; Serbia Fencing Team; Serbia Judo Team; Serbia Karate Team; Serbia Modern Pentathlon Team; Serbia Rowing Team; Serbia Sailing Team; Serbia Shooting Team; Serbia Swim Team; Serbia Tae Kwon Do Team; Serbia Triathlon Team; Serbia Weight Lifting Team; Serbia Wrestling Team

WINTER SPORTS

Serbia Alpine Ski Team; Serbia Bandy Team; Serbia Biathlon Team; Serbia Curling Team; Serbia Ice Hockey Team; Serbia Junior Ice Hockey Team; Serbia Luge Team; Serbia Skating Team

NATIONAL HEROES OR PERSONIFICATIONS

Milos Obilic, leader of an uprising against the Ottoman Empire; Vuk Stefanovic Karadjic, a linguist responsible for modernizing the Serbian language; Josip Broz Tito, communist leader of the partisans during World War II and ruler of Yugoslavia until 1980; Nikola Pasic, a Serbian politician during the Yugoslavia era in the early part of the 20th century

NATIONAL HOLIDAY/INDEPENDENCE DAY

National Day, February 15

FESTIVALS/FAIRS

State of Exit Festival, June; International Film Festival, February; Zajecar, April; Constantine Festival, June; Vrnjacka Banja Cultural Festival, June; Belgrade Summer Festival, July; Guca Trumpet Festival, August

SIGNIFICANT EVENTS IN FORMATION OF NATIONAL IDENTITY

Fourth century B.C.E.   Greek peoples colonize the southern part of the region, followed by Macedonians under Alexander the Great.

First century C.E.   Roman authority extends to most of the Balkans. After the retreat of the Romans, the eastern Romans or Byzantines control the region.

Sixth century   Slavs begin to settle on the edges of Byzantine territory in great numbers.

1389–1750   The Serbian nobility is devastated at the Battle of Kosovo Polje against the expanding Ottoman Empire. Serbia is absorbed into the Turkish Ottoman Empire for nearly four centuries.

1817   Serbia becomes an autonomous principality within the Ottoman Empire.

1878   War between Russia and the Ottoman Empire leads to full Serbian independence.

1918–1929   After the First World War, the related peoples of the Balkans create a South Slav state, the Kingdom of the Serbs, Croats and Slovenes, later known as Yugoslavia.

1940–1945   Yugoslavia is invaded by the Axis powers. Josip Broz Tito leads a largely communist partisan war against the invaders. At the end of the Second World War, he creates a communist republic in the former Yugoslavia.

1960–1980   Tito distances communist Yugoslavia from Soviet domination while firmly controlling dissent in the multicultural federation. Tito's death unleashes nationalist movements across the country.

1987–1991   Serbia comes under the control of old-line communists turned nationalists. Tensions between Serbia and the other Yugoslav republics lead to increasing violence. Nationalists demand the creation of a "Greater Serbia" out of Serb-populated areas of Yugoslavia, including parts of the other member states.

1991   Slovenia*, Croatia*, Macedonia, and Bosnia and Herzegovina* declare independence from Yugoslavia. The Serbian military, directed by Slobodan Milosevic, attacks Slovenia, Croatia, and Bosnia, with its large Serbian minority, extending war across the Balkans.

1992   The two republics of Serbia and Montenegro* form a federal republic.

1995–1997   Peace accords bring an end to the bloody Bosnian War. Slobodan Milosevic becomes president of Serbia under a radical nationalist government.

1998–1999   The Albanian population in the southern Serbian province of Kosovo* rebels against the Milosevic government. A brutal reprisal sends hundreds of thousands fleeing from Kosovo. Following NATO air strikes on Belgrade and other Serbian targets, Kosovo becomes a United Nations protectorate.

2000   Milosevic is accused of rigging the presidential election, mass demonstrations break out, and Milosevic is toppled from power. A reformist government introduces a democratic system.

2001–2006   Milosevic is extradited to stand trial on charges of war crimes stemming from atrocities committed during the Bosnian War. Milosevic dies in prison.

2003–2004   Ethnic violence breaks out between Serbs and Albanians in Kosovo.

2006   Montenegro secedes from the union to become an independent republic. Voters approve a new constitution that declares Kosovo an integral part of the republic.

2008   Kosovo declares its independence and is recognized by many countries. The former Bosnian Serb leader Radovan Karadzic, who is responsible for the Srebrenica massacre and other atrocities, is finally arrested in Serbia and extradited to the International Court at The Hague to stand trial.

2009   The Serbian people face an ongoing dilemma over the role of their country in Europe as a potential member of the European Union or as a close ally of Russia* and its more obstructionist politics.

SLOVAKIA

OFFICIAL NAME
Slovenská Republika (Slovak); Slovak Republic (English)

POPULATION
5,392,800 (2009e)

INHABITANTS' NAME/NICKNAME
Slovak(s)

LANGUAGE/LANGUAGES
Slovak (official); Hungarian, Romany, Ukrainian

RELIGION/RELIGIONS
Roman Catholic, 69 percent; Protestant, 10 percent; Greek Catholic, 4 percent; other or no religion

NATIONAL FLAG
The flag is a horizontal tricolor of white, blue, and red bearing the coat of arms, outlined in white, centered on the hoist side. The white, blue, and red are the traditional pan-Slav colors originally carried by the flag of Russia*. The coat of arms was added to the flag in 1992.

COAT OF ARMS/SEAL
The coat of arms is a red crest or shield composed of a silver (white) double cross elevated on the middle peak of three blue hills. The shield represents the Slovak nation and its history. The double cross is a symbol of the Christian religion of the country, and the hills symbolize the three famous Slovak peaks, Tatra, Fatra, and Matra.

MOTTO
Afferant montes pacem populo (Latin); May mountains bring people peace (English)

CAPITAL CITY
Bratislava

TYPE OF GOVERNMENT
Parliamentary republic

NATIONAL EMBLEM
Slovak double cross (patriarchal cross)

NATIONAL COLORS
Blue and white

NATIONAL ANTHEM
The anthem was first used in the 1840s and became official with the creation of Czechoslovakia after the First World War. It was played immediately after the Czech anthem. When Czechoslovakia was divided in 1993, it was retained as Slovakia's national anthem.

Nad Tatrou sa blýska (Slovak); Lightning over the Tatras (English)

Lightning flashes over the Tatra, the thunder pounds wildly,

Lightning flashes over the Tatra, the thunder pounds wildly.

Let us pause, brothers, they will surely disappear, the Slovaks will revive,

Let us pause, brothers, they will surely disappear, the Slovaks will revive.

This Slovakia of ours has been deeply asleep until now,

This Slovakia of ours has been deeply asleep until now.

But the thunder and lightning are encouraging it to come alive,

But the thunder and lightning are encouraging it to come alive.

PATRON SAINT

Our Lady of the Assumption

CURRENCY

Euro

INTERNET IDENTIFIER

.sk

VEHICLE IDENTIFICATION PLATES/STICKERS

SK

PASSPORT

The passport cover has name of the European Union and the name of the country in Slovak, the coat of arms, the Slovak word for passport, and the standard biometric symbol.

NATIONAL FLOWER

Rose

NATIONAL TREE

Small-leafed lime (linden)

NATIONAL RESOURCES

Natural resources include brown coal and lignite; small amounts of iron ore, copper, and manganese ore; salt; and arable land. Since the transition to a market economy, the country has seen sustained growth and increasing prosperity. Tourism, based on varied scenery, historic cities and monuments, spas, and ski resorts, has become a very important resource.

FOODS

Bryndzové halušky, a type of thick, soft, potato noodles or dumplings served with *bryndza,* a sheep's milk cheese, is the national dish. Other specialties include *sulance,* potato-dough turnovers filled with plum preserves; *strapačky,* potato dumplings with stewed sauerkraut; *bryndzové pyrchy,* a small pastry filled with minced meat and onions; *zemiakové placky,* potato pancakes fried in oil; *kapustnica,* a soup made of sauerkraut; *fazulová,* a bean and vegetable soup; and *orechovnik,* a sweet nut roll. *Slivovica,* a plum brandy, is the national drink.

SPORTS/SPORTS TEAMS

Association football (soccer) and ice hockey are the most popular sports. Slovakia national teams participate in many sports at an international level.

TEAM SPORTS

Badminton

Slovakia Badminton Team

Baseball

Slovakia Baseball Team; Slovakia Softball Team

Basketball

Slovakia Basketball Team; Slovakia Women's Basketball Team; Slovakia Wheelchair Basketball Team

Cricket

Slovakia Cricket Team

Football

Slovakia Football Team, nickname Bojovni Jondovci (the Fighting Jondas); Slovakia Women's Football Team, nickname Bojovni Jondovci (the Fighting Jondas); Slovakia Rugby Union Team; Slovakia American Football Team; Slovakia Futsal Team

Handball

Slovakia Handball Team; Slovakia Women's Handball Team; Slovakia Beach Handball Team; Slovakia Women's Beach Handball Team

Hockey

Slovakia Ice Hockey Team; Slovakia Junior Ice Hockey Team; Slovakia Women's Ice Hockey Team; Slovakia Field Hockey Team

Korfball

Slovakia Korfball Team

Racing

Slovakia Speedway Team

Table Tennis

Slovakia Table Tennis Team

Tennis

Slovakia Davis Cup Team; Slovakia Fed Cup Team

Volleyball

Slovakia Men's Beach Volleyball Team; Slovakia Women's Beach Volleyball Team; Slovakia Men's Volleyball Team; Slovakia Women's Volleyball Team

INDIVIDUAL SPORTS

Slovakia Aikido Team; Slovakia Amateur Boxing Team; Slovakia Archery Team; Slovakia Athletics Team; Slovakia Canoeing Team; Slovakia Cycling Team; Slovakia Equestrian Team; Slovakia Fencing Team; Slovakia Gymnastics Team; Slovakia Judo Team; Slovakia Karate Team: Slovakia Modern Pentathlon Team; Slovakia Rowing Team; Slovakia Sailing Team; Slovakia Shooting Team; Slovakia Swim Team; Slovakia Tae Kwon Do Team; Slovakia Triathlon Team; Slovakia Weight Lifting Team; Slovakia Wrestling Team

WINTER SPORTS

Slovakia Alpine Ski Team; Slovakia Biathlon Team; Slovakia Bobsleigh and Tobogganing Team; Slovakia Curling Team; Slovakia Ice Hockey Team; Slovakia Junior Ice Hockey Team; Slovakia Women's Ice Hockey Team; Slovakia Luge Team; Slovakia Skating Team

NATIONAL HEROES OR PERSONIFICATIONS

Janosik, a heroic figure who helped the poor by robbing the rich, is the national personification. He was finally caught and hanged by his rib.

Other national heroes include Ludovit Stur, the linguist and nationalist responsible for modernizing and standardizing the Slovak language; and Alexander Dubcek, the political leader of the crushed Prague Spring in 1968.

NATIONAL HOLIDAY/INDEPENDENCE DAY

Constitution Day, September 1

FESTIVALS/FAIRS

Nitra Music Festival, September–October; Ledermode, September; Coronation Festival, September; Cinematik, September; Interbeauty Fair, September

SIGNIFICANT EVENTS IN FORMATION OF NATIONAL IDENTITY

450 B.C.E.   The territory is settled by Celts, who coin the first money in the region.

8 B.C.E.–179 C.E.   A Suebian kingdom is established in the western and central parts of present Slovakia.

2 C.E. The Romans establish a chain of outposts along and north of the Danube amid near-constant skirmishing with the Germanic and Celtic tribes of the region.

Fifth century–eighth century Migrating Slavs settle the region from the east. Several Slavic states form, including the Principality of Nitra, with the first Christian church in Slovakia, dating from 828. The principality, along with Moravia, forms the core of the Great Moravian Empire.

863 Saints Cyril and Methodius, the inventors of the Cyrillic alphabet, arrive in the kingdom.

10th century Hungary* takes control of Slovakia, becoming the Kingdom of Hungary around 1100.

1241 The Mongol invasion leaves many districts virtually depopulated. A subsequent famine further devastates the population.

1536 The expansion of the Ottoman Empire into Hungary, including the conquest of the Hungarian capital, forces the kingdom's government to move to Pressburg (Bratislava).

18th century The Ottoman Turks retreat from Hungary, decreasing Slovakia's importance in the kingdom. The Slovak language is mostly spoken as a peasant language around the Hungarian-speaking towns and cities.

1848–1849 The Slovaks rise in support of Austria* against Hungary in the hope of forming a separate state within the Austrian Empire, which is not realized.

1863 The first cultural organization is founded to promote the Slovak language and culture and to nurture the dream of Slovak independence.

1867–1918 During the reign of the Austro-Hungarian Empire, the Slovaks experience severe oppression and forced assimilation into Hungarian culture.

1918 At the end of the First World War, the empire is divided into a number of independent states. The Slovaks and the neighboring Czechs form a joint republic, Czechoslovakia.

1938 Pressure on democratic Czechoslovakia by the fascist governments of Germany and Hungary leads to the dismemberment of the country. The Czech territories come under German control, while most of present Slovakia becomes an independent fascist puppet state with all the trappings, including harsh anti-Semitic laws.

1945–1948 The Czech and Slovak territories are again united. Under Soviet pressure, Czechoslovakia becomes a communist country, part of the Warsaw Pact.

1968 A liberalization of harsh communist rule known as the Prague Spring, led by Slovak Alexander Dubcek, is finally crushed by the invasion of the Warsaw Pact nations.

1989–1993 The one-party communist state is ended in a bloodless uprising called the Velvet Revolution. Tensions between the two member states of the Czechoslovakian federation lead to the peaceful separation of the Czech Republic* and Slovakia.

1994–1998 Populist governments spend on prestige projects as the economy, already damaged by decades of socialist experimentation, flounders.

1999–2004 A pro-Western government pursues membership in the North Atlantic Treaty Organization and the European Union (EU), which comes in 2004.

2007–2009 Slovakia withdraws its last troops from the coalition forces in Iraq. Slovakia's economic progress allows the country to adopt the Euro on January 1, 2009.

SLOVENIA

OFFICIAL NAME

Republika Slovenija (Slovene); Republic of Slovenia (English)

POPULATION

2,033,500 (2009e)

INHABITANTS' NAME/NICKNAME

Slovene(s); Slovenian(s)

LANGUAGE/LANGUAGES

Slovene (official); Italian, Hungarian, German, others

RELIGION/RELIGIONS

Roman Catholic, 57 percent; Muslim, 2.5 percent; Orthodox, 2.5 percent; other or no religion

NATIONAL FLAG

The flag is a horizontal tricolor of white, blue, and red bearing the coat of arms centered on the division between the white and blue stripes on the hoist side. The colors, although considered pan-Slav colors, come from the flag of Carniola, which included Slovenia, in the Austrian empire.

COAT OF ARMS/SEAL

The coat of arms is a shield of blue outlined in red on both sides with a depiction of the three-peaked Triglav, Slovenia's highest mountain, crossed by two wavy lines representing the sea and the country's rivers, and three yellow, six-pointed stars above. The device is taken from the arms of the counts of Celje, the most important family in Slovenian history.

CAPITAL CITY

Ljubljana

TYPE OF GOVERNMENT

Parliamentary republic

NATIONAL EMBLEM

Mount Triglav

NATIONAL COLORS

White and green

NATIONAL ANTHEM

The anthem, adopted in 1991, is based on a poem by France Preseren, Slovenia's national poet.

Zdravljica (Slovene); A Toast (English)

God's blessing on all nations,
Who long and work for that bright day,
When o'er earth's habitations
No war, no strife shall hold sway;
Who long to see
That all men are free
No more shall foes, but neighbors be.

PATRON SAINT

Saint Virgilius

CURRENCY

Euro

INTERNET IDENTIFIER

.si

VEHICLE IDENTIFICATION PLATES/STICKERS

SLO

PASSPORT

The passport cover has the name of the European Union and the country name in Slovene, the coat of arms, the word *passport* in Slovene, and the standard biometric symbol. Passports are also issued using regional language below the Slovenian names.

AIRLINE

Adria Airways

NATIONAL FLOWER

Carnation

NATIONAL TREE

Tilia (lime or linden)

NATIONAL ANIMAL

Brown bear, chamois; lynx (unofficial)

NATIONAL REPTILE

Olm (proteus)

NATIONAL RESOURCES

Natural resources include lignite coal, lead, zinc, building stone, hydropower, and timber. A well-educated population and access to European markets gives the country one of the highest per capita incomes in the European Union. Tourism, supported by varied scenery, historical cities and monuments, sandy beaches, and proximity to large population centers, is an important resource.

FOODS

Ajdovi zganci, a type of crumbled polenta made of buckwheat or cornmeal flour and served with sauerkraut and meats or with milk and sugar, is considered the national dish. Other specialties include *potica,* a sweet pastry rolled and filled with nuts or fruit; *goveji golaz,* beef goulash; *redrca v zelju,* spareribs cooked with sauerkraut; *nadevana paprika,* sweet green peppers stuffed with minced meat and rice; *jagnjetina na palckah,* spit-roasted lamb; and *sladko zelje z rezanci,* cabbage and noodles.

SPORTS/SPORTS TEAMS

Association football (soccer) and ice hockey are the most popular sports. Slovenia national teams participate in many sports at an international level.

TEAM SPORTS

Badminton

Slovenia Badminton Team

Baseball

Slovenia Baseball Team; Slovenia Softball Team

Basketball

Slovenia Basketball Team; Slovenia Women's Basketball Team; Slovenia Wheelchair Basketball Team

Cricket

Slovenia Cricket Team

Football

Slovenia Football Team; Slovenia Women's Football Team; Slovenia Under-21 Football Team; Slovenia Women's Under-19 Football Team; Slovenia Rugby Union Team; Slovenia American Football Team; Slovenia Futsal Team

Handball

Slovenia Handball Team; Slovenia Women's Handball Team

Hockey

Slovenia Ice Hockey Team, nickname Risi (the Lynx); Slovenia Women's Ice Hockey Team, nickname Risi (the Lynx); Slovenia Junior Ice Hockey Team, nickname Risi (the Lynx); Slovenia Field Hockey Team

Table Tennis

Slovenia Table Tennis Team

Tennis

Slovenia Davis Cup Team; Slovenia Fed Cup Team

Volleyball

Slovenia Men's Volleyball Team; Slovenia Women's Volleyball Team

INDIVIDUAL SPORTS

Slovenia Amateur Boxing Team; Slovenia Archery Team; Slovenia Athletics Team; Slovenia Canoeing Team; Slovenia Cycling Team; Slovenia Equestrian Team; Slovenia Fencing Team; Slovenia Judo Team; Slovenia Karate Team; Slovenia Rowing Team; Slovenia Sailing Team; Slovenia Shooting Team; Slovenia Swim Team; Slovenia Tae Kwon Do Team; Slovenia Triathlon Team; Slovenia Weight Lifting Team; Slovenia Wrestling Team

WINTER SPORTS

Slovenia Alpine Ski Team; Slovenia Biathlon Team; Slovenia Ice Hockey Team, nickname Risi (the Lynx); Slovenia Women's Ice Hockey Team, nickname Risi (the Lynx); Slovenia Junior Ice Hockey Team, nickname Risi (the Lynx); Slovenia Luge Team; Slovenia Skating Team

NATIONAL HEROES OR PERSONIFICATIONS

France Preseren, Slovenia's national poet; Leon Stukelj, six-time Olympic medal winner, honored at the Atlanta Olympics in 1996 as the oldest living Olympian; Primoz Trubar, the author of the first book printed in the Slovene language in 1550

NATIONAL HOLIDAY/INDEPENDENCE DAY

Independence Day/Statehood Day, June 25

FESTIVALS/FAIRS

Preseren Festival, February; Festival Ljubljana, June–August; City of Women Festival, October; Tartini Festival, August; Borstnik Meeting (Theater Festival), October; Lent Festival, June–July

SIGNIFICANT EVENTS IN FORMATION OF NATIONAL IDENTITY

500 B.C.E.–300 B.C.E. The region is inhabited by the Adriatic Veneti, related to the later inhabitants of Venice, with Illyrian peoples in the Sava Valley. Celts settle the region.

181 B.C.E.–115 B.C.E. The Romans conquer the various tribal groups.

Fifth century Germanic tribes invade the Roman territories.

Sixth century By 536, the region is incorporated into the Ostrogoth kingdom established in Italy*. The Slavs begin arriving in the region as part of the great Slav migrations between 550 and 595.

Ninth century The region forms part of Charlemagne's Frankish empire and later comes under Germanic rule.

1282 The Slovene territories come under Hapsburg rule.

1550 The first book in Slovene is printed, Primoz Trubar's primer and a catechism.

1840s Railroads are constructed connecting the Slovene territories to the rest of the Austrian Empire. The United Slovenia, the first political organization, is organized.

1914–1919 The First World War begins with fighting on the border with Italy. Slovenia joins with the other South Slav territories to form the Kingdom of the Serbs, Croats, and Slovenes, later called Yugoslavia.

1921 A new constitution institutionalizes Serbian domination of the South Slav state.

1941–1954 German, Italian, and Hungarian forces divide Slovenia in three parts during the Second World War. At the end of the war a communist government takes control of Yugoslavia under Josip Broz Tito.

1960s–1970s Nationalism again becomes a widely supported ideal, although suppression by the Tito government keeps it underground.

1980–1991 Tito dies, setting off national sentiments among the different peoples of Yugoslavia. The Slovenes vote to secede and declare independence. The Yugoslav Army invades, setting off the Ten-Day War.

1991–2000 The new government replaces communism with a market economy that quickly changes decades of mismanagement as prosperity returns to the country.

2004 Slovenia joins the North Atlantic Treaty Organization and the European Union, securing its security within the powerful alliances of European countries.

2007–2009 Economically the most advanced of the former Soviet bloc countries, Slovenia is allowed to adopt the euro. Slovenia takes over the six-month presidency of the European Union, the first of the former communist member states to do so.

SOUTH OSSETIA

OFFICIAL NAME

Khussar Iryston (Ossetian); Yuzhnaya Os-etiya (transliteration from Russian); Sam-khreti Oseti (Georgian); Republic of South Ossetia (English)

POPULATION

70,000 (2009e)

INHABITANTS' NAME/NICKNAME

Ossetian(s)

LANGUAGE/LANGUAGES

Ossetian, Russian, Georgian (official); others

RELIGION/RELIGIONS

Eastern Orthodox, Muslim, other or no religion

NATIONAL FLAG

The flag is a horizontal tricolor of white, red, and yellow. White symbolizes moral purity, red symbolizes martial courage, and yellow stands for wealth and prosperity.

COAT OF ARMS/SEAL

The coat of arms is a circle showing a yellow snow leopard on yellow ground against white mountains and a red sky. The colors are the colors of the national flag. The snow leopard is the national animal, and the seven mountains symbolize the Caucasus Mountains. Around the central disk is a border with the name of the country in Russian above and in Ossetian below.

CAPITAL CITY

Tskhinvali

TYPE OF GOVERNMENT

Republic

NATIONAL EMBLEM

Snow leopard

NATIONAL COLORS

White, red, and yellow

NATIONAL ANTHEM

The "Anthem of South Ossetia" was adopted as a national anthem in 1995, although it was originally written and composed while Georgia* and South Ossetia formed part of the Soviet Union. The lyrics are in the Latin alphabet version of Ossetian. No translation in English is available.

Respublikæ Hussar Irystony Paddzahadon Gimn (Ossetic); Anthem of South Ossetia (English)

Uarzon Iryston! Dæ nomy kadæn
Læuuæm cyrag au mah uyrdyg,
Dy dæ næ uarzty ænuson avdæn,
Dy—næ cin æmæ h yg!
Fæhæræm mah dæ zæhhæj ard,
Dæ nom dyn isæm bærzond,
Uduældaj dyn kænæm læggad,

Dæuæn u næ card nyvond!
Uæ, Styr Huycau! Dæ horzæh, Dæ arfæ—
Iry Uæzægæn Dy cardamond ratt!
Uæzzau uyd dæ ivg"uyd, Iry bæstæ,
Zyldi dæ fædyl sau fydoh,
Fælæ-iu uæddær dæ farny ræstæj
Kodtoj dæ zyntæ roh.
Cardy ruhsmæ ædzuh cydtæ,
Fydbonty næ sast dæ nyfs,
Særbærzond alkæddær uydtæ,
Ærgomæj razmæ cæuys!
Uæ, Uastyrdži! Dæ horzæh, Dæ arfæ—
Iry dzyllæjæn fændagamond ratt!
Fydælty ærdhæræn, Iry Uæzæg!
Zærdæjy tægtæj dæ nyvæzt,
Acy dunejy nyn masty uæzæj
Ma u dih æmæ uærst,
Dugæj dugmæ næræd dæ nom,
Bærzonddær kænæd dæ kad,
Dæ nyfsæj mah cæræm ængom,
Dæ færcy ruhs u næ card!
Uæ, Bæsty Farn! Dæ horzæh, Dæ arfæ—

Næ uarzon Iræn Dy iu amond ratt!
Nom æmæ jyn kad!

CURRENCY

Russian ruble

VEHICLE IDENTIFICATION PLATES/ STICKERS

GE Georgia (official); KI (Khussar Iryston) South Ossetia (unofficial)

PASSPORT

South Ossetians travel on Russian passports.

NATIONAL TREE

Oak

NATIONAL ANIMAL

Snow leopard

NATIONAL BIRD

Golden Eagle

NATIONAL RESOURCES

Natural resources include forests, hydropower, manganese, iron, and copper. The majority of the population lives by subsistence farming. The only economic asset is the Roki Tunnel that connects Georgia and Russia*, from which the government collects customs duties. Remittances from Ossetians living in Russia are an important source of foreign currency and investment.

FOODS

Ossetian pie, a type of bread made with potatoes and filled with meat and mushrooms, is the national dish. Ossetian flatbread is another local specialty.

NATIONAL HEROES OR PERSONIFICATIONS

Eduard Kokoity, the president of South Ossetia

NATIONAL HOLIDAY/INDEPENDENCE DAY

Independence Day, November 28

SIGNIFICANT EVENTS IN FORMATION OF NATIONAL IDENTITY

First century–ninth century C.E. The Alans, originally from Central Asia, settle in the lowlands north of the Caucasus Mountains. Waves of invaders push the Alans farther into the mountain valleys for protection.

Ninth century–13th century The Alans, also called Ossets or Ossetians, organize a state that maintains a precarious independence. Christianity is introduced.

15th century The Caucasus region is the scene of a fierce rivalry between the Persian and Ottoman empires.

16th century Russian expansion reaches the Caucasus and is welcomed by the Christian Ossetians as protection against Muslim neighbors.

1792–1850 Ossetia comes under direct Russian rule, and the Christian Ossetians are permitted to repopulate the plains to the north of the mountains. The Ossetians are favored by the Russian authorities over their Muslim neighbors.

1918 North Ossetia is declared an autonomous Soviet Republic. The South Ossetians rebel when Georgia declares independence, and the rebellion is put down with great brutality.

1922 South Ossetia is made an autonomous part of the new Soviet Republic of Georgia.

1953 The Georgian alphabet, used for the Ossetian language in South Ossetia, is changed to the Russian Cyrillic alphabet.

1970s Discrimination and the assimilation policies of the Soviet Georgian government force many to leave for North Ossetia in Russia.

1980s The liberalization of Soviet life in the late 1980s allows nationalism to once again gain support. The South Ossetian leaders demand secession and reunification with North Ossetia in 1988, setting off violent confrontations between Ossetians and Georgians. In 1990, the region's autonomous status is rescinded.

1991–2000 The disintegration of the Soviet Union results in the independence of Georgia, including South Ossetia. National leaders declare South Ossetia independent of Georgia. War breaks out, sending some 100,000 refugees fleeing from the fighting. Russian troops intervene, leading to a stalemate.

2008 Violent clashes break out between Ossetians and Georgians. Georgian forces invade South Ossetia but are stopped when Russian reinforcements arrive. The Russians drive the Georgian forces out and invade Georgian territory before the European Union (EU) arranges a ceasefire. Russia recognizes the independence of South Ossetia, becoming the first country to extend diplomatic recognition since independence was declared in 1991. Nicaragua* follows Russia's lead and extends recognition in September 2008.

2009 South Ossetia's president reiterates his goal of unification of South Ossetia with North Ossetia, one of the republics of the Russian Federation. In July, the last UN monitors leave the region following Russia's veto of an extension of their mandate. Venezuela's leader, Hugo Chavez, on a visit to Moscow in August, announces Venezuelan recognition of the independence of South Ossetia and Abkhazia*.

See also Georgia

SPAIN

OFFICIAL NAME
Reino de España (Spanish); Kingdom of Spain (English)

POPULATION
45,676,900 (2009e)

INHABITANTS' NAME/NICKNAME
Spanish; Spaniard(s)

LANGUAGE/LANGUAGES
Spanish (official); Catalan, Basque, Galician (co-official in Catalonia*, Euskal Herria*, and Galicia*, respectively); French, Portuguese, English, others

RELIGION/RELIGIONS
Roman Catholic, 76 percent; Muslim, 2.5 percent; other or no religion

NATIONAL FLAG
The flag has three horizontal stripes of red, yellow, and red, the yellow stripe twice the width of the red stripes. The national coat of arms is just to the left of center on the yellow stripe.

COAT OF ARMS/SEAL
The coat of arms is composed of six other arms and additional heraldic symbols representing the kingdoms of Castile, Leon, Aragon, Navarre, and Granada, the House of Bourbon (Anjou branch), the Pillars of Hercules, the imperial crown of the Holy Roman Empire, and the Spanish royal crown.

MOTTO
Plus ultra (Latin); Further Beyond (English)

CAPITAL CITY
Madrid

TYPE OF GOVERNMENT
Constitutional monarchy and parliamentary democracy

NATIONAL EMBLEM
Black bull

NATIONAL COLORS
Red, yellow, and blue

NATIONAL ANTHEM
The anthem was adopted as the royal anthem in 1770 and has remained since, except during the republic from 1936 to 1939.

Marcha Real (Spanish); Royal March (English)
Glory, glory, crown of the fatherland
sovereign light that in your standard is gold.

Life, life, future of the fatherland,
in your eyes it is an open heart

Purple and gold: immortal flag;
in your colors, together, flesh and soul is.
Purple and gold: to want and to achieve;
You are, flag, the sign of human effort.

Glory, glory, crown of the fatherland
sovereign light that in your standard is gold.
Purple and gold: immortal flag;
in your colors, together, flesh and soul is.

PATRON SAINT(S)

Saint James the Greater; Saint John of Avila;
Our Lady of Ransom; Immaculate Conception of Mary

CURRENCY

Euro

INTERNET IDENTIFIER

.es

VEHICLE IDENTIFICATION PLATES/STICKERS

E

PASSPORT

The passport cover has the names of the
European Union and Spain in Spanish, the
coat of arms, the Spanish word for passport,
pasaporte, and the standard biometric symbol. Three thin vertical lines run from the top
right to below the coat of arms, where they
run horizontally between the coat of arms
and the word *pasaporte,* and then continue
vertically to the bottom left.

AIRLINES

Iberia; Air Europa; Spanair

NATIONAL FLOWER

Carnation

NATIONAL ANIMAL

Black bull; lion

NATIONAL RESOURCES

Natural resources include coal, lignite, iron
ore, copper, lead, zinc, uranium, tungsten,
mercury, pyrites, magnesite, fluorspar, gypsum, sepiolite, kaolin, potash, hydropower,
and arable land. Sandy beaches, a pleasant climate, historic cities and monuments, a unique
culture, and proximity to large population
centers support the thriving tourist industry.
Tourism and construction, mostly along the
coasts, are the two largest industries.

FOODS

Cuisine in Spain is regional, with many different food styles and traditions. Tapas, various appetizers or small dishes, are considered
a national habit. Paella, from the Mediterranean region, a rice dish with seafood and
vegetables, is often considered the national
dish, as is *cocido,* a stew of meat and vegetables with many regional variations. Other
specialties include *bacalao vizcaina,* salt cod
with tomato sauce; *bunuelos,* codfish fritters;
caldo gallego, chicken soup from Galicia;
angulas, baby eels sautéed with garlic and
parsley; *cochinillo,* roast suckling pig from
Castile; and gazpacho, a cold vegetable soup
from Andalusia.

SPORTS/SPORTS TEAMS

Association football (soccer) is the most
popular sport, followed by basketball. Spain
national teams participate in many sports at
an international level.

TEAM SPORTS

Badminton

Spain Badminton Team

Baseball

Spain Baseball Team; Spain Softball Team

Basketball

Spain Basketball Team; Spain Women's Basketball Team; Spain Under-21 Basketball

Team; Spain Under-21 Basketball Team; Spain Under-19 Basketball Team; Spain Wheelchair Basketball Team

Cricket

Spain Cricket Team

Football

Spain Football Team, nickname La Furia Roja (the Red Fury) or La Selección Roja (the Red Team); Spain Women's Football Team; Spain Under-20 Football Team; Spain Rugby Union Team, nickname El XV del Leon (the Lion's Fifteen); Spain Women's Rugby Union Team, nickname La XV del Leon (the Lion's Fifteen); Spain Women's Under-19 Football Team; Spain Beach Soccer Team; Spain Youth Football Team; Spain Under-21 Football Team nickname La Furia (the Wrath); Spain Australian-Rules Football Team, nickname the Bulls; Spain American Football Team; Spain Beach Soccer Team; Spain Futsal Team; Spain Rugby Union Team (Sevens), nickname Spain Sevens or Spain 7s; Spain Women's Rugby Union Team (Sevens), nickname Spain Sevens or Spain 7s

Handball

Spain Handball Team; Spain Women's Handball Team; Spain Beach Handball Team; Spain Women's Beach Handball Team

Hockey

Spain Ice Hockey Team; Spain Junior Ice Hockey Team; Spain Field Hockey Team; Spain Women's Field Hockey Team; Spain Roller Hockey Team

Korfball

Spain Korfball Team

Racing

A-1 Team Spain; Spain Speedway Team

Polo

Spain Polo Team

Table Tennis

Spain Table Tennis Team

Tennis

Spain Davis Cup Team; Spain Fed Cup Team

Volleyball

Spain Men's Volleyball Team; Spain Women's Volleyball Team; Spain Fistball Team; Spain Men's Beach Volleyball Team; Spain Women's Beach Volleyball Team

Water Polo

Spain Men's Water Polo Team; Spain Women's Water Polo Team

INDIVIDUAL SPORTS

Spain Amateur Boxing Team; Spain Archery Team; Spain Athletics Team; Spain Cycling Team; Spain Equestrian Team; Spain Fencing Team; Spain Gymnastics Team; Spain Judo Team; Spain Karate Team: Spain Modern Pentathlon Team; Spain Rowing Team; Spain Shooting Team; Spain Swim Team; Spain Tae Kwon Do Team; Spain Triathlon Team; Spain Weight Lifting Team; Spain Wrestling Team

WINTER SPORTS

Spain Alpine Ski Team; Spain Bobsleigh and Tobogganing Team; Spain Curling Team; Spain Skating Team

NATIONAL HEROES OR PERSONIFICATIONS

Hispania is the national personification, a classical figure in Roman dress. Juan Español (John Spaniard) is the personification of the average man.

National heroes include Antoní Gaudí, famed architect at the turn of the 20th century; King Juan Carlos, who aided the transition to democracy in the 1970s; Federico Garcia Lorca, known as Spain's favorite author; Salvador Dali, an innovative, surrealist artist; and Pablo Picasso, leader of the avant garde artist movement.

NATIONAL HOLIDAY/INDEPENDENCE DAY

National Day, October 12

FESTIVALS/FAIRS

Semana Santa (Holy Week Festival), March–April; Tamborrada de San Sebastian (Drum Festival), January; Feria de Abril (April Fair), April; Bilbao Semana Grande, August: Catalonia Christmas Festival, December; Las Fallas de Valencia, March; Festival of San Fermin, July; San Sebastian Film Festival, September

SIGNIFICANT EVENTS IN FORMATION OF NATIONAL IDENTITY

1100 B.C.E. Phoenician traders establish the first colonies on the coast to trade with the native Iberians.

228 B.C.E.–218 B.C.E. Rome defeats Carthage in a rivalry for control of the Mediterranean. Roman legions occupy the Iberian Peninsula.

409 C.E. The collapse of Roman power allows Germanic Visigoths to conquer the peninsula.

711 A combined Arab and Berber army from North Africa conquers most of Christian Spain. An independent Muslim emirate is established.

913 The Christians, driven into the north, begin the reconquest of Spain.

1013 The Muslim state breaks up due to internal strife, and a number of small feuding kingdoms emerge.

1492 The last Muslim kingdom of Granada falls to the Spanish. Jews are forced to convert or are expelled from the kingdom. Christopher Columbus begins his first expedition to the New World, the first step to Spain's political and economic empire covering much of the Americas.

1702–1714 The War of the Spanish Succession pits region against region. Thousands die in the siege of Barcelona.

1808–1814 Napoleon Bonaparte conquers Spain and deposes the Spanish king. The Spanish rise against French rule. The events in Europe begin the breakup of the Spanish Empire in the Americas.

1898 The Spanish-America War begins. Spain loses its last colonies in Asia and the Americas.

1931 A revolution forces the abdication of the Spanish king. A republic is proclaimed and liberal laws are adopted.

1936–1939 Conservative military forces attack the republic, beginning the bloody Spanish Civil War. General Francisco Franco's victory ends the republic, and a fascist dictatorship is established.

1975–1986 Franco's death begins the transition to democracy. Spain's restive nationalities are granted limited autonomy. Spain joins the North Atlantic Treaty Organization (NATO) and the European Community, later the European Union (EU).

2004 Islamic terrorists bomb commuter trains in Madrid, killing hundreds of people. The incident precipitates a change of government.

2008 The Basques of Euskal Herria, the Basque Country, defy the government and plan a referendum on self-determination. Spain refuses to recognize the independence of Kosovo, fearing the effect on its own separatist Basque, Galician, and Catalan regions.

2009 The government unilaterally announces the withdrawal of its troops that form part of the NATO military contingent in Kosovo. The move, made without consultation with its allies, brings protests and criticism from other NATO members. Economic problems with high unemployment bring hardship after years of high economic growth.

See also Canary Islands; Catalonia; Euskal Herria; Galicia

SWEDEN

OFFICIAL NAME

Konungariket Sverige (Swedish); Kingdom of Sweden (English)

POPULATION

9,224,500 (2009e)

Inhabitants' Name/Nickname

Swede(s); Swedish

Language/Languages

Swedish (de facto official); English, Danish, Norwegian, Finnish, German; five regional languages recognized

Religion/Religions

Lutheran, 87 percent; Roman Catholic, Orthodox, other Protestant, other or no religion

National Flag

The flag has a blue field bearing a yellow Scandinavian cross. The design and colors come from the present coat of arms of 1442. Blue and yellow have been used as the national colors since at least 1275.

Coat of Arms/Seal

The lesser coat of arms is a blue shield charged with three gold crowns and a red and gold crown representing the monarchy. The greater coat of arms is the traditional emblem, with a quartered shield supported by two gold lions surrounded by a red, ermined cape draped from a royal crown.

Motto

Royal motto: *För Sverige—i tiden* (Swedish); For Sweden— with the times (English)

Capital City

Stockholm

Type of Government

Parliamentary democracy and constitutional monarchy

National Emblem

Three golden crowns

National Colors

Blue and yellow

National Anthem

The anthem is based on a folk tune and began to be used in the late 19th century, although it has never been officially adopted. Sweden also has a royal anthem.

> **Sång till Norden (Swedish); Song of the North (English) (unofficial as the anthem is not mentioned in the Swedish constitution)**
>
> You ancient, you free, you mountainous North
> You quiet, you joyful beauty!
> I greet you, fairest of the lands upon earth,
> Your sun, your sky, your meadows green.
>
> You rest upon memories of great olden days,
> When honored your name flew over the world,
> I know that you are and will be as you were,
> Yes, I want to live, I want to die in the north
>
> I forever will serve my beloved country,
> your faith until death will I swear,
> Your right will I protect with mind and with hand,
> your banner, great the feats it carries.
>
> With God shall I struggle (fight), for home and for hearth,
> for Sweden, the dear motherland.
> I trade you not, for anything in the world
> No, I want to live, I want to die in the north.

Patron Saint

Saint Eric of Sweden, Saint Birgitta

Currency

Swedish krona. In September 2003, Swedish voters turned down entry into the euro system, concerned about the impact on the economy and sovereignty.

Internet Identifier

.se

Vehicle Identification Plates/ Stickers

S

PASSPORT

The passport cover has the name of the European Union, the name of the country, and the word *passport* in Swedish; to the right is a stylized depiction of a compass, and below are a small coat of arms and the standard biometric symbol.

AIRLINES

SAS Scandinavian Airlines System (shared with Denmark* and Norway*); City Airlines

NATIONAL FLOWER

Twinflower

NATIONAL TREE

Pildamsparken (Swedish tree) (unofficial)

NATIONAL ANIMAL

Lion; elk

NATIONAL BIRD

Eurasian blackbird

NATIONAL RESOURCES

Natural resources include iron ore, copper, lead, zinc, gold, silver, tungsten, uranium, arsenic, feldspar, timber, and hydropower. The country's well-educated skilled workforce gives the country's one of the highest standards of living in the world. Tourism is also important, based on varied scenery, a unique culture, historic cities and monuments, and proximity to large population centers in Europe.

FOODS

Köttbullar, Swedish meatballs, served in gravy, are considered the national dish. *Smörgåsbord,* a buffet of various hot and cold dishes, is a national institution. *Ostkaka,* a type of cheesecake or curd cake, is the national dessert. Other specialties include *gravlax,* smoked salmon; *inglad sill,* pickled salt herring; and *pannkakor,* Swedish pancakes, eaten with sweet fillings for desserts or savory fillings for meals. *Glogg,* a mixture of red wine, vodka, brandy, port or Madeira, dried figs, spices, and beer, is a Christmas drink considered, along with *aquavit,* as a national drink.

SPORTS/SPORTS TEAMS

Ice hockey and association football (soccer) are the most popular sports. Sweden national teams participate in many sports at an international level.

TEAM SPORTS

Badminton

Sweden Badminton Team

Baseball

Sweden Baseball Team; Sweden Softball Team

Basketball

Sweden Basketball Team; Sweden Women's Basketball Team; Sweden Wheelchair Basketball Team; Sweden Women's Wheelchair Basketball Team

Cricket

Sweden Cricket Team

Football

Sweden Football Team, nickname Blågult (the Blue and Yellow); Sweden Women's Football Team, nickname Blågult (the Blue and Yellow); Sweden Rugby Union Team; Sweden Women's Rugby Union Team; Sweden Under-21 Football Team; Sweden Women's Under-19 Football Team; Sweden Australian-Rules Football Team, nickname the Elks; Sweden Wheelchair Rugby Team; Sweden American Football Team; Sweden Rugby League Team

Handball

Sweden Handball Team; Sweden Women's Handball Team; Sweden Beach Handball Team; Sweden Women's Beach Handball Team

Hockey

Sweden Men's Ice Hockey Team, nickname Tre Kronor (the Three Crowns); Sweden Women's Ice Hockey Team, nickname Tre Kronor (the Three Crowns); Sweden Junior Ice Hockey Team; Sweden Field Hockey Team

Korfball

Sweden Korfball Team

Lacrosse

Sweden Lacrosse Team

Table Tennis

Sweden Table Tennis Team

Tennis

Sweden Davis Cup Team; Sweden Fed Cup Team

Volleyball

Sweden Men's Volleyball Team; Sweden Women's Volleyball Team; Sweden Fistball Team; Sweden Men's Beach Volleyball Team; Sweden Women's Beach Volleyball Team

INDIVIDUAL SPORTS

Sweden Aikido Team; Sweden Amateur Boxing Team; Sweden Archery Team; Sweden Athletics Team; Sweden Canoeing Team; Sweden Cycling Team; Sweden Equestrian Team; Sweden Fencing Team; Sweden Gymnastics Team; Sweden Judo Team; Sweden Karate Team: Sweden Modern Pentathlon Team; Sweden Rowing Team; Sweden Sailing Team; Sweden Shooting Team; Sweden Swim Team; Sweden Tae Kwon Do Team;

Sweden Triathlon Team; Sweden Weight Lifting Team; Sweden Wrestling Team

WINTER SPORTS

Sweden Alpine Ski Team; Sweden Bandy Team; Sweden Biathlon Team; Sweden Bobsleigh and Tobogganing Team; Sweden Curling Team; Sweden Men's Ice Hockey Team, nickname Tre Kronor (the Three Crowns); Sweden Women's Ice Hockey Team, nickname Tre Kronor (the Three Crowns); Sweden Junior Ice Hockey Team; Sweden Luge Team; Sweden Skating Team

NATIONAL HEROES OR PERSONIFICATIONS

Mother Svea is the national personification, usually depicted as a shieldmaiden with one or two lions. Svensson is the Swedish common man.

National heroes include Gustavus Adolphus, the founder of the Swedish Empire in the 17th century; King Charles XI, the king who rebuilt the economy and the army in the late 17th century; Esaias Tegnér, considered the father of modern Swedish poetry; and Olof Palme, the prime minister murdered in 1986.

NATIONAL HOLIDAY/INDEPENDENCE DAY

National Day/Flag Day, June 6

FESTIVALS/FAIRS

Lucia Festival, December; Walpurgis, March; Midsummer Festival, July; Sweden Rock, June; Peace & Love Festival, July; Way Out West (Goteborg Festival), August

SIGNIFICANT EVENTS IN FORMATION OF NATIONAL IDENTITY

100 B.C.E.–100 C.E. Greater contact with Roman Europe begins a change in the life of the northern tribal peoples. Sweden is mentioned in the *Germania* of Tacitus in 98 C.E.

8th century–11th century Vikings expand from eastern Sweden to incorporate much of Scandinavia. Vikings travel and raid east into Russia, the

Mediterranean, and regions as far away as Baghdad and Constantinople.

1350 The Black Plague sweeps Scandinavia, killing a third of the population.

1397 The Union of Kalmar unites Denmark, Sweden, and Norway under a single monarch, with Denmark as the dominant power.

1523 Gustav I, known as Gustavus Adolphus, takes Sweden out of the union and begins the kingdom's territorial expansion.

1611–1720 Sweden's conquests in Finland*, the Baltic region, Poland*, and Germany* make the Swedish Empire one of the most powerful states in Europe.

1750–1800 Sweden declines as a leading power, losing territory to Russia*, which takes the last important part of the empire, Finland, in 1809.

1814 After the Napoleonic Wars, in which Sweden is a leading allied power against the French, the country adopts a policy of neutrality. Denmark cedes Norway to Swedish rule.

1850–1914 Over a million Swedes leave the kingdom, mostly for the United States* and Canada*.

1901 Alfred Nobel, the millionaire chemist and inventor of dynamite, initiates the Nobel prizes.

1905 Norway secedes and becomes a separate kingdom.

1914–1946 Sweden maintains armed neutrality during both world wars. After the Second World War, Sweden joins the United Nations in spite of its avowed neutrality.

1986 Olof Palme, the prime minister, is murdered on a Stockholm street.

1990–1995 Swedish voters narrowly approve membership in the European Union, which Sweden joins in 1995.

2003 A referendum vote goes against joining the single European currency.

2005–2009 Sweden remains active in United Nations peace efforts around the world but maintains its historic political neutrality.

See also Scania

SWITZERLAND

OFFICIAL NAME

Confoederatio Helvetica (Latin); Schweizerische Eidgenossenschaft (German); Confédération Suisse (French); Confederazione Svizzera (Italian); Confederaziun Svizra (Romansh); Swiss Confederation (English)

POPULATION

7,623,100 (2009e)

INHABITANTS' NAME/NICKNAME

Swiss

LANGUAGE/LANGUAGES

German, French, Italian, Romansh (official); English, Serbian, Albanian, Tamil, others

RELIGION/RELIGIONS

Roman Catholic, 41 percent; Protestant, 40 percent; Muslim, 5 percent; Orthodox, 1.5 percent; Jewish, other or no religion

NATIONAL FLAG

The flag is a red square bearing a centered equilateral white cross. The flag is one of the oldest in Europe, dating from the 13th or 14th century, and only one of two square national flags, the other belonging to the Vatican*.

COAT OF ARMS/SEAL

The coat of arms is a red shield charged with a white cross like that of the national flag.

MOTTO

Unus pro omnibus, omnes pro uno (Latin); One for all, all for one (English)

CAPITAL CITY

Bern

TYPE OF GOVERNMENT

Federal parliamentary republic

NATIONAL EMBLEM

White equilateral cross on a red field

NATIONAL COLORS
Red and white

NATIONAL ANTHEM

The song was written and composed in the 1840s, although it was only adopted as the official national anthem in 1981.

> **Schweizerpsalm (German); Cantique Suisse (French); Salmo Svizzero (Italian); Psalm Svizzer (Romansh); Swiss Psalm (English)**
>
> When the morning skies grow red
> And o'er us their radiance shed,
> Thou, O Lord, appearest in their light.
> When the Alps glow bright with splendor,
> Pray to God, to him surrender,
> For you feel and understand,
> That he dwelleth in this land.
>
> In the sunset thou art night
> And beyond the starry sky,
> Thou, O loving Father, ever near.
> When to heaven we are departing,
> Joy and bliss thou'lt be imparting,
> For we feel and understand
> That thou dwellest in this land.
>
> When dark clouds enshroud the hills
> And gray mist the valley fills,
> Yet thou art not hidden from thy sons.
> Pierce the gloom in which we cover
> With thy sunshine's cleansing power
> Then we'll feel and understand
> That God dwelleth in this land.
>
> Towards us in the wild storm coming,
> Thou thyself give us resistance and
>   stronghold,
> Thou, almighty ruling, rescuing!
> During horror and nights of thunderstorms
> Let us childlike trust him!
> Yes, we feel and understand
> Yes, we feel and understand
> That God dwelleth in this land
> That God dwelleth in this land.

PATRON SAINT
Saint Notbunga

CURRENCY
Swiss franc

INTERNET IDENTIFIER
.ch

VEHICLE IDENTIFICATION PLATES/ STICKERS
CH

PASSPORT

The passport cover, decorated with many small Swiss Crosses, has the words *Swiss Passport* in the four official languages and English, a larger white Swiss Cross, and the standard biometric symbol.

AIRLINE
Swiss International Airlines

NATIONAL FLOWER
Edelweiss

NATIONAL TREE
Murten lime (linden) (unofficial)

NATIONAL ANIMAL
Chamois (unofficial)

NATIONAL BIRD
Little ringed plover (unofficial)

NATIONAL REPTILE
Alpine salamander (unofficial)

NATIONAL RESOURCES

Natural resources include hydropower potential, timber, and salt. Switzerland's location in the heart of Western Europe, its well-educated, multilingual and highly skilled population, and an open economy gives the country one of the highest standards of living in the world. Tourism is an important resource, offering varied and mountain scenery, winter resorts, historic cities and monuments, unique cultures, and proximity to large European population centers.

FOODS

Rösti, a dish of grated potatoes shaped into rounds or patties and fried that originated in the German-speaking cantons, and fondue, a semiliquid cheese dish served with cubes of bread, ham, pickles, and other small bits for dipping that originated in the French-speaking western cantons, are considered the national dishes. Other Swiss specialties include *jägerschnitzel,* pounded pork cutlets dipped in an egg-and-breadcrumb batter and then fried and served with a sauce of diced bacon, onions, morels, tomato, and white wine; and *Birchermuesli,* a mixture of oats, dried berries or raisins, lemon juice, apple, coconut, yogurt, almonds, blackberries and honey, created by Dr. Bircher-Benner for patients in his Zurich clinic.

SPORTS/SPORTS TEAMS

Association football (soccer) is the most popular sport. Cycling and ice hockey are also very popular. Switzerland national teams participate in many sports at an international level.

TEAM SPORTS

Badminton
Switzerland Badminton Team

Baseball
Switzerland Baseball Team; Switzerland Softball Team

Basketball
Switzerland Basketball Team; Switzerland Women's Basketball Team; Switzerland Wheelchair Basketball Team

Cricket
Switzerland Cricket Team

Football
Switzerland Football Team, nickname Nati or Die Eidgenossen (the Comrades); Switzerland Women's Football Team, nickname Nati; Switzerland Under-20 Football Team; Switzerland Women's Under-19 Football Team; Switzerland Rugby Union Team; Switzerland Women's Rugby Union Team; Switzerland Wheelchair Rugby Team; American Football Team; Switzerland Beach Soccer Team

Golf
Switzerland Pitch and Putt Team

Handball
Switzerland Handball Team; Switzerland Women's Handball Team; Switzerland Beach Handball Team; Switzerland Women's Beach Handball Team

Hockey
Switzerland Ice Hockey Team; Switzerland Junior Ice Hockey Team; Switzerland Women's Ice Hockey Team; Switzerland Field Hockey Team; Switzerland Roller Hockey Team; Switzerland Women's Roller Hockey Team

Racing
A1 Team Switzerland; Switzerland Speedway Team

Table Tennis
Switzerland Table Tennis Team

Tennis
Switzerland Davis Cup Team; Switzerland Fed Cup Team

Volleyball
Switzerland Fistball Team; Switzerland Men's Volleyball Team; Switzerland Women's Volleyball Team; Switzerland Men's Beach Volleyball Team; Switzerland Women's Beach Volleyball Team

INDIVIDUAL SPORTS

Switzerland Aikido Team; Switzerland Amateur Boxing Team; Switzerland Archery Team; Switzerland Athletics Team; Switzerland Canoeing Team; Switzerland Equestrian Team; Switzerland Fencing Team; Switzerland Gymnastics Team; Switzerland Judo Team; Switzerland Karate Team; Switzerland Modern Pentathlon Team; Switzerland Rowing Team; Switzerland Sailing Team; Switzerland Shooting Team; Switzerland Swim Team; Switzerland Tae Kwon Do Team; Switzerland Triathlon Team; Switzerland Weight Lifting Team; Switzerland Wrestling Team

WINTER SPORTS

Switzerland Alpine Ski Team; Switzerland Bandy Team: Switzerland Biathlon Team; Switzerland Bobsleigh and Tobogganing Team; Switzerland Curling Team; Switzerland Ice Hockey Team; Switzerland Junior Ice Hockey Team; Switzerland Women's Ice Hockey Team; Switzerland Luge Team; Switzerland Skating Team

NATIONAL HEROES OR PERSONIFICATIONS

Helvetia, carrying a spear and a shield emblazoned with the red and white cross of the Swiss flag, is the national personification of Switzerland; Herr and Frau Schweitzer are the personification of the solid Swiss bourgeoisie; Colin Tampon is the Swiss everyman.

National heroes include Henry Dunant, founder of the International Red Cross; William Tell, who symbolized the bravery of the Alpine peoples in resisting oppression; and Henri Guisan, a military leader who strengthened Swiss defenses at the outbreak of the Second World War.

NATIONAL HOLIDAY/INDEPENDENCE DAY

Founding of the Swiss Confederation, August 1

FESTIVALS/FAIRS

Mardi Gras/Karneval/Fasnacht/Carnival, February–March; International Jazz Festival, March–May; Sechseläuten (Spring Festival), April; Berner Tanztage (Bern Dance Festival), June; Zurich Festival, June–July; Estival Jazz, July; Montreaux International Jazz Festival, July; Festa d'Autunno (Lugano Food and Wine Festival), October

SIGNIFICANT EVENTS IN FORMATION OF NATIONAL IDENTITY

500 B.C.E. Celtic tribes inhabit the region.

56 B.C.E. The Celtic Helvetii tribe submits, following defeat by the Romans under Julius Caesar.

Fourth century C.E. Germanic tribes overrun the region as Roman power disappears.

Seventh century The region forms a part of the Frankish kingdom. Christianity extends to even the remote alpine valleys.

9th century–13th century The region is included in Charlemagne's Holy Roman Empire. Many small states and fiefs emerge as the power of the empire declines in the 12th century. The Hapsburgs become the dominant power in the eastern region.

1291–1315 The small canton states of Schwyz, Uri, and Lower Unterwalden form a defensive confederation known as the Everlasting League to resist Hapsburg control. The confederation defeats the Hapsburg forces at the Battle of Morgarten in 1315. Lucern, Zurich, Basel, and other cantons join the Swiss Confederation, which becomes independent of Hapsburg rule.

1523–1529 The urbanized regions accept the Protestant Reformation, but rural cantons remain Roman Catholic.

1648 The Treaty of Westphalia recognizes the confederation's independence from the Holy Roman Empire.

1815 The Great Powers recognize the perpetual neutrality of Switzerland.

1845–1847   Seven predominately Roman Catholic cantons form the Sonderbund to resist any strengthening of the weak central government by liberals. Federal troops defeat the Sonderbund in a brief civil war.

1847–1874   The central government is strengthened, and the principal of popular referendum is introduced.

1920   The League of Nations selects neutral Geneva as its headquarters in the aftermath of the First World War.

1939–1945   Strict neutrality is maintained during the Second World War.

1960   Stepping back just a little from the policy of strict neutrality, Switzerland joins the new European Free Trade Association, which is considered a purely economic alliance.

1971   Women are granted the right to vote in federal elections.

1986   A proposal for Swiss membership in the United Nations is rejected in a national referendum.

2001   Proposed membership in the European Union (EU) is rejected in a national referendum, although it is approved in the French-speaking western cantons.

2002   The Swiss join the United Nations while maintaining their traditional neutrality.

2005–2009   Several new laws are approved by referendum to tighten the country's asylum and foreign worker laws. Some tax and banking laws are also revised in the face of international criticism.

TATARSTAN

OFFICIAL NAME

Respublika Tatarstan (transliteration from Tatar and Russian); Republic of Tatarstan (English)

POPULATION

3,841,200 (2009e)

INHABITANTS' NAME/NICKNAME

Tatar(s); Tatarstaner(s); Tatarstani(s)

LANGUAGE/LANGUAGES

Tatar, Russian (both official); Chuvash, Udmurt, Ukrainian, others

RELIGION/RELIGIONS

Sunni Muslim, Shia Muslim, Russian Orthodox, other or no religion

NATIONAL FLAG

The flag is a horizontal bicolor of green over red, the two stripes divided by a narrow white stripe across the center. The green represents the Muslim Tatars, the red stands for the Christians in the republic, and the white represents peace. The green also represents spring and revival and symbolizes hope, freedom and wealth; the white stands for purity, peace, concord, and the future; and the red represents maturity, energy, and the life force, as well as happiness, bravery, and courage.

COAT OF ARMS/SEAL

The coat of arms, called the *Aq Bars,* is a circular red disk bearing a white, winged snow leopard bearing a shield to protect the Tatars, because the wings signifying that it rules over land, water, and the heavens. The disk is bordered by a thin white circle and an outer green circle decorated in a traditional Tatar design, with the name of the country, Tatarstan, in the Cyrillic alphabet below the leopard. The *Aq Bars* is an ancient symbol of the Tatars, originally used by the Volga Bulgars, the ancestors of the Tatars, as their state symbol. The red disk represents the rising sun, a symbol of rebirth. The three rings represent the three historical stages of Tatar statehood: the Volga Bulgar khanate of the 9th to the 13th centuries, the Kazan Khanate of the 15th and 16th centuries, and modern Tatarstan.

MOTTO

Buldirabiz! (Tatar); We can! (English)

CAPITAL CITY

Kazan

TYPE OF GOVERNMENT

Parliamentary republic as a member state of the Russian Federation. Tatarstan, following a number of treaties signed in the 1990s, is officially an autonomous state in free association with the Russian Federation.

NATIONAL EMBLEMS

Aq Bars, the winged snow leopard; Kazan Kremlin

NATIONAL COLORS

Green, white, and red

NATIONAL ANTHEM

The anthem, originally written as a hymn, was officially adopted in 1993.

Tuğan yağım (Tatar); My Native Land (English)

I have walked so many roads and I have seen the world
And tender winds stroked my face.
But only when I return to you, my native land,
I am the happiest in the world.
And even if I leave you for just a day
I miss you with all my heart.
I think, my native land, that if you didn't exist,
I couldn't live in this world.

And even if I leave you for just a day
I feel as if I'm an orphan.
You are all the beauty of this endless world.
The graceful star that shines bright in the night.

PATRON SAINT

Saint Gregory the illuminator

CURRENCY

Russian ruble

VEHICLE IDENTIFICATION PLATES/STICKERS

RUS Russia (official); TAT Tatarstan (unofficial)

PASSPORT

Tatars are Russian citizens and travel on Russian passports.

AIRLINE

Tatarstan Airlines JSC

NATIONAL FLOWER

Aster; tulip

NATIONAL TREE

Silver birch (unofficial)

NATIONAL ANIMAL

Snow leopard

NATIONAL BIRD

Great tit (unofficial)

NATIONAL FISH

Volga sturgeon (unofficial)

NATIONAL RESOURCES

Natural resources include major deposits of petroleum and natural gas, abundant arable land, hydropower, fish, and timber. The major industry is the extraction of the republic's large oil and gas deposits, making it one of the largest producers in Europe. Tourism, based on the region's historic cities and monuments and the growth of cruise lines on the Volga River, is becoming an important industry.

FOODS

Balis, a dish of meat (mutton, beef, goose, or duck) mixed with barley or rice, is considered the national dish. Other traditional dishes include *pilman,* a type of ravioli served in a meat or vegetable broth; *shulpa,* a soup made of meat and noodles; *pilaw,* a rice dish with meat and vegetables; *quilama,* a type of meat pie; *ocpocmaq,* a triangular pastry stuffed with meat and onions; *qoymaq,* a tart type of fritter; and *bakkan,* pastries stuffed with vegetables.

Sports/Sports Teams

Ice hockey is the most popular sport, with Tatar participation at all levels of Russian league sports. Association football (soccer) is also very popular.

Team Sports

Football

Football Club Rubin Kazan is considered the Tatar national team, wearing Tatar national colors and symbols

National Heroes or Personifications

Rudolf Nureyev, famed ballet dancer; President Mintimer Shaimiev, who led Tatarstan after the collapse of the Soviet Union; Mohammad Amin, Tatarstan's 15th-century national poet; Aleksandr Butlerov, a scientist, one of the creators of the theory of chemical structure, for whom the crater Butlerov on the moon is named; Musa Dzhalil, a poet and freedom fighter; Tukai Gabdulla, a poet and writer regarded as the father of modern Tatar literature; Baqi Urmance, a painter and sculptor of the mid-20th century

National Holiday/Independence Day

Day of the Republic, August 30

Festivals/Fairs

Nureyev International Ballet Festival, annual; Republic Day festival, August; Tatar Zhyry (Tatar Song), June; Festival of Opera, February; Europe-Asia Festival of Modern Music, April; Republic Theater Festival, December; Tatarstan Exhibit, September.

Significant Events in Formation of National Identity

100 C.E. The Bulgar peoples are mentioned in historic records as nomadic tribes living around the Sea of Azov.

660 The Bulgars migrate to the lower Volga River valley. Other clans turn to the west to eventually settle along the Danube in central Europe.

Ninth century The Bulgars are the dominant tribe in a wide region of the lower Volga valley, incorporating into their state many Finno-Ugric and Turkic peoples.

922 According to Tatar tradition, Islam is introduced by travelers from Baghdad in 922.

1238–1430 The Bulgar Volga region falls to the invading Mongols of the Golden Horde. The mixture of the Mongol and Turkic invaders with the earlier inhabitants produces the Volga Tatars.

1430s The region becomes independent of the remnants of the Golden Horde. The Khanate of Kazan flourishes as a center of Muslim culture.

1552 Invading Russians conquer the khanate. Many Tatars are forcibly converted to Russian Orthodoxy. Churches are constructed in all Tatar cities and towns.

1593 The Russian government orders all mosques in the region to be destroyed and prohibits the building of new mosques.

1600–1700 The Tatars become the middlemen in Russia's dealings with the other Muslim peoples incorporated into the empire as its borders expand through military conquests.

1750–1800 The first mosque is rebuilt in 1766–1770 following the lifting of the prohibition by Catherine II. Tatar resistance to forced Russification and conversion to Christianity sparks a number of serious uprisings. Tens of thousands of Slavic colonists settle the Tatar lands.

19th century Tatarstan becomes a center of Jadidism, an Islamic sect that preaches tolerance and acceptance of other religions. The Tatars become famous in the Russian Empire for their advanced culture and easy tolerance of other peoples and other religions. A large middle class evolves in the 1880s, with a progressive outlook and an emphasis on education and publishing in the Tatar language.

1914–1919 The Russian Revolution, in the midst of World War I, spurs the rapid growth of Tatar nationalism. Leaders create the Idel-Ural republic with other regional ethnic groups, but the new state is quickly overrun by invading Bolshevik forces.

1920 The Tatar Autonomous Soviet Socialist Republic is formed as part of the Soviet Russian Federation. Although the Tatars are one of the largest ethnic groups in Russia*, the boundaries of the autonomous republic are drawn to include only about a third of the Tatar population. Unlike the other large ethnic groups, the Tatars are allowed to form a union republic as a member state of the new Soviet Union.

1940–1945 The discovery of large petroleum deposits during World War II brings a large influx of non-Tatars to the region.

1987–1990 The cultural and economic reforms introduced by Mikhail Gorbachev lead to the dissolution of the Soviet empire. Tatar leaders declare Tatarstan an autonomous republic in August 1990.

1991–1992 The complete collapse of the Soviet state triggers mass support for independence. A referendum is held, with 61 percent favoring immediate independence. The adoption of a new constitution as an independent republic is vehemently opposed by Russia.

1994 The Tatar government agrees to postpone full independence, but signs a number of treaties with Russia giving the republic full autonomy as an associate state of the Russian Federation. The standard of living becomes one of the highest in Russia.

1997 The war in the separatist republic of Chechnya* is a sobering example for nationalists who continue to demand secession and full independence.

2000 The Russian government revokes many of Tatarstan's powers of autonomy that contravene the Russian constitution.

2005–2009 The Tatars increase their unofficial diplomatic ties to the Muslim nations to the south and to the countries of Europe. Nationalism remains subdued, partly due to the prosperity brought to the region by its abundant petroleum and natural gas. The economic downturn in 2008–2009 begins to impact public opinion, with renewed calls for greater autonomy and control of the Tatarstan economy.

TRANSNISTRIA

OFFICIAL NAME

Republica Moldovenească Nistreană (Moldovan); Pridnestrovskaya Moldavskaya Respublika (transliteration from Russian); Pridnistrovs'ka Moldavs'ka Respublika (Ukrainian); Pridnestrovian Moldavian Republic (English)

POPULATION

538,400 (2009e)

INHABITANTS' NAME/NICKNAME

Transnistrian(s)

LANGUAGE/LANGUAGES

Moldovan (in its Cyrillic form), Russian, Ukrainian (all official); Romanian, Gagauz, others

RELIGION/RELIGIONS

Russian Orthodox, Protestant, others

NATIONAL FLAG

The flag has three equal horizontal stripes of red, green, and red, reflecting the former flag of Soviet Moldavia. The official state flag is the same three stripes with the addition of the hammer and sickle of communism and the red star outlined in yellow on the upper hoist.

COAT OF ARMS/SEAL

The coat of arms is a remodeled version of the emblem of the former Soviet Moldavia, showing the hammer and sickle in the center, a rising sun, garlands of agricultural products, and a red banner inscribed with the name of the country in the three official languages, all under a single five-pointed red star.

CAPITAL CITY

Tiraspol

TYPE OF GOVERNMENT

Unrecognized semipresidential republic

NATIONAL COLORS

Red and green

NATIONAL ANTHEM

The anthem was adopted in 1991 using the melody of the former Soviet anthem of Moldavia with new lyrics.

My Slavim Tjeba, Pridnestrov'je (Russian); We Sing the Praises of Transnistria (English)

We sing the praises of Transnistria
Where the friendship of peoples is strong.
We are connected to it for centuries to come
With great love as sons.
Let's praise gardens and factories,
Settlements, fields and cities—
Much effort has been put into them
For the sake of the motherland.

Chorus

Let's carry through the years
The name of the proud country.
We'll be faithful to the republic of freedom
As to the truth.

We praise the native valleys,
The banks of the grey Dniester.
We remember epic heroic deeds,
The glory of our fathers is dear to us.
We will praise everyone by the name
Who died for the fatherly home.
We take an oath to the motherland
In holy memory of the dead.

CURRENCY

Transnistrian ruble

INTERNET IDENTIFIER

.ru Russia (official);

VEHICLE IDENTIFICATION PLATES/ STICKERS

PMR Pridnestrovskaya Moldavskaya Respublika (transliteration from Russian) (unofficial)

PASSPORT

Between 300,000 and 400,000 Transnistrians had acquired Moldovan passports by 2008. No country recognizes passports issued by the Transnistrian government. Russia opened a consulate in Tiraspol (against the will of Moldova) and issued about 80,000 passports to Transnistrians by the end of 2006.

NATIONAL RESOURCES

The heavily industrialized region produces steel, electricity, and textiles but has limited natural resources.

FOODS

Borscht, a beet and beef soup that is popular in Moldova*, Russia*, and Ukraine*, is considered the national dish.

SPORTS/SPORTS TEAMS

Association football (soccer) is the most popular sport. The Transnistria national team participates in football at an international level.

TEAM SPORTS

Football

Transnistria Football Team, nickname the Red and Green

NATIONAL HEROES OR PERSONIFICATIONS

Alexander Suorov, the founder of modern Tiraspol; Pyotr Vershigora, a Soviet writer and a leader of the partisan movement during the Second World War; Igor Smirnov, leader of the Transnistria independence movement

NATIONAL HOLIDAY/INDEPENDENCE DAY

Independence Day, September 2

SIGNIFICANT EVENTS IN FORMATION OF NATIONAL IDENTITY

Seventh century C.E. The region is settled by Slavs during the great Slav migrations.

1242–1513 Devastated by the Mongol invasion, the largely depopulated region is settled by Romanians and forms part of the medieval Moldavian principality. The region comes under the rule of the Ottoman Empire.

1711–1792 Russian rule is established in the region, called Bessarabia. Tiraspol is founded as center of Slav colonization.

1917–1918 Romanian troops occupy the region when the Russian Revolution begins. The Red Army, victorious in the Russian Civil War, invades but is stopped by Romanian troops at the Dniester River.

1924 The east bank of the Dniester under Soviet control becomes the Moldavian Autonomous Soviet Socialist Republic within Soviet Ukraine as a showpiece for the export of communism to neighboring Romania*.

1939–1940 The Red Army occupies Romanian Bessarabia, which is annexed to the Soviet Union and combined with the small east-bank region to form the Moldavian Soviet Socialist Republic, over the protests of the Slav population on the east bank.

1987–1990 Moldovan nationalism spreads rapidly with the Soviet liberalization. A new Moldavian (Moldovan)–only language law alienates the republic's Slavs, who are vilified as foreigners and invaders by radical Moldovan nationalists. The Slav leadership declares the independence of Transnistria, to include all of former Soviet Moldavia east of the Dniester River.

1990–1991 Fighting breaks out along the Dniester River between Moldovans and Slav militias aided by the Soviet 14th Army, which is still in the region. Soviet Moldavia becomes independent Moldova, which is rejected by the east-bank Slavs. Heavy fighting spreads along the disputed border region.

1994 The new Moldovan government offers autonomy within a loose federation, but the separatist leaders reject the offer.

2003 The Russian government proposes a federation of Moldova and Transnistria, but a clause for a Russian military presence for 20 years leads to Moldovan rejection of the proposal.

2005–2008 The situation remains a military and political stalemate. Transnistria continues to function as a Soviet-era independent state, unrecognized but supported by the Russian government. Local leaders appeal to the Russian government for recognition, as has been extended to Abkhazia* and South Ossetia*.

2009 The world financial crisis and ongoing gas disputes between Russia and neighboring countries hurt the region's economy, although smuggling continues to flourish.

See also Moldova

TURKEY

OFFICIAL NAME

Türkiye Cumhuriyeti (Turkish); Republic of Turkey (English)

POPULATION

70,894,600 (2009e)

INHABITANTS' NAME/NICKNAME

Turk(s); Turkish

LANGUAGE/LANGUAGES

Turkish (official); Kurdish, Dimli (Zaza), Azeri, Kabardian, Armenian, Greek, others

RELIGION/RELIGIONS

Muslim, 97 percent; Christian, other or no religion

NATIONAL FLAG

The flag, known as *ay yildiz* (moon star), is a red field charged with a white crescent moon and a white five-pointed star offset to the hoist. The colors and design are probably ancient, although there are a number of legends concerning their origins. The flag, which was the flag of the Ottoman Empire, influenced many other flags in territories that once formed part of the empire.

COAT OF ARMS/SEAL

Turkey does not have an official coat of arms but uses a logo, a red oval containing a white crescent moon, points vertical, and a white five-pointed star, with the official name of the country, in white around the upper edge of the oval.

MOTTO

Yurtta sulh, cihanda sulh (Turkish); Peace at home, peace in the world (English)

CAPITAL CITY

Ankara

TYPE OF GOVERNMENT

Parliamentary republic

NATIONAL EMBLEM

Hagia Sofia in Istanbul

NATIONAL COLORS

Red and white

NATIONAL ANTHEM

The anthem is based on a poem of 10 verses, but only the first two are used. It was adopted as the official anthem in 1921.

Istiklâl Marşi (Turkish); Independence March (English)

Fear not! For the red flag that proudly ripples in this glorious twilight shall never fade,
Before the last fiery hearth that is burning for my nation is extinguished.
For that is the star of my nation, and it will forever shine;
It is mine; and solely belongs to my valiant nation.

Frown not, I beseech you, O thou fair crescent,
But smile upon my heroic race! Why the anger, why the rage?
Our blood that we shed for you will not be blessed otherwise,
For freedom is the absolute right of my God-worshiping nation.

PATRON SAINT

Saint John the Apostle (Asiatic region only)

CURRENCY

New Turkish lira

INTERNET IDENTIFIER

.tr

VEHICLE IDENTIFICATION PLATES/STICKERS

TR

PASSPORT

The passport cover has the name of the country in Turkish and, in smaller print, in English; the Turkish crescent and star; and the word *passport* in Turkish and English.

AIRLINES

Turkish Airlines; Pegasus Airlines

NATIONAL FLOWER

Tulipa (tulip)

NATIONAL TREE

Fig (unofficial)

NATIONAL ANIMAL

Gray wolf

NATIONAL BIRD

Redwing

NATIONAL RESOURCES

Natural resources include coal, iron ore, copper, chromium, antimony, mercury, gold, barite, borate, celestite (strontium), emery, feldspar, limestone, magnesite, marble, perlite, pumice, pyrites (sulfur), clay, arable land, and hydropower. Tourism, based on varied scenery, historic cities and monuments, sandy beaches, a pleasant climate, and a unique culture, is a very important resource. Remittances from Turks living outside the country are an important source of foreign currency and investment.

FOODS

Shish kebab, skewered and marinated meat or chicken cooked over charcoal, is considered the national dish. Other national specialties include *meze,* a variety of starters or appetizers; dolma, vine leaves stuffed with minced meat and onions; *sharma,* very thinly sliced meat or chicken served in pita bread with onions and yogurt; *köfte,* fried balls of minced meat, rice or bulgur, and onions, served with various condiments; and *pilav,* a dish of cracked wheat or rice browned in oil and then cooked in a season broth, often served with meat or vegetables. *Raki,* known as "lion's milk," because it clouds when water is added, is considered the national drink.

SPORTS/SPORTS TEAMS

The national sport is *yagli güres,* oiled wrestling. Association football (soccer) is the most popular sport. Turkey national teams participate in many sports at an international level.

TEAM SPORTS

Badminton

Turkey Badminton Team

Baseball

Turkey Baseball Team; Turkey Softball Team

Basketball

Turkey Basketball Team; Turkey Women's Basketball Team; Turkey Wheelchair Basketball Team

Cricket

Turkey Cricket Team

Football

Turkey Football Team, nickname Ay-Yildizlilar (the Crescent-Stars) or Türko; Turkey Women's Football Team, nickname Ay-Yildizlilar (the Crescent-Stars); Turkey Under-21 Football Team, nickname Umit Milli; Turkey Under-18 Football Team; Turkey Under-17 Football Team; Turkey B Football Team; Turkey Futsal Team, nickname Ay-Yildizlilar (The Crescent-Stars); Turkey American Football Team; Turkey Beach Soccer Team

Handball

Turkey Handball Team; Turkey Women's Handball Team; Turkey Beach Handball Team; Turkey Women's Beach Handball Team

Hockey

Turkey Ice Hockey Team; Turkey Women's Ice Hockey Team; Turkey Junior Ice Hockey Team; Turkey Field Hockey Team

Kabaddi

Turkey Kabaddi Team

Korfball

Turkey Korfball Team

Racing

Turkey Speedway Team

Table Tennis

Turkey Table Tennis Team

Tennis

Turkey Davis Cup Team; Turkey Fed Cup Team

Volleyball

Turkey Men's Volleyball Team; Turkey Women's Volleyball Team

INDIVIDUAL SPORTS

Turkey Amateur Boxing Team; Turkey Archery Team; Turkey Athletics Team; Turkey Canoeing Team; Turkey Cycling Team; Turkey Equestrian Team; Turkey Fencing Team; Turkey Gymnastics Team; Turkey Judo Team; Turkey Modern Pentathlon Team; Turkey Rowing Team; Turkey Sailing Team; Turkey Shooting Team; Turkey Swim Team; Turkey Tae Kwon Do Team; Turkey Triathlon Team; Turkey Weight Lifting Team; Turkey Wrestling Team

WINTER SPORTS

Turkey Alpine Ski Team; Turkey Ice Hockey Team; Turkey Women's Ice Hockey Team; Turkey Junior Ice Hockey Team; Turkey Skating Team

NATIONAL HEROES OR PERSONIFICATIONS

Mustafa Kemal, called Ataturk or father of the Turks, the military and political leader during and after the First World War; Rumi, the famous poet and Sufi mystic, famed for his acceptance of all religions and beliefs; Sultan Mehmet II, the conqueror of Constantinople in 1453; Enver Pasha, the ruler of Turkey during World War I

NATIONAL HOLIDAY/INDEPENDENCE DAY

Republic Day, October 29

FESTIVALS/FAIRS

Izmir International Fair, September; Nowruz (Turkish New Year), variable dates; Ankara International Film Festival, March; Istanbul Film Festival, April; Ankara Music Festival, April; Tulip Festival, April–May; Aspendos, June; Istanbul Jazz Festival, July

SIGNIFICANT EVENTS IN FORMATION OF NATIONAL IDENTITY

18th century B.C.E.–13th century B.C.E.   The Hittite Empire becomes the first of many states and empires in the Anatolia region.

Seventh century B.C.E.   The coast is settled by Ionians, one of the ancient Greek peoples.

Sixth century B.C.E.   Persians conquer and incorporate the entire region.

334 B.C.E.   Alexander the Great captures Anatolia from the Persians.

First century B.C.E.   Rome conquers the Greek states of Anatolia.

324 C.E.–395 C.E.   Roman emperor Constantine I chooses Greek Byzantium (Constantinople) as the new capital of the Roman Empire. Constantinople becomes the capital of the Eastern Roman or Byzantine Empire.

Ninth century   The Seljuk Turks begin migrating west from their Central Asian homeland.

1071–1300   The Turks defeat the Byzantines and take control of Anatolia. Mongols destroy the region in 1243. One of the smaller Turkish principalities, ruled by Osman I, begins to fill the political void in the region to become the Ottoman Empire.

16th century–17th century   The Ottoman Empire is one of the world's most powerful states, stretching from the Horn of Africa and the Middle East to North Africa and nearly to Vienna in Europe.

1914–1919   The empire enters World War I as a German ally. Up to 1.5 million Armenians die in a coordinated government operation in eastern Anatolia. The victorious Allied Powers dismember the empire, with even Anatolia divided into occupation zones, prompting the Turkish national movement under Mustafa Kemal.

1919–1923   Kemal leads the Turkish War of Independence against the European armies, which are expelled from Anatolia. The new Turkish Republic is proclaimed.

1928   Turkey is proclaimed a secular state. Islam is removed from the constitution as the state religion.

1938   Mustafa Kemal, known as Ataturk, dies after a decade as president.

1940–1952 Turkey remains neutral during the Second World War. Turkey holds its first open elections in 1950. Abandoning Ataturk's strict neutrality, the country joins the North Atlantic Treaty Organization.

1960 In the first of a number of military coups, the military seeks to preserve Ataturk's secular legacy.

1974 Turkish troops invade Cyprus*.

1984 Turkey formally recognizes the independence of Northern Cyprus*. A separatist war breaks out in the southeastern region of Kurdistan*.

1987 Turkey applies for full membership in the European Community.

1992–1995 Turkish offensives target the Kurds in northern Iraq*. Turkey becomes a major aid donor to the newly independent Turkic republics of the former Soviet Union.

2001 A diplomatic break with France* follows French recognition of the Armenian holocaust as genocide. Controversy begins over Islamic political parties in the government.

2002 Women are given equal legal status. Reforms aimed at securing entry into the European Union include abolishing the death sentence and ending restrictions on the Kurdish population. An Islamic party, victorious in general elections, promises to stick to Ataturk's secular tradition.

2004–2005 The first Kurdish-language programming begins on State Television. Talks on EU membership finally begin. Conflicts over women wearing the Islamic headscarf pit religious groups against supporters of the secular state.

2007 Tens of thousands march in Ankara in support of secularism. A diplomatic row opens with the United States* after a U.S. congressional committee recognizes the Armenian massacres as genocide.

2008 Large protests follow a new ruling allowing women to wear Islamic headscarves in universities. Attempts are made to ban political parties with Islamic roots, including the present governing party.

2009 The conflict between Islamist and secular forces continues to dominate the country. The Turks remain divided on the question of joining the European Union (EU) after decades of waiting for their application to be accepted.

UKRAINE

OFFICIAL NAME
Ukrayina (transliteration from Ukrainian); Ukraine (English)

POPULATION
46,341,500 (2009e)

INHABITANTS' NAME/NICKNAME
Ukrainian (s)

LANGUAGE/LANGUAGES
Ukrainian (official); Russian, Crimean Tatar, Hungarian, Romanian, others

RELIGION/RELIGIONS
Ukrainian Orthodox—Kiev Patriarchate, 51 percent; Russian Orthodox—Moscow Patriarchate, 26 percent; Uniate Greek Catholic, 8 percent; Ukrainian Autocephalous Orthodox, 7.5 percent; Roman Catholic, 2.5 percent; Protestant, 2. percent; Jewish, Muslim, other or no religion

NATIONAL FLAG
The flag is a horizontal bicolor of blue over yellow. The colors of the flag are pre-Christian symbols of water and fire. The historic flag was reversed, with the yellow at the top, so that Ukrainians continue to call the flag *zhovto-blakytnyy*, meaning the yellow and light blue. Blue and yellow, the colors of the sky, mountains, streams, and golden fields, symbolized Kievan Rus' long before the introduction of Christianity.

COAT OF ARMS/SEAL
The coat of arms is a yellow trident with a blue background. The history of the trident

symbol as featured in the present Ukrainian coat of arms is more than 1,000 years old.

CAPITAL CITY

Kyiv (Kiev)

TYPE OF GOVERNMENT

Semipresidential unitary republic

NATIONAL EMBLEM

Tryzub, the Ukrainian trident

NATIONAL COLORS

Pale blue and yellow

NATIONAL ANTHEM

The anthem is based on a choral work from 1864. It was adopted in 1917 but was banned after 1919 by the Soviet government. It was adopted when Ukraine regained its independence in 1991.

> **Shche ne Vmerla Ukrayiny (Ukrainian); Ukraine's Glory Has Not Yet Perished (English)**
>
> Ukraine's glory has not perished, neither her glory, nor her freedom
> Upon us, fellow compatriots, fate shall smile once more.
> Our enemies will vanish, like dew in the morning sun,
> And we too shall rule, brothers, in a free land of our own.
>
> **Chorus**
> We'll lay down our souls and bodies to attain our freedom,
> And we'll show that we, brothers, are of the Cossack nation.
> We'll lay down our souls and bodies to attain our freedom,
> And we'll show that we, brothers, are of the Cossack nation.
>
> We'll stand together for freedom, from the Sian to the Don,
> We will not allow others to rule in our motherland.

> The Black Sea will smile and grandfather Dnieper will rejoice,
> For in our own Ukraine fortune shall flourish again.
>
> **Chorus**
> Our persistence and our sincere toils will be rewarded,
> And freedom's song will resound throughout Ukraine.
> Echoing off the Carpathians, and rumbling across the steppes,
> Ukraine's fame and glory will be known among all nations.
>
> **Chorus**
> We'll lay down our souls and bodies to attain our freedom,
> And we'll show that we, brothers, are of the Cossack nation.
> We'll lay down our souls and bodies to attain our freedom,
> And we'll show that we, brothers, are of the Cossack nation.

PATRON SAINT

Saint Josaphat; Saint Andrew

CURRENCY

Ukrainian hryvnia

INTERNET IDENTIFIER

.ua

VEHICLE IDENTIFICATION PLATES/STICKERS

UA

PASSPORT

The passport cover has the coat of arms, the trident, the words *passport Ukraine* in Ukrainian and English, and the standard biometric symbol.

AIRLINES

Ukraine International Airlines; Aerosvit Airlines

NATIONAL FLOWER
Sunflower; Guelder rose (unofficial)

NATIONAL TREE
Viburnum; willow

NATIONAL ANIMAL
European bison (unofficial)

NATIONAL RESOURCES
Natural resources include iron ore, coal, manganese, natural gas, oil, salt, sulfur, graphite, titanium, magnesium, kaolin, nickel, mercury, timber, and arable land. The country has significant natural resources, but infrastructure remains outdated, bureaucracy slows development, and economic reforms are still not complete. A growing tourist industry is based on the country's historic cities and monuments, varied scenery, and cultural offerings.

FOODS
Varenyky (pierogi), dumplings of unleavened dough filled with potatoes, cheese, minced meat, vegetables, mushrooms, or sauerkraut, are considered a national dish. Borscht, a soup of beets, often with beef or other vegetables, is also considered a national dish. Other specialties include *holubtsi,* cabbage or vine leaves stuffed with minced meat and rice; *kasha hrechana zi shkvarkamy,* buckwheat cooked in seasoned broth served with chopped bacon and onion; *shpyndra,* a dish of pork and beets; *kollety,* minced meat or fish fritters; *huliash,* a meat and vegetable stew, from the Hungarian goulash; *vinihret,* red beet salad with peas, onions, and beans; and *pampushky,* a small fried pastry with sugar and cinnamon.

SPORTS/SPORTS TEAMS
Association football (soccer) and gymnastics are the most popular sports. Ukraine national teams participate in many sports at an international level

TEAM SPORTS
Badminton
Ukraine Badminton Team

Baseball
Ukraine Baseball Team; Ukraine Softball Team

Basketball
Ukraine Basketball Team; Ukraine Women's Basketball Team; Ukraine Wheelchair Basketball Team

Cricket
Ukraine Cricket Team

Football
Ukraine Football Team, nickname Zhovto-Blakytni (the Yellow and Blues) or Zbirna ("the Team" in Ukrainian)/Sbornaya ("the Team" in Russian); Ukraine Women's Football Team, nickname Zhinky; Ukraine Under-21 Football Team, nickname Zbirna or Molodizhka; Ukraine Women's Under-19 Football Team; Ukraine Under-16 Football Team; Ukraine Rugby Union Team; Ukraine Futsal Team; Ukraine American Football Team; Ukraine Beach Soccer Team; Ukraine Rugby League Team

Handball
Ukraine Handball Team; Ukraine Women's Handball Team; Ukraine Beach Handball Team; Ukraine Women's Beach Handball Team

Hockey
Ukraine Ice Hockey Team; Ukraine Junior Ice Hockey Team; Ukraine Field Hockey Team

Racing
Ukraine Speedway Team

Table Tennis

Ukraine Table Tennis Team

Tennis

Ukraine Davis Cup Team; Ukraine Fed Cup Team

Volleyball

Ukraine Men's Volleyball Team; Ukraine Women's Volleyball Team; Ukraine Fistball Team; Ukraine Men's Beach Volleyball Team; Ukraine Women's Beach Volleyball Team

INDIVIDUAL SPORTS

Ukraine Amateur Boxing Team; Ukraine Archery Team; Ukraine Athletics Team; Ukraine Cycling Team: Ukraine Equestrian Team; Ukraine Fencing Team; Ukraine Gymnastics Team; Ukraine Judo Team; Ukraine Karate Team: Ukraine Modern Pentathlon Team; Ukraine Rowing Team; Ukraine Sailing Team; Ukraine Shooting Team; Ukraine Swim Team; Ukraine Tae Kwon Do Team; Ukraine Triathlon Team; Ukraine Weight Lifting Team; Ukraine Wrestling Team

WINTER SPORTS

Ukraine Alpine Ski Team; Ukraine Bandy Team; Ukraine Curling Team; Ukraine Biathlon Team; Ukraine Ice Hockey Team; Ukraine Junior Ice Hockey Team; Ukraine Luge Team; Ukraine Skating Team

NATIONAL HEROES OR PERSONIFICATIONS

Taras Shevchenko, famed poet and nationalist leader of the cultural reawakening; Shlomo Aleichem, writer on Ukrainian themes; Leonid M. Kravchuk, first president of independent Ukraine in 1991; Ivan Franko, poet and nationalist; Bohdan Khmelnytsky, leader of the Cossack Ukrainian uprising in the 17th century; Mykhailo Hrushevsky, national leader during the Russian Revolution

NATIONAL HOLIDAY/INDEPENDENCE DAY

Independence Day, August 24; Unity Day, January 22

FESTIVALS/FAIRS

World Food Fair, October; DoJ Donetsk Jazz Festival, November; Kazantip, July; Kiev International Advertising Festival, May; Kotebel International Jazz Festival, July; Odessa Jazz Festival, September

SIGNIFICANT EVENTS IN FORMATION OF NATIONAL IDENTITY

Sixth century C.E.   Slavs settle the region as part of the great Slav migrations.

988   Christianity becomes the major religion after the conversion of Prince Vladimir at Kiev.

1054   The first important Slav state, Kievan Rus', is established. The Slav state becomes the leading power in Europe.

13th century   Kievan Rus' is overwhelmed by the Mongol invasion. The state disintegrates into a number of smaller states that fall prey to more powerful neighbors.

1386–1648   Western Ukraine is incorporated into Poland* by 1569. Bohdan Khmelnytsky leads a Cossack Ukrainian uprising against Polish rule.

1765–1774   Eastern Ukraine comes under Russian rule. Austria* takes Western Ukraine as part of the partitions of Poland.

19th century   Efforts to assimilate the Ukrainians into Russian culture stimulate a national awakening, resulting in the growth of nationalist sentiment.

1914–1917   Ukraine becomes a battleground during World War I. The Russian Revolution of 1917 ends Russian control. Ukraine declares independence and unites with Western Ukraine.

1920–1921   The Red Army, victorious in the Russian Civil War, defeats the new republic, which is incorporated into the new Soviet Union as a member republic. War between Poland and the Soviet Union ends with Polish control of Western Ukraine.

1929–1933 Collectivization is resisted in Ukraine. Determined to crush the Ukrainians forever, Stalin initiates a planned famine by confiscating all grain. An estimated 7 million Ukrainians perish during the campaign.

1932–1937 Mass executions, forced labor camps, and deportations devastate the educated classes. Purges eliminate every possible cultural and religious leader.

1939–1940 The Nazi-Soviet invasion of Poland brings Western Ukraine under Soviet rule. Mass deportations continue to target anticommunists, religious and political leaders, and intellectuals and their families.

1941–1944 The Nazis turn on their Soviet ally and invade the Soviet Union, quickly overrunning the Ukrainian republic. Over 5 million Ukrainians die in the fighting, and the nation's 1.5 million Jews are exterminated in the Holocaust. The Crimean Tatars, over 200,000 people, are deported from the Crimea.

1945–1954 The Soviet Union annexes Western Ukraine. The last resistance movements are wiped out.

1960s–1970s Soviet policy is to assimilate the Ukrainians into the Russian-speaking Soviet culture. Resistance begins to grow in the 1960s, leading to a brutal repression in 1972.

1986 A nuclear reactor at Chernobyl explodes, sending a radioactive cloud across Ukraine and Belarus*.

1987–1988 The relaxation of Soviet rule under Mikhail Gorbachev allows the organization of cultural groups and the first openly Ukrainian political movement since 1920.

1990 Mass demonstrations bring down the Ukrainian republican government. An attempted coup in Moscow begins the unraveling of the Soviet Union. Ukraine declares independence following a national referendum.

1990s About 250,000 Crimean Tatars are finally allowed to return to their homeland in the Crimea. Timid economic reforms and tensions with Russia* create economic hardships and instability.

2004 A flawed election leads to mass demonstrations and the occupation of central Kiev in the Orange Revolution. A second election is won by the opposition.

2006–2008 Political conflicts between pro-Russian and pro-Western factions continue governmental instability. The leaders of the North Atlantic Treaty Organization decide not to invite Ukraine to join the organization until its membership is reviewed in light of recent upheavals and Russian objections. Russia warns of dire consequences should Ukraine join the Western alliance.

2009 Russia stops all gas deliveries to Ukraine after the collapse of talks over prices and unpaid bills. The stoppages severely affect several other European nations.

UNITED KINGDOM

OFFICIAL NAME

United Kingdom of Great Britain and Northern Ireland

POPULATION

60,549,600 (2009e)

INHABITANTS' NAME/NICKNAME

British, Briton(s); Brit(s)

LANGUAGE/LANGUAGES

English (de facto); Scots, Scottish Gaelic, Welsh, Irish, Ulster Scots, Cornish (recognized regional languages)

RELIGION/RELIGIONS

Christian (Anglican, Roman Catholic, Presbyterian, Methodist), 72 percent; Muslim, 3 percent; Hindu, 1 percent; other or no religion

NATIONAL FLAG

The flag, popularly known as the Union Jack, is a blue field charged with a centered red cross outlined in white, the Cross of Saint

George, representing England, superimposed on the crosses of Saint Patrick, representing Northern Ireland*, and Saint Andrew, representing Scotland*.

COAT OF ARMS/SEAL

The coat of arms has a central crest or shield quartered, showing the arms of England, three gold lions on red, in the upper left and lower right quadrants; the arms of Scotland, a red lion and tressure on gold, on the upper right quadrant; and a gold harp on blue, to represent Northern Ireland, in the lower left. Above the shield are a heraldic helmet and a gold crowned lion. A gold lion, representing England, and white unicorn, representing Scotland, support the shield, and below is a banner inscribed with the royal motto.

MOTTO

Royal motto: *Dieu et mon droit* (French); God and my right (English)

CAPITAL CITY

London

TYPE OF GOVERNMENT

Parliamentary democracy and constitutional monarchy

NATIONAL EMBLEM

Big Ben

NATIONAL COLORS

Blue, white, and red

NATIONAL ANTHEM

The anthem was first performed in 1745 and has continued as "God Save the Queen" or "God Save the King" since that time. It is also the royal anthem of many of the member countries of the British Commonwealth.

God Save the Queen

God save our gracious Queen,
Long live our noble Queen,
God save the Queen:
Send her victorious,
Happy and glorious,
Long to reign over us:
God save the Queen.

O Lord, our God, arise,
Scatter her enemies,
And make them fall.
Confound their politics,
Frustrate their knavish tricks,
On thee our hopes we fix,
God save us all.

Thy choicest gifts in store,
On her be pleased to pour;
Long may she reign:
May she defend our laws,
And ever give us cause
To sing with heart and voice
God save the Queen.

PATRON SAINT

England: Saint George; Scotland: Saint Andrew; Northern Ireland: Saint Patrick; Cornwall*: Saint Pirin; Wales: Saint David

CURRENCY

British pound (pound sterling)

INTERNET IDENTIFIER

.gb

VEHICLE IDENTIFICATION PLATES/STICKERS

GB

PASSPORT

The passport cover has the name of the European Union, the full name of the kingdom, the coat of arms, the word *passport*, and the standard biometric symbol.

AIRLINES

British Airways; Virgin Atlantic Airways; British Midland BMI; EasyJet

NATIONAL FLOWER

Rose (England)

NATIONAL TREE

Oak (England)

NATIONAL ANIMALS

Lion and unicorn (official animals of the United Kingdom based on mythical animals introduced to European heraldry in the Middle Ages); red fox; bulldog; red deer (England)

NATIONAL BIRD

European robin (England)

NATIONAL FISH

Roach (England) (unofficial)

NATIONAL RESOURCES

Natural resources include coal, petroleum, natural gas, iron ore, lead, zinc, gold, tin, limestone, salt, clay, chalk, gypsum, potash, silica sand, slate, and arable land. A well-educated population, proximity to large population centers, and a long tradition as a banking center have made the United Kingdom the fifth-largest economy in the world. Tourism, based on historic affinities, monuments and historic cities, the British culture, and varied scenery, is one of the most important resources.

FOODS

Roast beef with Yorkshire pudding is considered the national dish. Fish and chips, fried battered fish and fried potatoes, is another well-known national dish. Other national specialties include chicken tikka masala, chicken cooked Indian-style; bubble and squeak, a dish of potatoes, cabbage, and onions, often served with bacon; cheese and onion pie; steak and kidney pie; bangers and mash, a dish of sausages and mashed potatoes; and toad in the hole, sausage wrapped in dough and then baked. Tea is the most famous national drink.

SPORTS/SPORTS TEAMS

Association football (soccer), cricket, and rugby are the most popular sports. Great Britain and United Kingdom national teams participate in many sports at an international level, as do teams from the individual countries that make up the United Kingdom, England, Northern Ireland, Scotland, and Wales.

TEAM SPORTS

Baseball

Great Britain Baseball Team; Great Britain Softball Team

Basketball

Great Britain Basketball Team; Great Britain Women's Basketball Team; Great Britain Wheelchair Basketball Team; Great Britain Women's Wheelchair Basketball Team

Football

Great Britain Australian-Rules Football Team, nickname the Bulldogs; Great Britain Rugby Union Team; Great Britain Women's Rugby Union Team; Great Britain Rugby League Team, nickname the Lions; Great Britain Women's Rugby League Team, nickname the Lionesses; Great Britain Wheelchair Rugby Team; Great Britain American Football Team

Golf

Great Britain Men's Pitch and Putt Team

Handball

Great Britain Handball Team

Hockey

Great Britain Ice Hockey Team; Great Britain Junior Ice Hockey Team; Great Britain

Women's Ice Hockey Team; Great Britain and Northern Ireland Field Hockey Team

Kabaddi

United Kingdom Kabaddi Team

Korfball

Great Britain Korfball Team

Racing

A1 Team Great Britain; Great Britain Speedway Team

Tennis

Great Britain Davis Cup Team; Great Britain Fed Cup Team

Volleyball

Great Britain Beach Volleyball Team; Great Britain Women's Beach Volleyball Team

Water Polo

Great Britain Water Polo Team; Great Britain Women's Water Polo Team

INDIVIDUAL SPORTS

Great Britain Aikido Team; Great Britain Archery Team; United Kingdom Athletics Team; Great Britain Canoeing Team; Great Britain Cycling Team; Great Britain Equestrian Team; Great Britain Fencing Team; Great Britain Gymnastics Team; Great Britain Judo Team; Great Britain Karate Team; Great Britain Modern Pentathlon Team; Great Britain Rowing Team; Great Britain Sailing Team; Great Britain Shooting Team; Great Britain Swim Team; Great Britain Tae Kwon Do Team; Great Britain Triathlon Team; Great Britain Weight Lifting Team; Great Britain Wrestling Team

WINTER SPORTS

Great Britain Alpine Ski Team; Great Britain Biathlon Team; United Kingdom Bobsleigh and Tobogganing Team; Great Britain Luge Team; Great Britain Skating Team

ENGLAND SPORTS/SPORTS TEAMS

England participates in many international sports as one of the individual British nations. For other teams, see Cornwall, Northern Ireland, Scotland, and Wales*.

Badminton

England Badminton Team

Bowls

England Bowls Team

Cricket

England Cricket Team; England Women's Cricket Team; England Lions Cricket Team

Football

England Football Team, nickname the Three Lions; England Women's Football Team, nickname the Three Lions; England Rugby Union Team, nickname the Red and Whites; England Under-19 Football Team, nickname the Lions: England Women's Under-19 Football Team, nickname the Lionesses; England Women's Rugby Union Team, nickname the Red and Whites; England Rugby League Team; Team; England Beach Soccer Team; England Futsal Team; England Touch Football Team; England Women's Touch Football Team; England Australian-Rules Football Team, nickname the Dragonslayers; England Rugby Union Team (Sevens), nickname England Sevens; England Women's Rugby Union Team (Sevens), nickname England Sevens or England 7s

Hockey

England Field Hockey Team; England Women's Field Hockey Team; England Ice Hockey Team; England Junior Ice Hockey Team

Kabaddi

England Kabaddi Team

Korfball

England Korfball Team

Lacrosse

England Lacrosse Team; England Women's Lacrosse Team; England Under-19 Lacrosse Team; England Women's Under-19 Lacrosse Team

Netball

England Netball Team

Polo

England Polo Team

Table Tennis

England Table Tennis Team

Volleyball

England Men's Volleyball Team; England Women's Volleyball Team; England Men's Beach Volleyball Team; England Women's Beach Volleyball Team

INDIVIDUAL SPORTS

England Amateur Boxing Team

WINTER SPORTS

England Curling Team; England Ice Hockey Team; England Junior Ice Hockey Team

NATIONAL HEROES OR PERSONIFICATIONS

Britannia is the classical personification of the British people; John Bull is a national personification of the United Kingdom and of England in particular: a stout man in a top hat, tailcoat, and bulging Union Jack vest.

National heroes include Winston Churchill, the prime minister during World War II; William Shakespeare, considered Britain's national author; Elizabeth Fry (Florence Nightingale), the inventor of modern nursing; and Sir Alexander Fleming, the discoverer of penicillin; Horatio Nelson, the admiral who led the British fleet to victory over the French during the Napoleonic wars.

NATIONAL HOLIDAY/INDEPENDENCE DAY

The United Kingdom does not celebrate one particular holiday on a national level; see Northern Ireland, Scotland, Wales.

FESTIVALS/FAIRS

Spring Olympia Fine Art and Antiques Fair, February; Guildford International Music Festival, March; Dorchester Festival, May; Covent Garden Festival, May; Brockley Max Festival, June; Chelsea Festival, June; Covent Garden Flower Festival, June; Henley Festival, July; The Mayor's Thames Festival, September

SIGNIFICANT EVENTS IN FORMATION OF NATIONAL IDENTITY

600 B.C.E.–100 B.C.E. Celtic tribes dominate the island, along with their Druid religion.

51 B.C.E. Romans conquer the southern part of the island, called Britannia, while the north, called Caledonia, is left to the Celts.

Fifth century–sixth century The end of Roman rule allows invasions by Angles and Saxons. The Celts are driven east to the peninsulas of Wales and Cornwall and across the channel to Brittany*.

1054 The Normans, descendants of Vikings settled in France*, invade and conquer the Anglo-Saxon kingdom.

1204 The King of England is forced to sign the Magna Carta, a statute of rights.

13th century–15th century Wars with Scotland continue intermittently. England becomes a Protestant kingdom. Wales becomes part of the kingdom in 1542.

17th century The monarchy is overthrown and the Commonwealth of England is established under Oliver Cromwell. The restoration of the kingdom follows in 1660.

1707–1801 England and Scotland join in the United Kingdom. The American colonies revolt. Ireland is added to the kingdom in 1801.

1900 The United Kingdom is the dominant world power, with an empire that covers a quarter of the world's landmass.

1914–1918 World War I breaks out, leading to the loss of most of a generation of young men.

1921 Ireland is partitioned. Northern Ireland remains part of the United Kingdom.

1939–1945 The Second World War begins with the German invasion of Poland*. Winston Churchill leads the country through the war, including the Blitz, the heavy bombing raids on London and other cities.

1955–1975 The era of decolonization begins, with the colonies gaining independence. Most remain in the Commonwealth.

1961 A U.K. bid to join the European Community is vetoed by France.

1973–1975 Britain joins the European Community, which is endorsed in a national referendum. North Sea oil production begins.

1982 The United Kingdom goes to war to expel invaders from Argentina* in the Falkland Islands*.

1997 Referendums in Wales and Scotland support the creation of separate legislatures. A political agreement ends decades of sectarian violence in Northern Ireland.

2001 Britain offers strong support to the United States* in the wake of the terrorist attacks on New York and Washington, D.C. The United Kingdom joins the United States in the invasion of Iraq*.

2005 Terrorist bombs kill 52 and injure over 700 in central London in a series of terrorist attacks.

2006–2008 Antiwar feeling grows, with calls to pull out of Iraq. The Church of England votes 2–1 to allow the ordination of women bishops.

2009 The Bank of England cuts interest rates to 1.5 percent, the lowest level in its 315-year history, as part of the government response to the international financial crisis.

VATICAN CITY

OFFICIAL NAME
Stato della Città del Vaticano (Italian); State of the Vatican City (English); Santa Sede (Italian); Holy See (English)

POPULATION
825 (2009e)

INHABITANTS' NAME/NICKNAME
Citizens of the Holy See

LANGUAGE/LANGUAGES
There is no official language in Vatican City, but the de facto official language is Italian. The language of the Swiss Guards is Swiss German. Latin is the language of the Holy See and is employed for formal pronouncements.

RELIGION/RELIGIONS
Roman Catholic

NATIONAL FLAG
The flag is a square vertical bicolor of gold and white charged with the crossed keys of Saint Peter and the Papal Tiara centered on the white field. The flag was adopted in 1929, modeled on the flag of the earlier Papal States. The two colors refer to the crossed keys of gold and silver. The keys represent the keys to heaven given by Jesus Christ to Saint Peter. The popes are regarded as the successors of Peter.

COAT OF ARMS/SEAL
The coat of arms is a red crest or shield charged with the crossed keys of Saint Peter and the Papal Tiara. The keys represent the keys of the kingdom of heaven promised to Saint Peter. The three-tiered tiara represents

the three powers of the Supreme Pontiff: sacred orders, jurisdiction, and magisterium. The personal coat of arms of Pope Benedict XVI has a central shield divided into three parts, a moor's head on a gold background on the upper left, a gold scallop shell on red in the center, and a brown bear on gold on the upper right. The Keys of St. Peter appear behind the shield, which is topped with the Episcopal mitre favored by the Pope.

CAPITAL CITY

Vatican City

TYPE OF GOVERNMENT

Theocratic absolute monarchy

NATIONAL EMBLEM

The crossed keys of Saint Peter

NATIONAL COLORS

Gold and white

NATIONAL ANTHEM

The anthem was originally written in Italian in 1857, but only the Latin translation, slightly modified in 1993, is now used.

Inno e Marcia Pontificale (Latin); Hymn and Pontifical March (English)

O happy Rome—O noble Rome
You are the seat of Peter, whose blood was
   shed in Rome,
Peter, to whom the keys of the kingdom of
   heaven were given.
Pontiff, you are the successor of Peter;
Pontiff, you are the teacher, you confirm your
   brethren;
Pontiff, you who are the servant of the ser-
   vants of God,
And fisher of men, are the shepherd of the
   flock,
Linking heaven and earth.
Pontiff, you are the vicar of Christ on earth,
A harbor amidst the waves, you are a beacon
   in the darkness;

You are the defender of peace; you are the
   guardian of unity,
Watchful defender of liberty; in you is the
   authority.
You, Pontiff, you are the unshakable rock,
   and on this rock
Was built the Church of God.
O happy Rome—O noble Rome.

PATRON SAINT

Saint Peter

CURRENCY

Euro

INTERNET IDENTIFIER

.va

VEHICLE IDENTIFICATION PLATES/ STICKERS

V

PASSPORT

Vatican City issues only diplomatic and official passports.

NATIONAL RESOURCES

Vatican City's unique, noncommercial economy is supported by contributions (part of which is known as Peter's Pence) from Roman Catholics throughout the world, fees from Vatican museums, and the sale of postage stamps, tourist souvenirs, and publications.

SPORTS/SPORTS TEAMS

Association football (soccer) and basketball are popular sports. Vatican City national teams participate in football and basketball at an international level.

TEAM SPORTS

Basketball

Vatican City Basketball Team

Football

Vatican City Football Team

NATIONAL HEROES OR PERSONIFICATIONS

The Pope is the personification of the Vatican.

National heroes include Giovanni Lorenzo Bernini, the designer of the quadruple colonnade in front of Saint Peter's Basilica; Michelangelo, the artist and inventor responsible for many of the most outstanding features of the Vatican; and many famous popes who are now revered

NATIONAL HOLIDAY/INDEPENDENCE DAY

Coronation Day of Pope Benedict XVI, April 24

SIGNIFICANT EVENTS IN FORMATION OF NATIONAL IDENTITY

30 C.E.–64 or 67 C.E.   Peter serves as the first pope. He is still noted as the longest serving, for a total of 34 or 37 years.

254   Pope Stephen institutes the rule that clerics should wear special clothes at their ministrations.

270   Bishop Valentine is killed by Emperor Claudius for refusing to acknowledge the monarch's outlawing of marriage. The Christians then make Valentine a symbol to oppose an ancient custom in honor of the god Lupercus, in which the names of teenage girls are put in a box and drawn by young men for use as sex toys until the next Lupercalia.

Fourth century   The celebration of Christ's birth on December 25 is gradually adopted.

325   The Council of Nicea establishes the doctrine of the Holy Trinity and decrees that priests are forbidden to marry after ordination.

356   Emperor Constantine II closes all non-Christian temples.

590–604   Pope Gregory claims to see an angel atop Hadrian's Mausoleum. The site is then reconstructed as a fortress called Castel Sant' Angelo. The popes are established as the de facto rulers of the territories of central Italy*, the Papal States. Gregory also establishes "God bless you" as the religiously correct response to a sneeze.

700   The Catholic holiday of All Saints' Day, set on November 1, is instituted to supplant the pagan All Hallows' Eve. The pagan festival survives and is transplanted to the United States* in the 1840s.

800   Pope Leo III crowns Charlemagne emperor of the Holy Roman Empire at Saint Peter's Basilica.

1054   Pope Leo IX brings the conflict between Rome and the eastern church into open conflict by excommunicating the Patriarch of Constantinople. The Roman and Orthodox churches split decisively.

1095   Pope Urban II, responding to false rumors of atrocities against Christians in the Holy Land, appeals to Christian knights to defeat the Muslims and recapture the Holy Sepulcher in Jerusalem.

1139   The use of the crossbow is outlawed, at least against Christians. Universal celibacy is enforced within the church.

1145–1159   The only English pope, Adrian IV, grants Ireland to Henry II, King of England*.

1198–1216   Pope Innocent III raises the papacy to the heights of its prestige and power. Catholic Europe comes close to a unified theocracy. He oversees two additional crusades against the Muslims in the Holy Land and establishes fees for indulgences to supplement the church's treasury. In 1205, he decrees that the Jews are doomed to perpetual servitude and subjugation due to their crucifixion of Jesus. In 1215, following a request from King John, he decrees that the Magna Carta is invalid.

1227   Holy Roman Emperor Frederick II is excommunicated because his expanding empire threatens theocratic rule in the Papal States.

1244   Pope Innocent III launches the Albigensian Crusade, leading to the extermination of the Cathars and the Troubadour culture. The nearly depopulated region stretching north from the Mediterranean becomes part of France*.

1267   Pope Clement IV creates the Inquisition.

1294   Pope Celestine V is so besieged by the political, social, and religious challenges that he becomes the first pope to resign. He is imprisoned by his successor and there he dies.

1300 The Jubilee Year celebrates 1,000 years of Christianity in Rome.

1378–1417 The Great Western Schism splits the Church, with rival popes and antipopes vying for power.

1484–1486 The *Malleus Maleficarum*, the "Witches' Hammer," becomes the definitive encyclopedia of demonology throughout Christian Europe. The usual result of the trial of a witch is burning.

1493 Pope Alexander VI issues decrees dividing the New World between Spain* and Portugal*.

1499 Michelangelo completes his *Pieta* for installation in the Vatican.

1506–1508 The Swiss Guard mercenaries, summoned to Rome to protect the pope and the Vatican, begin their military tradition. The first stone of the new Saint Peter's Basilica is laid. Michelangelo begins painting the ceiling of the Sistine Chapel.

1520–1521 Martin Luther publishes his religious beliefs and is excommunicated. The Inquisition bans Luther's books. King Henry VIII of England is declared Defender of the Faith for his rebuttals of Luther's writings.

1534 King Henry VIII, unable to obtain permission for a divorce, severs ties to the Church, and papal authority in England is abolished.

1534–1563 Pope Paul III commissions Michelangelo to paint *The Last Judgment*. The painting is ordered repainted to cover over many of the fresco's previously nude figures.

1536–1569 The Inquisition is extended to Portugal and Mexico*. The enslavement of native peoples in the New World is banned by papal decree. The Inquisition is launched against Protestants, with alleged heretics tried, tortured, and executed in an effort to stem the spread of the Reformation. The Inquisition is extended to South America.

1582 The Julian calendar is abandoned for the Gregorian calendar on papal orders. The Protes-

tant countries do not accept the change until after 1700.

1587 Pope Sixtus V proclaims a crusade against England, which is interrupted when Francis Drake destroys the Catholic fleet in Cadiz harbor.

1633–1640 Astronomer Galileo Galilei is put on trial before the Inquisition. Pope Urban VIII orders Spanish priests to stop smoking cigars.

1683 A combined Christian army, aided by Marco d'Aviano, sent by Pope Innocent XI, defeats the Ottoman Turks at Vienna. The fleeing Turks leave behind sacks of coffee, which the Christians find too bitter. After sweetening it with honey and milk, they call it *cappuccino* after d'Aviano's Capucin order of monks. An Austrian baker, to celebrate the victory over the Muslim crescent moon, creates a crescent pastry that is later carried to France as the croissant.

1731–1732 All Hebrew books in the Papal States are confiscated, and anti-Jewish laws are renewed.

1797–1809 The French invade the Papal States and arrest Pope Pius VI, who is exiled and dies in France. France annexes the Papal States, leading to Pope Pius VII excommunicating Napoleon.

1854–1864 Pope Pius IX proclaims the dogma of the Immaculate Conception. In 1864, he issues the Quanta Cura, which lists 70 errors in contemporary beliefs, including freedom of speech, freedom of religion, and separation of church and state.

1870 Pontifical infallibility is proclaimed. All papal pronouncements on matters of faith or morals cannot be mistaken and must be believed. Italian troops occupy the Papal States, completing the unification of Italy*.

1904 Pope Pius X bans low-cut dresses in the presence of churchmen. A papal encyclical denounces the separation of church and state.

1929 The sovereign State of Vatican City comes into existence through the Lateran Treaty with Italy. Italy reimburses the Vatican for territory seized in 1870.

1930 The Vatican rejects all birth control methods other than the rhythm method.

1933 The Vatican signs an accord with Adolf Hitler. An encyclical of Pius XI denounces Nazi paganism and racism.

1938 The Vatican recognizes Francisco Franco's fascist but Catholic Spain.

1942–1943 Japan establishes diplomatic relations with the Vatican, the first non-Catholic country to do so. Church leaders ask Pope Pius XII to condemn Nazi war crimes, but he refuses. He later issues a strong attack on Nazism, but without mentioning Jews. The Jews of Rome are rounded up for deportation to Auschwitz without a papal protest.

1949 Pope Pius XII excommunicates communist Catholic voters in Italy.

1962–1963 Pope John XXIII modernizes and reforms the church.

1965 Pope Paul VI becomes the first reigning pontiff to visit the Western Hemisphere when he visits New York to address the United Nations General Assembly.

1966–1970 A special dispensation is arranged for priests wishing to leave the priesthood. Thousands leave the ministry to marry.

1968 Pope Paul VI reaffirms the church's opposition to abortion and all contraception except the rhythm method.

1978–1979 Pope John Paul II, of Poland*, becomes the first non-Italian pope since 1523. He becomes the first pope to visit the White House and the first to attend an Orthodox service in over a thousand years.

1981 The Pope is shot and seriously wounded in Saint Peter's Square by a Turkish assailant, reportedly sponsored by the Soviet Union*.

1983 John Paul II makes the first visit by a pope to a Lutheran church. A church commission concludes that the 1632 condemnation of Galileo was in error.

1989 Soviet President Mikhail Gorbachev meets with Pope John Paul II at the Vatican. A new church law requires dioceses around the world to support the Holy See.

2000 The Pope begs God's forgiveness for sins committed or condoned by Roman Catholics over the past 2,000 years. The Vatican issues a statement declaring that efforts to depict all religions as equal are wrong and reasserts that the Catholic Church is the one true church.

2000–2005 The Pope issues apologies for sexual abuses perpetuated by priests in many countries. Pope John Paul II dies and is succeeded by Cardinal Joseph Ratzinger, Pope Benedict XVI, who pledges to enforce conservative policies.

2006 The Vatican issues a sweeping condemnation of contraception, abortion, in-vitro fertilization, and same-sex marriage. The Pope's remarks about Islam in a speech provoke outrage and calls for an apology. The Vatican opens the secret archives to researchers, involving millions of letters, private correspondence, and other church documents.

2007–2008 A U.S. judge declares that victims of clerical abuse can sue the Vatican for damages. The Pope reasserts the universal primacy of the Roman Catholic Church, asserting that Orthodox churches are defective and that other Christian denominations are not true churches.

2009 Church support for opponents of such issues as abortion or gay marriage brings into question of the separation of church and state in the United States* and several other nations.

WALES

OFFICIAL NAME
Cymru (Welsh); Wales (English)

POPULATION
3,009,400 (2009e)

INHABITANTS' NAME/NICKNAME
Welsh, Cymreig (Welsh)

LANGUAGE/LANGUAGES
Welsh, English (official); others

RELIGION/RELIGIONS

Methodist, Anglican, Roman Catholic, Jewish, Muslim, other or no religion

NATIONAL FLAG

The flag, known as *Y Ddraig Goch* (the Red Dragon), is a horizontal bicolor of white over green charged with a large, detailed depiction of a red dragon. The red dragon has been associated with Wales for many centuries.

COAT OF ARMS/SEAL

The royal badge of Wales, the arms of Owain Glyndwr, is a shield divided into quarters, showing a red lion on yellow in the upper right and lower left quadrants and a yellow lion on red at upper left and lower right. Above the shield is a red and gold imperial crown, and around the shield are the plant emblems of the four countries of the United Kingdom. The shield is enclosed in a green banner inscribed with the national motto.

MOTTO

Cymru am byth (Welsh); Wales forever (English)

Royal motto: *Pleidiol wyf im gwlad* (Welsh); I am true to my country (English)

CAPITAL CITY

Cardiff

TYPE OF GOVERNMENT

Constitutional monarchy as part of the United Kingdom

NATIONAL EMBLEM

The Red Dragon; daffodil

NATIONAL COLORS

Green, red, and white

NATIONAL ANTHEM

The anthem was written and composed in 1856. The royal anthem is the British "God Save the Queen."

Hen Wlad Fy Nhadau (Welsh); The Land of My Fathers (English)

The land of my fathers so dear to me
Old land where the minstrels are honored and free:
Its warring defenders, so gallant and brave,
For freedom their life's blood they gave

Chorus

Land! Land! True I am to my land!
While seas secure, this land so pure,
O may our old language endure.
O land of the mountains, the bard's paradise,
Whose precipice, valleys lone as the skies,
Green murmuring forest, far-echoing flood
Fire the fancy and quicken the blood

Chorus

For tho' the fierce foeman has ravaged your realm,
The old speech of Wales he cannot o'erwhelm,
Our passionate poets to silence command
Or banish the harp from your strand.

PATRON SAINT

Saint David

CURRENCY

British pound

INTERNET IDENTIFIER

.uk United Kingdom (official); .cym Wales (unofficial)

VEHICLE IDENTIFICATION PLATES/ STICKERS

GB Great Britain (official); CYM Wales (unofficial)

PASSPORT

The Welsh are British citizens and travel on British passports.

NATIONAL FLOWER

Daffodil

NATIONAL TREE

Sessile oak

NATIONAL PLANT

Leek

NATIONAL ANIMAL

Red dragon

NATIONAL BIRD

Red kite (unofficial)

NATIONAL FISH

Common carp (unofficial)

NATIONAL RESOURCES

Natural resources include coal, livestock grazing land, hydropower, and timber. Wales was heavily industrialized in the 19th century, but since the 1970s, it has diversified into finance, research and development, and tourism.

FOODS

Cawl, a traditional stew of lamb, leeks, and other vegetables, is considered the national dish. Other specialties include *bara brith,* a type of bread enriched with chopped dried fruit; *cennin,* leek soup; Welsh rarebit, a sauce made of cheese and mustard and served over bread or ham; Welsh cakes; *crempogs,* buttermilk pancakes; *faggots,* pork meatballs; *laverbread,* an edible seaweed boiled and then minced or pureed; Glamorgan sausage, a cheese log in the shape of a sausage rolled in breadcrumbs; and *lob scows,* a lamb or beef stew.

SPORTS/SPORTS TEAMS

Rugby union, cricket, and association football (soccer) are the most popular sports. Wales national teams participate in many sports at an international level.

TEAM SPORTS

Badminton

Wales Badminton Team

Basketball

Wales Basketball Team; Wales Women's Basketball Team

Bowls

Wales Bowls Team

Cricket

Wales Cricket Team; Wales Women's Cricket Team; Wales Women's Cricket Team

Football

Wales Football Team, nickname the Dragons; Wales Women's Football Team, nickname the Dragons; Wales Rugby Union Team; Wales Women's Rugby Union team; Wales Rugby League Team, nickname the Dragons; Wales Under-21 Football Team, nickname the Young Dragons; Wales Women's Under-19 Football Team; Wales Rugby Union (Sevens), nickname Wales Sevens; Wales Women's Rugby Union Team (Sevens), nickname Wales Sevens or Wales 7s; Wales Under-19 Football Team, nickname the Young Dragons; Wales Under-17 Football Team, nickname the Young Dragons; Wales Under-20 Rugby Union Team; Wales Under-18 Rugby Union Team; Wales Australian-Rules Football Team, nickname the Red Dragons; Wales Touch Football Team; Wales Women's Touch Football Team

Hockey

Wales Field Hockey Team

Korfball

Wales Korfball Team

Lacrosse

Wales Lacrosse Team; Wales Women's Lacrosse Team; Wales Under-19 Lacrosse Team; Wales Women's Under-19 Lacrosse Team

Netball

Wales Netball Team

Table Tennis

Wales Table Tennis Team

INDIVIDUAL SPORTS

Wales Amateur Boxing Team; Wales Weight Lifting Team

WINTER SPORTS

Wales Curling Team

NATIONAL HEROES OR PERSONIFICATIONS

Dame Wales (Mam Cymru) is the national personification of the country.

Owain Glyndwr, who restored Welsh independence briefly and became the last Welshman to hold the title Prince of Wales; Llywelyn Fawr, Llywelyn the Great, the founder of Wales in 1216; Aneurin Bevin, regarded as the father of the National Health Service in the United Kingdom; Tom Jones, the most famous singer Wales has ever produced; Dylan Thomas, considered Wales' national poet

NATIONAL HOLIDAY/INDEPENDENCE DAY

National Day (Saint David's Day), March 1

FESTIVALS/FAIRS

National Eisteddfod, August; Ruthin Festival, June–July; Welsh Food Festival, September; Maindee Festival, September; Celf Caerleon Arts Festival, July; Conwy River Festival, August

SIGNIFICANT EVENTS IN FORMATION OF NATIONAL IDENTITY

500 B.C.E.–100 B.C.E. Celts from northern Europe colonize and settle the region, which forms part of the great Celtic empire that stretches across the continent.

43 B.C.E.–383 C.E. The Romans extend their control, and a Celtic-Roman culture develops after fierce Celtic resistance is overcome. The Romans abandon Britain as the empire's power wanes.

400–600 Saxons and Angles, Germanic tribes from central Europe, invade Britain in large numbers. The Celts retreat west to the defendable peninsulas of Wales and Cornwall* and across the narrow channel to Brittany*.

800–1216 English encroachment and claims keep the region on constant alert. The unification of Wales begins under Gruffydd ap Llywelyn. His grandson, known as Llywelyn the Great, unifies all of Wales and becomes the first Prince of Wales.

1267–1284 The English recognize the principality and the title, but an English invasion ends Welsh independence in 1282. The English construct a series of great stone castles to better control the territory. The Statute of Rhuddian establishes the Principality of Wales.

1400–1415 A rebellion led by Owain Glyndwr briefly restores Welsh independence. Glyndwr is the last Welshman to hold the title Prince of Wales.

1536–1543 Henry VIII unites the principality with England.

1689 The separate Council of Wales is abolished, and autonomy is revoked.

1830 The last legal distinctions between Wales and England are removed.

1886–1896 A nationalist reawakening spreads across Wales. David Lloyd George leads a campaign for Welsh home rule.

1920–1926 The Anglican Church loses its official establishment status. The Welsh national party, Plaid Cymru, is created.

1950 A campaign begins for a separate parliament for Wales.

1964 The British government establishes the separate Welsh Office.

1973–1979 A Royal Commission recommends the establishment of a non-lawmaking Welsh assembly. Voters overwhelmingly reject the first assembly proposals.

1997–1999 A second referendum narrowly endorses devolution and the creation of a separate

Welsh legislature. Nationalists denounce the move. The National Assembly is established in Cardiff.

2006–2009 New laws allow the assembly to acquire lawmaking powers subject to a referendum. A convention is established to advise the assembly on the timing of another devolution referendum.

WALLONIA

OFFICIAL NAME

Région Wallonne (French); Wallonische Region (German); Walloon Region (English)
  Waloneye (Walloon); Wallonie (French); Wallonia (English)

POPULATION

3,417,300 (2009e)

INHABITANTS' NAME/NICKNAME

Walloon(s); Walon(s)

LANGUAGE/LANGUAGES

French, German (both official); Walloon, Picard, others

RELIGION/RELIGIONS

Roman Catholic, 54 percent; Protestant, 7 percent; other or no religion

NATIONAL FLAG

The flag has a yellow field charged with a red rooster with one leg lifted. The flag's nickname is *le coq hardi,* "the bold rooster." The rooster represents the Walloons' ties to the Gallic rooster of France*. The colors are derived from ancient flags used in the region.

COAT OF ARMS/SEAL

The coat of arms is a yellow crest or shield bearing the red *coq hardi.*

MOTTO

Walon todi (Walloon); Walloon Forever! (English)

CAPITAL CITY

Namur

TYPE OF GOVERNMENT

Autonomous region within the federal Kingdom of Belgium

NATIONAL EMBLEM

Le coq hardi, the "bold red rooster"

NATIONAL COLORS

Yellow and red

NATIONAL ANTHEM

The anthem dates from 1900 and has both French- and Walloon-language versions. It was adopted as the official anthem in 1998.

> **Li Chant des Wallons (French); Le Tchant des Walons (Walloon); The Song of the Walloons (English)**
>
> Of our land Wallonia we are proud.
> Her children are revered the world over.
> Behold the triumph of her industry,
> The grandeur of her arts!
> Though our land be small, still her science
> Surpasses that of many a populous nation
> What we yearn for most is our freedom.
> That is why we are proud to be Walloons!
>
> We Walloons are all brothers
> And comfort one another in distress
> We do good without boasting about it
> And try to keep it secret
> Charity visiting a poor cottage
> Goes by night and cautiously
> We may give little, but it comes from the
>   heart.
> That is why we are proud to be Walloons!
>
> O humble land of Wallonia,
> Modestly we hail thee, land of our hearts'
>   desire.
> We are saddened when men speak ill of thee.
> It truly breaks the heart!
> But fear not attacks from the enemy
> Thy children will defend thy high repute.
> Who dare affront our anger?
> That is why we are proud to be Walloons!

PATRON SAINT

Our Lady of Banneux

CURRENCY

Euro

INTERNET IDENTIFIER

.be Belgium (official); .wl Wallonia (unofficial)

VEHICLE IDENTIFICATION PLATES/ STICKERS

B Belgium (official); WAL Wallonia (unofficial)

PASSPORT

Walloons are Belgian citizens and travel on Belgian passports.

NATIONAL ANIMAL

Rooster

NATIONAL RESOURCES

Natural resources include silica sand, carbonates, arable land, and hydropower. Highly industrialized in the 19th century, Wallonia has since declined as industries changed and aged. Tourism is an important resource, supported by historic cities and monuments, varied scenery, and proximity to large population centers. Many Walloons, called *frontaliers*, work across the borders in France, Germany*, and Luxembourg*.

FOODS

Moules frites, mussels and fried potatoes, is a dish typical of the Brussels region. Other specialties include *salad liégeoise*, a salad of green beans, bacon, and onions; *anguilles au vert*, eel in a green herb sauce; *chicons au gratin*, chicory (Belgian endive) with béchamel sauce and cheese; *boudins*, a type of sausage, often accompanied by potatoes and apple sauce; *booyah*, a soup made of chicken, oxtail, and vegetables; *trippe*, a sausage of pork and cabbage; *jutte*, a dish of mashed potatoes and cabbage served with pork; and *flamiche*, a type of quiche with cheese and leeks.

SPORTS/SPORTS TEAMS

Association football (soccer) is the most popular sport. Wallonia national teams participate in football and basketball at an international level.

TEAM SPORTS

Basketball

Wallonia Basketball Team; Wallonia Women's Basketball Team

Football

Wallonia Football Team

NATIONAL HEROES OR PERSONIFICATIONS

Georges Simenon, Wallonia's writer, the creator of police commissioner Maigret; Adolphe Sax, the inventor of the saxophone; Robert Collignon, the president of the Walloon Parliament in the turbulent 1980s

NATIONAL HOLIDAY/INDEPENDENCE DAY

National Day, September 27

FESTIVALS/FAIRS

Kirk-Messe (Harvest Festival), November; Binche Carnival, February–March; Festival of Wallonia, June–October; Mons Ducasse, June

SIGNIFICANT EVENTS IN FORMATION OF NATIONAL IDENTITY

57 B.C.E. After seven years of resistance, the Celtic Belgae surrender to Julius Caesar.

358 C.E. An invasion of Germanic Franks pushes the Latin-speaking peoples south to a line approximating the present northern border of Wallonia.

845 The region divides into a number of small states and bishoprics.

1226 The Treaty of Mélun solidifies the French language and cultural domination of the southern Low Countries.

1477 The Low Countries pass to the rule of the Hapsburgs.

16th century The Low Countries, or the Netherlands*, become a center of world trade. In 1555, control of the region passes from the Austrian Hapsburgs to Spain*.

1815 In the aftermath of the French Revolution and the Napoleonic Wars, Roman Catholic Wallonia and Flanders* are united with the Protestant-majority Netherlands in a single kingdom.

1830–1831 The Catholic provinces revolt against Dutch rule. Wallonia and Flanders unite to form the Kingdom of Belgium*.

1830s–1910s Newly industrialized Wallonia dominates the new kingdom. French becomes the language of government and society.

1914–1917 German occupation and fighting devastate the region.

1920–1940 The industrial decline is accompanied by decline in religion, which makes language the center of Belgium's growing regional conflict. The Flemish struggle to gain linguistic and cultural equality.

1946–1950 After the Second World War, the economic center of Belgium shifts to Flanders and its ports. The economic and political shift to Flanders stimulates Flemish nationalism, with a corresponding movement in Wallonia.

1960s Demonstrations, often with violent confrontations, spread throughout the country. In 1963, three official languages are recognized, French, Flemish, and German.

1970s Attitudes harden, with both Walloons and Flemish demanding greater political and economic autonomy.

1989–1990 Wallonia and Flanders are made autonomous states, opening a bitter debate over control of Brussels, which is created the third autonomous state in Belgium. The ethnic divide makes Belgium all but ungovernable, as governments rise and fall on the linguistic question.

1990–1993 Proposals are published for the creation of a European capital district around Belgium, with Flanders and Wallonia becoming separate independent countries within the European Union. In 1993, the official devolution of powers effectively partitions Belgium.

2001–2009 The Lambermont Accord gives even more powers to the regions, leaving the Belgian government with just a few remaining powers that will eventually become the responsibility of the European Union.

See also Belgium